Poetics of Dance

Oxford Studies in Dance Theory

MARK FRANKO, Series Editor

French Moves: The Cultural Politics of le hip hop
Felicia McCarren

Watching Weimar Dance
Kate Elswit

Poetics of Dance: Body, Image, and Space in the Historical Avant-Gardes
Gabriele Brandstetter

Poetics of Dance

Body, Image, and Space
in the Historical Avant-Gardes

GABRIELE BRANDSTETTER

TRANSLATION FROM THE GERMAN
BY ELENA POLZER WITH MARK FRANKO

OXFORD
UNIVERSITY PRESS

OXFORD
UNIVERSITY PRESS

Oxford University Press is a department of the University of
Oxford. It furthers the University's objective of excellence in research,
scholarship, and education by publishing worldwide.

Oxford   New York
Auckland   Cape Town   Dar es Salaam   Hong Kong   Karachi
Kuala Lumpur   Madrid   Melbourne   Mexico City   Nairobi
New Delhi   Shanghai   Taipei   Toronto

With offices in
Argentina   Austria   Brazil   Chile   Czech Republic   France   Greece
Guatemala   Hungary   Italy   Japan   Poland   Portugal   Singapore
South Korea   Switzerland   Thailand   Turkey   Ukraine   Vietnam

Oxford is a registered trademark of Oxford University Press
in the UK and certain other countries.

Published in the United States of America by
Oxford University Press
198 Madison Avenue, New York, NY 10016

Originally published in German as *Tanz-Lektüren:
Körperbilder und Raumfiguren der Avantgarde* by
Fischer Taschenbuchverlag, 1995.

Library of Congress Cataloging-in-Publication Data
Brandstetter, Gabriele.
[Tanz-Lektüren. English] Poetics of dance: body, image, and space in the historical
avant-gardes / Gabriele Brandstetter; translation from the German by Elena Polzer.
    pages cm.—(Oxford studies in dance theory)
Includes bibliographical references and index.
ISBN 978-0-19-991655-9 (cloth: alk. paper)—ISBN 978-0-19-991657-3 (pbk.: alk. paper)
1. Modern dance—Philosophy.   2. Body schema.   I. Polzer, Elena, translator.   II. Title.
GV1783.B7313 2015
792.801—dc23
2014023180

How curious these humans are,
Explaining here what cannot be explained,
And reading there what never had been writ.

Hugo von Hofmannsthal, *Death and the Fool*

Unreadable this
world. All doubles.

Paul Celan, *Snow Part*

CONTENTS

SERIES EDITOR'S PREFACE

This translation of *Tanz-Lektüren: Körperbilder und Raumfiguren der Avantgarde (Poetics of Dance)* at last makes available to an Anglo-American audience Gabriele Brandstetter's groundbreaking work of dance scholarship that first appeared in German in 1995 but has remained little known outside the German-speaking world.[1] Although Brandstetter has published numerous articles in English since this time, *Tanz-Lektüren*—her *Habilitationsschrift*—represents the first opportunity for the English-speaking world to engage fully with the breadth and scope of Brandstetter's research, theory, historiography, and interpretation of dance and cultural history. As such, it is nothing short of a major event for the field of dance studies.

Gabriele Brandstetter recounts that Ruth St. Denis and Hugo von Hofmannsthal met in 1906 in Berlin. This was one of the many encounters between dance and literature crossing national boundaries and contributing to new visions of dance, literature, and visual culture at the turn of the century. The intersection of these arts brought about a radical reconceptualization of what Brandstetter calls the *body-image* thanks to which movement, text, and image could no longer be interpreted as existing in isolation one from the other. This collapse of boundaries was due in large part to a crisis of the subject that had scientific, psychoanalytic, linguistic, and colonialist dimensions. In *Poetics of Dance* we discover a masterful account of early European dance modernism and the avant-gardes at the turn of the century as catalyzed by the crises in subjectivity and language.

Many of Brandstetter's texts of reference are little known to Anglo-American audiences, and this is one aspect of this book that makes it a fresh discovery of

1. Gabriele Brandstetter, *Tanz-Lektüren. Körperbilder und Raumfiguren der AvantGarde* (Franfurt am Main: Fischer Verlag, 1995). The book has just been reissued in German (Freiburg, Berlin, Vienna: Rombach Verlag, 2013).

this period in dance history and criticism, a period that reaches symbolic closure in 1929, the year of Serge Diaghilev's death, but also the year of the death of Aby Warburg, the art historian whose theory Brandstetter not only uses to such great effect in the conception of her analysis, but whose work—itself highly interdisciplinary—she was one of the first German intellectuals to rediscover and explore for its methodological potential.[2] It is not unreasonable to say that Brandstetter uncovers the very basis of interdisciplinarity as critical praxis in the hermeneutics of modern aesthetic practices around the turn of the century.

In this, Brandstetter's use of Warburg's iconographic concepts—pathos formula (*Pathosformel*) and topos formula (*Toposformel*)—is inspired, and constitutes a *methodological proposal*[3] in itself as a protocol for reading wherein dance, literature, and visual culture interact in productive and revealing ways.[4] Notably, here, with respect to her methodology and terminology, the term *body-image (Körperbild)* is key in that it refers neither entirely to the body nor to the image per se, but to a concept of the visual and kinesthetic that marks modernity in all its brilliance and complexity.[5] This is the field that Brandstetter opens up to us as she investigates overarching cultural patterns or paradigms that re-emerged in avant-garde dance, but also in the visual arts, in theater, and in literature around 1900. Body-images are frequently derived from classical antiquity and herein lies their particular power of memory as social energy in the detours—essentially "rereadings"—of their new framings and activations. Their re-performance is itself dependent on movement through which memory both returns and transforms itself. Yet they are equally markers of exoticism and representations of cultural otherness.

The *Lektüre* of the original title—readings—has thus more than one meaning. It connotes the ways in which dance was read or deciphered by literary authors and philosophers, but also the ways in which dance itself "read"—remobilized as danced movement—specific, preexisting "formulas" of bodily expression that

---

2. Ernst Gombrich's *Aby Warburg: An Intellectual Biography* was available in German in the early nineties, but there was not yet a critical edition of Warburg's at that time. Georges Didi-Huberman has acknowledged Brandstetter's influence in his book on Warburg, *L'image survivante: Histoire de l'art et temps des fantômes, selon Aby Warburg* (Paris, Editions de Minuit, 2002).

3. Here I would evoke Fredric Jameson when he asserts that a methodological proposal is more than "a set of theses." *Late Marxism: Adorno or the Persistence of the Dialectic* (London & New York: Verso, 2007), 94.

4. We translate *Pathosformel* throughout as pathos formula although we recognize this important term was translated as emotive formula in Kurt Forster's edition of Warburg's *The Renewal of Pagan Antiquity: Contributions to the Cultural History of the European Renaissance (Texts & Documents)* (Los Angeles: Getty Center for the History of Art and the Humanities, 1999).

5. In this translation we occasionally also use the term *body imagery* for fluency.

are found chiefly in the visual arts: the reading is visual, kinesthetic, and textual all at once. Many of the literary texts so effectively put to use here are themselves of an ekphrastic nature, such as Rainer Maria Rilke's treatment of Rodin's rendering of the torso, which opens up to discussion at long last the significance of Rodin to dance modernism. Hence, literature triangulates this research into the creative impulse behind the historical avant-garde of dance. Although some of the critical and artistic reference points in *Poetics of Dance* may be unfamiliar to English-speaking readers, the expansion of the scope of the corpus now available to scholarship will be of enormous consequence to the field.

Given the growth of dance studies in Germany today we can appreciate the impact *Tanz-Lektüren* had at the time of its first appearance on dance as an academic field in the German university: it basically pioneered that field and the interdisciplinary discussion that has since become a touchstone of excellence in the German academy.[6] In the 1980s and early 1990s the dance studies field had just begun to take shape in the Anglo-American world but was virtually nonexistent in Germany. Prior to *Tanz-Lektüren* there were primarily monographs on individual artists or technical discussions of dance without extended cultural context. Brandstetter's argument for the rhetorical structure and cultural significance of dance changed that. But, even more significantly, it pointed the way to German cultural studies (*Kulturwissenschaft*) in that her reading was crafted around an impressively rich intertextual and intermedial network of reflections linking together literature, visual culture, philosophy, theater, fashion, and cultural theory.

The interdisciplinary methodology of *Poetics of Dance*—Brandstetter's ability to perceive the complex and transformative web connecting image, text, and movement—demonstrates a rich interdisciplinary perspective on dance.[7] *Poetics of Dance* thus represents not only a signal contribution to dance studies, performance studies, cultural studies, visual culture, and literary studies, but an effective expansion of the parameters and practices of each field in that it maps the means by which these fields interact with one another.

Mark Franko
Series Editor

---

6. See the discussion by Susan Manning and Lucia Ruprecht on the transition from *Germanistik* to *Kulturwissenshaft* in "New Dance Studies/New German Cultural Studies" in *New German Dance Studies*, edited by Susan Manning and Lucia Ruprecht (Urbana, Chicago & Springfield: University of Illinois Press, 2013), 2–4.

7. See the special issue, "Dance the Disciplines and Interdisciplinarity" of *Dance Research Journal* 41/1 (2009). Despite the trajectory of dance studies in the American university, interdisciplinarity as such has less respectability in the American university than in its German counterpart. See Louis Menand, *The Marketplace of Ideas: Reform and Resistance in the American University* (New York: W.W. Norton & Co., 2010).

AUTHOR'S PREFACE

Habent sua fata libelli

I completed *Tanz-Lektüren / Poetics of Dance* twenty years ago. It was my post-doctoral thesis, submitted to and accepted by the University of Bayreuth with the title "Lecture corporelle: Körperbilder und Raumfiguren der Avantgarde" (Lecture corporelle: Avant-Garde Images of the Body and Figurations of Space"). Much time has passed since then—time during which dance studies has produced extensive and highly differentiated research into many of the top-ics and issues examined in this book. It has not been possible to incorporate in this translation all these subsequent findings. The result would have been an entirely different book in more ways than one. The inexorable progression of dance history and dance discourse, as well as shifts in viewpoints and knowl-edge, brings with it new perspectives, and in so doing produces an altogether different text. Books such as this one have their own history. The publication of this book in English introduces it to a new international realm of interpretation and a wider community of readers. Twenty years after its first publication, it thus offers a renewed chance to revisit European dance modernity. I hope that the insights offered here into new facets of dance history and my accompanying analysis of the aesthetic discourse at the time will provide discursive impulses for dance studies as a whole.

The translation thus also and above all serves to demarcate and recall a spe-cific period in academic history. In the mid-1980s, when I was researching and beginning to write this book, academic dance studies were still at an early stage in the German-speaking world. Much has changed since then. Dance studies has successfully established itself at German universities and caught up with international research. When I published *Tanz-Lektüren* in the early 1990s one of my main goals was to provide a historical and systemic outline of the field and reveal specific approaches and possible contributions of dance studies to the interdisciplinary orchestra of cultural studies and art history. This book focuses on the period from 1900 until the early 1930s, when movement, rhythm, body, and space played a significant role in the aesthetics of European modernity. This was a historical phase in which dance in its various manifestations, transformations, shapes, and forms became recognized as the figuration of the very imaginary of cultural modernity.

The title *Tanz-Lektüren*—here translated as *Poetics of Dance*—gives an indication of my methodological and theoretical approach to the archival materials, texts, images, and documents used here. The concept of reading implies that dance in its cultural and performative form can be understood as a discursive formation. In her seminal study *Reading Dancing* (1986), Susan L. Foster demonstrates how transdisciplinary theories, ranging from historical studies to post-structuralism, can be applied to critical dance studies. The term *Tanz-Lektüren* used throughout this book follows a similar concept in some ways. However, the historical focus and the rhetorical and visual theoretical approach emphasize other aspects. *Lektüre*—that is, reading, interpretation, hermeneutics—is here defined as a conjunction of reading and writing, as an intertwined process. I here use the idea of a *lecture corporelle* analogously to the description of dance as *écriture corporelle*, which Stéphane Mallarmé developed in his poetics. This reading has a dual meaning: it describes the various ways in which authors, artists, philosophers, and academics read dance as part of a discourse on modernity. But it also describes reading as a physical process, in which dance and dancer become intertwined in their conscious and unconscious readings and rereadings of body and movement models, which preexist in and can be retrieved from visual memory, that is, the historical and imaginary storehouse of history. The book therefore has an interdisciplinary approach. It attempts to uncover and contextualize concepts of dance based on an analysis of general structures and recurring, transforming patterns found in the historical fabric of the art and culture of European modernity. Forms and models of dance are thereby regarded in terms of their figural and tropological constitution. Even twenty years after its original publication, this aspect—that is, the act of regarding dance movement as a process of re-membering and therefore as an art form that draws its energy in mnemonic form from cultural archives and discourses—constitutes a theoretical dimension of the book that is still open for further academic development.

The same applies in particular for my line of argumentation concerning the iconographic and mnemonic theories of art historian Aby W. Warburg. When I originally began writing *Tanz-Lektüren*, Warburg's work had been afforded little attention. Academic involvement with his work only increased and reached international circles in connection with the publication of Warburg's writings on art history and cultural studies from the mid-1990s on. Warburg's texts provide a fruitful, theoretical approach for the analysis of visual and historical-mnemonic cultural references in modern dance, which incidentally developed during Warburg's lifetime. Warburg's concept of the pathos formula and the mobile accessories (*bewegtes Beiwerk*) contains a poignant theory of the affective dynamics of movement expression. And his *Mnemosyne* project of a visual atlas traces the historical repercussions and force fields of *mnemic kinesis*. By this he meant that memory itself moves or is made up of movement. Thanks to Warburg, a guiding concept of his iconography, translated into the field of dance movement, corporeal history, and its gendered aspects—in association with questions of rhetoric and discourse analysis—structured the theoretical framework and the methodological approach of this book.

The English edition of the *Tanz-Lektüren*, the *Poetics of Dance*, would not have been possible without support from various sides. The ongoing interest in the book expressed by colleagues and students during conversations about international and interdisciplinary research provided the impetus and the motivation for initiating a translation of this book into English. I wish to thank all who had a part in this endeavor from the bottom of my heart. It is Mark Franko who deserves my greatest thanks. His initiative and his willingness to include *Poetics of Dance* in the series Oxford Studies in Dance Theory at Oxford University Press now give me the chance to make this book available for English-speaking readers. I enjoyed our professional discussions on the theoretical and methodological aspects of the book, as well his lucid and eloquent sensitivity for language as an editor. I have been grateful for his commitment in the whole process of translation, especially his translations from the French as well as transferring the original style of thinking and writing found in the *Tanz-Lektüren* into readable English academic prose. I am happy that Norman Hirschy has agreed to publish the book at Oxford University Press. And I wish to thank Elena Polzer and her office *ehrliche arbeit* for the heavy work of translation. Her professionalism, commitment, attention to linguistic detail, and know-how in the often difficult process of finding English translations for cited texts have given *Poetics of Dance* its *façon* in English. This has been an intense process, in which Mariama Diagne and Ann-Kathrin Reimers also played an important role. I would like to thank both of them for their editorial perusal, for the tracking down of remote text citations and bibliographic details (in English), for the numerous exciting critical comments, and for their great help in photo editing and copyright research. Since books are always also accompanied by visions and expectations, I sincerely hope that readers in the English-speaking dance world will profit from this book and that the ensuing dialogue may enrich the exciting history of dance studies.

Gabriele Brandstetter
Berlin, Summer 2013

Poetics of Dance

Introduction

In 1907 *Bühne und Welt* (*Stage and World*) published "The Geisha,"[1] a novella by cultural anthropologist and author Lafcadio Hearn. Embedded in a framing discussion of Japanese art and culture we find the tale of an encounter between a *shirabyoshi*—a geisha of Japan's Golden Age—and a painter. "The Geisha" is a "legend" in two senses of the term: it is a mythical story, but its reading contains a key to deciphering the relationship between dance, image, and text, a relationship also played out in the novella at various levels.

During a journey on foot through the countryside the painter wanders into a desolate clime. Coming upon a remote cottage that promises shelter for the night, he discovers a beautiful young woman who lives there in solitude. She offers him food and her humble bed. In the middle of the night, he is "awakened by a singular sound." He peers behind the screen and "what he saw astonished him extremely":

> Before her illuminated *butsudan* [house altar] the young woman, magnificently attired, was dancing all alone. Her costume he recognized as that of a shirabyoshi, though much richer than any he had ever seen worn by a professional dancer. Marvelously enhanced by it, her beauty, in that lonely time and place, appeared almost supernatural; but what seemed to him even more wonderful was her dancing. . . . the spectacle fascinated him. He felt, with not less pleasure than amazement that he was looking upon the most accomplished dancer he had ever seen. (490 et seq.)

1. Hearn 1907 (the following page numbers in the text refer to the German magazine edition 1906/1907). *Translator's note*: the German title of the novella "The Geisha" carries far more connotations than the original English title, "Of a Dancing Girl," published in 1894 in "Glimpses of an Unfamiliar Japan"; original text in public domain and fully available online.

The dancer discovers the observer and tells him her story: she was a celebrated *shirabyoshi*, who fled one day with her lover to this lonely region so that they could exist only for each other. Soon, however, her companion died and she continued to dance the dances that had once given her lover so much pleasure. She did so every night as a ceremony of remembrance in front of the house altar.

The story then jumps forty years ahead, when the painter has become famous. One day a nondescript old woman visits him and requests he paint her portrait. Opening her ragged bundle of belongings, "the wreck of a wonderful costume of other days, the attire of a shirabyoshi" is revealed; old images rise up in the painter's memory:

> In that soft shock of recollection, he saw again the lonely mountain dwell-
> ing in which he had received unremunerated hospitality—the tiny room .
> . . the faintly burning lamp before the Buddhist shrine, the strange beauty
> of one dancing there alone in the dead of the night. (493)

Suddenly, time ceased to exist. The dancer's body and her movements came to life again in the painter's mind.

He grants the geisha's wish to recreate her dance from memory. This painting would henceforth replace her daily dance-ceremony for her deceased lover, as she is now no longer able to dance it herself. The painter produces a masterpiece:

> Upon soft white silk the artist painted a picture of her. Yet not a picture
> of her as she seemed to the Master's pupils, but the memory of her as she
> had been in the days of her youth, bright-eyed as a bird, lithe as a bamboo,
> dazzling as a tennin in her raiment of silk and gold. (494)

Seeking her out the following day in her hut, he finds her dead, her face trans-figured by a "vague sweetness," his painting of her dancing on the wall before the shrine.

Lafcadio Hearn's story sets forth in exemplary fashion the most impor-tant features of a whole constellation of ideas in which dance and literature intersect throughout the early twentieth century: it suggests a fundamental crisis of perception. The crisis of perception has to do with a nature-culture divide, with the duality of dance on the one hand as a transitory art of the body, which is subject to mortality, and on the other as a culturally stable set of techniques for symbolic representation exercised by visual images and in liter-ary discourse. We come here upon the theme of *memoria* as an art of remem-brance with its power of metamorphosis as contained in the memory of an image of the body: its production and its disappearance. Hearn's "The Geisha" moreover addresses the role of the plastic arts as a medium of iconographic modeling that is operative [*wirksam*] in mediating encounters between dance and literature. We also find in this story the connection between myth with the ceremonial act of memory, the linking of individuality with ritual, and the meeting of spatial figures [*Raumfiguren*] of a topographical nature and body-images [*Körperbilder*] in motion. Finally, we note a tension between the fleeting quality of unrepeatable dance moments and the transcendence of the model of presentness in dance performance by situations that transgress this immediacy. There is, in other terms, a moment of aporia between the "now" of movement and the historicity of representation. It occurs in the story with the overstepping of the boundaries between death on the one hand and the symbolic suspension of movements in both the visual and the narrated image on the other.

In its contextualization, Lafcadio Hearn's short dance story moreover points out characteristic traits of the manner in which the relationship of dance and literature was embedded in culture and the history of thought around the turn of the century: the story of the "shirabyoshi" appears as part of the longer text "On a Dancing Girl," which is itself part of a collection of prose entitled *Izumo: Glimpses of an Unfamiliar Japan*. The narrative framework of "On a Dancing Girl" combines elements of cross-cultural comparative studies with an aesthetic treatise. It thus addresses issues that play a major role in the self-reflection of European modernity and its experience with foreignness and alienation during the crisis of perception around 1900. On the one hand, these issues touch on the topic of innovative aesthetics for that time: the development of antinaturalistic, "abstract" patterns of representation. From an example of Japanese painting, Hearn addresses an issue of perception that is of great urgency in the age of the mechanical reproduction of art: the work of Japanese painters is "impersonal" and devoid of individuality; he idealizes and stylizes the detail, "makes of his experience a memory" (459).

On the other hand, these same issues form a cluster around the fin de siècle theme of the encounter with foreign cultures. Here Hearn's text becomes part of the discourse on the dissolution of existing habits of perception regarding both one's own culture and that of others, as also explored by Hugo von Hofmannsthal (in a response to Hearn's writings) in his *Briefe des Zurückgekehrten (Letters of a Returnee)* and its critique of the "European mind," which was also published in 1907. In "On a Dancing Girl," the famous authority on Japan informs the European reader of the social patterns, the symbolism, the ceremonies, and the dance forms associated with the role of the geisha.

In doing so, Hearn's text paradigmatically exposes cultural conventions prevalent around 1900, in which the configurations of literature and dance, via body imagery and figurations in space, have become the focus of aesthetic discussion. The blurring of the boundaries between cultural commentary and fictional text, between aesthetic manifesto and literary work, as evident in Hearn's narrative interweaving of framing reflection and retold dance legends, is also symptomatic of the self-commentary and the self-reflection found in modern art.

However, Hearn's text about the dance of the "geisha" has above all an effect on the cultural landscape of the year 1907, in which a strong influence emanates from the mechanisms and constructs produced by the multiple forms in which dance and literature read and reread body imagery.

Hofmannsthal is an ardent reader of Hearn's writings. He writes a review of his book *Kokoro* and Hearn's obituary (on the occasion of his death in 1904) and repeatedly experiments with images of Japanese culture[2] in his preliminary sketches for *Letters of a Returnee*. Finally, he culls the concept of "preexistence" from a story by Hearn about Buddhist concepts of preexistence and the transmigration of souls[3] and later stylizes it to become the central formula underlying his own aesthetic identity. In the same year as the publication of Hearn's "Geisha" in German, a friendship was struck up between Hofmannsthal and the dancer Ruth St. Denis. St. Denis is an important representative of the new free dance (*freier Tanz*) movement and brought her specific stylization of exotic body imagery from the United States to Europe in 1906.[4]

Hofmannsthal is fascinated by the intense presence of St. Denis, the sensual performance of her "hieratic" style, which is free from all "European conventions." He composed the essay "The Incomparable Dancer," in which he expounded his interpretation of St. Denis's Indian dances.[5] The personal encounter with St. Denis, instigated by Harry Graf Kessler, was transmuted into an extensive written and spoken "Conversation with the Dancer"—the model for a new creative-aesthetic ideal in Hofmannsthal's work from 1907 onward

---

2. There are multiple references in Hofmannsthal's notes from the years before writing the *Letters of a Returnee* (1905/7) to his intention of drawing up a "Story of the Japanese Officer," linked to the idea of holism lost, which Hofmannsthal finally adopted as a kind of guiding principle in his fictive *Letters*: "The whole man must move at once." Hofmannsthal CW 1979, A III, 435; see also on this subject Coghlan 1985.

3. Hofmannsthal adopted the term and its corresponding distrust of Western concepts of individuality from the essay "The Idea of Preexistence" contained in the compendium *Kokoro* by Lafcadio Hearn.

4. On Ruth St. Denis and H. v. Hofmannsthal, see Brandstetter 1991b.

5. Hofmannsthal, CW 1978, A I, 496–501; see also Brandstetter 1991b.

and the source of multiple preliminary drafts for dance and theater pieces, as well as works of literature.

On the one hand, the images from the archives of cultural history thus become the substrate of readings of and dialogue on images of the body: the poet and the dancer in the museum.[6] And on the other hand, texts of various origins from the history of literature and culture became subtexts, the framework and scenarios for such a *lecture corporelle*.

In the conversations between Hofmannsthal and Ruth St. Denis, Lafcadio Hearn's story "On a Dancing Girl" also takes on the role of a "script" for the presentation of exotic body imagery through dance: in 1908 Ruth St. Denis presented a new solo in her London program entitled *A Shirabyoshi*[7]—most likely a result of her conversations with Hofmannsthal and inspired by Hearn's story. Her dance concentrates on the heart of the story, the ceremonial dance of the geisha in front of the shrine erected for her deceased lover. Alongside her solos "Radha," "The Cobra," and "The Nautch," which she developed along the lines of "Indian" dance styles, St. Denis here employed dance imagery that is defined as Japanese: a transformation and combination of body imagery and gestures and of free dance movement techniques. The contribution to modern dance aesthetics made by this and similar translations of specific readings of body imagery is revealed most potently in the reception of and interaction with those Far Eastern theatrical patterns of presentation, which exerted a strong influence on European intellectuals' perception of the foreign "other" beginning with the 1900 World Exhibition in Paris, for example, Sada Yakko's and Hanako's performances of Japanese dances and drama.[8]

The individual moments in which the visual patterns of such multireflected sequences of interpretation underwent transformation back and forth between dance, literature, drama, and the visual arts cannot always be traced. The focus of the following study thus lies not in verifying direct influences or confirming acts of reception; instead it seeks to reveal and analyze characteristic patterns of reading art, which—with regard to body imagery and figurations of

6. See corresponding explanations in Part I of this study.

7. Shelton 1981, 85; the critics in London praised St. Denis's solo *A Shirabyoshi* as "one of the most interesting among the many impressive and beautiful things, which this remarkable artist has to show" (cited in Shelton, 85). St. Denis had already gained first experiences with *Japonisme* on stage during the first phase of her career in the United States in performances of *Madame Butterfly* (the model for Puccini's opera of the same name) by David Belasco's troupe. *A Shirabyoshi* was her first dance creation incorporating Japanese aesthetics; it was later followed by *O Mika* (1912) and *White Jade* (1926).

8. On the performances of Sada Yakko and Hanako, with regard to the dance historical connections to Ruth St. Denis and Loïe Fuller, see Brandstetter and Ochaim 1989.

space—carry potential in the semiotic field of the disintegrating and newly reorganizing structures of the arts system.

|

The following study focuses on an exemplary analysis of those symptoms of the transformation process that found their expression in a fundamental upheaval of the semiotic systems of literature (in the so-called crisis of language), theater (in its aspirations toward a "retheatricalization of theater"), and dance (the extrication of "free dance" from the aesthetics of classical ballet) at the beginning of the twentieth century.

This far-reaching cultural crisis around 1900, which has alternately been described as a crisis of language, of knowledge, and of meaning, also appears— in light of developments in the natural sciences and the problems of legitimation faced by modern aesthetics—as a *crisis of representation*,[9] namely as an expression of a complex cognitive problem, which called into question the self-evident communicability of sensual experiences and their experience of sense or meaning through symbolic representation.

An essential aspect of these symptoms of crisis and disorder at the turn of the century is a constant discussion of "crisis" both in everyday discourse and in forms of artistic reflection.[10] Modernity creates for itself the *myth* of breaking with tradition: in Adorno's words, "[The experience of the modern] . . . does not negate previous artistic practices, as styles have done throughout the ages, but rather tradition itself."[11] And in the avant-garde's unceasing discussion of the term *art*, the crisis discourse, as cultivated by Nietzsche and Viennese modernism and elaborated by them into a complex rhetorical system, takes on a central role in the self-reflexive production of high art.

In the fields of literature and theatrical forms, this core criterion of modernity has been well described and much commented on.[12] However, "free dance"[13]

9. On the concept of perception see the corresponding section of Part I of this study, "The Break with Tradition and the Collapse of Memory."

10. A text that is exemplary for these symptoms of crisis and their role in the self-contextualization of art is Hugo von Hofmannsthal's famous text *Ein Brief* (1902), better known as the *Lord Chandos Letter*.

11. Adorno 1997, 21.

12. See Adorno 1997; Bürger 1974; taking Niklas Luhmann's systems theory as his point of reference, Georg Jäger attempts to define the avant-garde (Jäger 1991).

13. On the terminological delineation of "free dance" and "expressionist dance" see my notes at the end of this chapter.

has also and in particular been fundamentally dominated by a side branch of this crisis discourse, namely the unceasing reflection of its break with tradition and the aesthetic negation of the system of classical ballet. The reflection of the medium of dance itself, the development of both discourse and dance pieces that explore the construction and transformation of body imagery, patterns of movement, and concepts of meaning in free dance within the cultural landscape of upheaval around 1900, becomes a central criterion, evidence of modernity in a new understanding of dance at the beginning of the twentieth century. So far, there is no written theory of the avant-garde in dance; the following study seeks to provide some of the building blocks for such an endeavor and to do so on the basis of the reading of body imagery and figurations in space, as they have emerged in the interaction of literature and dance.

The line of inquiry followed by this study is thus based on the description and discussion of this crisis of perception: how can we gain a better understanding, on the basis of select examples, of the cross-references contained in literature and dance—while taking into consideration the theatrical reform movements of the moment—with regard to the representation of body imagery and figurations in space? Which new aesthetic (poetic and choreographic) solutions resulted from the self-referentiality and fluctuation of the symbolic systems of text and dance (movement) in crisis?

One of the goals of this historical, systematic, cultural, and semiotic analysis is to significantly contribute to a new academic understanding of the aesthetics of modernity and the avant-garde from a perspective hitherto not yet established in existing research on the history of literature and theater—namely a comparative study of the overlaps between dance, text, and the image.

The relationships between literature and dance and dance and literature only fully reveal themselves in their complex mediated quality against the backdrop of the culture-critical upheaval, the "threshold to the new era"[14] at the advent of the twentieth century. Theater, itself also in a fundamental phase of reformation, naturally appears—in the intermedial web of text, moving bodies, figurations of space, and concepts of staging—to take on the role of a mediator between developments in the avant-garde of literature and those of dance. The theatrical reform experiments of the avant-garde[15] will be taken into account in what follows only where, in exemplary cases, the innovations of modern dance and theater directly refer to one another. The reason is that, on the one hand, important impulses for the process described by the phrase "retheatricalization of the theater" came from the field of dance (in its emphasis on physical

---

14. See Gumbrecht and Link-Heer 1985; Herzog and Koselleck 1987.

15. See Brauneck 1984; Fiebach 1991; Fischer-Lichte 1983.

movement, gestural, rhythmicized movement, scenic choreography, and a choreography of the masses). On the other hand, because the paradigmatic shift
in modern dance lies not only in the development of a new model of the body
and movement, but also in the development of corresponding concepts for the
stage, which in many ways—for example, in the theatrical handling of space
and temporality, in its stylization of the body (via costumes, set, and lights), in
the abstraction of the contents of what is being represented, in the relationship
of solo and group choreographies—is closely related to the reforms taking place
in theater; a relationship, all of which shall be analyzed in part in futuristic
dance and its hitherto virtually unexamined ties to the theater and to the aesthetic and poetic program of futurism.

II

This study therefore proposes—via an analytical reconstruction of influential
visual structures—an archaeology of the general reading processes that form
the basis of a complex cross-referential web of signs and systematic violations
by literature, dance, and theater.

Of central importance to *Poetics of Dance* is the concept of reading in terms
of a *lecture corporelle*. This concept is itself in turn based on a definition of dance
as *écriture corporelle*[16] as expressed by Mallarmé in his *Divagations*. Mallarmé
emphasizes the aspect of signification, the body semiotics contained in the generation of movement signs in dance. The dancer simultaneously becomes both
the vehicle of the physical act of writing and the sign itself:

> *The dancer is not a woman dancing* . . . but a metaphor summing up one
> of the elementary aspects of our form . . . suggesting . . . a kind of corporal
> writing . . . a poem independent of any scribal apparatus.[17]

The transcription of *écriture* into *lecture* highlights the fact that the focus has
here left behind any perspective concentrating on the aesthetics of text production, for which the shifting configurations involved in the aesthetics of
perception and effect have been substituted. The process of deciphering body
imagery, its iconography, and their structures of organization—the possible
readings of a grammar of *écriture corporelle*—is what is focused on here. The
adjective *corporelle* hereby refers both to the act, that is, reading bodies as body

16. Mallarmé, "Ballets" (1945, 303–7).

17. Mallarmé 1945, 304; Mallarmé 2007, 130.

imagery and their figurations in space, and to a physical method of reading the specific cultural and artistic phenomena contained in images and text with the help of dance itself.

Existing academic theories on reading can only partially be taken into account in the research intended here, for almost all recent significant theories on reading, such as those by Hans Blumenberg, Jacques Derrida, and Paul de Man, are oriented toward writing as text (*Schrift*)[18] as an object and system of reading.

In our context however, reading should not be understood in terms of Hans Blumenberg's concept of the "readability of the world,"[19] in which the phenomena of reality—via the topos of the "world as a book"—become interpretable as text, but instead as a form of experiencing the body in motion through dance, hence as the independent act of reading a nondiscursive medium, on equal footing with the reading of text. I wish to focus here on the transfer occurring between these two forms of reading.

On the one hand, what is being read is dance itself; the writers decipher the dance, its forms of expression, body imagery, figurations in space, and the myth of new femininity contained therein. The *analytical* reading of these *literary* readings of dance is a part of the following study. On the other hand, dance itself is also a staged act of reading various "materials," images, and media. A hypothetical and analytically structured theory of reading processes best does justice to the fundamental dichotomy—dance and text, movement and writing—contained in this twofold object of investigation. For both the production and the reception of literature, as well as the creation and representation of dance movement, can be understood and described—with recourse to the tradition of pathognomy and iconographic patterns of depiction—as the deciphering of signs and symbolic systems.

From a methodological point of view, this model of analyzing specific readings of cultural signs offers the advantage—in comparison with concepts developed by research on intertextuality—of capturing not only the dialogue of the texts, but also the dialogue of nonverbal and unwritten codes—for instance, the kinetic signification processes of (dance/theater) performance and the iconographic structures of pictorial traditions.[20]

---

18. *Translator's note:* The German language differentiates between *Schrift* and *Schreiben*, which both translate as "writing" in English. *Schrift* stands for the material side of writing, i.e., text (typeface, font, script, etc.), whereas *Schreiben* indicates the actual physical act of writing.

19. Blumenberg 1981.

20. Here and in the following, I make use of the tools of iconographic and iconological analysis as defined by Erwin Panofsky and in his wake academic art history—whereby a precise differentiation of iconographic and iconological reflection, which Panofsky's own

The deconstructivist theory of "deciphering" developed by Jacques Derrida[21] ultimately also solely focuses on the textual and the phenomenon of *différance* in a steadily inscribing, "supplementing" process of reading and writing that makes note of differences and deferments (note the play of words in the use of the terms *différence/différance*). Terms such as *texte en général, écriture, marque,* or *trace* may no longer describe the subject matter of a distinct text; however, Derrida's theory of reading fails to take into account pathognomic phenomena, nor does he look at the reading of body imagery as text in the staging of movement. Instead, writing is so much the universalized metaphor of his theory that even reading appears as a form of unceasingly self-reproducing *écriture*:

> If reading and writing are one, as is easily thought these days, if reading *is* writing, this oneness designates neither undifferentiated (con)fusion nor identity at perfect rest; the *is* that couples writing must rip apart.[22]

The same applies to Paul de Man's concept of the *Allegories of Reading*.[23] His theory of literature—a concept in which modes of reading are mutually exclusive, hermeneutically inaccessible, and delimited by the figural language of literature—refers exclusively to written text. Even where de Man speaks about dance—for example, in his essay about Kleist's "On the Marionette Theater"[24]—he describes it as a figurative element of rhetorical practice, which cannot be transcended in the system of the ongoing *Allegories of Reading*: in any case, this concept of reading is not adaptable

definitions are equally unclear about, can here be disregarded; see Panofsky 1991, as well as Straten 1989.

21. Derrida 1976 and Derrida 1972.

22. Derrida 1981, 63–64.

23. See Paul de Man 1979. In his readings of Paul de Man, Derrida asks himself why de Man always preferred to speak of reading and not of "écriture"/text:

> Some have asked why Paul de Man always speaks of reading rather than of writing. Well, perhaps because the allegory of reading is writing—or the inverse. But perhaps also because every reading finds itself caught, engaged precisely by the promise of saying the truth, by a promise which will have taken place with the very first word, within a scene of signature which is a scene of writing. It is not enough to say, as we have so often done, that every reading is writing, it is necessary to demonstrate it: following, for example, this structure of the promise. *Allegory of Reading*—this means many things in the book which bears this title: the scene of reading represented in the abyssal structure of a text, the allegory of "unreadability," "textual allegory," etc. (Derrida 1986, 99–100)

24. See de Man 1984.

to a reading of body imagery and figurations of movement in dance as a kinetic-performative act.

In contrast to these deconstructive concepts of reading and writing, the theories on reading that have developed in the field of theater studies and more recently in dance studies are different. They are semiotic methods,[25] which largely define the analysis of theatrical staging in terms of subject matter and a theory of signs. In the field of theater studies, the semiotic model of "reading performance" studies aspects of reception and the relationship between performance and the reactions of an audience.[26] The theory behind the model highlights various aspects of semiotics and the aesthetics of reception as can be found in the relationship of dramatic text with its manifestation on stage in terms of the associated act of reading shared by author, director, performers, and audience.[27] In dance studies, Susan Leigh Foster's *Reading Dancing* has recently shown that a semiotic-structural approach to reading dance and movement theater is viable.[28] Her studies, however, largely refer to contemporary American dance, which is for a large part documented on film and video. She makes little mention of dance in relationship to other systems of signification, such as the visual arts or literature.

The difficulty of "reconstructing" theater and musical theater mise en scène due to their more or less incomplete documentation can be postulated for the historical study of the performing arts in general[29]—and is all the more prevalent in the study of dance history: the original work itself in its transitory singularity is no longer available for later analysis. While in drama—at least in the European tradition—we usually at least have the dramatic text handed down through time, which once served as the backdrop for the creation of a stage production according to the theatrical conventions of its day, dance for the most part lacks the specifications of choreographic notation. The problem faced by historical source materials in dance is the lack of methodology for making them

---

25. An overview can be found in Fischer-Lichte 1983.

26. Pavis 1988; Carlson 1990.

27. Wolfgang Iser's model of a theory of "empty spaces" in literary texts and Hans Robert Jauß's receptive-aesthetic theories and his concept of the "implied reader" have been adapted to a theory of reading suitable for theater studies, e.g., by Anne Ubersfeld (1978). The writings of Victor Turner on the relationship of ritual and theater (Turner 1982), as well as Iser's theories on fictionality and representation (Iser 1991) all fall within this same research context.

28. See Foster 1986; Foster draws on the semiotic theories of Charles S. Peirce, Roman Jakobson, and Roland Barthes.

29. See Steinbeck 1981; furthermore and taking into account a discussion of semiotic approaches and the history of mentalities: Bayerdörfer 1990.

accessible. The discussion of reconstruction, as it has surfaced again in recent years due to various practical attempts to reconstruct historical work in the field of dance and theater, does not fully take into account all the fundamental aspects relevant here. In the era of shifting paradigms that we will be looking at here—from classical ballet to free dance—both the concept of the dance work and methodological attempts at reconstruction seem in need of revision. For while the illusion of a consistent work was at least retained during the era of ballet in the nineteenth century, thanks to the conventions of presentation, the musical-theatrical composition of the stage—for example in Petipa's *Swan Lake*—and the rhetorical system of ballet as a whole, the basis for a virtual reconstruction of those dance events considered revolutionary around 1900 was considerably reduced with the emergence of free dance. This is due in part to a feature of free dance that is in itself noteworthy as a symptom of change and the emancipation of dance—namely the fact that the protagonists of free dance (which from its beginnings was presented as an avant-garde art initiated and maintained by women) acted simultaneously both as creators and performers rolled into one. The separation of "role" and interpreter-"actor," as prevalent not only in classical drama, but also in ballet, was abolished with the advent of work by Loïe Fuller, Isadora Duncan, Ruth St. Denis, and those who followed them. The habitus of the unique individual[30] in free dance, which was raised to the level of an aesthetic and ideological program—and in the case of almost all representatives of free dance was linked to a conspicuous dislike of documentation, sketches, or even notation of their dances—caused the conventional concept of the work to become almost obsolete.

Thus when we speak here of reading in regard to the questions posed in this study, our understanding of reading in no way aims at any form of reconstructing early twentieth-century works of dance. Instead *Poetics of Dance* seeks to describe the act of transmission (*Vermittlung*) contained in the construction and the deciphering of specific body imagery, which have been influential in dance, especially in the new plurality of styles that arose after its reformation. We are operating here with an indirect method of analysis, with the help of which we hope to evaluate, interpret, and organize heterogeneous source and documentary material (e.g., reviews, photo material, theoretical and aesthetic texts, program notes, autobiographical documents, and—in very rare cases—film) with regard to the line of inquiry described above.

---

30. The "individual" here differs from individuality in the (role) play of actors or dancers, who even in cases of strictly conventionalized form still retain a certain degree of leeway. Especially in strongly regimented theater systems—e.g., Japanese Noh—small nuances of presentation become the carriers of meaning in the dialogue between the connoisseur-viewer and the actors.

III

The terms *body-image* and *body imagery* are used in this study as set phrases to bridge the gap between dance and literature. They are based on the social-anthropological theory that our perception of the body, its "nature," and functions is flexible and socially constructed and thus reflects a specific historical context. The writings of anthropologist Mary Douglas, themselves based on the findings of Norbert Elias and Marcel Mauss, summarize this perspective on the social construction of the body as follows:

> The social body constrains the way the physical body is perceived. The physical experience of the body, always modified by the social categories through which it is known, sustains a particular view of society. There is a continual exchange of meanings between the two kinds of bodily experience so that each reinforces the categories of the other.[31]

The body-image in connection with this research is defined as a symbolic construct that migrates between scenic event and text. This enables access to pictorial as well as textual documents that influenced free dance iconography, without assuming the visual and the textual to be the same kind of evidence. When we introduce here an iconographically[32] oriented pattern of reading dance through the body-image and figurations in space—always doing so with the knowledge that, in the long run, all attempts to historically understand forms of dance, movement patterns, and the underlying mental images are of course interpretative constructs in themselves and thus merely attempts at making them understandable—it is done explicitly in order to avoid the (ultimately unrealizable) fiction of reconstruction. I do not attempt to discover the (no longer accessible) movement designs of the dances in my study of how body imagery and figurations in space are transmitted, but seek instead to unearth their visual paradigms—the *patterns* that form the deep underlying structure that shapes the foundation of dance at the turn of the century and which become tangible for us where they overlap with comparable phenomena in theater and in literature.

With the help of the body-image concept, we can link the question of *physical presence*, and of the presentation of the moving body as a shifting sign primarily situated in the nonverbal and nondiscursive symbolic field,

---

31. Douglas 2003, 93.

32. On the reading patterns of "pathos formula" and "topos formula" see the following explanations.

to the question of literary text and writing (*Schrift*): as a system of signs that seeks to evoke the presence of the corporeal in its representational deferment. Body imagery is thus also capable—as a type-oriented pattern of reading—of facilitating communication between the staged and the discursive, between dance-theater and literary text.

However, the flexible methodological concept of reading dance and literature introduced here—namely the formulas "body-image" and "figurations in space"—also takes on a more central role in light of our topic here: namely the *construction and deconstruction of the concept of the subject*[33] as itself central to discourse at the beginning of the twentieth century.

Thus there are two directions of inquiry in my argumentation, in the analyses of examples and in the questions posed concerning the intermedial relationships of dance, theater, and literature: one focuses on the respective concepts of the subject and the other on the relationship of the subject to the space surrounding him or her, as modified by our specific object of inquiry—namely the representations of the body in question in dance movement and their respective models of utilizing space.

The two main parts of this study will therefore also link concepts of the subject with an analysis of how this body imagery and these figurations of space, which are so characteristic of the newly emergent free dance and its readings in literature, developed.

In the process described, the *concept of the subject* seems to be closely related to a specific *concept of nature*: both concepts are central to an understanding of modern culture, and they document the manifestations and modifications of the social construction of reality; both the body imagery prevalent at the turn of the century and the full range of ideas implied by the term *nature* in correlation with the construction of this very body imagery reflect this situation.

The first part of this study brings together two topics that are are symptomatic for the crisis of culture around 1900: one is the issue of the subject in light of increasing disbelief in the idea of personality as a coherent unit; the other concerns the construction of body imagery in connection with the emergence of free dance.

For the iconographic representation and analysis of body imagery—in terms of the development of free dance at the beginning of the twentieth century—I

---

33. The term *deconstruction* is here used in two ways: on the one hand, it refers to forms of destruction and dissolution, as the antonym of construction (especially in regard to the presentation of the subject); on the other hand, it is understood as a term in the context of theories of "deconstruction," namely insofar as this term encompasses both operations—construction and deconstruction in flux—within a single formula of manifestation.

have recourse to Aby Warburg's theory of the "pathos formula."[34] The underlying principle behind the pathos formula—as a "primal expression of human passion"—is based on a theory of art that emphasizes the dynamics of expressive potential in sculpture and painting. According to Warburg, pathos formulas are visual inscriptions of collective cultural memory, "dynamograms," which still contain the imprint of cult ritual—as the origin of symbolic representation—and are constantly transformed anew in the receptive traditions of art.

In his anthropological and psychohistorically based theory, Warburg assumes that a process of culturally coping with primitive action by creating distance between oneself and the world—by binding it to the image—has found its symbolic expression in certain passionate emphatic gestures of art that are emotionally charged with "primal instinct."

In his introductory comments to the *Mnemosyne* project, Warburg writes:

It is this process of "undemonizing" the inherited store of impressions that fear had once created which embraces the whole gamut of expressions in the grip of emotions, from helpless brooding to murderous cannibalism. It also imparts to the dynamics of human expressive movements which lie between the extremes of orgiastic seizures—such as fighting, walking, running, dancing, grasping—the hallmark of an uncanny experience. It made the educated public of the Renaissance, brought up in the discipline of the Church, look upon this sphere as a forbidden region where only the godforsaken who indulged in unrestrained passions were permitted to run riot. It is this process which the Atlas *Mnemosyne* is intended to illustrate. It is concerned with the effort psychologically to absorb these pre-existent coinages for the rendering of life in movement.[35]

In the *Mnemosyne* atlas Warburg sought to produce a comprehensive inventory of images depicting the pathos formulas and to document their transformation over the course of the history of art and culture since antiquity. He hoped that an "atlas of emphatic gestures" as a systematically organized repertoire of gestures and movement patterns would reveal how the present is connected to the past—a history of "the mimetic human" (*mimischen Menschen*) in corporeal images. This archive of corporeal memory lists various manifestations of "primally expressing the dynamics of passion": traces of Dionysian frenzy, orgiastic ecstasy, religious awe, triumph, Olympian mirth, grief, sacrifice. Examples

34. See Gombrich 1984; see also Barta-Fliedl 1992.

35. Gombrich 1970, 291.

of these pathos formulas can be found in the dances of the Greek maenads, the gesticulations of Nike, and the Roman Victoria.

Warburg's model of the pathos formula—modified and adapted to the body imagery of modern dance—appears, as a pattern for reading subjective emotionally charged expressive acts and the iconographic topoi of the representation of affect (as a quasi-pictorial rhetoric), to be especially suited to analytically capturing the typical characteristics of "free dance" and "expressionist dance." The body imagery of dance at the beginning of the twentieth century—read as pathos formula—thus appears as symbolic figurations, within which the engrams of passionate dynamics come alive, hidden under and transformed by the self-interpretations of the modern subject.

Here the pathos formulas fulfill a dual function in their specific transformation of body imagery: they contribute both to the construction of concepts of the subject and to their dissolution.

The body imagery upon which movement models of dance are based—for example, the "Greek" pattern or the "exotic"—often appears as emphatically staged acts of liberation from cultural restraints: free dance is thus celebrated as an artistic antidote to the damage civilization has wrought. The act of reshaping the subject into a *neuer Mensch* [new person] with the help of the cultural and emancipatory effects of free dance paralleled contemporaneous theories and practices of the deconstructing, or even the destroying/destructuring, of elements previously held to be fundamental to notions of the integrity of the individual and self-definition.

However, alongside the subject-constituting functions of body imagery, we also find patterns of self-dispersal—as pathos formulas of dissolution in dance and literature: whirling dances, fire dances, ecstatic frenzies of movement address and reflect images of depersonalization and the destruction of the boundaries of self in movement, as well as render them accessible as body imagery.

In the second part of the study, I will focus not on the constitution of body imagery in dance—as in the first part of the study—but rather on its transcendence in a turn toward the spatial: I will address figurations of space that frame dance movements, the production of typical "spatial formulas." Not body imagery, but rather its metamorphosis into abstract figurations, its transcription into spatial patterns, will become legible—almost as a topology of dance.

The term *topos formula* is here derived from Warburg's concept of the pathos formula, the latter defined as a pictorial pattern of symbolically shaped expressions of movement, which can practically be retrieved as formulas from the inventory of cultural memory and transformed.

The term *topos formula* can be applied similarly: as a compound of topos and formula, whereby topos here describes the space, the site of (dance) movement in the literal sense of the word, and on the other hand, the places—"commonplaces" (Ernst Robert Curtius)[36]—as formulas that inventory perception, much as does the use of topoi in classical in rhetoric. The topos thus fulfills the function of linking figures of speech and figures of space in dance. Topos formulas condense and transform symbolic patterns of perceiving "socially identifiable empirical and theoretical knowledge" (Lothar Bornscheuer) into figurative spatial shapes.[37]

Space and the relationships between the kinetic parameters defining it are the subject and the medium of the topos formula; the concept of topos formula thus refers to formative figurations, formulas of spatial relationships in typical configurations of depicting a subject and its surrounding space. In contrast to a pathos formula, which transports the manifestations and the modern reformulations of affect engrams in the body and movement imagery of dance, topos formulas appear as specific variations of processes of abstraction in modern art.

Topos formulas prove to be well suited to patterns of abstraction, which broadly define the processes underlying twentieth-century modern art—processes that run contrary to those oriented on the body and its presentation in various forms through pathos formulas as described in the first part of this study—and yet they also enter into dialogue with each other: the relationship of corporeal movement to space.[38]

The special function of "emptiness," the tension-laden space between various elements of spatial composition, assumes central meaning in twentieth-century modern art, as well as in modern dance.[39] There is no longer one *obligatory* perspective. Instead the multidimensional, empirically intangible space detaches viewers from their orthogonal orientation; the figurations of movement, the kinetic elements, draws them into a multicentered spatial perspective as if through an underground system of tunnels.

Two examples of such topos formulas—the movement and spatial figurations of the labyrinth and the spiral—will thus be examined in the various

36. See Curtius 1967 on the term *topos* and the literary use of rhetorical topoi.

37. Bornscheuer 1976, 17. In his study on "topic," Bornscheuer attempts to differentiate "aspects of a social, productive, critical, and linguistic-symbolic imagination (habituality, potentiality, intentionality, symbolicity)" (23).

38. Here "space" is not meant in terms of its functional theatrical definition, not as the place of the stage, but in its diversely connoted, mythical, "auratic," specific aesthetic qualities.

39. See Brandstetter 1991c; on the function of weightlessness, the dispersal of the central perspective in modern visual art see Simmen 1990.

contexts of their representation in dance, theater, and literature as fundamental pivotal patterns of movement and figurations in space. The topos
formula hereby appears in various forms of metamorphosis: last, but not
least, as the dissolution of the subject in the spatial figuration of abstraction, in particularization, in the montage and disassembly of body imagery. With regard to the concept of the subject, this primarily involves the
destruction of holistic models of the individual as a natural unit of body,
mind, and soul.

Integrative models of *space* replace the holistic, integrative concept of the
subject: organizational structures and constructive principles underlying topol-
ogies, organic and abstract figurations of space, which are produced by movement and—in closed or open gestalt—multiplied or destroyed. Constructivism
and conceptualization both reference structural forms of topology as well
as its production by the "instrument"—meaning both the apparatus of the
dancer-body and the "machines" of the technological and media age.

The impact on the discussion of the nature of the subject is evident:

- A deindividualization of the body (shifting the focus from body imagery to its expression in dance)
- The deconstruction and de-formation of the individual: the disorgani-
  zation of body and movement is expressed in the hypertrophy of body
  parts and individual movements (as in grotesque dance), in the cloaking and reassembly of segmented bodies and body shapes (e.g., in Oskar
  Schlemmer's "Bauhaus dances," in "puppet" and "machine dances")

Phenomena of alienation are thus addressed in dance via the physical and the
mechanical. On the one hand, "individuality" disappears in the ornaments of
spatial formula, and on the other hand, it is defined by the impersonal gestures
of "constructed" bodies, especially in the avant-garde author-personality.

The "pathos formulas" communicate the appropriation and reformula-
tion of iconographically predefined affect engrams by the subject in the
movements of free dance. The emphasis lies in the *habitus of individuality*
in presentation: the emphatic self-fulfillment of the subject in the dance
solo, as also expressed in the rhetorical figure of the "lonely ego" in early
twentieth-century literature.

By contrast, the topos formulas apply to processes of abstraction in reference systems surrounding the subject and the space created by his movement: they apply equally to abstract figuration, the stereotyping of the
corporeal in spatial ornaments, and the dissolution of the subject in semiotic
space: all important aspects of avant-garde aesthetics in twentieth-century
dance and literature.

IV

To bring these introductory remarks to a close, I would like to elucidate certain *issues of terminology*,[40] namely those abstract concepts that are here repeatedly employed in a differentiated manner throughout this study, such as the terms *modernity* and the *avant-garde* in their various meanings in literature, theater, and dance; and the expressions "free dance" and "expressionist dance," which we must differentiate in order to better understand our subject of inquiry.

First, some remarks on the use of "free dance" and "expressionist dance," which seem useful to me at this point. The term *expressionist dance* is often used to describe, without any form of differentiation, all manifestations of dance after 1900 that cannot be subsumed under the system of classical dance. Even in dance studies itself, we have as yet no consistent terminology for the new forms of dance that emerged at the beginning of the twentieth century. The distinction that I wish to suggest here for the use of the terms *free dance* and *expressionist dance*, however, largely corresponds to their use in more recent dance studies publications.[41]

I use the term *free dance* in a different historical and aesthetic context than the term "expressionist dance." Free dance in central Europe emerged *before* expressionist dance. It begins with the reform initiatives of Loïe Fuller (1892) and Isadora Duncan (ca. 1900) and continues until far into the 1920s in the work of those who followed them and the activities of the many practitioners of this movement reform. A main characteristic of free dance as a new style is a "natural," simple manner of moving from the center of the body.

Expressionist dance, in the narrower sense of the word, historically and aesthetically describes that emphatic-expressionist school of modern dance, which programmatically and pedagogically revolves around the dancer and choreographer Rudolf von Laban and his movement theory. The first phase of expressionist dance (after a preliminary stage in Munich around 1910) lies in the period between 1914 and 1917, beginning with Laban's summer courses at Monte Verità. During World War I (as with the beginnings of Dadaism in

---

40. I do not wish to define here all the terms used in this study; partly because certain terms such as, *discourse* (which is in any case used sparingly) and *iconography* are used in consensus with the established terminology of literary research and art history; partly also because certain problems of representation—such as, e.g., movement descriptions, for which there is (as yet) no consistent terminology in dance studies—should not be determined beforehand in theory. For the sake of a more precise phenomenological and historical assessment, they will be developed on the basis of the given respective case (as in the aesthetic, technical-physical, and historical analysis of "whirling dances").

41. E.g., Müller 1986; Klein 1992.

"exile" in Switzerland), a dance model emerged that then became known in the 1920s as "German" expressionist dance (and in America as "German dance") and that developed its strongest potential for innovation in a combination of expressionism and elements of new objectivity (*Neue Sachlichkeit*). Important representatives of this dance form were Mary Wigman, Rudolf von Laban, Suzanne Perrottet, Sigurd Leeder, Kurt Jooss, Gret Palucca, Hanya Holm, Rosalia Chladek, and Dore Hoyer.

I would like to emphasize one specific aspect in the definition of expressionist dance—in terms of aesthetics, programmatic ethics, and physical dance technique—that has hitherto received almost no attention in its relevance for the avant-garde aesthetics of dance: the role of an "aesthetics of ugliness." Only after dance had examined ugliness and integrated it in an aesthetics of expression that no longer gave priority to beauty and grace, but showed interest in dynamics and the expression of "truth" as the aim of movement composition, only then did dance join the ranks of the "former beaux arts"— a movement that, in the case of literature, began as early as the nineteenth century. In the nineteenth century, ballet, the "beautiful art of dance,"[42] separated the ugly from an aesthetics of weightlessness via representations of the grotesque-humorous—mostly in roles *en travesti*. Free dance at the turn of the century combined the ideal of the beautiful body moving "naturally" and gracefully with concepts of the "new woman." In contrast, expressionist dance integrated expressive forms of representing ugliness, that is, the unbeautiful, for the first time in its aesthetics and design: in its theoretical-ethical program of shaping the "truth" of human existence; in its aesthetic theory of the power of movement and the experience of space; and in its technical emphasis of body weight and tension—"expression" was a modern movement language that no longer paid homage to beauty: as the pathos of terror and grief (Mary Wigman) and as social-critical manifestation of distortion in motion (Valeska Gert).

The expressions "modernity" and "avant-garde" are used in the following study to define and delineate specific eras in the same way as they are used by academic literary studies. In the definitions of time periods and aesthetics, it

---

42. This is the title of Verena Köhne-Kirsch's dance-phenomenological dissertation; the "beautiful" not only alludes to the aesthetic of ballet; in this respect, the study indirectly attests to the degree in which movement arts—in the context of the "beaux arts"—seem to cling to this aesthetic model (Köhne-Kirsch 1990). How ambivalently the integration of the "no (longer) beautiful" has been evaluated can be seen in the writings of Frank Thieß (1920, 110ff.) in his dance aesthetics: "Dance as an art form" has finally achieved the same appreciation as the other arts, and "so the not-beautiful also rightfully exists in dance"; and yet Thieß draws a line in the aesthetics of the ugly regarding the image of the body: the dancer's body must not be unattractive, that is, ugly.

is important for our subject of study that we take a closer look at the common terminology denoting names of epochs, as they appear in the study of literature, theater, and culture, in light of the developments and historical upheavals that took place in dance. From this comparative point of view, we can then differentiate and put into perspective the parallels and differences that occurred in each respective field.

"Modernity" here refers to an artistic-literary phase of development since the late nineteenth century, a phase of programmatic self-reflection in art in its confrontation with new media (beginning, for instance, with the age of photography). In his essay "Le peintre de la vie moderne" (1863) Charles Baudelaire links the attributes of the transitory (*le transitoire*), the fleeting (*le fugitif*), and the contingent (*le contingent*) to his concept of *modernité*: "By modernity I mean the ephemeral, the fugitive, the contingent" ('La modernité, c'est le transitoire, le fugitif, le contingent')."[43] This statement not only identifies criteria for a definition of modernity, but simultaneously describes the art of dance: the transitory, the ephemeral is a fundamental, idiosyncratic feature of dance as an especially revealing example of the performing arts. Contingency becomes a specific criterion of free dance *after* breaking away from the aesthetic paradigm of ballet—the emphasis on chance, on improvisation and the presentation of movement imagery as spontaneous expressions of feeling. Hence, dance embodies a fundamental pattern of aesthetics in modernity and thus rises from its position at the bottom rungs of art's hierarchy to the top: dance becomes a key symbol of modernity and the central medium of all arts seeking to reflect the new technological age as an era defined by movement.[44]

As with modernity, the term *avant-garde* is used in the same context—insofar as it refers to literature, the theater, or visual arts—as in the various respective disciplines. As in the case of the term *modernity*, I seek to avoid using the term *avant-garde* in a general theoretical way that expresses the endless polarity of old versus new, but instead utilize it to differentiate historically those schools of thought that—more or less situated between 1912 and 1935—are called the historical avant-garde.

In principle, modernity in the field of dance began somewhat later than in literature, theater, and visual arts. Not until the last decade of the nineteenth

---

43. Baudelaire 1954, 892; 1964, 12.

44. The decisive role played by the media of photography and film in this context of an aesthetic of modernity, having caused a shift in the intermedial relationships of the arts, is not the dominant subject of this study; it will however often be referred to; in Parts I and II, on the role of (chrono-)photography and in Part II, the role of dance, theater, and literature in the development of film.

century, to wit: with the arrival of Loïe Fuller in Paris in 1892 a process began that signaled a radical break with the hitherto reigning paradigm of concert dance in classical ballet through its confrontation with free dance.

As yet there has been no attempt in the field of dance studies to differentiate between the development of modernity in dance and the advent of an avant-garde, which in turn behaved negatively toward modernity—analogously to the relationship of modernity and the avant-garde in theater or in literature. Such specificities are not the paramount intention of this study. In our context, it seems of greater importance to remain aware of the fact that this question has as yet not been clarified and that all pertinent outcomes of this study (as a result of the analyses contained in the second part of this study, in which a number of criteria for a definition of avant-gardism in dance are put to the test) must merely be regarded as tentative research results on the subject of "modernity"/"avant-garde" in dance.

Finally, a few thoughts concerning the problem of historical and aesthetic definitions in dance history: if we compare literature, art, theater, and dance on the basis of their characteristic attributes, it will appear that modernity and the avant-garde are almost identical in the case of dance (from a historical and aesthetic point of view)—namely when measured against the most important criteria for defining the avant-garde as mapped out by Peter Bürger:

- A radical break with the traditions of art and its institutions
- The establishment of new aesthetic paradigms
- The announcement of the new through treatises and manifestos (which are themselves also part of this new aesthetic)
- The self-reflection and self-contexualization of the respective artistic medium, as well as the conceptualization of art and its production
- An altered relationship to the recipient, who is driven to abandon conventional patterns of behavior through shock and provocation and made to become an "active" viewer

All these criteria basically already apply to the early period of free dance. The beginning of modernity in dance thus appears, with the arrival of Loïe Fuller and Isadora Duncan, to be characterized by these "avant-gardistic" features:

- A radical break with tradition; with the hitherto reigning model of concert dance in ballet
- A rejection of established institutions in theater, opera, and affiliated ballet academies, as well as the search for new performance venues
- A negation of aesthetic premises and codes of representation as dictated by the ruling form of concert dance: ballet

- The self-reflection of dance as an art form, both in dance itself (through the constitution and exploration of body imagery) and in texts and programmatic treatises: Isadora Duncan, for example, often combined dances and manifesto-like lectures on the aesthetics of free dance in her performances[45]
- The activation of the viewer, not only through scandals, which were provoked by new images of the body (nakedness) and new patterns of movement (primitivism), but also through the merging of life and art, as suggested in the relationship between popular physical culture and gymnastics movement and the body and movement aesthetics of free dance

Against the backdrop and at the crossroads of the language crisis and the excesses of discourse, the wordless art of dance appears to offer more than simply an alternative solution to issues of legitimate authorship and work in its focus on body imagery and figurations in space. In an age that fundamentally calls into question the productive efficiency of language for the investigation and reflection of the changing constellations of twentieth-century awareness, the attributes of *modernité* in dance—of *transitoire, fugitif,* and *contingent* (Baudelaire)—shift the focus of poetics away from the description of text to the exploration of the medium and the materiality of signs. In literature (in Mallarmé, Hofmannsthal, and Musil) and in dance and theater (in Loïe Fuller, Valentine de Saint-Point, and Oskar Schlemmer), the self-reflection of the medium leads to processes of semiotic negativity: not signification, but designification—the emphatic demarcation of an emptiness of signs—becomes the epitome of *poiesis.* "Destruction has been my Beatrice" ("La Destruction fut ma Béatrice"), says Mallarmé[46]; destruction becomes the epitome of inspiration, as well as creation. Not the piece itself, the work of art, but the metamorphic process in the poetic play of finding and extinguishing form enters into the

---

45. An avant-garde conceptualization of dance oriented on the model of Futurism (including manifestos and performance elements) was developed by Valentine de Saint-Point in her creation *Métachorie* (1913); see its analysis in Part II of this study. Finally, I wish to also draw attention to the numerous autobiographical publications by the founders of free dance regarding the self-reflection of dance and dance aesthetics, many of which were written in a very early phase of development: e.g., Loïe Fuller (1913); Maud Allan (1908); Adorée Villany (1912); Grete Wiesenthal (*Der Aufstieg* [*The Ascent*], 1919); Isadora Duncan (1903, and memoirs 1928b); Valeska Gert (*Mein Weg* [*My Road*], 1930).

46. Mallarmé:

Je n'ai créé mon œuvre que par *élimination*, et toute vérité ne naissant que de la perte d'une impression qui, ayant étincelé, s'était consumée et me permettait, grâce à ses ténèbres dégagées, d'avancer plus profondément dans la sensation des Ténèbres Absolues. La Destruction fut ma Béatrice." (Letter to Lefébure, May 17, 1867, in Mallarmé 1985, 148.)

focus of aesthetic production and reflection. "Transition", the transitory and transgressive, becomes the formula of an art in which the image has disappeared: in a moment of (ultimate) transgression, transition combines *dance*, the play of signs indicating movement and physical transformation, with *death*—as in Lafcadio Hearn's story "Of a Dancing Girl." In the tale of the *shirabyoshi*, text (the narrative) and dance (the evening ritual) face each other as media of memory, as culturally stabilizing *memoria*. The text visualizes that ultimate moment of transformation which manifests itself in dance, as in no other art, as something completely other, as indescribable.

In this sense, free dance embodied, for poets such as Mallarmé and Valéry, Hofmannsthal and Rilke, the idea of a sophisticated form of poetics that aimed at the eloquent elimination of all signs, the staging of absolute silence.

The most extreme manifestation of this aesthetic is the "white page," that empty page, that challenge to the never-ending process of creativity, onto which the signs of absolute textuality—"Le Livre" (Mallarmé)—inscribe themselves. Dance is a manifestation of the white page of movement. George Rodenbach wrote, in reference Mallarmé's poetics, that dance—as the epitome of pure suggestion—gives birth, in the ephemeral play of its signs, to the perfect text of a "vivid, colorful, rhythmic poem," drawn in the empty space, translated into the medium of the body, just as into the white page of the endlessly evolving text of dance: "Plastic poem of colors, rhythms, wherein the body is nothing more than a blank page, a page upon which the poem is about to be written" (*Poème de plastique, de couleurs, de rythmes, où le corps n'est pas plus qu'une page blanche, la page où le poème va s'écrire*).[47]

---

47. G. Rodenbach, "Danseuses," *Le Figaro*, May 5, 1896. Translation: Mark Franko.

PART I

Pathos Formulas

Body-Image and Danced Figuration

PATHOS FORMULAS: ON THE ICONOGRAPHY
OF THE BODY-IMAGE IN DANCE

The first part of this book brings together two issues that are symptomatic of the crisis of culture around 1900. One is the question of the subject and the doubts that arose in this period concerning its existence as a coherent unit. The other issue concerns the construction of the body-image as associated with the emergence of free dance.

As a "formula" for grasping the historical frame of mind and the aesthetics of a specific era, body imagery contributes significantly to understanding specific concepts of the subject. As a tangible artistic indicator of prevalent concepts of individuality and of the limits of the individual, the body-image is a particularly valuable tool for analyzing an age of shifting beliefs in which new media giving preference to the image, such as photography and film, were just emerging. The reading of body-images offers not only clues for deciphering and interpreting culturally dominant concepts of the self, it also contributes decisively—through its applications to discourse—to the constitution of the typical mentality surrounding individuality and subjectivity.

For the iconographic representation and analysis of images of the body— in terms of the development of free dance at the beginning of the twentieth century—I have recourse to Aby Warburg's theory of the *pathos formula*.[1]

---

1. See Gombrich 1970; see also Pochat 1983, 76–87, as well as Barta Fliedl 1992.

Warburg's theory, conceived as a psychohistorical model, can also be applied from a semiotic, as well as anthropological, point of view to the analysis of body and movement. The underlying principle behind pathos formulas—as primal expressions of human passion—is based on a theory of art that emphasizes the *dynamics* of the expressive potential contained in sculpture and painting. According to Warburg, pathos formulas are visual inscriptions of collective cultural memory—dynamograms—that still retain the imprint of cult ritual—at the origin of symbolic representation—and are constantly transformed anew in the receptive traditions of art.

In his anthropological and psychohistorically based theory, Warburg postulates that certain passionate, emphatic gestures of art, which are emotionally charged with "primal instincts," are actually symbolic expressions of an attempt to cope culturally with primal trauma by creating distance between oneself and the world, that is, by binding it to the image. However, while the symbolic act of integrating, or rather containing, the frightening chaos of overwhelming primal instincts in specific images of the body seeks to partially moderate their ominous elements, this act of sublimation simultaneously preserves the trauma and reinserts it back into the present. The imprint of the "thiasotic cult" remains symbolically inscribed—as *engrams*—in the pathos of the images of the body:

> It is in the area of mass orgiastic seizure that one should seek the imprint that stamps the expressive forms of extreme inner possession on the memory with such intensity—inasmuch as it can be expressed through gesture—that these engrams of affective experience survive in the form of a heritage preserved in the memory. They serve as models that shape the outline drawn by the artist's hand, once the extreme values of the language of gesture appear in the daylight through the formative medium of the artist's hand.[2]

Warburg's concept of the symbol corresponds to the pattern of the *engram*. According to Gombrich, "In the symbol—in the widest sense of the term—we find preserved those energies of which it is, itself, the result."[3] In his notes on the *Mnemosyne* project, Warburg wrote that pathos formulas facilitate a historical phenomenology of the energetic formation of expressive values. The actual, "esoteric" part of the *Mnemosyne* is the "*transformatio energetica* as objects of research and proper functions of a comparative historical library of symbols

2. Warburg 2009, 278.

3. Warburg, cited in Gombrich 1970, 243.

(the symbol as catalytic quintessence)."[4] In other words, pathos formulas are the storehouses of cultural memory.[5]

Warburg's *Mnemosyne* project is but one specific manifestation of a typical turn-of-the-century "antiquity project." Warburg developed his theory of the pathos formula and the corresponding idea of establishing a *Mnemosyne* atlas of gestures during the first years of the twentieth century. This is the same period in which Isadora Duncan also initiated her own influential "antiquity project" of movement art by basing her dance style on the visual patterns of ancient sculpture.[6]

Warburg established an archive in Hamburg[7] in the 1920s as an iconographic storehouse and a storehouse for a pictorial atlas of pathos formulas. His goal was to document the evolution and transformation of these pathos formulas over the course of history. Warburg collected photographs and newspaper clippings depicting the movements of athletes, pilots, dancers, actors, and warfare. He believed that advertisements and sports coverage revealed the modified movement patterns of pathos formulas and that these transformations in particular, these inversions of the meanings of gestures and movement patterns, could lead to a revitalization and thus to new informative interpretations of the body-image. For our study of movement patterns in dance, it is this aspect in particular—the interpretative framework of pathos formulas—that appears particularly promising.

In turn-of-the-century dance, theater, fine arts, and literature, body-images can be isolated and analyzed as characteristic manifestations and transformations of pathos formulas.

In the following chapters, this book will mainly focus on exactly such representations of pathos formulas in dance, as well as their interpretation and their

4. Cited in Barta Fliedl 1992, 169. Translation: Elena Polzer.

5. The subject of *memoria*, the question of preserving or erasing cultural memory, has been repeatedly addressed in literary criticism and cultural studies; see Assmann and Hölscher 1988; Lachmann 1990; Haverkamp and Lachmann 1991; Assmann and Harth 1991a, 1991b; Schmidt 1991; Haverkamp/Lachmann (eds.) 1993.

6. Warburg's student Ernst Gombrich recounts how Warburg once saw a performance by Isadora Duncan and "made ironic comments about her naked feet and her 'holy expression'" (Gombrich 1984, 146). In my opinion, this does not, however, contradict my theory about the parallel development of a theory of pathos formulas in the fine arts and its actual materialization in dance. What is instead expressed in Warburg's reaction is Warburg's ambivalence, as described by Gombrich, toward tracking down pathos formulas as images of passion and the self-distancing rationalism of a historian.

7. Warburg was forced to transfer the archive to London in 1937 under the threat of the Nazi regime. The archive is still located there today as part of the Warburg Institute at the University of London.

expository function in the translation and transformation of specific, paradigmatic patterns of culture. I will hereby differentiate between two exemplary models of body imagery and the methods used to transport them:

- On the one hand, we have the *Greek model*; pathos formulas are reactivated as genuine patterns of nature and naturalness for the movement forms of free dance through the reinterpretation of images of antiquity in dance.
- On the other hand, there is the *exotic model*, images of the body that evolved out of various encounters with foreign cultures, as well as with the Other in one's own culture. In dance (but also in literature and in the fine arts), this movement imagery is mainly associated with the exotic, erotic femme fatale pattern of femininity.

Based on typical examples of body imagery in turn-of-the-century dance, I will describe and analyze Greek images of the body as embodied pathos formulas such as the statue of *Nike*, the image of the *Primavera*, and the *dance of the maenad*.

In the case of exotic images of the body in fin de siècle dance, two patterns seem especially characteristic: the exotic-erotic image of the dancing femme fatale Salome and the, thus far less researched, equally exemplary figure of the oriental dancer dancing the "bee dance."

These examples, these representative patterns of body imagery in dance (as well as their literary manifestations), demonstrate the dual function of pathos formulas. As specific transformations, they contribute both to the construction of the subject concept and to its deconstruction.

In free dance, the images of the body—both the Greek as well as the exotic—that these kinetic models of dance were based on often appeared, on the one hand, as emphatically staged acts of liberation from cultural restraint. Free dance was extolled as an artistic remedy for the damage done by civilization. The act of reshaping the subject into a *neuer Mensch* [new human] with the help of the cultural and emancipatory effects of *freier Tanz* [free dance] paralleled contemporaneous theories and practices of deconstructing, or even destroying/destructuring, elements that had previously been considered fundamental to notions of individuality and self-presentation. One such movement was the elimination of certain "supporting devices," which defined the appearance of the body during the late nineteenth century. These devices particularly applied to patterns of femininity, such as the corset, whose role in stylizing the body can only be properly acknowledged if we look at the pros and cons of contemporary aesthetic and hygienic discourse on dress reform and dance reform. This discourse clearly demonstrates that developments in dance costume and the emergence of a new freedom of movement for women were symbolically interrelated at the turn of the century—not only in dance.

On the other hand, representations of the individual in dance also reflected a perceived disintegration of the coherent subject—as discussed on various levels in the fields of medicine, psychiatry, and psychoanalysis, as well as in philosophy and literature. Whirling dances, fire dances, and other moments of ecstatic frenzy examined and reflected images of depersonalization and the attempt to abolish inner restraints *through* movement itself.

In terms of the constitution and representation of images of the body in dance, the concept of the subject is closely related to the concept of nature. What is defined as natural is subject to similarly construed concepts of the body and of space. Notions of body-nature and natural movement, which emerged in connection to the historical turn-of-the-century youth and reform movements, were linked to the development of Greek or exotic images of the body in free dance: these were modeled on both occidental-Christian traditions and foreign cultures. The idea of nature can therefore only be read and understood if we disentangle it from already symbolically formed patterns of body and movement. J. J. Winckelmann once wrote of Greek sculpture that its mere presence reawakens the viewer's ability to perceive nature. Likewise, the rediscovery of nature by young, modern, turn-of-the-century artists was a return to the archives of art and cultural history. Inspiration—in literature, as well as in dance (in both cases semiotic systems in crisis)—seemed characterized by enthusiastic reception, whose aura brought to life antiquity's imprint of pictorial history in the form of pathos formulas.[8]

In Aby Warburg's words, this enthusiasm for nature proved to be an "expedition to the wellsprings of European enthusiasm."[9]

8. See the chapter on Hofmannsthal's "Moments in Greece."

9. Gombrich 1984, 146. Translation: Elena Polzer.

Chapter 1

Dance in the Museum

Body and Memory

THE BREAK WITH TRADITION AND THE COLLAPSE OF MEMORY: THE CULTURAL CRISIS AROUND 1900. HOFMANNSTHAL'S *LORD CHANDOS LETTER*, READ WITH BOTHO STRAUß

As a way of pointing to the text-based manifestations of the "crisis of culture circa 1900,"[1] the phrase *language crisis* is still largely relevant for critical literary discourse today. In broader terms, this phrase also describes the upheavals that various cultural systems of signs and meaning underwent in the twentieth century, as well as the problems these upheavals provoked.

In Friedrich Nietzsche's critical diagnoses of culture, especially in his "Richard Wagner in Bayreuth," the fourth of his *Untimely Meditations,* and in *On Truth and Lies in a Nonmoral Sense*, the problem of the validity of language as truth emerges, a problem linked in turn to the self-understanding of the subject. In literature, the question of language henceforth became a central theme of self-reflection. Writers proclaimed a state of emergency of "civilization": "Everywhere language is sick, and the oppression of this tremendous sickness weighs on the whole of human development."[2]

When language is pressed into service by the forces of the rationalization of human intercourse in "civilization," language itself becomes unfit for the communication of feelings. Language has

become a power in its own right, which now embraces mankind with ghostly arms and impels it to where it does not really want to go. As

---

1. Sasse 1977; Koch 1989, 131ff.

2. Nietzsche 1997, 214 (further citations with page numbers in the text).

soon as men seek to come to an understanding with one another, and to unite for a common work, they are seized by the madness of universal concepts, indeed even by the mere sounds of words, and, as a consequence of this incapacity to communicate, everything they do together bears the mark of this lack of mutual understanding, inasmuch as it does not correspond to their real needs, but only to the hollowness of those tyrannical worlds and concepts: thus to all its other sufferings mankind adds suffering from convention, that is to say from a mutual agreement as to words and actions without a mutual agreement as to feelings. (215)

Hugo von Hofmannsthal's writings reflect this same problem of language and identity. Text culture, the terrible nightmare of the written word, results in indifferent perception and communication. The "accumulation of books on the reading desk," which Hofmannsthal describes in *Der Tisch mit den Büchern* (*The Table with the Books*, 1905), the immeasurable production of printed materials, drives the individual into a world of alienation. Books are no longer the mediators of culture, no longer the medium for interpreting reality, but signify instead the isolation of the subject. The inflationary nature of circulating texts allows the medium itself to replace reality:

That most unreal of all realms, most uncanny of all phantasmata, the so-called real world is crammed with them. Our existence is encrusted with books.[3]

The result is an entropic growth of information, a state of chaos. The circulation of incessantly self-duplicating texts causes a contagious flattening of all distinctions in "a system of madly whirling atoms of thoughts, seemingly interconnected in innumerable rotating funnels, while in truth incoherent" (339).

Similar formations of signs, such as the maelstroms of atomized thought described here by Hofmannsthal, are referred to by Botho Strauß at the end of the twentieth century—against the backdrop of chaos theory—as "patches" and "fog": as figurations of dissolution. I will return to the writings of Botho Strauß later.

Let us remain for now with Hofmannsthal. At the beginning of the twentieth century, Hofmannsthal's *Lord Chandos Letter* depicts dispersion as a

---

3. Hofmannsthal 1979, 337. (Page numbers will be cited hereafter in the text.) Translation: Elena Polzer.

phenomenon associated with how the self and the world are experienced. The language crisis of the subject is a result of the subject detaching himself or herself from the history of European civilization. Young Lord Chandos's incapacity to "speak or think coherently about anything" is evidently a failure to come to terms with the sight of the overflowing table of books in the archive of history. His plan—to write an "encyclopedic book" as a compendium of the history of civilization since antiquity, entitled *Nosce te ipsum*—proves to be impossible to carry out. His confrontation with the universe of language results not in self-awareness, as in a self-confirmation of the subject, but in a dissociation of the ego in a crisis of consciousness and language.

Hugo von Hofmannsthal's *Lord Chandos Letter* and his semiotic writings and cultural critiques written in 1907—*Die Briefe des Zurückgekehrten* (*Letters of a Returnee*), *Furcht* (*Fear*), *Die Wege und die Begegungen* (*The Paths and the Encounters*), *Der Tisch mit den Büchern* (*The Table with the Books*), *Der Dichter und seine Zeit* (*The Poet and His Time*)—are prime examples of early twentieth-century crisis literature. These texts, each stressing somewhat different aspects of the discourse, articulate the crisis of perception and knowledge by describing the decomposition of patterns of perception and interpretation as primary symptoms of disorder. The so-called crisis of language reveals itself in this light as above all a crisis of perception.[4] As summed up in a legendary statement by Lord Chandos, the collapse of thought and representation is a result of a disintegration of those forms, which are no longer recognizable as forming a whole, as being "coherent": the abstract terms of which the tongue must avail itself as a matter of course in order to voice a judgment—these terms crumbled in my mouth like moldy fungi."[5]

---

4. For the sake of terminological clarity, the term *perception* primarily applies in this study to the cognitive sensory process (*Wahrnehmung*); especially regarding those transformations of perception associated with the development of new technology and media (in particular: photography, film, and, later, electronic media). It also serves as a starting point for an analysis of the transformation and the crisis of perception around the turn of the century. In the sense that it always draws on existing concepts of meaning, *perception* cannot be distinguished from the creation of meaning: perception and production are therefore—whether in the field of language or in the field of dance (and body) imagery—caught up in a dynamic relationship. In the following chapters, e.g., in the chapters on "Dance of the Statues" (Part I) and on "Interruption" (Part II, chapter 5), my line of inquiry will focus primarily on this, especially when placing the art of modernity in perspective. On Husserl's interpretation of the intentionality of perception and its poetological consequences for literary modernity see Kleinschmidt 1992, 162ff.

5. Hofmannsthal, 1986.

Chandos continues with an eloquent portrayal of the dissociative experience, of the dissemination of meaning and of the dissolution of structure in the "maelstrom" of chaos:

> For me everything disintegrated into parts, those parts again into parts; no longer would anything let itself be encompassed by one idea. Single words floated round me; they congealed into eyes which stared at me and into which I was forced to stare back—whirlpools which gave me vertigo and, reeling incessantly, led into the void.[6]

In his book *Beginnlosigkeit: Reflexionen über Fleck und Linie* (*Beginninglessness: Reflections on Patch and Line*),[7] Botho Strauß reflects on the phenomenon of decomposition as a symptom of the crisis of modernity around 1900: the same phenomenon that modern literature described and analyzed historically as the disintegration of the subject,[8] or rather a manifestation of the dissolution of processes of perception from the perspective of postmodernism. In the age of electronic media, according to Botho Strauß, dissolution[9] no longer suggests the fin de siècle connotations of enfeeblement, cultural fatigue, and decadence. On the contrary, although the term *high resolution*—the capacity for precise differentiation—contains echoes of decomposition, it also now implies the ability to focus one's perception, "the minute density of the rendering that a technical image medium is capable of, the capacity of a (optical) device to distinguish and reproduce very fine details (117).

High resolution (*Auflösung*), as a phenomenon of dispersion, is the result of a new perspective of attention: a transformation of the gaze conducted by electronic media.

Strauß's late twentieth-century reading of Hofmannsthal's *Lord Chandos Letter* foregrounds the problematic of a "high-resolution consciousness" whose ultra-precise capacity for detail necessitates the "development of new fields of knowledge":

> That painful thrust of awareness, which Hofmannsthal's Lord Chandos endured at the beginning of the twentieth century, as words and things

---

6. Ibid.

7. Strauß 1992 (page numbers in the text). All citations are translation: Elena Polzer.

8. See Brinkmann 1961; Mauser 1961; Saße 1977.

9. *Translator's note*: Botho Strauß uses the German word *Auflösung*, which conveys the dual meaning of *dissolution* and disintegration/dispersal, as well as *resolution* in the sense of "high-resolution images."

fell to pieces in his hands and then again into even smaller pieces, proves in the end to be a parable of exuberant, of complex comprehension. It was not decay, but *dissipation*, not dissolution, but a shift in energy, which contributed to the development of new fields of knowledge. The path to the particles was the indispensable premise for experiencing the whole in more detail. (117)

Strauß's return to Hofmannsthal is more than mere aphoristic reference to a new "Arcades" project" à la Benjamin: the entire text is, in fact, a contrafactum of the *Lord Chandos Letter* and Hofmannsthal's epistemological *Erfundene Gespräche und Briefe (Fictional Conversations and Letters)* from around 1907.[10] The crisis of consciousness provoked by the scientific realization that the beginning of creation can be neither calculated nor proven forms the heart of Strauß's thoughts, which attempt to trace the lines of a cybernetic loop of simulated "beginninglessness" both as stylistic device and mental image. The consequent crisis-ridden central question around which revolves his *Reflexionen über Fleck und Linie (Reflections on Patch and Line)* is this:

How can humankind . . . with the knowledge of absolute beginninglessness . . . a beginninglessness of creation . . . of consciousness . . . of everything and everyone—how can humankind experience itself and the world, and what consequences does this inevitably have for everyone and everything? (8)

Yet it is precisely this knowledge of the "steady state" condition of the "moving ever present" posited by astrophysics that implies the very possibility of beginning. The historical pattern referred to here is the crisis experienced by early modernity around the year 1900—the Chandos model of dissipation, in which a new beginning is born as a form of *autopoiesis*. The subject reforms itself out of the ruins of collapsed memory, after it has lost its connection to tradition. Strauß goes on to examine the relationship between "epistemological collapse" and artistic creation, between the "world in pieces" and the beginning of a "creative act" (13). Here postmodern aestheticism suddenly seems ominously analogous to that fin de siècle aestheticism which in the long run became transformed into a semiotic crisis of modernity. Strauß describes postmodernism's obsession with detail as a reaction to the threat expressed by the chaos of endless clouds, fogs, permanent fluctuation. The result is a new form of

---

10. In Strauß's *Beginninglessness*, various intertextual passages refer to the following works by Hofmannsthal: *Ein Brief (A Letter)*, *Die Wege und die Begegungen (The Paths and the Encounters)*, and *Die Briefe des Zurückgekehrten (Letters of a Returnee)*.

aestheticism: structures emerging out of vast "nonintegrable" systems, anarchic turbulences, which, although not mathematical, nevertheless take the form of graphic figures and images. These formations of similar masses emerging from chaos have an aesthetic dimension. "Humankind wants to see fractal structures: what does a tree really look like? This could lead to new aesthetic bigotry, now on a Mandelbrot basis" (68).

However, this close-up of the "ornamentation of nature," the act of losing oneself in the "restless beauty of the fractal formations on the monitor in an endless game of self-similarity," (68) involves a form of revulsion that sparks a Chandos-like crisis of postmodern consciousness:

> First he didn't want to touch anything anymore, then he couldn't name anything anymore. He had fled from the things to the words, then from the designations to the correlations formed by the words among themselves. That which was to him comprehensible was what the words had put together among themselves and pointed out to him. People, actions, and objects lost their clear-cut contours; he saw nothing but patches and jumps, and instead of a shape or a distinct character set in a temporal or biographical continuity, he detected movement patterns of aimless, erratic changes both in his surroundings and in his inner concepts. His ability to comprehend a steady sequence was destroyed. But was it truly destruction? Was it not in fact the emergence of a different, suppressed sensitivity that forbade all explanations, summarizations, conclusions and that upgraded him to a state of incessant expectation (*Gewärtigen*)? (128)

The experience of decomposition results in a new definition of aesthetic perception and artistic beginnings: the loss of the ability to "comprehend a steady sequence"—the lost capacity to "think coherently" as experienced by Hofmannsthal's Lord Chandos and radicalized by chaos theory—leads, if productively interpreted, to a keener awareness of discontinuity, a sensitivity to the "scattered in every thing and action" (129). The inability to perceive form and select information consequently yields new patterns of production—"the emergence of a different, suppressed sense." The concept of expectation (*Gewärtigen*)—which Strauß balances in the limbo between presence (*Gegenwärtigkeit*) and readiness for the unexpected (*Gefaßtheit auf das Unerwartete*)—calls attention to the relationship of the subject to time and space as illustrated in the recursive visual structures of "line and patch" (the subtitle of Strauß's reflections). Sequence and succession are characteristic aspects of the "line." Simultaneity, collapse, and the vortex are temporal patterns of "patchiness." These two contrary aspects of the space-time experience exist in a relation of uncertainty to the observer's perspective. They overwhelm the observer's capacity to differentiate. However, they also challenge cognition's sense of order and, even more so, the poetic sense of a production of form. Mankind thus appears as a "compulsive producer of world images." "Creation and production, poetry and poiesis, as the continuation and criterion of cognitive operations," belong "to human nature like flight to birds" (12).

The ability to conceive of a beginning as well as an end amid the crisis of consciousness, in spite of the stigma of "beginninglessness," involves, for Botho Strauß, the affirmation of myth. Writing, the beginning of a production of text, thus means the expression of a desire for form in the face of chaotic diffusion. The "flights of fancy"—a state of consciousness repeatedly evoked by Strauß as a mirror image of the foggy patches of "high resolution" matter—accumulate into integral figurations of poetic beginnings. Writing thus means, as in the case of Hofmannsthal, the pictorial synchronization of recursive sequences of signs; the reassignment of chaotic movement patterns, of vortexes of fog and patches to linguistic figurations; the superimposition of "fractal ideography" (119) and lineaments of nature. Literature creates characters and molds images, topoi, and bodies, by revoking the "dying beginning" (36), with a yearning for an interaction of endings and beginnings, of destruction and creation, a desire to "collapse in a spot accompanied by the sizzlings of a beginning" (36).

Strauß's final allusions to Hofmannsthal's *Die Wege und die Begegnungen* (*The Paths and the Encounters*)—the image of a swallow in flight, scenes of beauty in nature—reveal clearly that the poetics of beginning and the crisis of consciousness are linked to aspects of remembering and forgetting posed as problems in Freud's *Civilization and Its Discontents*: "In order to acquire new knowledge, the human spirit must forget that it once knew the same in other symbols" (28).

For both authors, the dialectic of remembering and forgetting symbolizes a decisive moment in aesthetic production. Art appears as a phenomenon of emergence. It "steps into the world utterly unexpected" (Botho Strauß). Yet the "shadow of the chance to express oneself in a completely different way"[11] displaces the universe of written culture. Hofmannsthal's idea of developing a different form of communicating through signs in a "medium more immediate, more liquid, more glowing than words"[12] is not articulated as the negation of language and writing, but as the emergence of a different formative

11. Hofmannsthal 1979, A I, 339. Translation: Elena Polzer.

12. Hofsmannsthal 1986.

medium: images, created by corporeal signs, by the "beats of the blood" (339), based on the experience of physical movement:

> It, too, forms whirlpools, but of a sort that do not seem to lead, as the whirlpools of language, into the abyss, but into myself.[13]

Out of these chaotic whirlpools an as yet unknown language material takes form—not unlike thermodynamic turbulence, they are images and forms of a new poetic order. The structures of these figures suggest modes of interpretation; the pictograms of self-similar shapes appear, on the one hand, as pictorial landscapes, as topos formulas linked to the representation of spatial structures. On the other hand, they also take the form of body imagery, as pathos formulas, which can be read as the iconographic patterns of (affect) movements.

Between order and chaos, between structure and "turbulence," between remembering and forgetting, there arises a realm untouched by text culture in which the play of corporeal signs in motion—as dance—can take place. This is a way out, a detour away from the semiotic crisis of literature into a medium that seems to permit a different model of creativity[14]—a poetics of the corporeal, of gesture, of pantomime, of dance, which is characteristic of Hofmannsthal since the *Lord Chandos Letter*. It is a poetics that accomplishes the shift away from the textual archive of literary history to the pictorial inventory of pathos formulas via the medium of dance.

THE DANCER IN THE MUSEUM: THE BIRTH OF MODERN DANCE FROM THE ARCHIVES OF CLASSICAL ANTIQUITY

The break with nineteenth-century traditions took place in dance otherwise than in literature. In fin de siècle literature, the term *décadence*,[15] as Bourget and Nietzsche defined it, took on a glittering array of meanings interwoven with symbolist aestheticism. Hofmannsthal famously diagnosed it as follows:

---

13. Ibid.

14. See Brandstetter 1991b.

15. See Fischer 1978, 41ff. (especially for a differentiated comparison of the influences of Nietzsche's concept of decadence and of Bourget—via Hermann Bahr—as in the case of Heinrich and Thomas Mann—on literature); see also Koppen 1973; Borchmeyer 1989. For a summary of research on this topic, see also Bauer 1991.

We have nothing but sentimental memory, a crippled will and the uncanny gift of self-duplication. We watch ourselves live our lives; we empty the cup before its time and yet remain endlessly thirsty . . . we have virtually no roots in life and wander, as clear-sighted and yet day-blind shadows, among the children of life . . . To study the anatomy of one's own soul or simply dream. Reflection or fantasy, mirror image or visions in a dream. Old furniture and young nerves are modern. Modernity is to psychologically hear the grass growing and dabble in the purely fantastic world of wonders.[16]

The word itself was diagnosed as "sovereign": it sprang "forth from totality" (Nietzsche). A rift had opened up in culture, a gaping gulf between art and life: "There is no direct path from poetry to life, none from life to poetry" (Hofmannsthal).[17] "Words are everything"—this verdict formulates doubts that arose for the first time in literature concerning the power of language, from which also arose attempts to cope with the problem that literature is always a rewriting and, hence, nothing more than the product of other literature—in short, an endless proliferation of semiotic references and textual dialogue, a self-referential web disconnected from life. The silence of Lord Chandos—literary speech struck dumb—and, then, the "nameless dance"—the corporeal event of an alternative creativity[18] appear—against the backdrop of the crisis of literary discourse—to be mutually interrelated attempts to resolve the semiotic problem or to shift the problem onto another terrain: that of the medium of dance.

Around 1900, the term *decadence* was much more clearly defined in dance than in literature and, although rarely used, exclusively referred to a specific period of decline in classical ballet. Recent historiography still describes the artistic stagnation, the decay of dance culture, that took place at the Paris Opera during the last two decades of the nineteenth century as "La Décadence."[19] In the 1920s, prominent representatives of free dance and *Ausdruckstanz* (expressionistic dance), from Isadora Duncan to Hans Brandenburg, Max von Boehn, Frank Thieß, John Schikowski, and others, used the words *decadence* and *degeneration* often in their programmatic writings on dance when referring to the system and the stage presence of ballet.

16. Hofmannsthal, "Gabriele D'Annunzio," in 1978, A I, 175ff. Translation: Elena Polzer.

17. Hofmannsthal 1978, A I, 13–19. Translation: Elena Polzer.

18. See Brandstetter 1991b.

19. Guest 1976, 127ff.

In *The Dance of the Future* (1903), Isadora Duncan attacks the "unnatural quality" of the "distorted muscles" and the "body deformed" by ballet training, the "sterility" and the "degeneration" of ballet, as well as its incapacity for innovation and the "illusionism" of ballet's attempts to defy gravity:

> The school of the ballet of to-day vainly striving against the natural laws of gravitation or the natural will of the individual, and working in discord in its form and movement with the form and movement of nature, produces a sterile movement which gives no birth to future movements but dies as it is made. The expression of the modern school of ballet wherein each action is an end, and no movement, pose, or rhythm is successive or can be made to evolve succeeding action, is an expression of degeneration, of living death.[20]

When the paradigm shifted from ballet to free dance, it also involved a transition from a system of dance (the *danse d'école*) to a habitus—the habitus of the individual, which dance reform around 1900 typically associated with "natural" and "free" movement. "The dance of two people should never fully be the same," declared Isadora Duncan, and she based her interpretation of dance as the primary expression of individuality on the following—in this context somewhat far-fetched—reading of Schopenhauer's *The World as Will and Representation*: "The dance should simply be the natural gravitation of this will of the individual, which is in the end no more nor less than a human translation of the gravitation of the universe."[21]

At the turn of the century, a time when philosophy, psychology, and literature began seriously questioning the concept of the individual,[22] dance rediscovered individuality as an insignia of authenticity and of the liberating possibilities of the medium. In literature, the findings of Ernst Mach caused Goethe's phrase "individuum est ineffabile" to be replaced by the formula "The ego is irretrievable" (Hermann Bahr), while dance celebrated the individual as a medium capable of expressing the "movements of the cosmos," as a medium whose "individual body" (Isadora Duncan) reflected the harmony of greater nature.

More than two hundred years after the first *Querelle des anciens et des modernes* in seventeenth-century aesthetics, the second *Querelle des anciens et des modernes* at the turn of the century manifested itself in dance in an utterly different way than in literature, the fine arts, or music.

20. Duncan 1903, 13f.

21. Duncan 1903, 13.

22. See Bahr 1981, 147ff.

While modernist writers experienced the break with the tradition of bourgeois learning (*Bildungskultur*)[23] as a liberating step—as an avant-garde moment reminiscent of Hofmannsthal's act of erasing the cultural *memoria* from antiquity's hall of paintings—the modern dancer explored the museum as a storehouse of images. Dance's pursuit of the new at the turn of the century is inconceivable without the visual archives of occidental (as well as oriental) culture. Isadora Duncan and Maud Allen, Ruth St. Denis and Alexander Sakharoff, Mata Hari and Vaslav Nijinsky gathered their ideas for new dance concepts in the galleries of the Louvre and the museums of London and Berlin by gazing at the artworks of antiquity, at ancient Egyptian and Indian art, at Italian Renaissance painting and its successors, the Pre-Raphaelites.

By referring back to the great works of art history and transforming their pathos formulas into movement, these artists introduced a new dimension to early twentieth-century dance, a dimension that had until then been more or less aesthetically irrelevant: the realm of historicism as an active, interpretative act of referencing art history on the one hand and as a reflective recourse to the traditions of dance history on the other. One could even say that dance only truly became a modern art form because of these developments.

The dancer in the museum of art history—this basic formula for understanding the conceptual development of an aesthetics of body-image in dance is related to three distinct, but nonetheless related issues concerning the productive appropriation of historical models:

1. The interpretation of antiquity
2. The influence of Asian art, and
3. Theater's position as a model, that is, the communication of the pathos formula via fine arts and via theater: the actor's rhetorical storehouse of gestures

We should not underestimate the meaning of the "Greek phantasmata"[24] for the development of the body-image in modern dance. Even just a quick

23. On the constitution of self and traditional bourgeois education around 1900 under the influence of antiquity, see Wunberg 1989.

24. The reception of antiquity, the stylization of body imagery on the basis of Greek sculpture, the concept of nature and authenticity associated with Hellenism, bear the mark of a cultural phantasma, characteristic of fin de siècle mentality. As symptomatic for the appropriation and the patterns of redefining antiquity, we can draw on the arguments of historian Gustav Droysen, who emphasized that a true understanding of Greek art can only be gained from a study of mythology (e.g., the *Oresteia* by Aeschylus) and not of history. The art of antiquity must take effect through "emotional appreciation" and not critical historical interpretation—an approach to the function of myth that is itself closely linked to Richard Wagner's concept of myth. Contrary to the eighteenth-century "Greek phantasmata"

glance at the numerous contemporaneous historical, anthropological, ethno-logical, and psychohistorical publications on dance and on the way movement was depicted in the artworks of antiquity is highly revealing. Right at the turn of the century, the French journal *Le Théâtre* published a large article in the December 12, 1899, edition entitled "Théâtre Antique—Gestes Modernes. La Grèce,"[25] which elaborately compared Greek vase painting and sculpture with various modern, neoclassical theater, opera, and dance performances.

In addition to major studies such as Erwin Rohde's *Psyche* and Walter Pater's *Greek Studies*, approximately two dozen books were published at the turn of the century on this subject alone.[26]

In addition, a spate of articles in various journals widely popularized the ideal of the Greek statue as a prototype of the "naturally" beautiful body: not just in the form of artistic theory, but also as a hygienic practice. The "Greek phantasmata" played a key role in programs aimed at reforming the body of the modern woman, that is, at freeing her from the corset. The first volume of Kurt Vanselow's magazine *Die Schönheit (Beauty)* contains no less than twelve essays on the eponymous topic—whereby in almost all the articles beauty, that is, the *cult* of the body "then and now," is declared to be a legacy of the ancient ideal of *kalokagathia*, the quintessence of a "new" culture of femininity (figure 1), as also propagated similarly by Isadora Duncan. "Dance as humanity's language of beauty" (Marie-Luise Becker)[27] is seen as an aesthetic cure for a society that has "fallen ill" through the alienating effects of civilization. The path to health leads into the museum, into the halls of classical antiquity: "But only two cultures have since then consciously and artistically cultivated dance. First, the Greeks. And how they cultivated it! Our maenad in the Berlin museum: see how she dances!"[28]

---

of J. J. Winckelmann and Weimar classicism, the emphasis here mainly lies—apart from the entirely different historical situation—on the archaic, "Dionysian" side of antiquity; see also the following section on "Dance of the Maenad."

25. *Le Théâtre* 24 (December 1899): 9–18.

26. These include Maurice Emmanuel, *The Antique Greek Dance after sculptured and painted figures* (1895, English trans. 1916), H. Flach, *Der Tanz bei den Griechen (Dance of the Greeks)* (1880), Ruby Ginner, *The Revived Greek Dance, Its Art and Technique* (1936), Valentine Gross, *Mouvements de Danse de L'Antiquité à nos jours* (1914), Louis Séchan, *La Danse Grecque Antique* (1930), Carl Sittl, *Die Gebärden der Griechen and Römer (The Gestures of the Greeks and Romans)* (1890), Ethel L. Uriel, *Dancing Ancient and Modern* (1911), and Fritz Weege, *Der Tanz in der Antike (Dance in Antiquity)* (1926).

27. M.-L. Becker, "Tanz," in *Die Schönheit (Beauty)*, 1. Edition, 1903, 277–90: "Who can dance? Perhaps the prima ballerina at the opera? My god, spare me the sight! Or the hot, lumbering people in the steamy dance halls? Or the anemic fashion doll with the laced-up waist? Anyone can dance, who dances for the sake of dance itself and beauty. For dance is beauty come alive" (277). Translation: Elena Polzer.

28. Ibid., 279.

Figure 1 Olga Desmond in a three-
dimensional study *à la grecque* (1908).
SOURCE: Derra de Moroda Dance
Archives, Salzburg, Austria / © Derra de
Moroda Dance archives, University of
Salzburg, Austria.

The second culture referred to here is that of Isadora Duncan and turn-of-
the-century dance reform.

Dance of Antiquity and Modernity: Maurice Emmanuel

I would like to begin my study of "the dancer in the museum" with a key work of
theory on the reception of antiquity in dance: Maurice Emmanuel's comprehensive study *The Antique Greek Dance after Sculpted and Painted Figures*, which was
first published in French in 1895.[29] The book is a systematic catalog and analysis of
visual documents of Greek antiquity based on their depiction of dance and dance
gestures.

29. Maurice Emmanuel's book was translated into English by Harriet Jean Beauley in
1916 and is now available online in the public domain.

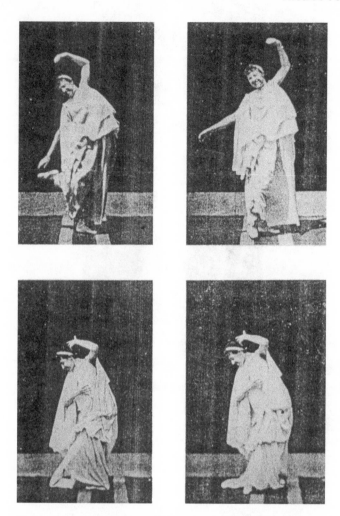

Figure 2 Sequence of images from M. Emmanuel, *La Danse
Grecque antique* (1895): chronophotographic shots of dance poses.
SOURCE: Derra de Moroda Dance Archives, Salzburg, Austria / © Derra
de Moroda Dance archives, University of Salzburg, Austria.

Emmanuel's documentation is in two ways a prime example of the second
Querelle des anciens et des modernes at the turn of the century. On the one
hand, Emmanuel employed the technical movement vocabulary of ballet[30] to
decode Greek vase paintings, bas-reliefs, and sculptures, their "*monuments
figurés*" (figural monuments). In other words, he based his study on a dance
paradigm, which was at that time already clearly in a period of decadence and

30. This technique of decoding Greek dance by comparing it to ballet was used again in 1965
in a study by Germaine Prudhommeau (inspired by the work of Maurice Emmanuel).

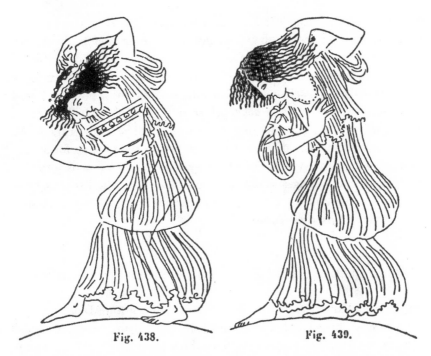

Figure 3 Sequence of images from M. Emmanuel, *La Danse Grecque antique* (1895): drawings in the fashion of images on Greek vases.
SOURCE: Derra de Moroda Dance Archives, Salzburg, Austria / © Derra de Moroda Dance archives, University of Salzburg, Austria.

decline and whose reform was being initiated on the basis of that very same recourse to antiquity.

On the other hand, Emmanuel's choice of media for reproducing and comparing these ancient images in his book—and herein lies the truly modern aspect of this publication—directly links the themes and motives of ancient dance to contemporaneous turn-of-the-century interpretations. In addition to graphic reproductions of Greek works of art, the book features multiple series of photographic reproductions, produced with help of a new technique invented by J. E. Marey.

Chronophotography[31] (see figures 2 and 3) is a form of movement photography, which uses a camera built along the same lines as a revolver, to photographically record split-second segments of movement in succession. Emmanuel's book includes multiple series of photos shot in this manner to depict the specific dance elements, poses, or steps described in the text—not unlike film stills. However, the ancient Greek movement patterns and gestures represented here by chronophotography are not compared to the *pas* or

31. See also my remarks on the effect of technology and new concepts of movements on avant-garde theater and dance in the chapter "Interruption" in Part II.

entrechats of ballet. Instead, the Greek dance images are portrayed in the photographs by a dancer dressed in an archaic, flowing tunic; that is, the images are translated into fin de siècle visual imagery. The theoretical derivative of antique dance cited here, the *modern*, is not ballet, but rather free dance—a dance form that based itself on models of antiquity and whose poses and steps were far removed from the *en dehors* (turn out) principle of ballet. This is all the more astonishing considering that it would still be many years before free dance found a wider audience thanks to Isadora Duncan's performances in London, Paris, and Berlin. Emmanuel systematizes the pathos formulas of Greek movement images into a language conveyed by bodily configurations: "Cette orchestique . . . est presque toujours un langage" [These orchestral movements are almost always a language].[32]

The Vitalist Interpretation of Greek Sculpture: Genevieve Stebbins

In an interview, American dancer Ruth St. Denis (born Ruth Dennis, 1879–1968) recalls visiting a Delsarte matinee[33] in 1892 at the Madison Square Theater in New York. Genevieve Stebbins, the leading American representative of the Delsarte system at the time, author of a well-known book about Delsarte[34] and director of the New York School of Expression, appeared on stage in the movement study *The Dance of the Day*. Her pose at the beginning of the piece—a sideways lying position, dressed in a Greek tunic—was based on the iconography of Olympia (by Titian) or of the Sleeping Venus: "Stebbins was sleeping à la Greek statuary at the back of the Stage. She unfolded from sleep—rose—got to noon—began to wilt at the setting sun until she slept in the opposite direction."[35]

For Ruth St. Denis, this simple movement sequence, and even more so Stebbins's intense and majestic presence, was an epiphany. It was the first time in the life of the budding dancer, in which the Delsarte exercises, which she had studied under the tutelage of her mother, gained artistic verisimilitude. Suddenly, the movement school's arduous exercise seemed to transform itself into art.

Stebbins's main contribution to the development of modern dance—her emphasis on the dynamics of dance movement—is still underestimated even

---

32. Emmanuel 1895 (1987), 82.

33. On the movement system of François Delsarte, see Shawn 1954; on its notation system Jeschke 1983; a good summary can be found in Casini Ropa 1988, 107–22.

34. See Stebbins 1885.

35. See the interview with Ruth St. Denis by Walter Terry, quoted in Shelton 1981, 14.

today. She was the first to no longer predominantly regard dance from the per-spective of dance technique, muscular training, or the systematic development of articulation, emphasizing instead its energetic principles. Stebbins's elabo-ration of the Delsarte system heralded a paradigm shift in twentieth-century modern dance in an attempt to redefine dance movement on the basis of a vitalist understanding of dynamics.

This dynamic movement model mainly focused on breath and situated the center of vitality in the diaphragm. All movements emanated from the region of the solar plexus and the breathing rhythm determined the temporal and dynamic patterns. Dance movement reflected the variations of rise and fall, expansion and contraction, tension and release. The flow of vital energy dic-tated the tonus of the muscles, as well as the tonus of the movement units contained in a single dance sequence, in harmony with the pulse of rhythmic breathing—contrary to the system of classical ballet, in which the principles of lightness demand a sustained degree of tension in the muscular apparatus.

In her book *Dynamic Breathing and Harmonic Gymnastics*, published in 1893, Stebbins developed an eclectic theory of vitalism on the basis of sources specially compiled for her interpretation of the Delsarte system. She consulted various ideological, religious, anthropological, and occult theories—studies on yoga and Buddhism, theosophy, Swedish gymnastics, oriental dance, as well as Delsarte's esoteric system of expression—in order to consolidate her concept of the driving power source of life as a model and translation of dance kine-matics. Her theories and line of reasoning resemble Henri Bergson's *élan vital*. His theory about the vital impetus[36] of organisms was itself based on Spencer's evolutionism[37] and Ernst Haeckel's monism.[38] Havelock Ellis later published a book entitled *The Dance of Life* that revived and popularized many of these same ideas—especially after its publication in German in 1928.[39]

36. Bergson 1912, 93.

37. M.-L. Becker, "Tanz," in *Die Schönheit* (*Beauty*), 1. Edition, 1903, 366ff.; on the subject of *vitalism*, especially on the eclecticism of natural philosophy in connection with the "func-tion of legitimating and concealing," which *Nature* was required to fulfill, see Gebhard 1984, 572ff.

38. Ernst Haeckel mainly played the role of a mentor and teacher in Isadora Duncan's evo-lutionist concepts; in her memoirs she recalls her personal encounter with the scientist-phi-losopher's impressive persona (Duncan 1927, 153ff.); Isadora reads his writings, and Haeckel in turn calls her dance "an expression of monism" (153ff). In *The Dance of the Future* (1903, 11) Duncan begins with the sentence: "I refer you to my most revered teachers Mr. Charles Darwin and Mr. Ernst Haeckel."

39. The German translation of *The Dance of Life* by the "great English sexologist Havelock Ellis" (originally Boston, 1923) is advertised in 1928 by his German publisher Felix Meiner: "Here, dance is a symbol of life and the world. It is the most primitive expression both of religion

Like these theorists and vitalists, Stebbins presumed a spiral of evolution and based her concept of dance on this three-dimensional movement pattern of vital dynamism:

There is no such thing as a straight line in the nascent life of nature . . . so the spiral motion is the type of life.[40]

Genevieve Stebbins was the first to clearly define this vitalistic model in her system of teaching. The same model would later go on to become an important discursive backdrop, argumentative-apologetic basis, and ideological-theoretical agenda for the development of the body-image in free dance and expressionistic dance. Its effects on the field of dance and on theater reform[41] in the early twentieth century were manifold and extensive. Isadora Duncan's idea of a dance of the future, Ruth St. Denis's spiritually accentuated concept of dance, the various schools of rhythmic gymnastics (Emile Jaques-Dalcroze, but also Rudolf Bode), and Rudolf von Laban's dominant theories on expressionistic dance were all based on a vitalistic belief in movement as a danced expression of the dynamics of life.

Individual elements of this theory also appeared in theories about acting propagated by theater reformers such as Copeau, Dullin, Meyerhold, Felix Emmel, and Artaud. Some of the most important aspects of these new movement concepts were these:

- The way movement is set in motion and accordingly a focus on the center of balance and its placement (equilibrium) with an emphasis on the significance of the breathing rhythm and the importance of the respiratory center as the center of the body, from which movement originates.
- The issue of dynamics, that is, the interaction of tension and release, swing and energy flow.
- And finally the relationship between body and space. "Harmonious" movement in "natural" corporeal and spatial patterns—the circle, the spiral[42] (and later in the case of Laban the dodecahedron and the

and love. It embodies strength and ordered harmony. It is thus in dance—as an ever so emphatic symbol, especially in our age—that Ellis develops his thoughts on the meaning and value of life." Translation: Elena Polzer.

40. See Shelton 1981, 14.

41. It also had a strong effect on theater, in particular on theories about the function of the actor by Copeau, Dullin, Artaud and many others; see Kirby 1972; see also Casini Ropa 1988, 122.

42. See the chapter on the topos formula of the spiral in Part II of this book.

icosahedron)—in flexion and torsion was considered elementary for the implementation of dance and choreography.

Genevieve Stebbins's movement repertory was definitive for most of twentieth-century free dance: symmetrical and asymmetrical arm and leg swings, parallel positioning and flexion of the feet, lateral bends, spirals and torsions of the torso, various forms of shifting weight and the center of gravity, use of body weight with the help of the floor.

Stebbins's movement theory and her pedagogical concept thus displayed fundamental elements of the new dance paradigm: a vitalist idea of dance, which concentrated on the dynamics of movement and was linked to primarily static body imagery that was oriented along the lines of ancient sculpture.

Stebbins described her adaptation of the expressive gestures of the Delsarte system as statue posing. Her catalog of movement exercises and sequences contained a pattern called the Athenian Drill, based on studies of the famous statue of Nike in the Louvre (Paris)—the Victory of Samothrace. Stebbins's physical appropriation of Greek models also influenced Duncan's idea of a reformation of dance. The origins of the dance-sculptural iconography in Duncan's interpretation of the *Marseillaise*—a depiction of Nike that merged the movement concept of free dance with the pathos of the revolution—can also be found in Stebbins's *Athenian Drill.*

In Hellerau near Dresden, Emile Jaques-Dalcroze likewise independently developed a dance-pedagogical concept of statue modeling (see figure 4), which he integrated into his training system of rhythmic gymnastics. The Dalcroze rhythmic gymnastics are a series of sculptural, mimetic dance exercises and poses, originally compiled under the name *plastique animée.*[43] In his article "Was die rhythmische Gymnastik Ihnen gibt und was sie von Ihnen fordert" (What rhythmic gymnastics can do for you and what it demands of you), Jaques-Dalcroze describes the significance of these exercises in connection with rhythmic training:

And although plasticity is not the goal of our studies, it is nevertheless and inevitably a result. You may criticize that I sometimes let you do purely plastic exercises whose only goal is the beauty of the movements. Certainly! . . . Embodied rhythm produces by definition a beautiful spectacle.[44]

43. See Perrottet 1989, 34.

44. Jaques-Dalcroze 1911, 47. Translation: Elena Polzer.

Figure 4 "Three-dimensional group" from *Orpheus* (1912/1913) in Hellerau by Emile Jacques-Dalcroze.
SOURCE: Author's archive.

The interpretation of antique sculpture in dance was simultaneously linked to a redefinition of the Greek phantasmata, namely a stylization of the ideal body as ostensibly represented by the Greek statue, into the image of the natural body. At the turn of the century, the ideal human form, as modeled and constructed by Greek sculpture on the basis of the mathematical ratio of harmonious proportions, assumed the guise of nature.[45] The focus shifted to that natural

45. In her essay *The Dance of the Future* (1903, 18) Isadora Duncan establishes a direct link between the body imagery of antiquity and the idea of nature: "Therefore dancing naked upon the earth I naturally fall into Greek positions, *for Greek positions are only earth positions.*"

On the concept of nature in the evolving discourse of free dance see the postscript on Isadora Duncan in the third, revised edition of Hans Brandenburg's book *Der Moderne Tanz* (*Modern Dance*) from 1921, in which he comments in a quite critical and nuanced manner on Duncan's concept of *nature*:

Beyond this undoubtedly great and incomparable skill, Duncan's *naturalness*, which liberated us from the soulless schematism of ballet, has advanced to the obligations of a conscious artistic style. We must become aware of the fact that the catchword *nature*, as important parole as it may be in battle, only contains a relative truth, which is that the

Figure 5 Vaslav Nijinsky in *L'Après-midi d'un Faune* (1912).
SOURCE: Editions Adam Biro, Paris, France.

quality of the human body, which was believed to have been lost in the process of civilization and in the advance of technological modernity in the big cities and which must be recovered in its physical-spiritual entirety by liberating the *body soul* (*Körperseele*)[46] in dance.

In his preface to Isadora Duncan's *The Dance of the Future*, Karl Federn—who introduced Duncan to Nietzsche's philosophy in 1902–03 and read *Zarathustra* with her—writes that Duncan's dance reveals the "struggle for the

human body, like nature in its entirety, is incessantly transformed by all kinds of determinates and conscious or unconscious demands, which are of course also *nature* and that our aversion to the *artificiality* of ballet only stems from the new determinates and demands, which surge forward to take the place of those now obsolete, only to also for their part transform nature. (Brandenburg 1921, 198f., translation: Elena Polzer). Here is already clearly described the exploratory phase of the early years and then a consolidating tendency of new dance in the period around 1920 to design a set code for the *new system* and to pass it on in corresponding pedagogic systems.

46. The term *Körperseele* [body soul] owes its wide dissemination to a book by Fritz Giese, *Körperseele* (1924); see Casini Ropa 1988, 95ff.

immediate expression of real life in conflict with conventions and tradition." Then he adds: "the number of statues that have come alive in her!"[47]

Here vitalism and classicism merge under the influences of Nietzsche and monistic philosophy to form a "Greek" pattern of thought as an epitome of the natural, whereby nature also always implies the image of primal human nature throwing off the restraints of civilization in a Dionysian frenzy of dance.

Hence, here we also have an alternative interpretation of antiquity as an expressive corporeal "poetic" counterprinciple to the ossified language of writing as extolled by Hofmannsthal, after seeing Nijinsky's portrayal of *The Afternoon of a Faun* (figure 5): the vision of an alternative, preclassical antiquity,

> which is entirely our own, nurtured by the great statuesque formations of the fifth century . . . with a vibrancy from destiny and tragedy up to the bucolic, equally far from Winckelmann's antiquity, Ingres's antiquity, as from the antiquity of Titian.[48]

The Body in Search of Greek Antiquity: Isadora Duncan

Upon her arrival in London in 1899, American dancer Isadora Duncan was eager to learn everything that old and new European culture had to offer in the form of cultural traditions and artistic treasures. She visited the museums, listened to lectures on ancient art, and studied the "Italian masters"[49] (including Titian) at the National Gallery. Her friend Charles Hallé, director of the New Gallery—meeting place of modern painters and poets—introduced her to the world of the Pre-Raphaelites, Rossetti, Burne-Jones, and William Morris. She enthusiastically absorbed everything in the form of mental and sensual stimuli provided by the circle of artists and intellectuals with whom she associated; incidentally, Ruth St. Denis was similarly introduced to the world of European history and culture and the archives of art and literature in Berlin in 1907 by Harry Graf Kessler and his circle.[50]

47. See the German introduction in Duncan 1903, 8. Translation: Elena Polzer.

48. Hofmannsthal 1978, A I, 509 (translation: Elena Polzer). Attempts to overlay the classical image of antiquity with more archaic stages of ancient Greece can also be found in the works of Nietzsche, Rohde, and R. Kassner. More recently, this image of antiquity has gained support from classical studies on antiquity, according to which (classical, European) antiquity is a construct, a myth of eighteenth- and nineteenth-century philhellenism; see Bernal 1992.

49. Duncan 1927, 49.

50. Harry Graf Kessler, who first called Hofmannsthal's attention to the dances of Ruth St. Denis in his letters, writes on November 20, 1906: "We will be exploring the museums here

Isadora Duncan read English translations of Winckelmann,[51] declared Rousseau, Nietzsche, and Whitman to be her "dance teachers," wandered with her brother Raymond through the museums under the well-informed guidance of the painter Alma-Tadema, and spent hours in the British Museum sketching the dance scenes of the bacchantes and maenads on the Greek vases and drinking bowls: "I tried to express them to whatever music seemed to me to be in harmony with the rhythms of the feet and Dionysiac set of the head, and the tossing of the thyrsis."[52]

At the dance recitals that Hallé arranged for Isadora in the courtyard of his gallery,[53] explanatory lectures were held on the subject of revitalizing dance, and even art itself, with the help of movement images gleaned from ancient sources: among the speakers were "Sir William Richmond, the painter . . . upon dancing in its relation to painting, Andrew Lang on dancing in its relation to the Greek myth, and Sir Hubert Parry on dancing in its relation to music" (62).

This is the environment that inspired Isadora Duncan to study the Dionysian by reading images and books on art history and then translating them into her own danced studies of Dionysus. Walter Pater's description of Titian's painting *Bacchus and Ariadne* visually references the Greek myth of Dionysus—quite in keeping with the pathos formulas that Aby Warburg defined for the affect engrams of antique portrayals of passion in Renaissance art:

> Of the whole story of Dionysus, it was the episode of his marriage with Ariadne about which ancient art concerned itself oftenest, and with most effect. Here, although the antiquarian may still detect circumstances which link the persons and incidents of the legend with the mystical life of the earth, as symbols of its annual change, yet the merely human interest of the story has prevailed over its earlier significance; the spiritual form of fire and dew has become a romantic lover. And as a story of romantic love, fullest perhaps of all the motives of classic legend of the pride of life, it survived with undiminished interest to a later world, two of the greatest masters of Italian painting having poured their whole power into it; Titian with greater space of ingathered shore and mountain, and solemn foliage,

over the next few days, as she is preparing new ancient, Egyptian dances." See the correspondence between Hofmannsthal and Kessler (1968, 134). Translation: Elena Polzer.

51. Duncan 1927, 51.

52. Duncan 1927, 55.

53. Isadora danced to poems by Omar Khayyam, Homer, and Theocritus, and to music by Mendelssohn (*Spring Song, Primavera*) and Nevin (*Narcissus and Ophelia*).

Figure 6 Isadora Duncan.
SOURCE: Author's archive.

and fiery animal life; Tintoret with profounder luxury of delight in the
nearness to each other, and imminent embrace, of glorious bodily presences; and both alike with consummate beauty of physical form.[54]

By transforming and physically reanimating the "world of Greek fantasy"
(Pater), Duncan's dancing conveyed an image of ephemeral sensuality lost
over the course of modern civilization: a key concept that fused concepts of
Hellenism and nature in a distinctly anticlassical, turn-of-the-century interpretation of antiquity that leaned toward the extreme affects of the Dionysian.
After her stay in London, Duncan (figures 6 and 7) moved to Paris just in time
for the World Exhibition in 1900. Again, she spent "many hours in the Louvre"
with her brother Raymond:

Raymond had already got a portfolio of drawings of all the Greek vases,
and we spent so much time in the Greek vase room that the guardian

54. Pater 1876.

Figure 7 Isadora Duncan, *Mouvement antique*,
drawn by Émile Antoine Bourdelle (1912).
SOURCE: Musée E. Bourdelle, Paris, France.

became suspicious and when I explained in pantomime that I had only
come there to dance, he decided that he had to do with harmless lunatics,
so he let us alone.[55]

Isadora Duncan's studies in the museum might suggest that her dance reform
amounted to little more than a mimetic adaptation of ancient movement
imagery. Some of her contemporaries and other critical voices accused her of
"governess-like" scholarliness in dance and sheer archaeological reconstruc-
tionism.[56] However, Duncan's intention and mission was to extract essential

55. Duncan 1927, 67.

56. Hans Brandenburg, who highly valued Duncan's achievements in free dance, also
expressed himself in similar terms (1921, 30): "With philological and archaeological reconstruction, she stringed together poses and performed copied moments of movement, instead
of real movement; and these moreover did not belong to dance, but to the fine arts" (translation: Elena Polzer).

images of the body from the condensed pathos formulas of ancient Greek art and to translate them—without recourse to the rhetorical code of ballet—into individualized dance movement. Over and over again, she emphasized that her interest lay not in "returning to the dances of the ancient Greeks." Instead, she sought a form of "new movement":

> No, the dance of the future will be a new movement, a consequence of the entire evolution which mankind has passed through. To return to the dances of the Greeks would be as impossible as it is unnecessary. We are not Greeks and cannot therefore dance Greek dances. But the dance of the future will have to become again a high religious art as it was with the Greeks. For art which is not religious is not art, is mere merchandise.[57]

Antiquity and Renaissance: Alexander Sakharoff's Dance Sketches

Like many of his contemporaries, dancer Alexander Sakharoff (1886–1963) drew visual inspiration for his choreographic work not only from ancient sculpture, but also from theater's formative repertoire of gestures. In his program booklet for the 1922 Paris season, Sakharoff wrote an essay entitled "Mes Maîtres," in which he emphasized that he owed his art to France: namely to Sarah Bernhardt, who embodied the epitome of theatrical art in fin de siècle France, and to the "Musée du Louvre," that is, the wealth of art that he first discovered while still a student at the Académie Julian.[58] These role models from the realms of fine art and theater taught him that audiences are most captivated and affected

---

57. Duncan 1903, 24.

58. In 1913, Alexander Sakharoff, a Ukrainian-born painter and dancer, met Clotilde von Derp (actually Clotilde von der Planitz, 1892–1974) at an artist's party in Munich. Soon afterward, they went to Lausanne and stayed in Switzerland during the war, where they performed together in dance recitals from 1917 onward and were enthusiastically received by the press as a couple, whose performances presented "the most accomplished union of physical charm and emotional expression," a "wealth of aesthetic-psychological and artistically-critical stimuli" (*Der Bund* [Bern], March 1, 1917). In the 1920s, they met with great acclaim in Paris. The dancer couple married in 1919 and developed their very own distinct style of modern dance—described by Alexander Sakharoff as "abstract pantomime"—in pieces such as *Florentine Spring, Bucolica, Chinoiserie, Pavane Royale, Bourrée fantasque,* and *Masques et Bergamasques.* The couple then toured for many years throughout the world, before settling down in Rome in 1953 and founding a school. For my analysis of their work, I studied the collection of program notes and reviews in the Rondel Collection at the Paris Bibliothèque de l'Arsenal, No. Ro 12755. See also the catalogue by Veroli (1991); and Sakharoff 1953.

Figure 8 Alexander Sakharoff in one of his first
Greek Dances (1910).
SOURCE: Author's archive.

by simple, natural, and unpretentious gestures. This realization prompted him to
follow his dream of embodying such corporeal images in dance—"la danse pure,"
as he writes. To reach his goal, he concentrated all his energies on developing his
capabilities as a dancer by studying classical and oriental dance, gymnastics, and
circus acrobatics.

A review in the Munich newspaper *Neuesten Nachrichten* describes a performance by Sakharoff in 1910 in which he danced the mythical characters of
Daphnis, Narcissus, and Orpheus. He celebrated a "Dionysian mass" (figure 8),
which Hans Brandenburg described in this way: "The recourse to antiquity, the
direct return to Greek sculpture, is reminiscent of Duncan and like her dance, this
one was also more a series of images than movement."[59]

Sakharoff's dances featured solemn gestures and poses to music by Thomas
von Hartmann. Every movement was set, down to the smallest detail. Early
indications of his later movement concepts can be found in the visual studies

59. Brandenburg 1917, 145. Translation: Elena Polzer.

that Sakharoff made during his apprenticeship as a student of the fine arts in Italy: in multiple small series of drawings, he sketched pathos formulas of antiquity, as transformed and adapted by Italian Renaissance art. Sakharoff's notebooks (ca. 1908) also contained studies of statues by Luca della Robbia and Andrea Pisano. Interestingly, these figurative sketches already appear—set in expressive gestures—to be designed as models for dance movement.

In his *Dionysos* studies in 1904, Walter Pater likewise described della Robbia's rondels as pathos formulas. He compared the chorus in Euripides' *Bacchae* with

> the spirit of some sculptured relief which, like Luca della Robbia's celebrated work for the organ-loft of the cathedral of Florence, worked by various subtleties of line, not in the lips and eyes only, but in the drapery and hands also, to a strange reality of impression of musical effect on visible things.[60]

In Sakharoff's notebooks, the reproductions of the paintings are immediately followed by sketches of exercises and stage directions for the first scene of a choreography about *Daphnis and Chloé*.[61]

In his unpublished essay "Über das Tanzkostüm" ("About Dance Costume"), Sakharoff emphasizes the significance of costume and the way fabric is draped for the body and movement imagery of dance. He first recognized the specific potential inherent in "the art of drapery" while developing his first dance studies of ancient sculpture:

> The great beauty, the great elegance, the great refinement of the Greek garments (as incidentally almost all garments of classical antiquity) consisted of the skillful arrangement of the folds.[62]

The arrangement of the folds and of gestures in ancient sculpture and Renaissance bas-reliefs configures the pathos formula of movements of the soul. Read by a dancer and choreographer, they become an expressive model of movement subsequently represented in dance.

Under these circumstances, della Robbia's bas-reliefs, created between 1432 and 1438 for the singers' tribune of the dome in Florence, acquired a similarly

60. Pater 2002, 15f. (German, 1904).

61. See the literary estate of Sakharoff in the collection of the Städtische Galerie im Lenbachhaus, Munich.

62. From an unpublished manuscript in the Lenbachhaus collection. Translation: Elena Polzer.

paradigmatic function to, for example, Sandro Botticelli's *Primavera* (1476–1478) or the *Nympha*, as Warburg called her, in Ghirlandaio's *Birth of John the Baptist* (1490).

As Walter Pater emphasized, these bas-reliefs were especially famous for their expressive combination of classical poise and Roman robes. The static quality of the sculptural forms and the dynamic motions of the moving folds of cloth produced a high degree of tension.

Luca della Robbia's images played a key role in the formation of body imagery and movement aesthetics in early twentieth-century dance. Alexander Sakharoff was not the only choreographer to base the movement patterns of his choreographies on the pathognomic studies of these bas-reliefs. Duncan also wrote about them in her memoirs. When she opened her dance school in 1904 in an old villa in Berlin-Grunewald, she furnished it with antique and Renaissance paintings, sculptures, and bas-reliefs, including reproductions of the "bas-reliefs of Luca della Robbia."[63]

Several years later, while preparing his *L'Après-midi d'un Faune* (1912), Vaslav Nijinsky likewise studied the bas-reliefs of Luca della Robbia.[64] Nijinsky used these sculptural reliefs, which had by then entered modern dance's iconographical canon of visual models, in order to develop the choreography and movement material for his innovative *Faune* in a sequence of poses and evocative danced relief-like effects (see figures 9 and 10).

These examples of the way Isadora Duncan, Alexander Sakharoff, and Vaslav Nijinsky interpreted della Robbia's bas-reliefs demonstrate how diverse were the artistic interpretations and transformations of the symbolic essence of even just a single work of art—made possible by the translation of pathos formula into the medium of dance[65] (figure 11).

In these dance readings, the Greek model acquired a particular, reflected quality especially in its relationship to twentieth-century avant-garde fine art—both

---

63. Duncan 1927, 173.

64. See C. Jeschke, "'Ein einfaches und logisches Mittel' Nijinskij, der Zeitgeist und *Faun*" ["Simple and logical means" Nijinsky, the zeitgeist, and *Faun*], in Nectoux 1989, 107f. The reason that Nijinsky consulted exactly this Renaissance piece for his work seems to me to lie in the paradigmatic function of Luca della Robbia's work explained above as a model for the pathos formulas of *ancient* gesture and movement expression.

65. In a way, it suits the aesthetic logic of the dynamic relationship of sculpture and dance, of ancient or rather antiqued bas-reliefs and choreographic work "in relief," that a retranslation of modern Greek dance into relief sculpture was undertaken by the fine arts around 1900: in 1911–13, Emile Antoine Bourdelle created a monumental haut-relief for the Théâtre des Champs-Elysées that featured Isadora Duncan and Vaslav Nijinsky in Greek poses and veiled-garments—a representation of the same two dance creators who translated the body imagery of antiquity into modernity. See fig. 11.

Figure 9 Scene from Nijinsky's *L'Après-midi d'un Faune* (1912).
SOURCE: Editions Adam Biro, Paris, France.

in the case of Nijinsky, who explored the Fauves, cubism, and "primitive" art in Paris and Berlin, as well as in the case of Sakharoff, who attended the social circles of the Münchner Künstlervereinigung (Munich Artist's Association) and collaborated with Wassily Kandinsky, Gabriele Münter, Alexander Jawlensky, and Marianne von Werefkin.

In the preface of a playbill for a 1910 Munich dance recital[66] almost exclusively inspired by ancient mythology and Renaissance imagery, Sakharoff writes about the *Tanz der Griechen* (Dance of the Greeks) as the "basis of all true artistic dance":

> It seems to me that such models can only be sought for in Greek antiquity, in a people that possessed and cultivated a natural and comprehensive training of the body like no other, in a culture that did not differentiate between body and mind.

He goes on to reflect gender differences in dance in general and in Greek round dances in particular and concludes:

66. The program notes list the "Tonhalle" in the Türkenstrasse 5 as venue for the performance on June 21, 1910; the program—to music by Thomas von Hartmann (for string quartet and two harps)—featured the dances *Daphnis, Bacchanale, Tanzstudie, Narcissus, Zwei Tanzstudien nach den Meistern der Frührenaissance, Orpheus, Dionysischer Gottesdienst.*

Figure 10 Relief of Nijinsky's *Faune* for the title page of the journal *Comoedia illustré*.
SOURCE: Derra de Moroda Dance Archives, Salzburg, Austria / © Derra de Moroda Dance archives, University of Salzburg, Austria.

It appears to me that neither the mature man nor the mature woman is ideally suited to dance as a pure and independent art form. Instead, it is youth still on the margin between both and still almost possessing in himself the possibilities of both sexes.[67]

Sakharoff's espousal of androgyny as the ideal embodiment of a form of free dance based on ancient models anticipated an aspect of his work that would later become a distinct feature of his joint performances with Clotilde

67. See the literary estate of Sakharoff, Lenbachhaus; translation: Elena Polzer.

Figure 11 E. A. Bourdelle: *La Danse: Isadora et Nijinsky,*
Haut-relief for the Théâtre des Champs-Elysées (1913).
SOURCE: Musée E. Bourdelle, Paris, France.

von Derp—namely their experimentation with gender. While in some of
Sakharoff's dances, especially in his Greek studies, the androgynous appeared
as an accentuation of the feminine, of gestures and movement patterns that
adapted contemporaneous signals of femininity, Clotilde, in contrast, appeared
boyish beside a partner so femininely stylized. Especially in her portrayal of
the *Faun* (a choreography from the 1920s to music by Debussy), the "severity"
(Brandenburg) of her charm merged with a soft sensuality.

In his description of the two dancers, Hans Brandenburg clearly expresses
his dislike of Sakharoff's experimentation with androgyny: "Arms and legs were
covered in white powder, as was the face, and in spite of his finely molded muscles, his appearance had something feminine about it" (145).[68]

In the long run, however, Brandenburg did not object to the performances
for reasons of bad dance technique or any aesthetic disagreement, but because
of his rigid attitude toward the representation of gender in dance. Sakharoff's
body-image did not comply with Brandenburg's preconception of gender

68. Translation: Elena Polzer.

difference. It did not appear "male" enough—in terms of "willpower, bravery, thirst for power" (146)—and, moreover, it incurred his displeasure because of the way Sakharoff proclaimed "dual sexuality even in words." Although Brandenburg rejected Sakharoff's experiments with the androgynous body and his epicene movements, as well as the chosen body imagery, he did nevertheless appreciate Sakharoff's contemplation of dance concepts, such as his attempts to redefine the meaning of the single step for dance:

> Sakharoff keeps asking himself even on the podium: what is a step? An artistic device? Not only my foot must know of it, but all my limbs as well. It has to be the kind of movement that likewise flows through relaxed parts [of the body], forming a whole from crown to sole. (151)[69]

For Brandenburg Sakharoff's merit was to be one of the first "form seekers" in modern dance. He attempted to assemble movements architecturally and by referencing historical material and employing the laws of music and of costuming with "sophisticated taste."

The study of ancient sculpture by dance thus produced that art of concentrated expressive tension, of precision in every movement and pose, of almost static-meditative boredom, in short, that art of delay which so fascinated Rainer Maria Rilke that he was moved to express it in his French poems. Rilke, who corresponded with both artists but was especially enchanted by Clotilde, dedicated the following verses to her in 1925:

> To dance: is it to fill an emptiness?
> Is it concealing the nature of a scream?
> It is the life of our fast stars
> Captured in slow motion . . .
> [Danser: est-ce remplir un vide?
> Est-ce taire l'essence d'un cri?
> C'est la vie de nos astres rapides
> Prises au ralenti . . .][70]

Dance in the Hall of Statues: Isadora Duncan and Mata Hari

The dancer in the museum: this formula describes not only the physical act of appropriating images from the archives of cultural history, but also the process

---

69. Translation: Elena Polzer.

70. Rilke 1955–66, 6: 1238. (English translation: Mark Franko and Elena Polzer.) On her name day in Paris on June 3, 1925, Rilke gave Clotilde an issue of Paul Valéry's magazine

of transforming the museal representation of works of art into the moving presentations of dance. In other words, the dancer not only goes to the museum
to study works of antiquity as visual models for his or her performances but is
also there—where they have been archived—in order to revive them as figures
of dance in contemporary memory.

The museum was chosen as a stage for dance for two reasons. First, the
choice of *performance space* was closely related to turn-of-the-century theater and dance reform. Alternative theater spaces and stage designs were
seen as free from the burden of the nineteenth-century illusionist theater
tradition. The recourse to ancient amphitheaters, festival halls, rotundas,
and all forms of experimental avant-garde theater architecture is not the
only indicator of attempts to change the institutional landscape. The conquest of new performance spaces also held similar significance for dance.
In addition to concert halls, artists' houses, and park terraces, galleries and
museum spaces were likewise turned into stages for modern presentations
of movement.

However, "dance in the museum" also played a programmatic aesthetic role.
By choosing to perform in art temples erected by the educated upper middle
class as monuments to a particular understanding of high art and culture,[71]
free dance acquired the dignity of an independent art form on equal footing
with other art forms.[72] By referencing the pictorial and sculptural works of
antiquity as models for the representation of movement, dance attempted to
uncover the immediate evidence of pathos formulas in the "animated statue."[73]
The dignified air of the performance space and the aesthetic reputation of the
surrounding "lofty" works of art invested dance with the aura of an "art form
of the future" (Duncan). Terpsichore, always on the lowest rung in the hierarchy of muses according to the aesthetic canon of philosophy from Aristotle to
Hegel, was suddenly raised to the allegory of twentieth-century art par excellence. One generation after dance first appeared in the museum of art, George

Commerce: Cahiers trimestrels (Fall 1924), in which his cycle of poems *La dormeuse* had been
published. In the magazine, he had written the dedication cited in French. This prolonged,
decelerated slow-motion precision and sculptural aspect of Sakharoff's dances was often
emphasized in reviews of his work.

71. The museum has also played an important role as a performance venue in postmodern
dance, for example in Merce Cunningham's events; in the case of postmodern dance, the
intention has, of course, no longer been to reacquire a dignified status for dance, but rather
to question the general dignity of art altogether; see Brandstetter 1991c, 243ff.

72. On modern dance aesthetics and the role of dance in artistic hierarchy, see Brandstetter
1992.

73. The motifs of *Pygmalion* and *Galatea* also belong to this trope of (modern) dance.

Balanchine's *Apollon Musagète* (1928) clearly reflected dance's newly matured self-confidence. And it took only one more generation for Maurice Béjart to finally proclaim the twentieth century as a century of dance and accordingly declare his company to be the Ballet du XXième siècle. At the turn of the century, dance in the museum became that special occasion that attracted a wide scene of artists and intellectuals.

Isadora Duncan danced her first recitals in the New Gallery in London.[74] Lectures, recitations, and conferences by renowned art historians and archaeologists framed her performances as a comprehensive antiquity project, in which "dance in the museum" actually replaced the aesthetic function of the Greek sculptures, instead of merely duplicating them.

In Vienna, Duncan appeared at the Künstlerhaus; likewise in Munich, where she associated with the likes of Kaulbach, Lenbach, and Stuck:

> Gross wished to arrange for my début in the Künstler Haus. Lembach [*sic*] and Karlbach [*sic*] were willing, only Stuck maintained that dancing was not appropriate to a Temple of Art like the Munich Künstler Haus. One morning I went to find Stuck at his house, in order to convince him of the worthiness of my Art. I took off my dress in his studio, donned my tunic, and danced for him, then talked to him for four hours without stopping, on the holiness of my mission and the possibility of the dance as an Art. He often told his friends afterward that he was never so astonished in his life. He said he felt as if a Dryad from Mount Olympus had suddenly appeared from another world. Of course he gave his consent, and my début at the Munich Künstler Haus was the greatest artistic event and sensation that the town had experienced in many years.[75]

Duncan's description—particularly its seemingly naïve narcissistic self-portrayal—gives us some idea of the *gestus* behind the act of conquering the museum as an art temple for dance, of the handling of ancient mythologems (the image of the dryad), and the unconditional soliciting of body and speech for the mission of free dance.

However, dance staged more in the museum than merely ancient Greek body imagery. Gallery spaces and art collections also became intimate stages for a model of exotic dance: the aura of the Other in the archives of text and image, the library and the museum—as if bringing the statues and texts to life and releasing them from their rigidity into a fantastic fairy-tale world of dance.

74. Duncan 1927, 61.

75. Duncan 1927, 110f.

Figure 12 Mata Hari, scene in the Musée Guimet, Paris (1905).
SOURCE: Musée Guimet, Paris, France.

On March 13, 1905, a small invited audience was exposed to exactly this kind of spectacle at the Musée Guimet in Paris. Its director, the industrialist and art collector Ernest Guimet from Lyon, had arranged for a very special kind of event in the library of his rich archive of Asian art. The small, pillared rotunda of the library had been transformed into a Hindu temple. An improvised altar stood in front of a wall hanging. Garlands of flowers were twined around the altar. There was a hint of sandalwood in the air and candlelight. The famous statue of the dancing Shiva from the Guimet collection sat behind the altar on an elevated pedestal. In stepped Mata Hari (figure 12), who presented her dances *The Poem of the Princess and the Magic Flower, The War Dance of Subramanya,* and *The Invocation of Shiva* framed by the topoi of the exotic.[76]

The subsequent newspaper reviews all described the event as an erotic sensation, rather than one particularly noteworthy for its dance qualities:

A tall dark figure glided in. Her arms were folded upon her breast beneath a mass of flowers. For a few seconds she stood motionless, her eyes fixed on a statue of Siva [*sic*] at the end of the room. Her olive skin blended with the curious jewels in their dead gold setting. A casque of worked gold was set upon her dark hair and a breastplate of similar workmanship beneath

76. See Gomez Carillo 1927; Waagenaar 1964; Keay 1987.

her arms, she wore a transparent white robe and a quaint clasp held a scarf around her hips. She was enshrouded in various veils of delicate hues, symbolizing beauty, youth, love, chastity, voluptuousness and passion.[77]

The performance was a mix of all those forms and images of the exotic that had accumulated in the visual memory of the belle époque since the Paris World Exposition—the Javanese ceremonial *serimpi*, erotic Hindu temple dances, the Egyptian-Arabic *baladi* (also called *danse du ventre* in France), and the Indian street dance *nautch*:

> With slow, undulating, tiger-like movements, she appealed to the Spirit of Evil to help her avenge a wrong. The movements became more and more intense, more feverish, more eager. She first threw the flowers, and then divested herself one by one of the veils . . . and finally, worked to a state of frenzy, she unclasped her belt and fell in a swoon at Siva's [*sic*] feet.[78]

The largely naked "Javanese" dancer, dressed only in a bejeweled *cache sexe* and a *breast shield*, became a sensation in the salons and the gossip columns of the press. Mata Hari's reputation as a courtesan came later, during World War I, during which she was accused of espionage. In 1917, the Dutch dancer, originally born in 1876 under the name of Margaretha Geertruida Zelle, was convicted by a French military court and condemned to death by firing squad.[79]

Mata Hari's performance in the library of the Musée Guimet was a theatrical amalgam of fiction, visual legends, and savvy business sense. Ernst Guimet first noticed the twenty-six-year-old hot-blooded and well-endowed young Dutch woman, who went by the name of Lady MacLeod, at a soirée. She had just recently divorced and moved to Paris. Her years spent in Java married to a Dutch officer who was despotic and an alcoholic were over, and she felt free to begin a new life. Her assets were her body and her memories of the Javanese dances that she had seen on various occasions during her stay in the "Dutch East Indies." However, she could only remember elements of the movement patterns and costumes and had no prior dance training.

When Guimet, one of the greatest aficionados of East Asian art at the time, saw her amateur performance, he decided to exhibit her—honed to

77. Keay 1987, 33.

78. Keay 1987, 33–34.

79. See Waagenaar 1964; to this day, it has still not been sufficiently clarified whether (and to what degree consciously) Mata Hari was truly an active agent (for Germany).

perfection—in his museum, rather than unmask her fiction of being an Indian dancer. He more or less modeled her into a mannequin of exotic dance born of the museum. The art treasures in his collection provided the real props for her dance fiction—fabrics and jewelry, statues and vessels. Together Guimet and the young woman invented a name and a personal history and launched them in the press. The name MacLeod was transformed into Mata Hari—*The Eye of the Morning*. Her biography was rewritten into an Indian legend: a Brahman daughter who had dedicated herself entirely to temple dancing as a labor of love until a Scottish (!) officer swept her away to Java.[80] The aura of the foreign, the world of oriental excess, which Mata Hari mystified in her name, in the legends spun around her, and in her dancing, and which she simultaneously confirmed as true by presenting the authenticity of her naked body, caused quite a sensation. Ernst Guimet's and Mata Hari's plans bore fruit: the museum director qua impresario had correctly assessed the desires of the beau monde, the arrogant Paris elite.

That performance in the Musée Guimet marked the birth of the myth of Mata Hari, a myth sprung from the museum of Asian art, produced as a fiction of name and body—*The Eye of the Morning*—and staged as dance in the library, the archive of fictions par excellence. It is through the consistency of its recurring medial transformations that the myth of Mata Hari, which weaves together the desire for beauty, passion, and adventure, continues to live on in today's cinema as the dominant medium of twentieth-century fictitious body imagery.[81]

The Dance Theater as Dance Museum: The Théâtre Loïe Fuller

The dialogue staged in the museum between the statues and the dancers who read them, between the visual model and the actual act of dance in the archives of pictorial cultural memory, continued and grew even more complex as the years went by. The dance theater simultaneously became a dance museum. The dancer appeared both as a performer and as a "statue" in her very own dance museum. This is one way to describe the experiments by some dancers at the

---

80. See Carillo 1927, 40–55.

81. In filmic representations, this combination of dance, love, and espionage provides ideal material for fiction; see, e.g., *Mata Hari* (1931) with Greta Garbo in the title role (directed by George Fitzmaurice) or *Mata Hari, Agent H. 21* (1966) with Jeanne Moreau (directed by Jean-Louis Richard); dance theater has also reappropriated the myth of the dancer, courtesan, spy: in 1992, Verena Weiss, a student of Carolyn Carlson, presented a piece entitled *Mata Hari* in Hamburg.

turn of the century, who sought to create theatrical spaces of their own, in which their dances could simultaneously be performed and archived. In the 1920s, Loïe Fuller, Charlotte Bara, and Akarova[82] had such "dance temples" built for them as buildings that combined the functions of both stage and museum, as performance spaces as well as places for documenting dance.

During the World Exposition in Paris in 1900, Loïe Fuller had a pavilion erected between the various theaters and cabarets in the Rue de Paris, the "street dedicated to Apollo and his muses." The dancer, whose *danses lumineuses* had been highly acclaimed in Paris since 1892,[83] commissioned the young architect Henri Sauvage (1873–1932) to construct the building. The sophisticated architectural design was meant to serve a dual purpose: the task was to house both a museum and a theater in a single structure. This dual function—namely that of a gallery, as well as a stage for dance—influenced not only the arrangement of the rooms, but also the plastic design of the building. The little theater became a gem of art nouveau architecture with rich, flowing lines and a façade that dissolved into organic-dynamic forms. In its integration of construction and ornament it resembled August Endell's Atelier Elvira (Munich 1898). Every detail reflected the spirit of Loïe Fuller's dances; the pavilion seemed to translate her serpentine dance into architecture.

The façade resembled the folds of her silk dress frozen in mid-turn—"des plis de sa robe on a pu tirer une architecture" [an architecture was derived from the pleats of her dress], wrote Alexandre Arsène in *Le Théâtre*.[84] The shimmering cascades of light, which illuminated the building at night and transformed the stucco façade into a glittering sea of light and shadows, corresponded to the lights and the *ombre* experiments of her dances. The polychromatic small windows along the lines of the roof, executed by Francis Jourdain, paraphrased Fuller's experiments with colorful panes of glass and mirrors: "Intérieurement, son théâtre est un kaleidoscope" [On the inside, her theater is a kaleidoscope] (Arsène).

On the one hand, the architecture represented an ornamental reproduction of Fuller's dances—the façade appeared almost as a metaphor for dance movement, as a visualization of the scene of theatrical representation. On the other hand, it fulfilled the function of reorganizing the spaces in which a distinct turn-of-the-century image of the female body—an image that materialized itself both in dance and in sculpture—was exhibited.

---

82. For more on the Belgian dancer Akarova, see the section "Lettres dansantes" in Part II.

83. See Brandstetter and Ochaim 1989; on the dances of Loïe Fuller, see also the corresponding section in chapter 2 of Part II of this book.

84. See Arsène, in *Le Théâtre* 40 (August 1900): 23f.

The arrangement of statues and bas-reliefs along the facade of Loïe Fuller's pavilion adhered to this principle, but also reflected the additional influences of representative architecture from the era of Napoleon II, such as Carpeaux's relief *The Dance* at the Paris Opera House. The no-longer-extant Loïe Fuller theater was decorated on the outside with a series of ceramic bas-relief portraits of the artist. Over the entrance, Pierre Roche[85] mounted a larger-than-life sculpture of the dancer in a winged pose that resembled the Nike of Samothrace, the *Victoire* at the Louvre.[86]

The layout of the inner rooms of the pavilion fully revealed the dual function of the museal theater and the theatrical museum. Sculptures and small statues, bas-reliefs, paintings, prints, drawings, and poster prints of Loïe Fuller's dances were exhibited in the lobby that preceded the auditorium and the stage and was lined in black like a magic lantern. The gallery space and the stage thus represented the antipodes of static and dynamic, of body and fabric, of restraint and release of the body in dance, of sculpture and dance, of museum and theater.

The Theater as an Archive of Gesture

So far, all my remarks on the subject of dance in the museum have concentrated on the institutional archives of art and theater and their function as mnemonic spaces for the representation of pathos formulas in sculpture and dance. The museum was transformed into a theater and the theater turned into a museum that housed the rhetorics of gestural expression as a space in which the expressive forms adopted from the artworks of antiquity were physically brought up to date and simultaneously inventoried. At the end of the nineteenth century, the three great fin de siècle actresses Ellen Terry, Sarah Bernhardt, and Eleonora Duse individualized and simultaneously generalized this expressive component in their performances to such a degree that they likewise became alternative visual models for modern dance on a par with the legacy of ancient statues.

In his essay "On Pantomime," Hugo von Hofmannsthal describes physical gesture as a language of the body that is "seemingly general, but in truth highly personal. Nor is it body that speaks to body, but the human whole that speaks to the whole"[87]—a symbolic, holistic reading of the pathos formula.

85. The ceramic prototypes were also by Pierre Roche. Moreover, he produced a number of impressive small statues of Loïe Fuller, depicting her, e.g., as Salome.

86. On the pathos formula of the Nike, see the corresponding section in the following chapter of Part I.

87. Hofmannsthal 1923, 261. No translator credited.

If we look more closely at the role played by ancient sculpture as a foil for the development of specific theatrical body codes at the turn of the century, we discover a hitherto almost unnoticed parallel development in avant-garde theater and avant-garde dance. In the period in which a new concept of expression was emerging in free dance, the techniques used by actors in theater also changed. Theater's attitude toward theatricality and acting shifted from a naturalistic-mimetic model to various patterns of stylization in representation. These changes also shaped the reform developments of free dance. On the one hand, they affected the theory and the construction of theatrical and dance spaces. On the other hand, they also influenced the way the body was used, the development of new body imagery, and the adaptation of (stylized, abstract) concepts of the body in acting and dance.

In fin de siècle theater, the individual styles of Terry, Bernhardt, and Duse were a prime formative influence. As distinctly as each of these heroines, who are today considered almost mythological figures of the theater era—especially as protagonists of a new, markedly individual notion of femininity— may have presented themselves, they also appeared, each in her own way, as the embodiments of the theatrical per se.[88] And the quasi-gestural-exalted quality of their styles likewise appeared to the founders and innovators of modern dance as a sculptural-theatrical expression of those pathos formulas that they had encountered in other forms in the statues housed in the museums of fine art.

Isadora Duncan, for example, regarded it as her greatest goal to achieve that same intensity of expression in her dance as Duse emanated on stage by simply standing motionless like a statue. Hofmannsthal wrote about Duse:

> She describes with a twitch of the lips, a movement of the shoulder, a flourish of tone, the ripening of a decision, the premonition of a train of thought, the whole psycho-physiological event that precedes the emergence of words. . . . Like nature itself, she emphasizes banalities and lets revelations fall to the ground.[89]

Hofmannsthal describes Duse's performance as "nature itself," as the ultimate embodiment of the high art of stylized representation. This equally applied— Stokes, Booth, and Bassnett—to the way the other two great actresses were received by audience and press: "It was often said at the time about each one of them that she was a 'natural' actress, but from our twentieth-century viewpoint

88. See Stokes, Booth, and Bassnett 1991.

89. Hofmannsthal 1978, A I, 471. Translation: Elena Polzer.

it is difficult to imagine exactly what an audience may have seen that was 'natural.'[90]

At the same time, the *natural* again appeared directly connected to ancient sculpture. One critic, for example, described Terry's appearance in Shakespeare's *Winter's Tale* as that of a "statue" cloaked in long, draped garments, who "recalled the Niobe of the Louvre. Every gesture seemed a memory of the sorrow and dignity written by sculptors in marble, of those long lines of statues stolen by Europe from Greece."[91]

This interpretation of the pathos formula of ancient sculpture resembles those influencing free dance as in the case of Duncan. Duncan first encountered Terry, the mother of her lover Edward Gordon Craig, during her first stay in London in 1899. She was inspired by the actress's "majestic beauty": "As for Ellen Terry, she became then, and ever after remained, the ideal of my life."[92]

But it was not only Duncan who studied the pathos formulas of intensely expressive body language both in the museum and in the theater. In a program booklet that accompanied his performances in Paris in the 1920s, Alexander Sakharoff also emphasized that both the ancient statues in the Louvre and Sarah Bernhardt had been his teachers.[93]

Here we have two mutually complementary visual archives as spaces of inspiration for modern dance: the theater with the living statues—the tableaux vivants of the great actresses—and the museum with its halls of ancient sculpture and bas-reliefs.

By the same token, modern dance also influenced theater, especially movement representation. The development of free dance in particular affected the theory and practice of physical technique and actor's training. John Martin, for example, emphasized the relationship between Duncan's concept of dynamic impulses and the spontaneous expression of emotion through movement and Konstantin Stanislavsky's system of actor's training, which "demanded from his actors the same kind of emotional truth, arising from the same kind of inner impulsion, that Isadora demanded from herself and all dancers."[94]

Hence, it was not the naturalistic imitation of affect, but rather the physical representation of human experience condensed into pathos formulas, that

90. Stokes, Booth, and Bassnett 1988, 3.

91. Ibid., 82.

92. Duncan 1927, 63.

93. See the program notes from the Rondel collection, Bibl. de l'Arsenal, Paris.

94. Martin in Magriel 1977, Part III, 8.

found its expression in both theater and dance: "It is the same truth that under-lies both their arts, for they are in essence only one art in different guises" (ibid.).

The truth referred to here is the truth of gesture, transmitted from the ges-tural inventory of theater and from the pathos formulas of ancient sculpture in the museums of art history.

DANCE OF THE STATUES: HUGO VON HOFMANNSTHAL'S "MOMENTS IN GREECE"

Hofmannsthal wrote his essay "Moments in Greece" after his return from a trip to Greece in spring 1908[95] in the company of Harry Graf Kessler and the sculptor Aristide Maillol. The text reflects the role of memory in culture, the meaning of the visual archive of antiquity for literature, and the importance of classical education from the perspective of modernity.

It is structured into three sections, which correspond to three approaches toward reading. The first part, "The Monastery of St. Luke," depicts the jour-ney to Greece as an encounter with nature.[96] The author experiences the Mediterranean landscape of current-day Greece, from which the traces of antiquity have been partially erased, as a landscape subsumed by the structures of Christian patriarchalism and the order of monastic hierarchy. The journey to the "crevices" of Delphi becomes a search for "submerged" knowledge: "You

95. Two circumstances gave the impetus for Hofmannsthal's text and influenced his plans to journey to Greece. First of all, there was Hofmannsthal's friendship with the dancer Ruth St. Denis, who prepared and performed her new Indian dances *Yogi* and *The Nautch*—an ecstatic whirling dance—in 1906–1907. Hofmannsthal wrote about them in a letter to Kessler on February 6, 1908 (correspondence, Hofmannsthal and Kessler 1968, 175); on the relationship between Hofmannsthal and Ruth St. Denis, see Brandstetter 1991b.

Second, Hofmannsthal's wish to travel to Greece in the spring was also influenced by Gerhart Hauptmann's short pamphlet *Greek Spring* (1908), compiled from his notes in a diary written during a journey to Greece in March–April 1907 and dedicated to Harry Graf Kessler. Once again, Hofmannsthal is caught up in a loose form of rivalry with Hauptmann—as incidentally also in the case of a dance libretto intended for Ruth St. Denis—in a situation contrived by Kessler; this may also explain Hofmannsthal's various attempts to create a dis-tance between them at a later point in time. In the case of his journey to Greece: the abrupt abortion of the trip after eleven days.

96. Hofmannsthal published the text just a few weeks after his return from Greece. In a letter to his sister, Kessler offers some possible reasons for Hofmannsthal's premature termination of the journey: "Hofmannsthal in Greece was a failure: il ne se retrouvait pas. He was almost always out of sorts, or out of temper, or out of feeling with the surroundings. After ten days of much suffering, he left us, to our mutual contentment . . . he said he could not stand the barrenness of the country; woods, rivers, and green fields were his lifeblood, etc." (corre-spondence, Hofmannsthal and Kessler 1968, 512). Translation: Elena Polzer.

gaze down into their centuries as into a cistern, and down there in dream-depths lies the Unreachable."[97]

Here we have the main theme of the text, namely the idea that memory, as an act of creativity, is only possible if cultural knowledge is first forgotten. Amnesia is the premise for an activation of *memoria* and the only way that the knowledge stored in memory can be recollected from the unconscious and the dream in order to ascend again as something subjective, that is, a new source of artistic creation. Hofmannsthal repeatedly returned to this subject in multiple texts written around 1907.

The second section, "The Wanderer," concentrates on the problem of reading human form when moving through unfamiliar surroundings and in foreign lands.[98] The traveler encounters a homeless "wanderer" and seeks to decipher his face and body. The focus now lies on reading the traces and cracks of history—as signs of *memoria* and the origins of the subject—in the human landscape of the body, rather than in the barren Greek landscape.

In a third step, the traveler's attempts to read the topography of the landscape, as well as the physiognomy and pathognomy of the wanderer, finally lead him to an encounter with the buried culture of ancient times. At first, the traces of the past culture likewise resist being read. Touch and sensual experience require the subject to step over a threshold contained within himself. This act of transgression provokes a crisis of perception: "Everything alive, every landscape, reveals itself once, and it its entirety: but only to a heart deeply moved" (93).

Hofmannsthal here depicts a specific pathos formula—a basic pattern of affect as defined by Aby Warburg—namely the gestalt of a man shaken to the core, as the frame of mind required in order to read and awaken images from the reservoir of cultural memory. In other words, a specific figuration of affect is postulated as the necessary precondition for encountering art. This pathos gestalt has an influence on how the artwork is received. In the section "The Statues," this process is illustrated in an encounter between the traveler and the ancient statues housed in a museum. In other texts by Hofmannsthal, we find a similar emphasis on the gaze as important for experiencing classical works of art,[99] for example, his interpretation of van Gogh's paintings in *Letters of a Returnee*.

---

97. Hofmannsthal 2008a, 85.

98. Kessler writes about this same encounter in a letter to his sister: "A very extraordinary meeting with a young German workingman, starved and nearly naked, in one of the wildest and most desert parts of the Greek mountains around Parnassus, at the very spot where Oedipus is supposed to have killed his father Laius."

99. See Renner 1991.

The search for traces of a buried culture continues in part 3 of "Moments in Greece," which is entitled "The Statues." In the twilight of evening, the traveler climbs up the hill of the Acropolis. Standing alone among the ruins of the pillared landscape, he senses a "whiff of mortality" blowing toward him as he gazes at the remains of the temple. "Magnificently self-composed, nevertheless, it stood there" (94).[100]

The attempt to retrieve the sunken world of antiquity from memory and reestablish it in the present fails:

These Greeks, I asked within myself, where are they? I tried to remember, but I remembered only memories. Names came floating near, figures; they merged into one another as though I had dissolved them into a greenish smoke wherein they appeared distorted. Because they had passed long ago I hated them, and also because they had passed so fast. (95)

Neither from the archaeology of the cultural landscape nor from the mythological world of ideas can a spark of imaginary encounter be gleaned: in the twilight of the sunset, the traveler fantasizes the figure of Plato, the "inventor of myths": "His glance revealed me to myself, and revealed him" (95).

Yet the phantom fades. In his Faustian insistence on intuitive sensual revelation, which separates him from all forms of Platonism, the traveler remains behind, disillusioned by the present. He sees himself condemned to plunge everything "into the terrible bath of time," always chasing after the "just-departed moment." The subjective knowledge of mortality and the experience of time as loss, as a decline into amnesia, as death reflects and multiplies itself in the monuments of a bygone culture: "It is your own weakness, I called to myself, you are unable to revive all this" (96).

Next the traveler attempts to penetrate antiquity's realm of memory with the help of literature. He pulls out Sophocles' *Philoctetes* and begins to read: "Clear and transparent, verse after verse stood before me, melodious and dreadful the wailings of the lonely man rose into the air" (96).

Yet a heightened experience of strangeness[101] denies him any understanding of the text: "All this was strange beyond measure and inaccessible. I could not read any further."

---

100. *Translator's note:* The translation of Hofmannsthal's "Moments in Greece" published in Hofmannsthal 2008a contains some slight variations from the original text by Hofmannsthal cited in the German version of this book.

101. The text here reflects the experience of strangeness—triggered and directed at writing itself—which so disturbed Hofmannsthal during his journey through Greece that he prematurely departed. While Kessler and Maillol experienced it as an encounter with the

The author's cognitive abilities seem clouded, his senses sealed shut. Neither the semiotic world of ancient culture nor the sensual enchantment of his surroundings can reach him. He breathes in the scents "of strawberries and acacias, of ripening wheat, of the dust of the roads and the open sea," yet he is unable to surrender himself to them. He remains resigned to the knowledge of "impossible antiquity, said I to myself, aimless searching" (97).

This feeling of resignation—the idea of unattainable access—establishes itself as a threshold of perception in his mind.

On entering the museum, the traveler attempts to transcend his inner limitations of perception. The transition from the cultural landscape into the archive of ancient art is literally staged as a liminal experience. However, this transgression in search of an "impossible antiquity" is also linked to an experience of disturbance. The late museum visitor sees himself beset by the clinging officiousness of a custodian, whose behavior reflects a *gestus* of ownership, of brash possessiveness, and of an unreserved didactic presentation of antiquity as object of cultural heritage. The traveler's sense of "demonic irony," which already overcame him facing the temple ruins in a futile search for the spirit of Hellenism, is now intensified by the sight of a grotesque "three-legged demon" from the "original temple of Athena," which is praised by the custodian as evidence of an unknown antiquity.

The traveler now steps out of this demonic sphere over the threshold of a third room: a room of statues, the korai. Here perception changes. The author's innermost self is prepared for that awe-inspiring affect, which—as described at the end of part 2, almost at the threshold of the "Statues" section—permits awareness of the Other as an act of revelation: the *fascinosum et tremendum* experienced in the face of the numinous. For this purpose, Hofmannsthal employs the traditional topos of contemplating the divine. The lightning bolt of enlightenment does not, however, penetrate the ego from without, but emanates from within the author's innermost self, from the abyss of the unconscious. Standing before the "statues in long garments," the visitor is seized by

an indescribable shock. It came not from outside, but from some immeasurable distance of an inner abyss: it was lightening: the room, as it was, rectangular with whitewashed walls and the statues that stood there, was suffused for an instant with a light utterly different from that which was

"homeland of art," Hofmannsthal saw himself exposed to "raw reality," "wild, primitive forces" that paralyzed his powers of perception (see correspondence, Hofmannsthal and Kessler 1968, 511). Only back in the safe surroundings of his home did the moments in Greece emerge—in an act of visualized reminiscence—as an *interior realm of literature*, while in reality he had only felt rejection and strangeness.

really there: the eyes of the statues were all at once turned toward me and an unspeakable smile came to their lips. (97–98)

The statue's gaze on the observer triggers a mystical experience. The subsequent passage is dedicated to describing this moment. The religious experience of art—that transsubstantiatory awareness which George Steiner attempted to reactivate in his writings on "real presence"[102]—is characterized by

- The experience of pure presence. The "contingencies of time" are suspended; the moment of mystical experience appears "without duration," as if "outside of time" (ibid.).
- The experience of time as déjà vu, as a moment of self-encounter: "I knew: I am not seeing this for the first time—in some other world—I have stood before them, had some kind of communion with them, and ever since then everything in me has been waiting for just this shock, and so dreadfully had I to be shaken thus within my innermost self in order to become again what I had been" (98).
- The experience of interconnectedness.

The distance between subject and object is seemingly overcome: the self is filled with a feeling of "being interwoven" with the statues standing vis-à-vis.

The aspect of "dynamization" is particularly significant in this act of visionary perception. In the moment of *unio mystica*, the static sculptures appear to vibrate with rhythmic movement: "From where else rose in me this foreboding of a departure, this rhythmical expansion of atmosphere, . . . this soundless tumult." The dynamic moment manifests itself in a dual form: on the one hand, as dance—as rhythmic movement, whose laws and motives evolve solely of their own accord and not as the results of music. On the other hand, the moment is illustrated by the image of a journey as the "rapt expectancy" of an outcome, intentionality as fulfillment, "this foreboding of a departure."

The journey into the realm of antiquity thus reveals itself to be a journey into archaic zones of the self, "for I am the priest, who will perform the ceremony—I, too, perhaps the victim that will be sacrificed" (98). The crossing of the threshold, which, we recall, refers to that boundary between archaic sacrificial ritual and symbolic substitution which symbolizes the genesis of culture—as Hofmannsthal explained in his *Gespräch über Gedichte* (*Conversation on Poetry*) in 1904: "Do you know what a symbol is? . . . can you attempt to

102. See Steiner 1989; see also Bohrer 1981.

imagine how sacrifice originally came about? . . . I mean the sacrificial animal, the sacrificed blood and life of a bull, a ram, a dove."[103]

The killing of an animal as a sacrifice to the gods, as a substitute for self-sacrifice, marks the transition to "symbolic sacrificial death." This is "the root of all poetry." The first human who sacrificed an animal may have believed for a moment that it was his own blood.

> He must have, for a moment, died in the animal. This is the only way that the animal could die for him. That the animal could die for him was a great mystery, a great mystical truth. Henceforth the animal died a symbolic sacrificial death. But everything was based on the fact that he had also died in the animal, just for a moment. That his existence, for the space of time that it takes to a single breath, vanished into a foreign existence.—This is the root of all poetry. (*SW*, 80)

This disintegration of the ego in another existence, this magic, this enchantment is an "incarnation of the symbols that overcome us." The symbols are compelling and overpowering through their sensual nature as *corporeal* experience. Sacrifice is not a metaphorical process, in which one thing takes the place of another, but rather a manifestation of the transubstantiating power of the symbol that carries that magic "which has the words, to touch our bodies, and to ceaselessly transform us."

Hofmannsthal's theory of the creation of the symbol out of ritual as stated in his *Conversation on Poetry* is very similar to Aby Warburg's thoughts on pathos formulas as the visual storehouses of collective memory in both an anthropological and a semiotic sense.

In his definition of the symbol, Warburg continues the arguments expounded by psychologist Richard Semon in *The Mneme* (1921)—the idea that engrams store the potential energy of an event in matter, in the body. In Warburg's psychohistorical concept of the mneme, the symbol corresponds with the engram: "In the symbol—in the widest sense of the term—we find preserved those energies of which it is, itself, the result."

This is how Ernst H. Gombrich, Warburg's student, put it in his monograph on Warburg.[104] "The symbol, in Warburg's reading, was the counterpart, in the collective mind, of the 'engram' in the nervous system of the individual" (260). It represents a shift in energy, a shift that takes effect upon contact. In light of this semiotic theory, the formulas of antique sculpture appear as

---

103. Hofmannsthal 1975–, 31: 80f. Translation: Elena Polzer.

104. See Gombrich 1970, 243.

dynamograms or—as Warburg explained in his notes—as expressions of that psychic energy which once shook "the Greek tribal community in the seizures of the Bacchic cults":

> Thus Mneme carries with it the relics of a mental state in which the ego was not yet master, a state of immediate reflex movements resulting in the abandonment to maenadic frenzy and barbarous struggles—a state, also, in which the difference between the self and the outer world was not yet perceived and in which the magic attitude to image and symbol held undisputed sway. (253–54)

In 1895, Warburg traveled to America, where he had the chance to take part in the tribal rituals of the Hopi during a three-day festival. Warburg observed and photographed the ceremonies and dances of these "primitive men." He believed himself to have found an answer to the question of the transition from the ritual to the symbolic in culture. The premise for a differentiation of human behavior, wrote Warburg in his notes, is the "corporalization of the sense impression" in religious ritual.

Gombrich aptly points out that Warburg's view of this encounter with the foreign was typical of his day and age. "As a convinced evolutionist, Warburg saw in the Indians of New Mexico a stage of civilization, which corresponded to the phase of paganism that ancient Greece left behind with the dawn of rationalism" (91). This comparison of a Native American culture as an incarnation of the primitive with the legacy of ancient Greece has a long tradition in cultural history. It reaches as far back as the eighteenth century, to Winckelmann and Voltaire.

For Warburg, his encounter with Indian ritual was important in the sense that it made paganism vivid and real to him. In the same way that Hofmannsthal derived the symbol concept from archaic sacrificial ritual in his *Conversations on Poetry*, Warburg explored the moment of transition from primitivism to the semiotic world of culture. This line of inquiry later led him to his theory of the development of rationality out of the fear of the demonic.

The degree to which this idea of a development of culture out of archaic rituals of sacrifice—purged or sublimated in the process of symbolization— influenced the thinking and visual fantasy of artists and scientists around 1914 reveals itself potently in Nijinsky's/Stravinsky's *Le Sacre du Printemps* (1913). The scandalized reactions to the "barbaric" piece at its world premiere in Paris and the excitement with which the barbarity of World War I, was integrated soon afterward into the conceptual perspective on sacrifice as a cultural-formative ritual are only apparently paradoxical. The ambivalence toward pagan cult and Christian culture, toward the unleashing and binding of "thiasotic base instincts," as revealed in reactions to these two phenomena, is also evident in the words of Jacques-Emile Blanche:

> During the scientific, chemical "cubist" warfare, on nights made terrible by air raids, I have often thought of the *Sacre*.[105]

For Aby Warburg, the fear of an invading barbarism, of the primitive, appears overcome, suspended in the symbol, within which the primal source of affect still nevertheless resonates. Works of art and sculpture retain a tangible echo of "deep devotion," as expressed in the thiasotic cult: an "unhindered release of expressive bodily movement" that encompasses the "entire range of dynamic expressions of the life of a humanity shaken by fear."[106]

This "imprint" of the cultic envelops the pathos formula—even in its modifications and inversions over the course of Western art. Warburg also attributes the creativity of the artist to the symbol's energetic potential as a dynamogram. It is here that the thoughts and emotions of images and metaphors unfold between magic and rationality.

The reconstructed history of the cultural theory of symbolism reveals a (Nietzschean) understanding of antiquity that has little in common with the classical Greece of the eighteenth century or that of Winckelmann in the nineteenth century in the works of both Hofmannsthal and Warburg. The focus has shifted to the emergence of so-called classicism from barbarism, the primitive cult traces of which can be found in and recalled from the visual memory of culture. Nietzsche's influence,[107] his dualistic model of the Apollonian and Dionysian as elaborated in *The Birth of Tragedy*, is also evident in the search for an alternative Greece, which Hofmannsthal alludes to in his review of Nijinsky's *Afternoon of a Faun*:

> A vision of antiquity that is entirely our own, nurtured by the great statuary figures of the fifth century, the Charioteer of Delphi, the archaic head of a youth in the Acropolis museum, with its oscillation between fate, tragedy and the bucolic, just as far from Winckelmann's antiquity, or that of Ingres as from that of Titian. (AI, 509)[108]

---

105. J.-E. Blanche, quoted in Eksteins 1989, 139.

106. Warburg 2009, 279.

107. Nietzsche's influence on dance and dance discourse at the turn of the century is summed up by Ernst Bloch as follows: "And the entire dance world—in the original itself, not only in its imitations—was equivocally dedicated to the Dionysian; in the sense that this form of new dance would never have been achieved without Nietzsche." Bloch 1959, 1: 462. Translation: Elena Polzer.

108. Translation Elena Polzer.

The *other* antiquity is that of the *Other* in culture. In "Moments in Greece," the autobiographical background of the essay, as well as the protagonist's futile attempts to read the landscape, human physiognomy, and ancient art, all testify to this experience. This foreign Other is likewise reflected in the gaze of the statues housed in the hall of the korai. The acquiescence of the ego corresponds to an experience of profound strangeness. The statues appear ominous. Their form expresses something both animalistic and divine: "Am I not standing before the strangest of the strange? Does not the eternal dread of chaos stare at me here from five virginal faces?" (98)

However, the moment also represents that transient step into another existence which Hofmannsthal previously emphasized in his *Conversation on Poetry* as the epitome of the compelling magic of symbolism: a form of cultural shamanism that reveals the "breathtaking sensual presence" of the symbol—of the statues as embodied images of cultural memory—in a moment of corporeal exchange. For the author, the bodies of the statues are "more convincing to me than my own. In this material there is a tension, so powerful that it creates in me a tautness, too" (99).

The solemn appeal of their physical form transforms the marble of the sculptures into a different aggregate state. The intentionality of the artwork translates the stone into something liquid, transforms static into dynamic, repose into yearning. The reverse structure of intentionality—from the recipient to artwork and back again—is, last but not least, also expressed in the image of the journey. It is no longer the explorer who has set out on a journey into the cultural past in search of antiquity, but rather antiquity itself, which has set forth on a journey into the present: "Did not the universe, for a fleeting moment, open up to me?" (99). The moment of arrival, the now of landing in the present, describes the situation between art and the reader as bilaterally *passing over* into another existence.

In his notes on the "Leser" (Reader),[109] Hofmannsthal writes: "The poem is blind without the reader" (*SW*, 327).[110]

The eyes of the Greek statues appear to see—appear to be reading their reader. In the eyes of the viewer, the statues represent more than the visual memory of "primal expressions of human passion" (Warburg). Instead, the hermeneutic gaze of the female statues exposes the author and onlooker as a representative of the pathos formula of ecstasy, spellbound in timeless communion with incarnations of the Greek ideal of beauty. The enigma of art unravels in

---

109. This essay was planned for various contexts, originally as a second part of the *Conversation on Poetry*. See Hofmannsthal 1975–, 31: 316f. and 327–35.

110. Translation: Elena Polzer.

a moment of rapture, in an act of mutual revelation. The enigmatic smile that Hofmannsthal saw expressed in the statues, in the countenance of the *Gioconda*, as well as in Ruth St. Denis's face when she was dancing,[111] represents the hieroglyphic nature of the body. In 1907, in a preliminary draft of *Die Tänzerin* (*The Dancer*), Hofmannsthal forges a link between Greek vase paintings, Bacchic forms of movement, and the "Primavera goddess of the wind"—the epitome of Warburg's pathos formula[112]:

> What she does with her body always seems impossible, inconceivable. It is only possible out of an entirety of nature. The individual word, the individual gesture, is worth nothing. We will no longer tolerate a message that is less complicated than that of a whole being. Equally so on an intellectual level: Beethoven, Nietzsche. We want to read all the hieroglyphs. (AIII, 490)[113]

The motto of this aesthetic based on the "rhythm of the body" is the paradigm of holism, as revealed in its recourse to Nietzsche and condensed in the formula "The whole man must move at once"[114]—a formula often used by Hofmannsthal.

The veil, however, confronts the topos of corporeal holism with the "dialectics of outside and inside" (Gaston Bachelard).[115] It represents the boundary

---

111. In his review, *Her Extraordinary Immediacy*, Hofmannsthal writes about the enigmatic smile of Ruth St. Denis: "Her motionless eyes continue to have the same mysterious smile: the smile of the statue of Buddha, a smile not of this world; an absolutely unfeminine smile; a smile that somehow is akin to the impenetrable smile of the paintings of da Vinci; a smile to which is impelled the soul of remarkable persons and which from the very first moment on and incessantly, alienates the heart of women and the sensual curiosity of many men" (1968, 38).

112. In his studies of Botticelli and Ghirlandaio's *Nympha*, Warburg developed the idea of pathos formulas as engrams of passion (the maenads), which continue to influence the forms of movement in Florentine Renaissance painting; see Gombrich 1970, 105–27 and 297–304; see here also the chapter on *Primavera*.

113. Translation: Elena Polzer.

114. This quotation is from the English author Richard Steele (1671–1729), taken from the journal *Spectator*, which he published together with Addison. Hofmannsthal copied this sentence—which was originally "The whole man is to move together"—from Lichtenberg, who attributed it to Addison. Hofmannsthal invoked this sentence several times in the period from ca. 1902 to 1907, e.g., in *On Characters in Novels and in Dramas*, in his notes on the *Andreas* novel, and in particular in his *Letters of a Returnee*. Here the idea takes on central importance in his cultural-critical line of argumentation; see Coghlan 1985.

115. See Bachelard on the "dialectic of outside and inside" in his *Poetics of Space* (1975, 242–62). However, Bachelard focuses on the phenomenon of the boundary, the threshold

between body and surrounding space, while simultaneously representing the "open secret" of the interpenetration of inside and outside:

> It is, I answer myself, unerringly like a dreamer, it is the secret of infinity in these garments. He who would truly be a match for them must approach them by means other than the eye, with greater reverence yet with more daring. And still, it is the eye that would have to bid him, beholding, absorbing, but then drooping, growing dim as with one overwhelmed. (99)

Goethe's "open secret"[116] is here translated into an artistic-religious model of relationships. The Arcanum not only conceals and reveals itself in the object, but also constitutes part of the subject. The veil therefore no longer symbolizes the boundaries between the hidden and the evident, between subject and object. Instead, it becomes a symbol of translucence, of transparency; a symbol that simultaneously envelopes the surface as well as the deeper layers underneath.

On his journey into the memory of antiquity, the traveler resembles the "novice of Sais" on a journey to himself—standing in rapture before the statues as a dreamer and dancer to whom the "meaning that stands above all meaning" is revealed in the very act of forgetting his classicistic ideal of education. Hofmannsthal's references to Novalis are based on his avid readings of Hardenberg, especially *The Novices of Sais* and the *Pollen* fragments, while writing *Conversation on Poetry*. His notes cite Novalis repeatedly on the process of art reception as an absorbing dialogue: "Novalis: Poetry dissolves the being of others in its own."[117] And in a significant modification of a passage from *The Novices of Sais*, Hofmannsthal writes: "Nature is the epitome of everything that moves us. In order to understand it, we must understand our body."[118]

This concept of a corporeal aesthetics of affect is further linked to a text passage by Novalis on the subject of *memoria*: "We are wrong to call memory the

---

between inside and outside in terms of both concrete and imaginary space. He does not include the body in his considerations.

116. On the subject of concealing and revealing, see, e.g., the following passage from *Wilhelm Meister's Travels*: "Certain secrets even if known to everyone, men find that they must still reverence by concealment and silence." Goethe 1827, 131–32.

117. See Hofmannsthal 1975–, 31: 323. Original in Novalis 1997, 56.

118. Translation: Elena Polzer. Novalis originally wrote: "The epitome of what stirs our feeling is called nature, hence nature stands in an immediate relation to the functions of our body that we call senses." Novalis 2005, 77. (For this quotation in Hofmannsthal's own notes see Hofmannsthal 1975–, 31: 346.)

poetic voice in us. However, we should acknowledge that it conjures eternal presence before us" (*SW*, 324).[119]

Hofmannsthal develops his idea of a movement relationship between an artwork and its beholder by combining a model of visionary perception, that is, an aesthetics of affect, with an aesthetics of creation that emphasizes corporeal immediacy. In order for us to be a match for works of art such as ancient sculpture, we "must approach them by means other than the eye, with greater reverence, yet with more daring" (99).

This idea leads us directly to *dance*. Dance—as *ceremony*[120]—replaces the distant gaze; the moving body becomes the eye of the observer.

By basing his art theory on the relationship of movement, Hofmannsthal emphasizes the distinct dialogical relationship of artwork and beholder. This form of dialogue is highly specific: the dynamograms are translated from static sculpture into dance movements. In other words, questions and answers pass between artwork and contemplative onlooker in a dynamic play of inside and outside. In his diary, Warburg describes this dialogical relationship as the "iconology of the space in-between."[121]

Hofmannsthal attempts to understand this dialogue in motion by examining the imprint and the effect of dynamograms in art by interweaving them in a new mixture of texts and arts that oscillates between signification and interpretation, between the discovery of signs and their eradication.

In winter 1903, this danced dialogue between Greek sculpture and solemn contemplation became reality. Isadora Duncan traveled to Greece to fulfill her long-cherished wish to set foot in that country, that cultural landscape, which she considered the cradle of her own art. In her memoirs,[122] she writes extensively about the deep impressions that this journey made on her, the "beauty too sacred for words," to which she gave herself with complete abandon—although the inhabitants of Athens were disconcerted at the sight of her dancing, her classical Greek clothing, and her construction of a temple and establishment of a school.

She danced at the Acropolis, in the "rhythm of the columns," in front of the Kore of Erechtheion: "This here is perfection: form, line, rhythm, this is my dance."[123]

---

119. Translation: Elena Polzer.

120. In his notes, Hofmannsthal comments on the relationship to dance as one of ceremony and individuality: "The meaning of the ceremony: it is a gesture, in which the individual acts for his predecessors and successors—the ceremony never befits the personal . . . *the ceremony is a noetic achievement of the body*" (GW 1979, A III, 537). Translation: Elena Polzer.

121. See Gombrich 1984, 343.

122. Duncan 1927, 116–35.

123. Niehaus 1981, 29. Translation: Elena Polzer.

Helene von Nostitz, Hofmannsthal's friend and correspondent, was in the audience, as Isadora danced in the moonlight at the Acropolis and in the Theater of Dionysus Eleuthereus[124] (see figure 28), to the recitations of Greek dramas by her older brother Augustin and to a choir of Greek boys singing. She writes:

> As usual, she filled the entire evening with her dance fantasies. The audience did not tire even for one moment, for here was expressed the abundance of life and of art. She danced the columns, which she had experienced by sunrise and under stars. She danced the holy awe of the temple, in which the incense rises up to the gods, danced the nymphs of the hills, woods and rivers and the bacchanalian joy of Dionysian celebrations.[125]

Duncan's dance appeared as the living manifestation of the dance of the Greek statues—come to life out of the memory of antiquity. von Nostitz's report seems almost like the libretto or scenario of Hofmannsthal's "Moments in Greece": the "rhythm of the columns," the mystical moment, the liquefaction of the stony silence in the dynamics of the creative dialogue between cultural monument and artist correspond to a poetics of dance and literature that is derived from the pathos of antiquity.

Von Nostitz's correspondence and conversations with Hofmannsthal clearly influenced the development of his text.[126] Nostitz and Hofmannsthal often mentioned the journey to Greece and shared their thoughts on his writings in the letters that they wrote between 1908 and 1912. The subject of the vitalized statue and the mysterious smile of the archaic women take on a special role in their communications. On April 6, 1912, von Nostitz writes

---

124. See Nostitz 1979, 99: "Here stood the temple of Dionysus and the mysteries. Only the torsos of the dancing maenads and the bacchanalian festive processions on the tombs still recount the fervor of religious joy. Yet we require a living being to convey to us the atmosphere that these stones still emanate. Suddenly to our surprise the dancer Isadora Duncan appeared: stepping out of the shadows of the columns, a red coat swirling around her against the backdrop of the blue sea. She believed herself to be alone. With dancing steps she flew through the abandoned room. Yet one could feel how she was filled with the spirit of some god. Her movements lost their restraint, slowed down, and the solemn gestures became a ministration to the mysteries—Dionysus received his due once more from a mortal soul. The grand dancer strode from stone to stone, listening to the voice of her soul and the salutations of the god; then she turned to face the sea and vanished from sight." Translation: Elena Polzer.

125. Nostitz 1979, 195. Translation: Elena Polzer.

126. See Nostitz 1991, 173.

to Hofmannsthal from Athens. Her letter cites elements from *Moments of Greece*—the subject of light and of the statues:

> There are moments in this country that are unforgettable, such as certain illuminations of the Parthenon, a day on the island of Aegina, the grandeur of Mycenae. . . . I like being in the small Acropolis museum in the morning, among the smiling archaic women. Possibly it is there that one comes closest to the sentiment of the age.[127]

But Hofmannsthal and Duncan share more than just the enthusiastic reconciliation of the temporal abyss between modernity and antiquity. They also document their experience of the collapse of that same bridge between the ages: the disenchantment of coming up against an "impossible antiquity":

> I remember the evening after the Royal performance I could not sleep and, at dawn, I went all by myself to the Acropolis. I entered the Theatre of Dionysus and danced. I felt it was for the last time. Then I ascended the Propylaea and stood before the Parthenon. Suddenly it seemed to me as if all our dreams burst like a glorious bubble, and we were not, nor ever could be, other than moderns. We could not have the feeling of the Ancient Greeks. This Temple of Athena before which I stood, had in other times known other colors. I was, after all, but a Scotch-Irish-American. Perhaps through some affinity nearer allied to the Red Indian that to the Greeks. The beautiful illusion of one year spent in Hellas seemed suddenly to break. The strains of Byzantine Greek music grew fainter and fainter, and through it all the great chords of the Death of Isolda floated upon my ears.[128]

As in Hofmannsthal's case, Duncan likewise—despite her naïve adoption of ancient pathos formulas—perceived the gulf faced by modernity as

---

127. Correspondence, Hofmannsthal and Nostitz 1965, 110f. Translation: Elena Polzer. Helene von Nostitz sent a photograph of one of these kore statues to Hofmannsthal (ibid., 122 and 186). O. v. Nostitz (1991, 173) recalls: "Hofmannsthal thanked me with the words: 'The picture will help me more than anything else in the word to write the third chapter— already all hopes of being able to finally bring to the light of day some uninterpretable inner voice are linked to this unreadable face.' The framed image of the kore hung in his study until he had completed his essay." References to the "smile of the archaic women" accompanied their correspondence as a kind of leitmotif in the period from 1908 to 1912. After attending the *Ariadne* together in Dresden and reading from the first part of "Moments in Greece" together, Helene von Nostitz noted: "Conversations about Archaic Women" (Hofmannsthal and Nostitz 1965, 185f.)

128. Duncan 1927, 134.

a break with classic aesthetics. As a consequence, her dances shifted their focus both in terms of the topics that she explored (e.g., from depictions of the *Primavera* to the dance of the maenad) and in the movement elements and dramaturgical ideas used (e.g., her choreography for the *Tannhäuser* Bacchanal, which the last sentence above already anticipates).

Hofmannsthal's "Mnemosyne" project as it appears in "Moments in Greece," as well as in other texts of his from this period—*The Path and the Encounters, Letters of a Returnée, Fear: A Dialogue*—however, fundamentally differs from Aby Warburg's *Mnemosyne* archive. While Warburg attempted to compile a large-scale visual inventory of pathos formulas and their transformations over the course of cultural and art history since antiquity, Hofmannsthal proceeded to suspend the idea of an archive altogether. He sought to *erase* the images—those topoi of antiquity that Warburg attempted to serially compile in an "atlas of mimicry"—from memory before they reappeared, rising up as animated movement, as immediate vitalized representation from a visionary dream. Remembering therefore becomes the result of forgetting. Only the collapse of memory can pave the way to *memoria*. The experience of an "impossible antiquity" is based on an awareness of the barrier impeding the search for an individualized access to the past—an obstacle faced in the attempt to continue reading Greek art as the epitome of European culture. A creative connection to history generated by the immediacy of the human body will first lead into the dark zone of the "unreachable" found in memory loss. Freud's theory of psychoanalysis multiplies the difficulties of remembering and forgetting.[129] Hofmannsthal's writings around 1907 reflect this in their experimentation with alternative creative aesthetics that are not limited to writing. The result is a poetics of remembering as forgetting. Loss of *memoria*, forgetting as the shedding of cultural memory, thus appears as the premise for memory to rise up from the unconscious as a quasi archetypal formula of cultural knowledge—in terms of Warburg's psychohistorical model, the dream as a vision of beginning.

The epilogue to the encounter with the statues in the museum of the Acropolis describes this relationship of remembering and forgetting as that moment of awareness in which the boundaries between the self and culture, between the body and the realm of signs, momentarily dissolve:

> I do not really embrace them as something present, but I call them to me from somewhere with continuous wonder, with a feeling anxiously sweet, like memory. It would be unthinkable to want to cling to their surface. This surface actually is not there—it grows by a continuous coming from

129. See Worbs 1983, 259–295.

inexhaustible depths They are there and are unattainable. So, too, am I. By this we communicate. And while I feel myself becoming stranger and under this one word "Eternal" forever losing more and more of myself, vibrating like a column of heated air above a conflagration, I ask myself, slowly fading like the lamp of bright daylight: if the Unattainable feeds on my innermost being and the Eternal builds out of me to eternity, what then still stands between me and the Deity? (99–100)

This moment of abandon, the moment of throwing off the mantle of culture, describes the dialectic of body and text, of nature and culture, while simultaneously representing a transgression of that demarcating line—"on the borderline of the body" (as described in the dialogue *Fear*)[130]—from which dance emerges as the ecstatic movement of the creative self.

Hofmannsthal's poetics of remembering as forgetting emphasizes other aspects than Warburg's *Mnemosyne* project. Both concepts of a revitalization of cultural memory share a psychohistorical approach: the attempt to link ontological and anthropological factors. For both—the author and the art historian—pathos formulas, as mediators between the subjectivity of expression and the iconic topoi of affect representation, and their reflection in images of the moving body are instrumental in their research. But while Warburg focuses on reconstructing an inventory of expressive values imprinted by the engram in the archive of cultural history, Hofmannsthal is occupied with their *deconstruction*: namely the deletion and reassignment, de- and transfiguration of images and rhetorical elements of conventionalized cultural memory.

For Hofmannsthal, only the eradication of signs allows their resignification. Ultimately, the act of signifying or finding signs is nothing more than a process of finding oneself, that is, of self-creation. The burden of cultural memory is forgotten in the self-abandon of the subject. The act of burying memory allows a new beginning to emerge from the chaos of "beginninglessness" (Botho Strauß). In Hofmannsthal's "Moments in Greece," the eradication of predetermined semiotic structures and their trajectories of meaning from cultural memory does not equal radical *deletion* as proposed by Thomas Bernhard. Instead, eradication here contains the implications of both liquidation and liquefaction: both the suspension of meaning and the liquefying of fixed semiotic and visual conventions in an act of visionary reading. This act is an act of movement, in which the "material" takes on "a liquid quality"—a moment in which the statues begin to dance.

130. See Brandstetter 1991b.

Chapter 2

Patterns of Femininity and the Body-Image of Dance

Around the turn of the century, the body-image of dance reflected contemporary patterns of femininity that were (largely) based on two key models: the model of ancient Greece and the model of the exotic. Occasionally, these models appeared in "pure" form as ideal types. Sometimes only fragments of them can be found in the wide spectrum of documented dance performances that are still available to us.

In the Greek model, pathos formulas were activated and transformed as genuine patterns of *nature* and *naturalness* of the movement forms of new dance by interpreting images of antiquity through dance. In the following chapter, I will illustrate this corporeal process of translation with the help of three exemplary pictorial motives: the *Primavera*, the *Nike*, and the *Maenad*.

In the exotic model, distinct body imagery developed in response to the encounter with foreign cultures and in response to the experience of the Other in one's own culture. Exotic images of the body were particularly linked to codes of exotic dress and erotic dance movement, which were associated with the femme fatale—as I will demonstrate in the cases of the oriental "bee dance" and the dance of Salome.

The recurrent theme that links these two models of body imagery is that of *fabric*, or rather the folds or drapery of dance textiles, both as expressions of fashion and as examples of costuming, in the form of the Greek tunic or of the exotic dancer's veil. On stage and in literature, fabric became the medium of movement figurations both in dance and in writing.

DRAPERY IN MOTION: DANCE DRESS
AND DANCE REFORM

The advent of distinct forms of body imagery and corresponding patterns of femininity, and the associated discourse on dance reform, coincided at the turn of the century with discussions of *dress reform*. In search of a new fashion image of the modern female body liberated from the corset in all its guises, the women's liberation movement and the physical culture movement discovered similar goals, which were also shared by the reformist aspirations of free dance, which was likewise experimenting with new forms of "costume" at the time.

In the following chapter, I will therefore attempt to take these parallel developments into account. However, it should be noted that it is not possible to strictly distinguish between (everyday) fashion and (theatrical) costume, between dress reform and dance reform, and thus between theater and salon since these are all spaces in which the new forms of "artistic" dress were exhibited.

Let me start with a short summary of the history and aesthetics of dress reform at the turn of the century (in terms of its relationship to dance) as well as a problem-oriented outline of the subject of *mode et modernité*, as it is played out in Stéphane Mallarmé's citations of fashion, which are also a literary and journalistic practice of fashion as citation. Then I turn to the theme of dance costume with respect to body imagery of antiquity and the exotic. The folds of freely flowing fabric, the pathos formula of "drapery in motion," play a paradigmatic role here: after an excursion into the semiotic function of the veil, I will present an exemplary case of dance dress as it presented itself both on the catwalk of fashion and on the avant-garde dance stage. I am here referring to the dresses of Mariano Fortuny, the basic structures of which were composed of a play of moving pleats—a model that in the writings of Proust and D'Annunzio became more than just motifs in the contexts of fashion and performance.

Dress Reform and Women's Bodies

Dance reform at the beginning of the twentieth century was inseparably linked to dress reform. Both were so closely associated in the public mind that Isadora Duncan's costume—a loosely draped "Greek" tunic worn over naked legs—became almost in itself a symbol of the newly emergent *freier Tanz* movement: illustrations but also caricatures of Isadora, for example in the magazine *Die Jugend* (*Youth*), attest to the interconnections of dress reform and dance reform.

The new "costume" that modern dance created for itself departed in every way from the traditional costume elements of ballet (leotard and tights, corsage, short tutu, and pointe shoes). In doing so, the avant-garde conspicuously accentuated the intent to distance itself from classical ballet, thus emphasizing the aesthetic of a new understanding of dance by changing its approach to textile design.

Dance reform was moreover closely linked to a more far-reaching social reform of women's clothing. Both reform movements had similar goals: they sought to liberate women[1] from old, antiquated constraints and establish alternative images of the female body, based on natural silhouettes and on the idea of restoring to the body its freedom of movement. Hygienic, emancipatory, and aesthetic arguments thus overlapped in the discourse surrounding dress reform.[2]

"Women's rights are largely impeded by women's dress," said Max von Boehn in his book *Bekleidungskunst und Mode* (*The Art of Apparel and Fashion*) in 1918.[3] Dress reformists sought to liberate women from the dictates of fashion, which—in the name of "accentuated" femininity—deformed, harmed, and disfigured the body by lacing the waist and by employing corsets or bustles. The fiercest ideological battles were fought against the corset—against its anatomical, hygienic, and aesthetic deformations. The main issue in fin de siècle fashion was the bustle. "Prisons pour Femmes" is the title of an article about corsets in *Le Théâtre* in 1899. In his manuscript *Die Kultur des weiblichen Körpers als Grundlage der Frauenkleidung* (*The Culture of the Female Body as the Basis of Women's Dress*, 1910), doctor and medical historian Paul Schultze-Naumburg valiantly advocated modeling the body on Greek sculpture (although he regrettably did so for reactionary reasons that were frighteningly well suited to the ideological schemata of National Socialism).

1. On the relationship between dance reform, *Ausdruckstanz*, and the emancipation movement, see Klein 1992; Klein emphasizes in particular the reactionary tendencies that can be found in the images of femininity and the body evoked by *Ausdruckstanz* (especially in the 1920s). In my opinion, however, the problem is more complicated, because progressive, as well as retrogressive, tendencies overlapped in the codification of the female body as nature, in its appropriation by women themselves (who appeared in dance and choreography not only as representatives of this new body imagery, but also as its producers).

2. I refer to Roland Barthes, *The Fashion System* (1990), in which he postulates that fashion only becomes a semiotic system through discourse; he therefore analyzes *talk* about fashion or rather the reading of fashion that is signified in this talk, the "vestimentary codes," rather than "fashion as such." His analysis of "the systems of written clothing" follows two complementary trains of thought: on the one hand, that "which I shall call the written vestimentary code or the terminological system" in terms of describing a function, and on the other hand an analysis of the organization of the signifiers among themselves (ibid, 34f.).

3. Boehn 1918, 97. Translation: Elena Polzer.

In the introduction to his manuscript, he emphasizes that his arguments shall strive to hold up to "inspection by the most accurate of scientific observation and the sharpest logical thinking"[4]:

> This is no matter of personal taste or of a vague general feeling, of which there is little to say in detail. That would not be the way of an aesthetic of the future. Instead, the cumulative knowledge of all anatomical, biological, motoric moments of the body produces an understanding of corporeal principles, which culminates in a vivid image of the ideal body.[5]

Schultze-Naumburg goes on to denounce the continued prevalence of wrong ideas about the body and to demand their rectification, for "years of bad habits have caused knowledge of the body to be lost; for centuries there has been no visible translation of that which is based on truth" (16). To substantiate his conviction that nature never intended tightly laced wasp waists, he references representations of the body found in ancient sculpture. Multiple photographic series of ancient statues such as the Venus de Milo and the *Vergine Vinitrice* from the collection of the Vatican contrast with drawings of laced torsos—the famous wasp waist. According to Schultze-Naumburg, the reason for molding the body with corsets lies in its eroticization of the female form. In contrast, loosely draped reform dress, which exerts no pressure, accentuates the body's "natural" shape.

We have here an antagonistic relationship of eroticism and nature that is more or less typical for the entire physical culture movement: the integration of the naked body in everyday life and recreation goes hand in hand with its desexualization—a phenomenon that especially characterizes discourse concerning the nudist movement.[6]

The development of a new awareness of the body (also in the form of an educational program for modern women) also provided the basis for changes in aesthetic appreciation.

One of the slogans of dress reform, issued by the leading American and British instigators of associations and magazines for modern female dress, was "Aesthetic, hygienic, practical, economical." Women's rights activists and designers, such as Anna Muthesius and Belle Armstrong Whitney and her book *What to Wear: A Book for Women* (1916), emphasized the possibilities that reform dress gave women to develop new forms of individuality and creativity.

4. Schultze-Naumburg 1910, 8f.

5. Schultze-Naumburg 1910, 11. Translation: Elena Polzer.

6. See Andritzky and Rautenberg 1989.

They encouraged women to discover their own "personal form of dressing" (Anna Muthesius), to design their clothes to reflect their own individual style (figure 13). This is also the artistic-individualized line of argumentation followed by Alfred Mohrbutter in his popular book *Das künstlerische Kleid der Frau* (*The Artistic Dress of Women*, 1904). Here we can clearly see how closely linked is the impulse of art nouveau to design dresses "artistically"—as is also the case for other objects of daily use—to an escape from the conformity of ready-made clothing:

Textile manufacturing (i.e., the coercion that it entails: here is the newest pattern, the latest innovation, the momentarily prescribed material, this is

Figure 13 Reform dress at the turn of the century.
SOURCE: Derra de Moroda Dance Archives, Salzburg, Austria / © Derra de Moroda Dance archives, University of Salzburg, Austria.

what you now all must wear, no matter what you look like and who you
are), this ready-to-wear clothing and its decorative trimmings, which are
unable to fulfill even a single desire and express nothing, is not compatible
with woman, who wisely and imperturbably states: this is what I like, what
suits me and my nature.[7]

Such nonconformity, however, remained an elite endeavor, as is evident in
the names of those artists who designed artistic clothing in the style of reform
dress, such as Henry van de Velde, Richard Riemerschmidt, Hermann Obrist,
Peter Behrens, Marie Hartmannn, and Else Oppler.

Nonetheless the "tricks of fashion"[8] soon caught up with reform dress and its
emphasis on individuality in opposition to the fashion industry, causing dress
reform to become an art nouveau fashion movement of short duration.

Mode et Modernité

A similar juxtaposition of art and everyday culture can also be found in the
work of Stéphane Mallarmé. In his journalistic texts, this author of hermetic
poetry combined thoughts on fashion with thoughts on modernity. In his
magazine *La Dernière Mode* (1874),[9] he put into practice that characteristic
perspective on fashion and on the aesthetics of fashion which Baudelaire
had already outlined in his major essay "The Painter of Modern Life" ("Le
Peintre de la via moderne") (1860). The artistic citation thus became the
decisive link between "la mode" and "la modernité." "Fashion cites art . . .
and assimilates it as decoration into the life of the sophisticated personality."[10] Elements of art and various artistic styles are made available as citation, a procedure committed as much to nineteenth-century historicism as
it is to aestheticism.

According to Mallarmé, modernity's "new" innovative potential only truly
reveals itself in talk about reflections of art in fashion: the new silhouette,
the lines and cascades of frills and drapery are pictorial citations that evoke

---

7. Mohrbutter 1904, 14. Translation: Elena Polzer.

8. See Bovenschen 1986.

9. Mallarmé was editor of this magazine for one year and wrote articles under various
pseudonyms on fashion, jewelry, theater, sports, and subjects such as menus and gossip in
the salons and at the beach; see Mallarmé 1945, 705ff.; see Goebel 1978.

10. Mallarmé 1945, 44. Translation: Elena Polzer.

antiquity, rococo, or the Second Empire. Modern life at the beach appears reflected in the mythical image of the nymph or the sea goddess ("*déité marine*").

In this configuration of artistic citation and fashion, modernity literally appears "robed" in femininity.[11]

Harry Graf Kessler, confident observer and interpreter of his age, gave his own interpretation of the subject of fashion and modernity in his diaries from 1907. For him the peculiarly ambivalent quality of modernity is a dominant sign of the times: the unresolved simultaneity of "yes and no," citing the old, while celebrating the new, the parallelism of refinement and pragmatism, of fashion and art:

> Spent the day at the dressmakers with Gee: Sœurs Callot, Doucet, Drecoll. Pretty girls in the newest fashions walk slowly past, twirl, show themselves from all sides, and disappear. The Byzantine orchid quality of today's evening gowns, the wide, enveloping gowns, the rare, refined, pale colors suited these slender, pale girls well. One sits as if watching a strange ballet, one that determines the physiognomy of the age. Short and smart street clothes are suddenly presented between the dreamy evening wear, fabrics and lines precisely calculated for rainy wet streets, trains, yachts, automobiles, a form of elegant interior decoration. It is this dichotomy of almost perverse esotericism and austere, but elegant utilitarianism that seems to me to characterize today's fashion and maybe even the age itself: in other words not the tendency toward refinement shared by all periods and both poles of our age. What is special is neither this refinement nor the exclusively practical aspect, but the simultaneous affirmation and denial of modern reality; yes and no belong to the character of the age as they do to modern fashion: they are the two sides of modernity. Vandevelde [*sic*] is wrong to allow only "yes" to be modern. One side of modernity ranges from brutally practical to elegant, the other from brutally gaudy to mystical; at the bottom we find autobus and emperor, at the top Vandevelde [*sic*] or Whistler and Baudelaire or Monticelli. Our day and age encompasses Byzantium and Chicago, Hagia Sophia and turbine halls; we will not understand them if we only wish to see one side.[12]

11. At this point I would like to at least mention Mallarmé's numerous poems about fans in which the semiotic game of "fashion" is projected onto the field of poetology (a dimension of "fan" metaphorics, which already appears in Goethe's *West-Eastern Divan*).

12. H.G. Kessler, diary entries from November 26, 1907; in: Kessler 2005, 371f. Translation: Elena Polzer.

Drapery in Motion: Fabrics of Dance and
Patterns of Textu(r)al Production

In his article "Dekorative Variationen" (Decorative variations, 1907/8), Felix Poppenberg dealt with the aesthetics of the *veil-shawl*. He regarded the subject as belonging to the "chapter on individualized female costume" in terms of reform dress and particularly emphasized its ornamental aspect:

> The idea is to allow the contours and the charms of rhythm to express themselves in softly flowing fabrics regardless of the dressmaker's pattern or style, simply through the shape of the body and through movement.[13]

He emphasized associations with images and figurations of "ancient cultures" and in his article referred both to classical antiquity and to Asian costume, both the "draped folds of Tanagra figurines" and "East-Asian kimonos" and "Indian Cashmere shawls."

Drapery not only plays with the act of alternately revealing and disguising the body, but also jumps from art to fashion and from fashion away again into forms of presentation in dance and theater: Poppenberg speaks of "etudes in a material rich in sculptural potential," whereby

> these veil and shawl costumes, which only develop . . . their full charm when in use, unceasingly shifting in their charms, while always serving as a logical-decorative expression of the natural body in motion, and thus hence must be considered elements of our cultural context and "constructive aesthetics."[14]

This conjunction of the dance movements contained in the folds of drapery with "constructive aesthetics" is also typical for the work of painter and dancer Alexander Sakharoff. In his unpublished essay "Über das Tanzkostüm" (About the Dance Costume),[15] Sakharoff emphasized the meaning of drapery for movement imagery and associated images of the body. The garment is not a "disguise," but a kind of dance skin. For Sakharoff, dance costumes were therefore not "copies" of a historical style, but rather abstract and nevertheless sensual fantasies, which came to life in the dance: "l'enveloppe matérielle de la danse."

13. Poppenberg 1907–8, 741. Translation: Elena Polzer.

14. Ibid., 742.

15. The typescript is stored in the Sakharoff collection of the Lenbachhaus, Munich; the following quotes are taken from this German-French manuscript.

This dance skin, this total mask, modified, transformed, and formed the very basis of the dance itself in the existence of the dancer's body. According to Sakharoff, two modes of creation mingle when designing a dance costume: the painted image and the mathematical play of proportions. "Form, color, line, space"—their coalescence in the creation of dance and dance costumes is "pure mathematics." The result is a "synthetic costume," a construct of image and number, sculptural form and the geometry of the pattern. In his drawings, Sakharoff deconstructed and segmented the complete images of the moving dresses into precise, "synthetic notations" as he called them. These were both dressmaking patterns and choreographic notations, a collage of movement sketches, numbers, writing, and applied pieces of fabric. Thus the construction of the "fabric of dance" also in turn produced new forms of sculptural art.

The deconstructed folds, the costume as a planar dressmaker's pattern—this prototype of clothing again references the simplest textile form of drapery: the shawl, the veil.

Shawl and Veil

In dance, the veil marks the boundary between expressiveness and impenetrability, between the dynamics of transient movement and the motionless structure of the body in space. The drapery of the veil[16] signifies a zone of transition; as in the case of dance itself, the veil unfurls a transitory act of creating and relocating meaning in motion. On the one hand, we have the body, which owes its visibility to the veil, as it almost impregnates the fabric and molds it with its "contours" (J. J. Winckelmann). On the other hand, we have the garment, the shawl, whose movements dissolve all contours in an abstract process—a process in which the body is quasi-transformed into the very texture of the fabric.

It is thus necessary to differentiate the dual function of the veil in dance performances:

- As a medium of concealing and dematerializing the body on the one hand, as exemplified in Loïe Fuller's *Serpentine Dance* (figure 40). This aspect of abstraction, the blending of the body with the surrounding space via the medium of orchestrated fabric, will be studied in the second part of this book.

16. On the subject of the veil see Perniola 1989; Perniola gives an iconographic-structuralist overview of sculpture from antiquity to the baroque; the central aspect of dance as relevant for the context of this book is of course not taken into account.

- And on the other hand, as a symbol for accentuating and erotically presenting the body or specific parts of the body—especially in traditional
  depictions of and in the iconography of exotic dance (figure 12) in the
  dance of the Bayadere, *Odalisque*, and, especially, in Salome's dance of
  the veils; hence with the goal of creating exotic body imagery, as I will
  elucidate more clearly in the following chapters.

In her dances, Loïe Fuller employed the veil in a revolutionary and highly
progressive manner as a medium of concealment, that is, as a medium through
which to obliterate all body images in a metamorphosis of moving fabric in
space.[17] This process of transformation, the act of folding the corporeal element into the spatial frame, resembles what Rainer Maria Rilke described in
his late "shawl" poems: "around this quiet center, the desire . . . the incredible
flower consummating all of itself within the swaying weave"[18]—in the first of
two poems entitled "Shawl" from 1923:

As for the virgin, from he who kneels before her,
names rush in unheard: spring, rose, house, star . . .
and as he has always known that the more names come
not one will be enough for what she means—
. . . so, while you look at the casually outspread center
of the cashmere shawl, reborn in black
from its flowered edge, a clearing in its frame,
creating a purer space for all of space . . . :
you realize: that names would be forever
wasted on it: for it is the center.
As, whatever pattern may guide our steps,
It is around a void like this we wander.[19]

The chain of signs—the names and the patterns of the steps—takes on the
shape of movements that create and relocate, replace and erase meaning. It
resembles the texture of a finely woven web, a web that creates a "purer space" by
dynamically referencing "center" and "edge," interior and periphery—a space that
absorbs both body and signs. Mallarmé described Fuller's veil dance as movement around an empty center, bringing forth space as a nonsignified realm.[20]

17. See the sections on Loïe Fuller and Stéphane Mallarmé in Part II of this book.

18. Rilke 2010, 93.

19. Ibid.

20. See the section on this subject in Part II.

In exotic dance (which I will analyze in the following chapters on the basis of examples of the "bee dance" and "Salome's dance"), the veil or the shawl—usually translucent and made of silk or finest chiffon—becomes the dominant symbol of physical representation. It is not a costume or a mere stage prop, but rather a moving texture that marks the "dark continent of the feminine" in an erotic game of concealment and unveiling, defining and shifting the boundaries between different zones of the body. It is neither the movement figurations, nor the choreography—the writing of movement itself—but rather the body of the dancer, textured in such a way through the lines of the fabric that it becomes an enigmatic image of desire. Gustave Moreau's depiction of Salome dancing before Herod (figure 35) is a portrayal of precisely this type of "veil dance." It is the artful "description" of the female body by the dancing lines, freezing the body into a statuesque pose, the engraving of moving traces of desire onto the body: the ornament of the veil dance. In his book *Le Ruban au Cou d'Olympia* (*The Necklace of Olympia*), Michel Leiris similarly attempts to trace the mechanisms of desire generated by this principle of describing the body, a principle that is a prerequisite for the eroticism of nakedness.[21]

In this cultural-historical context, the gowns of visual artist and costume designer Mariano Fortuny are ideal examples of the relation of fashion to modern forms of representation or movement citations in the fine arts and in dance.

Draped Folds: The Veils and Dance Gowns of Mariano Fortuny

The Spanish painter and designer Mariano Fortuny (1871–1949) was one of those artists at the turn of the century who designed clothes in such a novel style that they helped establish a new form of fashion. Fortuny's textile designs were not high fashion—Fortuny did not consider himself a couturier like Paul Poiret or Coco Chanel. Instead, his inspiration came from theater, as was very common at the time. And Fortuny is known in theater history not for his costumes and textile designs, but mainly for his design of a distinct lighting system, as well as for the invention of a unique type of cyclorama, the "Fortuny sky" or "Fortuny dome."[22]

However, in his lifetime he became famous for his clothes. "My dress is my fortuny" was the pun shared by women in the 1920s, who expressed their exquisite taste and their sense of the theatrical in fashion, by acquiring an extravagant

---

21. Leiris 1983.

22. On Mariano Fortuny, see *Fortuny e Caramba* 1987; *Mariano Fortuny* 1985.

wardrobe. Such a wardrobe simply had to contain, especially in artist and intellectual circles, at least one "Fortuny dress." To this day, the list of famous owners of Fortuny gowns and Fortuny shawls in theater, film, and dance history surrounds these textiles with an aura of the extraordinary and precious—Eleonora Duse, Isadora Duncan, Ruth St. Denis, Peggy Guggenheim, Martha Graham, and even Julie Christie and Geraldine Chaplin.

In the 1920s and 1930s, in a period already completely under the influence of a sophisticated and (to a limited degree) mechanized mass production of textiles, Fortuny's clothes became the epitome of the international fashion world— not least of all thanks to their refined fabrication by machines that Fortuny himself invented. The first, experimental phase of Fortuny's textile creations is closely linked to his decorative and technical work for the stage work and for dance.

Fortuny's passion for the theater ignited in 1892 in Paris when the twenty-one-year-old encountered the music of Wagner for the first time. Full of enthusiasm, he went to Bayreuth and was so overwhelmed by the impression the festival made on him that he exclusively designed sets for pieces by Wagner throughout the following years. The surviving designs for *Tristan and Isolde* and for *The Ring of the Nibelung* demonstrate a bold use of space and a sensitive use of color and light, which seems closely related to concepts propagated by Adolphe Appia in his manuscript *La Mise en Scène du Drame Wagnérien* (1895). Before arriving at his true calling, theater and textiles, Fortuny attempted to make his way—with little success—as a painter in the family tradition, which boasted a long genealogy of famous Spanish painters both on his mother's and on his father's side.

Mariano Fortuny y Madrazao was born in 1871 in Granada, as the son of the painter Mariano Fortuny y Marsal. His father died at the height of his career when Mariano was three years old. His mother, Dona Cecilia, then moved the family to Paris, where Fortuny's cousin Coco de Madrazao lived, who later wrote the libretto to the ballet *Le Dieu bleu* together with Jean Cocteau for Serge Diaghilev's Ballets Russes. Michel Fokine was responsible for the choreography, Reynaldo Hahn for the composition. Vaslav Nijinsky created the main character of the "blue God." Mariano Fortuny was also associated with the periphery of this group of artists. In Paris, he finally had everything that the fin de siècle and sophisticated society of the belle époque had to offer in terms of literature, arts, and theater, before going to Venice, where his truly creative period began. In 1899, he moved into the palazzo Pesaro Orfei, which was later renamed Palazzo Fortuny or "House of the Magician." Here, Fortuny showed, as Henry de Régnier recounts, his own first collection of textiles in September 1906.

Helene von Nostitz, who visited Fortuny in his palazzo in later years, remembers a collection of scarves and gowns, presented in the magnificent Venetian rooms as in a museum:

> There were ancient Mycenaean patterns and the garment of the charioteer of Delphi with its bold and noble drapery. The splendor of the garments glowed between the simple wooden pillars, like the sun setting on the lagoon; from deep orange to radiant carmine, the symphony of color played all tones. Fortuny stood next to them almost austere. All this had come into being he knew not how—these leaves and blossoms on the translucent fabrics, which clung as light and immaterial as clouds.[23]

The moving drapery of the "bold and noble drapery," translation of the pathos formula of ancient descriptions of the statuesque body, simultaneously revealed the static beauty of the sculpture and the agile beauty of the dancing body. The Greek prototypes and names of the modern gowns additionally indicate the semantic field of translating and transforming body imagery into a "textile" medium: the Mycenaean meander and labyrinth pattern on the "Knossos" shawl on the one hand, and the pleated folds of the charioteer's garment in the "Delphos" dress, on the other.

Fortuny had already fashioned clothes at an earlier point in time as costumes for the stage. His first important experience in designing costumes was for Eleonora Duse in Gabriele D'Annunzio's *Francesca da Rimini* (1901). After critics wrote that the dresses didn't show off the movements of the actress to her best advantage, he continued to experiment with various materials and varying degrees of freedom of movement. His goal became to harmoniously blend light and beautiful fabric, thus permitting the greatest possible freedom of movement. He finally succeeded in reaching this goal with the development the above-mentioned large silk scarves or shawls, the edges of which he printed with meandering patterns.

These "Fortuny shawls" were presented for the first time in a theatrical context in a ballet by Charles M. Widor, performed in Paris at the house of the Comtesse de Béarn. A photo of the performance shows a setting with a Z-formed catwalk rising upward diagonally across the stage along which the dancers were distributed in various poses. Both this catwalk, a bridge resembling the *hashigakari* of Noh theater, and the costumes, dresses made of long draped fabric—a mixture of geisha kimono and sari—contextualized the ballet

23. Nostiz 1979, 193. Translation: Elena Polzer.

as turn-of-the-century *Japonisme*.[24] The dancers wore wide printed shawls of translucent fabric stretched over the shoulders or draped diagonally across the midriff, spread wide or loosely slung.

This was ostensibly the first public presentation of those wide, rectangular Fortuny shawls, which the creator himself referred to as Knossos shawls. They were made of fine, transparent silk, printed with symmetrical, usually geo-metrical and meandering patterns resembling Minoan Cretan art. The topos formula of the labyrinth transformed itself in the "wrap" of the garment into a medium for defining the body and its lines through contours and movements. Incidentally, I would like to also mention here that the short piano pieces by Eric Satie titled "Gnossienne" (= Knossos) from 1890 to 1897 were also based on this same Cretan-Minoan ornament.[25]

Although his scarves immediately found an enthusiastic audience, Fortuny was initially far from applying himself exclusively to his textile creations. He was instead largely occupied during this period with perfecting his lighting experiments[26] and with the development of a cyclorama for the stage, which was installed at the Krolloper in Berlin and later also in Paris. Fortuny dem-onstrated his inventions by stretching giant canvas sails lengthwise in a large hall in order to achieve the ideal lighting and projection effects. In this way, he attempted to create scenery that integrated lights, fabrics, colors, and a dynamic use of space in order to facilitate communication between audience, prosce-nium, and stage. Ruth St. Denis gives a good impression of these presentations in her memoirs. The dancer, who was introduced to Fortuny in 1907 by Harry Graf Kessler, Hugo von Hofmannsthal, his brother-in-law Hans Schlesinger, and Max Reinhardt in Berlin, recalls one of these fantastically operated stage innovations in *An Unfinished Life*:

> His thoughts, at that time, were entirely bound up in what was called the Fortuny sky, a revolutionary innovation for the theatre. . . .
> His invention was a curious vacuum-like contraption, which gave you the impression of being inside a balloon. It consisted of two elaborate air-filled compartments under two great spheres of silk. At the left of the stage was a piano-like instrument to be used for the play of the lights.

24. In his review of Ruth St. Denis's presentation of Fortuny's veils and shawls, Felix Poppenberg also compares them to the "kimonos of East Asia" and to Japanese paper: "The Fortuny veils are of the most delicate of silk chiffon, patterned and with shaded threading, reminiscent in structure and in the crépon luster of the surface of fine Japanese silk paper" (1906–7, 741). Translation: Elena Polzer.

25. See Wehmeyer 1974; and Volta 1992.

26. See St. Denis 1939, 112.

Over the proscenium inside the stage was a color-trolley, which moved in front of these powerful lights. By a touch on three or four buttons of his instrument he could transform these spheres into a sky full of sunrise or moonlight. The effect was overwhelming. The moment he began to play his lights I cried, "Your reproduction of nature is so perfect that your actors will look artificial. This sky belongs to dancers because of the harmony of movement and abstract costuming." . . .

The influence of that sky is felt in every theatre in America whether it is known or not. Under its inspiration flies have been done away with, and a huge bowl substituted—in most cases of plaster instead of the silk of Fortuny. But his original conception of silk spheres was used by the Paris Opera and several other opera houses in Europe.[27]

Even by themselves, these demonstrations of Fortuny's "cupola" achieved an immensely theatrical effect—not just merely as a framework for performances on stage, but also as an almost independent form of theater for its own sake thanks to the scenery, the use of space, the textile draperies, and the lighting effects. This abstract "scenodrama" resembled the theatrical experiments of Loïe Fuller, but *without* a dancer as its rhythmic moving centerpiece. Ruth St. Denis recognized this dimension of Fortuny's designs with the practiced eye of a theater and movement expert. Her exclamation that the Fortuny cupola should have been designed for dancers, because of the harmony of its movements and abstract costume design, said as much.

This harmony of movement and this abstract costume design were also characteristic qualities of Fortuny's shawls. It is hardly surprising that St. Denis declared herself willing to present these shawls:

Before I left Berlin I demonstrated his Greek veils for him at the great Wertheim store. These veils were given their shape by wooden molds, the design of which were taken from bas-reliefs at Knossos. I can think of nothing more exquisite than these veils or his Greek gowns, which are the quintessence of chic to many fashionable ladies both in New York and in Europe, where he now has shops.[28]

Hugo von Hofmannsthal has even more detailed memories of this performance than St. Denis, especially of the peculiarities of the improvised dances. Hofmannsthal was first introduced to Fortuny by his brother-in-law Hans

27. Ibid.

28. See St. Denis 1939, 112.

Schlesinger, who was at the time entering into a romantic liaison with St. Denis. He had also declared himself happily willing, as he reports in a letter from Weimar on December 3, 1907, to his childhood friend Georg Freiherrn zu Franckenstein, to hold a small speech at the presentation of Fortuny's Knossos shawls:

> Yesterday morning before an invited audience, a presentation of Fortuny's Greek veils by St. Denis, who very charmingly improvised short dances in ordinary dress—I held a short conference before, 12 minutes completely effortlessly and entirely improvised, without having written down a single word—of course the locality was packed, the entire first set of journalism, and today columns of articles (which I won't be reading, by the way), while in Vienna they probably would have sent the courtroom reporter.[29]

Hofmannsthal's letter to Helene von Nostitz describes the dance in even more detail:

> The matinee was a great success for Fortuny, almost even more so for St. Denis—she was wonderful—she improvised short dances, whose charm I am (hopefully) never to forget, it was such a bizarre, heartrending contrast to the everyday visiting dress that she was wearing and these small and so endlessly intense gestures, in which she sometimes threw her entire soul upward, squandering her charm and her graciousness in a manner so completely free of "airs," without all pomp.[30]

Hofmannsthal's description clearly shows that St. Denis did not perform any of those Indian dances at the matinee that had made her so famous in Europe from 1906 to 1909: *Radha, The Incense, Yogi, The Nautch*. Her improvisations were instead a form of *freier Tanz* with "Greek" elements of movement—the same gestures and poses that so enchanted Hofmannsthal. For it was he who coaxed her toward the Greek, as he wrote in a letter to Kessler.[31] Of course, for St. Denis, these elements of *freier Tanz* were far from new, as they were part of the movement repertory at her disposal since the beginning of her career thanks to her Delsarte schooling.[32] What she improvised—out of this

29. Hofmannsthal 1937, 299f. Translation: Elena Polzer.

30. Hofmannsthal 1937, 301f.

31. On February 4, 1908, Hofmannsthal writes to Kessler that he is going to see the two "new Indian dances" by Ruth St. Denis (*Yogi* and *Nautch*) and will "also hopefully be able to encourage her to turn her attention to antiquity." Hofmannsthal and Kessler 1968, 174.

32. For more on the system of expressive training created by the French pedagogue François Delsarte, which was avidly propagated across the United States by his students Steele

movement repository—was a dance of flowing, undulating arm movements, soft torsions, and side positions of the body, showing the translucent veils and fabrics to their best advantage.

The possibilities of draping Fortuny's rectangular wide silk fabrics on the body were endless. They could be looped around the body, simultaneously revealing and concealing, shaping and glossing over curves. They clung to the body, gave it complete freedom of expression. These fabrics literally seemed to demand that they be danced in so as to fully unfold their potential. And freedom of movement, by now already inscribed into the public mind by free dance, likewise set the standard for how "new" women dressed: in clothing, which like Fortuny's Knossos shawls only truly unfolded its beauty in motion.

As in the language of the fan, the effect of a silk scarf oscillates between accessory and dress, between (dance) costume and fashion, between signifier and signified. The indefinable position of "in-betweenness," constantly resurveying the limbo between sign and signified through movement, is a typical characteristic of these textiles. They belong just as much to theater and to dance as to teatime and to fine evening gowns. It was not least of all Isadora Duncan's dances (herself an ardent devotee of Fortuny dresses)—in loosely falling tunica, which in no way restricted her freedom of movement and which she modeled on ancient Greek "chiton"—which helped to lay the groundwork for the fashion craze caused by Fortuny's dresses (figure 14). Soon they were not only presented in public as "tea gowns," but made appearances at a wide range of public events. Dance and theater were the catalysts for the spread of this textile art. Fortuny's excellent sense of material and form in the use of fabrics, his instinct for the artistic potential of textile design, came from his experience in theater and in painting.

His designs were neither merely decorative paintings on fabric nor revolutionary new concepts of assembling clothing into patterns. The secret behind his success lay instead in the development of designs that looked like works of art, but didn't overwhelm the wearer's personality. These dresses guaranteed singularity and individuality, while combining freedom of movement and harmony of color and form with the aura of precious heirlooms from ancient times—such as those depicted in paintings by the Pre-Raphaelites or by Klimt.

The Knossos shawl formed the nucleus of all of Fortuny's subsequent textile creations: his silk and velvet dresses, his heavy, brocade-like overdresses, as well

MacKaye and Genevieve Stebbins and had a major influence on the founders of modern free dance, Loïe Fuller, Isadora Duncan, and Ruth St. Denis, see the section on Stebbins. See also Shawn 1954; Casini Ropa 1988, 107–22.

Figure 14 Isadora Duncan in a Greek pleated dress à
la Fortuny (drawing by C. Barbier, 1913).
SOURCE: Derra de Moroda Dance Archives, Salzburg,
Austria / © Derra de Moroda Dance archives, University of
Salzburg, Austria.

as the long, sleeveless coats and translucent silk wraps. But it was a silk robe, both
simple and sophisticated, that became Fortuny's most famous creation after the
Knossos scarves. This garment was the one later intrinsically connected to his
name—Fortuny call it the "Delphos" robe, after the "Charioteer of Delphi."

The pleated pieces of fabric that tightly enveloped the bodies of the ancient
korai—those sixth-century statues that Hofmannsthal reanimated in his
"Moments in Greece"—likewise served as prototypes for Fortuny's textile creations. Fortuny was an enthusiastic photographer and owned an extensive collection of images of ancient statues from all periods in his photo archive.

It wasn't, however, so much Fortuny's reconstruction of Greek clothing that
played a decisive role in the enormous success of his Delphos as its peculiar
mix of familiar and foreign, of ancient and avant-garde—a mixture well suited
to the contemporaneous predilection for neoclassicism and "reform" designs
of all kinds. This field of connotations, which ranged from Hellenism to exoticism, from physical culture to women's liberation, produced fertile ground

both for Duncan's dance reforms and for the textile innovations by Fortuny and other dress reformers of the age such as Paul Poiret.[33] Poiret, the great Paris couturier of the 1910s and 1920s—who boasted about being the man who freed modern women from the corset—was a great admirer of Fortuny's creations and bought several Delphos dresses for his daughter. Poiret, who likewise designed for the great dancers of the age, for Duncan, Ida Rubenstein, and Anna Pavlova, created designs that seemed deliberately influenced by Fortuny's Delphos pleats.

Last but not least, elements of Fortuny's textile designs can also be detected in the fantastic costumes created by Léon Bakst for the performances of Serge Diaghilev's Ballets Russes in Paris, especially in the ballets based on subjects of antiquity such as *Narcisse* (1911), *Daphnis et Chloé* (1912), and *L'Après-midi d'un Faune* (1912). Bakst, the great costume designer, interpreted antiquity in his own way and in a much more theatrical-fantastic fashion than Fortuny, but both men utilized the contemporary topos of the "Grecian"—"Greek, everything must be Greek," as Diane Cooper formulated the trend—freely dealing with images of antiquity in a way typical for the age.

Here the pathos formula of drapery in motion, which Aby Warburg analyzed as the symbolic inscription of passionate movements of the soul in ancient sculpture (and in their transformations throughout art history), becomes a freely applicable iconographic element that links the theatrical choreography of dance with the everyday choreographies of fashion.

Fortuny's artistic textile creations were not those of the Paris haute couture, a world dominated by Charles Frederick Worth, Poiret, and Chanel—although these masters of fashion in turn adopted and further developed his ideas. His dresses always retained the air of theatrical costume. They owed their existence to his artistic work in the fields of theater and painting. They translated the phantasms and shifts of color and light in the Fortuny sky from the movement space of "scenery" onto the shape of a single woman, wrapping herself in a Delphos.

The immanent omnipresent double-encoding of the Fortuny dress, which (both as "Delphos" and as "Knossos") appeared as both a fashion garment and a costume, as both individualized attire that accentuated the personality and a historicizing signifier that transformed subjectivity, loaded with a reservoir of meaning for turn-of-the-century physical culture "in the spirit" of antiquity, made these textiles almost predestined for *freier Tanz*. Duncan, who probably first encountered the Fortuny Delphos during her visit to Venice in 1910, wore these designs not only in her dances (figure 14), but

---

33. On Poiret and the influence of his fashion on body imagery at the turn of the century, see Battersby 1969, 96–122.

also privately, up to her tragic death. There exists a photo by Man Ray of her student Catherine Hawley in a Fortuny dress, as well as of Natasha Rambova, the actress, designer, and wife of the great silent film star Rudolph Valentino. Even Martha Graham, student of St. Denis and founder of American modern dance, continued to make use of the theatrical properties of the Delphos costume on stage. St. Denis not only presented Fortuny's Knossos scarves very early on in her dances, as mentioned above, but also danced her first Egyptian dance *Egypta* only a few years later, in 1910, in a "Delphos."

This seemingly unproblematic, seamless shift from Greek to Egyptian, equally exoticized mythical spaces, manifested both in Fortuny's dresses—whose names already established the connection—and in the dances of St. Denis and Duncan. In the field of dance, it also clearly corresponded with a tendency to merge antiquity and the Orient, as von Hofmannsthal took it from Erwin Rohde's book *Psyche*, and from Rudolf Kassner's early essay "Über den indischen Idealismus" (On Indian idealism, 1903).[34]

In its first phase around 1900, certain characteristics of *freier Tanz* derived from this very conjunction of the Oriental and the classical and from their translation into models of movement. Oriental dance had already lent an exotic element to opera and nineteenth-century ballet, as in the dance of Almeh, the odalisque, or the *Bayadère*, patterns of dance that were now adopted for the first time as an independent art form by turn-of-the-century *freier Tanz* in line with the individual styles and personalities of the dancers.

The unique character and significance of Fortuny's textiles, of Delphos and the Knossos scarves—their enigmatic tendency to oscillate between dress and accessory, concealing and revealing, as a mediator between the theater and the intimate domestic female sphere, between antiquity and the avant-garde—was acutely perceived by various fin de siècle authors. They integrated Fortuny's dresses into their work for the representative poetic attributes. In the writings of Marcel Proust, von Hofmannsthal, Henry de Régnier, and D'Annunzio, Fortuny's textile creations take on multiple symbolic functions: the fabrics appear as "citations" translated into text from the level of everyday culture, from the dimension of theatrical-dance performance, citing antiquity, but also—in the pathos formula of the affect-laden folds—citing the rhetoric of a "modern" freedom of movement and freedom of the body. The gown thus enabled a variety of references to distinct, even contrary body-images: a woman or dancer wearing a Fortuny dress embodied simultaneously, if she so desired, the Nike and the *Primavera*. The very fabric

---

34. See Hofmannsthal 1978, A III, 461; in the notes, he mentions reading Kassner's *Über den Indischen Idealismus* (ibid.) several times.

of fashion, the codified text of the pleated fabric, allowing an individualized assertion of female identity out of a collage of movement citations. These citations in turn referenced the imprint of fine art, especially that of antiquity and its renaissances: first of all the renaissance of antiquity from the fifteenth to the sixteenth centuries; then, during the French Revolution (with its dress reform in the Directoire style); and finally the nineteenth century, as seen with the Pre-Raphaelites (who provided the basis for references to antiquity by *freier Tanz*, that is, by Duncan).

Fashion cited the fine arts—as did dance. In fashion's textile collage of citations, body imagery as it appeared in art itself become a model in turn for art: as symbols, which applied the classical idea of the *natural* to the dancer's body; as a medium for staging and constructing femininity as in the writings of Proust and D'Annunzio.

Marcel Proust: *The Prisoner*

Fortuny dresses are repeatedly mentioned in the volume *The Prisoner* of Marcel Proust's *A la recherché du temps perdu*. The jealous observations of narrator Marcel, tracing the paths and conversations of Albertine, are again and again grounded in a discourse involving the refinements of aesthetic education, especially in the fields of *savoir vivre*, sophisticated conversation and fashion. Over the course of the novel, the Duchess de Guermantes and her exquisitely crafted wardrobe designed by the finest couturiers become role models for Albertine's developing and increasingly sophisticated fashion sense. Marcel supports her in her desire to be desired. Fashion and the endless variations of its details appear increasingly indispensable to achieve this goal, but for that very reason, they also become symbols of the unattainable. In self-tormented devotion to his jealous fantasies, the narrator assumes the role of an aesthetic tutor, agent, messenger, and fashion journalist, who gleans dressmaking patterns, the particularities of detail, of accessories, of fabric and fabrication from the prototype of fashion—the unique model embodied by Madame de Guermantes—and attempts to transfer them onto the body of his lover. While Albertine is away on one of her long trips, Marcel goes to Madame de Guermantes and during the idle teatime conversation about art and society, he interrogates her, who willingly discloses in great detail all that he wants to know, on the particulars of the design of her wardrobe:

> And that loose gown you were wearing the other evening, the one that smells so strange, it's dark, velvety, with spots and golden streaks like a butterfly's wing?—Oh, that's a Fortuny dress. Your young friend can certainly wear that kind of thing at home. I have lots of them, I'll show you some, I

can even give you some if you like, But I'd really like you to see the one my cousin Talleyrand has. I must write and ask her to lend it to me.[35]

The Fortuny dresses play a particularly prominent role in this game of love and aesthetic education. They possess the air of something exquisite, one-of-a-kind, accentuating the individuality of their wearer on the one hand, while lending to her shape the aura of something belonging to another place and time on the other—as in the images of antiquity and the Renaissance, whose atmosphere the dress drapes around the female form like an ephemeral memory:

> Of all the gowns or tea-gowns that Mme de Guermantes wore, the ones which seemed most expressive of a particular intention, most endowed with special meaning, were those gowns with Fortuny based on ancient Venetian designs. Is it their historic appearance, is it rather the fact that each one is unique, which gives them such an individual character that the pose of the woman who is wearing one to wait for you, to talk with you, takes on an exceptional importance, as if this costume had been chosen after long deliberation and makes the conversation stand out from everyday life like a scene from a novel? In Balzac's novels we see the heroines choose particular costumes to wear on the days when they are to receive a particular visitor. The costumes of today have no such clearly defined character, with the exception of Fortuny dresses. There can be no vagueness in the novelist's description since this dress really exists, and the smallest elements of its design as unalterable as those of a work of art.[36]

The Fortuny dress described here—one of the designs for which the decor-artist printed patterns based on models from the Renaissance onto heavy velvet fabric in a specially developed technique—is depicted as an artwork, of nature seemingly reproducing art. In a reference to nineteenth-century realism, Proust reverses the mimetic principle of art imitating nature: it is not art that imitates nature, but rather nature that imitates art. The stylized lines of the female body clothed in a Fortuny dress are not in fact femininely natural, but appear instead as nature formed by the dictates of art.

Proust here makes use of the topos "reality imitates art," a "turn of the century figure of thought,"[37] that Oscar Wilde paradigmatically formulated in his

35. Proust 2003, 35.

36. Ibid., 25–26.

37. On this subject see the inspiring observations of Victor Žmegač (1989). On the meaning of this mimetic correlation of art and life in Proust see Curtius 1952, 36–41.

essay "The Decay of Lying" (1891). The body, defined and set in stylized motion by images of the Renaissance, thus appears not as "natura naturata," as a natural model of art, but rather as the product of an *imitation of art*. Images of art reveal themselves in the lines of the female form thus shaped and stylized by the Fortuny dress: the pathos formulas of love and jealousy come undone as passion in the folds of movement—caught between an obligation to remember and the desire to forget.

Gabriele D'Annunzio: *Forse che sì forse che no*

Both in Proust's text as well as in Gabriele D'Annunzio's novel *Forse che sì forse che no* (1910),[38] Renaissance art forms the setting for an aesthetic construction of body imagery presented by the semiotic structures of fashion—in the form of Fortuny gowns. In Proust, references to the Renaissance are loaded with connotations to and reflections on the relationship of art and nature.

D'Annunzio in turn develops the relationship between patterns of femininity and dance as an eclectic montage of heterogeneous visual motifs and their mythical interpretation. Ancient patterns (the Fortuny scarf), oriental body imagery (the bee dance), mythical spatial models (the labyrinth), and topographical structures overlap as corporeal landscapes in motion (in Isabella's dance and Paolo's flight) throughout the narrative of the novel.[39]

In one scene, the novel's female protagonist, Isabella Inghirami, whose name calls up images of Isabella d'Este and the age of the Renaissance duke Vicenzo Gonzaga, dances before her lover Paolo Tarsis. Dramatically lit by the rays of the setting sun, in front of a fantastic natural backdrop—at the mouth of the Arno, with the mountains of Pisa in the background and the broad glittering expanse of the Tyrrhenian Sea on the horizon—the dance unfolds as a kind of "natural phenomenon." The dress that Isabella has chosen for this occasion—a Fortuny gown—transposes the pathos of the scene onto her body in that the grandeur of the landscape with its luminous sunset is as if poured into the fabric.

---

38. There is no English translation to date of D'Annunzio's *Maybe Yes, Maybe No*. All quotations in the following section are translated by Elena Polzer on the basis of the German translation, *Vielleicht, vielleicht auch nicht*, by K. Vollmoeller, 1910. Page numbers are from the German edition. On the interpretation of Isabella's dance see also the chapter on the bee dance and a corresponding section in chapter 1 of Part II.

39. On erotic-exotic body-image and dance see the chapter on the bee dance; and on the relationship of dance costume and space, body landscape, and the abstraction of movement images see the section on "Dance Costume" in chapter 1, Part II.

Gazing upon the spectacle of nature, Isabella finds her desire to embody and transform natural phenomena through dance grows: "And now the sea transformed into the divine garment of evening, a garment of such wonderful pleats, that Isabella desired a piece of it. 'If I could dress myself in such silks, Aini!'" (196f.)

The wish to translate the dramatic lines of the topography into the pathos of the drapery, the fabric, and the movement patterns corresponds with a second image, in which another "phenomenon of nature" is imagined as enveloping the body. Isabella experiences the wealth of caresses bestowed on her by her lover as equivalent to the folds of a veil moving over her limbs—"she felt all caresses on her body overlapping like the petals of a full rose"—and uses the Fortuny dress to describe her reading of both patterns of naturally impassioned movement:

> She had draped one of those long shawls of oriental gauze around herself, which the magician Fortuny dipped in the mysterious dyes of his color troughs and draws out again laden with foreign dreams. . . .
>
> And the dance began. The first rhythmic notes seemed to lend life to the long, thin fabric covering her naked body. The dancer's skilled hands wandered up and down the seams and lent to them that floating motion, which incessantly rippled the disc-shaped outer edges of the medusas. Occasionally she gave them a spiral twist and then let go, and the veil continued its circling motion like a tornado of rosy sand, drooped and shortly before it threatened to collapse, the fleeting fingers revived and reawakened it to new movement, a new twirl. (197ff.)

Isabella's dance demonstrates the typical characteristics of *freier Tanz* at the beginning of the twentieth century:

> Her dance is a solo, an improvisation based only on a few, formulaic movement patterns (here: first, the "veil" or "sash dance" and later, the "bee dance"). It is staged as a private performance not in a theater, but amidst nature; the "simple nature of nature" (Helene von Nostitz), as glorified in exemplary fashion in physical culture and rhythmic gymnastics. And Isabella's dance is a "barefoot dance"; the costume—a long scarf over the naked body—permits maximum freedom of movement. Her dance thus corresponds with the program of movement reform, namely the presentation of "un-encoded" natural movement. At the same time, her dance also fulfills two visual patterns of *freier Tanz*: it cites both "Greek"— in the form of the Fortuny shawl—and exotic dance, as inspired by Ruth St. Denis.

After the first dance scene (described above), in which Isabella freely plays with the veil in a way reminiscent of Loïe Fuller's *Serpentine Dance*, the performance passes into a phase of oriental dance that is modeled on the odalisque or Almée erotic dance of the veils. By alternatively concealing and revealing individual parts of the body, Isabella imitates the "oriental dance of love," before presenting a pantomime bee dance as the final act of her performance.[40]

In Isabella's oriental dance, the Fortuny dress changes its function: while relatively "impersonal" in the first part (in terms of Mallarmé and Hofmannsthal),[41] the dancer's body absorbed in spiral and circular figurations of the naturalness translated into textile form, the second part of the dance is an expression of Isabella's erotic desire that deploys exotic body-images. On the one hand, her use of the Fortuny shawl follows the general pattern of a Bayadère veil dance. On the other, she inscribes specific modes of eroticism into the dance, which can only be deciphered by her solitary audience—Paolo—as idiosyncratic elements of Isabella's body and movements.

Hence, the dance lines of the Fortuny gown here do more than reveal the *ornatus* of the rhetoric of desire. The folds of Isabella's garment simultaneously appear stigmatized with the physical traces of her history, as a history of passion.

This becomes evident in the final part of the novel, as Isabella—marked by the entanglements of love, hate and guilt, incest with her brother, her sister's suicide—visits Paolo again in a bout of insanity. After a violent scene, in which Paolo strikes her, Isabella attempts—now disfigured by bloody injuries on lips and cheeks—to once more transform herself into the ardent dancer that had so enchanted him in the villa near the "Boca d'Arno."

She clothes herself in a Fortuny Delphos gown:

> As she stepped back into the room in which the little table stood prepared, she wore one of those garments with a thousand pleats, which shriveled without her body into a kind of tightly wound cord, and, as soon as she skillfully slipped into it head first, opened up like innumerable fans. The one that she wore now was blue-black with green veins. The seam had a red fruit pattern stenciled on it. (327)

Again the dress describes the movements of passion and thus it appears as a visual medium of affect. The pleats of silk wound to a rope, spreading over the

40. See D'Annunzio 1910.

41. See the section on Loïe Fuller and Mallarmé in chapter 1, Part II.

maltreated body like a fan; the midnight blue color citing the "insanity" of their passionate lovemaking; the lines of red fruit along the edge as ornaments of blood seeping from Isabella's wounds.

The texture of the garment, its folds and printed ornaments, thus become symbolic catalysts of feeling onto which the visual formulas of passionate movements of the soul are projected, a mnemonic text of passion.

BODY-IMAGE I: THE MODEL OF ANTIQUITY

The concept of antiquity, which influenced images of the body and concepts of nature around the turn of the century, emerged in several stages of looking back into history. The most prominent of these periods in time are themselves characterized by a distinct approach to "Hellas" that stylizes or mystifies a specific definition of the "archetype" of antiquity. The following phases in the history of Renaissance movements are significant for the role that they play in the relationship of dance to antiquity (looking backward in time from the beginning of the twentieth century):

- First, the art of the Pre-Raphaelites with their recourse to the Renaissance and beyond that to antiquity; this is, for example, how Isadora Duncan came into contact with the Renaissance, Botticelli, and Greek art via the paintings of the Pre-Raphaelites.
- Secondly, the eighteenth-century notion of Greece, as influenced in particular by J.J. Winckelmann's idealization of the beauty of the naked body in Greek sculpture (we can take Duncan again as an example, since she read English translations of Winckelmann's writing while in London 1898–99);
- And, finally, the idea of reincarnation in Renaissance art itself: an understanding of Greek and Roman ancient art and culture that deeply influenced the cultural identity of the fifteenth and sixteenth centuries.

When looking at these historical phases in the reception of antiquity, it seems necessary to emphasize that, both in the case of turn-of-the-century literature as well as in the case of dance, the preferred aesthetic model was not classicism (in the form of neoclassicism or neo-Renaissance), but rather a Nietzschean dichotomy of the Apollonian and the Dionysian. It was this dichotomous structure, that provided the formal framework for the popularity of antiquity. It was precisely this duality of the terms when raised to the status of cultural topoi—the simultaneity of antitheses as a characteristic trait of the ambivalence of modernity (Harry Graf Kessler)[42]—that became the typical aspect of the modern understanding of antiquity.

Greek images of the body, deduced from readings of vase paintings, bas-reliefs, and sculpture, embodied a phantasmata that appeared in concentrated form in modern *freier Tanz* as the restitution and transformation of pathos formulas into archetypical affect engrams. The image of the Renaissance composed by Jacob Burckhardt, Walter Pater, and Jules Michelet contained similar traces of mythical construction: "The Myth of the Renaissance," according to historian Peter Burke[43] in his analysis of the history of mentality, is the result of nineteenth-century notions of "Renaissance man" and the birth of individualism, as described by Burckhardt in the metaphors of awakening and rebirth.

Primavera, or The Dance of the Graces

One of the Italian Quattrocento works of art that became vital for an understanding of the Renaissance in the nineteenth century is Sandro Botticelli's *Primavera*, hanging in the Uffizi in Florence (1476–1478, figure 15).

In the eyes of the Pre-Raphaelites and the Symbolists, the painting's arrangement, the relationships between Venus, the Allegory of Spring strewing flowers, and the three dancing Graces, was considered an epitome of grace, "beauty in motion" (Friedrich Schiller), and an ideal of femininity. Edward Burne-Jones, for example, cited the three Graces in his paintings *Venus Concordia* (1871) and *Perseus and the Sea Nymphs*. The slender female figures seem to float; the flowing sweep of the folds of "antiquity" (loose dresses bound under the breast) trace the contours of the bodies. The lines of the gestures and the framework of mythological scenes emulate Renaissance models of depicting the body.

However, the pathos formulas of passionate affect here appear subdued, almost diluted by a sickly atmosphere of decadence:

Passions dissolve themselves in mime or meditations. The figures are portrayed from the front or from behind, inserted into scenes of parallel images. The heads are frequently turned sideways, lacking a conciliating

---

42. Kessler's diagnosis of modernity as noted in his diary is cited in the chapter on "Mode et Modernité"; it was also Kessler who (e.g., in his correspondence with Hofmannsthal) repeatedly proclaimed that one should not solely draw on Greek influences, but mix them with the oriental.

43. Burke 1990.

Figure 15 Dance of the three graces in Sandro Botticelli's painting
Primavera (1476–78).
SOURCE: Uffizi, Florence, Italy.

lateral posture: Burne-Jones avoids dramatic moments, instead he gives us
eurhythmic groups à la Botticelli.[44]

The above quote comes from Guenther Metken's description of the transformation of Renaissance patterns in his monograph on late nineteenth-century
Pre-Raphaelite art.

Aby Warburg first developed his fundamental idea of an anthropological,
psychocultural approach to the study of art during his studies of Renaissance

44. Metken 1974, 118. Translation: Elena Polzer.

art, particularly on Ghirlandaio and Botticelli, which he then methodologically consolidated into his symbol theory of pathos formulas. According to Warburg, the pathos formula reveals, as a symbolic representations of expressive values, the "continuation of ancient compositions of energy in Renaissance Europe."[45]

Warburg's *Mnemosyne* project aimed at reconstructing "the (a)wakening of the heathen gods in the age of European renaissance as energetic formation of expressive values"[46] in the images of the body as they appear in art. It is precisely this relationship of antiquity and Christianity in the iconographic compositions of Renaissance art, which forms the main focus of Edgar Wind's study *Pagan Mysteries in the Renaissance*.[47] The merging and overlapping of pathos formulas derived from antiquity and Christian iconography, as they appear, for example, in the work of Botticelli, finally became so widespread in the nineteenth century that the syncretic contamination of ancient and Christian imagery remains to this day fully ingrained in general knowledge as a pattern of citation, for example, in the double image of the *Venus Madonna*, as used by the Romantics from Heine to Hofmannsthal, from Richard Wagner to Heinrich Mann as a formula for a dualistic configured pattern of femininity.

Wind attributes the depictions of mythological figures in Botticelli's paintings *The Birth of Venus* and *Primavera* to the intellectual realm of Florentine Neoplatonism, according to which the three graces embody the trinity of beauty, chastity, and love. Venus appears—in the Neoplatonic interpretation of "Venus-Virgo"—as the personification of the triadic fragmentation of love into the dancing graces, so that the entire group represents the metamorphosis of the allegory of love: "Venus-Virgo unfurling in the Graces, the Graces enclosed in Venus-Virgo."[48]

In Wagner's Venusberg version of the *Tannhäuser* (1860) conceived for Paris, the three Graces appear, as Dieter Borchmeyer recalls,[49] as "vanquishers of the wild passions," which then are unleashed in a bacchanalian frenzy; the Graces

embody moderation in this erotic cosmos. In Wagner's complete design of the pantomime (May 30th, 1860), they almost seem to demand "the

45. Aby Warburg in his notebooks; see Gombrich 1970.

46. Ibid.

47. Wind 1981. Edgar Wind was also a student of Warburg. On the interpretation of Botticelli's *Primavera* by art history, in particular concerning Edgar Wind's reading, see Bredekamp 1990.

48. Wind 1981, 93. Translation: Elena Polzer.

49. Borchmeyer 1992, 108ff.

preservation of grace and sensitive propriety." The lewd fauns shrink back from the "severity of their expressions." The dance, which they then initiate takes on a "ever more solemn graceful character, in which the longings of love find only gentle and soft expression" (XI, p. 416f.)[50]

Borchmeyer verifies the visual reference to Botticelli's painting *La Primavera* and interprets the configuration of Venus and the Graces in Wagner's Venusberg pantomime with the help of Wind's theory of a "concordance" of ancient and Christian imagery in Renaissance art.

The *Primavera*'s function as a role model for the scene with the Graces and the "representation of Venus as a goddess of temperance" in Wagner's *Tannhäuser* "Bacchanal" also influenced Isadora Duncan's performance in Bayreuth 1904. Duncan developed her choreography for the Graces in keeping with Wagner's concept of the triadic dance of the Graces under the sign of temperance, as "melodic reserve"—not as temperance in terms of a Neoplatonic "castitas," but in the neo-heathen affirmation of her libertine philosophy of life as a tranquility of the contented senses.

In her ruminations on the *Tannhäuser* "Bacchanal," she describes the appearance of the Graces during a moment of calm after a "shocking eruption of desires," a moment in which "peace" sets in: "These are the Three Graces embodying the calm, the languor of satisfied amorous sensuality. In the dream of Tannhäuser, they are interlaced and separated and, joining themselves together, become alternately unified and parted."[51]

Two years before Duncan encountered the mythological world of Wagner's *Tannhäuser* in Bayreuth, Botticelli's *Primavera* had already become a leitmotif of her self-proclaimed identity as a dancer. And again it is the birth of the pathos formula of the "Dance of the Future" (as Duncan titled her aesthetic program from 1903 in reference to Wagner's essay *The Artwork of the Future*, 1849) from the visual archives of the museum. This time, the birthplace is not the Louvre's hall of ancient statues, but the ultimate Renaissance temple of art: the Uffizi in Florence. Like eighteenth- and nineteenth-century poets and painters before them, the founders of *freier Tanz* likewise experienced the journey to Italy as a formative moment. Duncan and Maud Allan both visited Florence during their trips to Italy and both reported experiencing a fundamental moment of inspiration at the sight of Botticelli's *Primavera*. Duncan writes:

50. Borchmeyer 1992, 108ff. Translation: Elena Polzer.

51. Duncan 1927, 145.

At that time it was Botticelli who attracted my youthful imagination. I sat for days before the Primavera, the famous painting of Botticelli. [. . .] I was enamoured of it. A nice old guardian brought me a stool, and viewed my adoration with kindly interest. I sat there until I actually saw the flowers growing, the naked feet dancing, the bodies swaying; until the messenger of joy came to me and I thought: "I will dance this picture and give to others this message of love, spring, procreation of life which had been given to me with such anguish. I will give them, through the dance, such ecstasy."[52]

Duncan's attempt to shape the message of this painting, the enigma of spring as a "message of love and the creation of life" into dance, culminated in her vision of a "Dance of the Future"—her mission to celebrate dance over and over again as a medium of love and individualized movement expression.

And so Duncan, who called herself Isadora (her birth name was actually Dora Angela) meaning "gift of the gods" and who retold the story of her birth as an almost mythical event[53] modeled on the *Birth of Venus*, appeared to later generations as the one true embodiment of Botticelli's painting. So much so that e.g., Maurice Lever's monograph of her is entitled *Primavera*.[54] Duncan attempted to translate her impressions of Botticelli's paintings at the Uffizi in Florence into dance movement (figure 16).[55]

Maud Allan's choreographic work inspired by Botticelli resembled Duncan's *Primavera*. She also modeled her dress, flower wreaths, and hair ornaments on Flora. In her memoirs, Allan writes about her visit to the Uffizi and of the inspiration she found in front of the *Spring* and the *Venus:*

One of the most inspiring and delightful trips was to Florence. My stay in Florence would have been a memory landmark to me if only for one impression made upon me by Botticelli's wonderful picture, "The Return

52. Ibid., 113.

53. In her memoirs, she describes her birth: "I was born by the sea, and I have noticed that all the great events of my life have taken place by the sea. My first idea of movement, of the dance, certainly came from the rhythm of the waves. I was born under the star of Aphrodite, Aphrodite who was also born on the sea, and when her star is in the ascendant, events are always propitious to me" (Duncan 1927, 10).

54. See Lever 1988.

55. See Duncan 1927, 113: "Inspired by this picture, I created a dance in which I endeavored to realize the soft and marvelous movements emanating from it; the soft undulation of the flower-covered earth, the circle of nymphs and the flight of the Zephyrs, all assembling about the central figure, half Aphrodite, half Madonna, who indicates the procreation of spring in one significant gesture."

Figure 16 Isadora Duncan, *Primavera* (around 1900).
SOURCE: Author's archive.

of Spring," [*sic!*] and the fact that as I stood before it, entranced by the
rhythm and the flowing lines of the dancing graces, all my indefinite longings and vague inspirations crystallized into a distinct idea.[56]

Botticelli's portrait became a paradigm for the expressive model of *freier
Tanz* and like Duncan, Allan equally based her credo of expressivity in dance
on the inspiring act of reading the *Primavera*.[57]

56. Allan 1908, 53.

57. Ibid. See also Allan's conversation with the violinist Joseph Joachim on expression in art,
in which she brings up Botticelli's *Primavera*: "Then once when studying Botticelli's 'Spring,'

The dancing Graces and the lightly striding Flora in Botticelli's *Primavera* embody leitmotifs of body imagery and movement prevalent in *freier Tanz* around the turn of the century. The ideal of beauty, of graceful movement, is particularly significant. The commitment of the aesthetics of *freier Tanz* to beauty, to grace and to lightness of movement (a quality that—while incorporated in a new code of movement—free dance incidentally shared with ballet, which it had so fought against) was seriously called into question and even partially suspended at the turning point of the avant-garde from 1912–13 onward.[58] *Ausdruckstanz* with its primacy of intensity, "truth," and expressivity in dance movement, in contrast explored the aesthetics of the ugly and grotesque.[59]

The dance of the Graces in Botticelli's painting, barefoot, in translucent, flowing veil-dresses that trace the forms of the body, symbolized—in the aesthetic understanding of *freier Tanz*—"antiquity" as sublimely beautiful "nature." Flora personified this beauty of feminine nature unfolding in dance; as described by Duncan's concept of the "Dancer of the Future": "one whose body and soul have grown so harmoniously together that the natural language of the soul will have become the movement of the body."[60]

In 1907, Hugo von Hofmannsthal was inspired by Ruth St. Denis and *freier Tanz* to intensely reflect on the expressive potential of the body[61] and it is in this year that he first jots down his thoughts on the visual impulses of antiquity and the Renaissance for dance: "The dancer," writes Hofmannsthal, "mimetically" draws inspiration either from a Greek vase painting or from the "wind goddess in *Primavera*, the bent hands forward and backward . . . striding over flowery meadows; head thrown back and stiffening with a twitch; fleeing."[62]

Here Hofmannsthal plays out the full sequence of dramatically climaxing pathos formulas in the form of a visual dance manifesto: from gesture to stride, from

a picture to me so vivid and beautiful that I could not gaze upon it without emotion, a thought impressed itself upon me. If I could only bring these beautiful women to life again it would be something for my world to be proud of" (Allan 1908, 77).

58. The years 1912–13, which are, among other things, the years in which Futurism was founded and Nijinsky's best choreographies for the Ballets Russes, the *Faune* and *Sacre*, performed, are generally considered a turning point in avant-garde art; see Fischer 1978.

59. See the section on *Ausdruckstanz* in the introduction. The pathos formula in the image of the *Primavera* nevertheless remains active in *Ausdruckstanz*: dancer Hilde Holger, for example, whose career began in the late 1920s and who was forced by the National Socialists to emigrate in 1939, named her daughter, who was born in exile, "Primavera"; see Hirschbach and Takvorian 1990, 39.

60. Duncan 1903, 24–25.

61. See Brandstetter 1991b.

62. Hofmannsthal 1978, A III, 489. Translation: Elena Polzer.

the wind-blown folds of the garment to the "hysterical" head movements of the dancing maenad, finally stiffening in catalepsy. Edgar Wind likewise describes in a similar way the movement relationships, "metamorphoses of love" in Botticelli's *Primavera*: "The fleeing nymph and the enamored zephyr unite in the beauty of Flora."[63]

While Hofmannsthal's notes on Botticelli aim toward an iconographic substantiation of expressive gesture in dance, Heinrich Mann's trilogy *Die Göttinnen* (*The Goddesses*, 1902) uses Botticelli's *Primavera* as a model of "mythological configurations" and their transformations.[64]

The epic structure of the novel itself is based on a triadic principle. The main character appears split into three symbolic mythological characters. Violante, the Duchess of Assy, devotes herself to a life dedicated—one after another—to the ideals of freedom, art, and love. Each of these stages in her life is associated with a different classical goddess: *Diana, Minerva* and *Venus* (these also being the individual titles of the three parts). The mythological configuration transforms the sequentiality of the triadic structure of the Duchess's life into a simultaneity: the three goddesses embody three sides of Violante's personality. In his use of the triad chastity (*Diana*), beauty (*Minerva*), and love (*Venus*), Mann cites the Graces in Botticelli's *Primavera*. And the stage in the Duchesses's life, which is dedicated to art under the patronage of *Minerva,* is particularly filled with images of the Renaissance (as interpreted by Burckhardt, whose texts Mann read in preparation for his novel), although Mann mistrusted the prominent image of "Renaissance man" as propagated around the turn of the century not least of all by Nietzsche and his commendation of the Borgia family in the notion of decadence and its subjugation.

Violante commissions the painter Jacob Halm to build her a palace in Venice in a pompous neo-Renaissance style. As he leads her and her entourage of poets and artists through the rooms of the palace, they linger in the hall of Minerva:

> I love this hall, it is silver. The gods are scheming above us on the ceiling . . . gods and goddesses are soft, curious and fickle. Their mouths smile at everything that smells sweetly, chimes and boasts . . . a silver air pours peace over us here. In the folds of the pale blue and silver banners between the columns, silent victories lie dreaming. These are the victories of Minerva. For this is her hall.

---

63. See Wind 1981, 139. Translation: Elena Polzer.

64. On the subject of visual citation see Ritter-Santini 1971; for an interpretation of *Die Göttinnen* that takes into account Wind's *Primavera* analysis see Wanner 1976; as well as Hilmes 1990, 177ff. Only the first volume of the trilogy has been translated into English: see Mann 1929.

Properzia says:

"That Minerva up there, Duchess, that is you."[65]

Art here appears as a guarantor of visions of beauty and love, extending beyond life and mortality. The aestheticism of a "hysterical Renaissance," as Jacob Halm critically described the type of neo-Renaissance that he himself influenced, reached its tipping point at exactly that moment in which the Duchess poses as Botticelli's *Venus* for a painter surrounded by decaying "ancient" statues overgrown with rampant plant life. The attempt to portray her fails, the painting cannot be completed; only the boy Nino, observing the Duchess, whom he adores, from his hiding place, sees in her the embodiment of Venus—that vision of beauty which appears reborn in the image of the Renaissance as the pathos formula of sublime nature from the art of antiquity.

Perhaps the most convincing direct embodiment of the mythological-allegorical idea of femininity symbolized by the *Primavera* was the young dancer Clotilde von Derp. Critics such as Hans Brandenburg and Fred Hildenbrand testified to her lovely and at the same time austere, chaste, and yet sensitive appearance on stage. However, the description that draws a direct line to Botticelli's *Primavera*, is from Alexander Sakharoff, her dance partner and later also her lover. Sakharoff, who studied painting during his stay in Florence (ca. 1908) and made sketches and copies of the most famous Renaissance paintings, recalls his first encounter with Clotilde. He saw in her at first sight a "woman of spring." Of her "performance" (ca. 1910), which was actually not really a dance performance, but something rather "banal," he writes: one would be hard put to "imagine anything more resembling spring":

> Instead of stepping out and immediately beginning to dance, the dancer appeared with a gigantic vase filled with flowers, strode across the entire stage and placed it on a pedestal. This was so unusual, unexpected and unique, the dancer so strong in her purity and sincerity that the effect remains unforgettable.[66]

Sakharoff reads the dancer's simple movements, the walking, the gesture of carrying the flowers, as a resurrected manifestation of *Flora*. The pathos formula of dance contained in the image of the *Primavera* lends an aura of ancient

---

65. Mann 1969, 2: 13. Translation: Elena Polzer.

66. These unpublished notes are preserved in the Sakharoff archive at the Lenbachhaus in Munich. Translation: Elena Polzer.

beauty to the feminine appearance in spite of her everyday clothes: "This simplicity breathes spring . . . more so, it represents its quintessence . . . . Once as I walked through the museum of Naples, I discovered the famous 'Flora.' I love this fresco very much."

And so he always remembers when he sees this painting: "Miss Clotilde's first performance."[67]

Here Sakharoff, on the one hand, reads the "Renaissance" into the body image of *freier Tanz*, i.e., the ancient pathos formula of Flora or Nympha (Aby Warburg),[68] while, on the other hand, simultaneously translating the movement images of modern turn-of-the-century *freier Tanz* back into an interpretation of ancient "prototypes of passionate movement." The figuration of Grace thus unfolds as an epitome of the natural in the flickering changes of perspective between patterns of the body and patterns of patterns, through confrontation and through dialogue, as a dispute between "des anciens et des modernes," out of the museum and in the theater.

Nike, or Dance of the Future

Nike, the winged statue, goddess of victory, and allegory of history progressing, appears in dance as the pathos formula of modernity per se. Again the energetic expressive potential of ancient statues is transformed from sculpture into dance and, again, the reading of a statue in a museum forms the starting point for dance and choreography.

Nike figures, or Nikai, are depicted in Greek art as mythological figures accompanying the victorious Athena. Especially on vase paintings, the Nike with outspread wings embodies the gift of victory the goddess Athena bestows on athletes and fighters. What is remarkable is that the Nike—unlike the Olympian gods of Greek mythology—is a pure personification of the desire for success, for "victory," that is, a goddess without any history of her own. In her excellent book *Monuments and Maidens: The Allegories of the Female Form*, Marina Warner describes the Nike, or "Goddess of Success,"[69] as "a goddess without a story":

> Nike belongs to the salubrious, sunlit, upper air, and her wings mark her
> out as otherworldly, at one with the sky above and a spirit of concord and

67. Ibid.

68. In 1904, E. G. Craig made a pastel drawing of Isadora Duncan composed exactly according to this image.

69. Warner 1985, 130.

Figure 17 Nike of Samothrace—*La Victoire*
(second century B.C.).
SOURCE: Louvre, Paris, France.

harmony, like Athena. . . . But, most importantly, she represents a power for whom speed is of the essence, yet who hallows and glorifies the spot of her temporary halt. This makes Nike resemble an aspect of time itself, or more precisely a way we see our relation to time. She represents the propitious event that interrupts the ordinary flow and singles out the lucky winner.[70]

As a personification of time, the Nike became a cult figure of steadily progressing modernity. She does not symbolize a continuous flow of time, but instead that exalted and auratic moment in which success, victory, and triumph over an achieved goal are celebrated.

One of the most famous examples of the Nike has been housed in the Louvre in Paris since 1867: the torso of the Nike of Samothrace (figure 17) from the second century B.C. was discovered by a team of archeologists on the island of Samothrace in 1863. The monumental statue was initially placed in the hall of

70. Warner 1985,133.

the caryatids. Finally in 1884, she was given a place on a pedestal on the first half-landing of the wide staircase at the entrance of the Louvre.

The effect of this statue—the epitome of iconographic representations of the late nineteenth century's fantasies of victory—is overwhelming. The arms and head of the Nike statue are missing; and yet—as in the case of the aura surrounding the *Archaic Torso of Apollo* in Rilke's lyrical phenomenology—the "fragmentary" quality of the Nike, the perfection of torso, legs, and wings, the emotional strength of the figure, the ecstatic whirls in the drapery of the garment, which swirls around the lines of the body tracing them so that the torso appears more than the mere fragment of a whole, lend this torso fragment of a statue[71] the aura of a prototype.

In the eyes of the zeitgeist of the belle époque, the Nike of Samothrace—or *Victoire* as she is nicknamed—became an allegory of victory, a personification of the cultural and technical achievements made at the turn of the century; and so she became a symbol for the advent of modernity.

There is a famous line from F. T. Marinetti's *Futurist Manifesto* (1909) that marks the beginnings of the avant-garde art as one of the mottos of Futurist aesthetics: "A racing automobile with its bonnet adorned with great tubes like serpents with explosive breath . . . a roaring motor car which seems to run on machine-gun fire, is more beautiful than the Victory of Samothrace."[72]

This often-cited formula, repeatedly commented on by literary and cultural studies, unites in an almost exemplary way the ambivalences of the avant-garde: that simultaneity of citing the old and celebrating the new, the "simultaneous yes and no," which Harry Graf Kessler so aptly diagnosed as being the "spirit of the age."[73]

Marinetti's programmatic formula also expresses the avant-garde's fundamental distrust of art as an institution concentrated on preserving culture and retaining traditions. Instead of organizing art and culture in archives and museums, objects of everyday life should replace art in the service of modern technological progress. The Futurists' call to arms, to blast open the museums, thus proves to be an anarchistic consequence of the attack on the institutionalization of art (a consequence, incidentally, cited by Thomas Bernhard in his novel *Extinction*).

However, the affirmative component of the Futurist's negation of *passé-iste* art, that is, of art dedicated to a historical tradition, cannot be ignored. The dialectics of the renewed, vehement avant-garde *querelle des anciens*

71. On the subject of the "torso" in the work of Rodin and Rilke see the end of this chapter.

72. Marinetti 1909; see the documentation in Baumgarth 1966.

73. See Kessler's unpublished diary entries, cited in detail in chapter, "Mode et Modernité."

et des modernes reveals itself not least in its existing attachment to what it
has negated. Although the Nike of Samothrace exhibited in the museum
is—according to Futuristic aesthetics—outdone by the "beauty" of modern
technology in the fascination with the automobile,[74] both ancient statue and
the modern technological object are nevertheless linked via the *tertium comparationis* of *Victoire*. As symbols of victory and history progressing, both
represent the dynamics and speed of movement. The allegorical meaning of
the Nike-*Victoire* acts as an intermediary between the moving beauty of the
ancient statue and the aesthetics of the modern body in motion propelled by
technology.

The full ambivalence of this Futurist aesthetic motto that says an automobile is more beautiful than the Nike of Samothrace is particularly evident in
the cult that surrounded the statue of the Nike as a figuration of "movement."
Umberto Boccioni had a model of the Nike from the Louvre standing in his
atelier, while working on his *Walking Man*. The dragging steps of the *Walking
Man* became more clearly tangible, when seen in contrast to the dynamic figure, that "unique form of continuity in space,"[75] taking form in the flight of the
Victoire.

In the aesthetic program of the avant-garde, the winged Nike symbolized
speed and lightness, the subjugation of gravity, the transgression of the natural
limits of movement (as promised by the automobile and the airplane).[76] She
merged with the iconogram of *Velocitas*, as the epitome of the driving force
of the twentieth century. For Futurism, the intoxication of renewal that came
with military victory, the pathos of triumph in the face of danger, in battle and
war became a particularly emphatic aestheticized paradigm. One of the earliest music-theater pieces by the Russian Cubo-Futurist avant-garde was written
under the sign of the *Victoire*. The opera *Victory over the Sun* (1913), composed
by M. W. Matyushin with a libretto by A. J. Kruchonykh and stage design by

---

74. The cult of the automobile was prevalent not only in Futurism, but also in expressionism;
dynamism, tempo, chrome, and the freedom of (fast) movement made the car the fetish of
the new anarchist individual. In the article "Das Automobil" by Marie Holzer, published in
the magazine *Aktion* in 1912, e.g.: "The automobile is the anarchist under the vehicles. It
races, spreading terror, through the world, detached from established laws. No tracks pre-
scribe its path. . . . It is the master of unlimited possibilities. . . . It is the victory of strength
over the pedantry of prescribed boundary posts, overtaking, skipping slower stages of
development. . . . It is the epitome of thought, which needs no paths. . . . The automobile
overcomes the structure of time itself, the cruelest timekeeper of our lives." *Die Aktion* 2 34
(1912): 1072–73. Translation: Elena Polzer.

75. Calvesi 1975, 7.

76. On the subject of avant-garde art and modern technology—especially aeronautics (in
terms of the use of space in dance)—see Part II of this book.

Kazimir Malevich, did, however, also critically reflect the appearance of the "Strong Men" and the subject of victory.

Let us take a closer look from this perspective at the turning point of the avant-garde movement shortly before the outbreak of World War I. If we take into account the avant-garde's critical, almost hostile relationship to artistic tradition, that is, to the fin de siècle cult of Nike, then it becomes clear that Marinetti's pamphlet was not aimed at the art of antiquity itself, but that his attacks were directed instead at turn-of-the-century conservative-neoclassic aestheticism, that is, at those educated classes visiting the museum en masse, drifting through the museum as art consumers, blindly fetishizing the Nike of Samothrace.

The poetic apotheosis of the Nike cult of the belle époque appears—accentuated in an aristocratic aestheticized way—in a sonnet by Gabriele D'Annunzio from 1896:

> Je vois soudain jaillir ton essor véhément,
> O Victoire, je vois ton marbre où le sang coule
> prendre soudain, du socle, un vol qui se déroule
> comme l'aube d'un astre au sein du firmament . . .
> L'Ame chante le choeur auguste d'Euripide;
> —Niké très vénérable, en le chemin rapide
> accompagne ma vie! Au but, couronne-là![77]

Marinetti, who was especially committed to D'Annunzio in his early work and therefore later a particularly adamant public opponent of D'Annunzio, posited the formula of "Automobile versus Nike" in opposition to such symbolist poetry. He sought to introduce a moment of shock into the cultural landscape of classicizing aesthetics.[78]

The Nike's complex iconography can only be touched on here and limited to the key points Marina Warner makes in *Monuments and Maidens*. There she not only traces the pictorial history of the Nike, from Greek sculpture intertwining Nike with the goddess Victoria of ancient Rome and continuing up to the influences of Christian iconography in familiar depictions of angels. She also attempts to demarcate the allegory of victory from the equally female personifications of fortune, success, and opportunity (Fortuna/Tyche, Fama/Renommée, Occasio/Opportunity). Finally, she elucidates the formidable role of the Nike as an allegory of success—as a "goddess of success"—at the turn of

---

77. From *Sonnets Cisalpins*, D'Annunzio 1946, 315.

78. D'Annunzio was a big fan of the newest technical achievements of locomotion, the racing car and the airplane (and in this sense actually quite in keeping with Marinetti's machine aesthetics); see the section on D'Annunzio's novel *Forse che sì forse che no* in Part II of this book.

the century. The so-called Victorian age, which already includes the word *victory* in its name, projects all economic and political, military and emancipatory aspects of progress into the female form of the winged goddess. Like the goddess of freedom and the "goddess of light," that is, electricity, who often appears in figures depicting the dancer Loïe Fuller as an allegory of composite female personifications of ideas, the Nike embodies the progressivism of the Industrial Revolution with its unbroken dynamics and optimism.

The different patterns of what this progress meant in various social or cultural subsystems merged with the physical image of the "winged victory" as a monument to military victory in the *Wellington Victory*[79] and as a symbol of speed in the hood ornament for Rolls Royce,[80] as a Nike suffragette representing the victorious emancipation of women, as a figurehead for the Vienna Succession, and as a naked nymph representing international high finance, that is, "The Spirit of Achievement," mounted on the entranceway of the Waldorf Astoria Hotel in New York City.[81]

The iconographic-iconological[82] interpretation of the Nike as an allegory, which Marina Warner undertakes in her comprehensive and knowledgeable book, focuses on the various meanings ascribed to the winged goddess of victory over the course of history—a perspective based on a more or less static semiotic model, on a relationship of signifier and signified.

In contrast, I want to emphasize that aspect of various Nike depictions and their readings which interprets the plastic dynamism of the figure not only as a symbol (for example of progress), but also as characteristic for the artistic medium itself, as a premise for the reading of e-motionality. Hence I seek to describe and interpret the anthropological-aesthetic dimension of the pathos formula embodied by the Nike. These two ways of reading the sculpture, as

---

79. See Warner 1985, 143.

80. See ibid.: "The 'Silver Lady' Charles Sykes modelled for Rolls-Royce was added to the apex of the car's radiator temple in 1911 as if it were an acroterium itself."

81. Warner writes (Warner 1985, 143):

Movements of all persuasions adopted Nike: she appears in the emblem Sylvia Pankhurst designed in 1908 for "Votes for Women," the weekly journal of the Women's Social and Political Union, as a suffragette angel in green and purple and white, blowing a trumpet with the bannerette "Freedom." Even the iconoclast architect Otto Wagner could not resist her symbolism: although the Sezessionists rejected the ornament, he included Nikai, standing erect with garlands, on the corners of his key building, the Post Office in Vienna. The Waldorf Astoria Hotel in New York appropriated her too: a naked, winged nymph, "The Spirit of Achievement," was created for their entrance by Nina Saemundsson in 1931.

82. For a differentiation of iconography and iconology and discussion on the use of these terms by art history, see Panofsky 1991; as well as Straten 1989.

allegory and as pathos formula, are not contradictory. They are merely two alternate perspectives, which accentuate different aspects and allow us to draw certain connections between them, as with the attempt to define *allegory* in Paul de Man's sense. Paul de Man defined it not as the attribute of an aesthetic object, but as a form of reading—in *Allegories of Reading*—which already, as such, defines the allegory as a formula for the movements executed during the repetitive meandering process of reading.

One aspect that has not been taken into consideration so far in research on Nike as a female allegory of victory is the affinity of this figure to dance and to the new approach of dance to representation at the beginning of the twentieth century. Like the Nike, free dance represented a model of the future, a corporeal image of femininity as the triumph of natural beauty, as the advance of physical freedom and autonomy, as the ecstatic victory of an unfettered expression of emotion in movement. In these utopian concepts of the "new human" as formulated by Isadora Duncan and Maud Allan, but also by Mary Wigman and Rudolf von Laban, dance itself takes on traits of an allegory of victory, of progress and so appears in the form of the moving Nike.

At the turn of the century, it was probably Loïe Fuller and her revolutionary moving sculptures composed of dance, fabrics, and light[83] that most impressively represented the dancing form of the Nike. Her performances were by no means mimetic reproductions of the Nike of Samothrace, but rather abstract formations of dance. In her performances, she draped wide white silk fabric into three-dimensional forms that resembled wind-filled sails and great curved wings, which invoked a completely idiosyncratic form of the Nike; a representation of the goddess in dance that was entirely born of Fuller's distinctly personal medium of movement.

The Nike in the Louvre, of course, consciously formed the backdrop of such figurations of dance. A photograph taken at the time documents Fuller presenting herself as Nike in a very theatrical pose, standing on the foremost edge of a steep rock, high above the sea, with her dress blowing in the wind like the billowing white wings of the *Victoire*, resembling a figurehead at the prow of a monumental ship.

This image of the Nike in motion as established by dance became in turn became a model for the sculptural arts. The sculptor Pierre Roche fashioned a larger-than-life statue depicting Fuller with wings in motion like the Nike, which was attached to the roof of the Loïe Fuller theater[84] in Paris as a *Couronnement* during the World Exposition in 1900.

---

83. On Loïe Fuller's dances see Part II of this book; for details of her career and her performances, and for reviews, see Brandstetter and Ochaim 1989.

84. On Fuller's theater, which combined stage and museum, see the section on the "Dancer in the Museum."

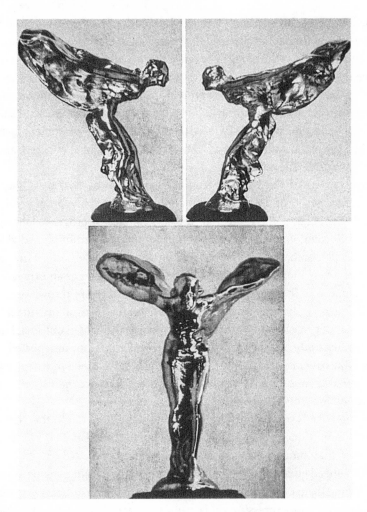

Figure 18 Charles Sykes, *Kneeling Lady*—model for the Rolls Royce
hood ornament (1934).
SOURCE: Gerhard Woeckel. 1970. *The Spirit of Extasy*, in: *Alte und Neue Kunst*
(*I und II*).

And Fuller's dances became a precursor of the creation of modern transformations of the Nike in other ways as well: the image of the winged "silver lady"
(figure 18) became a distinguished "mascot" on the hood of Rolls-Royce cars in
the serial production lines of the automobile industry. In a short essay on the
Rolls-Royce, Erwin Panofsky pointed out the resemblance of the modern "kneeling lady" to the *Victoire*,[85] and in a detailed study Gerhard Woeckel[86] established

85. See Panofsky 1963.

86. See Woeckel 1970.

the relationship of this statuette, designed by Charles Sykes in 1911, not only to the Nike of Samothrace, but also to Fuller's dances and Pierre Roche's statue of her.

"Spirit of ecstasy" is the name Sykes gave this modern Nike, which was meant to grace the luxury automobile as an artwork of the new era and as a new concept of movement. Here art and twentieth-century technology merged (as in the previously mentioned relationship of Nike and automobile as established by Marinetti) to become a symbol of movement. *Velocitas*, the movement formula, embodied the pathos of modern dynamics: ecstasy, the thrill of speed, and the dream of weightlessness in flight.

Interpretations of the Nike of Samothrace in dance—by Loïe Fuller and Isadora Duncan—broadened and shifted the iconographic program associated with the Nike by the Industrial Revolution's idea of progress. During the Industrial Revolution, the *Victoire* personified fantasies of triumph and glory in a pointedly patriarchal culture. By contrast, in dance the Nike became the pathos formula of a new movement that was defined as *female* and as an expression of *nature*. Duncan: "(In my dance) the artifices of dancing are thrown aside, the great Rhythms of Life are enabled to play through the physical instrument, the profundities of consciousness are given a channel to the light of our social day."[87]

During her study of Greek art in the Louvre in Paris, Duncan repeatedly visited the Nike of Samothrace. Her enthusiasm was also sparked by a depiction of the Nike that is considered a national monument in France, namely the group of figures by François Rude on the Arc de Triomphe in Paris.[88]

Here the Nike is transformed into a triumphant memorial to the victory of the Revolution: Rude's group is also known as *La Marseillaise* (1792). Warner has verified that Rude based them on ancient statues of the Nike.[89]

As the winged goddess of a triumphant revolution, the Nike stands amid the group, urging them onward to victory with her raised left hand. Her face resembles that of a gorgon, expressing wild emotion, nostrils flared, large eyes opened wide. The tempo of her movement symbolizes the strength, even the violence, of the Revolution, as revealed in the torsion of the body and the momentum of the wings. "Uncover that screaming woman, and the figure leaps into ferocious life" (Warner, 127).

In Duncan's dance piece *Marseillaise* (1915), this revolutionary figure—the Nike-Libertas—is brought "into ferocious life" by the dance (figures 19 and 20).

Both plastic models, the figure of the *Nike of Samothrace* and Rude's allegory of the revolution, are combined in Duncan's performance.

87. Duncan (1917), in Rosemont 1983, 51.

88. In her memoirs, Duncan writes: "I was especially entranced by the Carpeau group before the Opéra, and the Rude on the Arc de Triomphe" (Duncan 1927, 68).

89. Warner 1985, 127f.

Figure 19 Isadora Duncan, *La Marseillaise* (1916).
SOURCE: Derra de Moroda Dance Archives, Salzburg,
Austria / © Derra de Moroda Dance archives, University
of Salzburg, Austria.

An integral element of the myth behind the creation of Duncan's *Marseillaise*—an element unrelated to the sculptural models gleaned from the museums of cultural history—was born of an improvisation. Duncan performed this piece, which is considered one of the principal works of her late creative phase (ca. 1914–1927), at a show performed with students of hers at the Metropolitan Theater in New York in 1915. It was shortly before the United States entered into the world war and Duncan spontaneously interpreted a danced version of the *Marseillaise* as a finale—as an emphatic proclamation in the face of those atrocities of war that she had seen in Paris in the lazarets.[90] Her motive was a mixture of passionate patriotism, moral

90. Duncan writes in her memoirs: "One night, after a performance at the Metropolitan Opera House, I folded my red shawl around me and improvised the 'Marseillaise.' It was a call to the body of America to rise and protect the highest civilization of our epoch—that culture which has come to the world through France" (Duncan 1927, 316).

Figure 20 Isadora Duncan in a drawing by
E. A. Bourdelle bearing the title *Victoire* (1913).
SOURCE: Musée E. Bourdelle, Paris, France.

fighting spirit for the rights of oppressed minorities, and a pacifist mission aimed at securing a future of freedom, beauty, and autonomy. Her performance met with enthusiastic applause. Carl van Vechten recalls: "The audience stood up and scarcely restrained their impatience to cheer."[91] Even more overwhelming were the reactions after her performance of the *Marseillaise* in April 1916 at a charity event in the Paris Trocadéro before an audience of thousands: everyone of distinction and reputation was present. The poet Fernand Divoire spontaneously wrote an article about Duncan's aesthetic, and Auguste Rodin cried out spellbound: "This woman is a sublime temple."[92]

In this mere five-minute piece, Duncan embodies the ideals of the French Revolution to the music of the French national anthem: first, she stands motionless on stage dressed in a long, white "Greek" tunic, over which she threw a

91. Van Vechten, "The New Isadora," in Magriel 1977, 30.

92. See Niehaus 1981, 73.

blood-red shawl.[93] Van Vechten attempted to differentiate the patterns of representation: "Part of her effect is gained by gesture, part by the massing of her body, but the greater part by facial expression."[94]

In a series of statuesque motionless poses, arm gestures, and powerful strides, alternating repeatedly with expressive gestures, she developed a dramatic arc of suspense out of pathognomic expressions, which culminated in the grand gesture of "Aux armes, citoyens!"—arms outspread like the wings of the Nike of Samothrace, the red shawl unfolding like the torch of the *Victoire*.

Van Vechten directly compared this epiphany to the image of the Nike: "Finally we see the superb calm, the majestic flowing strength of the Victory of Samothrace."[95] And a critic visiting the performance in New York recalled François Rude's *Marseillaise* on the Arc de Triomphe:

> Her exalted poses were imitative of the classic figures on the Arc de Triomphe in Paris. Her shoulders were bare, and also one side, to the waist line, in one pose, as she thrilled the spectators with representation of the beautiful figures (of Rude) on the famous arch. The audience burst into cheers and bravas at the living representation of noble art.[96]

We have here in Duncan's dance a transformation of the Nike's allegorical figurations of the meaning. In *Marseillaise*, she lends a twist to the expressive movement gesture of the pathos formula by introducing contradictory elements and thus almost roughening up the contours of the expressive form. The shadowy sides of victory—outrage, despair, and death—step forward to stand beside images of the sublime, the pathos of *victoire* and of *gloire*. In her memoirs, Duncan recalls that some visitors were displeased at the "antithesis or dissonance of gesture against music": "It is strange that in all my Art career it has been these movements of despair and revolt that have most attracted me. In my red tunic I have constantly danced the Revolution and the call to arms of the oppressed."[97]

In its representation in dance and gesture of the antinomies of progress, Duncan's *Marseillaise* conveys a moving diagnosis of the physiognomy of

93. Later Duncan mainly performed the *Marseillaise* in a completely red garment: a beacon of the Revolution.

94. Van Vechten, loc. cit., 30.

95. Ibid., 31.

96. Duncan 1927, 317.

97. Ibid., 334.

modernity and with its revolutionary energy forms the near counterpart to the sacrificial idea behind *Le Sacre du Printemps*. The *Spring Sacrifice* and the *Marseillaise*, both created at the onset of World War I, can be read not only as complementary models of avant-garde dance aesthetics, but also as contrary ways to reflect the developments of the age via the medium of danced images of the body.

In Duncan's interpretation, the pathos formula of the Nike-*Marseillaise* unfolds its intensity of effect in a dynamic play of gesture, in the dramatic "usurpation" of individually eloquent body parts, as Carl van Vechten recalls: "At times, legs, arms, a leg or an arm, the throat, or the exposed breast assume an importance above that of the mass, suggesting the unfinished sculpture of Michel Angelo."[98]

The gestalt of the torso, in which the statue of the Nike of Samothrace appears auratically glorified in modernity's memory of antiquity, is translated in Duncan's dance into a rhetoric of dramatic gesture. The pathos formula of the Nike model reaches its greatest degree of suggestive strength in its *danced aposiopesis*: the pauses in the movement, the omission of deictic gesture, the spaces that the rhetorical movement ellipses unveil for the allegories of the reading beholder.

Van Vechten notes that Duncan's depiction of the Nike in the *Marseillaise* also activated "Rodin's inspiration,"[99] indicating the complex relationships between ancient sculpture, their interpretations in dance, and the transformations of both forms of representation in turn by modern sculpture as in the statues of Rodin, Maillol, or Bourdelle (figure 20).[100]

Rodin's enthusiastic commentary of Duncan's interpretation of the Nike-*Marseillaise* was based on his fundamental interest in the possibilities of representation provided by the body. However, Duncan's vivid shaping of the Nike as a *torso* in dance may have impressed him even more.

In his study on Rodin (1902), Rilke attempts to understand this same sculptural art as the rhythmic movement of light and shadow and moreover to grasp the meaning of the torso in Rodin's work as a form of condensing expression into the pathos of space unfolding. In doing so, he draws a comparison to the image of the Nike:

A man sat motionless before Rodin when he created this mask [the bust of *Homme au nez cassé*, 1864, G.B.], his expression calm and unmoved.

98. Van Vechten, loc. cit., 31.

99. Ibid.

100. On Bourdelle's drawings and statues of dance and dancers see Aveline and Dufet 1969.

But it was the countenance of a living person, and as he studied this face it became clear that it was full of motion, full of disquiet and crashing waves. There was movement in the course of the lines and in the grade of the planes. The shadows played as if in sleep, and light passed softly over the brow. There was, in short, no peace, not even in death. For even in decline, which is also motion, death was subordinate to life. There was always motion in nature, and art that wished to present a conscientious and faithful interpretation of nature could not idealize a motionlessness that exists nowhere. In reality there was no such ideal in antiquity. We have only to think of Nike. This sculpture gives us more than the motion of a lovely young woman going to meet her love; it is also an eternal representation of the wind of Greece, of its breadth and glory.[101]

At first, Rilke reads Rodin's sculpture as the art of the balance of the living planes in which a sense of weight is revealed by the shadow, by the moving surface of the statue. What is essential to Rilke is the way that Rodin deals with the contrasting effects of light and shadow, of repose and motion, of weight and lightness.

The resultant interpretation of the Nike as an archetype of movement—a movement of love, of nature, of life—is quite similar to the pathos formula in Duncan's danced reading of Nike, that is, to her understanding of the rhythmic flow of dance movement: "Dance waves, sound waves, light waves—all the same."[102]

This accumulation of gestural movement in the sculpture—of energetic expressive value in Aby Warburg's sense—intensifies as this gesture turns *inward*. In his interpretation of Rodin's work, Rilke does not mean this as a description of the *intention* behind the representation. Instead, the visual image of turning inward describes the realm of gestural *influence*, which appears so intense that it results in a reversal of the direction of movement, turning inward on itself.

Rodin returns again and again in his nude figures to this turn inward, to this intense listening to one's own depths. We see it in the extraordinary figure he called La Méditation, and in the unforgettable Voix intérieure, the softest voice of Victor Hugo's songs, which is almost concealed by the voice of anger in the monument to the poet. Never before has the human body been so concentrated around its interior, so shaped by its own soul

101. Rilke 2004, 42.

102. Duncan, in Rosemont 1983, 31.

and yet restrained by the elastic power of its blood. And the way the neck rises ever so slightly, stretching to hold the listening head above the distant rush of life, is so impressive and deeply felt that one has a difficult time remembering a gesture as moving or expressive. The arms are noticeably missing. In this case Rodin must have felt them to be too easy a solution to his problem, something not belonging to a body that wished to remain shrouded in itself, without any help from outside. One thinks of how Duse, left painfully alone in one of D'Annunzio's plays, tries to embrace without arms and to hold without hands. This scene, in which her body learned caress that extended far beyond itself, belongs to the unforgettable moments of her acting career. It conveyed the sense that arms are super-fluous, merely decorative effects common among the rich and excessive, which one could cast off in order to be completely poor. At that moment one did not have the sense that she had forfeited something important; rather she was like someone who has given her cup away in order to drink from the stream, like someone who is naked and still a bit awkward with the depth of the revelation. The same thing is true of Rodin's armless stat-ues: nothing essential is missing. Standing before them, one has the sense of profound wholeness, a completeness that allows for no addition.[103]

Compared to Eleonora Duse's dramatic acting of a "torso," Rilke interprets the Rodin torso as the artistic consequence of an extreme creative need. The "missing" arms do not appear, as in the case of the Nike of Samothrace, as an imperfection. Instead, the fragmentary form of the Rodin torso is what makes the modern aesthetic experience possible in the first place: "that an artistic whole doesn't necessarily coincide with the ordinary whole-being."[104]

In a late poem by Rilke, dedicated to Nanny Wunderly-Volkart "around Christmas 1920," entitled "Nike—on an Ancient Figure (little Nike on the Shoulder of the Hero),"[105] the connection between Rodin's statues and the movement figuration of the Nike is reproduced and even more clearly estab-lished as central to Rilke's poetics than in the Rodin essay itself. In this poem, the winged statuette is again described as a torso against the backdrop of an aesthetics of the fragment:[106]

---

103. Rilke 2004, 44.

104. Ibid., 45.

105. Rilke 1955–66, 2: 243f.; German title: "Nike—zu einer antiken Figur: (kleine Nike an der Schulter des Helden)." For a history of this Nike poem and its relationship to Rodin's statues see Hausmann 1991.

106. On the aesthetics of the fragment, see Dällenbach and Hart Nibbrig 1984.

The victor carried her. Was she heavy? She sways
like a premonition on the prow of his shoulder;
in her quiet flight that she installs in him
she presents to him the *empty* space, which he *fills with his accomplishment*.
She transforms the vastness into a vessel,
for his actions not to scatter in the wind.
She flew to god, and hesitated for his sake,
And for hers, he measures up to measure.[107]

According to Ulrich Hausmann, the Nike in Rilke's poem is based on a bronze statuette by Rodin from 1889, known under various names such as *Victoire* and *Man and His Genius* as well as described by Rilke himself as *Le Sculpteur et sa muse* (figure 21).[108] The statue is of a sitting, muscular male form, on whose shoulder a small, winged figurine, a torso without head and arms, floats in an expansive ascending movement that contrasts with the motionless of the resting hero. In a letter to Mrs. Wunderly-Volkart, Rilke explains the meaning that this statue has for him:

Niké, little Niké, goddess of victory, who can be portrayed so small and yet always bestows what is great, the great victory; I have often stood in front of such small figurines in museums and thought to myself how enchanting they are. They have infinite openness before them, the space of the victor, which begins slightly above his head.[109]

Two aspects of the poem appear to me especially striking in terms of the visual aspect of Nike-*Victoire*. First, the subject of the *relationship*: the *Nike* is not presented as a monodramatic representation of the pathos formula of lonely victory, but rather as the visual embodiment of a dialogue between moving

---

107. Rilke 1955–66, 2: 243f. Translation: Elena Polzer.

> Der Sieger trug sie. War sie schwer? Sie schwingt
> wie Vor-Gefühl an seinem Schulterbuge;
> in ihrem leis ihm eingeflößten Fluge
> bringt sie den Raum ihm leer, den er voll-bringt.
> Sie wandelt Weite um in ein Gefäß,
> damit sein Handeln nicht im Wind zerstiebe.
> Sie flog zum Gott –, und zögert ihm zu liebe,
> und ihr zu lieb wird er dem Maaß gemäß.

108. See Hausmann 1991, 82ff.; for a description of the figurine as *Victoire* in the catalogue of an exhibition in Paris in 1900, ibid., 92.

109. Cited in Hausmann 1991, 83. Translation: Elena Polzer.

Figure 21 Auguste Rodin, *Le Sculpteur et sa muse* (1889).
SOURCE: Nationalgalerie Berlin, Germany.

bodies. Second, there is the poetry of *space*, which was also explored in other poems by Rilke during this period, especially in his shawl poems.

In Rodin's statue, Nike appears as the hero's companion, symbolizing victory as in ancient depictions of Athena.[110] Hence, the statue visualizes a quasi deconstruction of the pathos formula of *Victoire* in dualistic male-female form. In this communion of sculptural form, the goddess of victory enters into a dialogue with him who fulfills the possibility of the victory that she has "suggested." Here

110. Warner calls attention to the fact that it was not only Athena who was accompanied by the winged Nike, but also Zeus, for instance: "Zeus' colossal statue of Olympia also carried a statue of the goddess of victory in the palm of his hand"; 1985, 129.

the dialogue between the sexes fulfills a quasi-Platonic turn of the Nike concept. Unity is conceived of as only being possible with a renewed synergy of the male and female form (which were formerly also *one*). Thus the little Nike—as a vessel for creating an empty and yet circumscribed framework of potential—embodies the act of providing, in a victorious gesture of achievement, the space necessary to be able to conceive of action at all. She provides a measure, a premonition of victory, which the hero is then forced to measure up to.

This image of an empty space generated by the gestures of the winged female form also points to a poetological aspect of Rodin's sculpture, namely the constellation of artist and muse in the form of the genius pathos formula via the myth of creation. The Nike muse is characterized by a gesture of "hesitation." Rilke comments on the "fleeting goddess striving to move on," her "already fading, no-longer-recognizable being" by recalling a statement made by Rodin, who once said to him the figurine embodied "l'inspiration qui se retire."[111]

The space, generated by the turning away of the fleeting muse, gains importance as a space of reference in the moment of loss. The transitory movement of flight resembles a gesture of concession (*Ein-räumung*), literally an act of allowing space to enter: not as a gift of inspiration, but as withdrawal, leaving behind in the empty space only the *condition* of a possibility of poetic creation.

Such a "turning" of the image—not in the realm of artistic creation, but rather in the mind's eye of history—was also evoked by Walter Benjamin in 1940 shortly before his suicide. In his reflections "On the Concept of History," Benjamin explicated his interpretation of Paul Klee's painting *Angelus Novus*. To Benjamin, Klee's painting bears the traits of a Nike who has passed through the metamorphosis of abstract art. In Benjamin's ekphrasis of the water color, the winged "angel of history" appears in the gestalt of Nike-*Victoire*, transformed by the physiognomy of horror in the age of Nazi terror. The dialectics of blindness and knowledge, of memory and suppression, of progression and ill-fated relapse into barbarity are disturbingly expressed in the visual image of progression portrayed by the winged and yet hunted figure, with its back turned toward the future:

> There is a painting by Klee called Angelus Novus. An angel is depicted there who looks as though he were about to distance himself from something, which he is staring at. His eyes are opened wide, his mouth stands open and his wings are outstretched. The Angel of History must look just so. His face is turned towards the past. . . . He would like to pause for a moment so fair [*verweilen*: a reference to Goethe's Faust], to awaken the

111. Rilke in a letter to Georg Reinhardt, cited in Hausmann 1991, 81. On the subject of muses, see Neumann 1993a.

dead and to piece together what has been smashed. But a storm is blowing from Paradise, it has caught itself up in his wings and is so strong that the Angel can no longer close them. The storm drives him irresistibly into the future, to which his back is turned, while the rubble-heap before him grows sky-high. That which we call progress is this storm.[112]

In his *Mnemosyne* project, Aby Warburg attempted to establish an archive of cultural memory, whose multiple serial images revealed the metamorphoses, transformations, and "inversions" of pathos formulas over the course of the history of art and culture. For Warburg, the golfer in a photo or on an advertising poster from the 1920s mirrored, for example, a movement gestalt similar to that of the *Nympha* in Ghirlandaio's painting *The Birth of John the Baptist* (1490).[113]

As the following two examples—one from the realm of fine arts and one from sports—will show, the pathos formula of *Victoire* likewise appears over and over again in patterns of twentieth-century art and culture up to the age of postmodernism.

First, we have the sculpture *Nike* by Haus-Rucker-Co, which was installed in Linz in 1977 (figure 22). A Nike of Samothrace is mounted high up at the end of a fire ladder, not as a "closed" sculpture, but hollow—ripped open length-wise so that the larger-than-life figure gapes open in front. The statue represents no more than the empty husk of the Nike, split into two parts, which now themselves look like wings. The empty space in between becomes visible, the steel construction of the supporting structure. *Victoire* appears only as a fragment of torso—as fragment of a fragment—as an empty shell. *Victory* is an empty promise of progress. Its "movement" deconstructed: "no future" and "stop making sense."

In contrast to this artistic manifestation of the "as-if" form of the Nike torso, Nike is omnipresent today in society's largest leisure sector: the field of sports. It appears here not in the form of cultural critique, but as the positive prospect of progress. Here Nike "steps in" to represent the traditional qualities of *Victoire*: victory, dynamics, speed, success, *velocitas*—a promise of triumph for every man and woman. The consumer is guaranteed that he or she will "be a winner." Nike is one of the fastest and strongest producers of sport shoes. Nike, embodiment of the pathos formula of victorious progress, now travels "in sneakers," as Sally Banes implied in the title of her book.[114]

112. Benjamin 2005, Part XI.

113. See Gombrich 1970, 301.

114. *Terpsichore in Sneakers* is the title of a book on postmodern dance by Banes (1980).

Figure 22 Haus-Rucker-Co: *Nike* (Linz, 1977).
SOURCE: Edition Cantz, Stuttgart, Germany.

The Dance of the Maenad

Like the Nike model of movement, the "dance of the maenad" is a turn-of-the-century cultural pattern that likewise adapted a distinct image of the body from antiquity and linked it to concepts of femininity, although in a different way.

While the winged *Victoire* reflected contradictory aspects of man's relationship to time, progress, and the memory of culture in the form of dance, the maenad embodied the movement patterns of hysteria.[115] It symbolized a

115. On hysteria as a cultural pattern of femininity and the construction of dramatic form, see Schaps 1982; Israël 1983; Irigaray 1985; Schneider 1985; Wilson 1989.

diagnosis of the modern age, using the catalogue of symptoms associated with hysteria (the metaphor of the pathological, theatricalized illness) to delineate modernity's transformations, its abrupt leap into a new century perceived as uncontrollable, as having unleashed unknown forces. This aspect of strangeness in one's own culture, the "discontent of the age" and its "uncanniness" (as Sigmund Freud called it), was ascribed to the feminine—especially in connection with concepts of nature and an ambivalent sense of the irrational. Marked as an expression of hysteria—as embodied in the pathos formula of the raving maenad—this construct of femininity appeared as a formula for interpreting aspects of modernity that were considered disconcerting and even threatening.

These connections will be briefly outlined with reference to the cultural-theoretical and anthropological writings of Otto Weininger, Sigmund Freud, Walter Pater, and Erwin Rohde.

Then I will turn to various forms of representing the dance of the maenad: as a movement model in dance at the turn of the century, especially in Isadora Duncan's performance and interpretation of this ancient image of the body, the "Dionysian," and as a pathos formula in theater and literature, for example in Hugo von Hofmannsthal's fragments of the *Bacchen* and of *Pentheus*, as well as in his dramatic concept of the dance in *Electra*.

I will also take a special look at how a prevalent, turn-of-the-century pattern of femininity—the femme fatale, the "animalistic woman"[116]—blended with a distinct model of cultural theory. The "character" of femininity, the aesthetic concept of the Dionysian, and the cultural theory of the modern[117] overlapped to produce an allegory of the age, whose iconography—in the words of Eugen Wolff—is described as follows: "she is an experienced, but pure woman, in rapid movement like the spirit of the age, with *fluttering garments* and *streaming hair* . . .—that is our new divine image: the *Modern*."[118]

This image of a goddess personifying the modern is a moving image, an image of movement, a dance of the maenad "in rapid movement," "with fluttering garments and streaming hair." The cited pathos formula of the Dionysian aspect of the dance of the maenad here simultaneously envisages the forward-striving movement of the *Victoire*. The ancient pictorial patterns of the Nike and the maenad seem to overlap as emblems of modernity.

116. See Taeger 1987; Hilmes 1990.

117. I use the term *the modern* here, as defined, e.g., by the Wiener Moderne versus the aestheticism of French Symbolism, as an alternative concept to "Décadence," to the culture of the belle époque and the fin de siècle; see Fischer 1978.

118. Wolff 1976, 41–42.

In his book *Sex and Character*,[119] Otto Weininger attempted to define the *female* not as a form of sexual identity or gender role, but as a cultural type. Weininger ultimately concluded that differences between the sexes are only minimally founded in biological functions. Instead, he believed that there is an endless and paradoxical number of ways in which aspects of masculinity and femininity can overlap and be combined. Weininger's understanding of sexual identity demonstrates a shift in awareness directly associated with the so-called cultural crisis around 1900. His text testifies to a new epistemic field of interest that—in a different discursive context and with other accents, but in a context similar to Freud's *Three Essays on the Theory of Sexuality* (1904–05)—will continue to influence the *gender* discussion[120] of modernity: namely whether and in what way concepts of masculinity and femininity can be considered mental constructs and whether and in what way their iconographic representations are to be interpreted.

Interest in socioculturally defined bisexuality increased in this period in particular. Awareness of this phenomenon was gradually growing more widespread, as is recognizable in the phenomenon of the effeminate male (especially in the form of the decadent artist) on the one hand and of the emancipated woman (in an appropriation of social roles, mentalities, and behavior previously defined as male) on the other.

One of the main difficulties that Freud worked through in his essays lay in reconciling the idea of (biological) bisexuality with the primacy of the phallus, which ostensibly applied to both sexes.[121] Psychoanalytic discourse on the one side and the misogynous rhetoric of writers like Nietzsche, Wedekind, Weininger, and Karl Kraus, which aimed at a restitution of gender polarity,[122]

119. See Weininger, *Sex and Character*, online at http://www.theabsolute.net/ottow/geschlecht.pdf with interlinear translation. In the following I will refer to an excellent summary by Jacques Le Rider (1985).

120. On feminist *gender* discourse, see Butler 1989.

121. "When you meet a human being, the first distinction you make is 'male or female'? and you are accustomed to make the distinction with unhesitating certainty. . . . Science next tells you something that runs counter to your expectations and is probably calculated to confuse your feelings. It draws your attention to the fact that portions of the male sexual apparatus also appear in women's bodies though in an atrophied state, and vice versa in the alternative case. It regards their occurrence as indications of bisexuality, as though an individual is not a man or woman but always both merely a certain amount more the one than the other. You will then be asked to make yourself familiar with the idea that the proportion in which masculine and feminine are mixed in an individual is subject to quite considerable fluctuations . . . and must conclude that what constitutes masculinity or femininity is an unknown characteristic which anatomy cannot lay hold of." See Freud 1965, 113f.

122. Karl Kraus repudiated modern, emancipated women, as did Frank Wedekind. Instead he glorified women as "creatures of nature," wild and erotic like "Lulu" and constructed, as

on the other, represented two models for dealing with the (reputed) danger of a growing culture of bisexuality.

Women here appeared as the true source of danger in this landscape of imaginary displacements of gender and culture. In discussions on bisexuality and on the difference between the sexes, the talk was of "femininity"[123] and of the "female aspect" (Weininger).

The concept of femininity and the culture of modernity thus appear linked in academic, critical-cultural, and literary discourse and through innumerable iconographic depictions. Weininger's book provides the key to the "great metaphor that bears the name *woman*" as interpreted by Jacques Le Rider:

> Femininity in "Sex and Character" is synonymous with unlimited pleasure, the lability of states of consciousness (which utterly forbid the possibility of conceiving a female *subject*: woman has no ego), with irrationality, the inability to make judgments, indifference toward the imperative of truth, an instinctive harmony with nature and life, the negation of monotheism and moral values, in brief, cultural chaos.[124]

Weininger's characteriology of femininity is largely based on Johann Jakob Bachofen's book *Das Mutterrecht: Eine Untersuchung über die Gynaikokratie der alten Welt nach ihrer religiösen und rechtlichen Natur* (1861—*Mother Right: An Investigation of the Religious and Juridical Character of Matriarchy in the Ancient World*).[125] A return to matriarchy, in the anthropological form described by Bachofen, met at the time with skepticism, as did the study itself: on the one hand, the cyclic restitution of matriarchy—under the reign of Dionysus, the "female god"—was believed to be accompanied by dangerous decadence. On the other hand, the crisis of meaning invoked in patriarchal culture by the return of matriarchy could provide a chance for the development of something new—a "revaluation of values," a project associated with Nietzsche one generation later.

Aside from Friedrich Nietzsche, it was the cultural historians Walter Pater and Erwin Rohde, in particular, who broadened the notion of antiquity by reintroducing the Dionysian as a counterpoint to the received image of classical antiquity. In their depictions of the mysteries of the Dionysus cult, the ecstatic

---

an idea of sexual difference, the pact between the nature of women ("Weibnatur") and the genius of the male mind; Wagner 1987.

123. Freud 1933.

124. Le Rider 1985, 243. Translation: Elena Polzer.

125. See (on reactions to Bachofen; on the subject of matriarchy) Göttner-Abendroth 1982. Hofmannsthal read Bachofen in the early 1890s; see Worbs 1983, 268 and 279f.

dances of the bacchantes and of the maenads appear as movement models for unbinding, the conglomeration of all those forces that threatened the order of civilization; models of being-beside-oneself that suspend the *principium individuationis*.

In his book *Psyche* (1893), Rohde writes that the dance of the maenads was very different from

> the measured movement of the dance-step in which Homer's Greeks advanced and turned about. . . . It was in frantic, whirling, headlong eddies and dance-circles that these inspired companies danced over the mountain slopes. They were mostly women who whirled round in these circular dances till the point of exhaustion was reached; they were strangely dressed; they wore *bassarai*, long flowing garments. . . . Their hair was allowed to float in the wind; they carried snakes sacred to Sabazios in their hands and brandished daggers or else thyrsos-wands. . . . In this fashion they raged wildly until every sense was wrought to the highest pitch of excitement, and in the "sacred frenzy" they fell upon the beast selected as their victim and tore their captured prey limb from limb. Then with their teeth they seized the bleeding flesh and devoured it raw.[126]

In his essay on Euripides' *Bacchae*, Walter Pater likewise situates the throng[127] of bacchanalian women in the sphere of the Dionysian, which he metaphorically subtitles the "essence of that fiery spirit in the flowing veins of the earth."[128] Pater anticipates Nietzsche's understanding of the dual character of Dionysus: the god's terrifying appearance as Dionysus Omophagos, reflected in the *sparagmos* of the maenads, and the enchantingly beautiful image of "Dionysus Meilichius," the "honey-sweet" god.

The Bacchanals are a "spring sacrifice" during which the women of Thebes head for the woods and mountains to celebrate the god. Heathen mysteries such as these spring rites often seem to Pater to be linked to forms of ecstasy in dance: a ceremony of nature worship, "that giddy, intoxicating sense of spring— that tingling in the veins, sympathetic with the yearning life of the earth, having, apparently, in all times and places, prompted some mode of wild dancing."[129]

The typical image of the ecstatically moving maenad, as interpreted in dance, in theater, and in literature is in its entirety, or in fundamental elements, deeply

---

126. Rohde 2001, 257.

127. See also the section on "Dance of the Bees": Pater compares the swarming of the bees with "raving" maenads.

128. Pater 1903 (2002), 1–48.

129. Pater 1903 (2002), 53f.

Figure 23 Maenad—Greek kylix (around 490 B.C.).
SOURCE: Staatliche Antikensammlungen, Munich, Germany.

influenced by Greek vase painting, for example, the image inside a white bowl
by the Brygos painter around 490 B.C. (figure 23). The female figure, barefoot
in a wide dance step, appears to look behind her in a motion of turning from
the waist. In her right hand she carries an ivy-covered thyrsus; in her left hand
she holds by its hind feet a leopard (the symbol of Dionysus). She is dressed
in a finely pleated garment, which flows around her body. A hissing snake is
wound about her streaming hair like a headband. In the Dionysus cult, beast
of prey and leopard pelt, snake and thyrsus symbolized untamed nature. The
powers of Eros and the conjunction of Eros and Thanatos are embodied in the
figure of Dionysus Omophagos and also expressed in the terrifying rage of the
maenads. Ecstasy, this being-beside-oneself of the maenads in "enthusiasmos,"
appears even more clearly depicted in ancient paintings—one example of which
can be found on a drinking bowl by Makron, circa 480 B.C., or an amphora by
the Kleophrades painter, circa 500 B.C.[130] The maenad dances with her upper

130. For depictions of Greek drinking bowls in the large collection of the Staatliche
Antikensammlung (State Collection of Antiques), Munich, see Vierneisel and Kaeser 1990.

body bent far back, head thrown deeply into the nape, hair open and wildly in motion, the facial expression—with open mouth and ecstatic look—in orgiastic devotion, the transparent chiton in swinging folds, presenting the body and movement as practically naked.

The raving maenad[131] appears as a wild moving beauty: not with the grace of the *Primavera* and not with the lofty winged step of the Nike-*Victoire*, but rather with a suggestive and enticing physical gesture of debauchery.

The following movement elements are characteristic for the dance of the maenads and representations of this type of body-image in terms of conscious dance movements and dynamics: a dynamic, often sweeping step; a deep arch backward of the upper body, sometimes combined with a torsion from the center of the body, head thrown far back with hair streaming outward, accentuating the ecstatic moment of the entire movement at the boundaries of balance. (The aspect of open, streaming hair consciously appears in the Maenad model of *freier Tanz* as a counteraesthetic to the ballerina's chignon tied closely to the head, which represents the discipline and "clarity" of the dance system of classical ballet).

In his systematic study *The Antique Greek Dance after Sculpted and Painted Figures* (*La Danse Grecque antique d'après le monuments figurés*) (1895),[132] Maurice Emmanuel analyzed the characteristic movement patterns of antiquity and compared them to modern ballet. From Greek vase paintings, he isolated a specific type of representation that he categorized as "Dances with the Body Bent Backward." In this pose, the body arches backward, which he described as the *cambrure* or "backward bend of the torso." According to his observations, the movement is often depicted in Greek vase paintings, but is especially prominent, as "exaggerated movements," in the dance of the bacchantes "suivantes de Dionysos": "The backward bend of the torso is often accompanied by backward bending head."[133]

Emmanuel contrasted his figurative sketches of ancient images of the dance of the maenads with a series of photographs by J.-E. Marey[134] depicting

---

131. On the iconography of the maenad, see Lindner 1987. In her historical research, Linder concentrates on the "symbolic formulation of structures of violence, which are discussed via the female encoded figure of transgression and representation in a confrontation of the sexes" (Linder 1987, 282). However, this general approach of linking the iconographic representation of pictorial formulas of unfettered femininity with the feministic intention of analyzing patriarchal structures of violence and their reversal by the "suppressive powers" of the feminine appears to me to be problematic.

132. Emmanuel 1916; on his system of comparing Greek dance and ballet, see the chapter on "The Dancer in the Museum."

133. Emmanuel 1916, 171.

134. On J.-E. Marey, inventor of chrono-photography, see the section on M. Emmanuel in Part I and the chapter "Interruption" in Part II in this book.

Figure 24 Drawing of the *cambrure* of a bacchantess in the fashion of images on Greek vases in M. Emmanuel's *La Danse Grecque antique* (1895).
SOURCE: Derra de Moroda Dance Archives, Salzburg, Austria / © Derra de Moroda Dance archives, University of Salzburg, Austria.

contemporary dancers dressed in Greek garments and imitating the bacchanalian poses and movements of the *cambrure*. In his description of a "bacchante" illustrating "the extreme limit of the pose,"[135] he alludes to something that is very revealing in terms of the meaning associated with the dance of the maenad as a cultural pattern of femininity (figure 24). Emmanuel associates the "extreme," orgiastic movements of the bacchante with a similar gestural pattern in hysteria:

> Here the backward bend of the torso is accompanied by a backward droop-ing Head . . . shows the length to which the pose was sometimes carried at the climax of the Bacchic dances. . . . If this dancer is not one of those made with hysteria, she certainly holds the pose indefinitely.[136]

Hence, the ecstatic *cambrure* of the bacchantes seems comparable to the movement repertory of hysterics, as described by Jean-Martin Charcot, especially regarding the movements of the "grand attaque," the body posture assumed in those phases of the "attaque" that Charcot analyzed as "passionate

135. Emmanuel 1916, 173, fig. 427.

136. Ibid.

attitudes."[137] The "grande arc-en-cercle" is a precise replica of the very dance posture described by Emmanuel as *cambrure* and often resembles a cataleptic pose frozen in time, which Charcot calls a "particularly expressive" element of convulsive ecstasy.[138]

Like Emmanuel, Charcot used photographs to document the various forms in which hysteria presented itself. He sought to systemize and archive the symptoms and the sequence of phases that accompany the grand hysterical attack, and in so doing he produced a museum of expressive images of the malady.[139] This institutionalization of the iconography of hysterical body imagery, which was produced in order to "decipher the manifestations of hysteria and possession expressed by the choreography of the nervous system," as Manfred Schneider put it, formed the basis for a construction of a culturally generated female pattern of hysteria through the medium of photographic reproduction: "The hysteria of the modern age is nothing more than the production and reproduction of codes of femininity."[140]

In the imagery of the medical terminology used to described the various phases and symptoms of the hysterical attack, we already see how closely related this so-called illness was to the physiognomy of the age: terms such as "antics," "demonic," "clownish," "expressive gesture," "simulation," clearly demonstrate how closely the body imagery of this disorder was linked to the theatrical realm. The "grande attaque" of the hysteric "Augustine" thus appeared, thanks to the expressiveness quality of her gestures, "beautiful" to her contemporaries. It became very difficult to distinguish drama, as the *pathognomic* presentation of ecstasy, from the attack, as its *pathological* expression. Hence, the hysteric appears as the prototype of an actress acting out her symptoms, as "la grande simulatrice": the description of a dimension of representation as "simulation," which Weininger in turn (misogynistically) generalized as the "amorality" of female character.

---

137. See Charcot and Richer, in Schneider 1988, 130.

138. On the sequence of individual phases of hysteria with descriptions of the corresponding theatrical "acts," e.g., the "demonic" and the "farce phase," see Charcot, in Schneider 1988, 115ff. The "passionate gestures" of the hysteric, also and in particular the "arch," are still diagnosed as hysterical signs of a sexual disorder of the body in some recent therapeutic procedures. In various models of physical therapy, e.g., in the method of Alexander Lowen's "bioenergetics," the arch is used in movement therapy in order to release tension and blockage in the abdomen, which manifests itself in sexual disorders ("blocking the free flow of energy").

139. "We own a pathological-anatomical museum with associated ateliers for photography and plaster casts." Ibid., 144.

140. Ibid., 141. Translation: Elena Polzer.

However, in his own study on hysteria and the physicality of "the possessed in art," Charcot finally came to the conclusion that "hysterical ecstasy per se is very similar in its special attributes to other variations of ecstasy."[141]

The phase that Charcot described as an element of the grand hysterical attack, as an expression of "passionate attitude," bears the traits of representation or even of an exemplary staging of pathos formulas of ecstasy. This is most strongly expressed in the arch as described by Charcot: the *arc en cercle*.

The arch in the dance of the maenad—a pose of passionate devotion and orgiastic enthusiasm—combines a characteristic movement pattern of free dance with a culturally encoded scenario of femininity as embodied in hysteria.

In this way, the creation of pathos formulas of ecstatic corporeal symbols wandered from the "closed" stage—the lecture hall of the Salpêtrière—onto the open stage of dance theater. The theatricality of the passionate gesture discovered its own possibilities of forming itself into a "language" (Mary Wigman) of the body through the expressive medium of dance.

Among the most impressive examples of such transformations of the "medium" and staged institutionalizations of the ecstatic, hysterical body were the performances of the so-called dream dancer Madeleine (1904). Her dance performances under hypnosis, staged by the Munich doctor and psychologist Freiherr von Schrenck-Notzing as part of the Munich "Psychological Society," were a sensation. They provoked an intense debate on whether the dancer was truly in trance or whether she was merely simulating the hypnosis and playing the somnambulist.[142] For many of her contemporaries, Madeleine's stage appearances and her "highly dramatic" movements were manifestations of hysteria on stage. Her performances—as unconscious trance phenomena or as the simulation of trance in a hysterical production of related corporeal signs—brought up fundamental aspects of a psychology of expression and of aesthetic production in dance and theater.

The so-called *arc en cercle*, the arch as an expressive gesture of the upper body leaning far backward from its center, literally became a signature gesture in the body-image of *free dance* and *Ausdruckstanz*. This movement pattern revealed all the innovations and "deviations" of new images of the body presented by these art forms, particularly in their attempts to differentiate themselves from the reigning codes of ballet. Leaving the symmetry of alignment behind, the pelvis swerves outward (to the side or to the back). The dancer

---

141. Ibid., 131. Translation: Elena Polzer.

142. On these questions, on the dance of the "sleep dancer" Madeleine and its connection to contemporary dance reform, see Brandstetter 1992.

defies the laws of balance and gravity to the point of instability. The head and arms are thrown backward and released in a backward arch that abandons all controlled composure.

These characteristic features of movement are visible in the work of a number of very different dancers depicted in the "maenad" posture of the grande arc: in Isadora Duncan, La Belle Otéro, Ruth St. Denis, Grete Wiesenthal, Rosalia Chladek, and Mary Wigman (figures 25–31). Each dancer executed the movement in a slightly different way and with varying degrees of bodily tension. The differences between the patterns of presentation reflect their respective personal styles and the specificities of *freier Tanz*, *Ausdruckstanz*, and modern dance.

The dances of the maenad, the ecstatic movement model of the Dionysian, were embodied in a particularly impressive way by Duncan: in her dances and likewise in her love life, which was uncompromisingly, almost programmatically devoted to the female-Dionysian. Duncan's perfect representation of the self-definition of modernity in a dancing female body seems to be the real reason behind her phenomenal success. She herself defined her dance as being in accordance with the pathos formula of the passionate dance of the maenad. In an open letter from 1903, published in the *Berliner Morgenpost*, she reacted to the queries "Can Miss Duncan Dance?" by referring to the likeness of an ancient maenad:

The dancer to whom I refer is the statue of the dancing Maenad in the Berlin Museum. Now will you kindly write again to the admirable masters and mistresses of the ballet and ask them, "Can the dancing Maenad dance?"[143]

According to Helene von Nostitz, Duncan also performed bacchanalian dances in front of the Dionysus temple in Athens (see figure 28):

Isadora danced the holy shiver of the temple, in which the incense rose upward to the gods, danced . . . the bacchanalian joy of Dionysian celebration. She danced the majestic sorrow of ancient tragedy. Then she raged again like a maenad.[144]

Duncan's interpretation of the pathos formula of the maenad maintained its continuity—over a period of almost twenty years—more from the embodiment

143. See Rosemont 1983, 34; see also the writings of Marie-Luise Becker on new free dance, which likewise refer to this "Maenad" sculpture in Berlin and Duncan's dance (1903, 279): "Our maenad in a Berlin museum: yes, she dances!" Translation: Elena Polzer.

144. See Nostitz 1979. Translation: Elena Polzer.

Figure 25 Ruth St. Denis in *Radha* (1906).
SOURCE: Author's archive.

of these guiding iconographic patterns than from her technical innovations in dance.[145]

The *moving* representation of this body imagery by the habitus of the individual in dance manifests itself in Duncan's performances as a characteristic symbol of modernity. Edward Gordon Craig, who in the first period of his relationship with Isadora (during the years 1904–05) put his own work aside and studied her performances and her stage[146] and movement concepts and reflected them both in drawings as well as in writing, wrote:

145. Duncan's success and in particular her inspiring effect were accompanied after a few years, and then repeatedly, by highly critical assessments by contemporaries, especially from experts in dance history; this is evident in statements by e.g., H. Brandenburg, F. Thieß, J. Schikowski, F. Böhme, and other dance critics.

146. Duncan presented her dances on an empty stage (i.e., without a set or other decor). Blue curtains were sometimes hung in the background and also in the wings; allegedly there was a "quarrel" between Duncan and Craig, who had "invented" this empty, blue-draped stage. Of greater importance to the history of theater than the solution of this—now mythical—dispute over "priorities" are, however, the parallels to modern aesthetical stage concepts in dance and theater.

Figure 26 La Belle Otéro in an Egyptian dance.
SOURCE: Author's archive.

It would be impossible to conceive the effect of Isadora's performances in Germany. In this period of her dance career she was undoubtedly *the* dancer of the age. Since Taglioni there has been no such thing, and since Isadora there has been no other and I doubt that Isadora has ever been more herself than in those years of 1905–1910![147]

A number of aspects in Duncan's life and work are particularly symptomatic of her personification of turn-of-the-century body imagery. The tendency of critics to trivialize the Duncan model from very early on as well as the

147. E. G. Craig, in Niehaus 1981, 40f. Translation: Elena Polzer.

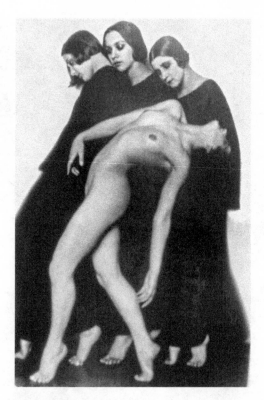

Figure 27 Rudolf Koppitz: Movement study
(around 1926).
SOURCE: Derra de Moroda Dance Archives, Salzburg,
Austria / © Derra de Moroda Dance archives,
University of Salzburg, Austria.

subsequent attempts of her followers to mythologize her work, which Duncan
herself also attempted to do, and finally the cult built up around her by admirers and biographers after her tragic death, all these made of Isadora the true
embodiment of the new dance.

In 1911–12, the sculptor and painter Emile Antoine Bourdelle produced a
whole series of drawings of Duncan dancing (as she danced in his atelier). In
his collection of sketches[148] depicting passionate expressive gestures—a true
inventory of Aby Warburg's pathos formulas—those ecstatic postures and
dance figurations are especially prevalent that resemble the "dance of the maenad" in the movement patterns of head, arms, and torso. Often they are titled
accordingly: *Ecstasy, Frénésie I–IV, Tourbillon* or *Rage*.

148. A large collection of these drawings, paintings, and statues is stored, looked after, and
inventorized by Madame Dufet-Bourdelle, the daughter of the artist, in the Musée Bourdelle
in Paris. Mme Dufet-Bourdelle was so kind as to give me access to the rare documents; see
Aveline and Dufet 1969.

Figure 28 Isadora Duncan dancing in the temple of Dionysus.
SOURCE: Bibliothèque de l'Arsenal, Paris, France.

The pathos of these patterns of embodiment and simultaneously their trivialization was reflected in the various neologisms and puns at the time, such as the term "Isadorables" for a group of Duncan's students, of which six[149] were finally "adopted" as Isadora's heirs in order to physically continue the Duncan genealogy through dance (not in writing, as was the case with Rudolf von Laban, who sought to pass on his system of expressive dance in the form of notation). Or "Duncanité" for those successors, who—such as Annabelle Gamson in the 1970s—attempted to reconstruct various dance movements based on the Isadora model.

Not only the numerous caricatures of Isadora's dances—probably best known are the drawings of Olaf Gulbransson in *Simplizissimus*—but also various texts,

149. The six students who were given permission to use the name "Duncan" are portrayed in a photo from 1917 by Arnold Genthe: Irma, Theresa, Anna, Lisa, Erica, and Margot.

Figure 29 Grete Wiesenthal, *Danube Waltz* (1908).
SOURCE: Historisches Museum der Stadt Wien, Vienna, Austria.

such as the following parody of the Berlin popular song the *Holzaktion*, demonstrate a humorous approach to the pathos formula of the dance of the maenad:

> In Grunewald, in Grunewald is dance class!
> Bare knees, naked calves
> and armpits exposed;
> Our classical maenads
> Are dancing today in the *Hundekehle* [dog's throat].
> Did they know much of Orpheus,
> Who to the maenads fell prey?—
> Gluck and other composers
> Are no more better off today.[150]

150. Cited in Niehaus 1981, 41; these verses, published in 1905 in the *Lustige Blätter* Berlin, refer to performances by the Duncan school, which Isadora founded in 1904 in Berlin-Grunewald and which was led, while Isadora was on tour, by her sister Elizabeth Duncan.
    Original German (English translation: Elena Polzer):

> Blanke Knie, nackte Waden
> Und entblößte Achselhöhle;
> Uns're klassischen Mänaden
> Tanzen heut' bei Hundekehle.

Figure 30 Rosalia Chladek, *Slavic Dance* (1923).
SOURCE: Derra de Moroda Dance Archives, Salzburg, Austria / © Derra de Moroda Dance archives, University of Salzburg, Austria.

Duncan incorporated characteristic poses and movement components of the "maenad dance" in various aspects of her work: in dance, for example, in her depiction of the *Marseillaise* (1915), in the *Trauermarsch* (to music by Chopin), and in her choreography of the Bacchae in Richard Wagner's *Tannhäuser* in Bayreuth, where she staged the female-Dionysian both in the theater and in her

Ob sie was von Orpheus wußten,
Der Mänaden fiel zur Beute?—
Gluck und andern Komponisten
Geht es auch nicht besser heute

Figure 31 Mary Wigman, *Allegro con brio from Slavic dances*
(1920).
SOURCE: Battenberg Verlag, Augsburg, Germany.

salon. The subject of the Dionysian, however, also repeatedly surfaced in her
writings and lectures as well as in anecdotes about her.

The dance *Bacchus and Ariadne* was already part of a program of Duncan's
early performances in London in 1899–1900. The piece was based on a famous
painting by Titian, hanging in the London National Gallery. She was probably
inspired to include this particular subject matter in her movement images and
intensify her aura as a "Dionysian dancer"—basing it in particular on Titian's
Bacchus and Ariadne—by Walter Pater's *A Study of Dionysus*. His *Greek Studies*
appeared in 1895 and were quite widely distributed.

Hugo von Hofmannsthal's dramatic concept for *Electra* and his fragments of both the *Bacchen* and *Pentheus* were also inspired by Pater's *Study of
Dionysus*.[151] Both in *Electra* and in the *Bacchen/Pentheus* fragments, the dance

151. Hugo von Hofmannsthal owned a copy of Pater's *Greek Studies* (1904); notes in the mar-
gins testify to the importance of this text, which aside from the writings of Nietzsche, especially
The Birth of Tragedy, can be considered the most important source for his planned rework-
ing of the *Bacchae* of Euripides, as well as the *Pentheus* fragment; see Hofmannsthal 1975–,

of the maenad appears as a pathos formula of transgression and takes on a central dramaturgical function: the trespassing of cultural structures of order. The character of Electra, in the tragic (1903) as well as in the later operatic version (1909), resembles a maenad, as described by Erwin Rohde, as well as by Pater: "In 'Thiasus', in a wild nocturnal procession through woods and hills," accompanied by lights and music, the maenads tear apart sacrificial animals—goats and "dappled fawn" (Pater).[152] Electra's excesses, her craving for the blood sacrifice[153] of *sparagmos*, her entire behavior alludes to the image of the maenad. A direct reference to the dance of the maenad can be found in the stage directions at the end of the tragedy: "She has thrown back her head like a maenad."[154]

After the bloody deed, after the murder of Clytemnestra and Aegisthus by Orestes, Electra feels as if she herself has been slain. She lingers in a state of cataleptic stupor, unable to move a single leaden limb. She is unable to command her body:

I know very well that they are waiting for me,
because I must lead the dance, and I cannot;
the ocean, the enormous twentyfold ocean
buries my every limb with its weight, I cannot
raise myself![155]

Yet as Electra rises, every one of her movements indicates extreme tension. The "nameless" dance, in which she—lonely and "solo," as she was wrapped up in memories until the murder—leads the "round" of an imaginary multitude of bacchanalian dancers,[156] is sustained by the pathos formula of

18: 379 and 384f. In 1904, the year in which the German translation was published, he reread Pater's "Bacchae" essay. Evidence of the close ties between *Electra* and the *Bacchae/Pentheus* can moreover be found in Hofmannsthal's notes concerning all three ancient dramas.

152. See Pater's essay "The Bacchanals of Euripides" (1878).

153. For Electra, the "eternal blood" of patricide can never be washed off the floorboards. Her existence is concentrated on never forgetting the bloody deed, keeping the memory of it alive until the murder of Agamemnon is avenged by the death of the mother Clytemnestra and her lover Aegisthus: "When the right victim falls beneath the axe, you will no longer dream." The entire piece is (literally) saturated with the blood motive, which appears around thirty times over the course of the drama; see Mayer 1993, 235f.

154. Hofmannsthal 1966, 139.

155. Ibid., 138–39.

156. On this matter, Reinhold Schlötterer's interpretation (1986) must be firmly objected to. Electra's dance is in no way based on the model of the ancient round dance "choros"; Schlötterer's concept, connected to his recommendation for the staging of *Electra* that "the restoration of social order, which Electra longs for, is for her connected with a round dance"

ecstatic movement—the arch, the thrown-back head, the throwing of
the limbs:

> Electra has risen. She comes striding down from the doorsill. She has
> thrown back her head like a maenad. She flings her knees up high, she
> stretches her arms out wide; it is a nameless dance in which she strides
> forward.[157]

After leading the imaginary round dance with the words "Be silent and
dance. . . . I bear the burden of happiness, and I dance before you. For him who
is happy as we, it behooves him to do only this: to be silent and dance!"[158] she
collapses at the climax of her "triumph." Here the passionate pattern of expression and movement found in the so-called great hysterical attack is linked to
the pathos formula of the dance of the maenad in order to depict the "eccentric"
aspect of this character in a drama about the loss of self.

In *Electra*, Hofmannsthal attempts to dramatize the "forbidden depths of
passion," those powers that erupt in the Dionysus mysteries as the "birth of
tragedy" (Nietzsche). Hofmannsthal's three ancient dramas, *Alcestis*, *Electra*,
and *Pentheus*, all share a preoccupation with a suspension of individuation in
the frenzy of Dionysian "enthusiasmos" as depicted in Nietzsche's essay on tragedy. Hofmannsthal writes:

> All three of my three ancient dramas are concerned with the dissolution of
> the concept of the individual. In Electra, the individual disintegrates in an
> empirical way—the substance of life bursts it apart from within like water
> transforming to ice inside an earthen jug. Electra is no longer Electra, sim-
> ply because she is trying so hard to be Electra through and through. The
> individual can only seemingly continue to exist when a compromise is
> reached between the common and the individual.[159]

However, the elements of "being-beside-oneself" as movement patterns of
the dance of the maenad already sporadically surface throughout the course of

---

(Schlötterer 1986, 56), also fails to understand, in my opinion, the meaning of dance in
the *Electra* tragedy. The solipsistic, purely imaginary concept of the round dance in particular, which culminates in the solo, in Electra's somewhat lonely ecstatic dance, lends
Hofmannsthal's composition of the ancient drama its modern character leveled at the "dissolution of the concept of the individual" (Hofmannsthal 1978, A III, 461).

157. Hofmannsthal 1966, 139.

158. Ibid.

159. Hofmannsthal 1978, A III, 461. Translation: Elena Polzer.

the tragedy,[160] even before Electra's dance at the end of the piece culminates in ecstasy and collapse.

Over and over again, other characters comment on the fact that Electra's movements appear uncoordinated and uncontrolled, dizzy (Aegisthus: "Why do you stagger back and forth with your light?"), animalistic and convulsively spasmodic, "ghastly," "like an animal in a cage" and "in wild drunkenness." These movement patterns of the raving maenad, the "hysteric" acting out an identity already burst apart from within, is however paired with that other trait of Electra's which—contrary to her physical appearance—seems to be an expression of complete control, namely her domination of language, in which the memory of the murder of Agamemnon is constantly kept alive.

While in the drama the ecstatic movement model of the dance of the maenad takes on the function of physically representing an act of stepping out of time—into ecstasy, into the passionate loss of control, finally into death—the rhetoric of memory indicates sovereignty over the memory of time, gained at the expense of life and love. Electra's clever words, her gift—in her long dialogue with Clytemnestra—of holding equivocal speech, her untiring vigilance—"for you are clever. In your head there is great skill. You speak of old events as if they had happened yesterday"[161]—demonstrates the other side of her nature: rationality, control, superiority.

The *lack of connection* between these two aspects of her character, almost like the split parallel existence of the actions of head and body, the responses of memory and the collapse of memory, the back and forth of intellectuality and maenad frenzy, reveals the truly modern and tragic side in this dramatic character.[162]

160. Hofmannsthal 1966, 101, 103, 132, 136.

161. Ibid., 91–92.

162. Unlike Mayer's interpretation of *Electra*, I base my observations on a model of dualism, expressed on the level of character configuration (e.g., the contrasts between the three women, Chrysothemis, Clytemnestra, Electra or Electra/Orestes) and in the character of Electra herself via the body imagery of the "Maenad", versus the memory of the mnemonist; on the level of dramatic poetics in the *unresolved and unconnected parallelism of language and corporeal action, of rhetoric as memory of horror and dance of the maenad as appalling talk of movement.* Mayer, however (1993, 243) interprets *Electra* as "a character reflecting the poet himself": Electra's silence after the "powerfully eloquent" climax of the drama anticipates the suspension of speech in music; the operatic version of Electra was more or less already present in Hofmannsthal's conception of the tragedy. Here Mayer reads *Electra* (without however explicitly pointing it out) against the backdrop of Nietzsche's understanding of (Wagner's) music drama as detailed in *The Birth of Tragedy*. However, this ultimately means the pursuit of a *synthesis* of the arts. In my opinion, such patterns of synthesis are not recognizable in the *Electra* piece (even if Hofmannsthal does strive toward such in his later work). Instead the contradictions are maintained until the end, and on an abstract dramatic

In his comments on *Electra*, Hofmannsthal mostly expressed himself quite reservedly about the piece, which to him—as he writes in a letter to his brother-in-law Hans Schlesinger—"would be entirely unbearable in its frantic imprisonment, its ghastly darkness," if he hadn't already drawn up before his mind's eye "the integrally inseparable second part of the *Orest in Delphi*"[163]—a plan that Hofmannsthal, however, never implemented.

In *Pentheus*, the two antagonistic characters—distributed in connection with *Electra* onto a dramatic diptych with the *Orestes* drama as a counterbalance—were meant to face each other in a single tragedy, in the form of Pentheus and his mother Agaue. The myth, as passed down by Euripides in the *Bacchae*, focuses on the Theban king Pentheus, who—like Orpheus—despises Dionysus and seeks to prohibit the orgiastic cult in honor of the god. The Theban women, among them his mother Agaue, take part in the Dionysian celebrations. Pentheus manages to capture Dionysus. The god convinces him to hide in the woods—dressed as a bacchante—and to observe the activities of the women engaged in the Dionysus cult. Pentheus is discovered and torn apart by the raving maenads—among them his mother, who doesn't recognize him.

After completing *Electra* in 1904, Hofmannsthal based his concept of the tragedy, which he first titled *Die Bacchen* (*The Bacchae*), later *Pentheus*, on a lucid, theatrical setting. The stage design was based on ideas of Appia, Fortuny, and Craig: an "almost naked stage," in which transformations merely took place "with the help of changing lights." The other basis for the tragedy was an underlying pattern of "relationship to art," which to Hofmannsthal seemed to provide the material of the ancient myth, namely that "of enthusiasm and of wild hatred" (*SW*, 377).

In his dramatic concept, which he also refers to as a "transcription based on antiquity" (*SW*, 59), Hofmannsthal did not refer to the ritualized "cult of Dionysus," its "gay, civilized" form, but instead sought to portray the dark side of the mystery cult.

The *Pentheus* drama is based on the subject of the disintegration of individuality and centers around the antagonistic relationship between the Dionysian, to which Agaue belongs, and the Apollonian, embodied by Pentheus: "Pentheus short-sightedly adheres to the indivisibility of the person, to the 'character.' When a person falls out of character, such as Agaue, then this is a crime, excess, affliction" (*SW*, 51).[164]

---

or rather poetological level—in terms of the antagonism and constantly gaping chasm of difference between acts of speech and physical action.

163. Hofmannsthal, *Briefe* (*Letters*), 2 1979: 132f.

164. Translation: Elena Polzer.

As in *Electra*, Hofmannsthal's dramatic conception for *Pentheus* is focused on the subject of dissociation in the individual ego.[165] In both tragedies, this schism—the duality of control and loss of control, of body and intellect, of cultural order and bacchanalian anarchy—references the dance of the maenad.

In contemporary interpretations of *Electra*, in statements made by Alfred Kerr, Hermann Bahr, or Theodor Gomperz, it is predominantly the hysterical aspect that is considered the psychologically interesting moment in Hofmannsthal's antiquity dramas.[166] In light of the forms and functions of how body imagery is culturally produced and interpreted, this drama is particularly impressive in its conjunction of antiquity and modernity: the interlacing of the pathos formula of the dance of the maenad with the ecstatic expressive gesture of the hysteric, staged as a construct of femininity.

BODY-IMAGE II: EXOTICISM

Exotic dance, wherein a female dancer presents her body to the male gaze in an erotic-seductive performance, provides a different but complementary model of the antique body-image. Dressed in the attire of an oriental dancer—Odalisque, Almeh, Bayadère, or Indian temple priestess—Woman appeared as the epitome of the fascinatingly foreign. Eroticism and dance, in these cases, were treated as almost synonymous. The phenomenon of exoticism played

---

165. The subject of dissociation of the ego repeatedly appears in Hofmannsthal's work even before he—in 1907—attempts to work directly with the psychiatrically documented model of a disruption of identity (in his fragments *Andreas* and *Dominik Heintl*, both conceived/initiated in 1907) based on his reading of Morton Prince's psychopathological study *The Dissociation of a Personality* (1906).

166. See Worbs 1983, 269ff.; in his study, Worbs explores the contemporary reception of "Electra as Hysteric." Alfred Kerr, for example, saw in Electra an "epileptic's private thirst for revenge"; Theodor Gomperz summed up the tendency of the drama with the word: "Hysterical!"; and Hermann Bahr praised the "hysterical tone" of Electra impersonator Gertrud Eysoldt. Hofmannsthal wrote (in his *Letters*, 2: 384) that he read Erwin Rohde's *Psyche* (1893) and the *Studies on Hysteria* (1895) by Sigmund Freud and Josef Breuer, while writing *Electra*.

It is for this reason that "hysteria" has been adhered to for so long in literary studies as a basis for interpreting the pathological feminine in *Electra*. But in doing so, the outlines of patterns of femininity associated with the character of the hysteric as were prevalent around the turn of the century have continuously been reproduced without critically questioning the associated, historically situated, mythicizing construction of body imagery (and pathos formulas: such as the *dance of the maenad*). Wolfgang Nehring (1991) gives a quick overview of the "hysteria" debate in literary studies on *Electra* from Politzer (1973), Urban (1978), and Worbs (1983) to Lorna Martens (1987).

an important cultural role in explorations of images of the Other undertaken in nineteenth- and early twentieth-century fine arts, musical theater, and literature.

However, the roots of those forms of exotic-erotic dance that flourished in particular around the turn of the century are to be found in nineteenth-century Romantic ballet. It is here that we have the dichotomy of the fairylike, pure dancer and the erotic-sensual "worldly" dancer. Théophile Gautier called them the "Christian" versus the "heathen" ballerina, as embodied by Marie Taglioni and Fanny Elßler (who was famous for her sensual and temperamental performances of the *cachucha, cracovienne,* and *tarantelle*). Other variations of the two-faced image of Madonna and Venus, of the Blessed Virgin and the whore, appeared in *La Sylphide* and *La Bayadère.*

At the turn of the century—in an age just setting off into the hidden worlds of the psyche, an era in which the norms governing relationships between the sexes were changing—exotic dance gained a striking popularity. Modern dance in particular with its free, vivid movement vocabulary—developed out of the body's center by dancers as distinct from one another as Isadora Duncan, Ruth St. Denis, Maud Allen, and Grete Wiesenthal—offered new possibilities for representing the lascivious, the erotic, and the foreign. Naked dancing, the so-called beauty dance, and pantomime-oriental dance—for example, by Mata Hari, Olga Desmond, Anita Berber, Adorée Villany, or Sent M'ahesa—conquered stages and the media. The World Exposition in Paris in 1900 and the performances presented there by Javanese, Cambodian, and Japanese dance and theater groups were a major factor in the popularization of such dance performances. To an intellectual landscape weary of Europe and marked by *décadence* and colonialism, the confrontation with the Other, especially with the body and movement imagery of other cultures, provided new aesthetic stimuli and incentives.

However, looking at European culture through foreign eyes also served to confirm a skeptical perspective on Western civilization, that is, by interpreting familiar European body imagery as proof an indication of the alienated Western identity. Hofmannsthal's *Letters of the Returnee* (1907), for example, clearly reflects this kind of cultural criticism: the "evil eye" is directed at symbols of modern civilization—"the curse of European nature." The "form of quiet contamination, a hidden creeping infection that seems to lie in wait in the European air for him who returns from afar, after being away for very long, perhaps too long,"[167] is an indicator of a fundamental experience of splitting as an "existential sensation." Based on faith in that *one* unconscious "seamless" gesture that reveals the subject as being "at one

167. Hofmannsthal 1978, E, 562f. Translation: Elena Polzer

with himself,[168] the motto "the whole man must move at once"[169] emerged as a countermovement to this experience of alienation. The celebration of exotic dance in the European world reflected this yearning for the Other, for mysterious foreignness, as described by Hofmannsthal in his review of Ruth St. Denis's Indian dance *Radha* (1906):[170] "It presents us with something totally strange, without pretending to be ethnographic or sensational. It is there simply for the sake of its beauty";[171] here the act of "suffusing European imagination with Asiatic beauty" is given shape in a dance, whose gestures appear as "eternal emanations"[172] of the sensual, removed from all conventions.

"Dance of the Bees"

One example of the juxtaposition of exotic images of the body with pathos formulas of antiquity is the "dance of the bees": the whirring dance of the bees represents the ecstatic movement character of the maenad and simultaneously symbolizes the "erotic pantomime" (Hofmannsthal) of the oriental dancer.

The imagery in the "dance of the bees" thus attaches itself to the previously elucidated pathos formula of the dance of the maenad. Walter Pater compared this "wild" dance of the "swarming" maenads to a flight of bees. Inspired by Pater's essay, Hofmannsthal developed an even more complex set of images by comparing the maenad's dance with swarming bees. The bee metaphor for the dancing women in the Dionysus cult is juxtaposed with the image of a drone, symbolizing the ecstatic self-sacrifice of a maenad drunk with bloodlust. Hofmannsthal notes in his plans for the *Bacchae*:

> The chosen ones set out with the queen, delighted homage of all toward their queen; as bees toward theirs.
> The bee = drone motif interwoven.
> Daughters of the City: called the Bees.[173]

168. Ibid., E, 550.

169. For more on this sentence, often cited by Hofmannsthal and accredited by Lichtenberg to the British author Addison, see Coghlan 1985.

170. On Ruth St. Denis's Indian dances, her connection to Harry Graf Kessler, and Hofmannsthal, see Brandstetter 1991b, 38–44.

171. Hofmannsthal 1968, 37.

172. Ibid., 38.

173. See Hofmannsthal 1975–, 18: 60. Translation: Elena Polzer.

The visual matrix of bees/dance of the drones here unfolds in an intertextual connection with Pater's study of the *Bacchanals*. In Hofmannsthal's own work it indicates a link between the ancient dramas of *Electra* and *Pentheus*. This is evident in Hofmannsthal's notes that he wrote in 1904 describing the "nameless dance," which ends in collapse, at the close of *Electra*:

> That she can no longer go on living, that when the deed is done her life and innards must gush from her, just as life and innards along with the fertilizing sting must gush from the drone when the queen has been fertilized.[174]

In the passage of Pater's study on the *Bacchanals* of Euripides used by Hofmannsthal, Pater compares Coleridge's translation of the Greek term for "being-beside-oneself"—for "enthusiasm" in religious ecstasy—to the German word *Schwärmerei*,[175] thus comparing the image of swarming bees with the dance of the Bacchic women and the wild, whirling frenzy of the maenads:

> Coleridge, in one of his fantastic speculations, refining on the German word for enthusiasm—*Schwärmerei*, swarming, as he says, "like the swarming of bees together"—has explained how the sympathies of mere numbers, as such, the random catching on fire of one here and another there, when people are collected together, generates as if by mere contact, some new and rapturous spirit, not traceable in the individual units of a multitude. Such swarming was the essence of that strange dance of the Bacchic women: literally like winged things, they follow, with motives, we may suppose, never quite made clear even to themselves, their new, strange, romantic god.[176]

This interpretation of the dance of the bees as a metaphor for "the essence of that strange dance of the Bacchic women" differs both from the conventional meaning of the bee dance in the history of dance and from the symbolism of the bee motif and the dance of the bees in literature.[177]

---

174. Translated in Scott 2005, 32.

175. *Translator's note*: The word contains *Schwarm* as in *insect swarm*, but actually means *infatuation*.

176. Pater (1878) uses this ecstatic dance to link the bacchants of the Dionysus cult to the maenads, the "Later sisters of Centaur and Amazon . . . as they beat the earth in strange sympathy with its waking up from sleep."

177. See Neumann 1993b.

In literature from Ovid and Lichtenberg to Nietzsche, the bee, as a collector and transformer of the essence of blossoms—as honey gatherer—symbolizes the poet. As a "prudent" architect and, moreover, as a creature organized in social colonies, the bee embodies the principles of enlightenment. The perfect, functional stereometric design of the honeycomb as well as the ornamental "language" of the bee dance (Karl von Frisch) lead the bee to be associated with basic anthropological patterns of orientation. Architecture and dance, as found in the orderly structures of production and reproduction in nature, become symbols of spatial and temporal orientation and of communicating clearly encoded information about the structures of one's environment. The bee dance thus becomes a metaphor for sign language and the "art forms of nature" (Ernst Haeckel).

However, when it comes to the dance of the bees in the context of nine-teenth- and early twentieth-century theatrical dance I do not claim *this* semantic horizon of bee iconography to be operative. Here, an entirely differ-ent connotative field of the motif is translated into dance: not the bee's rational and functional capacities of orientation, which could be the choreographic aspect of their dance, but—to the contrary—the emotional side of the bee motif, suggested by a *loss* of orientation: (seemingly) uncontrolled movement, the "rage" of ecstasy, the frightened motion of flight, and self-intoxication in a whirling dance.

The bee dance appeared in nineteenth-century ballet as a specific manifes-tation of theatrical exoticism. At the time, the Orient and performances of exotic motifs of femininity were evident in various forms in the fine arts (e.g., in Ingres's painting *Bain turc*), in literature (e.g., Flaubert's travel novels), and in opera and ballet.[178] In ballet, libretto material based on oriental fairy tales provided the framework for opulent, exotic stage scenery and choreographies of dances in fantasy costumes based on oriental images, as in pieces such as *Le Dieu et la Bayadère* (1830; choreography by Filippo Taglioni; music by Daniel F. Auber), *Lalla Rookh* (1846; choreography by Jules Perrot; music by Cesare Pugni, based on Félician David's paradigmatic "orientalizing" symphonic ode *Le Désert*), and *La Péri* (1843; choreography by Jean Coralli; music by J. F. Burgmüller). The bee dance was composed of a mixture of pantomime ele-ments, spirited dancing, erotic veils, and risqué performance. Not only in ballet, but in opera as well, the inclusion of a bee dance in the general plot ensured a nice dose of oriental atmosphere, as in Karl Goldmark's *The Queen of Sheba* (1875).

178. See the catalog *Exotische Welten, europäische Phantasien* (*Exotic Worlds, European Fantasies*) (Pollig 1987); however, the bee dance is not mentioned here or in the study on oriental dance by W. Buonaventura 1990, 1994.

In his *Handbuch des Tanzes* (*Handbook of Dance*), Viktor Junk writes in 1930 about the bee dance: "The dancer removes parts of her costume bit by bit, as she attempts to find the insect in the folds of her dress, thus presenting the slender form of her body."[179]

This description is already influenced by depictions of the bee dance found in some dances and works of literature at the beginning of the twentieth century, which treat it largely as a slightly more sophisticated form of striptease.

In turn-of-the-century encyclopedias and handbook articles, the bee dance is characterized in a similar fashion. In his *Schule des Tanzes* (1907—*School of Dance*), W. K. von Jolizza describes the bee dance alongside the dance of the odalisques and the Egyptian "ghaziya" in his chapter "People of the Orient and Far East."[180] By contrast, A. Diringer emphasizes the resemblance of the "raving" maenad-like elements of the bee dance to a St. Vitus's dance, in the third edition of *Die Tanzkunst* (*The Art of Dance*) published in 1899:

A new Egyptian solo dance. A dancer expresses in various, sometimes very frank positions, the pain of having been stung by a bee. This is followed by wild raging movement gestures of searching for the insect, which often gets so out of hand that the dancer falls down utterly exhausted.[181]

Two aspects of this text are particularly noteworthy: on the one hand, it attempts to convey lexical cultural-historical knowledge and, on the other, it seeks simultaneously to provide instructions for dance classes. Here we have compelling evidence that it was early twentieth-century ballroom dancing in particular that absorbed elements of "oriental" dance. The isolations, the multi-centric mobilization of the limbs, as typical of the shimmy and the Charleston, have their origins not only—as often described[182]—in Afro-American jazz dance, but were equally influenced by the oriental patterns of the "beledi."[183] And the same censors who placed those ballrooms in which the newest social dances whirled over the dance floor under police control in the 1910s and 1920s[184] also exerted their influence on the first cinematic images of the *danse*

179. Junk 1930, 32. Translation: Elena Polzer.

180. Jolizza 1907.

181. Diringer 1899, 50. Translation: Elena Polzer.

182. See, e.g., the work of H. Günther (1969), who is very knowledgeable in the field of jazz dance.

183. See Buonaventura 1990, 16f.

184. See Eichstedt and Polster 1985.

du ventre (belly dance) in 1896. It is worth noting that the first cases of censorship in cinema involved "exotic" dance performance.[185] Even in the mid-nineteenth century, exotic dance was considered quite risqué, as is documented by reviews of the ballet *La Péri*, in which dancer Carlotta Grisi celebrated multiple triumphs not least of all for her captivating rendition of the bee dance, "Pas de l'abeille." In his book *Meister des Balletts*[186] (*Masters of Ballet*) André Levinson writes that the "Pas de l'abeille"—that very bee dance in which Grisi had shined so brilliantly—was deleted in the revival of the piece. Théophile Gautier recalls:

> If you knew with what chaste clumsiness Carlotta freed herself from her long white veil; how her pose, when she kneels under the translucent folds of the fabric, resembles a classical Venus, smiling at us from her mother of pearl seashell; what child-like fear grips her, when the irritated bee flies up from the blossom! How well she accentuates her hopes, her fears, the alternating coincidences of the struggle! How the corsage, the sash, the skirt, wherever the bee seems to penetrate, flies left and right in haste, to disappear in the tempest of the dance! (192)[187]

According to Levinson, this scene of the bee dance fell victim to the censors, who argued that such elements of "ethnographic choreography" had no prospect of lasting success on the "prudish opera stage." The subsumption of the exotic under the category of "ethnographical" here provides us with a clue to a shift in patterns of reading and interpreting the "foreign" (as the erotic female) that were occurring at the beginning of the 1920s. In 1906, Hugo von Hofmannsthal still praised Ruth St. Denis's Indian dance *Radha* (performed in a similar costume as in the case of the bee dance) in his review as "something totally strange, without pretending to be ethnographic," as "suffusing European imagination with Asiatic beauty."[188]

During the wave of exoticism that swept Europe at the beginning of the twentieth century and blended with the body imagery of *freier Tanz*, elements of Egyptian *beledi*[189] entered the bee dance. By now, the bee dances' patterns of presentation had been detached from the context of ballet. The

---

185. See Buonaventura 1990, 102f.; this belly dance, "Fatima's Dance," which fell victim to censorship, was available for viewing in a film automat along the beach promenade of Atlantic City around 1896.

186. Levinson 1923.

187. Translation: Elena Polzer.

188. Hofmannsthal 1968, 37, 38.

189. See Buonaventura 1990, 99ff.

beledi, known in Europe under the name *danse du ventre*, became the epitome of erotic dance. The mysterious female figure, her dress, her nakedness, but especially the *beledi*'s distinct style of movement, were enormously fascinating to European artists and audiences, as we can see in Gustave Flaubert's *Hérodias* and *La Tentation de Saint Antoine*,[190] in Ernst Hardt's *Fatema* (1909), Alexander Castell's *Die mysteriöse Tänzerin* (1911), or Charles Gobineau's *La danseuse de Shamakha* (1926).

European performers of exoticism, such as Mata Hari, Adorée Villany, and Ruth St. Denis, however, never truly adopted or only hinted at those typical oriental movements that were perceived as especially erotic: the isolation of the hips, ceaselessly "dancing" in rolling, circling, thrusting movements, in slow and also quick vibrating impulses, while the dancer remains largely in one spot and the arms and the head follow a slower pattern of movement of their own, isolated from the motions of the body. It was this division of the body into an upper and lower section, connected with a lack of movement in space and a certain degree of monotony in the flow of the performance, that made up the unique, entrancing quality of the *beledi*.[191]

Stasia Napierkowska: *Pas de l'Abeille*

Stasia Napierkowska was one of those turn-of-the-century free dancers who exhibited a particularly broad range of work and forms of expression.[192] In her three-part solo *de l'Abeille* (1911), she combined various patterns of representation: elements of pantomime, which still harked back to nineteenth-century ballet versions of the bee dance; movement forms taken from *freier Tanz*; and

190. Kutchuk Hanem (= "little princess") was one of the few *ghaziya* (i.e., professional Egyptian dancers and courtesans) whose names were known (usually they danced anonymously). On her dance and how it was received by Western travelers, see Buonaventura 1990, 68–75. The American journalist J. W. Curtis made Kutchuk Hanem known in the West through his descriptions in 1851. Gustave Flaubert also visited Kutchuk Hanem twice during his travels. He used his detailed notes for his depictions of the dance in *Salammbô*, in *Hérodias*, and in *The Temptation of Saint Anthony*, as being that moment in which the Queen of Sheba attempts to seduce the holy man with her dancing.

191. Charles Gobineau describes the hypnotic effect of this dance on the audience in his novella *La danseuse de Shamakha*, 1926: "Hours pass and it is difficult to tear oneself away. This is the way the motions of the dancing girls of Asia affect the senses. There is no variety or vivacity, and seldom is there a variation through any sudden movement, but the rhythmic wheeling exhales a delightful torpor upon the soul, like an almost hypnotic intoxication." See http://www.zehara.co.uk/bdfactsorientalism.htm.

192. See Brandstetter 1988.

Figure 32 Stasia Napierkowska, *Pas de l'Abeille* (1911).
SOURCE: Derra de Moroda Dance Archives, Salzburg, Austria / © Derra de
Moroda Dance archives, University of Salzburg, Austria.

eclectic components of "exotic" dance, resembling the poses used by Mata Hari
and postures that imitated images of Indian gods and goddesses.

In the November 22, 1911, issue a series of photographic images entitled
Attitudes of Napierkowska depicting her performance *The Bee* was published in a
supplement of the magazine *The Sketch*. The photos are a kind of chrono-photo-
graphical documentation of her dance (see figure 32). Napierkowska wore an out-
fit typical for the theatrical presentation of the Oriental *beledi* in dance:[193] a short

193. See Buonaventura 1990, 113ff. In the cabarets, in the revues, and soon also in film, a
surprisingly uniform pattern of costume established itself in exotic dance, especially at the
beginning of the twentieth century; the costume itself took on a symbolic function for the

brassiere edged with rhinestones; a skirt tightly gathered around the hips, turning into broad, long tassels from the thighs downward, with naked legs showing through; a decorated headband and a long, white, translucent veil, which was thrown off toward the end of the dance.

The program booklet described the following scene:

> After a long day's travel a party of Arabs arrive at an oasis. Their chief has made captive a Maroccan [*sic*] Princess, who is bound. The girl beseeches the chief to release her, and he consents upon the condition that she will dance for him . . . she complies with "La Danse de l'Abeille." A young girl is gathering flowers, from one of which a bee finds its way beneath her clothing. Terrified, she tries to find the bee beneath the folds of her dress, but is unsuccessful. Some of her draperies are removed in the process of the search. The chief, forgetting his promise of freedom, makes passionate love to his captive, and she, in an agony of terror, wounds him with the sword of one of the tribe. . . . In death she sees freedom. She chooses "La Danse du Feu." It is a human sacrifice. The captive offers up her life upon an altar of fire, which, gradually enveloping her writhing form brings the release for which she has prayed.[194]

By adding a framework plot to the subject matter and especially by introducing the sacrifice motif of a "fire dance," Napierkowska's bee dance abandons conventional exotic patterns of the nineteenth-century *pas de l'abeille* in favor of a type of dance theater, which even resembles in some ways Hofmannsthal's *Pentheus*.

Napierkowska's performance somewhat reflects the bee dance genre itself—the structural elements of swarming, flight, the sting of the bee. The sexual connotations contained in the dance of seduction before the Arab chieftain simultaneously appear fragmented and dramaticized. The dancer, who is at first merely occupied with the imaginary bee, finally ends up embodying the insect herself. The erotic component of the dance transforms itself under male threat into a deadly act of defense. At first the woman's aggressive gestures are directed at the man in an act of "stinging" him. Then however, she turns the sting against herself in an auto-aggressive gesture of self-sacrifice, culminating in the ecstasy of a "Danse du Feu." She is consumed by a raging fire—a prime element of metamorphosis.

In this dramatic turn of events, Napierkowska's piece, that is, the visual function of her bee dance, resembles Hofmannsthal's "drone motif" in *Pentheus*

---

semantic context: female, exotic, erotic, mysterious, desirable, sexually passionate, fatal—in short as a semiotic system of fashion for the exotic variety of the femme fatale.

194. Cited from *The Sketch*, supplement, November 22, 1911.

and in *Electra*. Electra "can no longer go on living when the deed is done." Her "life and innards must gush from her" together with the sting. Electra's final maenadic dance—the "nameless dance," which is also a consumptive "fire dance"—symbolizes the disintegration of the individual collapsing after being released from cataleptic stupor. It is the dissolution of a subject under the enormous pressures of attempting to maintain the central maxim of extreme individualism, which is "to remain true to oneself": "Electra is no longer Electra, simply because she is trying so hard to be Electra through and through."[195]

By entirely transforming her individuality into movement, the dancer is consumed by the fire of the dance.

Nuronihar, a pantomime written by Carl Einstein for Stasia Napierkowska, ends in a similar glowing ecstasy of self-sacrifice. We do not know how intense or impressive Napierkowska's performance of the bee dance described above was; nor do we know whether it was this piece that so enchanted Einstein that he wrote an enthusiastic open letter to the dancer in 1911, which reads like a manifesto of new *freier Tanz*.[196]

Major structural components of Napierkowska's *Danse de l'Abeille* were also the basis for *Nuronihar*. The "exotic" subject matter of the elaborate poetical scenario—a dramatized rendering of William Beckford's "Arabian story" *Vathek*—features Nuronihar dancing seductively before Vathek in a "dance of disrobing." This is then followed by a "dance of conjuring," which ends with the dancer being consumed by flames. The erotic dance before Vathek begins in a childlike and austere manner, but then unfolds to become "free and lascivious." Nuronihar gathers together "all her erotic abilities into a single culmination" "like an elemental creature." She begins the dance of disrobing, which completely conquers the caliph Vathek:

> She removes a garment and threw it down beside the caliph, who stoops to grasp it. Whereupon the stooped figure is wantonly dragged into the darkness like an animal. . . . Nuronihar performs the dance of disrobing as if alone, without coquetry; she is delighted with her own body and thereby forgets her surroundings.[197]

195. Hofmannsthal 1978, A III, 461. Translation: Elena Polzer.

196. See Brandstetter 1988. In all likelihood, Einstein saw Napierkowska in an exotic dance (although her repertory covered a very large number of other dance styles), also with performances at the Paris Opéra-Comique; at the peak of her dance career (she later switched to film), in the years 1910–1913, she was much sought after for "exotic" roles; Serge Diaghilev, for example, considered casting Napierkowska for a role in 1912 during his Berlin season (as an alternative to Mata Hari).

197. Einstein, *Nuronihar: Eine Pantomime* (Nuronihar: A Pantomime), in Einstein 1980, 173–83. Translation: Elena Polzer.

But then she dances "tantalizing and sophisticated between his knees."

The subsequent dance of conjuring culminates in a furious whirling movement in a pool of light that emanates from a blazing sphere. Nuronihar moves toward the fiery orb as if drawn to it by magic. Whirling in place, she dances in its pool of light: "then it lowered itself over her and covered her. She burns within it crackling in an utterly ecstatic agonizing dance."[198]

As in the "Danse du feu" of the final scene of *La Danse de l'Abeille*, the ecstasy of the flames and the movements of light itself consume Nuronihar in the fire dance. The dancer is a mythical image of the modern psyche, with allegorical traits of the furious motions of the new age. Modernity's pool of light here reminds us of the cold ecstasy of light symbolized by the arc lamp in Einstein's *Bebuquin*.

Gabriele D'Annunzio: Isabella's "Bee Dance"

Isabella's bee dance in Gabriele D'Annunzio's *Forse che sì forse che no* (1910)[199] is closely related to Stasia Napierkowska's *Danse de l'Abeille* and Carl Einstein's interpretation of this dance in his pantomime *Nuronihar*. In the narrative framework of the novel, this dance takes on a central role in its retrospective and anticipatory functions. Isabella, a typical D'Annunzio femme fatale[200] who celebrates love out of an ecstatic passion for life, spends a week with her lover, the pilot Paolo Tarsis, filled with the exaltations of their ardor in a villa at the mouth of the Arno. One evening, she surprises Paolo with a musical box from her childhood. Dressed only in a long Fortuny shawl, she begins to dance an increasingly ecstatic dance to the sounds of the little jukebox. The description of her movements recalls the patterns of free dance and exotic body imagery that D'Annunzio had seen in performances in Rome, Milan, and since 1910 in Paris: dances by Isadora Duncan, Loïe Fuller, Ruth St. Denis, and Napierkowska.

At first, Isabella's movements are slow, lasciviously gathering up the fabric in wide spiral motions. With her movements, she "weaves a fabric" that is just as

198. Einstein, *Nuronihar: Eine Pantomime* (Nuronihar: A Pantomime), in Einstein 1980, 173–83. Translation: Elena Polzer.

199. There is no English translation to date of D'Annunzio's *Maybe Yes, Maybe No*. All quotations in the following section are translated by Elena Polzer on the basis of the German translation *Vielleicht, vielleicht auch nicht* by K. Vollmoeller, 1910. Page numbers in the text are from the German edition.

200. Isabella was not modeled, as in the novels *Il fuoco* and *Il piacere*, on Eleonora Duse (although traits of this great actress are recognizable), but on Donatella Cross (Nathalie de Goloubev, wife of the Russian art historian and collector of oriental and Far Eastern art, Victor de Goloubev); see Germain 1954, 172–236.

translucent and enchanting as the veil that she wears around her body. For the first dance sequence, D'Annunzio chooses the metaphor of text as texture:

> Like a weaver, she chooses with alternating gestures from the multiple colorful strands, the threads for her work, and pulls them out. She seemed thus to take the most beautiful lines from the things near and far and to unite them into this creation of ephemeral beauty. (199)

A turning point is reached when Isabella meets the resting gaze of the man: the diction of the dance changes register—from a dancer's soliloquy to a direct address to her audience. Art as the ornamentation of steps in space is replaced by seduction, the body's swaying movements in place as in the oriental veil dance:

> She covered her face with a corner of the veil, hid her entire body under the volutes of gauze. She resembled an unfulfilled metamorphosis with all limbs transformed into clouds. Only the feet were still human. Then her prior nature seemed to shine through the clouds again and trembled: half of the face bashfully reappeared and immediately disappeared again, a hand, a hip, a shoulder appeared and immediately disappeared again. She imitated the love dance of oriental dancers: shame, fear, resistance, desire, abandonment. (200)

After this sequence, in which erotic elements of the odalisque veil dance are juxtaposed with the body-concealing metamorphoses of Fuller's *Serpentine Dance*, the bee dance-pantomime begins.[201] It carries her, as in Napierkowska's *Danse de l'Abeille*, directly into the embrace of the man watching:

> "A bee!" she suddenly cried with a small scream and made a gesture of fending it off like in front of the gates of the Palace in Mantua. The memory rose vividly in Paolo's mind. In her dance, she reproduced the moment of childlike terror, her tiny hops, taking flight, dodging, her gestures of fending off the irate bee as if it were still threatening to sting her. The veil curved over her head in a wide arc, fluttered, floated, fell in on itself, inflated again, now trailed far behind.
>
> "Ahi, ahi!" she cried out miserably, stood still, pulled her legs tightly together, so that her body appeared in its entire divine length and slenderness, bent her upper body backward, threw her head with the half-loosened

---

201. This bee pantomime is already anticipated in the text at the beginning of the dance scene, namely by the sounds of the music box: the cylinder of the music automat produces sounds that resemble the whirring sounds of insects, like "a wasp's nest" (198).

plaits behind her. Her first cry truly sounded like an expression of pain. . . .
The sound that she then produced was a familiar cry of lust, dull and wild.
She pushed up against him on the pillows.

"That is where she stung me."

His lips kissed the spot. (200f.)

The pose adopted by Isabella, before her performance of the bee dance
modulates into lovemaking with Paolo, is consonant with the visual patterns
of the maenad's dance: the elongated body—an almost mannerist lengthen-
ing of the silhouette—and the thrown-back head with the streaming hair.
With this pose consciously presented as the habitus of exaltation, the dance
ends. The statuesque pose of ecstasy forms a transitional motif from mono-
logical dance to the sexual dialogue of two bodies. In the next level of "erotic
pantomime" (Hofmannsthal), the spectator Paolo is involved as a co-actor.
The bee dance henceforth takes on the function of a semiotic allusion to a
crucial moment at the beginning of Isabella and Paolo's love affair. Memory
is condensed into dance. The past becomes symbolically legible through its
transformation into gesture. The bee dance, located almost exactly in the
middle of the three-part text, takes on central importance for the entire
novel thanks to the cross-references, which connect the dance motif as a
form of visual and movement choreography to key scenes in the first and last
part of the book.

The bee sting in Isabella's dance and in her lovemaking with Paolo already
anticipates the cruel, frightening, and guilt-ridden sphere of incest in the
novel: Isabella's bee dance becomes a mnemonic motif of the incest initiated
later in a bout of bloody kisses of Isabella and her younger brother Aldo.
Isabella's pantomime before Paolo recalls a prior incident at the Palazzo
Ducale in Mantua, which also summarizes the conflict-ridden configuration of the four protagonists: the lovers, Isabella and Paolo; Vana, Isabella's
sister, who is desperately in love with Paolo; and Aldo, who worships his
sister and hates Paolo with the same degree of ardor. This quartet wanders
through the rooms and corridors of the labyrinthine Palazzo of the Gonzaga.
Each of them is preoccupied with contradictory feelings and desires, caught
up in an uncertain and dangerous game, the motto of which they find written on the wooden ceiling of a room along the edge of a painted labyrinth[202]
in a line by Vincenzo Gonzaga: "Forse che sì forse che no" (Perhaps yes,
perhaps no).

202. See the section on the labyrinth and D'Annunzio in Part II of this book.

The atmosphere (the corridors and suites of the palace) and the image (the drawing of the labyrinth on the ceiling) all reflect the contradictory feelings of the four characters. The mad course of desire is already laid out, the uncertainty of the entangled paths that—like the riddle under Vincenzo Gonzaga's labyrinth-emblem—might or might not allow them to escape.

The labyrinth motif is not only expressed by the space and the image, but also by the dance: the long translucent Fortuny shawl, which Isabella drapes around her body as a dance costume, is known by the name of Knossos—after the ornaments and meander print along its edge, patterned after the ground plan of the palace of Knossos.

As they move dreamlike through the Palazzo in Mantua, Isabella begins an imaginary game with her brother—a "perverse frenzy" half in play and half already in madness (which will be her fateful end). She assumes the role of Isabella d'Este, transporting herself back into ages past, taking all the rooms, pictures, shrines, and treasures of the palace into her possession. In a fantastic dialogue with Aldo, who plays along with Isabella's simultaneously charming and erotically provocative game, she "remembers" the events of a story never experienced. The entire theatrical mise en scène is characterized by a mixture of fiction and a form of reinterpreted reality that requires an audience (as is typical for the hysteric). As in her later accounts of erotic adventures, as in her performance of the bee dance, Isabella forces Paolo into the role of the observer—not as the distanced onlooker of a staged piece, but as one tormented by the sting of jealousy.

The fantasy acted out by Isabella takes on a dramatic turn when a bee flies into the palace from the rose garden. The scene is now as if laid out for Isabella's bee dance, in which—as in her speech—reality and imagination overlap. She flees, using those same gestures of fear and defense that Paolo later recognizes again in her dance. The bee stings the heel of her hand and her brother sucks the poison out with a kiss: these events already anticipate the third part of the novel.

The path through the labyrinth of feelings stretches from "Isabella's Paradiso"—Aldo's name for Isabella's apartments in the Palazzo—to the "inferno" of incest in an Etruscan burial chamber and Isabella's insanity.

Paolo Tarsis, the pilot, who is over and over again pushed from the inner circle of passion into the role of observer at the edge of the winding paths, finally detaches himself from the dimension of the labyrinthine pathways on the ground. In the mythical role of Icarus, he throws himself as victorious hero toward the sky, flying into the sun. According to myth, Daedalus invented not only the labyrinth as a dancing ground for Ariadne, but also the flying apparatus—an instrument of both hubris and domination of nature, capable of freeing mankind from the shackles of gravity. Likewise D'Annunzio steers his hero, whose name (Paolo) and that of his airplane (named after the crane) cite Dante's "Inferno" from the *Divina Commedia*,[203] over the maze in a spiraling dance of flight. In the key role assumed by the act of flight, its sense of orientation in a new dimension and as symbol of the new movement technology of the modern era, we here have some indication of a connection between D'Annunzio's novel and basic Futurist concepts—something that will be examined in the second part of this book in further detail.

Isabella's bee dance configures the course of events by translating it from the inner realm of feeling and thought into visible movements of the body. Its symbolic representation by predetermined patterns of dance—those of the bee dance—reassemble the fragments of shattered identities into a form that is ostensibly transpersonal:

- As a pathos formula of ecstasy in Isabella's oriental, maenadic, exalted image of the body
- As the spatial figuration of the "maze" in the dialogue of bodies, ending in a collapse in the "center," symbolized by the labyrinth

The Dance of Salome

The biblical-mythical prototype of seductive dance is the dance of Salome. In the nineteenth century, the femme fatale figure of Salome, which was often juxtaposed with traits of Herodias, fascinated Symbolist artists. There is much that can be said on the subject of this motif, but in the following chapter I will restrict myself to those structural elements of the Salome myth that are relevant to my discussion of exotic body-images in dance.

Salome was the preferred subject of fin de siècle aesthetics, not only in literature, as in the case of Heine, Mallarmé, Flaubert, Huysmans, Oscar Wilde, and Arthur Symons, but also in the fine arts, as with Gustave Moreau, Max Klinger, Aubrey Beardsley, and Franz von Stuck (figure 33) and in numerous music dramas, for example, in Jules Massenet's opera *Hérodiade* (1881), in Richard Strauss's *Salome* (1905), and in Florent Schmitt's *La Tragédie de Salomé* (1907).

In the work of Heinrich Heine, the typical features of the fin de siècle Salome—the beautiful, passionate, and cruel femme fatale—were combined for the first time with the psychologically inspired idea that Salome's motivation

---

203. The matrix of meanings contained in the name "Paolo" is simultaneously a reference by D'Annunzio to another work of his: the drama *Francesca da Rimini* (1901), written for Eleonora Duse (and based on Dante).

Figure 33 Franz von Stuck, *Salomé* (1906).
SOURCE: Städtische Galerie im Lenbachhaus, Munich, Germany.

for wishing John the Baptist dead was that she desired him sexually. In other words, her incentive for cruelly demanding the prophet's head was disappointed sexual desire. By contrast, the interpretation mainly prevalent in the Middle Ages[204] was "superbia," the offended pride of Herodias. Heine replaced this with a *jungdeutsch*[205] "heathen" line of argumentation, which emphasized the sensual. In this interpretation mother and daughter—the innocently

204. On the iconography of Salome depictions, especially in the fine arts from the Middle Ages, Renaissance, and baroque, see Merkel 1990.

205. *Translator's note*: "Jungdeutsche" or "Junges Deutschland" (Young Germany) is the name given to a group of German writers, of whom Heine was the most famous, that in the third decade of the nineteenth century initiated a revolt against the prevailing spirit of

unknowing dancing Salome and the immoral Herodias, who seeks revenge from the prophet because he warned her to change her ways—are thus no longer pitted against each other. Instead both characters merge to become one person as in the poem *Atta Troll*, chapter 19:

> Yes, she really was a princess,
> Was the queen of all Judea,
>   And the lovely wife of Herod,
> Who the baptist's head did covet.
> For this blood-guilt must she also
>   Be accursed; she must, as Night-Spook,
>   'Til the very Day of Judgement,
> Ride along with this Wild Hunt.
>   In her hands she bears forever
> That sad platter, with the head of
> John the Baptist, which she kisses;
>   Yes, she'll kiss the head with fervor.
> For, at one time, she loved John—
>   It's not found within the Bible,
> Yet the people keep the saga
> Of Herodias' bloody loving—
>   Otherwise, 'twere no explaining
> The attraction of that lady—
> Would a woman crave the head of
> Someone, if she does not love him?[206]

Heine's interpretation of Salome's dance in *Pomare*[207] also combines, as does his interpretation of the Herodias kiss, the traits of the "belle dame sans merci" with the depiction of her desire in an erotic dance. Whenever a woman is "fetching" in dance, seductively beautiful and cruel, then the basic scenario of Salome's dance repeats itself in this old, ever new game of woman against man:

romanticism in the national literature, which had resulted in a total separation of literature from the actualities of life. Against the dominant spirit of absolutism in politics and obscurantism in religion the writers of this school maintained the principles of democracy, socialism, and rationalism. Among many things they advocated the separation of church and state, the emancipation of the Jews, and the raising of the political and social position of women. See http://en.wikisource.org/wiki/The_New_International_Encyclopædia/Young_Germany.

206. Available online in English at http://davidsbuendler.freehostia.com.

207. Pomaré was the stage name of Paris Cancan dancer Elise Sergent (1825–1846); on Heine and dance see B. v. Wiese, "Das tanzende Universum" (The dancing universe), in Wiese 1976, 67–133.

She dances. It is the same dance
That Herodias' daughter danced once
To Herod. And while she dances,
Her eyes cast their deadly glances.
She'll dance me frantic—she cast a spell—
  What do you desire, I pray you tell?
You smile? Quick runner! Do not delay!
  I want the Baptist's head right away.[208]

Here the dance of Salome appears as a pathos formula that is interpreted ironically—as the pathos of passion and cruelty—and in its generalization admits to being a cliché of female behavior.

In most cases, however, the dance itself was only negligibly touched on by literary figurations of the Salome subject. Salome's dance was merely treated as an atmospheric side element. Instead, the more decisive aspect was its meaning for the dramatic configuration of the characters or for the general role of the dance in the structure of the text, as in Flaubert's *Hérodias* or Joris-Karl Huysmans's Salome in *A Rebours*. Frequently, Salome's veil dance marks an empty space in the text, as in Mallarmé's poem *Hérodiade* or in Wilde's drama, where the substance of the dance is left to the respective choreographer or director of the piece in the form of pragmatic stage directions—"Salome dances the dance of the seven veils."

Not the dance itself, but its effect—the dramaturgical function of the juxtaposition of seduction and bloodlust, the constellation of Herodes-Herodias-Salome, the atmosphere of decadence—is what literary depictions focus on. Even in Flaubert's *Hérodias* text from the *Trois Contes*, in which Salome's dance at the center of the celebrations simultaneously marks the literary climax of a narrative *lecture corporelle* of oriental dance, Salome's dance is merely an ornamental element in the much larger topography of political power. In this context, in the convoluted scheme for dominance, Salome appears as a simple tool in the calculations of a power-hungry Herodias. As Salome begins her dance at the climax of the feast in the form of a performance minutely planned by Herodias in terms of its composition and its erotic effect on the attending men, she appears as a lovely, younger duplicate of her mother. In its careful composition, the dance follows a theatrical-corporeal rhetoric of the erotic, which Flaubert assembles out of various images of dance: on the one hand, medieval depictions of Salome's dance on pillars and tympanum reliefs in Romanesque cathedrals and, on the other, experiences of his own with oriental dance in Egypt, especially with the *beledi*, the *danse du ventre* of the famous dancer Kutchuk-Hanem.

208. Available online in English at http://www.heinrich-heine.net/haupt.htm; here section 2.

In the story *Hérodias*, Salome, dressed as the spitting image of the oriental *ghaziya* dancer, begins a slow swinging bell dance, which gradually transforms into increasingly ecstatic forms of movement:

> Her bosom heaved with sighs, and her whole being expressed profound languor, although it was not clear whether she sighed for an absent swain or was expiring of love in his embrace. With half-closed eyes and quivering form, she caused mysterious undulations to flow downward over her whole body, like rippling waves, while her face remained impassive and her twinkling feet still moved in their intricate steps. . . . And now the graceful dancer appeared transported with the very delirium of love and passion. She danced like the priestesses of India, like the Nubians of the cataracts, or like the Bacchantes of Lydia. She whirled about like a flower blown by the tempest. The jewels in her ears sparkled, her swift movements made the colors of her draperies appear to run into one another. Her arms, her feet, her clothing even, seemed to emit streams of magnetism that set the spectators' blood on fire.[209]

Salome's dance becomes a frantic whirl, the audience "gazed upon her with dilated nostrils," the Tetrarch is beside himself and offers her "half of my kingdom." Salome's final pose forms the climax of the dramatic erotic performance:

> She threw herself upon the palms of her hands, while her feet rose straight up into the air. In this bizarre pose she moved about upon the floor like a gigantic beetle; then stood motionless.
>
> The nape of her neck formed a right angle with her vertebrae. The full silken skirts of pale hues that enveloped her limbs when she stood erect, now fell to her shoulders and surrounded her face like a rainbow. Her lips were tinted a deep crimson, her arched eyebrows were black as jet, her glowing eyes had an almost terrible radiance; and the tiny drops of perspiration on her forehead looked like dew upon white marble.[210]

In this final pose, Flaubert contaminates the snakelike dance movements of Egyptian dance with representations of Salome in medieval reliefs (as in the tympanum of the Cathedral in Rouen) that portray her as pausing in an acrobatic backward arch in a pathos formula of erotic exaltation. Flaubert's travel notes on performances by the dancer Aziza in the late 1840s

209. Flaubert n.d.

210. Ibid.

demonstrate that he combined these images very early on in his observations of oriental dance:

> Her Dance is savage and makes one think involuntarily of the negroes of central Africa. . . . She held out her two long arms, black and glistening, shaking them from shoulder to wrist with an imperceptible quivering, moving them apart with soft and quick motions like those of the wings of a hovering eagle. Sometimes she bent over completely backwards, supporting herself on her hands in the position of the dancing Salome over the left portal of the Rouen cathedral.[211]

The character of Salome and her relationship to the character of the prophet, which oscillates between desire and disgust, appear in a wide range of forms and genres in literature. Salome is either depicted as a type of cruel, cold femme fatale, in a characteristic mixture of being "saturated with animal odors . . . exuding incense and myrrh" (Huysmans), as in the poem cycle *Salome* by Eugenio de Castro[212]; or as the *femme fragile*, chaste, untouchable, trapped in the narcissistic space of her "chasteté" and "impassibilité," as in the case of Jules Laforgue. In *Hérodias*, Mallarmé describes her as "mon corps solitaire le glace/D'horreur," "le frisson blanc de ma nudité," and "ma pudeur grelottante d'étoile"[213]; as "froide enfant," so completely self-contained that she can only bear the "sight" of the gazeless man, Jean. A similar case is Théodore de Banville's sonnet on the dancer "Salomé," *La Danseuse* (1870), dedicated to Henry Regnault.[214]

Arthur Symons's Salome poems are prime evidence of the way in which the Salome subject—in the perspective of a woman coveting a man and her attempt to annihilate his male gaze—finally reached the poetic dimension of "reading"

211. Cited in Buonaventura 1994, 72; on Flaubert and his experiences in the Orient, especially concerning dance, see Mustacchi 1981.

212. See Castro 1934; in Castro's poem Salome strolls in lavish-exotic surroundings between lions; and as with her lions, she also attempts to "domesticate" John the Baptist in the cage:

> Poucos se afoitam a passar diante dêle,
> E se alguem passa, é a fugir, em doido anseio;
> Apenas salomé, a princesinha imbele,
> Se aproxima da jaula, sem receio . . .
> . . .
> E Joao, que para os pitros é feroz,
> É para ela um dócil cordeirinho; . . .
> Salomé ama Joao. (Castro 1934, 23)

213. Mallarmé 1945, 41ff.

214. See Banville 1926, 259f.

and "directing the gaze" of the reader in literature. His verses repeatedly feature Salome and the dance of Salome, beginning with his early poems in the 1890s, up to the second decade of the twentieth century (as the Salome fashion already began to wane in dance).[215]

Symons's handling of the subject, even more so than Huysmans's or Wilde's depictions of Salome iconography, is an exploration of *alternative* texts and images of Salome. He weaves a complex intertextual web, in which Salome becomes a mere sign, a character embodying the pure *l'art pour l'art* principle.

Under the influence of Wilde's *Salome* and particularly the Beardsley illustrations (Symons dedicated a few of his poems directly to Beardsley and his art), Symons was inspired to attempt several approaches to the Salome material from various angles. In the cycle *Images of Good and Evil,* the body and the dance "engage" in a dialogue of seven deadly sins (*The Dance of the Seven Sins*). In *The Dance of the Daughters of Herodias,*[216] the myth of seduction in the enchantment of the dance appears, as in the case of Heinrich Heine, evoked by femininity, the multiple manifestations of Salome. In his cycle of poems *Studies in Strange Sins* (after Beardsley's designs), Symons adapts the fin de siècle subject of exquisite immorality (as featured in the writings of Wilde and Huysmans). The poems "Salome's Lament," "John and Salome," "Enter Herodias," and "The Eyes of Herode"[217] form a lyrical commentary to the *Salome* of Wilde and Beardsley.

The poems appear as metatexts of other Salome texts—repeated attestations of the Salome myth in the moving words, finally culminating in 1915 in the condensed poem "Salome,"[218] which contains all the traits of the turn-of-the-century Salome myth—the metamorphoses of the dancing figure, whose morbid features seem never to pale:

> When Salome lifting up
> In her painted hands the cup,
> Symbol of her virginity,
> Her perverse, pure eyes malign
> See, instead of signs of wine,
> Frantic, to her vision, blood.
> One foot twisted in advance
> In the rhythm of the dance
> Beats upon the perfumed floor.

215. See the poems in volumes 2 and 3 of the *Collected Works*: Symons 1924.

216. Symons 1924, 2: 36–40 or also *Images of Good and Evil*, Symons 1899, 42–48.

217. Symons 1924, 2: 276–80.

218. Symons 1924, 3: 239 f.

The dance of Salome found its ideal theatrical frame at the turn of the century in the fields of free dance and exotic dance. In 1895, long before Strauss's successful opera, Loïe Fuller created her *Salomé* to the music of Gabriel Pierné as a full-length dance drama. Armand Silvestre and Charles Henry Meltzer wrote the libretto. The premiere took place at the Théâtre de l'Athenée in Paris. However, it met with only moderate success, not least of all because of Fuller's concept of the body imagery of Salome. She was probably inspired by the Salomé idea of Massenet's opera *Hérodiade* (1881) to endow the exotic-decadent femme fatale with extra-innocently sweet features. This resulted in an ambivalent performance.

Nevertheless, Fuller returned to the same subject in 1907, which was the same year that Strauss's opera *Salome* (1905) premiered in Paris. With a libretto by Robert D'Humières and vividly colorful music by Florent Schmitt, *La Tragédie de Salomé* (1907) was much more haunting and convincing—both choreographically, as well as scenographically—than her first Salome dance drama. This time, Fuller attempted to combine her own style of lighting technique, which had gained in virtuosity over the years, with the Salome material by projecting colored lights onto wide, moving fabric surfaces. This Salome was not merely a dramatization of Salome's dance—as an erotic presentation of the body—but a drama of desire and guilt clothed in phantasmagorical images. The psychological drama was reflected in elements of the landscape—in cloud formations, the play of light on the Moab mountains, the elements of light and water—as in the moment after Salome's dance on the palace terrace high above the Dead Sea:

> She wins her guerdon. She casts the prophet's head into the sea. And lo! It is now a sea of blood and Salome seeing, quakes. She turns to flee, but everywhere on the great terrace is the head, grisly, piteous, menacing. She is in frenzy, and in frenzy the wild nature about her answers. Riven trees splinter and crash. The mountains dart fire, the very earth shakes. Frenzy and fear overwhelm each other.[219]

The lighting effects seem to have been especially impressive in this scene, including a "dance on a panel of glass lighted from below," as Harry Graf Kessler noted in his diary.[220]

---

219. *Boston Evening Transcript*, November 29, 1913, Part 2.

220. Kessler visited a performance of *La Tragédie de Salomé* on November 26, 1907. Although he was impressed by Fuller's lighting concept, he was disappointed by her embodiment of Salome, because Fuller did not conform to the image of the slim, lithe dancer, see Kessler's unpublished diaries in the Archive for Literature in Marbach/Neckar; I wish to thank Ulrich Ott for granting me access to them.

Fuller's *Tragédie de Salomé* combines the most important Salome motifs in fin de siècle literature and painting. The character of Salomé unites traits of the lascivious indolence of Wilde's princess, the aloofness of the "froide enfant" in Mallarmé's *Hérodiade*, and the sultry sensuality of Joris-Karl Huysmans's literary interpretation of Salome from Gustave Moreau's painting *L'Apparition* (figure 15). D'Humières and Florent Schmitt's technique of suggesting rather than picturing the *atmosphere* of inherited sin and decadence is likewise evident in Fuller's choreography.

In the years before World War I, danced performances of the cruel and beautiful Salome, ironically named "Salomania," proliferated in various sorts of depictions of her, her dance of seven veils and—as the climax of the plot often on the borderline of kitsch—her dancing with a platter carrying the severed head of John the Baptist. Ida Rubinstein, Maud Allen, Adorée Villany, Nathalia Trouhanova, Tamara Karsavina, Valeska Gert, and Martha Graham all danced the Salome in various choreographies. Hofmannsthal planned a Salome libretto for Ruth St. Denis—a proposal that the dancer turned down because of her aversion to anything that was too fashionable. In 1908, Rubinstein caused a sensation with her interpretation of Salome in a performance of Wilde's drama in St. Petersburg. She celebrated the dance of the seven veils as a scene of disrobing described by contemporaries as highly risqué,[221] in a choreography (music by Alexander Glazunov) created for her by Michel Fokine. Rubinstein, who was not a trained dancer, fanatically rehearsed every detail of her physical presentation as femme fatale with the greatest care. The critics were impressed—some by her spectacular performance, some merely by her mysterious and erotic presence.[222]

If we take a closer look at two very different interpretations of Salome in dance—one by Valeska Gert (1923) and one by Martha Graham—we will see more clearly what transformations the representation of Salome went through in the wake of art nouveau's version of the exotic femme fatale. Graham's interpretation of Salome in *Hérodiade* (1944) coincides with the concept underlying other pieces the 1940s, such as *Cave of the Heart* (1946) and *Night Journey* (1947): the exploration of mythology in dance by translating archetypal images from the mnemonic space of the psyche into figures of movement. The original title of her *Hérodiade* (music by Paul Hindemith)—*Mirror before Me*—also reflects the introspective-psychological side of her choreography, in which she interpreted the Salome subject as a problem of narcissistic incarceration.

---

221. See Cossart 1987, 11–14.

222. Ibid., 10.

Twenty years earlier, on April 20, 1923, Valeska Gert premiered a completely different *Salome* (based on Wilde) in Berlin. In it, she explored a new, grotesquely shrill method of representing the physical femme fatale image. In a radically alienated, ruthlessly garish performance, the beautiful, exotic-attractive art nouveau Salome was presented as an outdated cliché of femininity:

> I wanted to play Salome. I slashed Oscar Wilde's text down to an extract. . . . I wanted bloody life, a thousand colors and spontaneity. . . . There was no set, a black curtain for a backdrop, two black upholsteries as furniture. We squeezed into tight shirts, I had a bright red one, Herodes's was bright blue, Herodias's was a bilious green, the young Syrian was in an orange-colored pajama and the long scrawny Jochanaan was sewn into a gray sack. . . . I danced without music, to the girls rhythmically howling like bitches in heat, while standing behind the curtain.[223]

Gert's *Salome* marked the avant-garde transformation of a pet subject of the Decadent movement. It was almost a parody: "Compared to her Salome, Oscar Wilde's pales to a docile Helena," critics wrote:[224]

> Gert's Salome is one of a kind and will never be repeated. . . . Her version is simultaneously a supremely animalistic and supremely divine affair. The animal, as instinct, in her cannot be broken. Her thighs of such fantastic juicy plumpness emit sparks. Blood screams through the rouge on her lips and transforms them into flews.[225]

But let us return from such deconstructed exotic body imagery to what is perhaps the most famous turn-of-the-century interpretation of Salome in dance: the performance of Maud Allan (1873–1956).[226]

The world premiere of Allan's *The Vision of Salomé* (figure 34), to music by Marcel Rémy, took place on December 2, 1906, at the Carl-Theater in Vienna. In London in 1908, the piece later had a particularly successful long run at the Palace Theater. Canadian-born Maud Allan moved to Berlin

---

223. Gert 1978, 48f. Translation: Elena Polzer.

224. Richard Meyer, cited in Peter 1987, 45. Translation: Elena Polzer.

225. Ibid.

226. On Maud Allan see Cherniavsky 1983a, 1983b, 1984a, 1984b; the visual documents and magazines, which the following descriptions are based on, can be found in the archives of the Bibliothèque de l'Arsenal Paris, Collection Rondel.

Figure 34 Maud Allan, *The Vision of Salomé* (1906).
SOURCE: Author's archive.

in 1903 in order to study music, but then began a career as a dancer in the new free style—based on training in the Delsarte system. In her Salome interpretation, she surpassed by far all other dancers, who likewise turned their attentions to this fashionable subject matter. It was not only for this reason that the clever Ruth St. Denis, who clearly recognized the situation, thus resolutely declined Harry Graf Kessler's suggestion[227] to bring together

227. When Kessler wrote his letter to Hofmannsthal on November 24, 1906, giving more details about Ruth St. Denis and his intention of developing a dance-pantomime version of Salome, for which Hofmannsthal should write the libretto, he had himself already written up the exposé of the dance drama: the starting point was a banquet at which Herodes and Herodias sat with their guests around a circular table in a lofty hall of columns. Salome's

dancer and poet, namely Hofmannsthal, for the creation of a dance piece about Salome. She had, writes Kessler, "numerous doubts," especially concerning Oscar Wilde's *Salome*, for it was "anyhow a purely literary piece, in which dance can always only be extra." The "mistake made by Wilde's piece" lay in the fact "that Salome's dance is without dramatic effect; it plays no role in the conflict, or only coincidentally. It should, however, on the contrary be seen as the very climax of the conflict and plot."[228]

The particular success of Maud Allan's *Salomé* lay—aside from the intensity of her dance—in her discovery of an interpretative model for Salome, which offered a completely independent solution both in terms of its dramaturgical concept and in its composition of patterns of femininity. It clearly distanced itself from Oscar Wilde's drama, which had served as the prototype for all turn-of-the-century Salome interpretations so far, and was very convincing in its specific conception as a dance monodrama.

Maud Allan's *Salomé* appears on stage when the proper "drama"—as handed down in the Bible and also described in Wilde's one-act play—is already over. In her version, Salome is (still) juvenile and innocent, in contrast to Wilde's version. Salome has obediently "completed" the dance that her stepfather, whom she objects to, demanded from her. At her mother's behest, she has requested the head of John the Baptist as her prize and the Tetrarch has grudgingly fulfilled his oath. As the head is brought out on a platter and handed to the princess, she flees, disgusted and horrified, out into the open, onto the garden terrace of the palace.

This is the when Maud Allan's dance *The Vision of Salomé* begins: as the embodiment of an inner drama, which now, after the external events have passed, rises up from memory and is relived in Salome's fantasy. In Allan's

dance is conceived in various phases that gradually grow in intensity, as a demonstration "at the center of the circle." "She dances various dances, one after another, driving Herodes more and more wild, until he finally pledges his oath in a complete frenzy. *During* the dance the lights continue to dim, the banquet grows darker, until only the faces of the guests shine in the darkness . . . out of this sinister darkness comes the oath of Herodes. Then the curtain closes for a moment and opens again to reveal an atmosphere of *yonder morn* (dawn) and Salome strides in with the head of John the Baptist." (Correspondence Hofmannsthal and Kessler 1968, 135f.—translation: Elena Polzer.)

The interesting aspect of this plan, which clearly comes from Kessler (for St. Denis refused to be convinced of the Salome subject matter) is the remarkable resemblance of its dramaturgical concept to the *Josephslegende* (1912–14) later written by Kessler for Diaghilev's Ballets Russes: the banquet of the reigning couple, the innocent dancer in the inner circle in front of the couple and their guests; the awakening of desire (Herodes/wife of Potiphar); the suspension of the "price" as extortion and finally the "victim" with the apotheosis as finale.

228. Hofmannsthal and Kessler 1968, 135ff. Translation: Elena Polzer.

dance, the central motif of the Salome interpretation is not the "dance in the dance" or the dance in the drama, not the dance of seven veils so frenetically applauded in Wilde or in Strauss's opera, but a shift in perspective by a girl fleeing into an inner realm of imagination at the sight of the decapitated John.

In the form of a psychodrama, by reliving the traumatic initiation experience from girl to woman, the princess again lives through the moment of coming face to face with the horrifying severed head of the Baptist:

> And a pale, sublime face with its mass of long black hair arises before her—the head of John the Baptist! There is a sudden crash. She is horror stricken! Suddenly a wild desire takes possession of her. Why, ah! why, should her mother have longed for this man's end?[229]

At first, Salome sees the head of John the Baptist only as a trophy of her childish obedience to her mother, but she now desires this man to gaze on her once more. She wishes to know her mother's secrets. She rebels against motherly governance, against the control enforced by the rivalry that her mother feels at the sight of her beautiful daughter—a sense of rivalry that ultimately finds its expression in her instructions to her daughter, instructions to demand the head of the prophet as a prize for erotic dance. This mother-daughter conflict of dependency and independence becomes part of the Salome-Herodias constellation in a dramatic scene of inner development.[230] "What passes in those few moments through this excited, half-terror-stricken, half-stubborn brain makes of little Salomé a woman!"[231]

In short moments of insight, in moments of frenzied dancing before the dead, unseeing head, a specific desire awakens in Salome: "Now, instead of wanting to conquer, she wants to be conquered. . . . Salomé, seeking an understanding, and knowing not how to obtain it, presses her warm, vibrating lips to the cold lifeless ones of the Baptist!"

---

229. In her memoirs, Maud Allan herself describes the scenario of *The Vision of Salomé* in these words; Allan 1908, 126.

230. In this regard, it is interesting to note that Maud Allan, who published her memoirs in 1908, when her *Salomé* was at the height of success in London, dedicated the book to her mother with the words: "Darling Mother:—At the last moment I am told that my book requires a Dedication. Of course it does. This is it, Your devoted, Maud. London, October 1908." Allan was not the only one very close to her mother, who was always nearby as her confidante, travel companion, organizer. It was the same with Isadora Duncan, Loïe Fuller, and other protagonists of *freier Tanz*. It would be worth examining these constellations and their connection to the body imagery of dance, patterns of femininity, and theories of "the feminine" in dance in a separate, dance-sociological study.

231. Allan 1908, 127.

Fear, a feeling of loneliness, and the desire for salvation take possession of her until she finally collapses under the impression that she will not be able to shake off the sin of John's death: "It is the atonement of her mother's awful sin!"

Various newspaper reviews and a series of now famous photos of Allan's *The Vision of Salomé* give an impression of her gestural art, of the intensity of expression contained in her movement vocabulary and the way in which her interpretation of the role was based in posture and dress on models of oriental dance. Two aspects are particularly noteworthy, namely the composition of the dance and the way in which the exotic body-image was presented.

What was typical for Allan's depiction of Salome was the combination of dramatic pantomime and dance elements, which were themselves a mixture of movement forms from *freier Tanz* and elements borrowed from the oriental *beledi*.[232] The dramatic suggestiveness of Allan's vision of Salome expressed itself in the tension that arose between a movement vocabulary, which mainly emphasized motions of the arms and upper body, and transitioned from one level of movement to another, in particular the incorporation of the floor. A particularly impressive scene in which Salome, stretched out sideways on the floor in a half-sitting, half-lying position, fixes her gaze on the severed head of the Baptist combined, for example, an animalistic and a visionary aesthetic.

The subject of the gaze, in combination with the performance of the *Vision*, directs our attention to the realm of the imaginary: to that dimension of the phantasmal "apparition" of the prophet's head before the eyes of Salome, which Gustave Moreau also depicted, almost as the "face" of the dancer, in his painting *L'Apparition* (1876) (figure 35).

The consequences that such dramatizations of the vision of Salome had on the general interpretation of the subject are clear—and not least of all through the suggestive effect of Allan's dance solo. By staging "Salome's vision" as a drama of imagination, Allen incorporates the audience perspective into the Salome scenario and simultaneously dramatized. By gazing on a dancing female body, on a woman dancing her desire, while simultaneously evading the desires of the audience, Herodes's perspective and that of the audience merge along a line of sight that is focused on the "apparition." Thus the *Vision of Salome*, as depicted by Allan in her solo, manages to project a reflection of events that have already become memory in a monodramatic visualization of the occurrence. The dancer's body becomes the medium of the vision, as in Moreau's picture *L'Apparition*. The body of the dancer is "tattooed" with the lineaments of the phantasmagoria, which permeates the space.

232. On the *beledi*, the traditional Arabic-Egyptian dance, known as belly dance in the West, on its typical movement patterns and the historical background, see the chapter on the bee dance, as well as Buonaventura 1994.

Figure 35 Gustave Moreau, *L'Apparition* (1876).
SOURCE: Musée Gustave Moreau, Paris, France.

It is impossible to prove whether Moreau's Salome paintings, which inspired
Wilde's Salome, also served as visual models for Allan's danced vision. However,
the perspective of the audience on her dance monodrama can easily be compared to that corporeal reading of Salome which Des Esseintes conducts in
Joris-Karl Huysmans's novel *A Rebours*. Standing in front of Moreau's painting
L'Apparition, he translates the motif of the phantasmal gaze between Salome
and the "apparition" into rhetorical figures.[233]

233. On J.-K. Huysmans's concept of Salome, see Taeger 1987, 38–44. Taeger's interpretation
of Huysmans's depiction of Salome in *A Rebours* remains on a sexual-psychological level,
as already formulated in the text itself—as a reading of the "phallic" Salome in Moreau's oil
painting—as the perceptual pattern of the contemplating Des Esseintes. In my opinion, the

The severed head of the saint stared lividly on the charger resting on the slabs; the mouth was discolored and open, the neck crimson, and tears fell from the eyes. The face was encircled by an aureole worked in mosaic, which shot rays of light under the porticos and illuminated the horrible ascension of the head, brightening the glassy orbs of the contracted eyes which were fixed with a ghastly stare upon the dancer.

With a gesture of terror, Salomé thrusts from her the horrible vision which transfixes her, motionless, to the ground. . . .

Like the old king, Des Esseintes remained dumbfounded, overwhelmed and seized with giddiness, in the presence of this dancer.[234]

In its presentation of exotic-erotic body imagery, Allan's piece corresponds with patterns found in fin de siècle paintings and travel accounts: an unspecific femme fatale pattern of femininity gleaned from the world of oriental fantasy fairy tales, distinguishable as "Byzantine," "Egyptian," or "Arabian" only with regard to costume depending on the materiality of the depicted subject. Des Esseintes's description of Moreau's "Salome" perpetuates the basic configuration of dressed and nude, of veil and bejeweled corselet, of sparkling necklaces and naked skin:

She is almost nude. In the ardor of the dance, her veils had become loosened. She is garbed only in gold-wrought stuffs and limpid stones; a neck-piece clasps her as a corselet does the body and, like a superb buckle, a marvelous jewel sparkles on the hollow between her breasts. A girdle encircles her hips, concealing the upper part of her thighs, against which beats a gigantic pendant streaming with carbuncles and emeralds.

All the facets of the jewels kindle under the ardent shafts of light escaping from the head of the Baptist. The stones grow warm, outlining the woman's body with incandescent rays, striking her neck, feet and arms with tongues of fire,—vermilions like coals, violets like jets of gas, blues like flames of alcohol, and whites like star light.[235]

The erotic pathos formulas of the naked body, which provoked sensations and scandals at the beginning of the twentieth century, upon their presentation

question of the gaze, brought up in the fragmentation via the reading of the image, opens up an additional approach to interpretation especially regarding a multiple perspectivization of the Salome topic.

234. Huysmans 2006, 36.

235. Ibid.

on stage, in plays, in opera, or in dance, had already been housed in the visual storehouses of painting and literature since the nineteenth century, especially depictions of the exotic femme fatale.

The influence of Salome's dance, hence, resided mainly—as I return in my closing remarks to the aspect of reading exotic body imagery—on its function as a symbol for a way of presenting the naked female body in theater: almost all reviews of Salome performances were dominated by discussions of how the body was revealed and concealed, how the veil dance was composed, that is, the question of how liberal the theatrical representation of erotic physicality should be.

One example is an article by Marie-Luise Becker in the journal *Bühne und Welt* from 1907, in which she compiled an overview of "Salome imper- sonators on the modern stage."[236] Becker concentrates on those Salome per- formers who have made a career in Wilde's drama and in Strauss's opera on various German-speaking stages. After noting that Salome was "wasted on the public prosecutor during the first years of the new century" and "arrived at the theaters of the court" only thanks to Strauss's setting it to music, she analyzes the work of actresses and singers such as Gertrud Eysoldt, the "clas- sical representation of the role," Hedwig Reicher, Tilla Durieux, Lotti Sarow, Hedwig Lange, Marie Wittich, Anna Sutter, Emmy Destin, Lili Marberg, and Thyra Larsen. Becker compares each case in terms of its various rep- resentations of the exotic body-image, the "oriental fabrics," "Indian silks," and "Byzantine costume," but her main interest pertains to the performance of "a naked or to all appearances naked Salome" in the dance of the seven veils, for an audience "taking a short jaunt toward the indecent in a 'Salome' performance."[237]

Becker's comments, on whether the depictions of Salome in paintings served as models for their theatrical embodiment or only had an effect on the images in the minds of the educated audience, simultaneously illustrate specific forma- tions of exotic body imagery:

> He who has seen Lenbach's Salome will find a strong similarity to the concept of this painting in Ms. Reicher's performance and interpretation, while Mrs. Eysoldt is closest also in her acting to the Salome of Louis [*sic*] Korinth.[238]

---

236. M.-L. Becker, *Bühne und Welt* 1.9 (October 1906–March 1907): 439–47. Translation: Elena Polzer.

237. Ibid., 440.

238. Ibid.

This brings up the motif of the veil again, in connection with the erotic presentation of the female body in the dance of the seven veils in terms of the pathos formula of passionately moving folds of fabric. Becker sums up all arguments concerning the "lively debated question of costume from a critic's perspective." She concludes that this veil dance "of the oriental female, covering the body" is predominantly "Greek," which is why Salome interpreters should be advised as to "a slight leaning toward the Greek-Roman costume—which was surely also worn at the court of Herodes"[239]; for "The ladies of Athens and Rome knew how to conceal and reveal themselves with great finery, without relinquishing the charms of dress. They had a distinct form of being naked while actually clothed."[240]

This particular manner of appearing naked when dressed—of revealing the body in moving folds of fabric—links "Greek" body imagery to exotic images of the body in a pathos formula, whose seductive potential is directed at the audience when embodied in dance. The theater audience's perception of Salome's dance corresponds with Herodes's perspective of this seductive-narcissistic act of self-presentation, of the erotic play of unveiling and concealing. And Becker thus also returns in her book to the first interpretation of Salome in dance: Fuller's performance, the "vision" of Salome rising up from the imagination *not* by presenting nakedness, but rather by playing with the gaze and fantasy of the audience:

> Loïe Fuller, who danced Salome as a great pantomime, has in this sense chosen an ancient Greek jacket dance, which projects to the audience only the illusion that a naked woman is dancing in this whirling jacket. She only opened the jacket for a few seconds in front of Herodes and played with the fantasy of the audience in the most exciting way. She danced the Salome upon a lit glass floor. This is the Salome dance that appears to me, of all those that I have seen, to be the most sophisticated and most gripping.[241]

Here again, we can clearly see how models of the "Greek" and the "exotic" operate as constructs of cultural patterns. The reasons for or goal of these mental schemata is neither a historiographic knowledge of antiquity nor an ethnological understanding of those cultures subsumed under the umbrella term of the exotic.

---

239. M.-L. Becker, *Bühne und Welt* 1.9 (October 1906—March 1907): 445f.

240. Ibid., 446.

241. Ibid.

In the case of early twentieth-century free dance, these "imagines"[242] fulfill a complex function that is both general typecasting as well as cultural-sociological. They provide frameworks through which the Other in nature—as nature of the body—can be transferred into Western "modernity's" patterns of cultural self-interpretation via the culturally defined Other, namely the exotic and antiquity as *imagines* of the natural. The costume—the draped, enveloping fabric as pathos formula of body-nature revealing itself in movement—appears thus as a marker for the shifting boundary between nature and culture. The body of the dancer, dressed or concealed, presented as Greek or exotic, becomes a medium of staging exactly this difference of nature and culture.

242. "Imagines" refers here in a broader sense to mental constructs operating in the reception of intra- and intercultural patterns of interpretation. The field of "imagology" in the comparative literature studies of the so-called Aachen School has developed a definition of the term that may be too narrow. In my opinion, the basic idea, however, offers a sensible approach for comparative studies reaching beyond literature studies into further areas of art and culture on questions concerning the history of mentality.

Chapter 3

Delirium of Movement and Trance Dance

The pathos formulas expressed in specific transformations of body imagery in free dance having been explored in the previous chapters, the following section will focus on an analysis of movement patterns that physically represent concepts of what is described as "nature" in terms of a precultural space in which all norms are suspended: trance, ecstasy, hypnosis, and bacchanal. I will therefore explore those pathos formulas of the ecstatic that essentially express the problem of control and loss of control, of dissociation and dissolution of the ego.

By addressing the subject of trance in various forms of whirling dances and rituals such as the bacchanal, expressionist dancers articulated the idea that nature—as a lost state of "primitiveness" and wholeness of the subject—can be reattained by dissolving the ego into a transpersonal unit (*Einheit*) in corporeal movement.

Their goal was use trance dance movement to recover and expose what had been buried in the process of civilization: the individual or collective unconscious as a storehouse of archaic forms of human creativity. Ecstatic dance, or rather the representation of ecstasy by free dance, thus became "the place and practice of producing the precultural in culture."[1]

The ecstatic, moreover, took on the function of a meta-aesthetic: in the field of dance, in its reflections on possibilities of representing the liberation of the body in and through movement, as well as in literature, in a poetics of metamorphosis—as whirling dance and as "fire dance," in the dissolution, transformation, and mediality of individual corporeality and its associated transformations of the creative subject.

1. Baxmann 1991, 319.

"WHIRLING DANCE": MOVEMENTS
OF SELF-DISSOLUTION

Ritual and Trance

In her social-anthropological studies on ritual and body symbolism,[2] Mary Douglas differentiates between two social dispositions, which lead either to the formation of *ritual* forms of communication or to the "religious rapture" of *trance*. Ritual and trance are thus defined as opposites: while ritual is the incarnation of controlled action, loss of control is particularly important for trance.

According to Douglas, ritualism corresponds to a "religion of control"—whereby the definition of ritual and its social function is far from limited to the narrow field of the cultic, as Hans-Georg Soeffner describes in his study on ritual as a form "of visible elements necessary to correlate and orient a uniform symbolic interpretation of reality."[3] The correlation of "rituals of enactment" (Soeffner) and encoded bodies as forms of symbolic order is of particular significance in our context here. A society that defines the body and its forms of expression through ritual is, for Douglas, highly sophisticated and equipped with a broad spectrum of social roles that govern interpersonal relationships, and with a strong and complex system of exerting control over its members. This also reveals itself in the forms and general framework of the symbolic order: in the differentiation of roles and situations, in the strong appreciation of a controlled mind, in the assignment of magical meaning to symbolic acts.[4] Western-Christian culture, especially modern industrial society, conforms to this model of a control-oriented system with a related symbolic order.

In the same way that this basic pattern is characterized by strong formalization, so does its antithesis, the "religion of ecstasy" in "trance cultures," appear

---

2. See Douglas 2003. In the chapter "The Two Bodies," Douglas reflects—in reference to Marcel Mauss and Talcott Parsons—on the relationship of ritual and trance regarding "body symbolism." While the underlying concept of the symbol is not further differentiated and neither theoretically nor semiotically delineated, her arguments on the body as a social construct do reflect fundamental insights, which I will refer to in the following text—insofar as the discussion touches on social-anthropological aspects.

3. Soeffner 1989, 158–84. Soeffner's definition of *ritual* transfers Douglas's concept of the ritual, which is more oriented toward the cultic, into a more general framework of symbolic forms of organization and interpretation in the social construction of reality. "The ritual, the linking of symbols and symbolic gestures into a consistent and prestructured chain of action, can be understood as a text composed of symbolic acts, represented and structured by actions" (178). Translation: Elena Polzer.

4. See Douglas 2003, 123: "magical efficacy attributed to symbolic acts" (e.g., sin and sacraments).

to be dominated by the informal.[5] Douglas's observation that we "tend to find trance-like states feared as dangerous where the social dimension is strongly controlled" leads her to the thesis that "as trance is a form of dissociation, it will be more approved and welcomed the weaker the structuring of society."[6] Control and the relinquishment of control, a strong or weak structure of society, formal or informal definition of roles and the symbolic order thus distinguish ritual culture and trance culture from one another.

Keeping this in mind, I would like to posit the following questions concerning the early twentieth century:

- What role does ritual—as a controlled form of communication in structured systems—play in theater, dance, and literature, considering that Hugo von Hofmannsthal, Richard Beer-Hofmann, Georg Fuchs, Rudolf von Laban, William B. Yeats, Max Reinhardt, Antonin Artaud, and others emphasized the need to revitalize modern art with the help of ritual?[7]
- And why do these same authors simultaneously fantasize in various texts and contexts about models of dissociation in various forms of trance? If we do not wish to restrict ourselves to whether or not a diffuse terminology of "ritual" and "trance" here merges with the mutual connotation of (religious) festivity, that sociocultural state of exception,[8] then we must clarify how this opposition of formal determination, social control, and structure coincides with the breakdown of these factors of order in trance in a discourse that emphasizes the connecting moment of ritual and trance as *informalization*.

The imprecise terminology,[9] the "confusion" apparent in the lack of differentiation, is already in itself characteristic of the "cultural crisis" around 1900.

5. In contrast to structured, formal social conditions, informal behavior is rated higher in less-structured societies. Cf. Douglas 2003, 82: "The less highly structured, the more the value on informality, the more the tendency to abandon reason and to follow panics or crazes, and the more the permitted scope for bodily expressions of abandonment."

6. Ibid., 83.

7. On the subject of "ritual," see Schechner 1990; Turner 1982.

8. See in this context Haug and Warning 1989; what is striking and in my opinion typical for institutionalized academia in Germany is that this volume contains no contribution at all from the field of dance studies on the subject of "festivity."

9. During the first third of the twentieth century, this terminological imprecision, and the use of ritual and trance as synonyms, can quite often be found in texts and also in dance performances; the following examples in this book also document this mental mix-up.

On the one hand, the aim of the artists was to revitalize "ritual" as the main cultural element of a supposedly disturbed, incoherent symbolic interpretation of reality. On the other hand, new forms of ecstatic dance were developed in order to experiment with a suspension of control. This is probably a good indicator—from a cultural-sociological perspective—of a situation in which the social system is no longer sufficiently stabilized by corresponding symbolic forms, such as rituals and formulas of distancing, while simultaneously still far too caught up in the taboos and constraints of obsolete structures to be able to handle an integration of the informal. Forms of ecstasy (fictive, as in literary narratives; or symbolic-representative, as in theatrical presentation) such as whirling dances compensated the need for a "loss of control" in the still "formally" organized social subsystems by providing anarchic experiences of dissociation.

Soeffner points out two further aspects of symbolic representation in ritual that are important here for the further course of my argumentation:

- On the one hand, we have ritual's function of creating distance through the "representation of a uniform configuration of meaning," or rather the creation of a "uniform framework of interpretation and action." This distance allows the dignity of the sacred (especially in the field of religion and cult), the "Arcanum," to be protected by the symbolic order of the ritual, which transcends individuality, time, and place.[10]
- On the other hand, ritual's provision of orientation and its effectivity are not influenced by (cumulative) semantic ambiguity: "The more so as inconsistency, overdetermination and multiplicity of meaning anyhow belong to the semantics of the symbol."[11]

Trance Dance: "Orgiasm" and Hypnosis

The concept of "dance as a state of delirium achieved through movement" appears in Georg Fuchs's definition as the main general characteristic of dance:

I define dance as the rhythmic movement of the body in space, practiced in a creative drive toward a harmonious life experience of the world in motion. This exhilarating and intoxicating experience is that of a sublime

10. Soeffner 1989, 181.

11. Ibid., 180f. Translation: Elena Polzer

order that we do not conceive to be harmonious in itself but that can still be experienced as satisfying and intoxicating.[12]

Fuchs sought to revive the "orgiastic dances" of ancient sacrificial mysteries and the "cultic dance orgies" of the "ancient peoples" in his reform theater: "For us, dance can be nothing other than the onrush of experience reaching ecstatic orgasm in its rhythmic powers through corporeality."[13]

As an ardent admirer of Nietzsche, Fuchs developed a theater model based on Nietzsche's model of the Dionysian.[14] One year after Nietzsche's death, Fuchs staged his pageant *Das Zeichen* (*The Sign*, 1900), as an example of mass theater being the "drama of the people,"[15] an idea that he continued to propagate over the following years. Fuchs aimed to produce theater that would "cause thousands upon thousands to fall into a state of delirium."[16]

The ecstatic dances of the "dream dancer Madeleine G.," who performed her sensational trance dance séances in Munich in 1904,[17] seemed to prove Fuchs's point that "great dramatic art" was once again possible. In his eyes, the way to achieve such "festive, rhythmic stagecraft" was orgiastic dance. The *Bacchantes* of Euripides, which Fuchs attempted to stage a few years later at the Künstlertheater in Munich, seemed to him resurrected in the movement hypnosis of Madeleine's dance, in a "Dionysian delirium of the cultic dancer's doubtlessly somnambulist state of sleep."[18]

The Parisian "dream dancer" Madeleine—often also ironically labeled the "sleeping dancer"[19]—was "presented" by Munich doctor and psychologist Freiherr von Schrenck-Notzing under hypnosis. The scientist and therapist staged and commented on the trance dance himself and explained the

12. Fuchs 1906, 6f. Translation: Elena Polzer.

13. Ibid., 21. Translation: Elena Polzer.

14. See Fuchs 1906.

15. Prütting 1971, 265ff.

16. Fuchs 1906, 29.

17. See Brandstetter 1992.

18. Fuchs 1906, 28.

19. An author by the name of Arthur Silbergleit published the following commentary in the journal *Das Theater* 1. 6 (November 1909): "Have you seen a sleeping dancer before? On the twilight stage of our subconscious, our fate, she lives the most attentive existence, our deepest, our own life, on the watershed of day and dreaming, between sleep and slaughter. And we sit in the audience and follow this act. Some only see its awakening and know nothing of its semi-somnolent state. Others see its dreaming and know nothing of its awakening" (135). Translation: Elena Polzer.

"artistic significance of expressive movement in hysteria and under hypno-sis."[20] In this context, hypnosis fulfilled the task of rendering the body ecstatic, that is, liberating the ego from its socially acquired inhibitions and releas-ing the free creative "natural" essence from its cultural form. According to Schrenck-Notzing, this act exposed the dancer's innate "mimetic choreo-graphic disposition" expressed by an "intuitive immediacy of the soul, which finds its adequate ideoplastic means of expression in the body." The dance of the somnambulist is the embodiment of an authentic expression of natural beauty freed from its physical form. For Fuchs, the issue of "hypnosis and hysteria," as discussed among psychologists, neurologists, and cultural crit-ics at the time, was of secondary importance concerning Madeleine's trance dance. Instead, he considered her dance to be an artistic revelation. It was precisely this power of "suggestion," this somnambulant state, that correlated with the exalted creative trance previously sought for in the ecstatic cultic union with the divine.[21]

And yet, like others, Fuchs vacillates between the various discourses sur-rounding Madeleine's dance as a paradigm of free movement, of the unre-strained ecstatic beauty of the unconscious, of natural movement:

- On the one hand, cultural-historical and anthropological discourses on the archetype of orgiastic cultic dance forms of antiquity and "primi-tive" people; in this context, the hypnotized dancer's solo was paradoxi-cally regarded as a reverberation of the group trance of archaic ritual.
- On the other hand, the medical-psychological discourse: the theory that the inhibition threshold of consciousness as acquired over the course of socialization becomes permeable under hypnosis for the powers of the subconscious, so that trance movement allows "what happens there in

---

20. This is also the title of a publication by psychologist Schrenck-Notzing from 1904; cf. Brandstetter 1992. Translation: Elena Polzer.

21. Fuchs draws comparisons—drawing on information available from travel accounts and anthropological studies—to the orgiastic rituals of "primitive peoples." Trance practices in dance achieve the same effect as hypnosis, namely a kind of anesthetic insensitivity (e.g., to pain), which in his opinion proved that the "corybantic-maenadic state of intoxication is an essential premise for dance" (1906, 22f.). In his account "Von der Lola Montez zur Saharet, Duncan und Madeleine, Die Wiedergeburt der deutschen Bühne aus dem Rhythmus" (From Lola Montez to Saharet, Duncan and Madeleine: The rebirth of German theater out of rhythm) from his memoirs *Sturm und Drang in München um die Jahrhundertwende* (*Sturm and Drang in Munich around the Turn of the Century*) (1936, 232–46), Fuchs is already much more reserved about Madeleine being a "slightly prudish, conventionally emotional" woman, but sticks to his opinion that her dance, as that of a "tragic muse," reveals the Dionysian as a decisive dimension of new "cultic theater."

the dark country, in the 'untrodden, untreadable,'"[22] to become visible. The trance-dream dance reveals, as it were, the royal road to the "dark continent" of the (female!) soul via the presentation of the female body in hypnotically (male) induced movement.

- Third: the iconography of patterns of femininity both present in Madeleine's dance and read into it call up—as gestures of the "tragic muse"—almost all mythical images of women from antiquity and Christianity: Eva, Judith, Salome, the angel Gabriel, Clytemnestra, Helena, Cassandra, Medusa.[23]

However, it was not only in the field of theater that hypnotically induced trance dance became a pathos formula of the "authentic" movements of nature hidden under the incrustations of culture. The idea that physical expression in trance unearths truths lost to modern culture also gained ground in the fine arts, encouraged by the flourishing occultism of the age. Graphic artist and painter Alfons Mucha worked with a model, Lina de Ferkel, who was hypnotized and photographed in melodramatic expressive poses.[24] Mucha employed this method in a search for "dissolving views" that translated the symbolic language of the subconscious into images via the medium of the female body.

Here I can only touch on this fashion of hypnosis in the arts at the beginning of the twentieth century. Aside from painting, photography, and film (e.g., Wiene's *Dr. Caligari*), it also played a role in dance, theater, and cabaret, as well as in literature. To name just a few examples: Arthur Schnitzler's one-act play *Questioning Fate* from the "Anatol" cycle, Max Mell's pantomime *Pierrot Hypnotizer*, and Hofmannsthal's pantomime *The Student*.

Finally in the 1920s, the hypnosis model of trance dance provided the framework for a popular-scientific "dream stage" put on by Dr. E. Schertel. It was more or less a publicly performed form of therapy, in which the subject transcribed his or her dreams into movement while in a state of trance.[25] According to the dance author Egon Vietta, trance and ecstasy are expressed most strongly in dance by a

depersonalized body that seems to have stepped out of itself. In ecstasy, in the individual act of "stepping out of oneself," mankind is lifted into a

22. Fuchs 1906, 25. Translation: Elena Polzer.

23. Ibid., 25f. Translation: Elena Polzer.

24. See Loers 1987, 8ff.

25. See Baxmann 1991, 329ff.

realm entirely different from the world as we know it. We experience this *ekstasis* as liberation, as a letting go of the world, similar to a separation of body and soul, and indeed it is the most corporeal of embodiments that lends us this exhilarating feeling of freedom, as if the dancer were absolved from this earth into a true life. It is a form of liberation, related to the greatest sense of philosophical bliss.[26]

Whirling Dances: From Dance of the Dervishes to Expressionistic Dance

One of the trance dance models that gained paradigmatic significance both in literature as well as in contemporary dance discourse and in the works of expressionistic dancers is the whirling dance, the "dance of the dervishes."

John Schikowski, one of the most prominent authors of dance discourse aside from Hans Brandenburg, Fritz Böhme, Max von Boehn, Frank Thieß, and Ernst Schur, writes about the dervish dance in the chapter on "oriental dances" in his *Geschichte des modernen Tanzes* (*History of Modern Dance*, 1926):

> The religious dance of the spinning dervishes, which goes by the name of Sema, is an ecstatic whirl, which nine, eleven, or thirteen persons perform with bare feet, closed eyes, and outspread arms on the right heel. It is danced on Tuesdays and Fridays with singing in the mosque and supposedly, according to Mohammedan legend, can be ascribed to David's dance in front of the Ark of Covenant.[27]

The Mevlana-Rumi order of the dancing dervishes, which is still a distinguished religious order today, is based in Konya. Dancing dervishes rotate "counter-sunwise." The act of pivoting around the body's central axis in meditative trance symbolizes a gesture of inspiration: "receiving from the heavens, scattering on the earth."[28]

Actors (not the dervishes, who spend eight hours a day praying and meditating) perform the "whirling dance of the dervishes" for tourist audiences—a practice that became widely known in central Europe during the nineteenth

---

26. Vietta 1938, 50. Translation: Elena Polzer.

27. Schikowski 1926, 99. Translation: Elena Polzer.

28. See Wosien 1972: "Thus the primal qualities of mankind . . . are 'brought into rotation.' . . . . This center cannot be directly accessed, it can only be circled around and it must be circled around until the center shines." Translation: Elena Polzer.

century thanks to various publicized travel accounts. What is interesting in terms of the "rotating moment" in the movement is that the spinning dance of the dervishes was often compared to the waltz, as in a text from 1928. "Waltzing," which was introduced to the ballroom in the eighteenth century as a symbolic movement pattern of bourgeois freedom, the freedom to experience the passionate tumult of emotion,[29] is here compared to the whirling dance of the dervishes.

According to this account, thirteen dervishes assemble in the hall and, after sitting motionless in prayer and bowing to the emir,

> slowly begin to waltz. You would think that this could not be watched without laughing, but such is not the case. To first see these men sit there so motionless and symmetrically and then see them waltz just so, are two groups of singular beauty and therefore deeply touching. When they waltz, it is as if they were marionettes, being turned by a machine hidden underground. The faces are rapt, the eyes closed, arms extended at the shoulders, their skirts spread outward and downward in a funnel shape. The steps are slow and so small that it must take three minutes until they have circled around the room once. This dance lasts around ten minutes, then there is a short pause, after which the waltzing begins again and so it continues three times. Then the emir prays to fatherland and monarch, whereupon the dervishes depart in the same way as they appeared, the emir being last.
>
> The founder of this order to said to have introduced this whirling dance, not only to find God, who can be found at all sides, as he is everywhere, but also because the constant shifting of one's position symbolizes breaking away from the mortal things, which should not induce us to stand still.[30]

---

29. Ballroom dancing reflects the changes in social etiquette and in behavior between the sexes: the revolution of the waltz in bourgeois ballrooms is a prime example of one such change. With its rise in popularity in the mid-eighteenth century, this new dance with its swaying 3/4-time rhythm expressed the mental attitude of the generation that followed Rousseau, who—like the generation around 1900—elevated nature and passion to key elements of their own identity. The minuet was passé, for it embodied courtly tradition and the conventions of the outdated etiquette of the dancing master in the meeting of the sexes stylized as dialogue, in the rhetoric of its movement figurations and steps. The waltz, however, was a provocation. It reverberated with the challenge of breaking free from feudalistic forms of representation in dance. The intoxicating floating whirl of the tightly embracing couple became a symbol for passionate freedom. The waltz in Goethe's *Werther*, danced by Lotte and Werther, isolates a moment of happy intimacy in the whirl of shared movement from the context of a story of unrequited love.

30. Anonymous report from 1828, cited in Gallwitz 1981.

This association of rotating waltz with trance is also evident in titles such as the *Delirium Waltz*, a composition by Josef Strauss (1827–1870), in which the narcotic intoxicating effect of the dance is already implied in the waltz itself. The rise of the waltz fell into a period of transition that ended in turn-of-the-century decadence. This decadence celebrated itself in the form of the fin de siècle fast polka, composed in 1899 by Adolf Müller—a symbol of the frantic "gallop" of historical turmoil. And it was also the waltz with which Grete Wiesenthal's whirling dance captured the attention of enthusiastic audiences. Wiesenthal's so-called spheric momentum, the expansive waltzing rotation out of a deeply backward-bent upper body (figure 29) conveyed the stirring charm, the buoyant, ecstatic quality in Wiesenthal's dances.[31]

However, the fascination that the dance of the dervishes, this religious dance from the Orient, held for the central European avant-garde lay in those attributes in particular that seemed to situate it entirely beyond the artistic context of the theatrical. It is precisely the seemingly "primitive," the nonelaborated, nonvirtuosic aspect of this religious cult that so appealed to the artists of the avant-garde; especially the way it called into question the limitations of the "as if" conventions of artistic illusion. By continuously rotating around our own axis, we destabilize our ordinary perception of reality. The boundaries of the surrounding space, as well as the boundaries of the self, are lost in the transpersonal experience of trance. Hence, whirling dance offers a model of experiencing immediacy that contradicts the (theatrical-symbolic) representation of movement.

The trance achieved by the monotonous ritual of incessant rotation reveals a realm of transcendence. The goal and fruition of the movement ritual lies in achieving union with the divine in a moment of ecstasy. "At the climax of ecstasy, the dancer glides out of himself: God enters the dancer's body."[32]

In his book *Psyche*, which was so important for the turn-of-the-century interpretation of antiquity, Erwin Rohde mentions the oriental dance of the dervishes in connection with mystery cults:

31. The specificity of Wiesenthal's whirling trance dance lay exactly in this form of waltzing rotation, which also distinguishes it from the expressionist patterns of representation in the work of Mary Wigman and Dore Hoyer (analyzed below). Wiesenthal herself saw an ecstatic trance moment in her Strauss waltzes, in her whirling dances, which she described accordingly: "In the waltz as artistic dance, it seems to me that the boundaries of the form have to be drawn somewhat wider. It was not only the primitive-buoyant joie de vivre, but also the Dionysian-ecstatic and divinely carefree that expressed itself in these musical creations." (Cited from an unpublished typescript by G. Wiesenthal. I am indebted to Mr. Martin Lang for permitting access to this document.) Translation: Elena Polzer.

32. Vietta 1938, 69. Translation: Elena Polzer.

The dervishes of the Orient whirl round in their violent dances to the rattle of the drums, and the sound of flutes till the last stages of excitement and exhaustion are reached. The purpose of it all is vividly expressed by the most fearless of all the mystics, Jelaleddin Rumi, in the words: "He that knows the power of dance dwells in God; for he has learnt that Love can slay. Allah hu!"[33]

Hugo von Hofmannsthal may have had this same excerpt from Rohde's book in mind when he wrote the following lines of the libretto for *Electra*: "Ah! Love kills! But nobody passes on without having known love!"[34]

In this key line, which links the fulfillment of love with the transgression of death's boundaries, the text offers a decisive clue to the interpretation of Electra's dance.[35] The transition from individual to transpersonal is embodied in Electra's "nameless" dance.

Inspired by his encounter with Richard Strauss in 1906, Hofmannsthal reworked his drama *Electra* (1904) into an opera. Hofmannsthal's acquaintance with the dancer Ruth St. Denis and her Indian-inspired dances also falls into the same period as his first collaboration with Strauss. In her solo program, which Hofmannsthal saw during a matinee in fall 1906, organized by Harry Graf Kessler,[36] she presented an ecstatic "nautch" dance, in addition to the meditative ritual *Incense*, and the temple dance *Radha*. The *Nautch* was an Indian variation of the Arabian whirling dance and had likewise become popular around the turn of the century thanks to various travel accounts.

There were a series of central aspects, which influenced the discussion and handling of the oriental trance whirling dance either explicitly or in the form of subtexts. A decisive fact was that the dance of the dervishes is of religious-ritualistic origin and not an invention of theater or dance. This was important not only for how it was received in cultural-anthropological discourse, as was the case with Rohde and F. M. Böhme, Hermann Graf von Keyserling, and in Ernst Bloch's

33. Rohde 1925 (2001), 6: 262–63.

34. Hofmannsthal, *Electra*; cited in English in Puffet 1989, 31. There is evidence that Hofmannsthal knew Rohde's book well. Hofmannsthal cites the above passage from Rohde's *Psyche* in his essay on Oscar Wilde, "Sebastian Melmoth." "Everything is everywhere. Everything partakes of the dance of life. In the words of Jala-ud-din Rumi, 'He that knows the power of the dance of life fears not death. For he knows that love kills.'" Hofmannsthal 2008b, 146.

35. See the sections on "Dance of the Maenad" and "Fire Dance."

36. On Hofmannsthal and St. Denis, on *Conversation with the Dancer* and the related dialogue *Furcht* (*Fear*, 1907) and the review "Her Extraordinary Immediacy," see Brandstetter 1991b.

Principle of Hope. In its adaptation and transformation by *Ausdruckstänzer,* in their interpretative and productive treatment of the whirling dance pattern—particularly in solo work—the moment of immediacy also played an important role.

The subject of trance dance in the whirling ritual of the religious dervish dances is connected to one of the most important fundamental ideas underlying theater reform at the beginning of the twentieth century. By having recourse to the anarchistic, to myth and ritual, theater reform sought to renew the theatrical. In the 1910s and 1920s, Nietzsche and Wagner were cited by a younger generation seeking to legitimize its aspirations toward theatricality and festivity, theater architecture and mass choreography, as well as audience-oriented acting freed from illusionist principles. Among those who referenced ritual and "ceremony" (Hofmannsthal) in their work—despite all the differences in their theoretical and practical theatrical concepts—were Romain Rolland, Max Reinhardt, William B. Yeats, Hugo von Hofmannsthal, Edward Gordon Craig, Adolphe Appia, Emile Jaques-Dalcroze, Isadora Duncan, Ruth St. Denis, Mary Wigman, Rudolf von Laban, Georg Fuchs and the Munich Artist's Theater, and last but not least the Munich Cosmic Circle with their Dionysian Festivities, as well as other authors close to them such as Hans Brandenburg and Albert Talhoff, whose "Choreo-Dramas" aimed at renewing theater with the help of dance and the choric movements of the masses.[37]

However, these reform concepts of retheatricalizing theater with the help of ritual contain one contradictory moment in their references to trance dance. This contradiction is linked to the role of the *subject* of representation: Why was whirling dance, as an archaic group ritual of religious practice, understood and executed in modern art, both in dance and in literature, largely as a *solo?*

What significance is here awarded to trance and ritual as models of experiencing and performing symbolic representation? Is the staging of trance dance a celebration of the cult of the lonely ego? And does this indicate an inherent criticism of the mechanisms underlying emergent mass society? Do we have here self-presentation by visionary artists or a playful exploration of the fascination produced by psychological states of transgression—in light of a disintegration of value systems and a relativization of parallel, yet contradictory, ideologies?

All these questions are linked to the issue of subjectivation in solo trance dance and the simultaneous destruction of individuality in the dissolution

---

37. Albert Talhoff, *Das Totenmal* (*The Funeral Banquet,* 1920), subtitled "A dramatic choric vision of words dance light," written in memoriam for the dead of World War I, not choreographed until June–September 1930 by Mary Wigman, was performed at the Chorische Bühne in Munich; Hans Brandenburg, *Der Sieg des Opfers* (*The Triumph of Sacrifice,* 1914), whose performance of the piece, choreographed and directed by Rudolf von Laban, was abandoned when the war broke out.

of the boundaries within the ego. Whirling dance represents an experience evoked by movement, which Freud aptly described in his *Civilization and Its Discontents* (1929) as "oceanic," a religious sensation (here Freud is referring to Romain Rolland) of "eternity," "as of something limitless, unbounded."[38]

In modern literature as well as in modern dance, trance dance was predominantly presented as a solo. The whirling dance of the dervishes is, however, a group activity by members of a religious community. Each individual is by himself in the rotation, but the experience of self-renunciation and the union with the numinous takes place in the shared space of a ritual community of kindred spirits.

Georg Heym described the dance of the dervishes in his poem "Barra Hei . . ." (1911).[39]

38. Freud 1989, 11.

39.

Barra Hei. Barra Hei.
Und die Derwische tanzen zu Korta el Dei,
Tanzen wie rote Flammen im Sand,
Rund gedreht, wie Säulen aus Brand.

Der Weite Blau. Und der Wüste Gold.
Ist wie ein großer Teppich gerollt.
Und sie tanzen davor wie ein brennender Kreis
Rot gelb blau, schwankender Turbane Weiß.

. . .

Barra Hei. Barra Hei. Barra Hei.
Im unendlichen Himmel gellt ihr Geschrei.
Immer schneller <gedreht>, immer weißer der Tanz
Tausend <Leiber> gedreht, wie ein loderner Kranz.

. . .

Die Welt versank. Und die ewige Ewigkeit
Hängt wie ein Kleid von ihren Lenden so weit.
Keine Zeit mehr. Unendliche Ewigkeit.
Ewig in Gott, und ewig vom Leben befreit.

Keine Qual mehr. Sie sind auf <einmal ein Funke bloß>.
Ein goldenes Nichts in der Ewigkeit Schoß.
Wie die Lilien, in Gottes Händen so leicht,
Darüber der blaue Atem der Weite streicht.

Barra Hei. Barra Hei.
Leise wie Kinderlallen wird ihr Geschrei.
Und plötzlich zerschellt
Stürzt <einer> und fällt.

Der Gott hat ihn erfaßt.
Er ist schrecklich erblaßt.
Sein Kinn klappert und saust.

The whirling rapture in the dance of the dervishes resembles a form of prayer. The rotation around one's own axis, the vertical movement and the moment of elevation in trance achieved by overcoming the physical sensation of gravity, also influenced solo whirling dances. Mary Wigman describes the moment of elevation in trance with words similar to those used by Georg Heym in his poem: "Suddenly something peculiar occurred: she rose above the ground, stood still in the air, quietly floating . . . she floated, so lightly, carrying great bliss."[40]

Heym translated the elevation movement triggered by the force of the rotation in the whirling dance around the vertical axis from the microcosm into the macrocosm by using the metaphor of time and space: "And they rise upward to the sky free," "float above the world" with the "lightness" of the "golden stars" in the universe, "alone in infinite space" and "outside of time."

The ecstatic experience of time and space, "infinity" and "endlessness," transforms the dance into a "communion with space" (Wigman), and it allows the dancer (as well as the empathic onlooker) to take part for a moment in a mystical experience of union, to be the "center of the world," "center of a great occurrence of movement, part of the pulsating body of the world."[41]

Besides St. Denis, whose *Nautch* dance was based on Indian models, Alexander Sakharoff,[42] Alexander von Swaine,[43] Jean Börlin, Mary Wigman, and Dore Hoyer also included whirling dances in their programs.

One of Jean Börlin's earliest choreographies is the five-minute whirling dance *Dervishes* (1920) (figure 36).[44] Inspired by the Muslim trance ritual of the dervishes, Börlin staged an oriental prayer ceremony. The movement sequence is typical for the way it combines all elements that apply to whirling dance as

Alla <il>. Der Gott braust.

Gott braust. Wie er lächelt, seht,
Seine Augen sind aus den Höhlen gedreht.
Rücklings liegt er da. Und des Bartes Flaum
Füllt sich wie Schnee <an> mit weißem Schaum.

Heym 1964, 1: 367f.

40. Wigman, "Prosa-Dichtung" (Prose-Poetry), in Sorell 1986, 280. Translation: Elena Polzer.

41. Ibid., 280. Translation: Elena Polzer.

42. See Veroli 1991.

43. See Müller, Peter, and Schuldt 1992, 98.

44. *Derviches* premiered in Paris on November 18, 1920. Choreography, J. Börlin; music, Glazunow; scenography and costumes, Börlin. The short piece was designed as the middle part of a program between *El Greco* and *Les Vierges folles*; see Häger 1989, 111f.

Figure 36 Jean Börlin, *Dervishes* (1920).
SOURCE: Bibliothèque de l'Opéra, Paris, France.

ecstatic movement: elevation, climaxing rotation, loss of self in religious rapture, and finally the fall.

Nevertheless, the first impression is not one of the depiction and introduction of "primitive" trance rituals into dance, but rather—as in the better known Ballets Russes productions—that of a theatrical adaptation of the dervish dances as an *exotic sujet*. The scenography (a golden mosque), costume (fez, bolero jacket, and a long, wide, circular skirt with a heavy edge, which "stood" like a cone in the rotation),[45] and group choreography (Jean Börlin was joined in the dance by a total of five male dancers) conveyed to the mimetic theatrical representation an atmosphere of the oriental—a dance of the dervishes. Börlin's choreography seems to have been less committed to monotonous absolute trance dance than to the principles of illusion in pictorial representation, almost like a belated theatrical illustration of Georg Heym's poem "Barra Hei." It is not surprising that critics of this mise en scène of ecstatic whirling dance particularly emphasized the "virtuosité" of the "exercice de rotation."

45. See the images in Häger 1989, 110, 111, 113.

Contrary to choreographic depictions of the dervish dance as a religious community ritual, trance dance appeared in solos, such as those by Mary Wigman, as representations of the solipsism of the modern subject. Instead of expressing the security of a religious practice, these "ecstatic dances" (Wigman) conveyed a longing to connect the isolated self with transpersonal powers of nature and the cosmos. The solo act of rotating around one's own central axis, connecting body and space, allowed the transgression of barriers of subjectivity to become tangible in a representation of ritual action.

Whirling dances, as staged trance dance, demanded a fundamentally different perspective, and conditions different from other forms of free dance, which developed their material out of the moment of movement discovery. Here the dominant principle was that of repetition. The "monotony" of steady movement was produced by a base ostinato of rotation. The spindle pattern of the rotation created a degree of intensity that cast a spell not only over the dancers, but also over the audience.

In 1917, Wigman produced *The Dervish* for her solo series *Ecstatic Dances*. She created this choreography during a period of working with Rudolf von Laban on Monte Verità near Ascona. Her preoccupation with esotericism—a colorful coexistence of vegetarians and theosophists, "Lebenreform" followers, anarchists, spiritists, naturists, and followers of the *Lichtkörperkultur* (body of light culture) was characteristic of the colony located on the "Mountain of Truth" since the turn of the century[46]—intensified in summer 1917, when freemasons, occultists, theosophists, and anthroposophists came from all over the world to a congress of the esoteric order Ordo Templi Orientis, founded by Theodor Reuß.[47] Extensive festivities were staged to express the practice of dance ritual as well as Laban's *Weltanschauung des Tänzers* (*Philosophy of a Dancer*) based on the philosophies of Ludwig Klages and Friedrich Nietzsche.[48] Wigman's cycle of *Ecstatic Dances* also featured a religious theme: the mystical devotion of the individual to a higher power. For Wigman, the turn to "primitive" belief, to forms of "foreign," corporeal ritual (in contrast to the hostility to the body found in the cult of Christian liturgy) was of great importance. Although Wigman still used gestural elements from oriental temple ceremonies in her *Dervish* and although she still, in her choice of costume and bearded mask,[49] presented a theatrical representation of dervish dancing, the

---

46. See Landmann 1979; Szeemann 1980; Andritzky and Rautenberg 1989.

47. See Landmann 1979, 144 ff.

48. In summer 1917, Laban's three part *Tanzhymne* "Das Sonnenfest" (Dance hymn, "Celebration of the Sun") was celebrated in the form of a ritual prayer to the sun. On the subject of prayer to the sun and to the light (Fidus), see Frecot, Geist, and Kerbs 1972.

49. Wigman's colleague and friend, the dancer Berthe Trümpy, described *The Dervish* as follows: "The Dervish—there he sits in a stiff squat—red Turkish trousers, pointy green cap,

Figure 37 Mary Wigman, *Drehmonotonie* (1926).
SOURCE: Battenberg Verlag, Augsburg, Germany.

solo already featured fundamental choreographic elements of her later, pure dance transformation of ecstasy: the wild rotation around her own axis and movements in a bent-over, squatting position (as in her *Witch Dance* in 1914–1920).

In 1926, she developed the solo *Drehmonotonie* (*Monotony Whirl*) (figure 37), which she later included in the series *Die Feier II* (*The Celebration II*) (1927). The solos' evocative effect was not least of all due to Wigman's choice of music. While Dore Hoyer, twelve years after Wigman, used Maurice Ravel's *Boléro* for her whirling dance, Wigman chose a simple movement sequence accompanied by piano and drum: "In constant repetition a short, Oriental-like motif . . . and

brown wool beard. He raises his hands, lays them on his back, fulfils the prescribed gestures of the ritual almost indifferently. Slowly he rises—now horror enters the steel-blue eyes resting above the wooly beard, with deep steps he throws himself into the circle, staggering to the wall in sudden stupor—now eternity has forced itself upon him, like a wound, he feels the dread of endlessness, the magical eight takes hold of him, he attempts to flee from himself, back into calm, again he attempts the ritual gestures, but never again does he attain familiarity with them bringing calm, the deep wound of eternity rips him apart, destroys him." In Müller 1986, 63. Translation: Elena Polzer.

with it, the exciting uninterrupted taps, raps, and the urgency of the muted drumbeats."[50]

The whirling dance was produced by spiral-shaped floor paths, which circled the middle of the space in large expansive steps, accompanied by rhythmic arm movements. Wigman emphasized the gravitational pull of the center that was created and enhanced by her continuous circling around her own axis.

> Fixed to the same spot and spinning in the monotony of the whirling movement, one lost oneself gradually in it until the turns seemed to detach themselves from the body, and the world around it started to turn. Not turning oneself, but being turned, being the center, being the quiet pole in the vortex of rotation![51]

In her description, Wigman emphasizes the constitutive moments of the dance: the "monotony" of simple movements repeated in a distinct rhythm, corresponding to the ostinato in the music; the extremely self-referential situation and sudden transition into loss of self in the rotation around her own axis; her arrival at a center and the wandering outward movement of the center in the form of "surrounding space"[52]—and the moment of self-loss as a loss of body and space. The subject disappears *in* the center. The ultimate climax of this ex-centric movement is the disintegration of the self and the associated physical collapse analogous to a state of insanity. Wigman's description states the pleasure and fear found in endless rotation, the horror and the ecstasy of being unable to stop, as dangers inherent to this dance:

> Will it never end? Why does no one speak the redeeming word, stopping this madness? With a last desperate exertion, control over one's willpower is found again. A jerk pierces the body, compelling it to stand still at the moment of the fastest turn; . . . and then the sudden letting go, the fall of the relaxed body into the depth with only one sensation still alive: that of a complete incorporeal state.[53]

50. Wigman 1966, 39.

51. Ibid.

52. In her text on *Die Tänzerin* (*The Dancer*), she expresses this relationship between rotating body and space even more clearly: "The pulsating rotation is passed on to the dancing space; the walls turn, first clearly discernible, then gradually blurring more and more, endlessly expanding into a single frantic whirl." In Sorell 1989, 280. Translation: Elena Polzer.

53. Ibid. Translation: Elena Polzer.

Wigman describes the "sense of inescapability" as an experience of death. The individual's devotion to movement, as expression of a mythical entity, is a pivotal element of Wigman's philosophy of expressionistic dance; artistic dogma and credo of her ideology rolled into one.

This model of self-dissolution in trance movement is linked over and over again in Wigman's work to two basic motifs: the subject of sacrifice and death on the one hand and the subject of festivity and the depiction of cult in dance on the other.[54] *Drehmonotonie*, originally composed as a solo, fulfills its full representative function for the pathos of rise and fall, of emerging and passing, of birth and death only in the context of the larger subject of ritual "festivity": the whirling around one's own axis, the transition from collapse to return into the orderly world, is interpreted by Wigman in her manuscript notes[55] as the act of becoming one with the cosmos in dance: "Over and over again, I have delivered myself up to the ecstasy of experience, this almost lascivious annihilation of corporeality, in which I become one with the events of the cosmos for a few seconds."

Collapse as the termination of ecstatic rotation combines loss of control and repose as a premise and state of transition for regaining orientation on another level. The subject tumbles out of the axis-emphasized spiral movement, from vertical transcendental elevation, and falls to the depths.

Wigman used this contrasting effect of monotonous rotating movement of the body versus sudden transition from the lateral axis to the surface of the floor to produce the dramatic climax of *Drehmonotonie*. Dore Hoyer's *Drehtanz* was different. Early versions of this piece set to Ravel's *Boléro* were presented in 1938 and 1939.[56]

In *Drehtanz*, Hoyer employed the basic concept of Ravel's *Boléro* by resorting to an abstract form of dance, free from any kind of "plot" and entirely focused on the whirling dance itself. Ravel's *Boléro* composition was conceived from the onset as a whirling dance. Ida Rubinstein, who wanted a ballet with a Spanish flair for the program of *Les Ballets Ida Rubinstein*,[57]

---

54. See Müller 1986, 192.

55. According to ibid., 193. Translation: Elena Polzer.

56. In program notes from 1938, the dance is still entitled *Nach einem Bolero* (*Based on a Bolero*). In the first two versions of the piece, one of Hoyer's most successful solos, she still had—according to dance sketches—planned wider floor paths in circular and spiral patterns. In the 1950s version, she finally narrowed it down to the rotation. Cf. Müller, Peter, and Schuldt 1992, 93–99.

57. In 1925, pantomime and dancer Ida Rubinstein (1885–1960), who had become famous for her roles in productions by the Ballets Russes, e.g., in *Cléopâtre* (1910) and *Le Martyre de San Sébastian* (1991), founded her own company, Le Ballets Ida Rubinstein, and engaged Bronislawa Nijinska as chef-choreographer and ballet mistress; see Cossart 1987.

asked Ravel in 1928 to orchestrate a few pieces from Isaac Albeniz's piano suite *Iberia*. Ravel accepted the commission, but the rights had already been acquired by the Spanish dancer La Argentina.[58] Ravel therefore developed his idea of a two-part syncopic rhythmic theme that was repetitive in its alternation of instrumentation and done in the same style as popular compositions by Pedilla (the author of the *Valencia* melody), into a piece for the dance ensemble Ida Rubinstein.

At first, Ravel had in mind a dramatic ballet similar to Bizet's *Carmen*. In a reflection of the two-part theme, which loops on and on like a chain or the assembly line in a factory, he envisioned men and women leaving their workplaces and uniting in a general dance. This group would be confronted with a trio, stuck in a jealous drama between a woman, a toreador, and a deceived husband.[59]

The first draft of the plot was dropped, but Ravel's original idea of emphasizing the "Arabian" aspect in an obstinate repetition of entwining sections of the theme was retained and translated into choreography. The confrontation of group and soloists, the polarity of female trance dance and its hypnotic effect on the male gaze, the reduction of the movement vocabulary to that of a spinning rotation based on "Arabian" dervish dances, was already established.

Rubinstein's biographer Michael de Cossart describes the world premiere on November 11, 1928, choreographed by Bronislawa Nijinska, as follows:

> A dancer tries out some steps on a large table in the centre of the room. The men pay no attention at first. But as the slow stately dance gradually begins to evolve and the rhythm becomes more insistent and the dance becomes more frenetic, they start to take an animated interest in her. Their excitement reaches fever-pitch as the dancer brings her improvisation to an abrupt climatic end.[60]

On a gloomy stage designed by Alexandre Benois and modeled on Goya, the eyes of the audience focused on a tavern, in which a group of men sat over cards

---

58. On the origins of the *Boléro*, see Cossart 1987, 127–32. Composer Enrique Arbós undertook the instrumentation for the dancer La Argentina. Pianist and composer Joaquin Nin (father of author Anaïs Nin) reports on the precise context of Ravel's Boléro composition (1938).

59. This basic scenario, in terms of a meeting between the protagonists and the group in the tavern, reappeared in the structure of Roland Petit's choreography *Carmen* (1949).

60. Cossart 1987, 128. The basic framework of the choreography, the dance on the table, and the configurations of solo and group also govern Maurice Béjart's choreography of *Boléro* (1960).

and wine. The critic's reactions were mixed. Serge Diaghilev, who feared competition from Rubinstein and her company for his Ballets Russes, complained about the choreography and Rubinstein's lack of skill as a dancer—she had chosen to perform the solo on the table herself.[61]

However, the reactions of music critic Henry Prunières reflected the audience's enthusiasm for the magical effect of Ravel's music. Prunières saw in Rubinstein's performance a visual projection of the evocative, hypnotic monotony of the composition.[62]

Dore Hoyer, the great lone wolf of second-generation expressionistic dance, developed a deconstructivist reading of Rubinstein's *Boléro* and its "Spanish couleur locale" in an entirely uncompromising choreography. In her movement composition, she uncovered the basic structure of the music piece as a whirling dance.

While her first versions from 1938 and 1939 (figure 38) still incorporated floor paths, the new version from 1950, which became part of the series *Südamerikanische Reise* (*South American Journey*), concentrated entirely on the act of rotating upon a 2-meter-high, pyramid-like platform 2.5 meters by 2.5 meters. The solo, which traced the approximately eighteen minutes of Ravel's music—the perpetually accumulating layers of sound, which finally condense into a uniform bolero rhythm,[63] resembled a "single great accumulation. Self-intoxication" (Hoyer).[64] Her *Boléro*, in the words of essayist and dance critic Egon Vietta, was a "furious rotation, marked out by the hands as an extreme outer circle, a dervish dance, a hymnic spinning, a whirlwind, a primal image of rapture in dance."[65]

The motorics of the whirling dance consisted of a steady rotation around the lateral or rather vertical axis of the body. The limbs stabilized the overall destabilized physical structure. The legs and feet transferred weight in small steps. The arms were held more or less close to the torso, mostly in a symmetrical position, and regulated not only balance, but also the dynamics, the intensification, and the alternation of accelerando and decelerando.

61. Diaghilev supposedly said: "Still with the inevitable red coiffure, she spent a quarter of an hour clumsily turning on a table as large as the whole stage of the Monte Carlo Opera." Cossart 1987, 132.

62. Cossart 1987, 132. Ravel himself is said to have dryly answered an older lady in the audience who constantly cried out "Crazy! Crazy!": "It's okay, she got it."

63. Hoyer used the piano version of Ravel's *Boléro*. My description of this piece is based, if not otherwise noted, on a detailed (oral) account by Carl Rick, who worked with her as a dancer and watched the *Boléro* numerous times up to its last performance in Berlin.

64. Müller, Peter, and Schuldt 1992, 93. Translation: Elena Polzer.

65. Ibid., 98.

Figure 38 Dore Hoyer, *Drehtanz* (1939).
SOURCE: Deutsches Tanzarchiv Köln / (c)Deutsches
Tanzarchiv Köln, Cologne, Germany.

The incorporation of the head plays an important role in whirling, which
leads to trance, or better still, *represents* trance as in the solos of expressionistic
dance. The head is "taken along" in the rotation, meaning that it is integrated in
the entire body and the axis. The eyes glide along in the whirling motion without fixating a single point in space, thus leading more or less to the loss of optical orientation in space. The "diffuse gaze" technically prevents motion sickness
and simultaneously conveys a state of rapture to the audience. The surrounding
space becomes a circular band around the rotating axis of the dancer. According
to Mary Wigman, this creates the sensation of passing the rotation on to "the
dance space," to the "encircling walls," which merge one into the other.[66]

The position of the head is what fundamentally distinguishes rotation in a
trancelike whirling dance from the pirouette in classical ballet. In the latter,

66. Sorell 1986, 280.

spatial orientation is maintained by isolating the head in the rotation: a specific spot in the room—along the line of the pirouette—is visually fixated and
kept in the line of vision during the rotation of torso and limbs. The head is
thus isolated (held still) and only catches up with the rotation at the end of the
pirouette, in a swift motion, only to immediately return to fixing a point in
space in order to retain orientation. As a rational, rhetorical, and geometrical
system, ballet techniques and aesthetics particularly accentuate labile positions
and movement elements such as the pirouette, dance *sur pointe*, and attitudes
as moments of virtuosic body control. It is exactly this virtuosity in ballet that
expressionistic dance rejected as empty effect.

One of the fundamental differences between free dance and expressionistic dance lay in their attitudes toward the meaning of balance and its technical employ in connection with ballet. The art of equilibrating (Oscar Bie) is
related to the way in which the body's center of gravity is positioned. Without
going into more detail concerning the finer aspects of these relationships and
differences, I merely wish to emphasize the special manifestations of movement reflected in these contrary models of rotation in ballet and expressionistic dancer. While the pirouette in ballet seeks to achieve stability and ideal
spatial orientation by using a corresponding technique of rotation that isolates
the head, the ultimate goal of whirling expressionistic dance was loss of control
(i.e., loss of orientation)[67]—albeit the loss of control was "calculated" and "presented" as staged dance.

What is remarkable here is the shift in attitudes toward lability, toward risk-
ing the total destabilization of the subject in the displacement of the center of
gravity up to a point of identity loss and dissolution of the self. Mary Wigman's
and Dore Hoyer's whirling dances explore the externalization of the subject in
dance and the complete destruction of orientation, of course—and this must
be emphasized—with the help of a (new) dance movement technique, which
evoked trance while simultaneously representing it in an artistically controlled
way. What these dancers presented in their whirling dance solos was to all
extents and purposes the artistic control of the uncontrollable—and they did so
in every performance with the utmost intensity and the real risk of truly losing
themselves in ecstasy, an aspect that did not fail to have a deep effect on their
audiences.

---

67. In her remarks on trance dance, Kaye Hoffmann emphasizes the mythical meaning of
"losing one's head," movement "without head": "Every sense of identity seems disabled, but
this does not necessarily mean unconsciousness. Beyond all associations that produce identity, provide a structuring principle that takes effect in the body and does not require willpower . . . there seems to exist an outer-conscious borderline state of being." Hofmann 1984,
105f. Translation: Elena Polzer.

However, Hoyer was more occupied with the subject of "possession" in her whirling dance than was Wigman.[68] In her third version of *Boléro* (1950), the choreographic material was extremely reduced. Unlike Wigman, she practically excluded all paths in space: she rotated around her own axis upon a pedestal, while the ensemble danced contrapuntal circles around her in the background. This constellation cited the Nijinska/Rubinstein *Boléro* version from 1928 and, in turn, inspired Maurice Béjart to his own choreography of Ravel's *Boléro*.[69]

Hoyer's carefully elaborated foot technique—rotating on the flat foot, in small steps placed outward to the right—formed a kind of movement ostinato analogous to the bolero rhythm in the free figuration of the upper body, the head, and the arms. The climax to the passionate whirling was expressed in gradually intensified and increasingly complex interaction between transformations of the upper body and movements of the head and various arm gestures. The growing intensity of the rotation was supported by the color of the dress, which was divided into three layers of red—an orange-red section from the floor to the hips, a blazing red stripe up to the tips of the breasts, and a dark red arm and shoulder section: a "fire dance" rising upward as a beacon of passion in frantic whirling rotation.

In her steady spin, the dancer seemed to slip out of her body, seemed to fully become a vessel of transpersonal power. Contemporary critics saw in Hoyer's "dance of divine possession" a physical manifestation of "that existential sensation of being-thrown-into-the-world which we are so often confronted with today."[70]

The finale of *Boléro* did not culminate in a fall, like most other whirling dances. Hoyer instead ended it unpretentiously and—very impressively after such a long rotation—in an abrupt halt. This ending of the whirling

68. Hoyer's dance *Tanz der göttlichen Besessenheit* (*Dance of Divine Possession*) from the series *Der große Gesang* (*The Great Song*), which premiered 1948 in Dresden, was similar to the *Boléro* in its subject matter and composition. Unlike her later piece, we have detailed documentation of the spatial paths and the movement elements used in *Tanz der göttlichen Besessenheit* (see Müller, Peter, and Schuldt 1992, 135–41). The music, composed by Dimitri Wiatowitsch, was made up of a continuous rhythmic ostinato, like Ravel's *Boléro*. The space was an endlessly large circle. Herein lies the difference from the third version of *Boléro*, a whirling dance in one spot on a narrow pedestal.

69. Maurice Béjart's *Boléro* also exists in several versions. Although he used an entirely different movement vocabulary than Hoyer, what is of structural importance is the composition of a solo on a raised (round table) contrasted with circular group movements in the distance.

70. Reviews by W. Paul in the *Sächsische Tageblatt*; see Müller, Peter, and Schuldt 1992, 140. Translation: Elena Polzer.

movement in a "standing" calm—which still contained the ex-centric dissolution of what had gone before, allowing it to reverberate in erect centricity—was preceded, shortly before the finale, by a sudden interruption of the continual legato rotation. It was a final climax to the demonic rotation in a movement that disintegrated into a spasmodic staccato at exactly that point in Ravel's music in which the triumphantly resounding fanfares mark the transition of the hitherto consistently repetitive Bolero theme to the final apotheosis. In its gestural form, Hoyer's standstill at the end of the ecstatic rotation—with outstretched arms, still in an open state of rapture and yet returned from trance into the clearly outlined physical form of the self-conscious subject—sums up one last time the subject of her *Boléro*: "mankind, rotating in the crossfire of passions," in search not of self-dissolution, but of knowledge of its own limitations.

In the conscious employ and uncompromising sophistication of its dance devices, Hoyer's *Boléro* goes beyond the mere adaptation of an existential subject in expressionistic dance. Unlike Wigman, Hoyer did not interpret the subject of trance movement as the ego experiencing its affinity with the cosmos through a transpersonal dissolution of self, but as an ego aware of its limitations, aware of the fundamental loneliness of existence and consequently of its responsibilities, especially and particularly of the boundary to identity loss. The differences in Wigman's and Hoyer's approaches reflect the shift from *expressionism* to *existentialism*.

In Hoyer's exploration of the possibilities of corporeal representations of ecstasy, rotation itself became the subject of movement. Her *Boléro* tested and revealed the possibilities and constantly new variations of composing movement within tightly set motoric and choreographic confines, predetermined by the movement repertory of whirling dances. *Boléro* thus becomes a piece about whirling dance—an investigation of the inherent paradox of "dance ecstasy," as a composed and controlled exploration of the uncontrollable through dance.

FIRE DANCE: MOVEMENT PATTERNS OF METAMORPHOSIS

The various forms of trance, whirling dance, and hypnosis dance described in this chapter represent patterns of a suggestive or auto-suggestive purging of alert consciousness. They are methods for producing ecstasy through movement that loosens and opens up the stable structures of the ego in order to facilitate the return of a memory of archaic creative powers, which are "normally" (according to the theories of the psychologists) buried under and restrained beneath a layer of formalized living conditions and the generalized encoding of all (corporeal) expressions of the subject.

The partial dissolution of cultural and individual memory in trance appears to facilitate the release of primal "artistic" (Schrenck-Notzing) powers, which have their origin in the body. Whirling dance, hypnosis, and dance ecstasy thus become states of transition from the individual self to a transpersonal state of being.

In *Fear: A Dialogue* (1909), subtitled *Conversation between Dancers*, Hugo von Hofmannsthal uses the pathos formula of ecstatic dance as a model for developing a poetics "along the body's boundaries."[71] In a fictitious archaic dance, he outlines an aesthetic of creation that forms an antithesis to the Western cultural tradition of writing. The spell of the written word is broken in dance by the idea that creation is grounded in corporeality. The horizon widens to include the "Other"—the foreign in other cultures and the foreign and strange in one's own cultural sphere. In a dialogue that is structured in a way similar to Lukian's *Dialogues of the Hetaerae*, two dancers—Laidion and Hymnis—discuss the dream image of an unknown dance. In this "barbaric" ritual, the alienation of the body, perceived as a cultural product of restraint, is suspended by the experience of the primal state and integrity of the self in trancelike dance movement:

> They dance this way once a year. The young men crouch on the ground and the maidens of the Island stand together before them, their bodies uniformly still as if the limbs of one collective body. They dance and thereafter must, against their will, give themselves over to the boys, who make the young ladies theirs by grabbing them: They do it in the name of the gods, and they are blessed for it.[72]

Laidion fantasizes about the primitive dance as a ritual of initiation, as a spring sacrifice. Her vision of dance as an ecstatic act of communion is the result of feeling alienated within her own culture, of her desire "to shed the skin." Her body, torn between two worlds, feigns a physical journey into a precultural realm, a mythical existence "along the body's boundaries," which the word, the culturally encoded sign, cannot overcome. Finally, Laidion begins to dance, abandoning herself to her vision of an ecstatic primitive ritual:

---

71. Hofmannsthal 1952; on the various versions and subtitles of the dialogue as well as an overview of the dance-historical and intertextual references, see Brandstetter 1991b.

72. Hofmannsthal, *Furcht*, 575. Translation: Alessio Franko.

In this moment, Laidion begins to no longer resemble herself. Within her manic strokes hides something monstrous, menacing, and for that matter undying: the presence of a barbaric deity. Her arms flail up and down to an infernal rhythm, like swinging maces threatening lethal force. Her eyes sparkle as she closes in on ultimate bliss, the suspense intolerable.[73]

However, both Laidion's *dance* and her *vision* of an "altered state of life" (as a mystical experience quite in keeping with Musil's definition of the term) is a solo affair: the consciousness of the modern subject, its "discontent of civilization," the knowledge that alienation can only be suspended in rare moments, persists as a "stinging feeling of hope":

LAIDION: Hymnis, Hymnis! I lie there and know it—but I cannot have it! I want to scream and bite into my pillow. I want to bite into my arm and see my blood because such a thing exists, but *I cannot have it*! It shall, as a red-hot coal, burn deep inside me . . . that somewhere lies an Island where they dance and are blissful without the stinging feeling of hope. For that is what it is, Hymnis, that is everything—everything, Hymnis! Bliss in the absence of hope.[74]

This knowledge—that the moment of the loss of boundaries, the fleeting instant in which the difference between subject and object is suspended, cannot provide permanent relief, that the gap will only be even more tangible after having experienced sublime union in the transitory process of transformation in dance—this knowledge is the main topic in representations of trance dance by Hofmannsthal, Rilke, and Valéry.

However, what matters here is that the world of signs and of symbolic representation seems insurmountable—even in the representation of trance—no matter how strong the desire for an original state of being might be. The transition to a realm of the "informal,"[75] as represented by ecstatic dance, that is, the desire to reach a nonencoded space of expressivity via an expression of corporeal authenticity, is itself symbolically represented: both in the form of trance that is presented as dance, and in the talk produced by literary fiction about the unfettered body in ecstatic dance.

As a mental image, trance as dance ecstasy thus takes on a poetological function: the pathos formula of ek-stasis becomes the aesthetic model of a medial

73. Ibid.

74. Ibid.

75. The term is used here as defined in Douglas 2003.

process, namely that of metamorphosis. Transformation, as a principle of artistic production, as well as of dialogue and of the reciprocal readings of text and dance, creates links, suspends differences, liquefies the rigid boundaries between the media. In mythology (e.g., in the writings of Ovid) as well as in the natural sciences (e.g., Goethe and Romantic natural philosophy) we find descriptions of very different metamorphic phenomena and their effects.

However, the paradigm of metamorphosis is unmistakably—since the age of ancient natural philosophy—the element of fire.

In his brilliant book *The Psychoanalysis of Fire*,[76] Gaston Bachelard develops the concept that "from a primitive point of view, only those changes that are caused by fire are the deep, striking, swift, marvelous and definitive changes."[77]

Bachelard analyzes the "enormous poetic production of fire images" and explains that "fire is, among the makers of images, the one that is most dialecticized. It alone is *subject and object*."[78] The principle of contradiction is constitutive. In this "ambiguity," fire, metaphor of metaphors, appears symbolically situated between the myth of Prometheus and that of Empedocles, thus implying, in Bachelard's opinion, an option, "To seize fire or to give oneself to fire, to annihilate or to be annihilated" (112).

In the dialectic of self-abandonment and violence, love and death, fire becomes a symbol of the liminal and simultaneously "the connecting link for all symbols": "It unites matter and spirit, vice and virtue. It idealizes materialistic knowledge; it materializes idealistic knowledge. It is the principle of an essential ambiguity" (55).

This manifestation of an embodied and yet consistently shape-shifting symbolic ambivalence predestines "fire" to be a mediator between spirit and matter, between body and sign. It symbolizes the process of movement by connecting the worlds of the body and of the imagination—thus becoming the epitome of dance.

The fire dance is the concentrated image of ultimate transformation as complete consumption, even extinction of (corporeal) substance. In this process, imagined as self-exhausting movement, the elemental movements of fire represent the act of creation and simultaneously the destruction of what has been created.

Loïe Fuller's solo *Danse du Feu* (1894) is a prime example of how the metamorphosis of fire has been staged *in dance*.[79] By dancing on a panel

---

76. Bachelard 1964.

77. Ibid., 57.

78. Ibid., 111.

79. For a detailed description of the stage machinery and dance technique, as well as the historical context, see Brandstetter and Ochaim 1989.

of glass inserted in the stage floor and illuminating it with colored lights from below, Fuller combined the metamorphic moment, which was typical for her dance style with its constant transformations of moving fabric, lights and colors, with the allusion of fire. Cascades of light ranging from yellow-white and orange to flaming red traveled across her dress like the tongues of a flame, and glowing clouds surrounded her, as if she were standing in the middle of a fire. Fuller's *Danse du Feu*, dramatically presented to Richard Wagner's *Ride of the Valkyries*, conveyed the impression that her dance embodied the twitching frenetic movement of the fire element itself.

Isadora Duncan, who fully sought to combine dance and life into an individual *Gesamtkunstwerk*, once described her entire life as a fire dance. In a speech held in 1924, she spoke of herself as follows:

Like the family of the Atreids there are strains of blood whose life seems continuously enveloped in tragedy. The gods sell their gifts dearly. For every joy there is a corresponding agony. For what they give of Fame, Wealth, Love, they extract Blood and Tears and grinding sorrow. I am continually surrounded by flames.[80]

Hofmannsthal's *Electra*

Fire dance also plays a role in Hofmannsthal's Atreides tragedy *Electra* (1904). Electra's movements are restless, fierce, self-consuming. Electra's entire physiognomy of movement—interpreted as fire dance—reveals itself long before her "nameless" dance of triumph at the end of her long petrified wait in a state of vigilance—remembering and anticipating.

Electra's memories, which dominate the entire drama like evocative, ritual acts of voodoo magic, themselves resemble a fire dance,[81] in the sense that

---

80. Rosemont 1983, 26; Duncan is here referring to the tragic events in her life, e.g., the death of her two young children Deidre and Patrick, who drowned in a car accident in the Seine.

In other ways, fire dance also plays an important role as a subject matter in expressionistic dance. In the 1930s, for example, Lisa Czobel created the solo *Fire Dance*. The idea of a ritual fire dance, "Danza ritual de fuego," mainly gained notoriety thanks to Manuel de Falla's music for the dance piece *El amor brujo* (*Love the Magician*, 1915), which was inspired by flamenco motifs.

81. In this fire dance, Electra assumes the role of the maenad, presenting herself in a state of catalepsy and passionate "animalistic" expressive gesture; on the body imagery of the dance of the maenad, as regards Hofmannsthal's *Electra*, see the section on the "Dance of the Maenad." A short summary of the most important aspects of research concerning the

Electra is allowing her entire being, her potential in life, the entire structure of meaning in her existence, to be consumed by a process of incessant remembering in the twilight zone of death, caught up between patricide and matricide until she finally extinguishes herself in the end.

Hence, the fire dance here also takes on a key function in the visual imagery of Hofmannsthal's drama—both in the stage directions and in the language of the characters. During the entire course of the tragedy, the pathos formula of the fire dance is present as a gestural model, image of movement, and virtual energetic symbol. The semantic spectrum of fire is thus—in keeping with the affect structure of Hofmannsthal's concept of the tragic—directed at the utmost extremes of symbolic meaning (without the middle field of warmth).[82] The movement figuration of the self-consuming flame becomes a pathos formula for the ek-statis of this most intensive of affects. The motif of fire links— like the motif of blood, which has been given more attention in research on *Electra*[83]—life and death, love and hate, self-discovery and loss of self in the ecstatic moment.

Electra's wild, demonic, animalistic movements are conspicuously and frequently illuminated by the fiery glow of torchlight. Thus they appear as a reflection (in the dual sense) of gigantically magnified, delayed, and grotesquely distorted shadows. In her major entrance monologue, Electra envisions the goal and outcome of her endeavors as a bloody deed of vengeance for the patricide and her dance of triumph as a grim, bloodstained performance of sublime shadow theater held for the dead father:

> We, your blood, will dance around your grave:
> and above the dead men I will lift my knee
> high in the air, step by step, and they
> who will see me dance, yes, even they
> who will see my shadow only from afar
> dancing so, they will say: for a great king
> this royal pageantry is being held

interpretation of *Electra* in terms of "hysteria" can be found in Wolfgang Nehring's "Electra and Oedipus" (1991, 130f.).

82. Bachelard particularly emphasizes the aspect of warmth in the iconographic spectrum of fire; the development of the quasi-domesticated (hearth) fire on the one hand, and the image of love, as "inner" warmth on the other: "Where the eye cannot go, there warmth insinuates itself" (1964, 40).

83. On the blood motif, see Mayer 1993, 235 ff.

by his flesh and blood, and happy is he
who has children that dance such royal dances
of victory around his noble grave![84]

At the end of a highly affect-laden dialogue between Electra and Clytemnestra, in which Electra confronts her mother with her desire to murder her, Electra stands before her "in the wildest intoxication." Clytemnestra summons servants. Torches are lit so that "a red-yellow glare floods the walls" (103). Electra's fire dance becomes ever more violent and appears in the dramatic climax of a dense sequence of images toward the end of the "deed." After having already extolled the beauty of the deed in an image of "flames"[85] to her brother Orestes and envisioned her part in the murder of the murderers—"blessed . . . who holds the torch for him"—she executes a "fire dance" in front of Aegisthus. Swaying back and forth in an eerie "dance" and speaking in riddles, she leads him to the threshold behind which death waits for him: a demonic game in the presence of horrors.

Electra leads the dance of death by taking "the torch out of the ring," bowing before Aegisthus, so that he is frightened by the "disheveled figure in the flickering light": "Why do you stagger / back and forth with your light! . . . What are you dancing for? / Watch the way." Electra's distorted movements in the flickering flames suddenly appear as ambiguous as her words: as a fire dance, as ecstatic, seemingly uncontrolled and uncontrollable affectivity on the one hand and as the coldly ironic, accurate, and conscious "performance" of a dancer of death fully aware of her final goal on the other:

Electra *as she circles around him in a kind of weird dance, suddenly*
bowing very low
Here! the steps,
lest you fall. . . .
They are the men
who want to wait on you in person, my lord. (137)

In this manner, Electra's flame-driven movements climax in her "nameless dance" at the end of the drama: in a final, ultimate blaze of affect and the subsequent extinguishing of the fire.

84. Hofmannsthal 1966, 76–77.

85. Ibid., 130: "Blessed is he / who may do a deed! The deed is like . . . a bed of balsam, to rest the soul / which is a wound, a blight, an ulcer, / and a flame!"

The dramatic version of *Electra* merely represents this moment of heightened suspense *as dance*—as an ephemeral, highly intense corporeal gesture symbolized by silence and by a lack of words, but the operatic version from 1908 translates the subject of fire back from the ecstatic movement image of dance into the *linguistic gesture of text*:[86]

> The seeds of darkness did I sow
> and reap joy upon joy.
> A blackened corpse once was I
> Among the living and this glad hour
> The flame of life hath made me,
> And my fierce flame consumeth
> The gloom of all the world.
> And my face must glow far whiter
> Than the moonlight when
> it glows most white.
> And who so beholds me
> Must unto death be stricken
> Or be lost in pain of joy.
> See ye all not my face?
> See ye that light
> That from me doth shine?[87]

And at the end of the operatic version, trance is *cited as dance* in an allusion to the whirling dance of the dervishes by using the words of Jelaleddin Rumi—"Ah! Love kills! But nobody passes on without having known love!"[88]

Rilke's "Spanish Dancer"

In his depiction of flamenco in the poem "Spanish Dancer," Rainer Maria Rilke composed a fire dance as drama en miniature. Unlike Hofmannsthal's *Electra*,

86. This shift is, of course, linked to the change of theatrical genres, from drama to opera; a subject that—especially regarding the finale of *Electra*—requires interpretation of its own, while taking into account Richard Strauss's composition, as well as the practical and historical contexts of the performance; for a discussion of the opera finale, I would like to mention Carl Dahlhaus's theories on the divergence of the text's structure of argumentation and structure of affect (as subtext) as representative for more recent research on *Electra*: Dahlhaus 1991.

87. Hofmannsthal 1910, 57; full libretto online: http://www.archive.org/stream/elektratragedyin00strauoft/elektratragedyin00strauoft_djvu.txt.

88. Hofmannsthal probably discovered this sentence in Erwin Rohde's book *Psyche*. He also made use of it in his Oscar Wilde study, "Sebastian Melmoth."

which uses the pathos formula of fire dance to revisit as classic Greek tragedy in the form of a psychodrama about the modern subject,[89] Rilke's flamenco dancer expresses the entire dramatic spectrum of love and hate, of passion aroused and extinguished, of passion's dangerous game of control and loss of control—in short, the precisely measured and perfectly focused movement vocabulary of the "Spanish (fire) dance."

Rilke's description of flamenco is entirely based on fire imagery. He uses a theatrical metaphor to sustain the idea of dance as flame through the entire poem in an associative series of images:

> As in one's hand a sulphur match, whitely,
> Before it comes aflame, to every side
> Darts twitching tongues—: within the circle
> Of close watchers hasty, bright and hot
> Her round dance begins twitching to spread itself.
> And suddenly it is altogether flame.
> With her glance she sets light her hair
> and all at once with daring art
> whirls her whole dress within this conflagration,
> out of which her naked arms upstretch
> like startled snakes awake and rattling
> And then: as though the fire were tightening round her,
> she gathers it all in one and casts it off
> very haughtily, with imperious gesture
> and watches: it lies there raging on the ground
> and still flames and will not give in—.
> Yet conquering, sure and with a sweet
> Greeting smile she lifts her countenance
> And stamps it out with little sturdy feet.[90]

The poem demarcates the space created by the dancer in the dance movement: an imaginary space, in which the typical motions of flamenco stretch outward into the space—hard accentuated, violent turns of the head and torso alternating with soft arm movements, the powerful rhythmic footwork of the *zapateado*. The text explores, almost as a linguistic flamenco partner,

89. The transformation of the great mythical themes of Greek tragedy into psychodramas (not in terms of the therapeutic form of Moreno's psychodrama, but rather as a relocation of dramatic structures into the "vast landscape" of the soul of the subject) can also be found in Martha Graham's major pieces on antiquity; see the description of her piece *Errand into the Maze* in the section on the topos formula labyrinth in Part II of this book.

90. Rilke 1962, 177.

the suppleness of dance language in the rhythm of the lines and the change of meter—hard idioms and soft enjambment in a delayed gestural turn. Unlike in Hofmannsthal's *Electra*, the moment in which control is lost in the play with fire appears here to be no more than a tiny moment of danger. The sensual, artistic presentation of confident dance movement, of body control and the act of spellbinding the audience through movement, prevails. With the help of the theatrical metaphor, Rilke assigns the attribute of Spanish temperament—via the image of the "fiery" dancer[91]—to the movement and to the subject of the movement. In the dance, the dancer simultaneously becomes the flame and its keeper.

Rilke's poem, moreover, provides an exposition of the most important aspects of dance and dance-texts: dance dramaturgy as a succession and climax of movement elements; the contrast between controlled and released gesture, between discipline and ecstasy as models of discovering and losing oneself as an individual; the duality of nature and culture, of movement and stasis, of the ephemeral versus the eternal in the transitory process of signification and designification.

Valéry's *Dance and the Soul*

The processual aspect of metamorphosis as a productive aesthetic principle along with the transitory aspect of dance thus appear as two mutually related sides of a poetics of creation, which can be understood—according to Paul Valéry—as an open-ended act of expenditure and self-generating, as well as "self-consuming," signification. According to this philosophy of expenditure, dance and poetry are combined in the movement image of the flame:

> Or our philosopher may just as well compare the dancer to a flame or, for that matter, to any phenomenon that is visibly sustained by the intense consumption of a superior energy. [Notre philosophe peut aussi bien comparer la danseuse à une flamme, et, en somme, à tout phénomène visiblement entretenu, par la consommation intense d'une énergie de qualité supérieure].[92]

---

91. Rilke drew his inspiration for this poem from two very different artistic experiences: one being the performance of a "Spanish dancer" presented by the "Gitana" Carmela at the atelier of Zuloaga during a party, and the other being a painting by Goya, *La Ballerina Carmen, la Gitana*, which was exhibited on this same occasion. For Rilke, both images merge in the "Spanish dancer," both the moving image and the one affixed to the picture frame.

92. Valéry, "Philosophie de la danse," in Valéry 1960, 1: 1396; English in Valéry 1964a.

In Valéry's text *Dance and the Soul*[93]—which, like Hofmannsthal's *Fear*, is composed as a dialogue about dance following the Platonic models—Valéry steers the conversation on dance to a climax in which the dancer fully seems to embody the flame.

The Socratic dialogue about a female dancer and various aspects of dance between a philosopher (Socrates), a doctor (Eryximachus), and a scientist (Phaedrus) ultimately begets dance itself in an image of fire as a pure phenomenon of transformation. First, however, various arguments and hypotheses are introduced in a game of questions and answers and discussed while watching the Hetaera perform a dance during the philosopher's banquet:

> The problematic relationship of language and body, of truth and falsehood in expression; the subject of the gaze—concerning the perspective of the onlooker; the correlation of mimesis, rhetoric and hermeneutics; finally, the specific role that art places in the production of knowledge—in the "Socratic art" of dance, which reveals the unconscious aspect of everyday movement when reflected in dance movement.

The conversation focuses on the subject of metamorphosis as regards the dancer Athikte. Her dance, so says Socrates, is a "pure act of metamorphosis." Dance movement brings the body to "vie in speed and variety with its own soul" and so "this whirling into the greatest agility humanly possible, . . . [has] the virtues and powers of flame" (77).

In Athikte's dance, the game of transformation manifests as the dialectic of form and moments of pure presence: "she is showing us the instant" and "the instant begets form, and form shows us the instant."[94]

Socrates uses the image of fire to describe this model of metamorphosis, in which pure presence and the transitory in time and movement are paradoxically and inextricably connected: the dancer appears "as if she were living quite at her ease, in an element comparable to fire" (196), in ecstasy and an intensity of the fusion of everything corporeal in movement, which has "the virtues and powers of flame":

> But what is a flame, my friends, if not *the moment itself?*—All that is mad and joyous and awful in the very moment itself! . . . Flame is the act of the moment which is between earth and Heaven. O my friends, all that

93. Valéry, 1964b. All quotations here were taken from this translation unless otherwise noted; page numbers in the text.

94. Valéry 1951, 89.

passes from the state of heaviness to the state of subtlety, passes through the moment of fire and light. (79)

And flame too, is it not the intangible and haughty form of the noblest destruction?—What will never happen again happens magnificently before our eyes!—What will never happen again is bound to happen as magnificently as possible!—As the voice sings passionately, as the flame sings madly between matter and ether—and rushes and roars furiously from matter to ether—so, is not the great Dancing, my friends, the liberation of our bodies, which is wholly possessed by the spirit of falsehood, and by music which is falsehood too, and drunk with the denial of non-reality?—Look at that body leaping like flame replacing flame, look how it treads and tramples on reality. How furiously and joyously it destroys the very place where it happens to be, and how intoxicated it becomes with the excess of its changes! (197)

Caught up in the movements of the fire dance, which is commented on by the philosopher, the dancer falls into trance, at the mercy of that process which harbors the "secret of the energy emanations" (Gaston Bachelard) and glides over into the insanity of a whirling dance. Valéry lets the silent dance of Athikte, "bespoken" by the three partners in the philosophical conversation, end in the vortex of a whirling dance and finally in collapse—like Laidion's dance in Hofmannsthal's *Fear* and like Electra's dance:

She turns . . .
One would think this could last forever.
She could die, thus . . .
She would rest motionless in the very center of her movement. Alone,
Alone to herself, like the axis of the world . . .
She turns and turns . . . She is falling! (*Dialogues* 1958, 60–61)

And like Laidion, Athikte awakens from her trance state to experience the paradox of simultaneous joy and wise sorrow over the ex-centricity of the moment of ecstasy in the vortex. Words emerge from the paradox. Athikte speaks: "Refuge, refuge, O my refuge, O Whirlwind! I was in thee, I movement—outside all things" (*Dialogues* 1958, 62).

Valéry gives the dancer the final say in the philosophical dialogue: the awareness of difference gives birth to self-reflection in language.

The metamorphosis in the consuming flames thus appears as a transition from body-image to text.[95] The fire dance itself already implies, as Bachelard

95. On this aspect of the transition from body to text, the relationship of poet and dancer, of image (photography) and dance, see the section on Valéry in the chapter "The Dancer as Muse."

notes, the fundamental ambiguity of the metamorphic concept of the flame. The image of fire connects "the soul and the dance" in the transformation process of the body, in the expenditure of movement.[96]

The idiosyncrasy of dance as an art form manifests itself in the metamorphosis of the moving body into signs. The dancer writes rhythmic symbols into the space in a temporal order established by the movement. The sequentiality of the dance movements condenses into a figuration in the moment, in aesthetic perception as "momental sensation" (Wilhelm Heinse). Hence, it is the transitory aspect of dance events, the interwoven antitheses of body and sign, of nature and culture linked solely in the moment, that determines the idiosyncrasy of dance. This moment of transformation at its most extreme, this moment that dance allows to *manifest* as something entirely different, nonsignifiable as in no other art form, explains the special fascination that this art form holds for poets: those masters of language who, by immortalizing themselves for eternity in writing, are secretly envious of the living magic of the fleeting corporeal art.

In the context and chiasm of language crises and proliferations of discourse, the wordless art of dance does not just appear to offer an alternative to the question of legitimate authorship—"Who is speaking?" More importantly, Terpsichore tempts the poet with his probably greatest and most silent desire: the longing for eloquent silence. The phantasm of dance gives form to the expressive moment, in which all signs are extinguished, the emphatic lapse into silence.

Rilke, in his poem "Spanish Dancer," and Valéry in his dialogue *Dance and the Soul*, evoke the image of the flame to describe a dancer entirely consumed by the intensity of the moment. Consuming fire or pure light describes the total transformation of the corporeal, the standstill of movement at the center of the vortex, the blinding empty space of dissipation: the nonsign at the heart of dance.

---

96. Gerhart Hauptmann and Carl Einstein also explored the subject of the fire dance: in Hauptmann's glasswork tale "And Pippa Dances," the graceful character of Pippa embodies a "spark of the great fire" in her dance between the heavy glass furnaces, which control the fire. Pippa appears as a winged creature, as Psyche, in contrast to the aggressive violence of her counterpart, the old Huhn. And in the pantomime *Nuronihar*, previously mentioned in the chapter on bee dance, fire also takes on the ambiguous function of a gigantic celestial body. Ambiguity likewise characterizes Nuronihar's dance: the magic of the ecstatic movement and the scorching heat consume dance and dancer in the end.

Chapter 4

The Dancer as Muse

THE PATHOS FORMULA OF PAUL VALÉRY'S *INSPIRATRICE*

The turn-of-the-century crisis of the subject, which challenged the saying about individualism valid since Goethe's time—"individuum est ineffabile"—also significantly affected the subject of artistic production. With the onset of modernity, traditional notions surrounding the conditions and forms of creative expression—notably this idea that "ingenium est ineffabile"[1]—were called into question, and the pretense of the myth of artistic creativity as a function of inspiration was tarnished and even shattered in various ways.

At the beginning of the twentieth century new forms of knowledge and scientific discourse arose that contributed in particular to a disenchantment with the aura of inspiration surrounding the creative act: these included studies of the role of memory, and research on the structure of the imagination in psychology and psychoanalysis. The muse's kiss, probably the pathos formula of artistic creativity par excellence, was discarded from the rhetorical repertory of aesthetic production. The self-definition of the creative subject—especially the literary subject—no longer relied upon the traditional topoi of invoking the muse. In the crisis surrounding the legitimate authorship of art—the crisis of artistic identity itself—alternative concepts of creativity appeared as ways around such clichés or as mediating constructions.

Dance, as a new poetic role model, took on a central role in the dissolution of conventional concepts of creativity. Dance, in fact, offered an alternative figuration of the creative, one that transcends writing per se. As a medium of the transitory production of signs, dance movement drew attention to the

---

1. On the subject of creativity, theories of inspiration, and representations of the creative in nineteenth-century literature, cf. Blamberger 1991.

processual character of creativity, to the self-referentiality of the system; and to the dialogical quality of structures and media involved in the creative process. The function of the author and the prominent role of the artwork itself as a unified whole thus faded into the background. Consequently, as dance redefined and reconstituted itself as an independent art form at the beginning of the twentieth century, it simultaneously inspired new criteria for a sophisticated aesthetics of literature.

In this way, dance became the "inspiratrice" of the early twentieth-century artistic avant-garde. For writers, the dancer embodied the pathos formula of the muse in a new way through her act of transformation and ultimately of dissolution into intangible images and symbols of pure movement.

This relationship of poet and dancer manifested itself in various ways. For Hugo von Hofmannsthal, for example, the solistic role of the poet in the "icy silent tower chamber of his loneliness" amid a "universe of books"[2] transformed itself through contact with the medium of dance into a redeeming conversation, a "duet." For the poet, the artistic dialogue with dancers such as Ruth St. Denis and Grete Wiesenthal became a wellspring of alternative creative aesthetics, which transcended the bind of the written word and raised the corporeal art of dance to the status of antithesis to the written word.[3] In these conversations, the author ascribed to himself the role of reader attempting to decipher the moving expression contained in the body of the dancer. Physiognomy and pathognomy thus became patterns of interpretation, as well as sources of inspiration, especially for literature, because of the way that they rejected language's archive of citations and created instead a poetic vision out of the very ephemeral art of the corporeal. In this constellation of "conversation with the dancer," Hofmannsthal interpreted the author as the reader of movement and, as librettist, as the director of movement scenarios. The act of inspiration and creativity took place as a dynamic process between media, in a dialogue of text and dance, of body and word.

Unlike Hofmannsthal, Stéphane Mallarmé defined dance as a kind of autopoetic system: not as a creative process transpiring in the interaction between poet and dance maker, but as a kind of generation of semiotic structures that—hermetically sealed off against all conventional semantics—are entirely self-referential and generate themselves autonomously. For Mallarmé, dance—in particular Loïe Fuller's *Serpentine Dance*—brings forth figurations of movement that weave a texture of corporeal and textual signs into the empty space.

2. Hofmannsthal, *Der Tisch mit den Büchern* (*The Table with the Books*), 1979, A I, 339. Translation: Elena Polzer.

3. On the historical and aesthetic contexts, see Brandstetter 1991b.

Within this space the dancer herself as creator of these signs disappears.[4] This process of continuous destruction, becoming, and metamorphosis of the movement figures of dance became, for Mallarmé, the model of a pure poetry (*poésie pure*). The author vanishes in the text; the web of signs continues to exist of its own accord as a pulsating, "vibratory" generation of meaning structures produced by the dancer in the transitory act of her fleeting, temporal performance.

Last, but not least, Paul Valéry developed a poetic model based on the complementarity of dance and text, of movement and immobility, of ecstasy and analysis. The assumption of multiple perspectives by the beholder emerges as a paradigm not only for scientific epistemology, but also as a model for a poetics swinging back and forth between analysis and myth, seeking to combine the developments of technology and media with the ecstasy of artistic inspiration.

In the Laboratory of Signs: Biomechanics and Poetics of Dance in the Writings of Paul Valéry

In his essay "Degas Dance Drawing" (1936), Valéry sketches, by way of a series of excursions, digressions, "sayings," and anecdotes, far more than just the portrait of the painter Edgar Degas, whom he much admired. In light of Degas's work, his ascetic and uncompromising notion of art, his steady will for perfection and his dislike of any form of sentimentality or modernist aestheticism, Valéry develops a theory of art that provides a key to understanding his own poetry as well. In the short chapter "De la Danse," Degas, the illustrator, painter, and sculptor of dancers, provides the impetus for a theory of dance that becomes, despite its rambling line of argumentation, a model for advanced poetic theory. The constellation of semiotic *systems*—image, dance, text—and the semiotic and compositional *elements*—line, surface, space, time—take on a complementary relationship. Dance, which the poet observes and translates from the perspective of the visual artist as line and modeling, oscillates between image and text. In his "Philosophy of the Dance," Valéry outlines this intermedial, processual definition of dance, which ". . . sometimes changes [. . .] brusquely into a whirlwind, spinning faster and faster, then suddenly stops, crystallized into a statue, adorned with an alien smile."[5]

In "Degas Dance Drawing," Valéry draws near to an aesthetic determination of what dance is ("What in reality *is* dance?")[6] as a theory of dissipation.

4. On Mallarmé's dance-oriented poetology, cf. Brandstetter and Ochaim 1989, 140–47; and Brandstetter 1991a.

5. Valéry 1964a, 206.

6. Valéry 1951, 49.

He understands the art of movement from the perspective of energetic factors, explaining it with respect to an economy of drives and affect.[7] For Valéry, dance movements are the opposite of utilitarian everyday movements, which are determined by intentional and reproductive factors and efficiency. "Most of our movements are voluntary and have an external action as an end. . . . Once the goal is attained . . . our movement . . . ceases."[8]

As Valéry argues, the definitive factor is, above all, "our body's relation to the object and to our intention."[9] The functional allocation of movement is simultaneously its demarcation. Economy and energy are crucial for utilitarian and purpose-oriented movements: "This kind of movement always takes place according to a law of the economy of forces . . . which is in control of our energy expenditure."[10] These goal-oriented movements governed by a rationally organized economy of energy expenditure contrast with movements developed "of their own accord," without a spatially determined purpose and without a limiting aim—as forms of dissipation: "Instead of being subject to economic conditions, it seems to the contrary, that they have the dissipation of energy as their object."[11]

Movement for movement's sake, movement whose only goal is itself and the creation of a distinct state, is characterized by repetition. Movements, such as those generated by affects of joy or anger, are born of prodigality and terminate in fatigue. At this point in his reflection Valéry formulates his thoughts on the physiology of movement in light of the ordering function of time and the meaning of repetition. From this angle, movement is based on

a cycle of muscular acts that reproduce themselves, as if the conclusion or the accomplishment of the act in each case engendered the impulse to the next act. On this model, our members can execute a series of movements each one of which leads uninterruptedly to the next, and the frequency of which is productive of a sort of inebriation that goes from languor to delirium, from a sort of hypnotic abandon to a sort of furor.[12]

7. Valéry's ideas on energy expenditure and exhaustion are similar to the theories of Georges Bataille (in his *Eroticism*) and to those of Jean Baudrillard (in *Symbolic Exchange and Death*); cf. the previous chapter on "Delirium of Movement."

8. Valéry, "Degas Danse Dessin" (1960, 2: 1170). Translation: Mark Franko.

9. Ibid.. For more on Valéry and his philosophy of dance, see Sasportes 1989, 61–77.

10. Ibid.

11. Ibid.

12. Ibid., 1171.

Valéry understands ecstasy as that state proper to dance, that delirious state of movement which Roger Caillois describes in his book *Man, Play and Games* (1961) as a cultic manifestation of "vertigo." Everything, from mask to vertigo, is "delirium, ecstasy, trance, convulsion."[13]

For Valéry, what precedes this idea of dance as a state (*état*) is the shift from purely muscular to expressive movement, from physiology to art—a speculative conclusion that attempts to deduce the idiosyncrasy of dance, the state of ecstasy, from a "biomechanically" formulated hypothesis. If such exact empirical studies already exist in the natural sciences, in physiology, according to Valéry, then dance can be ascribed to a "neuromuscular phenomenon," related to the physical phenomenon of "resonance." The rhythmic repetition in the motor process of "muscle activity," the succession of figurations thus initiated and assembling themselves in a syntax of movements, correlates in this line of thought with physical laws of resonance. Vibrations and feedback processes, reflected in waves and loops, become the figurative models of dance movement: the buildup into "a frenzy," the intensification of the resonance curve from movement and excitement to a "kind of raving madness"—analogous to cybernetic processes in physics.

Valéry's excursion into the scientific deduction of the movement art—in a form of analogizing speculation—was not, however, aimed at providing *scientific proof* of an aesthetic phenomenon, but rather at formulating *poetic evidence*.

By reducing dance to its motor functions and to a physiology of movement, with recourse to physical laws of resonance and feedback, Valéry attempted to develop a scientifically substantiated poetics as the fundamental basis of an aesthetic, which incidentally also anticipated the same structures of recurrence and chaos theory that would later become decisive for the aesthetics of postmodernism.[14]

In his study on Valéry,[15] Karl Löwith points out that the poet's characterization of modernity, namely the oscillation between the "two chasms of order and chaos," is what also constituted the crisis of the European mind. Löwith stresses Valéry's Cartesianism as being the fundamental philosophical concept underlying his work with its emphasis on the automatism of living beings ("animal machine") and Valéry's distinctive transformation of Descartes's "Cogito, ergo sum" into the formula: "Je fonctionne, donc je suis" (I function, therefore I am).[16]

---

13. Caillois 1961, 102.

14. On the relationship between chaos theory and postmodern poetics (and aesthetics), see the writings of Botho Strauß and the previous section on "Collapse of Memory" in this book.

15. Löwith 1991.

16. Valéry 1957–61, 7: 838.

In his reflections on dance—in both "Degas Dance Drawing" and *Dance and the Soul*—this Cartesianism plays an important role. Valéry "constructs"[17] his poetics of dance on the basis of a (bio)mechanics of the locomotive system. In the section "Horse, Dance, and Photography," he relates photography and painting to dance en pointe and horse dressage.[18] Degas, who was a great painter not only of dancers, but also of horses (in the tradition of Géricault), "was one of the first to study the real appearance of this noble animal through the snapshots of a Major Muybridge."[19]

Eadweard Muybridge's chronophotography,[20] his series of images of horses, birds, and athletes in motion,[21] assembled in a photo book entitled *Animal Locomotion*,[22] resulted in a new awareness of the flow of physical locomotion: "Muybridge's shots revealed the errors into which all sculptors and painters fell when representing the different ways of locomotion of horses."[23]

However, when Valéry points out such mimetic deficiencies, he is not concerned with naturalistic representation, but rather with the consequences of an alternative theory of perception that is based on the technology of photography. This new, more precise medium of documenting movement reveals the fictions

17. On Valéry's concept of "construiere," cf. Schmidt-Radefeldt 1986.

18. Cf. Valéry 1951, 69–75; regarding Degas's representation of body and movement, animal and dancers, Valéry begins his remarks with the conceit: "The horse walks on his toes. Four hoofs support him. No animal resembles the leading dancer, the star of the ballet like a thoroughbred horse seemingly suspended in perfect balance by the hand of his rider, and walking slowly in full sunlight" (1948, 35). Valéry does not cite a drawing of Degas, but a text by Degas; a line of verse from a sonnet in which Degas dealt with everything at once, "its training, speed, the bets and frauds, its beauty and supreme elegance": "Nervously nude in his dress of silk" [Tout nerveusement nu danse sa robe de soie] (35).

19. Valéry 1948, 36. *Translator's note*: This translation is highly unreliable in that it eliminates large swaths of text without calling itself an abridged edition. Notably, all Valéry's thoughts on dance are deleted from this publication. I have therefore translated some quotations from this essay directly from the Edition de la Pléiade.

20. Cf. Zglinicki 1979, 166–85, and Frizot 1984; on the relationship of movement photography, film, and war technique, see Kittler 1999, 124: "In order to focus on and fix objects moving through space, such as people, there are two procedures: to shoot and to film."

21. On serial exposure and its meaning for the development of modern dance, see Brandstetter and Ochaim 1989, 123ff.

22. Muybridge 1881–1885. In it are pictured, e.g., on plate 370, the "battement" movements of a (naked) gymnast, on plate 193, the dance movements of a young girl, in a long translucent shirtdress, hair loose, dancing barefoot, in the Delsarte style of Genevieve Stebbins and anticipating Isadora Duncan's reform style; cf. also Emmanuel 1895.

23. Valéry 1960, 2: 1191. Translation: Mark Franko.

of the "inventive eye."[24] When reading movement, the eye of the viewer completes and interprets as a figuration of meaning that which is merely present as "raw, unconnected events" and irreconcilable opposites in a "world merely composed of blots."[25]

The *idea* of movement, in which *conventions* of perception fill in the gaps left by sensory perception, generally creates—as Valéry says—pictures of movement or moving images. Those phenomena that we "sum up as space, time, matter and movement"[26] are thus merely products of common opinion, of convention, which allow us to believe in the "congruity, transitions, transformations" of such events. Conventionalized perception consequently shapes the general idea we have of movement:

> And perhaps, if we could examine this representation of the past with enough subtlety, we might be able to find the *law* of its unconscious falsifications, that which allows us to draw moments of the flights of birds or the gallop of horses as if we were actually at leisure to observe them: but these interpolated moments are imaginary. One only attributed *probable* figures to these speedily moving bodies and it would not lack interest in a comparative study of such documents to grasp this order of creation in which understanding fills in the gaps left by our senses.[27]

This is the form of deception—emerging from the blind spots of a conventionalized, desensitized gaze and from predetermined perspectives—that the artist attempts to dissolve on the basis of a new approach to perception that allows insight into the mechanics of movement through the medium of technology, the serial pictograms of chronophotography.

The *unmasking* of a priori blueprints and patterns of perception and *construction* based on biomechanical analysis are the operations performed in the laboratory of the modern artist.

Like Degas, who used Muybridge's photos as models for his movement studies, Valéry enlists Etienne-Jules Marey's chronophotograph series for his poetics of dance. Marey improved Muybridge's photographic technique by developing a "chronophotographic gun." With the help of this photographic rifle, which worked like a double-action revolver, movement sequences that

24. Valéry 1960, 2: 1191. Translation: Mark Franko. "On vit alors combien l'oeil est inventif."

25. On the problems of "patchiness" in perception, cf. Botho Strauß and his ideas based on chaos theory in *Beginnlosigkeit*, 1992.

26. Valéry 1960, 2, 1192. Translation: Mark Franko.

27. Ibid.

were not discernable to the naked eye in their individual moments, could now be analyzed and recorded (figure 51). Marey published his chronophotograph experiments in 1873 under the title *La machine animale*, the same study that also influenced Valéry's theory of perception. In a letter to Louis Séchan in August 1930, in which he explains after the fact the development of *Dance and the Soul*, Valéry writes that his only inspirations for the dialogue were books by Maurice Emmanuel on Greek dance[28] and Marey's book, which he had owned since the 1930s and had lying open on his desk.[29]

The recourse to photographic studies, which reconnected dance as an art form to mechanics and the physiological functionality of movement, indicates the ambivalent structure of Valéry's aesthetic reflections, in the pendular movement of his thoughts in the *Cahiers*, alternating between a "sensibilité" of the mind and studies on the vital functions of the body: "The constant thought of the Dialogue [*Dance and the Soul*] is physiological" [La pensée constante du Dialogue est physiologique].[30]

In his reflections on dance, Valéry mainly focuses on the reactions of the sympathetic and vegetative nervous system, as well as the biomechanics of movement. For him, the surplus of art can be defined from this "animalistic" perspective only when the abstract and the sensual gradually merge in ecstasy.[31]

Valéry's model of physiology and the biomechanics of movement became the starting point and the configuring referential framework of a constructivist aesthetics: construction, and hence dance, is a method to escape the vegetative life dominated by physiological procedures.

This premise of a semiotically founded line of reasoning, based on a poetics of movement rooted in physiology and biomechanics, suggests comparison with Vsevolod Meyerhold's concept of biomechanics as developed for avant-garde theater.[32]

28. See Emmanuel 1916.

29. See Valéry 1960, 1: 1407. Translation: Mark Franko: "As a matter of fact, I limited myself to leafing through Emmanuel's book at the Library and I also left open on my table the Marey book I have had for thirty years now. These draughts of jumping and walking, some memories of ballets were my essential resources." On the specifics of Marey's chronophotography, which—unlike Muybridge's—(sometimes) presented the movement phases not side by side, but in a single photograph, see Frizot 1984.

30. Valéry 1960, 1: 1408. Translation: Mark Franko.

31. As in a ballet, writes Valéry of this text, "the abstract and the sensuous take turns leading and finally blend in vertigo" [L'abstrait et la sensible mènent tour à tour et s'unissent enfin dans le vertige]. Paul Valéry letter to Louis Séchan (1930) reproduced in 1960, 1: 1408 (translation: Mark Franko).

32. On Meyerhold's concept of biomechanics, on the subject of the body in avant-garde theater and dance, see the section on "Interruption" in Part II of this book.

Biomechanics here refers to the term used by Meyerhold to describe his method of training actors[33]—a method that he developed in an attempt to distance himself from Stanislavsky's psycho-technical concept of representation. Meyerhold argued that actors must "study the mechanics of the body." The "physical foundation" of corporeal representation must be laid by movement studies such as "gymnastics, acrobatics, dance, rhythmics, boxing and fencing":

> All psychological states are determined by specific physiological processes. By correctly resolving the nature of his state physically, the actor reaches the point where he experiences the *excitation*, which communicates itself to the spectator.[34]

Meyerhold's goal was to develop an approach of "outside-in," a materialistic, quasi-physiotechnical model—which later also played an important role in the physical culture movement—that has a "scientific basis."[35] In his constructivist aesthetics, Meyerhold attempted to draw parallels between art and the technology found in modern industrial labor. Hence, he mainly addressed the organization of material. According to Meyerhold, the artist always also takes on the role of the engineer. The conscious disposition of his "material," of the body and movements as semiotic factors of performance, necessarily demands a study of the "laws of biomechanics."

Like Valéry's thinking, which is based on mechanical and energetic processes of movement and includes the economy of everyday movements, Meyerhold reflected the effort involved in movement, the factor of time, the economy of working motions. In brief, he translated Taylorism into theater:

> If we observe a skilled worked in action, we notice the following in his movements: (1) an absence of superfluous, unproductive movements: (2) rhythm; (3) the correct positioning of the body's center of gravity; (4) stability. Movements based on these criteria are distinguished by their dance-like quality; a skilled worker at work invariably reminds one of a dancer; thus work borders on art.[36]

---

33. For a summary of the basic principles of "biomechanics," cf. Meyerhold's essay "The Actor of the Future and Biomechanics" (1922 [1969]).

34. Cited in Braun 1978, 199.

35. Cited in Brauneck 1984, 249. One of the principles of Meyerhold's "biomechanics" was Bechterev's reflexology; see Fischer-Lichte 1989a, 474.

36. Cited in Braun 1978, 198.

The forms and principles of operation of "economic"[37] movement, which Meyerhold lists here, correspond with the central terms that define the work of dancers: "rhythm," balance as a "positioning of the body's centre of gravity," stamina. By correlating work and art—based on "science" and labor technology—Meyerhold sought to establish an aesthetics of movement and movement signs that linked life and art. Their formalization produces new conditions for producing meaning in theater: by detaching themselves from the sign language of psychological realism, the body and the actor's movements undergo "an incredible growth in semioticity: they are now capable of producing signs for random objects, persons, relationships. They have become material for random semiotic processes."[38]

Meyerhold's theory of a "Taylorization of Theater," his thoughts on rhythmic movement as economic movement, his comparison of the beauty of skilled working motions with the aesthetics of dance, adapted theories already voiced by Karl Bücher in his widely read *Work and Rhythm* (1897), which was republished in 1924 in its sixth edition. Unlike anthropological theories of culture, which ascribe dance to play or seek its origins in ritual,[39] Bücher's basic hypothesis is that the origins of dance lie in rhythmic working movements that combine function and aesthetics. This idea had a great influence on the German *Rhythmusbewegung* [rhythm movement],[40] although leading rhythm pedagogues such as Rudolf Bode, Max Merz, and Rudolf von Laban did not deduce a theory of Taylorization of dance from it, but rather developed a *Weltanschauung des Tänzers* [a philosophy of the dancer] that was wary of civilization and hostile toward technology.[41]

The *Rhythmusbewegung* likewise based its theories and pedagogical system on the teachings of leading psychologists and physiologists such as Wilhelm Wundt and Melchior Palágyi. However, it is interesting to note in passing—in order to shed some light on the range of contrary ambivalent tendencies prevalent in contemporaneous avant-garde movements at the time—that the effects of this new knowledge on the movements and the conclusions that it

37. Meyerhold's concept of a Taylorization of the theater refers not only to movement, but also to the economy of time in theater, for example, the time required for putting on makeup, dressing, intermissions, and plot of the play.

38. Fischer-Lichte 1989a, 477. Translation: Elena Polzer.

39. See D. Günther 1962; Thieß 1920.

40. On the "German rhythm movement" and the development of an associated "völkisch," national socialist ideology of rhythm and gymnastics, see Günther 1983.

41. See, e.g. (as one example of many others), Mary Wigman 1966, 10: "When the emotion of the dancing man frees the impulse to make visible his yet invisible images, then it is through bodily movement that these images manifest themselves in their first stages."

drew are entirely contrary to the abstractionist models of "constructing" movement signs developed by Meyerhold and Valéry.

Rhythmic dance movement fulfilled a quasi-compensatory function in
the romantic-restorative philosophy of *Ausdruckstanz*. The semioticity of the
body was oriented toward a holistic effect. The concept of a rhythmic danced
expression of the human body-mind-soul unit almost represented a coun-
terprogram to Meyerhold's semiotization of the biomechanically schooled
actor's body.[42]

After this excursion into simultaneously operating waves of rhythm theories,
each of which spawned distinct holistic concepts of the body, I return now to
Valéry's poetics of dance. Valéry isolated and staged a holistic semiotic string of
dance motions much in the style of the chronophotographic serialization of the
"animal machine" movements:

> From these same members composing, decomposing, and recompos-
> ing figures, or movements corresponding to equal and harmonic inter-
> vals, there arises an *ornament of duration* as, with the repetition of motifs
> in space or of their symmetries, there also arises an *ornament of spatial
> extension*.[43]

For Valéry, the separation and relinking of rhythmic movement signs represents a model of modern poetry. Dance becomes the role model for an advanced
poetics. The poet turns into a director and operator of procedural ornaments
of signs. Valéry already voiced similar concepts concerning the emancipation
of the signifier in a reference to Mallarmé, in a review of Michel Bréal's *Essai de
Sémantique* in 1898:

> Every single word seems to come loose from its form, to win its freedom,
> to open itself up, to become, all by itself, a threshold to the entire spirit.
> Every page, one after another, appears as an endlessly linked system, an
> incalculable web.[44]

---

42. At first glance, one exception to this statement seems to be the rhythmic gymnastics
of Emile Jaques-Dalcroze, whose system teaches isolation of the limbs and polyrhythmics.
These exercises were, however, only developed as training and awareness-building levels in
a holistic, rhythmic-dance pedagogical system. See Perrottet 1989 and *Der Rhythmus: Ein
Jahrbuch* (Hellerau) 1913; Günther 1983.

43. Valéry 1960, 2: 1172. Translation: Mark Franko.

44. See Valéry, "The 'Semantics' of Michel Bréal" (1898). Translated by Elena Polzer from
the German.

Just as the dissolution of syntax emancipates words from the straitjacket of semantics, so semiotic strings of movement become released into time and space, interlocking and coming undone again as ornaments of duration and of spatial extension.[45] As an epitome of the transitory, these semiotic strings of movement patterns simultaneously embody and transcend the syntactic order; their nature is that of representation. But at the same time, they are constantly in motion. Here Valéry's aesthetics postulates a perceptual change from a body "whose mechanics and human forces permit it to stand upright"[46] to a restless system of incessantly transforming attitudes and configurations, a change that only art is able to bring about.

Such surplus of (potential meaning)—operating in dance as a form of energetic expenditure—signals the breakdown between actions whose aims are comprehensible on the one hand and the hermeticism of art on the other.

Muse-Medusa: Dance as a Medium of Metamorphosis

At this point in his reflections, Valéry shifts his perspective in the fabricated scenario of his meditations on dance from a reading of movement ornaments to a sympathetic comprehension of the ecstatic state inside the dance vortex.

By changing his perspective in this way, Valéry emphasizes a pattern of reading that is decisive for his aesthetic: the adoption of various perspectives from complementary angles or levels. Aware that two forms of receptive access cannot take place simultaneously—analogously to Heisenberg's uncertainty principle of quantum physics[47]—the author oscillates between observation and empathy, between the analytical "interruptive" principle of scientific perception and the act of gliding in the ecstatic temporal flow of incessant displacement. On the threshold of expenditure, in light of the hermetic fascination with physical exhaustion in (trance) dance, the analytical gaze of the author reverses, turns away from the diagnosis of semiotic processes and their segmentation, to the center of the "laboratory": where the mystery of inspiration's myth of creation lies hidden.

The poet, who experiences a state of extremes (*"un corps surexcité"*)[48] as the form of expenditure in dance takes, himself takes part—as a recipient—in that

---

45. Valéry 1960, 2: 1172. Translation: Mark Franko.

46. Ibid.

47. On the relationship of twentieth-century natural sciences and avant-garde poetics, see Kleinschmidt 1992, 178ff.

48. Valéry 1960, 2: 1172. Translation: Mark Franko.

poetic state ("état poétique") which he, as an author of absolute poetry, attempts likewise to place his readers in, an oscillation between body of sound ("son") and sense ("sens"):

> A state that cannot be prolonged, that puts us outside of or far from our-selves, and in which nonetheless the *unstable* supports us whereas the *stable* only appears as by accident, this is what gives us the idea of another existence capable of the rarest moments of that which is ours, composed entirely of *limit-values* to which our faculties can subscribe. I think of what one calls vulgarly *inspiration*.[49]

This talk of an ecstatic state of inspiration remains, on the one hand, part of the topos of enthusiastic poetic writing—a motif that stretches back to anti-quity. On the other hand, it also attempts to delimit the rhetorical visualization of the creative condition. The notion of the origins of production in "limit-values" ultimately aims—like Mallarmé's poetics of the self-inscribing book—at eliminating the author as the medium of creation. The text, as movement text, thus appears wrought of an infinitesimal process, coordinating restless units of body-time-space-text that are consistently decomposing themselves into new relations. In the transitory moment of danced movement, the production and erasure of signs merge and the state of inspiration—an "alternate state" (Robert Musil)—appears as "ekstasis" by falling out of the continuum of an organized awareness of time and space.

Of course, to speak of such states of inspiration, which are striving toward limit-values of experience, is no longer the responsibility of the author. In such processes, in the dissolution of the boundaries of destabilized perception and decomposing semiotic and signifying relationships, the legitimacy of the author seems misplaced. It is delegated to an abstract, absolute principle, namely that of "pure movement." Dance thus becomes the key to a *poésie pure*; the dancer becomes the muse.

This model of incessant transformation, also and especially in repetition, appears in Valéry's train of thought as the prevalent characteristic of a poetics of dance; a movement process that appears as dance, as an act,

> brings forth these beautiful transformations of her form in space; who now moves, but without really going anywhere; now metamorphoses her-self on the spot, displaying herself in every aspect; who sometimes skill-fully modulates successive appearances as though in controlled phases.[50]

49. Valéry 1960, 2: 1172. Translation: Mark Franko.

50. Valéry 1964a, 206.

The concept of metamorphosis becomes the dominant aspect of Valéry's poetics of transformation, and dance embodies for him the idea of metamorphosis per se. In his study on Valéry, Ernst Robert Curtius points out:

> Transformation, metamorphosis, transfiguration—this is the fundamental ideational schemata in Paul Valéry's art. In mathematics, it appears as an algorithm of abstraction and transformation. But in Valéry's case we find it in all areas of his thinking. His thought is a universal theory of transformation.[51]

This model of metamorphosis, namely the characteristic attachment of dance to the transitory, appears in Valéry's writings as the movement concept per se—especially with respect to those unforeseeable, irregular, chance-regulated, infinitesimal units of perception that are so significant for Valéry's poetics and also reveal themselves in the movement patterns of the elements: in fire and in water.

In the natural sciences, appearances of thermodynamic movement patterns such as the flickering of flames, whirlpools, or cloud formations are considered phenomena that cannot be precisely calculated. They are classified as so-called nonlinear systems, whose "chaotic" behavior proves to be "nonintegrable" in terms of mathematical analysis.

Fire and water are metamorphic elements. They symbolize the liminal experiences of every process of creation—as Valéry attempts to describe in his philosophy of dance. In *Dance and the Soul*, fire symbolizes the endless transformation of dance movement.

In "Degas Dance Drawing," however, it is water that acts as the medium of metamorphosis. The eddies, the tumult of movement in the depths, the white crests of the waves, these "indiscernible," constantly transforming effects—as expressed by Karl Löwith in his study on Valéry—are more important for Valéry than the great events of history. The poet was fascinated by the "sea" and the "foam of things."

The sea and its dancer, the Medusa (the jellyfish) appear—at the end of Valéry's reflections on dance in "Degas Dance Drawing"—as visualizations of a poetics of metamorphosis that has been transformed into the impersonal of creation.

Valéry begins with Mallarmé's paradigmatic "judgment" or "axiom" in the essay "Ballets" from the *Divagations*:

> Namely, that the dancer is *not a woman dancing* for these juxtaposed reasons: that *she is not woman*, but a metaphor summing up one of the

---

51. Curtius 1991, 235. Translation: Elena Polzer.

elementary aspects of our form . . . and that *she is not dancing*, but suggesting, through the miracle of bends and leaps, a kind of corporal writing.[52]

Valéry paraphrases this "profound remark": "Mallarmé says that the dancer
is not a woman who dances, for she is not a woman, and she does not dance."[53]

This sentence contains the key formula for a poetics of dance—for a dance of
metamorphosis and of the transformation of semiotic structures. In brief: dance
as a semiotic model of avant-garde aesthetics. The concepts of grammatical decomposition that Mallarmé developed in his poetic reflections already
anticipate the Futurists' operations of "parole in libertà" in their programmatic
uncoupling of medium and message.

By quoting Mallarmé, Valéry confirms his poetic claims. In the subsequent
text, he revisits them and translates them into twentieth-century forms of
media and discourse by transferring the images from text onto the screen of the
new media—film—and by introducing as a subtext the epistemological models
of natural science to the sophisticated poetological discourse:

not women at all, but beings of an incomparable substance, translucent
and sensuous, flesh of a highly reactive glass dome of floating silks, crystalline crowns, long living thongs permeated with rapid swells, fringes
and creases that she folds, unfolds even as they invert themselves and
become deformed, fly off as fluidly as the thick fluid by which they are
pressed, which weds them, holds them together at every end, yields in
face of the slightest modulation and restores them in their form. There,
in the incompressible fullness of water that seems to offer them no resistance, these creatures have access to an ideal mobility as they spread and
draw back into themselves their radiant symmetry. There is no ground,
nothing solid for these absolute dancers; no floor; but a medium in which
every point gives way to the desire to move. No solid in their bodies of
crystal elasticity, no bones, no joints, fixed connections, parts that can be
numbered. . . .

Never did a human dancer, inflamed woman, drunk with movement,
with the poison of her own overwrought energy, with the ardent presence
of gazes charged by desire, ever express the imperious offering of sex, the
mimetic call to be prostituted, like this giant Medusa, which, with undulating shocks in its waves of festooned skirts that she hikes up and drops
with a strange and lewd insistence, transforms herself into a dream of Eros;

52. Mallarmé 2007, 130.

53. Valéry 1960, 2: 1173. Translation: Mark Franko.

and then, suddenly flinging back all these vibrating furbelows, her gown mutates into separable lips, falls backward to expose itself, furiously open.[54]

The dancers that Valéry sets forth here, these "absolute dancers," correspond to Mallarmé's model in which the dancer is not "woman," but pure sign. Valéry describes the "dance of the medusas" as the "the freest, most supple and most voluptuous of possible dances." By poetically constructing the Medusa as dancer, Valéry switches the medium in two ways: on the one hand, the medium of the corporeality of dance movement, as pertains to its "biomechanics," and, on the other hand, the framing medium of representation, shifting from (theatrical) space to the screen.

The Medusa, the great, translucent jellyfish floating in the water and equipped with a fringe of short tentacles and long appendages, embodies pure, unconscious, animalistic movement, the rhythmic pulse of that vegetative state, which Valéry called "la vie végétative"[55]: the unlimited mobility of simply gliding along in a "pre-existent" state. Hence, "she" evokes the phantasm of precultural, shameless animalistic sexuality. At the chiasmus between nature and culture, presentation and prostitution, the Medusa appears as a cancan dancer fervidly gathering up her skirts, and the "human dancer" becomes, by the same token, a creature of nature, which "expose(s) itself furiously open" as pure sex.

Here the technical reproduction of film serves as the medium for the presentation of the dancing body. Dance appears—not in the contemplation of nature, but through its appreciation on the silver screen, where both body and space are simulated as illusions—as the *simulation of dance*: "not as women, and they do not dance."

Hence, dance is a construct of "transcription," a moving metaphor, read by the poet and deduced from general movement patterns.

And it is out of such associational readings of the simulated natural body that the myth of the creative moment emerges: namely out of the semantic aura surrounding the word "Medusa," that is, the key image for that prominent moment of inspiration, that state of "striving toward threshold values." This moment occurs between the flow and standstill of time, between the gliding motion of liquefied signs and their ossification, between the rhythmic floating of the Medusa-jellyfish and the petrifying gaze of the Medusa-Gorgon.

This double meaning of the word "Medusa," as a zoological term for translucent giant deep-sea jellyfish and name of the third and mortal of the three

---

54. Valéry 1960, 2: 1173ff. Translation: Mark Franko.

55. Valéry 1960, 1: 1407. Translation: Mark Franko.

snake-haired Gorgons in Greek mythology, becomes a pictorial wellspring for Valéry's theory of inspiration. The *tertium comparationis* of the two levels of meaning in the term *Medusa*—the zoological term and the mythological tale—lies in the image of the snake-tentacle-hair of the Medusa character, that element of her body which suggests animalistic movement. While the image of the Medusa-jellyfish (*medusa* means "jellyfish" in French—Trans.) is represented as a *dance of nature* with oceanic feelings of total interconnectedness in trancelike movement, the "trickery of heroes" in the tale of the mythological Medusa symbolizes the *origins of art*, that is, Perseus emancipating himself from female domination by deflecting Medusa's petrifying gaze with the mirror of his shield and then killing her. Out of the carcass of the beheaded Medusa flies the winged Pegasus—emblem of poetry and male self-assertion all rolled into one.

The dancing Medusa is assigned two roles in Valéry's text: that of the gliding aquatic animal and that of the disembodied creature of the air, which rises up "like a fire balloon into the luminous forbidden region where reigns the star and deadly air."[56] Hence, the poet himself assumes the role of Perseus at the end of his dance-text. He transplants the dancer-medusa into the sphere of abstract space, as a "star" between the constellations of mythology. He posits her in a space that he has construed—by killing the Medusa and bringing Pegasus to light—as artistic. The deadly dance of the Medusa thus becomes both a source and a theory of poetry: the dance, the dancer as *inspiratrice*.

Valéry's poetics thus takes its bearings from both the biomechanics of vegetative life and the visual storehouse of myth. The inspirational moment lies in the infinitesimal process of convergence, in the limit-values of this dual perception—creation as deduction. "This is my alphabet and something of my syntax" [Voilà mon alphabet et déjà un peu de ma syntaxe]. So Valéry on the cleavage of dance language into a paradigmatic and a syntagmatic sphere—into "alphabet" and "syntax"—or into a reservoir of movement signs and a grammar of movement arrangements. Silence lies at the root of such poetological reflections, sections, and differentiations—beyond the realms of sound and image. In the act of separation, in the gap of difference exposed by reading and the doubling of semiotic production in Valéry's operation of complementarity, these two languages—the *poésie pure* of semiotic strings in dance and the expressive gestures of desire—expose the space in which silence, the mystical moment of quiet, enters.

---

56. Valéry 1960, 2: 1173. Translation: Mark Franko.

PATHOS OF REPOSE

The Dancer, Who Doesn't Dance

The two contrary dance models and their images of transformation—the dissolution of the body in abstract dance movement and the direct presence of the body in sculptural movement—merge in the ultimate distillation of the gesture, in the concentration of movement in the moment, or as Hofmannsthal called it, in the "mimetic-poetic work." Literature and dance, mimetic and poetic work join in the creation of manifestations of body imagery and movement signs.

The image of the dancer as muse, whose corporeal art is celebrated as an epitome of moving and transforming linguistic creation, is confronted—in dialectic interaction—by that other image of the body which *fails to correspond* to the light and effortless movement of dance. These other models of a language of body and movement focus not on the ecstatic delirium of movement, not on the configurative formula of metamorphosis in dance, but rather on the pathos of repose: the act of standing still, motionless amid the vortex—and in the end, also the fragmentation of the figural order of choreography and dance.

At the utmost climax of *l'art pour l'art* aesthetics—the abstraction of the body into pure movement signs—a younger generation of poets turned away from the dancer and her skillful self-presentation in semiotic spirals of dance. Instead, they shifted their focus—both in postmodern dance and in literature— to those moments beyond art in which the art-body is no longer required.

The *dance* of the ballerina became most expressive not when she sought to communicate through movement, but rather when she *didn't* dance: in moments of repose, those moments of preparation before stepping out on stage, in the exhaustion after the dance—hence those situations in which the collapsing façade of effortlessly sustained body control becomes tangible.

In the same way that painter Edgar Degas observed ballet dancers behind the scenes, resting after rehearsals or massaging their feet, a number of modern authors now focused on the figure of the dancer—but without focusing on dance itself.

Hofmannsthal described his "Conversation with the Dancer" as a productive dialogue between woman and man, between body and text, between dance and literature—a dialogue between the arts.

Robert Walser also sought such a dialogue of the arts. He attempted to achieve this dialogue in his writing and, in doing so, failed more often than he succeeded. One example is his text *Über das Russische Ballett* (*On the Russian Ballet*, 1909) about Anna Pavlova. In this short piece of prose on the dance of the Ballets Russes, he writes about the "great dancer" Anna Pavlova. To do so, he chooses the perspective of a person who knows little of dance and who is actually unable to speak about dance:

> There is no doubt a touch of parvenu effrontery in this desire on the part of someone of my ilk, who has never studied dance, to engage in scribbling and scrabbling on the theme, topic and subject of dancing. And yet my sympathies are so vibrant that I cannot possibly bring myself to say: "No, I shall not write."[57]

And so Walser feigns the character of a poet, sitting at his desk and musing about the beauty of dance in the ironic prim tone of the unspeakable: "How beautifully she danced, this great artist, Anna Pavlova, is beyond me. . . . Ah, her smile!"[58]

Finally—"sitting" almost eye to eye with the dancer—the writer's enthusiasm concentrates on the dancer's gestures: Pavlova's greatest charm unfolds when "she sits."

In her text *Unvollkommene Liebesgeschichte* (*Incomplete Love Story*), Isabella Nadolny likewise tells the tale of a man meeting a former dancer. In his story "Irene Holm," Hermann Bang describes the hard-working life of a simple dance teacher who dreamed of becoming a prima ballerina and is now forced to make her way arduously teaching ballroom dancing to village youths.

In one poem (1922) from the *Sonnets to Orpheus*, Rainer Maria Rilke praises the dancer's walk, that seemingly natural and purposeful everyday movement which allows simplicity to manifest itself in an exalted and distilled presence after having, as it were, passed through the art form of dance:

> O dancer: your steps translating
> all vanishing into act: what lines they traced?
> And the final spin, that tree of motion,
> did it not whirl into itself the fleeting year?
> Did it not put forth its crown of stillness—so that
> your earlier figures might swarm within it? And up above
> was it not summer, was it not sun—all that heat
> from you, that measureless radiant warmth?
> But it bore too, it bore, your tree of ecstasy.
> Are not these its quiet fruits: the jug,
> with its ripening stripes, and the fully ripened vase?

57. Walser 2012, 40.

58. Ibid., 42.

And in the pictures: does not the drawing remain,
That dark stroke of your eyebrows
sketched swiftly on the wall of their turning?[59]

In his "Sonnett auf die Tanzende" (Sonnet for a dancing girl),[60] Rudolf Borchardt attempts to read the traces of the dancer's suffering in the language of body and face—in the "glory, after the dance"—and to decipher those signs of the body that are not determined by the artificial code of dance (the eloquent corners of the mouth, the shoulders, the bend of the neck) as a story of deadly overexertion in dance, whose swaying and rotations still resonate in the rhythm of the poetic language.

Thomas Bernhard likewise joined the ranks of those storytellers who have attempted to confront the artistic dream of the perfect body with an ironic perspective on the infirmities and fragility of the world. In an anecdote in *The Voice Imitator*, Bernhard describes a dancer in a wheelchair who has been paralyzed since he stumbled when reflecting on his steps in the ballet *Rapheal* [*sic*]—a fallen angel of dance:

In Maloja we made the acquaintance of a once-famous male dancer in the Paris Opera, who was brought in a wheelchair into our hotel one evening by a young Italian from Castasegna whom the dancer had engaged for a

---

59. Rilke, Sonnet 18, *Sonnets to Orpheus* (2004b, 95).

60.

Ave Atque Vale

Sonett auf die Tanzende

Der ganze mächtige Tanz war nur ein Leiden.
Was aber war das Ruhn, das nach dem Tanze?
In den Mundwinkeln trug sie doch das ganze
Qualvolle Reden, das nun in den beiden
Zu süßen Schultern schwieg—das nicht im Meiden
und wonnigen Wiederkehren, nicht im Glanze
Der Arme lag: sondern, im tiefen Kranze
Wohnte sie wie im Schlaf, daraus zu scheiden
Ein Leiden, Reisen, Abschiednehmen war –
Als sie zu trinken auf den Becher Wasser
Den Hals so fallen ließ als ob ihr Haar
Von hinten eine Hand mit Tod belüde,
War sie nicht nur vom halben Lichte blasser:
Die schönen Kränze wurden an ihr müde.

Borchardt 1957, 39.

period of several years. As we learned from the dancer, he had collapsed in mid-performance on the first night of Handel's *Rapheal*, which had been specially choreographed for him by Béjart, and he had been paralyzed ever since. The dancers said he had suddenly lost consciousness and only two days later had come to. It was possible, according to the dancer, who was wrapped in very expensive nutria fur, that his misfortune could be traced back to the fact that for the first time in his career he had thought about the complexity of a combination of steps that he had been afraid of for the whole fifteen years of his career and that had taken him to all the great opera houses of the world. A dancer, in his opinion, ought never to think about his dance while he is dancing; he should only dance, nothing else.[61]

In a parody of Kleist's *On the Marionette Theater*, Bernhard goes through the original sin of reflection, fall, and paralysis of movement and as well the slip of the tongue (Raph*ea*l instead of Raph*ae*l)—a scenario of modern worldly theater, as celebrated by Maurice Béjart's idea of dance as being the art of the twentieth century—in Bernhard's case, of course, without any prospect of a return to lost grace.

Via the pathos formulas of expressive movement, the body imagery of dance provides basic patterns that appear characteristic for forms of self-formation, but also for the dissolution of the subject in modernity. The constellations and structures of reciprocal readings of dance and literature range from the construct of a "progressive" human being in the movement image of the *Victoire* to the disintegration of the self in the intoxicating motions of the bacchanal, from the signature of modernity as being an age of femininity—in the pathos formula of the dancing maenad—to forms of metamorphosis in dance as figurations of inspiration.

The disruption of such intermedial chains of signs, as signified by the last few examples from Robert Walser to Thomas Bernhard, indicate—even in the dissolution of body imagery and its movement patterns—a never-ending search for noncodified images and figurations of expression in body and language.

This disruption also simultaneously points to a broadening of definitions of art by the avant-garde and postmodernism as a result of new technologies and media in transportation, telecommunications, and film. From this point onward, body imagery finds itself in a characteristic relationship and rivalry with the surrounding space, with new concepts of space and simulations of movement in the medial world of the twentieth century. The second part of this book will now focus on this very change of perspective from body to space.

61. Bernhard 1997, 45.

PART II

Topos Formulas

Dance Movement and Figurations of Space

The second part of this book focuses on the transformation and deconstruction of body imagery. I will not examine the constitution of body imagery in dance here—as in the first part of the study—but rather their transcendence in the spatial by reflecting the spaces that surround movement, the way in which typical *spatial formulas* are produced in dance. In the following section, I will therefore illustrate the metamorphosis of body imagery into abstract figurations, that is, their translation into spatial patterns—as it were, a topology of dance—based on characteristic examples from the early twentieth century.

Space and the relationships between the kinetic parameters that define it are the subject and the medium of *topos formulas* in modern dance. The term thus describes formative configurations, that is, the formulas of spatial relationships as they appear in the typical configurations of representation in avant-garde physical theater. Unlike pathos formulas, which transport the manifestations and the modern reformulations of affect engrams in the body and movement imagery of dance, topos formulas appear in modern art as specific processes of abstraction.

At the beginning of the twentieth century, the postulate of abstraction in art led to a new emphasis on individual elements of composition. The individual parameters and forms of art and their relationships to one another obeyed a distinct logic of their own, motivated by a multiplicity of potential perspectives. The structures of space were no longer defined by organizing them around a central perspective or balancing parts to a whole, but rather by an emancipation of indi-vidual elements and the disintegration of figure and ground in a dissolution of the illusion of concrete, functional space, in a dispersion of form into weightless-ness. The dominant gaze was one oriented to all dimensions, which demanded new patterns of reading art in order to compensate for altered visual habits that had developed through modern technology, transportation, and media. One of the consequences of these new perspectives was a disappearance of the concepts of *up* and *down*, as Russian artist Kazimir Malevich noted. And Erwin Panofsky described the relationships of forms in abstract art as a "suspension in emptiness."

Emptiness and the in-between spaces that bear the weight of the tension between the individual elements of a spatial composition played a prominent role in twentieth-century modern art, as well as in modern dance.[1]

The rise of modernity paralleled the decline of the *single* dominant, authoritative perspective. The viewer was detached from an orthogonal point of reference and set adrift in a multidimensional, no longer empirically tangible space. The move-ment figurations, the kinetic elements steered the viewer through the maze of mul-ticentric spatial perspectives as if through an underground system of tunnels and caves.

The labyrinth, its spatial paths oscillating between orientation and disorien-tation, thus became a major figuration of movement in the exploration of the abstract. The spatial formulas of the labyrinth and the spiral, in which the pro-cesses of dematerialization and metamorphosis present themselves in movement, manifest as models of abstraction in dance.

LABYRINTH AND SPIRAL

The following section explores the subject of reading topos formulas. The labyrinth and the spiral are examined as symbolic figurations that represent the transition from body to space, from individual to group, and from movement to symbols.

Topos formulas are patterns of abstraction that define a process in modern dance and track its development—a process that runs contrary to an emphasis on the body and its presentation via pathos formulas as elucidated in the first part of this book. And yet pathos formulas and topos formulas must be regarded as being engaged in dialogue: the relationship of physical movement to space, whereby *space*—in dance and theater—is not meant in terms of its function, not as a place on stage, but rather in its diverse connotative, symbolic, mythical, and "auratic" aesthetic qualities.

1. See Brandstetter 1991c; on the function of weightlessness, the elimination of the central perspective in modern painting, see Simmen 1990.

Figure 39 Basic drawing of a labyrinth.
SOURCE: Hermann Kern. 1982. Labyrinthe. München, p. 175.

Labyrinth

The labyrinth is a mythical *figuration* of space that can be defined either as the outline of a spatial structure or as an abstract figuration of movement (figure 39).

In his *Labyrinth-Studien* (*Labyrinth Studies*),[2] Karl Kerényi ascribes the significance of a *spatial formula* to these winding paths of spatial organization. The labyrinth, a spatial figuration born of archaic cultures, appears as the "linear reflection of a mythological idea." As with Aby Warburg in his *Mnemosyne* project, Kerényi's analysis is concerned with an anthropological subject matter of comparable cultural-historical scope. Here, too, the focus lies on a kind of

2. See Kerényi 1950. Hermann Kern's book *Through the Labyrinth* (2000), the most comprehensive and thorough work on this subject to date, is based on Kerényi's studies, in particular his interpretation of the labyrinth dance. For a photographic documentation of "mazes" all over the world, see Fisher 1990.

pathos formula, although no longer as a model of expressing representations of the body, not as body imagery, but rather as an abstract figuration of movement represented in spatial form.

The labyrinth is a document of visual thought, a "visual formulation" (Hermann Kern) of a mythical concept. I wish to emphasize three aspects in the iconographic interpretation of the labyrinth for my line of argumentation in the second part of this book, namely:

- The labyrinth as a spiral pattern of transition, or as a passageway from the center of the body into space; in the microcosmic corporeal figuration of viscera[3] on the one hand; and in the macrocosmic movement figurations of celestial bodies on the other.[4]
- The labyrinth as a graphic, linear figuration that can be read as the outline of a spatial structure. For our context here, the aspects of abstraction, space, and ornament are of particular interest in connection with this definition of the labyrinth. Kerényi defines the labyrinth—whether mythical or decorative as an "artistic exercise"—as a "spiraling form": every spiral that appears merely decorative, simply drawn for its own sake or formed as a meander, is a labyrinth, as soon as we imagine it to be a path and place ourselves, as it were, in it at an inevitable entrance or passageway. (13)[5]

Kern's essay, however, advocates a more strictly limited definition of the term *labyrinth*, as a "tortuous structure"—a definition whose origins may even lie before the Hellenic period, and includes neither the metaphor for a confusing situation so often used today, nor the open graphic structure of an ornament (e.g., a knotted labyrinth).[6]

---

3. Kerényi refers to Mesopotamian depictions of labyrinths and cuneiform texts. In the viscera of sacrificial animals [*translator's note*: the practice of using anomalies in animal entrails to predict or divine future events] the labyrinth becomes a "mythological reality" of transition: "In each palpable and physically individual case, a different reality shines through: something mythological that is also cited in the inscriptions. A palace came into view, a 'palace of entrails'" (14). Translation: Elena Polzer.

4. The cosmological aspect of the labyrinth relates to the trajectories of celestial bodies: their pathways become the movements in and the paths of the labyrinth from which various sun and moon dances are derived (Kern 2000, 32ff.). The mythological and symbolic meanings of the topos formula of the labyrinth have also been interpreted as a "cosmic wedding" between Father Sun and Mother Earth (e.g., among the Hopi Indians), or sexually as a symbolic place of sexual union—as a "love labyrinth."

5. For all Kerényi quotes, the page numbers are in the text. All Kerényi quotes are translated from German by Elena Polzer.

6. Kern 2000, 23f. Kern defines the labyrinth in a "formal" way; he only accepts those geometric forms whose paths and lines lead inward toward a center beginning at one single

- And finally, a third and crucial aspect of the labyrinth: the labyrinth as a figuration of dance movement. Both Kerényi and Kern believe that the oldest manifestations of the labyrinth had a choreographic function. Using the "Hainuwele mythologem" as an example, Kerényi illustrates that the abduction of the maiden was not presented as a form of pantomime, but rather as a dance whose spiral lines simultaneously symbolized "the outline of a gateway leading to the goddess of the underworld" (20f.). In the context of initiation rites, in the enactment of symbolic death and rebirth, the labyrinth appears as a figuration of movement, as a dance and equally as a spatial "linear reflection of an implicit mythological idea."

As a spatial formula of initiation rites, the labyrinth symbolizes the path to oneself, the process of individuation. There is only one entrance (and exit) to the labyrinth. The spiraling or meandering forms of the path isolate an interior space that is clearly distinguished from the exterior space. A certain level of maturity, orientation, and stamina is required of the initiand who ventures into this isolated environment, to navigate the winding labyrinthine paths. Upon reaching the center, the individual is alone and can only turn back on himself, pass through the center—the center that symbolizes self-confrontation—in order to correctly return to the outside world. At the center, according to Kern, the individual encounters himself, "a divine principle, a Minotaur."[7]

In Cretan mythology, the path through the labyrinth was linked to a ritual of sacrifice: every year, seven youths and maids had to be sacrificed in a "spring rite" to the monstrous Minotaur trapped in the labyrinth. The ingenious craftsman Daedalus was commissioned by the Cretan king Minos to create the labyrinth as a mythical prison for Ariadne's half-brother, the horrific half-bull, half-man Minotaur.[8] According to myth, those who entered the deadly maze never found their way out again. Only the hero Theseus, who succeeds in killing the Minotaur and freeing the sacrificial youths, is able to make his way out of the labyrinth with the help of his lover Ariadne and her thread.

starting point, with turns and twists, but without any intersections. Upon reaching the center, the traveler reverses direction and is finally led back out again through the same entranceway.

7. Kern 2000, 30.

8. Ariadne, who helps the hero Theseus kill the Minotaur, is later abandoned by him; Dionysus approaches the lamenting woman and takes her as his wife. It is worth noting here that another name for the Minotaur is "Asterios" and that his followers worshipped him as a star. Asterios is, however, also the name under which Dionysus is revered in his child form, as the reincarnated god in the Mysteries. Thus, the abandoned Ariadne resurrects her ("suppressed," murdered) brother in her union with Dionysus.

However, Daedalus not only created the Palace of Knossos and gave Ariadne the thread as a means of orientation in the lineaments of the labyrinth. According to myth, he also created a dancing place for Ariadne—in the form of a labyrinth.

In the eighteenth book of the *Iliad*, Homer describes the shield that Hephaestus made for Achilles. On it, a *choros* is depicted, which Homer compares to the dance, that is, the "dancing ground" that Daedalus once skillfully fashioned in Knossos:

> On it the renowned lame god embellished
> A dancing ground, like the one Daedalus
> Made for the ringleted Ariadne in wide Cnossus.
> Young men and girls in their prime of beauty
> Were dancing there, hands clasped around wrists.
> The girls wore delicate linens, and the men
> Finespun tunics glistening softly with oil.
> Flowers crowned the girls' heads, and the men
> Had golden knives hung from silver straps.
> They ran on feet that knew how to run
> With the greatest ease, like a potter's wheel
> When he stoops to cup it in the palms of his hands
> And gives it a spin to see how it runs. Then they
> Would run in lines that weaved in and out.
> A large crowd stood round the beguiling dance,
> Enjoying themselves, and two acrobats
> Somersaulted among them on cue to the music.
> On it he put the great strength of the River Ocean
> Lapping the outermost rim of the massive shield.[9]

Researchers agree that, according to Kerényi's theory, the topos formula of the labyrinth—especially in its form as a visual engram, ornament, and architectural structure—originally first developed as a figuration of choreography.[10] Hermann Kern discusses both forms of the mythical labyrinth, namely as a building and as a dance, that is, as a form of dance that has been preserved in the so-called *geranos* or ritual crane dance,[11] which Theseus is supposed to have performed in Delos:

9. Homer, *Iliad* 18, 590–606, p. 186.

10. See Kern 2000, 27: "As I have already indicated, I believe that the original manifestation of the labyrinth was a dance pattern.... The earliest literary reference is the *choros* on Achilles's shield in book 18 of the *Iliad*."

11. On the crane dance, see Kerényi 1950 and Kern 2000, 44ff.

Both labyrinth forms, a structure and a dance, exhibit parallels . . . namely, that the labyrinth design is intelligible only as an outline; that the lines between the paths are characteristically pendular and—as "walls"—cannot be stepped over; and that Daedalus, who personified "artistry," is attributed with having created both the labyrinth and the labyrinth dance.[12]

What is significant here for this book is the dual codification of the labyrinth as a topos formula: in contrast to the spiral, which follows a single, rotating line, the underlying movement figuration of the labyrinth is that of a pendulum. The path is laid out "with the maximum possible number of twists and turns," with the walker repeatedly approaching the goal, only to be led away from it again. Inevitably he reaches the center. I wish therefore to emphasize two aspects: on the one hand, the apparently aimless, disorienting, expansive "choreography" and, on the other hand, the structuring organization of the paths, which demand orientation in their constant change of direction. Disorientation and orientation, the dissolution and reorganization of the spatial movement structure, all equally play a role in the topos formula of the labyrinth. As a spatial formula, it combines the floating form of meandering and rambling pathways with a structuring perspective as a model that represents self-reflection in a danced figuration of movement.

Spiral

The second topos formula that is highly significant for the relationship of dance and space is the figuration of the spiral. Like the labyrinth, the spiral is an archaic form and perhaps, aside from the circle, the most ancient choreographic figuration of all. And like the labyrinth, the spiral draws its function as a universal figure of meaning from the visual realm of myth.

   The spiral is often interpreted as a symbol of "primeval forms of life," found, for example, in the paths of celestial bodies, orbiting planets, and spiral mists or natural forms, such as snail shells or curling fern leaves[13]—as a way of reading the "art forms of nature" (Ernst Haeckel),[14] so characteristic for the mindscapes of vitalism and art nouveau.

   In its symbolic-cultic association with rites of passage, the spiral, like the paths of the labyrinth, represents the act of turning inward on oneself as a model

---

12. Kern 2000, 44.

13. On symbolism, see Riedel 1985 and Gombrich 1984.

14. On the relationship of morphology and monism in Haeckel, see Gebhard 1984, 300ff.

for passing into another stage of existence, as a figuration of the transition from life to death, from birth to rebirth. The spiral as a mythical-ritual pattern of movement unfolds on the horizon of mythic thought as a linear reflection of the endless process of metamorphosis.

In esoteric religious and ancient lore, the spiral represents the path of life. Helena Petrovna Blavatsky, the founder of theosophy, dealt with this in the second volume of her book *The Secret Doctrine*[15] in an extensive explanation of "the development of symbolism" and in the third volume in her discussion "On Occult and Modern Science," in which she examines various topics of the natural sciences such as gravitation, rotation, energy, and theories on cosmic mist from an esoteric point of view.

The founders of modern dance, such as the Delsarte student Genevieve Stebbins, eclectically referenced the lore and knowledge of esotericism, various world religions, Darwinism, vitalism, and *Lebensphilosophie* in an attempt to establish modern dance as a holistic system. Ralph Waldo Emerson, William James, Henri Bergson, Ernst Haeckel, and others served to firmly install dance as a practice of vitalism. The role of the spiral in this process was that of a topos formula for metamorphosis, the embodiment of the theorem of *élan vital* in dance. Stebbins projected the spiral of evolution as a figuration of the river of life onto the movement patterns of dance: "There is no such thing as a straight line in the nascent life of nature . . . so the spiral motion is the type of life."[16]

As a topos formula for dance movement, the spiral takes on two forms:

- On the one hand, the two-dimensional, lying spiral: it rests on the surface, appears in natural form (sand patterns) and in cult form (rock carvings and mosaics); an ideogram, associated with the movement patterns of furling and unfurling, or of paths on the ground.

---

15. Helena Petrovna Blavatsky (1831–1891) founded the Theosophical Society together with Henry Steel Scott on November 17, 1874, in New York. Its declared goals included the formation of a universal brotherhood, a "comparative theology," and the exploration of unexplained phenomena and laws of nature. Blavatsky's opus magnum (after her popular book *Isis Unveiled*, 1872) was the four volumes of *The Secret Doctrine*, published in 1888 by Theosophical University Press. In the preface, Blavatsky stated the motto "Satyāt nāsti paro dharmah" [There is no religion higher than truth].

Rudolf Steiner's anthroposophy was a result of his attempt to differentiate his doctrines from theosophy. Admittedly, morphology played a fundamental role in Steiner's thinking (especially in Steiner's writings on Goethe's studies of natural science: for Goethe, the spiral represented *the* basic form of organic life); the spiral appears, for example, also as a "figuration" of this morpheme in the dance movements of Steiner's "eurhythmics."

16. Shelton 1981, 14.

- On the other hand, the three-dimensional spiral that winds itself into space (as appears in nature in the form of tornados, whirlpools of water or sand, plant growth); in an upward motion as an image of transcendence and downward in the image of the vortex, the epitome of regression.

In turn-of-the-century dance, we encounter the spiral in its two- and three-dimensional characteristic forms: as a pattern of paths—for example in the prevalent circle and chain dances associated with dance reform and rhythmic gymnastics—and as a spatial pattern, in various avant-garde dance and scenographic experiments, such as Loïe Fuller's spiral dances and the Futurists' *aerodanza* scenarios.

In its path-like pattern—a serial line of dance movements consisting of inward or outward rotations—the spiral fundamentally differs from the topos formula of the labyrinth despite its ornamental similarity. While the lineaments of the spiral mirror a virtually endless, constantly flowing progression of movements, the movement pattern reflected in the figuration of the labyrinth forces the dancer to pause, to reorient herself when changing direction. The flow of movement is interrupted by a moment of reflection, which takes place *in* the movement. A moment of self-reflection is thus integrated in the interaction of orientation and disorientation in space. The topos formula of the labyrinth consequently appears as a figuration of self-reflection in dance. In the *interruption*, in the exploration of possibilities of structuring, dissolving, and restructuring movement patterns, the ornamental choreography of the labyrinth permits both meandering paths and figurations of order.

By contrast, the spiral, as a topos formula of unbroken, nonsegmented flowing movement, does not induce a differentiation or interruption of movement as in the case of the labyrinth. It does not mirror an incisive moment of reflection. Instead, it generates a holistic pattern that maps the union of subject and figuration of movement, of body and figuration of space. The union-inducing lineaments of the spiral serve as a transition from the spatial formula to the pathos formula of movement as a subjective gesture of expression. The spatial path of the spiral and the spiral-like rotation of the body in whirling dance culminate in the irreversible pattern of trance.

In Martha Graham's choreography *Errand into the Maze* (1947),[17] the entire dance drama is built on these two topos formulas of labyrinth and spiral as the basic patterns of movement. Graham's choreographic study of the labyrinth,

---

17. *Errand into the Maze*, 1947; choreography, Martha Graham; music, Gina Carlo Menotti; scenography, Isamo Noguchi.

like all her works based on ancient mythology,[18] is conceived from the female perspective: an exploration of myth with the means of dance, a reinterpretation of its archetypal constellations from a female point of view.

Therefore, it is not Theseus who appears as the Attic hero conquering the Minotaur with Ariadne's help, but instead Ariadne herself who confronts the beast. *Errand into the Maze* is a piece about a woman facing her own fear. It is a portrayal of her fight with the monstrosity within herself.[19] The path into the labyrinth—as a path into the depths of her own soul, toward a confrontation with a schismatic and suppressed part of herself—is accompanied by movements and moments of orientation and disorientation. The thread of the lineaments of the "maze" runs across Ariadne's dress[20]; the path leading into depths of the labyrinth thus inscribes itself onto her body, while simultaneously laid out as a path of ropes on the floor. Her dance movements *before* she enters the unknown space reflect the ambivalence of control and surrender, of orientation and confusion, symbolized in the oscillation between the topos formulas of a labyrinthine movement of interruption and spiral movements of flowing rotation.

At first, the dancer moves in extremely strained, almost convulsive motions along a rectangular, broken, zigzagging path. Then she succumbs to the vertigo of her fear in a long whirling sequence. Having thus become familiar with the impending path into the unknown, she dares to enter the labyrinth: a path

18. For example, *Cave of the Heart*, 1946 (on Medea); *Night Journey*, 1947 (the myth of Jocaste and Oedipus); *Clytemnestra*, 1958 (the Clytemnestra-Orestes tragedy.)

19. The Minotaur, the shackled male principle, is portrayed by a dancer whose arms are laid across a yoke: his movements therefore appear bound and are reduced to legs and rump. Imprisoned in the labyrinth, the Minotaur is ultimately only mobile in the region of the torso (and almost only as a "torso"). Ariadne's fear, her battle with desire, literally affects her relationship to the (body) center. In that moment in which she is able to accept her sexuality, the spasmodic "contractions" cease—a fundamental principle of Graham's movement technique that is used here on a metalevel for representation. Ariadne conquers the Minotaur by climbing onto his thighs, bracing herself against the yoke and—while gradually becoming aware of her own strength—slowly forcing him to the ground; emancipation as a form of erotic union.

20. The spatial figuration of the choreography, the labyrinth, drawn on the dance costume, and its inversion via dance movement into the structure of the choreographic space reflects—in Graham's work *Errand into the Maze*—the function of a topos formula for modern dance. For Graham, Japanese theater played an important role in terms of the significance it ascribes to costume, scenography, and specific forms of movement. In her "notebooks" she often made references to Noh theater. She was familiar with touring productions by Kabuki actor Tokojiro Tsutui in New York (1930), with the work of Japanese dancer-choreographer Michio Ito, who worked on the concept and staging of W. B. Yeats's *At the Hawk's Well*, and with the work of the famous Chinese actor Mei-Lan Fang, who also inspired Brecht; see Jowitt 1988, 214ff.

of self-orientating interruptions at a high staccato pace across the rope, until finally, the thread of orientation becomes superfluous and she is caught up in it.

In contrast, the spiral line in space mainly appears in early twentieth-century avant-garde dance as a movement pattern of abstraction: as a dissimulation of the corporeal *in* movement itself, as a dissolution of the body in the spiral movement, as the disappearance of the subject in the lineaments of figurations of space. Loïe Fuller's dance is paradigmatic for this type of dance. Variations in this basic formula range from figurations of dance as iconograms of topographical figurations (as in the case of Gabriele D'Annunzio) to the spirals of *aerodanza* found in the experimental catenae of Futurist avant-garde aesthetics.

Chapter 1

Dance Costume and Movement Space

Spatial Formulas and Their Metamorphoses into Fabric

The dancer appears in space—in the functionally determined cubic space of the stage and in the imaginary space created by his movements—as a *Kunstfigur* [art figure]. His "costume" assumes various functions. From a structural perspective, dance costume can disguise the conditions of representation, by concealing the artificiality of the performance and positing the movements of the body as *natural*—thus communicating a pathos formula of passionate expression in the draped fabric of e-motion. Or dance costume becomes a medium of transforming the dancing body: by enveloping, transforming, deconstructing, and rewriting its form and its relationship with the space.

Hence, dance costume appears—either by revealing the body and its expressive movement or by transforming the form into a figuration of abstraction—as a medium of metamorphosis and simultaneously as an indicator of a specific aesthetic when combined with dance as

- a mimetic art of expression in "cultic soul dance" (Oskar Schlemmer) or
- abstraction and constructivism in the "aesthetic masquerade" (Schlemmer) of scenic "sculptural costumes," which mask the dancer's body.

In this chapter, I will examine the subject of *dance costume* and *spatial sculpture* in these terms.

In his article "Man and Art Figure" (1925), Oskar Schlemmer reflects the fundamental historical conditions leading to the conception of the dancer-performer as *art figure* in avant-garde theater: "The history of the theater is the history of the transfiguration of the human form. It is the history of *man* as the actor of physical and spiritual events, ranging from naïveté to reflection, from naturalness to artifice."[1]

The dancer is transfigured by the development of a "constructive configuration" that envelops, conceals, and causes his distinct form to disappear. This process involves the most prominent devices of avant-garde art: abstraction, construction, mechanization, technization, and montage. Schlemmer summarizes these aspects as they pertain to the establishment of "the stage as image of our time," on which these artistic goals are to be realized:

> One of the emblems of our time is *abstraction*. It functions, on the one hand, to disconnect components from an existing and persisting whole, either to lead them individually *ad absurdum* or to elevate them to their greatest potential. On the other hand, abstraction can result in generalizations and summation, in the construction in bold outline of a new totality.
>
> A further emblem of our time is *mechanization*, the inexorable process which now lays claim to every sphere of life and art. Everything which can be mechanized *is* mechanized. The result: our recognition of that which can *not* be mechanized.
>
> And last, but not the least, among the emblems of our time are the new potentials of technology and invention which we can use to create altogether new hypotheses. (359)

Hence, these conditions and fantasies are meant to represent not only an "image of our time" on stage, but also the utopia of a new age.

At the beginning of the twentieth century, space and time no longer guaranteed a uniform framework of order for dance, as was still the case in nineteenth-century ballet. The temporal configuration of nineteenth-century ballet was determined by the (fairy tale) plot, specially composed music, and the sequence of solo, pas de deux, and ensemble appearances, which followed a traditional choreographic schema. The space was structured by the principle of elevation, which strove toward the vertical in an expression of ballet's ideal of weightless flotation, and by the geometry of the choreography, which was aligned along a central perspective and whose fundamental principles of composition reach back as far as ballet's original development at the court of Louis XIV.

The dissolution of classical ballet's traditional order of space and time is as characteristic of twentieth-century modern dance as the renouncement of the central perspective by modern visual art in cubism and abstract painting.

---

1. Schlemmer 1925 (2002). (Further page numbers in the text.)

The growing dominance of technology and media and thus the fundamentally altered perception of space and time in their relationship to the moving body caused a profound change in twentieth-century dance. Avant-garde fine arts coined the phrase "There is no art, only arts" and likewise, we could say the same of twentieth-century modern dance: there is no dance, only dance performances—with a nearly infinite number of diverse, parallel, rapidly transforming dance styles and choreographic concepts. And what is closely related to these developments is that, instead of a predetermined dance space, dance could choose from a multiplicity of dance spaces—each so different that every dance, every new choreographic style produced its own space. Dance dress, costume, the body mask frequently became an additional medium of "creating space" in dance and through dance. Moreover it appeared—beyond acting as mere decoration—as moving scenography.

LOÏE FULLER AND STÉPHANE MALLARMÉ

Initiator and inventor of this new groundbreaking development in the relationship of movement and space in twentieth-century dance was the American artist Loïe Fuller.[2]

As principal media for a new conception of space through dance, Fuller used fabric (dance costumes as moving scenography) on the one hand, and colored lights (as a factor of space) on the other. It was her theatrical concept of abstract movement, which structured the space in combination with the newest in (lighting) technology, that made her dances so seminal for the twentieth century.

From 1892 onward, her *Serpentine Dance* conquered ballet-weary audiences across Europe and ushered in a paradigm shift on the dance stage. Artists and intellectuals celebrated "La Loïe"—whose dancing came to symbolize an entire era—as the "Fée de l'Electricité," a magician of light and of dancing colors. The novelty of her dance lay not in a specific "technique" of virtuosic physical movement, but in the creation of an utterly transformed, artificial semiotic space with the help of an almost entirely abstract scenic play of fabric, moving lights, colors, and music. The metamorphoses of Fuller's dances embodied that dream of perfect synesthesia, which was so often invoked by the poets of symbolism, from Baudelaire to Mallarmé, from Yeats to Valéry.

The fantastic element of the *Serpentine Dance* and dances such as the *Butterfly Dance, Lily Dance,* and *Fire Dance* (all created in Paris between 1892 and 1894)

2. See Brandstetter and Ochaim 1989.

was a figuration of draped fabric: a very expansive, white silk dress, into which two long bamboo rods were sewn. Loïe Fuller designed it herself and it was fabricated according to a patented special pattern.[3] On a stage lined in black fabric, to the music of Gounod, Massenet, Grieg, Debussy, and Stravinsky, she moved the fabric in spirals, circles, waves, loops, and twists to form ephemeral sculptural figurations, which partly resembled natural shapes, partly abstract sculpture (figure 40). Her movement figurations created topos formulas, that is, produced the texture of the scenes with the help of a textile medium.

Fuller's choreographies dispensed with "plots" and instead told stories through the silent art of gesture in a dance that staged movement itself as a shimmering phantom. The ephemerality of the incessantly transforming fabric—in which every movement impulse was slightly delayed before it perpetuated itself in space, thus keeping the audience in constant anticipation of new, floating, transient visual associations—communicated the fascination of nonrecurring, improvised movement, although every step, every movement was fixed in a rigorous rehearsal process.

Critic and art historian Julius Meier-Graefe wrote of the sensation caused by Fuller's dances in the third edition of *Insel*, 1900:

> But her ornaments remain the most striking. In one of the wild dances, where it is almost impossible to follow the colors and lines . . . only this rise and fall of the veils, she suddenly disappears, extinguishes. All is dark, but something moves in the darkness, it is tiny brilliant points that dance, it is a dance of fireflies, like stars. They form large, brilliant circles that merge into luminous mountains side by side, wriggling through, only spots; not an iota of human movement, of anything corporeal; ornaments, so bold, so pure, so mystical . . . it takes one's breath away. *La Danse Mystique!*[4]

Meier-Graefe's review addresses another decisive factor in the creation of a new dance space: in addition to the element of moving fabric, Fuller employed light as a medium of transforming body movement into spatial effects. She even became a lighting expert herself and experimented extensively in the development of new techniques for projecting colored light, which evoked, in shifting patterns and nuances of color, a "play of light" on the moving, reflecting silk fabric. Radiant colors, such as the cascades of light in the *Fire Dance* that ranging from orange to flaming red, leapt upward from a specially constructed glass panel in the stage floor, were just as typical for Fuller's dances as the finely

---

3. See the photographs in Brandstetter and Ochaim 1989, 25ff.

4. Julius Meier-Graefe, "Loïe Fuller," *Die Insel* 3.1 (1900): 105. Translation: Elena Polzer.

Figure 40 Loïe Fuller, *La Danse du Lys* (around 1898).
SOURCE: Author's archive.

graded shades of colored light reflected on the pearly-iridescent lengths of silk, which spiraled upward into a blossom in *La Danse du Lys* (1894).

Fuller's pieces were the celebration of a cult of dancing color—not on the painter's canvas, but in the theater. Reflections of light and color, glittering in floating swarms of sparks on endless meters of shimmering fabric, gave the impression that the artistic achievements of impressionism had been translated from the canvas into three-dimensional space, onto the moving silk fabric of the stage.

In her abstract, sophisticatedly balanced compositions of fabric, lights, color, and movement, which solely adhered to the laws of contrast and dynamics, Fuller discovered, for dance, what Kandinsky's first abstract paintings introduced to the fine arts. Kandinsky painted his first abstract picture in 1910 and interestingly gave one series of these paintings the title *Improvisations*. Kandinsky collaborated with the dancer Alexander Sakharoff around the same time that the Blaue Reiter was founded in Munich. This, but also Kandinsky's remarks on "abstract" composition in *Point and Line to Plane* (1926), which was itself based on a movement study by the dancer Gret Palucca, testifies to how closely these artworks were associated with the movement patterns of dance.

Fuller's innovations of movement in space, of "painted light," of the abstract stage, were created years before the seminal works of the stage reformers Adolphe Appia and Edward Gordon Craig.[5]

Fuller's background in American theater entertainment, from vaudeville, variety theater, and "musical comedy" to music hall, points out another fundamental aspect in the paradigm shift from nineteenth-century dance to that of the twentieth century: in addition to the standoff between free dance and classical ballet, *dance* as an art form gradually began to open up and incorporate elements from the entertainment sector, that is, vaudeville, revue, show. Many innovations in avant-garde dance would not have been possible without such transgressions of boundaries. The *space* and the *time* of twentieth-century dance owed its diversity and multimediality not least of all to the formal, as well as technical, principles of segmentation—the "editing" technique—of revue and film.

As one of the pioneers of new dance aside from Isadora Duncan and Ruth St. Denis, Loïe Fuller took a different path than her companions and followers. While Duncan and St. Denis presented and propagated the expressiveness of the female body as liberated from the shackles of ballet, Fuller preferred to draw attention to the surrounding space by staging the disappearance of the body in endless metamorphoses of enveloping silk fabric. While Duncan and St. Denis, as well as the subsequent generation of "art dance" and expressionistic dance, sought to rediscover the *nature* of the body and its archetypical expressive potential in ancient mythology or in the rituals of Asian temple dance, Fuller pursued a dematerialization of the corporeal with the help of modern technology.

The principle of metamorphosis governed the spatial formulas of all her dances. Of her work Fuller said, "Je sculpte de la lumière."[6] The paradox in her aspiration to form light instead of forming the body, to utilize the wave—both in textile form and in the form of electrical light—as an artistic sign vehicle, instead of matter,

5. See Brandstetter and Ochaim 1989, 113–19.

6. See Fuller 1908; 1913.

reveals the full scope, the eminent modernity of her work. It is thus quite in keeping with her work that film later took on a highly significant role in her oeuvre.[7]

Fuller's dances and her experiments with lighting technique and film as media of new art placed her at the center of the early twentieth-century avant-garde, of artistic reflections on forms of signification in the era of modernism. No one perceived this more clearly than Stéphane Mallarmé. In his text "Autre Etude de Danse" (Another dance study) from the collection *Divagations*,[8] Mallarmé writes about Fuller's dances (which he had seen at the Folies-Bergères in 1893):

> In the fearsome bath of the materials swoons—radiant and cold—the interpreter who illustrates many gyratory themes towards which stretches a thread in full bloom: an unfolding, like giant petals or butterflies, all very clear and straightforward. . . .

> That a woman should like the flight of clothes with a powerful or vast dance to the point of lifting them, infinitely high, like the expansion of her own being—*The lesson* is to be found in this spiritual effect. (114)

Mallarmé envisions Fuller—that is, not the dancer, but rather the upward-surging motion of her skirts, that is, "l'envolée de vêtements"—to be a manifestation of his muse. The *inspiratrice* reveals to him the relationship of clothes and body—analogous to the association of text and meaning. In order to specially emphasize the distinctness of Fuller's innovation, Mallarmé contrasts it with classical ballet's models of ideography and corporeal signs: the *écriture corporelle* of the ballerina appears, like the conventional rhetorical attribute of ornament, as "ornatus" and the text's intellectual core.

According to Mallarmé, the production of signs in dance is in principle impersonal[9]—the body becomes sign when stripped of its individuality. Hence, the dancer appears not as woman (she is not "une femme qui danse"), but as a *metaphor*. Her movements are not "dance," but a *symbol* of "dance"—a metaphor giving form to the *écriture corporelle*.

The dance is a "poem set free of any scribe's apparatus" (109). Mallarmé finds the disappearance of the author, which distinctly characterizes his poetology,

---

7. See Brandstetter and Ochaim 1989, 68ff. and 123.

8. Mallarmé 2001a. Page numbers for the following quotations in the text.

9. This—the idea of "dance's impersonal nature"—is an *axiom* (according to Mallarmé) that was adopted, e.g., by Hofmannsthal (in his essay "On Pantomime" in 1910), but also by other authors and critics and became a fixed formula in discourse on dance aesthetics.

embodied in the dance of fabrics in Fuller's *Serpentine Dance*. The creator of the choreography disappears. The billowing waves of silk and light dance around an "empty space," a "nothingness," which the wealth of fabric envelops like the gossamer weave of an abstract text.

Mallarmé compares the dancer to a magical spider, who generates the text of her art from within as the moving "tissue" of a veil, which she then draws back into herself—thus concealing herself at the heart of the texture.

The metamorphosis of the figurations causes the space to open up and change its appearance with the help of the fabric. As the veil ornaments circle around an empty center, they release a play of the imaginary, the topos formulas of moving spirals unleash cascades of images, which in turn glide into empty, spatial figurations of fantasy that evade interpretation: "All emotion comes from you, creating a milieu; or swoops down upon you, incorporating it" (115).

The result is "visions scattered as soon as they are recognized." The space, in which the pure signs of dance poetry unfold and lose themselves, remains "free to follow the fictions, a stage whispered into being by the game of a veil" (115).

For Mallarmé, Loïe Fuller's dance contained the birth of the absolute metaphor, the theatrical equivalent to his idea of a *poésie pure*. He interpreted Fuller's dance of light as a dramatic play of absolute signs, pulsating in that empty space in which the creator of the moving signs herself also ultimately disappears in the spiraling fabric—in the silks, that is, in the "texture." This movement around a concealed center, which stands for itself, empty, without meaning, brings forth the absolute arabesque, twining upward out of itself without referential connection to the signified.

The work—that is, both the dance and Mallarmé's own poetry—constitutes itself as rhythmic vibrating movement in a constant state of coming-into-being. For Mallarmé, the real creative dynamics of Fuller's dance lay in this pulsation of pure movement, of color and light around a corporeal center, which dissolves in the process, disappears into nothingness, leaving behind the absolute work of art.

The disappearance of the author[10] in the process of writing the absolute book *Le Livre* implies the production and the destruction of text as a virtually endless act of writing and reading. Fuller's dance, the constant metamorphoses of textile spatial formulas destroying the body—sign and creator of signs all in one—make up, as it were, a theatricalization of Mallarmé's notion of text: a philosophy of producing and reading of texts, a basic pattern that Roland Barthes describes as epitome of the modern experience of signs:

---

10. On the subject of the author and the absolute book, see Ingold 1988, as well as Ingold and Wunderlich 1992.

Text means *tissue*; but whereas hitherto we have always taken this tissue as a product, a ready-made veil, behind which lies, more or less hidden, meaning (truth), we are now emphasizing, in the tissue, the generative idea that the text is made, is worked out in a perpetual interweaving; lost in this tissue, this texture the subject unmakes himself, like a spider dissolving in the constructive secretions of its web. Were we fond of neologisms, we might define the theory of the text as a *hyphology* (*hyphos* is the tissue and the spider's web).[11]

Mariano Fortuny and Gabriele D'Annunzio

In his novel *Forse che sì forse che no*, Gabriele D'Annunzio describes a dance quite similar to Loïe Fuller's *Serpentine Dance*: the development of a moving theatrical space through the employ of a veil. In one scene, the protagonist Isabella spontaneously improvises a dance in front of her lover Paolo as gesture of love and seduction. She develops her performance entirely out of the possibilities suggested to her by her "dance costume." She wraps one of the famous Fortuny Knossos shawls around her naked body and begins to dance.

Mariano Fortuny—Spanish painter and set and costume designer—was the creator of robes that were considered the epitome of a new, flowing style of early twentieth-century dress. These dresses combined harmony of movement in the drapery of the fabric with the patterns of abstract ideograms. They were made of the finest translucent silk, stenciled with symmetrical, largely geometric or meandering patterns based on Minoan Cretan art. These rectangular wide silk fabrics allowed themselves to be draped and wrapped around the body in endless variations. They simultaneously served to reveal, conceal, shape, and improve the physical form. They clung to the body, giving it total freedom of expression. These fabrics seemed literally to demand that they be danced in so as to fully unfold their potential. Felix Poppenberg's review of the *Decorative Variations* in Ruth St. Denis's dance with the Fortuny shawls conveys an impression of the properties these textiles had as a medium of dance:

Charm of lines and rhythms in softly flowing fabrics. . . . Ruth St. Denis . . . presented variations of these veils, études in a material very rich in theatrical potential, and she demonstrated how fanciful women talented in the

11. Barthes 1975, 64.

graceful arts can endlessly engage their playful instincts in these suites of veils.[12]

Such is the "playfulness" that Isabella unfolds in her erotic performance for Paolo Tarsis: "She had draped one of those long shawls of oriental gauze around herself, which the magician Fortuny dipped in the mysterious lyes of his color troughs and draws out again laden with foreign dreams."
It is the "long thin fabric" of the veil that "dances."
Isabella sets the fabric in

that floating motion which incessantly rippled the disc-shaped outer edges of the medusas. Occasionally she gave them a spiral twist and then let go, and the veil continued its circling motion like a tornado of rosy sand, drooped, and shortly before it threatened to collapse, the fleeting fingers revived and reawakened it to new movement, a new twirl.[13]

The metaphor of water and the rhythmic movements of the Medusa-like fringe (as in Valéry's dance essay "Degas Dance Drawing"), the topos formulas of the circle and the spiral convey an image of the spatiality of this dance, which is already influenced by the pattern of Fuller's work: movement emanating from the body, perpetuating itself in slightly delayed, spiraling panels of fabric, constantly bringing forth new abstract formation in an act of continuous metamorphosis. In her intimate performance, Isabella even uses a lighting effect typical of Fuller's dances—an alternating play of colors:

The unsteady light, in which the gold of the moon mixed with the intensity of the night sky, seemed to transform her into a mediatrix between day and night. Her naked feet moved as if along a narrow and invisible isthmus, which separated the sea of day from that of the night. (200)

D'Annunzio's epic staging of the dance appears as a mixture of intimate private performance and theatricalization of the natural surroundings: an "open-air" piece, as envisioned by turn-of-the-century theater reformers, such as Georg Fuchs, Max Reinhardt, and Harry Graf Kessler in other forms of open-air theater modeled on the amphitheaters of antiquity.

12. Poppenberg 1907–08, 741f. Translation: Elena Polzer.

13. D'Annunzio 1910, 199. (Further quotations in the text.) All quotations are from the German version of *Forse che sì forse che no* and translated by Elena Polzer.

Unlike Fuller's dances of light, which unfolded their effect on the dark stage, the play of lights on Isabella's dancing veil is created by the reflection of the sun setting over the mouth of the Arno. Under open skies, against the splendid backdrop of the Pisan mountains and the broad glittering expanse of the Tyrrhenian sea, the movements of the dance stand out in stark relief— themselves an element of the landscape's play of lines and colors, as the dramatic rays of the sunset are transformed in the silk fabric of the dancing costume:

> The insentient moon rose without a single ray like a large water flower out of the cloudy haze of the Pisan mountains, while opposite on the outermost edge of the Tyrrhenian sea, the disc of the sun, not much larger, burned up in such wild fire that it immediately burned up into ashes. The lower dense strips of clouds covered it like a layer of ashes that drops off and forms anew. In the same way that the line of the water divided the disc in half, it was as if only a last heap of embers remained behind, which now faded. And now the sea transformed into the divine garment of evening, a garment of such wonderful pleats, that Isabella desired a piece of it. "If I could dress myself in such silks." (196f.)

Isabella's erotic dance is sparked by the dying "fire dance" of the sun as a spectacle of nature. The pathos of the sunset and the topos formulas of the landscape are transposed onto the scenery of the moving silks. The natural forms of the surrounding environment are translated into dance as figurations of Isabella's own individual movements and reinterpreted into expressive gestures of shared passion. Behind Isabella

> the extremity of the sickle-shaped curving coast appeared. The wood-covered coast of Versilia and the country of Luni, the mountains of Carrara in such fragrance that they also seemed like figures in the dance, a chain of high virgins, leaning toward the East to the rhythms of the choir. (199)

The intensity of the sensual perception of nature's beauty transforms itself into dance in the creation of movement: the dancer gathers the lines and circles of the landscape into her steps and gestures—she collects and interprets—integrating them into a fabric of fleeting spatial phenomena. Both the iridescent changing lights and the stony backdrop of the marble cliffs of Carrara (these ancient witnesses to the history of sculpture) are transformed into figurations of movement and abstracted from their concrete form. Thus they represent an imaginary choir that seems to comment on the dance—entirely in accord with

Nietzsche's *Birth of Tragedy* and the pathos of that tragedy which the dancer faces in her near future.

D'Annunzio compares the dancer to an "embroiderer" who "chooses and pulls out in alternating gestures the threads for her work from the numerous colorful skeins" and unifies the lines of the space both near and far into a "creation of ephemeral beauty."[14] In the dance, all lines appear to converge, those of the horizon and those of the vertical axis: "From the battlements of the marble mountains to the top of the low, sandy promontory, all flowed together in this play of manifestations and found expression in this flight of invention" (199f.).

In this creation of movement, which transforms nature and landscape as topos formulas into figurations of dance, the dancer appears in dual form. On the one hand, she is a culturally defined character, a medium between nature and art. By gathering up the surrounding space in her dance, she takes on the role of a reader, a carrier of knowledge and an interpreter, who translates images and symbols gleaned from the book of nature into movements of the body.

On the other hand, she also appears as a mythical character. Isabella's dance, which stitches together transience and permanence into a texture of lines, is reminiscent of the Norse Norns, in whose hands the threads of human fate converge. And her demonic features, the association of her physical form with nature and with the cycle of the seasons, recall traits of an archaic mother goddess.

Moreover, the aura of the mythical is emphasized by the veil's horizon of meaning—that veil in which Isabella dances and through which she transforms herself into a medium of the dancing natural landscape. Like the shimmering reflection of a mirage, the moving silk fabric reflects the phantasmagoria of desire.

The Fortuny shawl, which Isabella drapes around her body, with the ornaments and meander print of the Knossos palace, the Cretan labyrinth of the Minotaur, becomes the topos of "a linear reflection of a mythological idea" (Karl Kerényi). Not only the natural spectacle of the sun setting over the mouth of the Arno—a topography that is compared over the course of the novel with the "Inferno"—is inscribed in the silk scarf, but also the lines of

14. D'Annunzio 1910, 199. There is a similar relationship of "text-texture" to dance text in Mallarmé (see above): in the exposition of a poetics of dance in the *Divagations*, the dancer is compared to a spider who draws the threads of her web out of her body into movement, into the dance space, and artfully weaves them together; in D'Annunzio, dance poetics is conceived (here however with a turn into the mythological) in an analog image of the "embroiderer."

the labyrinth.[15] In this way, the mythical topos formula of the Minoan dance palace that Daedalus created for Ariadne is interwoven with the fabric of the veil and with the dancer. She traces the "dance steps" of Ariadne, while simultaneously embodying Ariadne's half-brother—the Minotaur, who has been banned to the center of the labyrinth.[16]

Isabella's devouring femininity is contrasted by D'Annunzio with the rational masculinity of the *superuomo* Paolo Tarsis. The record-breaking pilot and hero Paolo—a narcissistic self-portrait of the author—who is addicted to race cars and airplanes, frees himself from the clutches of erotic passion by fleeing into flight. He breaks away from the dimensions of the labyrinthine paths on the ground. In the mythical role of Icarus, he takes to the air as a victorious, death-defying hero, striving in flight toward the sun. Isabella's dance costume, transformed into the scenery of the topography, changes in Paolo's flight into the soaring flight of a bird, whose wings "clothe" the dance in the third dimension.

Like Daedalus—who not only invented the labyrinth as a dancing ground for Ariadne, but was also the inventor of a flying apparatus that released humankind from the shackles of gravity—D'Annunzio raises his hero above the earthly paths of folly into the spirals of an aerial dance:

> How big and masculine the sky is today. . . . He feels again how his body commands the entire machine, that the same air circulates within its wings and in the hollow bones of birds as in his own lungs. Again he is overcome by the feeling of no longer being a man in a machine, but a single giant body joined together. The sensation of the outrageously new animates every one of his movements. He flies along as if on his own rising air. "The heron! Tarsis!"
>
> He sees the disc rising on the signal mast that marks his victory, hears the roar of the sea, which rises up towards him, looks down, surveys the gray mass of the crowd with a thousand white faces, a thousand outstretched hands. And although he sinks downward in a curve toward his destination, it nevertheless seems to him as if he were rising to giddy heights over the rigid watchtower. He shoots downward, turns, flies past in

15. In the context of the novel, the motif of the labyrinth takes on a *nodal* meaning as leitmotif, in the formula "Forse che sì forse che no" written along the drawing of a labyrinth on the ceiling of the palace of the Gonzaga, which is later linked to Isabella's dance with the Knossos shawl; see the section on the bee dance in Part I of this book.

16. The incestuous moments already inherent in the Ariadne-Minotaur myth are activated in D'Annunzio's novel—as well as mythically grounded in the labyrinth motif—in Isabella's relationship to her brother.

a roar of victory, a whirl of radiance, white and light, glistening brass and
steel, a herald of the ultimate life. (80ff.)[17]

The airplane becomes one with the pilot. The Icarian hero is glorified as a
mythical flying creature, as an epitome of male heroism—"a herald of the ultimate life." The mythologization of the aviator in D'Annunzio's novel is a translation of the achievements of modern aeronautics into literature. On the one
hand, Paolo Tarsis is depicted as a confident flight technician based on the
model of pilots such as Blériot, Cambiaso, and Curtiss. On the other hand, the
aura of his character evolves out of a juxtaposition of various literary patterns,
namely allusions and quotations of texts, which can be interpreted as celebrating the pilot as a national hero and superhuman.

Aside from Homer's version of the myth of Icarus, D'Annunzio's novel also contains quotations from Dante's *Divine Comedy* and Nietzsche's "Aeronauts of the
Spirit" from the last part of *The Dawn* (1881). This comparison of the pilot, his corporeal unit with a flying apparatus, with a bird—"ornitio" is the victorious cry of a
pilot chasing through the ether—is introduced in D'Annunzio's novel in the form
of multiple motifs.[18] In a double citation of Dante's *Divine Comedy*, D'Annunzio
evokes the anthropomorphic form of a bird in flight. The allusion is to that episode
with Paolo (the name here also appears as a quotation) and Francesca in the fifth
canto of the *Inferno* in which the lovers "as cranes, chanting their dol'rous notes,
traverse the sky"[19] and the "witless flight" of Ulysses from the twenty-sixth canto:

> All the sudden there awakened in the clans of Italy the memory of that first
> pair of wings to plunge into the Greek sea, the Icarian wings, fashioned of
> hazel rods, joined with the sinew of cattle, winged with vultures' feathers.
> "Un-ala sul mare è solitaria!" the poet's call rang out from the tower.
> *Chi la racoglierà? Chi con più forte*
> *Lega saprà rigiugnere le penne*
> *Sparse per ritenare il folle volo?*

17. On the subject of literature and aviation, and for an interpretation of D'Annunzio's aviator
novel against the backdrop of the historical development of aviation, see Ingold 1980, 28ff.

18. For example, the motif of the swallow, which Isabella finds trapped in her room and sets
free.

19. Dante Alighieri, 2004.

> As cranes,
> Chanting their dol'rous notes, traverse the sky,
> Stretch'd out in long array: so I beheld
> Spirits, who came loud wailing, hurried on
> By their dire doom.

And all of the sudden they remembered the dream of the Niflung, which already hovered over Leonardo's cradle, the new Daedalus, the creator of art and machines, the new Prometheus unfettered. (54f.)

For the aviator, the "new Prometheus unfettered," the D'Annunzian super-human, the ether becomes the unwritten space from which he brings forth the "outrageously new" with every spiral of his movements.[20] The figurations, which he draws in the airspace, are the true purpose of his great dance, an autoerotic vertical movement. The grandeur of the male choreography in flight forms a contrafacture to Isabella's earthbound female "labyrinthine dance."

In D'Annunzio's work the Icarian hero is not just "influenced by the Nietzschean myth of an authoritarian aristocratic super-humanity."[21] In F. T. Marinetti's novel *Mafarka le Futuriste* (1910),[22] published in the same year as D'Annunzio's *Forse che sì forse che no*, the aerial hero, Gazourmah—"le héros sans sommeil"—also demonstrates traits of a grotesque-gigantic, exaggerated mythical creature. Gazourmah, Mafarka's son—his body is made of wood, the wings of metal, his heart is an airplane engine—celebrates himself as "l'invincible, maître de l'espace, le géant aux vastes ailes oranges." He embodies the myth of the machine creature: a centaur of the age of modern aviation.

Der Zentaur (The Centaur) is the title of an aviator novel by Frank Thieß, published circa 1931.[23] The cult of the aviator, this aristocrat of the airspace, justifies, as in D'Annunzio's and Marinetti's novels, the use of words such as "heroes," "fame," "victory," "death defying," "valor." The "Dream of Centaurs," which the aeronautical engineer and pilot Almquist[24] dreams in his youth—during a stay in Italy—is a phantasm of initiation, of the birth of the hero as leader. In the night before this dream, Almquist encounters a Greek-clad female dancer in a part of the city filled with ancient architecture and sculpture: the beauty of her body, the effect of her dance as an epitome of erotic-female movement figurations, evokes the image of the centaur as a counterfantasy, the demonic

---

20. On *aerodance*, the aesthetics of Futurist *aerodanza*, and how they are connected to D'Annunzio's treatment of the subject of flight, as well as the way Nietzsche is referred to in the writings of Marinetti, Morasso, and Azari, see the section on "Aerodance" in Part II of this book.

21. Ingold 1980, 38. Translation: Elena Polzer.

22. See Ingold 1980, 76ff.; see also Riesz, who specially emphasizes the depiction of decline as a gigantic "spectacle" of war and its associated experimentation with an "écriture fasciste" (Riesz 1983, 85–99).

23. See Schwerte 1991, 275–93.

24. This character in the novel is based on the real-life Swiss aviator Mittelholzer, a "wiry sportsman and likewise author"; see Schwerte 1991.

corporeality of men. As in D'Annunzio's novel, the male protagonist attempts to distinguish himself from the pathos formula of femininity by fleeing into the movement figuration of flight.

Ten years before writing his novel *Der Zentaur*, Thieß published his aesthetics of dance, *Der Tanz als Kunstwerk* (*Dance as Work of Art*).[25] In it he systematically defines the fundamental aesthetic principles of modern dance as being distinct from classical ballet. One of the categories of his dance aesthetic is *elevation*. In an extensive chapter titled "Overcoming Gravity," Thieß discusses the fundamental meaning of the principle of elevation for modern dance. He states that, although the virtuosity of the ballerina has led to "empty performances,"

> none the less, this demand for conquest of gravity was based on a correct conception of the nature of dance; for its main tendency is always to surmount the bonds of massive weight, and lightness of movement is, perhaps, the cardinal demand one has to make on a dancer. . . . It is, after all, nothing but the conquest of material resistance as such.[26]

The principle of elevation[27] marks the coincidence of dance movement and the spatial figuration of flight. What remains unresolved here is the final observation that the spatial formula of dance and flight choreography become mere ornaments in the configuration of hero and masses—both in the "fascist" flight novels of D'Annunzio and Marinetti, as well as in Thieß's descriptions of the aviator hero as the potential "true leader."

Léon Bakst and Carl Einstein

Carl Einstein once described Léon Bakst (1866–1924), the epochal set and costume designer for Serge Diaghilev's Ballets Russes, as the "Maquilleur of Space" and as a "great mime of color."[28] Einstein dedicated an introductory essay to the Russian painter and stage designer in a bibliophile edition of sketches and figurines, published in 1927 by the Berlin Wasmuth Verlag. Bakst (actually Lew Samojlowitsch Rosenberg) grew up in St. Petersburg, where he studied painting. He soon, however, left the Academy and founded the journal *Mir Iskusstwa* (*World*

25. Thieß 1920.

26. Ibid., cited in Langer 1983, 40.

27. See Brandstetter 1984; Rothe 1979, 60ff.

28. Einstein, "Léon Bakst," in Einstein 1981, 341–68.

of Art) together with Alexandre Benois and Diaghilev. The artists and intellectuals associated with *Mir Iskusstwa* organized, for example, exhibitions of Western avant-garde art; Bakst designed the magazine's book decorations. He became a master in the art of décor, which *Jugendstil* and art nouveau had developed to a degree of exquisite refinement—in book decorations, borders, and arabesques, for example, by Aubrey Beardsley, William Bradley, Alfons Mucha, Eugène Grasset, Peter Behrens, Otto Eckmann, Koloman Moser, and Henry van de Velde. Later the activities of *Mir Iskusstwa* shifted to the presentation of Russian art treasures: the Secessionists became explorers of the archives of Russian art history. They collected icons and family portraits, folk paintings, and old furniture. Herein lay the roots of Bakst's eclecticism, that protean capacity of transformation which benefited the "spatial actor" (Einstein). Einstein aptly describes the mixture of styles that Bakst had at his disposal: "This dandy and archaeologist presents himself as a careful Fauve. A bit of Munich *Jugend*, a little crafty ornamentation, and Beardsley's shadow reveal themselves occasionally."[29]

In 1900, Bakst turned to theater. His first scenography was for a performance at the Hermitage of the French pantomime *The Heart of the Marquise*. Stage décor and costume design now became his true artistic calling, although he still continued to paint.

Ten years later Bakst triumphed with a pompous-exotic mise en scène for the ballet *Shéhérazade* (1910) in Paris. Diaghilev engaged the services of the versatile artist as scenographer for the productions of his Ballets Russes in the West. Bakst created, for example, the set design and decorations for *Cléopâtre* (1909), *Le Carnaval* (1910), *Shéhérazade* (1910), *Le Spectre de la Rose* (1911), *Narcisse* (1911), *Le Dieu bleu* (1912), *Thamar* (1912), *L'Après-midi d'un Faune* (1912), *Daphnis et Chloé* (1912), *Papillons* (1914), *Josephslegende* (1914), and *The Sleeping Princess* (1921).

The ballet historian André Levinson, a Russian emigrant like Bakst and Diaghilev and author of the first monograph about Bakst (1922), described the scenography for *Shéhérazade* as a masterpiece of Bakst's oriental works:

> The reason for it is the fact that this Persian ballet, which adapts the prologue of the *Thousand and One Nights* to a subtle and decorative score composed by Rimsky-Korsakoff, the eminent colorist, is the affirmation and, what is still more important, the realization of a great principle—the optic unity of a production. The sides of a large green tent enriched with gold and black encase and encircle the ladies' apartment which is peopled with a crowd dressed in orange, pink and green clothes, who surround

---

29. Einstein, "Léon Bakst," in Einstein 1981, 341–68 (further quotations in the text). All Einstein quotations on Bakst: translated by Elena Polzer.

the single royal jewel, the Sultana Zobeide, a blue sapphire in a setting of rubies and emeralds. Thus the costumes either blend with the scenery in an infinity of fine shades and gradations of value that have been carefully studied out, or they contrast with the scenery in accordance with the visible logic of complementary colors. Is the result, then, a ballet? It is a living scenery with interchangeable elements.[30]

Levinson already emphasizes here those basic characteristics of Bakst's scenographic art that Einstein later incorporated in his text[31] and embellished into a poetology of the spatial mask. These characteristics are

- An orgiastic use of color in the form of fabrics (costumes and stage curtains)
- An opulent stylized exoticism
- A scenic, animated quality in the "texture" of the costumes and the scenography
- The decomposition of the cubic perspective of space into textile ornaments that oscillated between line, surface, and space.[32]

In his analysis, Einstein emphasizes that Bakst's scenography leaves the realm of mere décor, the decorative and the illustrative, behind. Bakst's scenography is the "mask of the drama": the dance costumes provoke a dramatization of the space. The lights, the gestures and colors function as quasi codirectors, as "dramatic stimuli" (354). "The mask of the spaces acts out the drama, actively takes part in the action, and the play of color tracks every reverberation thanks to the power of the reflectors" (356).

Hence, Einstein emphasizes the difference of Bakst's scenography from the decorative and the illustrative, which still influenced Bakst's earlier works. At this point in time, *Ornament and Crime* (1910), Adolf Loos's pamphlet against the "excessive ornamentation" of art nouveau, was, of course, already so outdated that a reappraisal of Bakst's scenographies from before 1914 from the perspective of

30. Levinson 1971, 158.

31. It is very likely that Einstein knew Levinson's Bakst monograph; there are indications of this in the analogies between Levinson's description of *Shéhérazade* and Einstein's texts on dance; e.g., in the depiction of the "tent" (see Einstein's account, 1981, 358) and in the detail of the great glowing globe, which found its way as a motif into Einstein's pantomime *Nuronihar*.

32. This blurring of the scene's two- and three-dimensionality particularly characterizes Bakst's stage design for *L'Après-midi d'un Faune* (1912); see Levinson 1983, 125. The aesthetic of two-dimensionality in the representation (of the space) must be seen in the context of an interpretation of Japanese woodblock prints; see Gebhard 1988.

the 1920s literally imposed itself on Einstein (also in the face of his own prewar writings). *Ornament* now no longer meant, as in the case of Loos, an enslavement of the surface. Instead, in Bakst's scenography, the ornament became a figuration that itself created space. The decor, as it were, emancipated itself from its illustrative function to become an independent actor in the piece: "The scenography used to be no more than the framework of the plot," but now, since Wagner's concept of the *Gesamtkunstwerk*, the scenography had become "a collaborator" (356).

Like the scenographic wrappers of moving fabric, which represented "theatricality" in Loïe Fuller's dance costumes, Bakst's tents unfurled in the space like "precious robes." "Flowing drapery," moving colors transformed the scene into a spatial mask, animated by dance movement:

> More than anything else, Bakst loved to build compartments, to pitch tents, which enveloped the dancers and actors like gleaming, decorative shawls. These tents are often the final festive fabric coverings, which sheath performers and scenery. Bakst is very skilled in wrapping a few squares of dramatic space in flowing folds and contrasting colors. These wide masks consolidate the moving and swirling colors of the dancers. (357f.)

The metaphor of envelopment—of the "wrap," "coat," the "robe," the "mask"—paraphrases and modifies the basic concept behind that spatial and corporeal formula which Einstein sees substantiated in Bakst's work: the concept of scenography as *dance costume*.

In this visual realm of staged dance costumes, Bakst is the "great couturier of fairy tales" (figure 41): "He dresses pantomimes like living bodies." However, these acts of metamorphosis, which place the scenography in the position of the true "dancing" protagonist of the dramatic action, also transform, dissipate, dissolve the body of the dancer. In a chapter entitled "Tanzende Gewänder" (Dancing robes) in reference to Bakst's scenography for *Shéhérazade*,[33] Einstein translates Bakst's ornamental poetry of textile art into *textual* art.

> In dimly lit tents, colorful robes circle, a red and green billowing pair of pants jumps over velvet blue silvery robes, the ornaments of the costumes rotate between the colorful decorations, the entire space swirls upward in a rhythmic moving ornament of color. A woman dances and whirls in a whirr of gold and green stripes, the suns on her dress roll with her; it is this robe that allows the

33. Here Einstein not only translates the dance-scenographic event from *Shéhérazade* into literature, he also weaves other intertextual threads into his reflections on the "text" of the scene: the section in which Einstein refers to *Shéhérazade* clearly shows influences from corresponding text passages in Levinson (see the previously quoted sections from Levinson 1983, 110f.); on the aspect of "poetic texture" in Einstein's aesthetics, see Kleinschmidt 1992, 200ff.

Figure 41 Léon Bakst, *Bacchantess* (costume sketch, 1911).
SOURCE: Bibliothèque de l'Opéra, Paris, France

dancing to appear big and bold. The colors reveal even the smallest rhythmic variation, the robe dances and the dancer almost seems to disappear inside it. The robe is the only thing that makes her enchantingly visible. (358)

"The robe dances": the dancer disappears in the moving lines of the fabric. Here, it is not the body that performs the dance, but rather the textile ornament of the dance costume. Dance only becomes a visible element of the spatial composition thanks to the movements of the fabric. While the dance dissolves in the labyrinthine spatial formula of the texture, the space itself becomes the true subject of dance, as a "rhythmically moving ornament of color."

The individual form of the dancing body vanishes in a scenography activated by textile masks and movements. The dissolution of the dancer's body resembles its fragmentation by the ornament: "This dancer is divided into pieces by the ornaments of the costume. It is not a human dancing, but rather an ornament, forms flying and whirling" (358).

The metamorphosis of the body—from figure to ornament, from image to symbol—resembles a process of abstraction sprung from movement. The form is fragmented, deconstructed. The text of textiles and colors weaves the body into the dancing spatial mask.

Scenography, costume, and movements are thus arranged into a *theatrical tatouage*: the dancer-body is tattooed by the moving ornaments of the fabric. Dance movement inscribes itself in the space through the "textile tattoo," the inseparably soldered signifier-signified-link of body and symbol, of skin and ornament.

The poetry of the spatial mask, which Einstein sees implemented in Bakst's moving scenography, stands in direct contrast to Einstein's thoughts on the sculptural mask in his essay "Negro Sculpture" (1915).[34] Sculpture is frozen movement: "It absorbs time, by integrating into its form what we experience as movement" (131). The absorption of the temporal dimension into the sculpturally configured space transforms the mask into a medium between space and dance: "the kinetic act must be arrested, must be fixed to become an unconditionality" (132). The mask represents "fixed ecstasy."

However, the dancing, moving, scenographic spatial masks in the works of Bakst communicate a theatrical liberation from such fixations—"the wonderful performed masks," whose glamorous era ended with the Ballets Russes: "After them came the age of exercising girls and ballets mécaniques."[35]

Oskar Schlemmer and the "Spatial-Plastic" Costume

Abstract dance, as first anticipated by Loïe Fuller's "Danses lumineuses," was later adopted and further developed in a new direction by the artist Oskar Schlemmer.

Fuller's works emphasized the abstract line in space, the dancing textile surface, a constant transformation of the space with the help of moving sculptures of light and dance, whereas Schlemmer experimented in

34. Einstein 2004.

35. Einstein 1981, 363. Translation: Elena Polzer.

his *Triadic Ballet* (1922)[36] with a constructivist model of transforming the body with the help of costume, by converting dance movements into spatial sculpture. Schlemmer experimented with the possibilities of new materials to replace textile costumes. He particularly scorned the "inevitable veil" as a medium of staging movement: "stiff, concealed forms, metal, for example, light aluminum, but also rubber, celluloid, flexible, unbreakable glass—the arsenal of all materials known and used to date only by industry and by science."[37]

Schlemmer's concepts of form, from which he transposed his "mathematics of dance" into ballet, stemmed from geometry and stereometry:

> The laws of cubical space are the invisible linear network of planimetric and stereometric relationships. The mathematic corresponds to the inherent mathematic of the human body and creates its balance by means of movements, which by their very nature are determined *mechanically and rationally*.[38]

Like Edward Gordon Craig and his theory of the *Übermarionette*, Schlemmer emphasized the rational, mechanical presentation of body and movement on stage, free from the pathos formulas of affect: the actor or the dancer should not appear as a human being representing a human being, but as an *art figure*.

The direct result of the art figure interacting with the "cubical, abstract space of the stage" is *Raumtanz* [spatial dance]—literally,

> the space as a whole is dancing, i.e., it is moved mechanically.
>
> A "space dance" is what we once called the form of movement theatre, which was performed on the Bauhaus's stage. . . . the space itself became intensely expressive, yet this was only due to the dancers' variations in the speed of their kinetic actions.[39]

Schlemmer's Bauhaus dances were a sequel to that spatial concept, which he had already based his *Triadic Ballet* on.[40] The piece was called *triadic* because

---

36. On the work of Oskar Schlemmer, especially concerning his theatrical pieces, see Maur 1977 and Scheper 1988.

37. Schlemmer 1986, 274–77. Translation: Elena Polzer.

38. Schlemmer 2002, 364.

39. Schlemmer 1990, 18.

40. Schlemmer wrote down his first ideas for a synaesthetic *Gesamtkunstwerk* as early as 1912, inspired by Scriabin's *Promethée* (1911) and Kandinsky's theater project *The Yellow Sound*.

of its threefold formal structure and color symbolism. It was structured into triads, three series of spatial-plastic costume dances, each with its own color horizon: the citrus yellow, the pink, and the black "series."

For this theatrical experiment, which Schlemmer also called a "mechanical ballet," he resorted to the potential of physical transformation inherent in costumes and masks (figure 42). He treated these "spatial-plastic costumes" not as a form of dress modeled on the body, but as a total enveloping body mask—designed according to the general laws of movement and space. The *Triadic Ballet* was an antiballet: Schlemmer's model of theater was not influenced by the physical techniques and spatial perspective of ballet, but by the materialization of abstract principles of space and movement in the total mask of the costume.

In his conception of these body masks for the stage, Schlemmer employed (what he called) a *Differenziermenschen* [differentiated man].[41] The associated image of the body is an analytical-abstract one. This is also reflected in the terminology and metaphors used by Schlemmer to describe his sketches and illustrations: "marionette," "mechanics of the joints," "technical organism," "ambulant architecture," "figure and linear network of space," and "egocentric linear network of space"—whereas the final term also brings up the subject of deindividualization in the relationship of figure and space. The "ego," here standing at the center of an imaginary space symbolized by a network of lines (figure 43), is not the ego of an individual human being, but the transpersonal topos of an "art-ego," in which the lines of space that transverse the cubic stage intersect.

The spatial-plastic costume links the abstract laws of the static space to the body's temporal, dynamic laws of movement. These general mechanical principles of movement were elaborated in the basic design of those distinctly color-coordinated space-body masks, which shaped the basic character of each of the three "series" in the *Triadic Ballet*:

- Part 1: costumes that transfer the laws of the surrounding cubical to the body ("ambulant architecture")
- Part 2: costumes that emphasize the mechanics of body movement in the form of a jointed doll ("marionette")
- Part 3: costumes that transform the laws of motion of the human body in space—rotation, intersection of space—into a kinetic mask ("technical organism")

In this early phase of development, the concept still displayed strongly symbolist traits. At its premiere in 1916 in Stuttgart (performed by the dancer couple Albert Burger and Elsa Hötzel), it had become a piece that the critics described as "cubist" and "Futurist." The completed piece was finally performed under the title *Triadic Ballet* on September 30, 1922, at the Württembergische Landestheater Stuttgart; see Maur 1977, 198; Scheper 1988, 53–56.

41. See Maur 1977, 282.

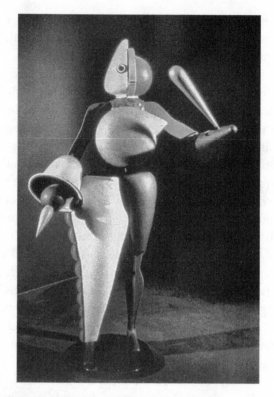

Figure 42 Oskar Schlemmer, *Das Triadische Ballett* (1922). Figurine "Der Abstrakte."
SOURCE: Photoarchiv C. Raman Schlemmer, 28050 Oggebio, Italy / © 1994 Oskar Schlemmer, Theater-Nachlaß, 79410 Badenweiler, Germany.

Schlemmer describes his attempts to transform the spatiotemporal art of dance into sculpture as an act of "molding the space":

> If one were to imagine a space filled with a soft, pliable substance in which the figures of the sequences of the dancer's movements were to harden as a negative form.[42]

The costume is thus the negative of the path drawn by dance through space, transformed out of its temporal dynamics into static sculpture. It forms a solidified container for the dance, which now surrounds the dancer as a plastic manifestation of his own movements, which have been reflected back on himself and in

42. Schlemmer 1969, 118.

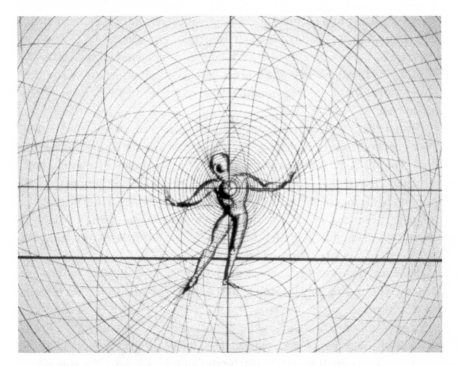

Figure 43 Oskar Schlemmer, *Egozentrische Raumlineatur* (Study of figure and space, around 1925).
SOURCE: Photoarchiv C. Raman Schlemmer, 28050 Oggebio, Italy / © 1994 Oskar Schlemmer, Theater-Nachlaß, 79410 Badenweiler, Germany.

doing so been reintegrated into the dance space. Henceforth, the dancer's movements are molded by the costume. The plastic "dance costume" envelops him like a shell. Not only in his "cocooned" form thus visually alienated; his movement possibilities are also altered by the limitations imposed by the costume. These movements likewise appear alien, dissociated, not "organically" related to the body—a result of their dialogue with the materiality of the body mask.

The dancer's body is visually alienated and moreover limited in its possibilities of movement both by the material (cardboard, papier-mâché, fabric padding, rubber, glass, aluminum) and by the abstract form—sphere, cylinder, hoops, spiral, and cube. The use of negative space, the limitation and alienation of movement, produces a study of what dance could be if defined as a kinetic phenomenon. The spatial-plastic costume allows both the dancer and the audience to experience the principles of dance movement in space in a different way. Schlemmer's *Triadic Ballet* is a reflection *on* dance *by* dance.

Schlemmer's analytical-constructivist approach, his concept of a "mathematics of dance," which he developed out of an analysis of space, body, and movement, featured a distinct fascination with technical-mechanical structures. Of course, this is not the same as a naïve enthusiasm for technology in the age of the machine. Instead, Schlemmer was interested in consciously reflecting the inevitable ongoing process of mechanization and medialization of modern life in art, in order to ultimately recognize "that which can *not* be mechanized."[43]

Schlemmer's perspective formulated in *Man and Art Figure*—the fundamental idea of utopian art—is related to Heinrich von Kleist's *On the Marionette Theater* and E. T. A. Hoffmann's depictions of automatons. By quoting both authors in the text (the term *art figure* is itself of Romance origin, namely an invention of Clemens Brentano),[44] Schlemmer interprets the terms *marionette, art figure, automaton,* and *the mechanical* in a positive way: namely as images symbolizing mankind's liberation from his "physical bondages," to "heighten his freedom of movement beyond his native potential."[45]

Schlemmer also saw his concept of the art figure confirmed by Edward Gordon Craig and his insistence on allowing the *Übermarionette* to act in place of actors.

Craig's manifesto *The Actor and the Übermarionette*,[46] published in 1908, is the result of a rejection of stage realism and illusionary theater, particularly as regards the function of the actor. The underlying idea behind the concept of the marionette is thus entirely committed to an aesthetic strictly opposed to all principles of "naturalism" or mimesis. According to Craig, art cannot be produced by nature. The human body, that is, the actor and his representative function, cannot be the material and medium of art. For the actor is "a living figure in which the weakness and tremors of the flesh are perceptible."[47] As art may not suffer chance nor the irrational, the human body is "by nature unfit as material for art."

For this reason, the actor must be replaced by the *Übermarionette*, where the prefix *über* also implies, similar to the prefixes *trans-* and *meta-,* overcoming common misconceptions of the marionette or puppet theater: "All puppets are now but low comedians. . . . Their bodies have lost their grave grace, they have become stiff" (ibid.).

43. Schlemmer 2002, 359.

44. In a late version of Brentano's *Märchen von Gockel, Hinkel und Gackeleia*, the term *art figure* plays a central, and also poetological, role.

45. Schlemmer 2002, 368.

46. Ibid., 159–65; on Craig, see Bablet 1965; on Craig's theatrical concept of an "autonomy of nonillusionary theater," see Fiebach 1991, 83–116.

47. Schlemmer 2002, 159.

The marionettes that Craig has in mind as role models are the puppets of a "beautiful art of a past civilization." Craig refers to Asian forms of puppet theater, Cambodian shadow puppets, and the marionettes of Japanese bunraku, but also to examples from Africa. For him, the marionette embodies more than merely the technical aspect of the mechanical-artificial. Instead, the puppet represents the renewal of theater out of ritual, out of old patterns of the ceremonial. The hieratic function here ascribed to the *Übermarionette* is that of a transfiguration of the actor/dancer body.

Hence, the *puppet* also symbolizes the Other in acts of (corporeal) dissociation and abstraction. The *Übermarionette* represents the transpersonal, the impersonal on stage—a topos that played a significant role in discourse surrounding theater reform, by Mallarmé, Hofmannsthal,[48] Kessler, Craig, and others, and that also defined how actors and dancers should perform on stage. The art figure, the marionette, is, moreover, the only "body" still able to display the craftsmanship of the artist. The marionette is the medium through which *art* can manifest itself on stage as more than the mere representation of *life* by a corporeal medium such as the actor:

And who knows whether the puppet shall not once again become the faithful medium for the beautiful thoughts of the artist. May we not look forward with hope to that day which shall bring back to us once more the figure, or symbolic creature, made also by the cunning of the artists, so that we can gain once more the "noble artificiality" which the old writer speaks of?[49]

The formula of "noble artificiality," which the marionette is meant to represent on the stage of the future, must be understood as a rebuttal of J. J. Winckelmann's aesthetics of "noble simplicity," that is, the explicit classicistic interpretation of ancient sculpture as the (ideal) representation of nature. The contemplation of Greek statues, the knowledge of a "noble simplicity and quiet grandeur" that they reveal, is that which transports the experience of "nature" via pathos formulas as corporeal engrams of human sensibility. Isadora Duncan, who strongly influenced Craig's work from 1904 to 1908, in the same period that Craig wrote his essay on the *Übermarionette*, likewise attempted to express this concept of Greek art as nature in her dancing as a form of (feminine)

---

48. See Hofmannsthal's text on the dances of Ruth St. Denis: "Die unvergleichliche Tänzerin" (published in English as "Her Extraordinary Immediacy" in *Dance Magazine* 1968) written in 1906, hence, in a period in which Hofmannsthal, Kessler, and Reinhardt were in contact with Craig about various (though ultimately not implemented) plans for new pieces.

49. Craig in Huxley and Witts 2002, 161.

theater of the future.[50] In doing so, she was of course quite at odds with Craig's anticlassical/antimimetic aesthetic, which accentuated the *artificial* in art and attempted to stage it in theater.[51] In her dancing, she programmatically embodied (and was interestingly praised by Craig in numerous articles in *The Mask!*) the mimic-pathognomic representation of (lost) unspoiled nature—that very model which Craig had rejected for himself.

Regarding this abstract pattern of representing the body and movement on stage, this emphasis on the "noble artificiality" of the marionette, Craig's concept seems related to Schlemmer's notions of the art figure, the mask as a medium of transforming the *natural* in art.

In his manifesto *Ballet?* published in 1922 to explain his concept of dance at the world premiere of the *Triadic Ballet*, Schlemmer contrasted "aesthetic mummery" with "cultic soul dance." The "mummery" of the body, the cloaking of the individual, is in itself what enables—via an awareness of one's own "physical bondage"—the symbolic transcendence of mankind's attachment to space and time. As a sculptor and painter, Schlemmer accessed a new approach to understanding issues of space and figuration through dance and theater. It allowed him to acquire tangible knowledge of the human form as a "being bewitched by space"[52] and henceforth transform it in his art. Beyond exploring an analytical-constructivist handling of space and the relationships of space to the art figure of the dancer, his reflections projected themselves far into the magic of space: in the conception of an imaginary space, a "metaphysical revue."

Schlemmer and his preference for typecasting, mechanization, and tectonic transmutation and abstraction preceded other tendencies, which characterized the European avant-garde in all areas of art, in painting and in literature, in theater, dance, and film. Karin von Maur summarizes Schlemmer's specific contribution to concepts of puppetry and symbolism in avant-garde dance and theater:

> Schlemmer thus managed—as Chaplin likewise did in other ways—the synthesis of man and marionette, of nature figure and art figure, into

---

50. On the subject of Duncan's dances, regarding the pathos formulas (Warburg) of Greek art, see the corresponding section in Part I of this book.

51. To my knowledge, this contradiction has not so far been registered in any relevant academic research; the opposite poles of abstraction and an aesthetic of *embodiment*, regarding associated images of movement and the body, have not been afforded any attention aside from references to the solitary aspect that the theater reform model emphasized dance and that Duncan's influence was substantial in this respect. See for a comparison Fiebach 1991, 85ff.

52. See Maur 1977, 24. Translation: Elena Polzer.

which he could pour his entire range of expressive possibilities: from weightless grace to monumental vehemence, from grotesque drollery to hieratic embodiment.[53]

In the fine arts, Schlemmer's concept of the "body-space-plastic" sparked a wide range of reactions, such as the robot-like, garishly colored characters in Jean Dubuffet's *Coucou Bazar*—his answer to Schlemmer's *Triadic Ballet*.

In dance, Gerhard Bohner continued Schlemmer's model in his *Abstract Dances* (1986). Bohner received significant inspiration from the *Triadic Ballet*, which he reconstructed in 1977, as well as from Schlemmer's Bauhaus dances, in which stage and body of the dancer were "clothed" completely in black similar to a black box, thus producing a "negative" space that allowed a staging of "abstract" movement and in which reflecting "hoop, rod and metal dances" unfolded a moving dynamic of their own as if suspended in a void. Bohner transferred this principle back into the body, by using paint and reflecting materials to emphasize individual body parts—in combination with black— and permit others to visually "disappear," thus situating the body as a moving asymmetrical abstract figuration in space.

In America, Alwin Nikolais experimented in the 1950s with a combination of space and body masks, abstract dance movements, and a surreal transformation of space in his piece *Masks, Props, and Mobiles* (1953). While Schlemmer still referenced Heinrich von Kleist's essay *On the Marionette Theater* and E. T. A. Hoffmann's automatons in his "mechanical ballets" and designed his abstract dance figuration in a semblance of Craig's concept of the *Übermarionette*, Nikolais's dance pieces also drew on other, less "classical" sources of inspiration—American Halloween pumpkin masks, the psychedelic spatial and color effects of LSD happenings, shaman dances, and bizarre models of extraterrestrial science fiction creatures.

In *Sanctum*, the dancers were all encased in seamless fabric tubes open on both sides. On the one hand, the audience saw the dancers in action— stretching the fabric, bending over, reaching out, molding it with head, feet, hands, and body. And on the other hand, they also saw asymmetrical, abstract plastic structures in space, which resembled bizarre, irregular trapezoids. Nikolais's spatial dance experiments thus oscillated between organic and geometrical body shapes, which manifested themselves not just in the wearing of costumes, but also in their removal, in masking and unmasking, in a play with the illusion of abstract forms in space. The magic of corporeality was thus made visible on stage in new ways and not only as metamorphosis and dematerialization.

53. Maur 1977, 200. Translation: Elena Polzer.

Chapter 2

Dance-Text

Transformations of Choreography

The process of abstracting the corporeal in dance—as opposed to a demonstrative presentation of the body—can be observed throughout the development of modern twentieth-century choreography from Loïe Fuller, Valentine de Saint-Point and Futurist dance, and Oskar Schlemmer's *Triadic Ballet* and the Bauhaus dances through to Alwin Nikolais, Merce Cunningham, and postmodern dance.

On the one hand, *abstraction* refers here to the entire ensemble of theatrical signs, and on the other, in a stricter dance-aesthetical sense, to a definition of the body as symbol.

In an overall dance-theatrical context, *abstraction* refers to far more than its common use as a term for *stylization*; it concerns the act of both

- Detaching oneself from a mimetic concept of theatrical performance, and
- Splitting up traditionally established complexes of collaboration between the arts in theater (e.g., stage design and costume design, dance, and music).

As the individual arts involved in staging theater became more autonomous, the range of possible applications for art and media broadened considerably. As paradoxical as it might seem, the abstraction of theater and the theatricalization of theater are closely linked. Moreover, abstraction in modern dance leads to different forms of *disembodiment*, not only in terms of a stylization of the dancer-body into a symbol of weightlessness (as in Romantic ballet), but also as a radical act of reassignment—in the deconstruction or even obliteration of the body as *body*—with the goal of eliciting a pure symbol of movement.

THE FEMALE BODY AND ABSTRACT DANCE: TOWARD
AN AMBIVALENCE OF INTERPRETATION

The body imagery of the female dancer (in the nineteenth and early twenti-eth centuries) was shaped by a cultural paradigm that was predominantly con-stituted and documented by the male gaze. Thus it emerged in dual form: on the one hand, as a signifier for the beautiful female body, presenting herself in dance to the admiring, desiring gaze and, on the other hand, in the syntax of choreography, as a purely kinetic signifier, from which all sexual connotations had been removed. Abstract forms of avant-garde dance disrupted this multi-plication of the semiotic function. The body of the dancer no longer appeared as *body*, as female form. It disappeared in the moving scenography of fabric and colored light, as in Loïe Fuller's dances, or appeared as a cipher in a web of texts and geometrical forms, as in Valentine de Saint-Point's *Métachorie*.

Métachorie, a neologism, was the name Saint-Point gave her concept and dance-creation of a synthetic movement art, which was meant to surpass all existing ideas about and forms of choreography. *Meta-choros*, moreover, implies the inclusion of self-reflection in dance on a metalevel of theory.

Despite this disruptive function of avant-garde self-reflection and self-presentation, conventional patterns of viewing the female dancer were pre-served in their dual form, even when dance attempted to blur the image of the body as an embodiment of the sexual and when this body image was altered from signifier of femininity to blank space. The *return* of the body as a topos of desire was the result of a *negation* of the body in an act of its transcendence. In this topos, the corporeal image of femininity condensed into an epitome of the erotic.

Detached from the actual figure of the female dancer, the semiotic constel-lation "female body–dance–erotic object" filled the blank space of the body in abstract dance as a schema of interpretation that took on a life of its own. We see this, for example, in one particular pattern of how Fuller's *Serpentine Dance* was read by her peers: the posters of artists ranging from Jules Cheret to Orazi, as well as the bronze sculptures, lamps, and figurines of Raoul Larche, Pierre Roche, and François Rupert Carabin present Fuller's physical form—in reality quite plump and rather corpulent, as photos of the time prove—only as slender and well-endowed, with all the markings of a sexually attractive being: the naked, slightly backward arching back, the wide skirt in translucent form or clinging to the contours of the body. The truly revolutionary aspect of her innovative dances—the sculptural movements of fabric, which concealed the moving body from sight—was retranslated in these patterns of interpretation back into a semiotic form of the feminine body. Undoubtedly, Fuller's dances were so fascinating in their process of transforming corporeality into a medium of its own that that moment, in particular, in which the body mysteriously disappeared in the movement, contained an intensely erotic element. However, it revealed itself merely to be imaginary potential: desire itself and not a true reflection of the actual object of desire.

Georges Rodenbach once wrote that the imaginary aspect of the erotic is that which unfolds from the magic of the dancer, whose body resembles "the rhythm on which everything depends, but which hides itself"[1]:

> Dance is pure allusion. For this very reason, it is the most accomplished of all poems. A plastic, colorful, rhythmic poem, in which the body is no more than a blank page, that page in which the poem writes itself.[2]

A distinct ambivalence of interpretation—in confrontation, on the one hand, with a new dance aesthetic and, on the other, in diversion of attention from artistic innovation to an affirmation of traditional attributions of the body—was also characteristic for most reactions to Valentine de Saint-Point's performance of her dance concept *Métachorie*.

After the premiere, some of the perplexed critics took refuge in emphasizing the "graceful" poses, the beautiful body of the dancer, praising legs, thighs, waistline, and "derrière." The standardized repertoire of reactions, which critics and the audience resorted to—in light of the strangeness of this production, which Saint-Point referred to as "danse idéiste"—ranged from, as it were, a quietly whistled appreciation of her body to a misogynistic denigration of female creativity. In a review by Jean-Jacques Brousson in *Gil Blas* from December 19, 1913,[3] the choreographer and dancer appears only in a few sentences. She is introduced as the grand-niece (*petite-nièce*) of the famous Lamartine. Already a prominent writer in her own right, she is now trying her hand at dancing. However, the critic gives practically no information about the dance itself or about Saint-Point's implementation of the novel theatrical concept that she had given the name *Métachorie*. In lieu thereof, he quotes a hymn to corporeal beauty from the Song of Songs and finally feigns a dialogue about women per se between Rodin[4] and Anatole France, ending with the statement: "Psyche is a little woman, who displays her bottom in thirty-six different ways."

1. Georges Rodenbach, cited in McCarren 1998, 124.

2. Rodenbach "Danseuse," in *Le Figaro*, May 5, 1896. Cited in Brandstetter and Ochaim 1989, 197. Translation: Elena Polzer.

3. Citations of this and all other documents concerning Saint-Point are, where not otherwise noted, from the files of the Rondel collection in the Bibliothèque de l'Arsenal, Paris; shelf number Ro 11973. All quotations cited here are translated by Elena Polzer from German.

4. Auguste Rodin was present during the rehearsals and at the premiere. Saint-Point considered herself one of Rodin's students; her collection of poems *Poèmes d'Orgueil* (Paris, 1908) contains two poems "à Rodin": "Ses Mains" and "Le Penseur."

By employing the old equation of dancer equals whore, the reviewer avoids confrontation with an avant-garde work of art choreographed by a woman. Instead, he restores (in a feigned dialogue between a sculptor and a poet) man in his role as Pygmalion—as creator and gourmet of the female form.

Saint-Point's intellectual aspirations toward the creation of a new concept of dance—her *Métachorie*, which she even dared to publish as a manifesto in spite of being a woman—provoked particularly cynical reactions from critics. Michel Georges-Michel writes in *Pall Mall*, Paris, December 13, 1913:

> No, not a dancer! A Métachorist. . . . But I'll leave the manifesto aside and speak directly of the festival.

And Georges Ploch ironically remarked in the January 1914 issue of the *Revue des Œuvres nouvelles* that women used to become dancers in order to entertain, to love, and to pray, but now

> they dance in order to think. About time too: philosophy was missing its legs. Let us thus turn to the "Métachorie" and Mme. de Saint-Point, its prophet.

The reviews of Colette (who, like Saint-Point, appeared in public as both a dancer and a writer) are by contrast very different. Her endorsement and her critique of Saint-Point's work are stated as concrete arguments. She praises the evocative performance and the intelligent choreography, but expresses her reservations about the principle of simultaneity, the juxtapositioning of dance, text, and projected symbols, as well as the "Merovingian" costume, which she considers to be an expression of naïve nationalism.

VALENTINE DE SAINT-POINT'S *MÉTACHORIE*

Who was Valentine de Saint-Point?[5] And what did the controversial dance piece *Métachorie* actually look like?

Saint-Point is doubtless one of the most exceptional artists of the avant-garde. Her oeuvre had many facets: as a visual artist, writer, and author of texts

5. Cf. the materials: program booklets, reviews in the file Ro 11973 mentioned above; cf. also Henri Le Bret 1923. Most often Saint-Point's avant-garde dance work is mentioned in connection with Futurism, to whose circles she is counted because of her manifestos on the "Futurist Woman" and "Lust," e.g., Bentivoglio 1984, 61–82; see also Lea Vergine 1980, 78f.; although the close association with Italian Futurism is contestable. On this see Le Bret, 40; he stresses that Marinetti's influence on Saint-Point is overestimated; that the influence of Nietzsche was more important; and, regarding her poetry, that her role model was Lamartine. See Volta 1992, 41f.

on art theory, as a dancer and performance artist, as well as, after 1934, a journalist and author of political texts.

Nevertheless: she is not included in any of the major reference works, neither
in *Grand Larousse Universel*, nor in German or Italian encyclopedias.[6] Valentine
de Saint-Point was the pseudonym of Anne-Jeanne-Valentine-Marianne
Desglans de Cessiat-Vercell, born on February 16, 1875, as the grand-niece of
Lamartine in Lyon. (She died on March 28, 1953, in Cairo.)

In her choice of pseudonym, Saint-Point drew a connection to her ancestors
in Burgundy. "Saint-Point" is a small town in the Mâconnais, in the Cluny area,
in whose fifteenth-century castle Lamartine liked to stay.

Valentine de Saint-Point began her eclectic career as a writer and painter. In
1904, she studied fine arts with Alfons Mucha, who painted multiple portraits
of her. In the following year, her first volume of poetry, *Poèmes de la Mer et du
Soleil* (1905), was published. In the ensuing years, her *Trilogie de l'Amour et de
la Mort* was released and in 1908 the volume *Poèmes d'Orgueil*. Her early poems
reveal the influences of Lamartine and of the philosophies of Schopenhauer
and Nietzsche. In Parisian artistic and literary circles—her admirers called her
"Jeune Dieu" or "Muse Pourpre" or, like D'Annunzio, "Fille du Soleil"—she
came into contact with F. T. Marinetti and Ricciotto Canudo, to whose group,
centered around the journal *Montjoie!* she belonged in 1913. Initially in accord
with the aesthetics of Futurism, she absorbed and transformed—in her concept of the *Métachorie*—Canudo's idea of *Cérébrisme* into her personal model
of an "ideistic" art. Canudo's maxim from the "Manifeste de l'Art cérébriste"
(Manifesto of cerebrist art) was

> We want a form of art that is more noble and more pure; which doesn't
> touch the heart, but instead moves the mind: which doesn't enchant, but
> causes one to think.[7]

It was from this aesthetic model that Valentine de Saint-Point extracted the
key impulses that she then developed further.

Between 1908 and 1913, Saint-Point formulated an independent concept of female avant-garde aesthetics in various genres: the piece *Le Théâtre
de la Femme* (*Theater of the Woman*), which was planned as a dramatic trilogy, remained unfinished. The drama *Le Déchu* (1909) was performed at the
Théâtre des Arts in the year of its creation. Over the following years, Saint-Point
wrote and published *Une femme et le Désir* (1910), *La Femme dans la littérature*

---

6. Biographical information can be found in Séché 1909; and in Reboul 1912.

7. Cited in Le Bret 1923, 29. Translation: Elena Polzer.

italienne (*Women in Italian Literature,* 1911), and finally—in a "response to Marinetti"—*Il Manifesto della donna futurista* (*Manifesto of the Futurist Woman,* 1912) and *Il Manifesto futurista della Lussuria* (*Futurist Manifesto of Lust,* 1913). Her scenic opus magnum, *La Métachorie—Drames idéistes* (1913), must be seen against the backdrop of this development in her career.

On the basis of a mixed lot of existing reviews and images, we are able to roughly reconstruct the following description of her dance solo, which premiered on December 18, 1913, at the Théâtre des Champs-Elysées, Salle Léon Poirier.

At the beginning of the performance, clouds of perfume[8] wafted across the red auditorium. After the curtain was lifted, the actor Georges Saillard read a text by Saint-Point on her notion of *Métachorie.* Then the dancer appeared in a "Byzantine" robe, her face covered with a veil, her legs bare. She moved in a manner "toujours héraldiquement," while behind her another actor, Edouard de Max, recited poems by Saint-Point—one after another from the *Poèmes d'Amour* (to music by Roland Manuel), from the *Poèmes d'Atmosphère,* and from the *Poèmes de la Guerre.* As the subject matter changed, the lights shifted from blue, pink to red and orange. At the same time, geometric forms—lines, circles, and triangles—were projected onto a screen. Maurice Droeghmans conducted music by Debussy, Ravel, Florent Schmitt, and Erik Satie. Satie had created the composition *Les Patins Dansent* (1913)[9] especially for Saint-Point—a "Poème ironique," which, like the title *Métachorie,* elevated the entire choreography to a metalevel, a quasi-synthetic self-reflection.

Saint-Point's dances, in "Merovingian" and "exotic" costume, were not really impressive in terms of virtuosity or technical brilliance. Instead, they seem to have been composed of a very simple movement vocabulary. Insofar as reviews describe details, the dancing mainly comprised various movements of the arms, twists of the torso, small steps forward and backward, and frequent forward bends.[10] The kinetic vocabulary looked a lot like gymnastics, like a presentation by the physical culture movement. Critics compared it to the rhythmic gymnastics of Emile Jaques-Dalcroze, to "Swedish" and J. P. Müller's gymnastics. If we look at photos that were published in an article in the journal *Le Miroir* (January 11, 1914), the angular form of the poses and movements are moreover particularly striking (figure 44). They show the same bent arm and leg postures prevalent in some examples of exotic dance, for example, in the "Egyptian" dances of Sent M'ahesa. However, in the case of Saint-Point, they are clearly

8. The program booklet lists "Parfum de Bichara."

9. See Wehmeyer 1974; and Volta 1992, 41f.

10. Ironically alluding to the tour de force of ballet virtuosity, the mastery of thirty-two fouettées, reviewers felt disposed to remark that the dancer was very adept at showing her backside in just as many ways.

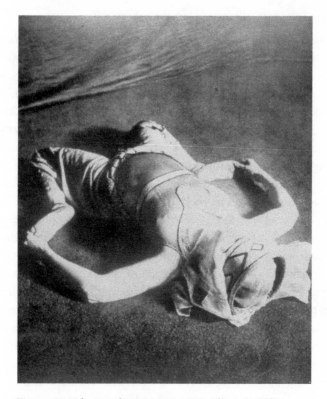

Figure 44 Valentine de Saint-Point, *Métachorie* (1913).
SOURCE: Bibliothèque de l'Arsenal, Paris, France.

intended as a consistently abstract, body-modifying pattern of representation, for example, dancing to Alexandrine rhythms in the poems on "war," "upon an octagonal frame adorned with volutes." And her interpretation of the *Poèmes d'Atmosphère* achieved a "synthesis defined by geometrochoreographical mimicry," for example, in a dance presented parallel to a recitation of the "Hymne au soleil" with verses such as these:

> Sun, masculinity of the earth, power of mankind,
> Rut of the beasts, king of the gods, take this name!
> You promise life and death and love,
> Warmth, light, time giving rhythm to night and day.[11]

11. Saint-Point 1905, 21ff.

> Soleil, mâle de la terre, Force de l'homme,
> Rut des bêtes, Roi des dieux, accueillez ce nome!
> Dispensateur de vie et de mort et d'amour,
> Chaleur, Lumière, Temps rythmant la nuit le jour.

This roughly reconstructed image of the performance demonstrates that the concept of *Métachorie* defined dance as being more than merely corporeal movement on stage. Instead, dance only obtains its distinct function when combined with the other performance elements. The innovative aspect of the *Métachorie* concept—whose historical significance was underappreciated at the time—is its designation of dance as the pivotal and framing art form within a comprehensive intermedial model of theater. Not Diaghilev's concept of a *Gesamtkunstwerk* (at the height of its popularity in the same year that Saint-Point premiered her *danses idéistes*) as implemented in his Ballets Russes, not as a balletic-theatrical integration of the arts, but rather as a multifactorial theatrical composition based on the superior idea of dance as abstract art.

Aside from the traditional theater arts—set and costume design, lights and music—three further elements were integrated here into the new theatrical framework:

- An olfactory component: fragrance—as related to the model of synesthesia, primarily developed by French and Belgian Symbolism, Baudelaire's poetry, Huysmans's novels, and Paul Fort's dramas
- Projected images—an interpretation and transformation of the colored lights and patterns projected by Loïe Fuller in her dances
- Text—a recitation of manifestos and poetry. The integration of texts, concerning images of sun, ether, and war, as well as the intentional nationalist leaning that motivated the choice of costume, reveals the proximity of the piece to performances of the Futurists.

In accordance with Futurist aesthetics,[12] the *manifesto* appears in the presentation as an integral component of the theatrical work. It does not serve as theoretical legitimation, but rather collaborates as a production element in the implementation of the *danses idéistes*. Theory, consequently, becomes an element of the artistic process itself. As a result, the explicit avant-garde dance aesthetic formulated by the manifesto enters, in the work itself, into a dialogue with an immanent aesthetic (which is thoroughly divergent from the explicit one). This is where the severance from nineteenth-century dance traditions and the advent of modernity were reflected: inside the dance-theatrical context itself.

This self-reflection of the art form ruptured and modified in turn the theoretical confrontation with tradition, which played an important role in Saint-Point's *Métachorie* manifesto.

---

12. See Schultz 1981.

Dance as Line and Text: The *Métachorie* Manifesto

On December 14, 1913, the Parisian newspaper *Tribune Libre* printed Valentine de Saint-Point's manifesto of *Métachorie* just in time for the premiere.[13] In compliance with the rhetoric of manifestos, Saint-Point begins her text with a direct attack on established art, which, in keeping with Futurist *passatismo*, is radically rejected. Classical ballet is denounced as a stagnating art form that cannot be reformed from within. But modern *freier Tanz*, insofar as it has established itself, also already appears to be in need of reformation. Saint-Point dismisses dance reform in the spirit of Hellenism, as embodied by Isadora Duncan, because of how her aesthetics relates to the body and to intuition, to the union of body and soul. For Saint-Point, the goal of *Métachorie* is not a holistic model of dance, not psychology, not an expression of the soul, but rather an understanding of dance as an intellectual, abstract art, "tout cérébrale":

> My métachorie creates ideistic dances, a dance that not only releases the plastic rhythm from the human sense of music, but also a dance that expresses an idea, held tight in strict lines like music in the meter of the counterpoint.

Aside from the influence of Marinetti's futurism, the concept of ideism was especially important for the theory of *Métachorie*—a version of *Cérébrisme*, as propagated by Canudo, which Saint-Point developed further for dance:

> We want a form of art that is more noble and more pure; which doesn't touch the heart, but instead moves the mind: which doesn't enchant, but causes one to think.

Statements such as these from Canudo's *Manifeste de l'Art cérébriste* were simultaneously an incitement and a challenge to Saint-Point's presentation of ideistic dance:

- Incitement—in the accentuation of the cerebral vis-à-vis the expression of emotions, as an approach, also found in German literature, for example, in Gottfried Benn's poetology roughly around the same time.
- And challenge, as Valentine de Saint-Point attempted in her *Métachorie* to transfer *ideistic/cerebrist* aesthetics from literature to dance: a risk

13. In 1914, Saint-Point's text on her concept of *Métachorie* appeared in the January edition of *Montjoie!*; at the height of her career, she performed the piece one more time in 1917 at the Metropolitan Opera House in New York.

and a provocation, in the sense that the *danses idéiste* were an attempt to stage the "cerebrism of the body."

The paradox of presenting the body as *thought*, dance as *idea* seems remarkable if we consider its aesthetic, as well as semiotic, implications. The aesthetic aspects pertain to an artistic exposition of new formalism and, accordingly, a redefinition of the traditional terminology of sensualism, as well as the development of an alternative *Gesamtkunstwerk* concept, which differed from all that had been articulated and presented before.

The semiotic aspect addresses the relationship of body and text, developed alongside the concept of *Métachorie*.

Cérébrisme and the Aesthetics of Lust

Saint-Point's aesthetic of an expulsion of the carnal from dance, her attempt to eliminate "every degree of sensuality,"[14] her affirmation of "muscle" and line, was by no means rooted in prudishness.

The *Métachorie* evolves "based entirely on the muscle and not on the flesh." Behind this commitment to line (contra the "flesh") lay the aim to liberate dance from the cultural connotative pattern of exhibiting female corporeality. What Saint-Point wanted to call into question was not sensuality itself (which, on the contrary, she more or less celebrated in her comprehensive concept of synesthesia and in her *Manifesto of Lust*), but rather entrenched *patterns of perceiving the sensual*: "*Lust is a carnal search into the unknown*, just as thought is the mind's search into the unknown. Lust is the act of creating, and is creation."[15]

What lies behind the reinvestiture of *cérébralité* is the idea of positing the formal in place of expression. Even before *Ausdruckstanz* expressionist dance in the stricter sense[16] had truly begun, its goals and mode of representation were already being repudiated. Valentine de Saint-Point developed her antiexpressive, ideistic model in reaction to the dominant idea that modern dance was a corporeal expression of movements of the soul. This was the banner under which Duncan had presented and defined her mission of a "dance of the future." And with this call for liberation, modern dance was able, in the first decade of the twentieth century, to gradually assert itself against the stylized bodies of classical ballet and to gain recognition as the art form of "new dance."

14. Le Bret 1923, 31.

15. Rainey, Poggi, and Wittman 2009, 130.

16. See my definition of *Ausdruckstanz* and its historical phases in the introduction to this book.

But no less than ten years after Duncan's first performances, the pendulum had already swung back in the other direction. Although not entirely superseded and replaced by the new alternative paradigm of a stylization of the body and the mediated abstraction of movement, the aggregate formula of "nature and dance," the relationship between expressive movement and corporeal representation (as an integral path of personal self-discovery), did, however, grow brittle through the avant-garde shocks of the prewar years.

The stylized elements in Saint-Point's *danse idéiste* mainly focused on the way in which the body and movement were presented. In order to suggest the *impassibilité* of "cerebrist" theory, she danced with a veil in front of her face. She thereby took into account the observation that facial expressions often seem to be the decisive expressive factor of expression, especially in poignant *freier Tanz*[17]: "The face with its flexible expressivity communicates ideas or feelings a lot faster than the movements of the body."[18]

Tellingly, Saint-Point's use of the veil in her ideistic dance demarcates the zone in which the relationships of expression and impenetrability, head and body, mime and pantomime were reversed. In the iconography of the veil, so historically important for the presentation of the body in dance, this travesty of concealing and revealing takes on a new role. In the history of dance, the veil served a dual function: either disguising and dematerializing the body, for example, the Sylph's veil in Romantic ballet, or accentuating and erotically presenting the body or particular parts of the body parts, for example, most notably in the performance tradition and iconography of exotic dance—the dance of the Bayadére, odalisque, and especially in Salome's dance of the veils. Here the veil or scarf emerges as the most important symbol of exotic dance: not as a costume or mere stage prop, but rather as a moving texture, which demarcates and displaces the boundaries of the female body in an erotic game of concealing and revealing. Hence it is neither the movement figurations nor the choreography—the writing of movement itself—but rather the body of the dancer, textured in such a way by the lines of fabric, that becomes the enigmatic image of desire.[19] Gustave Moreau's depiction of Salome dancing before Herod (figure 35) is a portrayal of exactly this type of veil dance: dancing lines artfully "notating" a female body fixed in a statuesque pose, the

---

17. Corporeal and facial expressions here contrast with the conventions of ballet, in which the movements of face, eyes, etc., are exactly defined and the smiling mask, moreover, represents the physiognomic equivalent of the pathognomonic imperative of weightlessness.

18. Le Bret 1923, 31. Translation: Elena Polzer.

19. In his study of the necklace of Olympia (*Le ruban au cou d'Olympia*), Michel Leiris attempts to track down the origins of mechanisms of desire, in which the principles of demarcating the body produce an eroticism of nakedness; Leiris 1983.

engraving of moving traces of desire on the body: the ornament of the veil dance.

Hence, this pictorial tradition of dance and veil contains all those associative components of the "sensual," that very model of the female sexuality which Saint-Point sought to thwart with her concept of ideism. The persistence, nevertheless, of these imprinted sexual connotations in the image of the female dancing body is evident in the reviews quoted above. The theory of *Métachorie* thus was conceived in antithesis to the aesthetics of *Ausdruckstanz*. Body movement and facial expressions should not reveal the movements of the soul. The covering of the face, the shaping of the body with the help of lights (from outside, not from "within") indicates principles of formalization, deindividualization, and depsychologization. In his essay from 1923 (from which we gather that he clearly didn't see the 1913, but rather the 1917, New York performance of *Métachorie*), Le Bret elucidates this aspect more clearly: *Métachorie* is not really a dance, if one adheres to the common notion that dance is a plastic art form, a rhythmical movement of flesh ("chair"). *Métachorie* deals completely with muscle and in no way with the flesh: "She imparts all with the muscle and nothing with the flesh" (ibid., 31), muscle meaning the spatial play of volume and line. However, the flesh is connoted by exactly that context of expression, which the concept of *danse idéiste* discarded as "triviale et inesthétique." The ideistic, antisentimental program in the *Manifeste de la Femme futuriste* from 1912 is the extreme form of an aesthetic of female heroism—almost a new position for women in art, for which Saint-Point cites her own poetry as examples, in particular the *Poèmes d'Orgueil*.[20]

GESAMTKUNSTWERK OR MULTICENTRIC PRODUCTION

In her concept of *Métachorie*, Valentine de Saint-Point developed a personal vision of the *Gesamtkunstwerk*. Part of this endeavor—in accordance with the avant-garde desire for a destruction of *passatistic* art and art theory—was the complete denial of all influences from the history of the *Gesamtkunstwerk*. Nevertheless, a connection to tradition is clearly evident in Saint-Point's work, in particular to Wagner's musical dramas. Her novel *Trilogie de l'Amour et de la Mort* (1906)[21] demonstrates a detailed knowledge of Wagner's work.

20. Cf. the collection Ro 11973.

21. Saint-Point 1906; the following citations are based on this edition with page numbers in the text.

In a fictional dialogue, the lovers in this epistolary novel speak of *The Flying Dutchman, Tristan and Isolde, The Valkyrie, Siegfried*, and *Götterdämmerung*. The writer of the letters, l'Amante, compares herself several times with female characters from Wagner's music dramas, for instance with Brünhilde—"You remind me of Brünhilde, goddess and woman" (16). She evokes the ecstasy of the *Liebestod* in *Tristan und Isolde*—"The great wisdom of death is in this oeuvre" (189)—and simultaneously celebrates the cult of the hero's birth by giving her son the name Siegfried. In the second part of the trilogy, replacing Wagner's sibling incest with the Oedipus myth, she describes a case of incest between mother and son. In contemporary evaluations of the novel, for example in Jacques Rebouls's *Note sur la morale d'une Annonciatrice* (1912),[22] who expresses his surprise that the author of the "Inceste" would be "doux et tranquille," the comparison is drawn to D'Annunzio's novel *Il fuoco*. There exists also a thematic proximity to the depiction of the incest motive in Thomas Mann's almost contemporaneous novella *Wälsungenblut* (*Blood of the Wälsungs*), based on Wagner's interpretation of the myth.

It is precisely this detailed knowledge of Wagner's work—and of his writings, which Saint-Point received from reading Baudelaire and Nietzsche[23]—that caused her, in an intensive involvement with the material, to develop a counterconcept, in which the fundamental ideas of Wagner's theories of *Gesamtkunstwerk*, even in their negation, are still noticeably apparent. Not only her idea of merging the arts (albeit organized in a different way and with a significant demotion of the importance of music) into a theatrical unit, but also the universalization of the artist as creator of not one but all arts, involved in the work reveals itself as a reverence to Wagner.

Saint-Point illustrated this synthesis of roles in her *Métachorie* by simultaneously appearing as a poet, painter, dancer, choreographer, costume designer, and set designer, as well as theorist and public relations agent all in one, "true to the principle that creation cannot occur except by dint of its creator."[24]

She herself embodied the idea of her *Gesamtkunstwerk* to some extent as Bohémienne and "Annonciatrice" (Reboul) of a new female aesthetic.

Yet Wagner's theories were not the only bone of contention for Saint-Point's *Métachorie*. A very successfully implemented, newer form of *Gesamtkunstwerk* (which can incidentally also be traced back to Wagner) also displeased her: the productions of the Ballets Russes. Her key objection to the epochal theatrical

22. Reboul 1912.

23. Cf. Saint-Point 1906, especially the numerous Nietzsche quotations and the recourse to the Nietzsche-Wagner relationship in the *Trilogie*, e.g., 145ff.

24. Cf. Le Bret 1923, 32. Translation: Elena Polzer.

synthesis of the Ballets Russes, which manifested itself in that very act of cooperation between top-level artists and works of art which she was calling for, concerned the relationship of music and dance. According to Saint-Point, dance was still merely a manifestation of music in these productions: "Dance is always a function of the music."[25]

What she could not predict was that her *Métachorie* would be performed at exactly the same time, in the same year as the premiere of the most revolutionary work of the Ballets Russes, *Le Sacre du Printemps* (*The Rite of Spring*), with a disjunction of music and dance that split the camps of critics and audiences alike. Such a coincidence of similar phenomena, both breaking with tradition, allows us to perceive in an even clearer light the aesthetic crisis that occurred shortly before World War I.[26]

Saint-Point's *Métachorie* was based on an aesthetic model that rearranged the traditional Beaux Arts system of classification. She thus also addressed the "Laocoön" problem anew and approached the problematic relationship of poetry and fine arts in terms of their representation of (psychological and physical) movement from an entirely different angle, namely from the perspective of dance as a temporal and spatial art.

In her aesthetic writings from 1911, she differentiates two groups of the arts, the mobile and immobile. "L'Art immobile" is governed by geometry and includes architecture (which she writes about in *La Musique de la Pierre, Symphonies architecturales*, and *L'Art hispano-arabe*), sculpture, and painting.

"L'Art mobile" is characterized by numbers and applies to poetry, music, and dance. The synthesis of these opposing groups of mobile and immobile art, of number and geometry, of symbol and line seeks—as Le Bret summarizes—to establish a new work of art, "un Art total et suprême" (29).

This corresponds with the term *Métachorie*, a neologism that is meant to signal and verify the idea of "trans" or "meta" art. In the end, it again refers back—although in deconstructed form—to the model of ancient tragedy (and thus again to the aesthetics of Wagner and Nietzsche). According to Le Bret, *Métachorie* means "beyond the chorus." The category of "meta" or "trans" applies to the chorus in Greek tragedy, to its function of commenting on the destiny and emotions of the protagonists. In a modern era, however—one in which science has replaced myth and the private ego stages its own "drama" far from the suprapersonal authority of destiny—the term *méta-chorie* appears very apt. The formula of "meta" designates not only a transgression of the boundaries of modern subjectivity, but also the self-reflexivity of art.

25. Ibid.

26. See Eksteins 1990.

CIPHERS OF DANCE

Saint-Point's *Métachorie* is therefore the result of a dual act of opposition: against the aesthetics of classical ballet and its associated system of dance rhetoric; and against the reform aesthetics of new "free" dance, with its habitus of individual expressive movement.

This dual act of breaking with prevailing models of artistic dance leads to a rejection of the principles of *plasticity* and *rhythm* in dance, those same two constituents that particularly shaped the body and movement imagery of dance at the beginning of the twentieth century: the principle of plasticity or sculpture, for example, in Duncan's "Greek" dances, but also in Nijinsky's *Faune*; the principle of rhythm in the "rhythmic gymnastics" of Jaques-Dalcroze, in the entire "rhythm" movement and in *Ausdruckstanz*.

In place of sculpture and rhythm, Valentine de Saint-Point posits the *idea* as *the* formative motor in dance. The principle of abstraction in her *danses idéiste* replaces sculpture, which emphasized the body as a semiotic form, and rhythm, which focused on the temporal component of movement as an expression of the rhythm of life, with the *line*—"la ligne totale de la danse." Of course, line here does not mean "ornament" (in terms of the art and aesthetics of art nouveau and *Jugendstil*), but rather an abstract basic pattern, a meta-choreo-graphy of the scenic event of "dance" and its immanent movement dramaturgy: a formula for both movement and space.

Just as the step ("pas") constitutes the primary unit of the entire syntax of ballet for the classical ballerina and the modulation of the body from the body's center lies at the heart of the movement language of *Ausdruckstanz*, "the dramatic scheme, which the body, dancing, draws on the scene,"[27] is of decisive importance for *Métachorie*—as Saint-Point explains in her "manifesto" in the *Figaro*.

The line, which is accentuated here, refers not only to the spatial line of dance movement, but also to the kinesphere of the body. Further elements that are also based on the formal principle of the line and relevant for the performance are:

- The geometric line
- Geometric shapes projected onto the backdrop, which are confronted with the stereometric, transitory lines of the dancers; and finally
- The line of writing, which, as text and image, is intertwined with the texture of the choreography. Saint-Point transcribed those poems that she had selected from her published cycles into geometric forms for the performance of *Métachorie*—"like an orchestra score" (Le Bret, 32).

27. See Collection Ro 11973.

As the configuration of a score—as performance text and stage design all in one—the poems assume that very structure which on a second, formal level fulfills the requirements of *Cérébrisme*: the translation of literature into graphic art.

In accordance with Futurist aesthetics,[28] the *manifesto* appears in the presentation as an integral component of the theatrical work. It does not serve as theoretical legitimation, but rather collaborates as a production element in the implementation of the *danses idéistes*. Theory, consequently, becomes an element of the artistic process itself. As a result, the explicit avant-garde dance aesthetic formulated by the manifesto enters, in the work itself, into a dialogue with an immanent aesthetic (which is thoroughly divergent from the explicit one). This is where the severance from nineteenth-century dance traditions and the advent of modernity were reflected: inside the dance-theatrical context itself.

Nevertheless, the recitation of manifesto and poetry at the same time as the dance should in no way be considered a duplication. Writing and dancing are in fact understood by Saint-Point as interrelated acts of semiotic play arising from the same gesture: "Je n'extériorise pas la lettre mais l'esprit." Writing and dancing, symbols and the body are not in disjunction. Saint-Point *writes* her dance as *Métachorie*. The body (as the individual dancer-body) disappears in this process of writing-contact with dance-line and text.

The preoccupation of some reviewers of Saint-Point's work with the female dancer's body as an erotic object reduced to a few prominent body parts bears witness to an effacement of the individual (and the "salvation" of the corporeal) *ex negativo*. The subject is concealed by the paravent of the danced *schème dramatique*. It loses itself between the seams of a union of coequal arts and their sensual suggestions—in music, fragrance, text as writing and sound, light and color, geometric and architectural figurations—all based on dance as the superior spatiotemporal art.

The simultaneity of coequal, independently staged arts—of dance, music, that is, sound, and scenic space—not only anticipates the happenings of the Futurists and Dadaists, and similar aspirations toward an independence of dance from music in the work of Laban, Wigman, and other contemporaries, but also foresees Merce Cunningham's radical neo-avant-garde aesthetic of isolated simultaneity.

28. See Schultz 1981.

Chapter 3

Aerodance

Futurist Dance and Aviation

"The dream of flight" is not only the source of countless myths and fantasies. The desire to overcome gravity has also had its effects on dance. The pursuit of elevation, of the illusion of weightlessness, and of a dematerialization of the body is constitutive for the aesthetics of classical ballet. The ballerina en pointe represents the ideal of weightlessness, and the flying machines still used in the nineteenth century to evoke the theatrical illusion of hovering sylphs as a symbol for liberation from the bonds of gravity testify to the fact that utmost virtuosity in dance is and was always embodied by the dream of flight. Vaslav Nijinsky's legendary leaps—in *Le Spectre de la Rose* (1911) and in *Shéhérazade* (1910)—came to signify the fascination exerted by elevation and the "ballon" of the leap.

"If the fin de siècle had a dream, then it was the achievement of human flight," wrote Karl Clausberg on the parallelism of occult flying projects and aviation technology.[1]

A comparable parallel development also occurred in the corporeal-metaphoric transcription of "flying bodies" on the one hand, and the projections of mechanical mobility and perfection of movement in dance on the other, particularly in Futurist and Russian constructivist concepts of dance.

Ironically, around the same time that the floating dreams of abstract art developed, that is, sundered the direct connection between likeness and reality in favor of optical levitations of pure dynamics, expressionistic dance discovered gravity and body weight as central aspects of its aesthetics.

Body weight and an increased emphasis on the use of the floor became an antithesis to elevation in ballet.

---

1. See Clausberg1988. Translation: Elena Polzer.

But at the same time, parallel and in contrast to these developments in expressionistic dance, further alternative artistic concepts of abstraction in dance, such as Valentine de Saint-Point's *Métachorie*, already aspired to formal, constructivist configurations.

As a governing perspective, flight applied differently to the weightlessness of abstraction than to the aesthetic of elevation in ballet, for here the gaze of the aviator reigned supreme. It stretched out to encompass all dimensions and, as a new model of reading artistic production, steered altered viewing habits. The Russian artist Kazimir Malevich once formulated the idea that one consequence of this new perspective was a disappearance of the notions of up and down, and Erwin Panofsky described this weightlessness of abstraction in the arts as the "suspension in nothingness."

As that art form which seeks to control space and time through movement, to master gravity with the help of corporeal virtuosity, dance appears—against the backdrop of Futurist *teatro aereo*—as the twin art of aviation, which celebrates the mythical conquest of new movement spaces for twentieth-century culture by the Icarus-like heroes of modern aeronautics.

THE AESTHETICS OF FUTURIST DANCE

It is in this context that we must regard Marinetti's "Manifesto della danza futurista" (Manifesto of futurist dance), which has so far not received much scholarly attention compared to other manifestos on Futurist theater and variety theater.[2]

The "Manifesto of Futurist Dance" was first published in 1917. Its French translation soon followed in 1920.[3] What strikes us most on our first reading is that the manifesto is worded in a very different tone from other Futurist pamphlets. Only in the end is there an indication of the usual militant style— the proclamation of new dance based on an aesthetic that negates the traditions of beauty, grace, and symmetry. Apparently, the shock of the new was

2. One of the few works on Futurism and Futurist dance is the comprehensive overview (though lacking in individual case analyses) by Leonetta Bentivoglio 1984. Also on Futurism, see (e.g.), Apollonio 1972; Azari 1970; Baumgarth 1966; Demetz 1990; Depero 1988; Eltz 1986; Fagiolo dell'Arco 1988; Finter 1980; Landes 1989; Lista 1973, 1976, 1977, and 1988; Riesz 1976; Verdone 1969.

3. The most widely available version of Marinetti's text in French can be found in Lista 1973, 264–68; a comprehensive collection of Futurist manifestos in English, including the "Manifesto of Futurist Dance" (234–39), was published in 2009 by Rainey, Poggi, and Wittman.

difficult to provoke in this field of the arts, save as a cynical negation of ballet as a whole, as a "passatistic" model of theater, for example, as in Francesco Cangiullo's happening-like "piece" *Detonation: A Synthesis of All Modern Theatre*.[4] The piece, itself already a parody on Futurist *teatro sintetico*, was nothing more than a minute of silence and a gunshot. The "tattilismo" of the Futurist concept of theater culminated in a cynicism that aestheticized modern warfare—in the performance of a "detonation." Modris Eksteins at least ascribes a certain "witty-comical element" to these theatrical acts, which were so typical for Futurist art theory—artistic "rites of war." The fascination of violence, especially in images of explosions, expressed itself not only in Marinetti's call to blow up all museums and libraries, but also in the way technology and media were used programmatically. Wyndham Lewis, for example, gave his newly founded journal the name *Blast* in order to "express his intentions."[5] The provocative "framework" of Cangiullo's *Detonation*, the allocation of cast and character of the piece, which presented itself as a "shot at" the conventions of theater institutions, was announced as "a bullet"—a pun on both projectile and "ballet," which ironically references both aspects of the performance as de-tonation.

The dilemma in Marinetti's manifesto of an as yet undreamed-of novelty that would naturally distinguish any forthcoming forms of Futurist dance, is clear: the *New* already *existed* in dance; the break with tradition had already taken place. Hence, a Futurist aesthetic of dance was reduced to radicalizing and exalting those paradigms of avant-garde dance which had already been set into motion.

Marinetti also sketches in great length the historical situation of dance around the turn of the century and turns to talk about the possibilities of a Futurist style of dance only in the last fifth of the short manifesto. He sorts the diversity of dance styles, which developed around 1900, into a simple antithetic schema that once more demonstrates his excellent analytical eye for contemporary art and cultural phenomena. In one corner, he situates that basic form of dance which is sensual, erotic, and sexually evocative and in the other, as its opponent, abstract, geometrical, *mathematical* dance. The first model appears in Arabic and Persian (belly) dancing or in South American dances: "the furious spasmodic tango from Argentina, the zamacueca from Chile, the maxixe from Brazil," all places where dance is equivalent to sensual rapture, delirium, vertigo.

---

4. See "Futurist Performance," edited and introduced by Michael Kirby, in *The Drama Review* 1970, 131.

5. See Eksteins 1990, 134; Kiefer 1991.

In contrast, the "rational" paradigm of stylized dance—symbolizing the body and geometry of space, repeating the "rotating movements of the stars," can be found—according to Marinetti—in Cambodian and Javanese forms of religious dance (which were presented at the International Exposition in Paris in 1900) as well as in classical ballet, in the "glorious Italian ballet" (though not in the Ballets Russes).[6]

In order to further clarify his line of argumentation, Marinetti applies his antithetical model to the dances of Duncan and Nijinsky, two key figures of modern dance. Duncan here embodies erotic dance, free dance, as an expression of passionate, feminine movement language. Marinetti repeatedly emphasizes the aspect of freedom and improvisation in Duncan's work, as if drawing parallels to Futurist "free verse." And indeed, the transition from the "bound" style, which dominated both ballet and poetry, to a freer style represented cutting-edge avant-garde innovation in both art forms.

In the eyes of Marinetti, however, Nijinsky embodied "dance's pure geometry," free of imitation or sexual stimulation. Here Marinetti's reading of Nijinsky provides an interesting contrast to widespread contemporaneous opinion. Nijinsky's animalistic movements and bewildering (androgynous) sexual charisma had in themselves become a certain topos among critics. Marinetti, however, focuses on that area of dance which corresponds to the interests of Futurism in the relationship between dynamism and abstract styles of movement, between mechanical-kinetic principles and energetic (force) lines: Nijinsky's incredible corporeal capacities as a dancer—as a "muscular system elevated to divinity."

Both artists—Duncan and Nijinsky—contributed in their own way to the emancipation of dance, to its independence from music. In Marinetti's opinion, however, the steps that they took toward a "Dance of the Future" (so the title of Duncan's programmatic text from 1903) did not go far enough, any more than the rhythmic gymnastic of Emile Jaques-Dalcroze. Marinetti clearly

6. This attribution of the wise astronomical order of stars to the "glorious Italian ballet" might have been affected by one of the most famous Italian works of ballet at the turn of the century: Luigi Manzotti's *Excelsior* (music, Romualdo Marenco; premiere, Milan 1881). It was a ballet that toured extensively abroad for a long period of time because of its large number of staff and immense technical complexity. The subject of ballet, the homage to technological progress portrayed in the allegories of, e.g., electricity and telegraphy, may have played a particularly precursory role in Futurist aesthetics. Marinetti's theater piece *Poupées électriques* (Paris, 1909), created in the same year as the publication of the founding manifesto of Futurism, gives some idea of the influence of this subject matter (the glorification of electricity and hence electric technology); Marinetti separated the intermezzo, which focuses on a mysterious relationship of dolls and humans, from the main text for the premiere on January 13, 1909, in Turin, at first as *Elettricità*, then *Elettricità sessuale*, and finally *Fantocci elettrici* (*Electric Marionettes*).

recognizes the limitations of the Hellerau model regarding the development of a new aesthetic in dance: although endowed with "much more modern ambitions," Jaques-Dalcroze's system was, for him, much too focused on "muscular hygiene" and pedagogy to produce avant-garde dance.

For Marinetti, the only (female) dancer worthy of attention as the inventor of aesthetic principles of dance relevant for Futurism was Fuller: "We Futurists prefer Loie Fuller and the African American 'cakewalk' (utilization of electric lights and mechanical movements)."[7]

Only variety theater and music hall, which the Futurists pitted against (traditional) theater, provide valid models for a theater of the future. Marinetti's text "The Variety Theater" (1913) was thus published as the first manifesto on theater two years before "The Futurist Synthetic Theater."

The shop-window quality of variety theater as a panorama of the "Futurist marvelous," the simultaneity and the dynamicism of "overpowering dance rhythms"; the fast-paced succession of acts, the illogical structure of the scenic fragments; the play with sensationalism, the "fisicofollia," the amazement and the participation of the audience; and finally the clear focus on the technical (electricity) and media-related (utilization of film) possibilities provided by the entertainment industry—it was these elements that made variety theater, as a melting pot of the theatrical, serve as a prelude to the aesthetics of Futurist theater.[8]

The cakewalk is cited here as a principle of grotesque movement: representing the nonbeautiful, the primitivism of Futurist "barbarismo," the offensive and a form of movement aesthetics that accentuates the technical concept of *interruption* (i.e., the angular, jerky, syncopated movement rhythms of the cakewalk), rather than organic flow—as later demonstrated in Marinetti and Bragaglia's *Cabaret epilettico* (1922–23).

Saint-Point likewise implemented, to some extent and much later than Fuller, elements of Futurist aesthetic in her abstract, dynamic, emotionless style of dance. She intermittently belonged to the inner circle of the Italian Futurists. According to Marinetti, she conceived

an abstract, metaphysical dance that was supposed to embody pure thought without sentimentality or sexual excitement. Her metachorie

7. Rainey, Poggi, and Wittmann 2009, 236.

8. In the manifesto "The Futurist Synthetic Theatre" (Marinetti, Settimelli, and Corra 1915), the main features of this vaudeville program have been adopted, substantiated by the "sensibility" of Futurism: "our frenzied passion for real, swift, elegant, complicated, cynical, muscular, fugitive, Futurist life."

consists of mimed and danced poetry . . . abstractions danced but static, arid, cold, emotionless. (ibid.)

Marinetti's idea of Futurist dance attempted to go beyond Saint-Point's concept, especially his approximation of those aesthetic premises that determined the coordinate system of Futurist avant-gardism:

- The dynamics and kinetics of technical-mechanical movement, as body machine
- The energy, speed, simultaneity of different rhythms and theatrical actions on stage
- The primitive, "le bruitisme," culminating in the "wonderful, greater barbarism" of Futurist man

Marinetti summarizes his "Manifesto of Futurist Dance" as follows:

Futurist dance will be

antiharmonic—ill-mannered   antigracious—asymmetrical—synthetic— dynamic—free-wordist.

This program of Futurist dance aesthetics met with little response from ongoing discourse on modern dance, mainly because of its relatively close proximity to contemporaneous patterns of innovation in free, experimental, and absolute dance. In his study *Der tanzende Schwerpunkt* (*The Dancing Center of Gravity*, 1923),[9] L. W. Rochowanski welcomes—from a similarly critical point of view on the situation of dance—a Futurist aesthetic that demands "that dance be ungraceful, asymmetrical and dynamic." However, he clearly does not classify the dance-theatrical experiments of the Futurists as avant-garde:

Yes, yes, yes! Asymmetrical, ungraceful, angular, yes, yes, yes! Wonderful! Finally! A few dynamic slaps in the face of the dozing beauty-sentimentalist (whose body is so beautiful that it's impossible to visit a public bath), whose "intoxicated" eye is always looking for curves (because his artistic sense is on edge), who gets drunk off a stiff toe, on which a female dancer stalks for minutes on end! (22f.)[10]

9. Rochowanski 1923.

10. Translation: Elena Polzer.

FUTURIST DANCE AS PANTOMIME OF FLIGHT:
MARINETTI'S *DANCE OF THE AVIATRIX*

The exemplary short Futurist dance scenarios published at the end of Marinetti's dance manifesto provide some idea of what Futurist dance was meant to look like: *Dance of the Aviatrix, The Shrapnel Dance*, and *The Machine-Gun Dance.*[11] The configuration of these three dance pieces, which were written—like the dance manifesto—in 1917, during the war and at the height of Marinetti's aestheticization of technology and warfare, corresponds precisely to the programmatic construction of the Futurist "superuomo,"[12] which is defined by

- Union with the machine (*aviatrix*)
- A vitalist enthusiasm for explosive dynamics, for danger (in war, shrapnel), and for the speed and "fire" of (military) technology (the machine gun).

The *Dance of the Aviatrix* appears, in its historical context, not only as a pattern of Futurist dance, that is, as a theatrical representation of the manifesto's catalogue of criteria. From a historical perspective, this document also reveals itself to be an extremely heterogeneous, synthesized dance-theater performance, in which the avant-garde pose abruptly confronts the remnants of a demonized tradition—the allegedly vanquished *danse passatistes*. The intended break with tradition appears less as a break with the movement codes of free dance than as a break with its traditions of theatrical representation. The movement paradigm of dance in particular is not—according to the usual Futurist program—revoked and liberated in new procedures and forms of representation. Futurist dance innovation focuses not on "la danza in libertà," not on unleashing the body and its movement possibilities. Loïe Fuller and Isadora Duncan, expressionistic dance, Oskar Schlemmer's *Triadic Ballet,* and the experiments of the Zurich Dadaists (with their consequent negation of dance) were by far more progressive in this regard. Instead, the innovative intentions are focused on embodying central motifs of Futurist aesthetics in theatrical dance. The

---

11. See Rainey, Poggi, and Wittmann 2009, 237–39; all following quotations are based on this anthology.

12. The Futurist concept of *superuomo* is first of all the result of an interpretation of Nietzsche's idea of the *Übermensch*, but, second, was propagated mainly as a counterconcept to Nietzsche. Hence Umberto Boccioni, in his manifesto "Futurist Painting and Sculpture" (1914), accuses Nietzsche of developing his term *Übermensch* out of a glorification of antiquity, born of the "dust of the libraries"; whereas the Futurist *superuomo* is an "enemy of books" and a "student of the machine."

emphasis thus lies far more on achieving an aesthetic revolution in the theatrical field, rather than in dance itself.

I would like to emphasize the need to make such a differentiation here, in
order to resituate the significance of various works and stagings of Futurist
"dance" experimentation in the field of avant-garde theater.

The most significant Futurist impulse for the stage came from the field of
set design and scenography. Enrico Prampolini's manifesto "Scenografia e
Coreografia futurista" (Futurist stage design, 1915) envisioned a "Teatro del
Colore," in which light, color, and architectural forms appear as the sole actors
in an abstract dynamic form of theater performed in a "poly-dimensional stage
space." In addition to Prampolini, this form of Futurist experimental theater—
situated between fine arts and technical scenography—drew its most important
inspiration from the work of Fortunato Depero and Giacomo Balla. In 1916–
17, Depero created a series of drawings for Stravinsky's *Le Chant du rossignol*
as a ballet for Diaghilev and the dancer and choreographer Léonide Massine:
an abstract spectacle, in which geometrical and stereometrical forms—cones,
disks, and plantlike structures—were designed as a kind of moving architecture. This concept was resumed in Depero's *Balli plastici* (figure 45), performed
in Rome in 1918 with moving scenery and marionettes and in Balla's futur-
ist-abstract scenography for Stravinsky's *Feu d'artifice*, designed for Diaghilev
and premiered in Rome in 1917—in the same year as the world premiere of
Massine's "cubist" ballet *Parade*, likewise choreographed for Diaghilev's Ballets
Russes.

The examples given above, to which other similar works of abstract, plastic-
scenographic choreography can be added, such as Ivo Pannagi's *Ballo meccanico* (1922),[13] up until the 1920s and 1930s also and in particular demonstrate
an accentuation of the visual-theatrical level in those works of Futurist dance
that were entitled *Balli, Ballet, Phantomime, or Coreografia*. The central motif of
"dynamismo" led to a genuine interest in movement, in dance. As Depero writes:

> My completely rhythmic style has brought me fatefully to dance, because
> dance is nothing more than a stylized motion sequence, and since I have
> combined every flower, animal, and human element in a rhythmic-colorist
> and formal uniformity, the logical consequence is that every one of their
> movements, their transformations, or their vibrations is homogeneous,

13. Pannaggi's *Mechanisches Ballett* (*Mechanical Ballet*), performed by the Russian dancers
Ikar and Ivanov, premiered on June 2, 1922, in Rome; the costumes were made of cardboard,
colorful shiny paper, and cardboard tubes in such a manner that the dancers appeared to
be mechanical figurines; instead of music there was a "rhythmic polyphony" of the sounds
made by two motor bikes.

Figure 45 Fortunato Depero, *Balli plastici*
(poster, 1918).
SOURCE: Revue d'esthétique 22/92, Paris, France / © VG
Bild-Kunst, Bonn, Germany.

rhythmic, and stylistic, allowing me to open up a broad horizon for future
dances.[14]

The Futurists' *teatro visivo* was more interested in the *implications of dance*
than in the genuine conception of an avant-garde aesthetic that treated dance
as an independent phenomenon of movement and space. This was also evident in experimental variations of perspective, such as aerodance, as well as in
Marinetti's *Dance of the Aviatrix*.[15]

14. Depero 1988. Translation: Elena Polzer.

15. The representation of all three allegoric motifs in Futurist dances—flight, explosion of
bombs, and instruments of warfare—by a female dancer corresponds to the definition of
the "Futurist woman": Saint-Point's manifesto emphasizes exactly these fierce, virile sides
of the female sex as the Futurist pattern of femininity in order to make her equal to the
superuomo.

In this pantomime for one dancer, which consists of six "movements," the focus lies on one of the key subjects of Futurism: the accomplishments of modern aviation. The flight to the stars is portrayed both as the technical act of flying and as a symbolic configuration of mankind's ability to command nature. In accordance with the Futurist aesthetic of the human machine, the female dancer embodies both the pilot and the plane. Her body takes on the form of an Icarian flying machine. The costume designed by Balla supported this impression of metamorphosis from a body covered by a veil into a streamlined "splendore meccanico":

> The danseuse must create a continual palpitation of blue veils. On her chest, like a flower, a large celluloid propeller constructed so that it vibrates with every bodily movement. Her face dead white under a white hat shaped like a monoplane. (Marinetti, *Dance of the Aviatrix*)

Surprisingly, the kinetic embodiment, the danced representation of the flight to the stars, actually closely adhered to pantomimic conventions, from the "takeoff" of aircraft's female body (the erotic obsessions of Futurist aviation fantasies are also evident here) up to her entry into the interstellar choreography of the *étoiles d'or*—the stage directions at the end state "gay ironic thoughtless." The requested irony may also be referring to the "étoile" with the status of *Première danseuse* in the ballet hierarchy of the Paris Opera.

The actual pantomime itself is simple: the dancer opens her arms to imitate wings; a few *soubresauts*, waving movements of the torso, and a series of increasingly intense *frémissements* symbolize the running motors, the takeoff, and finally, constant vibrating movements of the body (which become more intense, "frenzied, mechanical" in the moment of danger) embodying the machine in flight.

Marinetti's simple choreographic instructions contain no descriptions of steps, paths in space, or modes of movement. However, what is clearly apparent is that the technical transformations of the scene are just as important as the "dance" itself for the concept: the movements of the scenography, the lighting, the metamorphosis of the space—the same elements to which most theater reform models assigned a new and distinct role at the turn of the century. Marinetti's admiration for Loïe Fuller is apparent in the allusions to her metamorphosis of body and space, in the "costume," the concealing silk veil of the aviatrix-dancer and the lighting scenarios, especially in Movement 5, in the flight through the clouds[16], which is a clear reference to Fuller's famous

---

16. The fifth "movement" in Marinetti's scenario:

With organized noises imitate the rain and howling of the wind and, with continual interruptions of the electric lighting, imitate flashes of lightning. Meanwhile the danseuse will

choreography *Nuages* (1914), performed to a piece by Debussy of the same name.[17]

The space, constituted by the interaction of flight pantomime and moving scenography, corresponds—like the dance itself, like costume and set design—to the Futurist concept of *teatro sintetico*: a mixture of heterogeneous factors of spatial configuration, which simultaneously present the traditional and the innovative (a historic aspect of *simultaneità*, which is often overlooked).

The spatial design of the pantomime reflects the perspective of the pilot: on the one hand, looking down to the earth as unto the flat surface of a map (from an aerial perspective like a "grande carte géographique") and on the other, gazing into the aerial space, this third dimension to which the aspirations of elevation in dance and modern aviation both equally apply. Both realms of movement appear cartographically abstract—not as natural spaces, but as semiotic fields of spatial measurement, translated into a topographical system of orientation. The dance begins "sur une grande carte géographique," onto which the landscape and major traffic points are schematically drawn.

Dance and topography are juxtaposed in a reversal of perspective and its magnification into an extreme perceptual situation. In his 1934 text on *aeropainting*, Ruggero Vasari summarizes the meaning of topography: the "rigid perspective on the ground" is discarded in favor of a position that revives awareness of individual parts and the whole through constant movement and from a great distance—in a long shot "from above." The polycentric scattered elements of the landscape appear "flattened, artificial, makeshift, suddenly fallen from the sky."[18]

In Marinetti's *Dance of the Aviatrix*, the third dimension of air space is represented by two competing symbolic scenographic systems, namely digital and analog structures of representation. The digital signification of the space corresponds to the "technical" paradigm of writing by inscribing the act of measuring into the dance space with the help of signs indicating altitude:

> Movement 2: The danseuse, still straight, will shake a sign printed in red: 300 meters—3 spins—a climb. Then, right away, a second sign: 600 meters—avoid mountain.

raise up a frame that is covered with red vellum paper in the form of a cloud at sunset, and will break through it in a graceful leap (grand and low melancholy waves of sound). (Rainey, Poggi, and Wittmann 2009, 239)

17. See Brandstetter and Ochaim 1989, 150.

18. Vasari 1990. Translation: Elena Polzer.

The analog performance adheres to a mimetic model, namely a color-coded representation of individual visual elements: "green" for depictions of the landscape ("The danseuse will heap up a lot of green cloth to simulate a green mountain"), "golden" for the sun ("will wave in front of herself a large sun made of gilded cardboard"), the use of lights for changes of weather ("with continual interruptions of the electric lighting, imitate flashes of lightning"), rosy cloud formations covering the sun ("frame that is covered with red vellum paper in the form of a cloud at sunset").

The depiction of nature here is, in fact—in an homage to Loïe Fuller in dance and the stage reformers Adolphe Appia, Edward Gordon Craig, and others who followed them at the turn of the century—transformed into a play of color and light.

This technical aspect of the *Dance of the Aviatrix*, especially the lighting design, is very similar to the scenography of *Feu d'artifice*, a piece that Balla designed for Diaghilev to the music of Stravinsky in 1917—in the same year as *Dance of the Aviatrix*. This abstract "mise-en-scène without performers," a ballet *without* dancers, paradoxically commissioned by the impresario of the most-glamorous ballet company of the time, premiered on April 12, 1917, at the Teatro Costanzi in Rome. Richard Buckle describes the decor of this "colore in movimento," which had more than sixty lighting changes in fifteen minutes:

> Balla built a composition of jagged and curved shapes, surmounted by a stylized flower or Catherine-wheel, and lit both from without and within. There were fifty lighting cues, worked out by Balla and Diaghilev. The coloring was as violent as that of Pop Art in the 1960s, mainly scarlet and emerald green. Whether this glowing, flashing object was a help or a hindrance to the appreciation of Stravinsky's vertiginous little piece, it was the sort of adventure that made Diaghilev feel the opposite of stagnant.[19]

In his small scenario *Riesenpantomime mit Fesselballons* (*Giant Pantomime with Captive Balloons*), published in the journal *Das Theater 1910*, Paul Scheerbart parodies such abstract Futurist "balletti" and pantomimes, the subject of aerodance and the use of puppets or moving objects, (Craig's) theory of the *Übermarionette* and the continually discussed principle of illusionary theater.[20]

19. See Buckle 1979, 327.

20. Scheerbart 1909–10. Scheerbart was critical and skeptical of the general enthusiasm for aviation, where it merely represented a naïve homage to technology and progress; the complex relationship of fantasies of flight to modern aviation is also the subject of his novel *Lesabéndio* (1913).

In June of this year, I was visiting Prince Saburoff in Finland. One day the prince arranged a merry garden party and told his guests that he would also be performing a giant pantomime. Goliath and his wife—so the title of the pantomime, he said with a very mischievous expression.

A "colossal" scenery was erected. The giants appeared: "head and body of the giant were two hot air balloons." Everything, even the boots of the servant, was gigantic, "making the illusion perfect."

The pantomime consisted of a giant quarrel between the hot air balloon couple. In an act of reconciliation, they finally dance a "droll little minuet, without lifting their legs."

However, so the narrator and observer in the end, "the whole action could have taken place midair. But sadly nobody listened to what I was saying."

AERODANZA

Futurist movement aesthetics surged out beyond the restrictive confines of the stage. Experimental Futurist dance, such as Marinetti's *Dance of the Aviatrix*, staged with the help of theatrical means—with pantomime and moving objects, alienating costumes, elaborate lighting, and sound collages—that subject which most fascinated the Marinetti group, the subject that seemed to unite all aspects of revolutionary avant-garde art: the subject of flight, the beauty of modern aviation.

The "modernolatria" of the Futurists found its most consistent expression in the aesthetics of an "art of aviation" on par with the technological achievements of the twentieth century. This *aereo*-art was of course, aside from the "aeropaintings," not in the least oriented at having any substantial effect. Its implementations were just as transitory as dance. Here, the "passatismo" of traditional institutions of art and education seemed the furthest overcome.

The concept of Futurist *aerial art* applied to all areas of representation—flight as theater, dance, painting, and poetry; a kind of three-dimensional *Gesamtkunstwerk* established in manifestos and "aero"-acts. However, in the end the *danse aérienne* of the Futurists always aspired toward literature: the spirals and ellipses—the figurations of aerodance in space—formed various theatrical textures (as the final texts in this chapter will demonstrate).

In 1912, Marinetti published "Le Monoplan du Pape," a lyrical apotheosis of flight and the aerial perspective of Italy. In roughly the same period, Paolo Buzzi's *Aeroplani* poems on flight were published, as well as a series of texts on the same subject (that were however ignored by the Futurists) by a number of authors between 1909 and 1911, that is, around the time of the first international air meeting in Brescia in 1909,[21] such as Franz Kafka's "Die Aeroplane in Brescia" (The airplanes at Brescia, 1909) and D'Annunzio's novel *Forse che sì forse che no* (1910).

In 1919, Fedele Azari published his manifesto "Il teatro aereo futurista" (Futurist aerial theater); ten years later, Balla, Benedetta, Depero, Dottori, Fillìa, Marinetti, Prampolini, Somenzi, and Tota signed the "Manifesto dell'aeropittura" (Manifesto of aeropainting, 1929);[22] and finally in 1931, Marinetti wrote his "Manifesto dell'aeropoesia" (Manifesto of aeropoetry).

Gravity and duration were the hallmarks of a conservative, "passéist" approach. Futurism answered with an aesthetic of dynamism, mobility, technology: "We have lost our predilection for the monumental, the heavy, the static, and we have enriched our sensibility with a *taste for the light, the practical, the ephemeral and the swift*."[23]

Azari regarded his *aerial theater* as being related to dance and in fact emphasized its superiority—the superiority of flight over dance, the superiority of nature's stage versus the limited space of theater:

> The artistic form that we create with flight is analogous to dance, but is infinitely superior because of its grandiose background, its superlative dynamism, and the greatly varied possibilities which it permits, though we must complete the evolutions according to the three dimensions of space.[24]

Azari, himself a pilot during the war, had already performed a few expressive flights and examples of aerial theater over Busto Arsizio in 1918. His manifesto documents the transition from wartime into a phase of history under the sway of aviation as the "art of the future"; a work of art corresponding to the Futurist passion for the "real, swift, elegant, complicated, cynical, muscular, fugitive"—so Marinetti in his manifesto on "synthetic theater."[25] Aerial theater was characterized by speed and energy, dynamism and simultaneity, in a way otherwise only found in variety theater, whose emergence at the same time as electricity in itself already qualified it as a role model for Futurist theater.

21. See Ingold 1980.

22. Gerardo Dottori exhibited his aerial paintings—as wall and ceiling paintings—at the airport in Ostia in 1929.

23. St. Elia 1914.

24. Azari 1970, 128–30; the following citations are, unless marked otherwise, from this translation.

25. See Marinetti, Settimelli, and Corra 1915.

"Simultaneità," the staging of speed, of moving force lines in aerial theater meant "Vols dialogues," "Tableaux futuristes aériens," the creation, measurement, realization of synthetic spaces in "dialogue" with the landscape, the light, with other airplanes: "Pour nous autres aviateurs futuristes, le ciel devient un véritable théâtre."[26]

The sky as the true space of theater appears not as a limitless open space, as the ether, through which the Icarian-mythical hero flies toward the sun like Paolo Tarsis in D'Annunzio's *Forse che sì forse che no*, but as a gigantic stage, citing the baroque-mannerist *theatrum mundi*, whose "set" consists of colorful zones of smoke by day and of dancing constellations of light produced by the airplanes and the projections of strong colorful floodlights at night. The space of Futurist aerodance combined the synthetic structure of cubist painting with dynamism, the preferred energetic principle of Futurism. "Vivere pericoloso"—the Futurist slogan, in which the experience of danger is pitted against "comfort as ideology"—is intensely substantiated in flight. Flying, as a sport and new instrument of warfare, thus became the emblem of the Futurist's passion for danger, the "ecstasy of combat", and the glorification of violence and warfare.

In the propagation of such paroles and theatrical models, the Futurists in fact merely radicalized a widespread tendency to equate the avant-garde (the term originally also came from the military sector) in art and warfare. Jacques-Emile Blanche, who like Misia Sert belonged to the Parisian supporters of the Ballets Russes, apparently once said about the destruction of war: "These props of terror belong in the theatre" and Sert likened the war to a Secessionist poster. Modris Eksteins summarized it as: "The inclination here was to regard the war as a form of art, as a superior representation of life."[27]

Not only was Azari's aerial theater a truly consequent implementation "of the Futurist's love of technology and machines . . . in aesthetic production,"[28] but it also entirely derived from an aestheticization of modern technological warfare (and in this regard in close proximity to Ernst Jünger's position)[29]: the spirals of looping airplanes, illuminated by the floodlights of the *teatro aereo*, make no pretense at all of their birth from the aerial battles of World War I, not even in the context of aero-theater.

26. Azari: "Theatre aérien futuriste" (1919); cited in Lista 1973, 271.

27. Eksteins 2000, 210.

28. Brauneck 1984, 180. Translation: Elena Polzer.

29. See Theweleit 1982, vol. 2.

Occasionally the theatrical elements of these performances appeared merely as citations, as applications of almost conventional scenographic devices of the stage, translated and metaphorically represented by actors in aerial performances. According to Azari's manifesto, the airplanes were supposed to be painted on by Futurist artists—almost like war heroes dressing up for a costume show. The "music" was generated by an aircraft engine, designed especially for the performance by Azari and Luigi Russolo, the inventor of Futurist "intona-rumori."[30] Aside from grandstands built for paying onlookers, the audience had free access to this theater for the masses: this performance of the "premier theater vraiment démocratique" (first truly democratic theater) by a heroic elite.

Aside from the construction and function of the space, it also seems necessary to more closely examine the presentation of the actor, the "subject" of aero-theater, and the patterns of signification, the symbolic forms of *aero-choreography*, in order to uncover all elements needed for a comprehensive reading of Futurist aerodance.

The actor in the *teatro aereo* is neither the pilot nor the airplane, but a union of both. Their coalescence into a centaurian creature takes on its own full artistic reality as vehicle of a new art form only in this theater of the ether. This mechanical human, who plays a central role in the aesthetics of Futurism, especially in the form of mechanical and robot figures in avant-garde theater and Futurist pantomimes (such as the *Dance of the Aviatrix* analyzed above), has its immediate predecessors in the novels of D'Annunzio (Paolo Tarsis in *Forse che sì forse che no*), in Marinetti's *Mafarka le Futuriste* (1910),[31] and emerging almost at the same time, but slightly before these novels, the mythical machine-human-hybrid in Mario Morasso's *La nuova arma: La macchina* (*The New Weapon: The Machine*, 1905).[32]

Morasso envisioned that mankind would

bit by bit become one with his machine, forming a single body. He becomes a strange creature, yet unknown to legend, that poets have not yet sung about in fantastic ballads: a being half-man, half-iron structure, an assembled monstrosity, a centaur, a siren, unknown to myth, a phantasmata with rigid and gigantic lines, belonging not to the past, but to the future.[33]

30. On Luigi Russolo and his concept of "Art des bruits", see Lista 1988, 45–48; and Wehmeyer 1974, 187–92.

31. See Ingold 1980, 75ff.

32. See Baumgarth 1966, 135.

33. Ibid. Translation: Elena Polzer.

Azari modified this modern centaur for the actors of aerial theater:

It was easy for the spectators to follow all the nuances of the aviator's state of mind, given the absolute identification between the pilot and his airplane, which became like an extension of his body: his bones, tendons, muscles, and nerves extended into longerons and metallic wires.[34]

The essential premise for this theater of aviation was the *mechanization of the body* and the *embodiment of the mechanical*. This process implied all aspects developed by Futurist theories about literature and theater in order to identify the modern, "Futurist" subject:

> The destruction of the ego: here, the Futurists address the crisis of the subject, although relatively late in comparison to the turn-of-the-century "crisis of perception"; the destruction of the ego, its deterioration into multiple layers, the disintegration of the identity of the subject—that phenomenon which most strongly characterized modern European literature and first emerged in the late nineteenth century. Marinetti, who was well versed in late nineteenth-century French literature, who performed lyrical works by French Symbolists in touring recitals and whose first works were written exclusively in French, titled his first collection of poems *Destruction* (1905), in an allusion to Mallarmé.
> The emergence of the multiplied man, the "uomo moltiplicato," the fragmentation of the body,[35] the abstraction of the person and of the actor's physical form.

One of the consequences of this destruction and abstraction of the (theatrical) subject was its sexual neutralization. The technical aerial body of the actor performing an aero-choreography is gender-neutral. This, in fact, contradicts the pointedly misogynist Futurist aesthetic of excessive virility glorified in the new heroes of violence.

The image of the *superuomo* takes on clear contours only against the backdrop of gender difference, in *contrast* to femininity. Thus it is not very surprising and almost paradoxically consistent that Azari's manifesto suggests a new gender differentiation among the actors of aerial theater, almost a "resexualization"

---

34. Azari 1970, 129.

35. See, e.g., the fragmentation of the body in Marinetti's pantomimes and theater pieces: one of these works "deals" only with feet, *Jambes*; another, written by Marinetti and Corra, is merely entitled *Mains* (*Hands*).

of the gender-neutral flying machines by corresponding male-female codified semiotic structures:

> In our flight dialogues, in our aerial *parole in libertà*, a sense of character-ization will be given by the type of airplane, the voice of the motor, and the diverse lines of flight. For example, a SVA, which has a regular fixed motor of 200 HP and climbs with continual majestic zooming, is evidently masculine, while an Henriot, which has a rotating motor of 110 HP and flies with a rhythmic swaying from side to side, has all the characteristics of femininity. (130)

The recourse to traditional corporeal and movement stereotypes of mas-culine and feminine—the "majestic" lines on the one hand and the rhythmic waves on the other—appears, however, no longer bound to the subject, but releases in its abstract function as signifier. The feminine and the masculine emerge as pure structures of differentiation, while, of course, still reconstructed from traditional gender symbols. This resexualization of the machine via the reading of emphatically accentuated expressive gestures illustrates the irony of Futurist radicalism, not least of all in the divergence of an avant-garde under-standing of art and conventional patterns of thought.

However, the instructions for interpretation that Azari's manifesto contains are concerned not only with the outward appearance of the theatrical aerial artificial body, but also with the expressive functions of its movement. We have here a process of de- and reconstructing semiotic motifs similar to the constitu-tion of the aerial theater actor. Whereas in the latter case, a sexual neutraliza-tion of the human-machine challenged the reconstruction of abstract gender symbols in a process that is the reverse of abstraction, representation is in aero-dance, according to Azari, directed at yet another form of "differentiation": in the opposition of abstract aero-choreography and the semantics of their aerial figurations, they become objects of a specific pathognomy, as a form of reading movements and their meaning.

In his *teatro aereo*, Azari sought to simultaneously portray two models of a symbolic understanding of movement: on the one hand, the *movements of abstract figures* and, on the other, the *expression of movements of affects*—more or less pathos formulas and topos formulas rolled into one. Generalized affect formulas translated onto figurations of space thereby took the place of indi-vidual physiognomy.

The simultaneously staging of both models, the *deciphering of figurations* and the *interpretation of affects*, was meant to produce the multi-expressivity of the Futurist *Gesamtkunstwerk*. The dynamics of abstract line and plane—as in similar concepts of abstraction found in Kandinsky's and Schlemmer's scenographic compositions[36]—appears in the "aero-scena's" colorful random surfaces of smoke, in the projections of light, in the forms of movement in flight. The loops, rolls, dives, spirals testify to a play of intertwining and shifting pure "aviational" strings of signs. "Bizarre zig-zags" and "hieroglyphs" formulate an ephemeral and hermetic movement language, which is described in Azari's manifesto using a combination of flight and dance terminology:

> We futurist aviators love to roar up perpendicularly and dive vertically into the void, to turn in the intoxication of yawing with our bodies glued to the small seats by the centrifugal force, and to abandon ourselves to the whirl of spirals that press around the spiral staircase embedded in the void; to turn over two, three, ten times in increasingly happy loops, and to lean over in whirling barrel rolls; to swirl, skidding, to rock ourselves into long falls like dead leaves, or to stun ourselves with a breathless series of spins: in short, to roll, to rock, to flip over on the invisible trapezes of the atmosphere, to form with our airplanes a great aerial pinwheel.[37]

Here aerial theater appears as a technical transformation of the abstract movement principles of dance, while simultaneously citing the movement language of "expressionist dance" in a "pantomime aérienne." The movements of the aircraft are, according to Azari, "a precise expression of the pilot's state of mind," and specific lines, trajectories of flight, can be assigned to affects such as joy, impatience, anger:

> In fact, looping denotes happiness and spins denote impatience or irritation, while the repeated alternation of wings from right to left indicates light-heartedness, and long falls, like dead leaves, give a sense of nostalgia or fatigue. The sudden halts, followed by more or less prolonged zooming, dives, loops—all the infinite varieties of maneuvers joined and coordinated in a planned succession—give the spectator an immediate and clear comprehension of how much the aviator wishes to represent or declaim with the airplane. (129)

By assigning specific movement patterns carried out by the aviator to specific, clearly delineated expressive contents, Azari (re)constructs an *affect theory*

36. The contacts maintained by Futurists to Bauhaus testify to a mutual and reciprocal influence; likewise the relationship of Futurism and Russian constructivism (its theatrical concepts were, e.g., greatly influenced by the Futurist manifesto of variety theater).

37. Azari 1970.

of the (aero-)technical arts; or in other words, he superimposes the pathos formulas of expressive gestures onto the topos formulas of flight movement. The rules of aesthetic representation and the deciphering of aerial art conform to a pathognomic pattern of reading—a pathognomy similar to the *expressive movement of the machine*.

The theoretical background of this retheorization of an art that presents itself as pointedly technology-oriented, pointedly antiemotional, is the concept of a *new sensitivity* of Futurist man. This is not the same as the sensitivity of the Décadents in fin de siècle aesthetics. On the contrary: Marinetti deduces this new sensitivity from the development of technology and media, which require a new awareness of distance and space, of time and of speed.[38] As a result, Futurist *dynamism* is a reaction to these new experiences of energy and space, and a precept of perceiving and representing "simultaneity" as a consequence of altered attitudes toward time.

This new affect paradigm, derived from the *new sensitivity* and its rhetorical organization, did not refer to individual expressions of temperament. The focus lay not on the subject and its expression of affects, but on an "inhumane and mechanical type" of the multiplied man,[39] who, nonsentimental, with an "inexhaustible supply of vital energy," creates himself as the human of the future solely out of the force of his own will. Lamarckism and a popular understanding of Nietzsche's *Übermensch* and his "will to power" are here combined into a hybrid synthesis.

To this effect, *expression*, the rhetorical representation of affect in the specific variation of aerodance, manifested itself not as expressive movements of an organic body, but as the mechanical movements of a technical aerial body. According to Azari's theory, the (informed) spectator interpreted the trajectories drawn on the "invisible trapezes of the atmosphere" in order to gain an idea of the performer's "état d'âme": pathognomy as an interpretation of the exhibitionism of the heroic Futurist "uomo universale." However, nowhere is it stated under which conditions the millions of spectators could adequately perform this act of deciphering movement. More crucial than the reading of the message in a precise conjunction of aircraft movement and affect rhetoric is the more general proclamation (of the special qualities) of the "uomo moltiplicato," in whose flesh "wings are waiting to be awakened" (Marinetti). His auto-representation in the sphere of the third dimension—mastery of nature through willpower and technology, not only represented, but also embodied

38. See Baumgarth 1966, 132ff.

39. See Marinetti, "Multiplied Man and the Reign of the Machine" (1911), in Rainey, Poggi, and Wittmann 2009, 89ff.

in the paradigm of flight—demonstratively demanded an unlimited arena of airspace for the constitution of the multi-expressive genius of the avant-garde.

"MOTS EN LIBERTÉ AÉRIENS": FLIGHT AND WRITING

The subtitle of Azari's manifesto "Mots en liberté aériens" (Flight as an artistic expression of states of mind)[40] includes aerodance in the Futurist program of a *parole in libertà*. The double encoding of aero-choreography—as abstract graphemes on the one hand, and as affect language on the other—made it possible to stage the two fundamental aspects of a poetology of "liberated" language (of dance), namely *aesthetic* freedom from the limitations of traditional linguistic norms on the one hand, and *technical* freedom from the constraints of gravity and corporeality on the other.

In literature, Marinetti's *parole in libertà*, which he first introduced in his "Technical Manifesto of Futurist Literature" (Manifesto tecnico della letteratura futurista, 1912), represented a second, even more radical step in avant-garde literature. It was an answer to the demand for an elimination of all rules of versification, a liberation from rhyme and meter as stated in the "verso libero" of the first literary manifesto.

Parole in libertà referred to the deconstruction of all basic grammatical structures in literature. In his manifesto, Marinetti called for a destruction of syntax, an abolition of declination and conjugation, attributive adjectives and adverbs, as well as an eradication of punctuation as a logical consequence of the dissolution of structural functions.

Yet *libertà* involves even more, namely the dissolution of the boundaries of literature, the transition of language into a synthetical work of art. The visual dimension of writing shifts to the pictorial dimension of graphic art and the image through the use of mathematical symbols, through calligraphic and bold typography, while vice versa the fine arts and theater integrate writing as a symbolic element. In addition, the phonetic dimension of language as sound and "noise" is emphasized: onomatopoeia and declamation accentuate the acoustic experience of language. Gestures and facial expressions of the reciting author produce a theatricalization of literature—as in the staged performances of Hugo Ball and Tristan Tzara at the Zurich Café "Voltaire" as vanguards of today's contemporary "happenings."[41]

40. English translation Azari 1970.

41. Similar juxtapositions of linguistic and symbolic elements—of images, text, sound/noise, costumes, and movement were also staged, e.g., by the Berlin Dada group around Richard Huelsenbeck and Hanna Höch (see Bergius 1989); both the "staging" of literature and the

The various processes of visualization, staging, and theatricalization of language shifted the boundaries between literature, fine arts, and theater—and they attempted to open the gates between art and life. On the aesthetic side of production, this process of synesthetic osmosis matched the overriding importance awarded to associative imagination, not only on the level of individual pronunciation, but also in its function as a dynamic-constructivist technique of linking multiple pictorial and semiotic levels. In his "Technical Manifesto of Futurist Literature," Marinetti explains the function of an analogy, whereby the term *analogy* must be read in a way similar, and with effect similar, to comparable ideas by Russian constructivists, such as Sergei Eisenstein's *Montage of Attractions*.[42]

Analogy is nothing other than the deep love that binds together things that are remote, seemingly diverse or inimical. The life of matter can be embraced only by an orchestral style, at once polychromatic, polyphonic, and polymorphous, by means of the most extensive analogies. . . . To render the successive movements of an object, it is imperative to render the chain of analogies, which it evokes, each condensed and concentrated into one essential word. . . . To catch and gather whatever is most evanescent and ineffable in matter, it is imperative to shape strict nets of images or analogies, which will then be cast into the mysterious sea of phenomena.[43]

The process of agglutination, the serial construction of paratactical nouns that follow the snowball system of association (Marinetti gives an example: "battle = weight + smell," i.e., the literature of war) not only exceeds all conventions of understanding language and literature. From the perspective of Futurism, it reveals a pathway from the imaginary of the image to the formative structures of language. The Futurist technique of using words, developed out of a play of *analogies*, lays claim to another status of poetics that is more than just a variation of "telegraphic style."

Marinetti's technique of using words borders, on the one hand, on Dada's experiments with the absurd and nonsense, as well as on the *écriture automatique* of the surrealists. On the other hand, it is linked—via the model of association—to various theories and techniques in the fine arts, to cubism, Futurism, and constructivism. In the dynamism of paintings by Boccioni, Balla, Depero,

reactions of the audience were part of the Futurist concept of literature and language (see Riesz 1976). See also Finter 1980.

42. See here also the chapter on "Interruption," Part II.

43. Marinetti, "Technical Manifesto of Futurist Literature" (1912), in Rainey, Poggi, and Wittmann 2009, 119ff.

Figure 46 Gino Severini: *Female Dancer + Sea =
Bouquet of Flowers* (1913).
SOURCE: Privatsammlung, New York, USA / © VG
Bild-Kunst, Bonn, Germany.

and Severini, the principle of analogy controlled by the process of association
becomes a fundamental structuring element. The most famous example of this
technique is Gino Severini's *Dancer + Sea = Bouquet of Flowers* (1913, figure 46):

> So, using analogies, we can penetrate the most expressive part of reality and
> simultaneously render matter and will in their most intensive and expan-
> sive action. . . . For example: the sea dancing, with its zigzag movements
> and sparkling contrasts of silver and emerald, within my plastic sensibility
> evokes the distant vision of a dancer covered in sparkling sequins in her
> world of light, noise, and sound.
>   Therefore: sea = dancer.
>   . . . the plastic expression of the same sea, which through real analogy
> has evoked a dancer for me, by a process of apparent analogy evokes for
> me a vision of a large bunch of flowers.[44]

44. Severini 2009, 166–67.

The fact that *dance* is here chosen as an example reflects Futurist strategies of dissolving the static via principles of dynamism and simultaneity. As Depero's works reveal, even Futurist painting ultimately made use of the aesthetics of movement arts in a consequent translation of the dynamic spatial-rhythmical principles of representation found in dance, in "magical theater," and in film.[45] This is also evident in the conspicuously large number of Futurist paintings depicting dance and dancers,[46] such as Severini's *La danseuse obsédante* (1911), *Danzatrice gialla* (1912), *Ballarina blu* (1912), or Depero's *Macchinismo di ballerina; Ballerina + Idolo* (1917) and *Ballerina meccanica* (1918).[47]

The creation of a dense web of analogies, the denial of syntactical structure—the "antigrammatical" process[48] of the Futurist "rhetoric of the presence," the arrangement of words and figures of speech in an "immaginazione senza fili" ("wireless imagination")—simultaneously aimed toward a revolution of poetological standards and the propagation of a literary theory of the avant-garde. Texts such as the "Technical Manifesto of Futurist Literature," the "supplement" to the "Technical Manifesto," and the essay "Let's Murder the Moonshine" combine theory and practice of a radically performative approach to language. They *stage* the Futurist definition of art. They demonstrate the cracks emerging in the walls erected by the aestheticism of fin de siècle literature between art and life—cracks produced by the shock effect of violence, the theatricalization of technology, the diversification of sensual ways of experiencing art.

Futurist manifestos can therefore, as János Riesz emphasizes,[49] be understood as nonauthentic texts: not as theoretical manifestos, whose postulates are yet to be realized—as Alfred Döblin defined them in his answer to Marinetti's "Technical Manifesto of Futurist Literature," published in the *Sturm* under the title "Futuristische Worttechnik" (Futurist word technique) in 1912[50]—but as authentic mediums of avant-garde representation and self-commentary.

---

45. See Lista 1988.

46. The dancers in Futurist paintings are often portrayed as mechanized, as dolls or mechanical figurines.

47. The Futurists' preference for vaudeville, i.e., variety theater, could, as Maurizio Calvesi suggests, be the reason for such dancer portraits—not based on "an interest in the subject matter", i.e., an enthusiasm for the milieu, as in the case of Toulouse-Lautrec's vaudeville and music hall paintings, but out of dynamistic motives directed against the established high-art system, which predestined vaudeville to become an alternative to traditional theater.

48. See Finter 1980, 196ff.

49. See Riesz 1976, 260; Schultz 1981.

50. See Demetz 1990.

For the context of dance as a mechanized construction of body and space, and for Futurist poetology, this means the interpretation of these constructs becomes in itself a discourse on avant-garde aesthetics that is already theatricalized in the manifestos—as demonstrated, for example by Azari's manifesto of aerial theater or Marinetti's manifesto of Futurist dance. This process of interpretation does not aim at the "implementation" of its agenda. Instead, the text of art and modern technical everyday life already itself appears theatricalized in the manifesto.

Marinetti's "Technical Manifesto of Futurist Literature" is a prime example of the figurative nature of these manifestos, whose depictions adhere to an *analogical* principle, namely in the form of an *illogical* fictional structure. In Marinetti's case, the ironic "narrative voice" of the text is that of an aircraft propeller, which provides the conjunction between the poetological agenda and a reading of the technological body of modernity. Hence, the fictional framework *analogically* presents in a single image what the Futurist rhetoric of breaking the rules proclaims to be the poetology of the avant-garde: the destruction of existing structures and the establishment of the new as the voice of the machine. The propeller says:

> Sitting astride the fuel tank of an airplane, my stomach warmed by the aviator's head, I felt the ridiculous inanity of the old syntax inherited from Homer. A raging need to liberate words, dragging them out from the prison of the Latin period. . . . This is what the swirling propeller told me. . . . And the propeller added: 1. It is imperative to destroy syntax and scatter one's nouns at random, just as they are born.[51]

The fragmentation of the syntax creates a *libertà* that releases the specific cohesive powers of the analogical web. Only through deconstruction can there be construction, that is, a Futurist "reconstruction of the universe": not as an act of creation by a subject, but as a chain of associated terms, a series of logograms and ideograms; a "road of metaphors" that strings together abstract forms and colors, as well as nouns in a theatrical "equivalenti paro-libertà." Dance, as the play of movement by depersonalized abstract bodies, hereby represents the concatenative modus operandi of analogies. The audience—as actors amid the dynamism of associative imagination—is accorded the role of a producer of "free" figurations, for which "dance" offers an archive of model forms of movement, of color and lighting dynamics, and of time as noise-sound.

51. Marinetti in Rainey, Poggi, and Wittmann 2009, 119.

ELLIPSE AND SPIRAL: THE RHETORIC
OF THE SPATIAL FORMULA

The spiral and the ellipse, as essential spatial formulas in the dynamic movement aesthetics of Futurism, take on a special significance in these stagings
of abstract form. The formal and rhythmical movement aspects of the spiral
and the ellipse not only seem to determine the form of the space and the choreography, but also define the plasticity of the costume and the elements of a
scenography dramaticized by the dynamics of color, lights, and movement, as
in Depero's *Balli plastici*.

The winding spirals wrapped around the dancer's body represent architectural structures of moving colored veils. The references to the spatial-sculptural
scenography of Loïe Fuller's costumes are again very distinct. There is also a
medial aspect in the dynamics of these spatial moving spiral forms, alongside
their merely mechanical components and the physical laws of rotation and cen-
trifugal force: that of psychographic transference, the concretization of emotional states, unleashed in the process of reading the spiral as a pattern of energy.
Hence the spiral, as the archetype of life in esoteric lore and as a figuration of
space in macro- and microcosmic forms of nature, transfers the *élan vital* into
symbols of movement and into technical apparatuses—in the same way that the
Futurist terminology of energetic and dynamic states likewise oscillates between
technical, mechanical-rational and psychic-, biological-metaphysical levels.

The *pittura metafisica* attempted by Futurist painting under the influence of
Giorgio de Chirico clearly corresponds to the *danza metafisica*, which in turn
also applies further, via the figurations of the spiral and the ellipse, to the ethe-
ric texts of *aeropittura* and *aerodanza*.

The movement figurations of the spiral and the ellipse represent the conceptual framework of a scenic writing of *parole in libertá*; they summarize and
integrate the decisive poetological arguments as rhetoric figures:

- The dynamics of destruction and reconstruction
- The destruction of the "ego," its disappearance in the curves of the spirals, in the gaps of the ellipse/ellipsis
- The "reconstruction of the universe" out of the energy of light and
  movement, and finally
- The transformation and regeneration of language analogous to the rhetorical figures of the ellipsis and the "loop," as a figure of speech and as
  writing

The vitalistic side of Futurism is expressed in the spiral as an endlessly self-
perpetuating cycle of life. References to Bergson's *Creative Evolution* reappear

frequently in Futurist manifestos, for example, in Severini's "Le analogie plas-
tiche del dinamismo" (The plastic analogies of dynamism, 1913):

> Furthermore, the spiraling shapes and beautiful contrasts of yellow and
> blue that were intuitively felt one evening while experiencing the move-
> ments of a danseuse may be found again later, through a process of plastic
> affinities or aversions, or through a combination of both, in the concentric
> circling of an airplane or in the onrush of an express train.[52]

The multitude of rhythmical spiral forms in Futurist paintings (but also in
the "Orphism" works of Sonja and Robert Delaunay) mirrors the relationship of movement to the dynamics of the curve. The figurations of the spiral
and the ellipse play a central, almost exemplary role in Paolo Buzzi's novel
L'Elisse e la Spirale (Milan, 1915), as basic models of a cosmic-universal utopian dynamism.

As *figures of speech*, the spiral and the ellipsis take on the function of *tertium
comparationis* in the analogical principle underlying the *parole in libertá* of aerial theater, dance, and poetry. This means that the abstract patterns of dynamic
movement take on the role of mutually complementary basic rhetorical figurations in the poetology of Futurist literature.

The curve of the *spiral* obeys the endless movement of associative figures of
speech. It corresponds to the "elastic intuitions" (Marinetti) of self-reproducing
metonymic chains of analogies.

In contrast, the *ellipsis* plays with the spatial formula of the gap, the space
in-between, the rhetoric of omission. Its main principle is the segmentation and
elimination of linguistic elements, that is, the abolishment of adverbs, adjectives, and punctuation as demanded in the "Technical Manifesto." According
to Marinetti, the intentional destruction of style, of the harmony of linguistic
structure, produces—thanks to the omissions created by the "technical" procedure of the ellipsis—"magnetic waves" between "words freed," the radiance of a
"dynamism of thought."[53]

The symbols of the spiral and the ellipse, on their transitory trajectory
through space, appear, on the one hand, as spatial choreographies of experimental aerial theater, an aerial theater, however, that staged its greatest performances during World War I. In *War and Cinema*, Paul Virilio describes the
aesthetization of military aviation in the squadrons instituted by the infamous

---

52. Severini 2009, 165.

53. See the item on the adverb in Marinetti's "Technical Manifest": "Adverbs must be abolished, old buckles strapping together two words. Adverbs give a sentence a tedious unity of
tone" (Rainey, Poggi, and Wittmann 2009, 120).

cavalry captain Manfred von Richthofen, also known as the "Red Baron," to implement his "flying circus" tactics in 1917:

> In principle there was no longer an above or below, no longer any visual polarity. War pilots already had their own special effects, which they called "looping," "falling-leaf roll," "figure of eight," and so on. Airborne vision now escaped that Euclidian neutralization which was so acutely felt by ground troops in the trenches; it opened endoscopic tunnels and even brought "blind spots" within the most astounding topological field—vistas whose precursors could be found in the bog wheels and other fairground attractions of the nineteenth century and which were later developed in the roller-coasters and scenic railways of post-war funfairs, especially in Berlin.[54]

On the other hand, spirals and ellipses also appear as abbreviations of a poetology in which writing and the preservation of a culture of writing are categorized—against the backdrop of the world war's potential for destruction—*differently* than in Futurism's aesthetics of destruction.

Two entirely different examples of such reassessments of writing as transitory aerial trajectories of a dubious semiotic nature are the poems of Jean Cocteau (*Cape of Good Hope*, 1919), and Bertolt Brecht's "Mit Weissem Rauch" (With white smoke) and "Das Rauchzeichen" (The smoke sign).

Cocteau's verse poems, created between 1916 and 1919, focus on the real-life persona of the French pilot Roland Garros—who, shortly before World War I, managed to cross the Mediterranean and who died in an accident in 1918—in a web of aerial mythology and aerial figures in human history:

Grip tight Garros
hold on to my shoulder
Dante and Virgil
crouched over abysses
I will take you up now in

---

54. Virilio 1989, 18–19. The image of the "falling leaf" as a figuration of flight actually deserves an individual study of its own. It appears in the context of the metaphorics of artistic aerobatics, of the "danse aérienne." Like Richthofen, Azari used the image of the "feuilles mortes" as an aerial-rhetorical formula for a specific movement through space, namely the "rocking into long falls" (see above, in the section on *aerodanza*). It would be worth a study of its own how this image—which was initially a symbol of decadent literature (and as such appears in poems by Rilke, then in Trakl, and as the title of a composition from Debussy's *Préludes*)—was transformed into a figuration of movement in technical military "aerial art."

my turn
familiar ink,
and here are my loopings
my records of high altitude.[55]

Like D'Annunzio, Cocteau evokes the act of flight in Dante and Virgil as an act of floating above the abyss of the inferno. On the verge of crashing to earth, the poet himself initiates, as "familiar ink," the trajectory of his writing as a looping into uncertainty. The roles of pilot and poet are not, however, interchangeable: the poet is left only with the "song of obedience," with the "exiguous slave's role" that immortalizes the death of the hero by memorializing the fleeting ethereal traces of flying in the "loopings" of the text:

here is the song of obedience
our exiguous slave's role
and you
leaden angel Garros
your great sad epic
poor friend we are so heavy

"Poor friend we are so heavy": the gravity of writing, which only immortalizes the flight of thoughts, is not suited as an equivalent to Icarian elevation. Cocteau's sorrow over the lack of lightness in writing also expressed itself in his many artistic activities that went beyond literature: in the spiral lines of his drawings, in his work with various media, with photography, and especially with film, and finally in his affinity for concert dance. In 1923–24, Cocteau wrote a scenario for Diaghilev's Ballets Russes, entitled *Le Train bleu* (*The Blue Train*),[56] which not only portrayed sports as the leisure activity of a young dynamic generation, but also featured the train and the airplane as symbols of a new relationship to space in an age of technology and media.

Unlike Cocteau's affectedly melancholic gestural reflections on writing, the spirals of aerial writing in both of the following poems by Bertolt Brecht (created between 1939 and 1947) are a plea in favor of a political mandate of literature.

The first poem:

With white smoke in great sweeps

55. See Cocteau 1921.

56. *Le Train Bleu*, Paris, 1924; libretto, Jean Cocteau; choreography, Bronislawa Nijinska; music, Darius Milhaud.

An aviator inscribes the sky over four cities.
For a moment
V for "victory" appears. Then the wind,
Not noticeable below, rattles this sign
And it transforms into something crinkly.[57]

The second poem:

The Smoke Sign

The aviator, who described the sky today
With white smoke in great sweeps
Proceeded, so that the wind, not noticeable below
Could not clump his sign.
That teaches us, I thought to myself, how we must write.[58]

Both poems, which complement each other like two opposing sides of a coin, address the dialectic of writing between ephemerality and permanence, between the symbolic image and the trajectory of ideas.

The first poem describes the moment of letters emerging out of the spiraling curves drawn by the pilot on the ethereal blackboard, and the random moment in which they disappear again: written on the wind. Becoming and passing as two sides of creation are ironically represented in a reflection of the impermanence of power structures that rely solely on victory and defeat. Their corresponding symbols are ephemeral, as is that which is being signified. This is what the smoke symbols in the sky illustrate—rattled by the wind, the power of nature, they lose their contours as sensual and meaningful emblems of victory.

---

57. Brecht 1967, Supplement vol. 4, 368. Translation: Elena Polzer.

Mit weissem Rauch in großen Bogen
Beschreibt ein Flieger nun den Himmel der vier Städte.
Für einen Augenblick
Erscheint ein V für ›victory‹. Dann schüttelt
Der Wind, nicht spürbar unten, dieses Zeichen
Und es verwandelt sich in etwas Krauses

58. Ibid.

Das Rauchzeichen

Der Flieger, der den Himmel heut beschrieb
Mit weißem Rauch in ungeheuren Bögen
Verfuhr, daß ihm der Wind, nicht spürbar unten
Sein Zeichen nicht zusammenwerfen konnte.
Der lehrt uns, dacht ich, wie wir schreiben müssen.

The clarity of conventional symbols transforms into something "crinkly"—a literary fantasy, which is linked in Brecht's poetry to the reoccurring images of smoke, clouds, wind—and thus appears not only as a play of chance, but as the true task of writing: to distrust "victories" and the permanent consolidation of power.

The second poem, on the "smoke sign," focuses on the necessity of pursuing writing as an act of enlightenment in comparison with the pilot's act of aerial writing. Here an analogy is made not to the contents or objects of such texts, but rather to the process behind their production. Just as the pilot draws his curves, so that the wind (as a dissipating force not noticeable on the ground) cannot "clump his sign," so the author should choose a technique that makes his voice heard, his signs accessible to readers. This lesson on ideal production processes, which the author learned from observing this model of aerial writing, already in fact contains its own subversive counterforce.[59] Even the most skillful aerial technique will not avert the gradual disintegration of the smoke symbols. Politics and poetry are, although situated in different contexts of life, both located in the identical realm of an ephemeral production of signs, whose destructive forces, whether immanent or operating from the outside, deny being controlled by the author. However, this may be an impetus to appeal to the reader's solidarity and willingness to cooperate.

59. Here Brecht's ambivalence is conspicuously evident in the idea that symbols of power can be dispersed; this also applies to the symbols of literature, whose continuity can only be ensured by repeated reading.

Chapter 4

Writing Dance and Spatial Writing

Between Alphabet and Topos Formula

The reading of dance as moving signs—as kinetic ideograms in space—confronts the choreograph "writer" as well as the reader with the subject of writing: as written dance and as a medium of the space "described" by dance.

The volatile smoke signs in the sky in the poems of Bertolt Brecht cited in the previous chapter now become symbols of ephemerality, that is, symbols of that basic structure of dance characterized by the transitory nature of dance figurations and of the appearance and disappearance of its structures in space.

The individual signs, the quasi-graphemes of dance, and their placement in space—the differentiating con-figuration of figure and background, of positive and negative space—become a matter of meta-choreographic reflection: in the theory and practice of written dance, of systems of notation concerned with corporeal movement and choreography.

First attempts to encode dance in written form date back to the Renaissance.[1] The forms and structures, as well as the history of these systems of notation—which were never fully formulated into obligatory systems or widely used alphabets[2]—simultaneously reflect the respective aesthetics and cultural status of dance at the time. Semiotic reflections on the relationship of signifier and signified in written dance, on the proportion of images (as mimetic signs, e.g., spatial paths) to abstract conventional symbols, left their mark in more forms than simply as semiotic texts on dance.[3]

---

1. For a summary of the most important notation systems in historical order, see Jeschke 1983.

2. Labanotation, a notation system based on Rudolph von Laban's *kinetography*, is a recent exception to this rule. See also the following section on Laban.

3. See Foster 1986.

Both modern dance as well as the fine arts were influenced by the spatial pat-terns and designs produced by the symbols and figurations of these notations (systems),[4] as is evident e.g., in collaborations between choreographer Merce Cunningham and the painters Robert Rauschenberg and Jasper Johns,[5] or in Lucinda Childs's pixel graphics.

In early twentieth-century choreographic and scenographic productions, these semiotic aspects of dance frequently surfaced on the level of self-reflective dance practice, for example, in the play with "dancing ciphers," in particular during the period of transition from classical ballet to the various *free* styles.

In this book, I use the term *Schrifttanz*[6] [written dance] in three different, yet interrelated ways. In its most restricted sense, the term refers to a specific form of *Tanzschrift* [dance notation], namely Rudolph von Laban's attempt to translate dance and movement into writing in order to make it readable and reproducible. The system, developed by Laban together with Albrecht Knust, as well as subsequent activities meant to elaborate and distribute this notation system—*kinetography*—were often described at the time as written dance: espe-cially in connection with publications about dance writing. Many of these texts appeared in the journal *Schrifttanz*, which was specifically founded to address such issues.[7]

If we take a closer look at the period from 1928 to 1932 (in which the journal appeared four times a year), written dance also stood for the potential power of notation systems to create dances based on a written system—in other words, the power not to produce dance primarily on the basis of observations of the body and of experimentation with movement in space (as primary modes of dance production), but rather to *compose choreography with the help of graph-emes*. In Laban's own words, "the final artistic objective of kinetography is . . . not a notation system but dance literacy."[8]

4. See Louppe 1991.

5. See d'Offay's documentation on Cunningham and Johns, 1991.

6. *Translator's note*: the German terms *Schrift* and *Schreiben* both translate as *writing* in English. *Schrift* stands for the material side of writing, i.e., text (typeface, font, script, etc.), while *Schreiben* refers to the actual physical act of writing.

7. *Schrifttanz* was a quarterly published by the Gesellschaft für Schrifttanz (Society for Written Dance) from 1928 to 1932. The editor-in-chief was Alfred Schlee. The journal was published by the music publishing house Universal Edition in Vienna. The need for such a publication on written dance was explained in the first edition editorial: "Many questions arise, on the one hand from the effect on dance itself of the creation and the development of dance documentation, on the other hand from the effect of a notation on music, theatre, etc., and these will be looked at by this quarterly journal." Preston-Dunlop and Lahusen 1990, 29.

8. Laban in Preston-Dunlop and Lahusen 1990, 34.

Finally, written dance, in a broader and more general dance-related and poetological sense, is also used to describe "dancing texts," abstract figurations of signs, and graphemes in motion: *Lettres dansantes*.

LETTRES DANSANTES: MICHEL FOKINE'S BALLET *CARNAVAL*

In *Carnaval*,[9] choreographed by Michel Fokine for the 1910 season of the Ballets Russes in Berlin, one episode is entitled "Lettres dansantes." The storyline is conveyed with the help of pantomime and dance as is typical for narrative or fairy-tale ballets. Pierrot appears and dances a quick waltz, while tightly holding on to his hat. He believes it still holds "Papillon," whom he caught earlier. But his butterfly of love is gone and the hat is empty.

The ballet is danced to Robert Schumann's *Carnaval: Scènes mignonnes sur quatre notes* (1835). The movement "Lettres dansantes" is one of fifteen (in the twenty-one-movement work), in which the "four notes" simultaneously also stand for the four letters that form the basis of the composition. The four letters A-S-C-H determine the structure. The *Scènes mignonnes* vary either the three- or four-note version of the letter game, either as-c-h or a-es-c-h. The alphabetical notation contains encoded scenes from the life of the composer. All letters have a secret meaning: Schumann's first bride, Ernestine von Fricken, was from Asch in Bohemia. The letters can also all be found in Schumann's last name. The musical anagram therefore contains an encrypted erotic element.

It is exactly this aspect of the alphabetic game, namely the movement patterns of flirtation, that Fokine subsequently translated into choreography. *Carnaval* depicts the hide-and-seek of couples in a remote corner of a garden during a masquerade ball. The characters find and lose each other in rapid succession. The atmosphere of the piece is determined by the gaiety of the characters, who are modeled after the commedia dell'arte and cite the enthusiastically ironic and romantic air of Jean Paul.

LETTRES DANSANTES: AKAROVA'S CHOREOGRAPHY

The *lettres dansantes* reappeared in the early 1920s in the work of the Belgian dancer Akarova, who transformed them into a theatrical constructivist dance

---

9. *Le Carnaval: Ballet-pantomime en un acte*, premiered May 20, 1910, in Berlin (choreography, Michel Fokine; music, Robert Schumann, *Carnaval*, 1835, orchestral version of the piano piece); the ballet later became a standard in the Ballets Russes repertoire.

experiment—again to music by Schumann. The solo, which she created for herself—like all of her works—premiered in Brussels on October 10, 1924.

Akarova, born as Marguerite Acarin on March 30, 1904, in Brussels, is one
of the most important avant-garde artists of the 1920s. Her work has only
recently been rediscovered and given the attention it deserves.[10] Akarova created her very own, distinctly peculiar dance style in a syncretistic play with
those innovations and forms of dance that were popular at the time. She condensed her correspondence with Raymond Duncan, Isadora's brother, and
her study of the Ballets Russes and the Ballets Suédois, expressionist dance,
and Rudolph von Laban's kinesphere[11] into highly idiosyncratic spatial plastic forms. Her dances were always very rational and deliberately *sculptural*.
They frequently featured a particular emphasis on slow and bound movement, as well as the presentation of strange or surprising perspectives. This
was augmented by a particularly elaborate use of lighting—which she developed under the influence of the theater reformers working at that time at the
La Cambre stage in Brussels. For her lighting effects, Akarova also employed
film technology by using lights and shadows in a cinematographic way to
produce various nuances of gray, as well as by applying various pale or bright
cropped spotlights that lent the dance plasticity by sharpening or softening
the contours. In her productions, Akarova thus mobilized the entire ensemble of theatrical parameters into quasi-linguistic compositions, that is, every
element was assigned a function of its own in the semiotic system. At the
same time, she simultaneously single-handedly embodied the roles of dancer,
choreographer, and costume and set designer, as well as director. Aside from
lighting, the use of color was also of great importance to Akarova—both on
stage and in the color of the lights, as well as in the accurate designs of her
costumes. Her choreographies were always also *chromo-kinetic productions*.

Her syncretism in choice of media and role models also reveals itself
in her transformation of elements taken from East Asian theater. Critics
described Akarova's choreography and portrayal of Darius Milhaud's *L'Orestie*
(March 1931):

This is a European equivalent of the Noh, the Japanese lyrical drama: materialization of music through dance and gestures. The effect is all the more

---

10. See Akarova 1988.

11. Marie-Louise Van Veen introduced Akarova, among other things, to Laban's concept of
"Space Harmony," his theories on space and the icosahedron; see the following section for
more on Laban.

powerful in that the stage is small and any small movement by the actor is enough to modify its whole layout.[12]

In the 1920s, Akarova was closely connected to a leading group of Belgian stage reformers mainly associated with La Cambre theater. This small stage—built by Henry van de Velde—was equipped with a cyclorama inspired by Mariano Fortuny's *Fortuny Sky*. The theater, directed by Herman Teirlinck, was the Belgian answer to other European experimental avant-garde stages such as the Teatro Sperimentale degli Independenti in Rome under Anton Giulio Bragaglia, or Claude Autant-Lara's Laboratoire Art in Action in Paris.

After her first experiences with La Cambre, Akarova commissioned the architect Jean-Jules Eggericx to design a small theater in which she could best realize her ideas about dance. As in the case of Henri Sauvage, who built a theater for Loïe Fuller in 1900[13] that was fully adapted to her theatrical and lighting needs, Eggericx built a similarly distinct studio-stage in Akarova's house on Jean d'Ardenne Street in Brussels.[14] This space gave Akarova the chance to situate her sublime mimoplastic solos in a context that adequately conveyed the movement structures both functionally in terms of the architecture of the stage, and *spherically*, by allowing the kinetic figures sufficient room to emanate outward.

Akarova's dance and theater pieces reflected the two main functions that she ascribed to the stage as a space for experimentation: on the one hand, the theater is a *studio* or rather an *atelier* and on the other hand, a laboratory. This term has been revived in recent, processual concepts such as the *theater lab*[15] to describe the workshop nature of dance productions. However, in Akarova's case the word *laboratory* invokes the constructivist aspects of her work, almost the *Bauhaus* principle[16] and the machine model. This is also evident in her dances, for example, in Akarova's solo *Pacific 2-3-1* (1923), performed to an eponymous composition by Arthur Honegger. It was a machine dance, performed to Honegger's musical homage to the locomotive. Akarova's use of the body in this

12. Akarova 1988, 265.

13. See Brandstetter and Ochain 1989.

14. This stage still exists in Akarova's former house, while Fuller's theater has been destroyed.

15. E.g., George Tabori's *Theaterlabor* experiment in Bremen 1976.

16. Here "Bauhaus" is used to describe the general architectural principle behind her spatial compositions, but also in a narrower sense, her connection to the ideas of Bauhaus artists, who were just as important to Akarova as the Russian constructivists of the 1920s; see Akarova 1988.

piece, as well as its decor—rotating discs, pointed and obtuse garish geometric shapes—evoked Russian stage designs, such as those of Alexandra Exter or Foregger's *Maschinentänze* [machine dances].[17]

In an interview, Akarova recalled that after the premiere of *Pacific* some visitors spread rumors that she was a communist:

> The choreography of the latter dance was intended to suggest liberation through work. I danced in a simple black leotard in front of a red decor with hammer and sickle, using the strongly rhythmic movements. In the auditorium I heard whispering, "That's the communist!"[18]

The theater as *studio*, on the other hand, points to the propinquity of Akarova's dances to the fine arts. Just as Grete Wiesenthal's path to free dance could not have been possible without the Vienna Secession, Akarova was influenced by her encounters with Belgian and international avant-garde artists. Sonja Delaunay, Ivan Puni, Henry van de Velde, the pioneers of the art journal *7 Arts* (1922–1928) and Marcel Baugniet,[19] with whom she worked intensely for over five years, were all associated with Akarova's work. In addition to her dances, she also produced paintings and sculptures and designed the patterns of her own costumes. These dance costumes resembled sculptures, which enveloped the body, or transformed its shape and form like abstract paintings. Some of the costumes are reminiscent of the imagery and fabrics of Sophie Taeuber-Arp and Sonja Delaunay, that is, their scenography for the revival of *Cléopâtre* by the Ballets Russes during the 1920s.

As *studio* and *laboratory*, this stage provided the framework for Akarova's solo dances. One of these experiments, namely *Lettres dansantes*,[20] actually had its origins in the choreographer's own name. Marcel Baugniet recalls transforming the name "Acarin" into "Akarova" in an anagrammatic process closely related to his own art:

> In 1924, I published an album of linocuts, Kaloprosopies, inspired by her choreography. I was the one who invented her stage name for her. Her real

17. See the following chapter on "Interruption."

18. Akarova 1988, 130.

19. Baugniet (born 1986) was one of the most important representatives of constructivism in Belgium, before he turned to the "Plastic Pure" movement, which also influenced Akarova's dance style; he was her companion from 1922 to 1927; see Baugniet's catalogue essay in Akarova 1988.

20. For a contemporary contextualization of the piece, see Fabrice van de Kerckhove, "'Lettres dansantes': Akarova and the Beginning Theatrical Avantgarde," in Akarova 1988, 333ff.

name is Marguerite Acarin, but at the time, the fashion was the "Ballets Russes." Russian dancers were considered the best and having a Russian name was an extra trump card if one wanted to carve a place in the dance world. That's why I transformed Acarin into Akarova.[21]

The play with graphemes, the substitution of letters from Acarin to Akarova is here an artistic act in itself (Baugniet uses the metaphor of the linocut or xylography)—the transformation of an individual entity into a dancer persona. The Russian-sounding name is "cut" into the theater world: a postulated reinscription. It is this act of stylization that best expresses the individuality of Akarova's dancing and not her personal gestural expressivity. Her choreography in "Lettres dansantes" also follows this model.

The commedia dell'arte characters—which Fokine assembled into a fabric of alternating, ephemeral duets, crisscrossing as a metaphor for "elective affinities"—are now, in Akarova's solo, entirely abstract: elements of text set in motion. The relationships and affinities are represented by single graphemes, something like *kinetic anagrams*. They dance over the body and the contours of the dancer. The costume is a short tunic, made of white silk, onto which blue and red letters have been asymmetrically arranged. The movements constantly produce new combinations of logograms, like a game Scrabble. The kinetic process scatters and re-collects the graphic images. The dancer's body becomes a screen onto which the ciphers of dance are projected (figure 47). The dance is a literal translation of multi-perspectivity of figure and background. The stage curtain, which is also covered in letters and geometric forms, additionally emphasizes the flickering effect as the viewer's gaze shifts back and forth between the two-dimensional patterns and three-dimensional figure in space.

Compared to Fuller's *Serpentine Dance*, Akarova's *Lettres dansantes* took a very different approach to making the body disappear. In Loïe Fuller's work, the dancer is hidden in expansive folds of fabric, which are draped into spirals and volutes. In Akarova's case, the body disappears among the dancing graphemes, in the figurative signs and visual backdrop of the dance-text. While in the first case the body is absorbed in an endless whirl of spiraling fabric, the abstraction of the corporeal shape in *Lettres dansantes* resembles the leaps made by individual parts of a kaleidoscope—a jumble of letters against a black background.

Dances such as *Lettres dansantes* resembled what Mallarmé described in *Coup de dés* as a poetic game of dice. According to Maurice Blanchot in *The Book to Come*, "the throw of the dice" "is the outcome of a new concept of

21. Baugniet, in Akarova 1988, 188.

Figure 47 Costume drawing by Marcel-Louis Baugniet of
Akarova's *Lettres dansantes* (1923).
SOURCE: Archives d'Architecture Moderne, Brüssel, Belgium /
© VG Bild-Kunst, Bonn.

literary space as a space where a new rhythmic order would give rise to a new
system of correspondences"[22] and hence also give rise to a new language as
"a system of highly complex spatial relations," both by dint of "dispersal" and
"concentration"[23]—both being movement relationships.

This pattern, which Akarova first explored in *Lettres dansantes*, later formed
the basis for her entire choreographic work. Over and over again, in works such as
Golly Wogg's Cake-Walk (1924, to Debussy's *Children's Corner*), *Prélude à l'Après-
Midi d'un Faune* (1935, music, Debussy),[24] and *Jazz Music* (1933, music, Marcel

22. Blanchot 1982, 237.

23. Ibid.

24. Akarova's stage paintings and painted costumes feature colorful, stylized shapes against
a dark background. The playful composition of the paintings is reminiscent of Niki de
Saint-Phalle: an androgynous "faun" moving through an artificial paradise. This interpretation
is related to the two-dimensional quality of the scenery designed by Léon Bakst for Nijinsky's
Faune. However, Bakst lent his backdrop the lushness of a Mediterranean wilderness.

Poot), she used various visual patterns to consciously integrate and explore different models of perception in her choreographic concepts: by suddenly redirecting
the gaze from the figure in the foreground to the background, from line and plane
to spatial depth, from a detail to its framework. The gaze, lost in figurations and
perspectives, is captivated and confounded, repeatedly caught up in the dance only
to be diverted again by the seemingly moving abstract figurations of the space.
Akarova translated the "tossing motion" of Scrabble into kinetic visual formulas.
She activated the concepts of close-up and wide shot, zooming in and out as in
photography and film.

The movements of the body and the dance of abstract figurations and signs
mutually complemented each other. The complexity and homogeneity of these
dance pieces activated the viewer's ability to simultaneously perceive different foci in the theatrical space and to quickly shift attention while watching—
an ability that John Cage referred to as "polyattentiveness." In fact, several
elements of Akarova's theatrical compositions anticipate the work of Merce
Cunningham: for example, his dance piece *Summerspace* (1958), in which the
audience was confronted with a colorful pointillist image of indistinct forms
and shapes and had to reassemble the figures and the background, the space,
horizon, and the movements in their own minds. Robert Rauschenberg's
set design (small, brightly colored dots spattered over the dancer's leotards
and filling the stage as spots of light) radicalized a concept also employed
by Akarova: to merge body and space with the help of visual and lighting
effects into a planar perspective, causing a mimicry-like fusion of body and
background.

The abstract figurations in motion, the *lettres dansantes*, are a "concrete
poetry" of dance.

Avant-garde theater and dance produced a semiotic and textual kinesis similar to the concrete poetry and sound poetry generated by the happenings of the
Futurists, Dada, and surrealists.

In 1916, Giacomo Balla also designed a dance piece on the subject of *Lettres
dansantes*. The graphic movement designs, the costumes, and the set design of
this *Balletto Tipografico* reveal a distinct affinity to the theatrical experiments
of the 1920s, but also to fine art, poster art, and the typographic concepts of
Dada groups in Zurich and Berlin. In 1922, Ivan Puni (Yvan Pougny)[25] presented a *Buchstaben Ballett (Alphabet Ballet)* at the *Sturm* party in Berlin. Kurt
Schwitters' *Merz*-concept and Hugo Ball's sound poems, the *Verse ohne Worte*
(*Verses without Words*), performed in cubist costumes in 1917 at the Cabaret
Voltaire in Zurich, were also closely related to the *Lettres dansantes* choreographies. Ball describes the construction of an elementary alphabet in dance,
based on a "cubist dance" by Sophie Taeuber-Arp (1917), in which "individual

25. Puni 1993. For Ivan Puni, see Bergius 1989, 302f.

word particles" merged to form a moving syntax and a "poetic sequence of sounds":

> Abstract dances: a gong beat is enough to stimulate the dancer's body to make the most fantastic movements. The dance has become an end in itself. The nervous system exhausts all the vibrations of the sound, and perhaps all the hidden emotion of the gong beater too, and turns them into an image. Here, in this special case, a poetic sequence of sounds was enough to make each of the individual word particles produce the strangest visible effect on the hundred-jointed body of the dancer. From a *Gesang der Flugfische und Seepferdchen* [*Song of the Flying Fish and Seahorses*] there came a dance full of flashes and edges, full of dazzling light and penetrating intensity.[26]

CORPOREAL WRITING AND SPATIAL SIGNS:
RUDOLF VON LABAN'S KINETOGRAPHY

In their exploration of moving letters and semiotic patterns, constructivist and Dadaist performances focused on fragmentation. They attempted to destroy semiotic systems such as syntax or movement codes in order to liberate the elementary particles of these semiotic systems and then playfully recombine them. In contrast, Rudolf von Laban's written dance sought to establish a system for structuring movement based on holistically, philosophically, and ideologically substantiated theory. In literature and in the fine arts, the collapse of symbolic systems triggered a development of avant-garde aesthetics. Twenty years later, however, the same revolution in dance led to a system of transcription (except in the case of constructivist dance concepts as mentioned above). The goal was to use writing to achieve a standardization, specification, and notation of dance—in particular *Ausdruckstanz*—thus also making it possible to teach it in a uniform manner. In *Mitteilungen der deutschen Gesellschaft für Schrifttanz* (*Notes from the German Society for Written Dance*), the expectations regarding kinetography are described:

> This new form of writing dance captures every movement, whether harmonious or grotesque, ballet dance, folk dance, social dance, exotic dance.

---

26. Ball 1996, 102. His "Gesang der Flugfische und Seepferdchen" (Song of the Flying Fish and Sea Horses) was recited in accompaniment to Sophie Taeuber's dance; Ball's summary highlights the abstract suspense of Taeuber's dance, which disassembled the text into "word particles."

A form of notating all forms of dance by Pavlova, Fokine, Laban, Wigman, Bereska, Terpis, Kröller, and others . . . a system of writing suitable for preserving and transmitting valuable ways of teaching dance, able to record historical dances and notate new dances.[27]

As the inventor of a new form of dance notation, Laban endeavored to incorporate corporeal symbols and spatial figurations in the canon of cultural education as written dance, thus earning him the title of "father of new German dance."

The breadth of his influence on the development of German *Ausdruckstanz*, from its early stages at Monte Verità in Ascona to the continued effect of his training system even today, especially of his dance notation system, confirms the validity of this byname. From a historical perspective, Laban's significance for dance does not lie so much in his creation of an independently new dance or movement style. This was the pioneering achievement of the female founders of modern free dance, who came from the United States: Loïe Fuller, Isadora Duncan, and Ruth St. Denis. Rather, it was his ability to consolidate the multiple branches of dance reform and condense them into an abstract and didactic system. Albrecht Knust, Laban's student and collaborator, who later continued to refine the notation system of kinetography, once pointed out that the highly heterogeneous *Ausdruckstanz* community, which drew on a wide range of sources, converged in Laban's comprehensive attempts to encompass everything from theatrical dance to amateur movement choirs.

From the outset, Laban was interested in two fundamental issues. The first was to understand and analyze the relationship of the dancing body to the surrounding space. As a result, he developed his theory of space harmony. His second interest concerned the possibilities of a notation system that not only translated corporeal movement and spatial trace-forms into symbols, but also incorporated the aspects of time, duration, and rhythm. This was the basis of the Laban system: a merging of the space-time model with movement notation, its fixation in complex theory and its elaboration into the viable system of dance notation still widely used and known today as Labanotation.

Rudolf Laban de Varalja, born in Pozsony, now Bratislava, on December 15, 1879, began his career as a dancer at the theater in his hometown and in 1895 started working as a stage designer. Between 1900 and 1910, he studied fine arts in Vienna, Munich, and Paris, while continuing his manifold activities in the field of dance, the body culture movement, and at dance festivals. In 1902, he commenced studying architecture. Laban's preoccupation with historic forms of recording

---

27. *Schrifttanz* 1 (1928): 16. Translation: Elena Polzer.

choreography began sometime during this period. During his stay from 1911 to 1917 in the artist retreat and *Lebensreform* (life reform) colony at Monte Verità, Laban experimented for the first time with what would later become his theory of space harmony, laying a foundation for free dance, which articulated a heightened awareness of body and space, the "spatial-rhythmic sensation."

His movement analysis was based on the space surrounding the dancer. In Laban's construct, the abstract lines representing the movements of the body in space form a typical structure: the icosahedron as a stereometrical model for the portrayal of spatial laws and the moving body. Laban considered both regular crystalline structures—the dodecahedron and the icosahedron—to be spatial structures useful for formalizing the angles of body movement in space. The angle and direction of movement in the three basic ring swings—high-deep, right-left, front-back—were inscribed into the crystals. Laban used the icosahedron model not only to visualize the relationships of body and space, but also as a didactic tool to teach dancers precise spatial intention.

Laban's struggle to put his model of spatial dance into writing led to the development of so-called swallow-tail writing (figure 48). It mainly recorded inclination and degree of tension, as well as movement direction, with the help of symbols and a series of movement scales. In 1926, Laban published the book *Choreographie*, based on his new findings. The publishing house announced it thus:

> This book will provide a scientific basis for the definition of dance forms based on a new invention by Laban, namely dance notation. This book will elicit something similar to the invention of musical notes for mankind. Something new will enter our culture![28]

Laban was aware of the fundamental problem behind dance notation as either an *analog* or a *digital* system. Analog notation depicts body movements and/or spatial pathways as symbols, as stylized graphic signs. Hence, they convey an iconography of corporeal movements (e.g., the model of the marionette)[29] and trace-forms. Laban's first attempts to capture the three-dimensional icosahedral movements of the body in space on two-dimensional paper and to develop graphemes for spatial direction were initially based on a static analog relationship of dance and symbols.

28. Translation: Elena Polzer.

29. The marionette not only appears in Oskar Schlemmer's drawings of sculptural costume (see also part II, chapter 1 this volume); Laban also used the image of the marionette to illustrate the development of his kinetography in the journal *Schrifttanz*; see *Schrifttanz* 2 (1928): fig. 4-10.

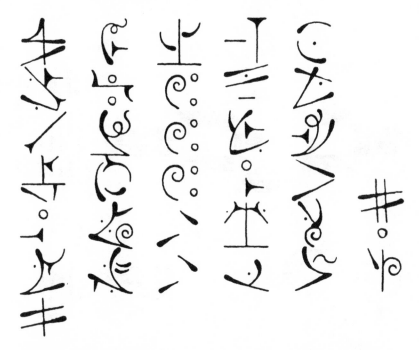

Figure 48 Rudolf von Laban: "Choreography," scale-notation in the so-called "Swallow's tail papers" (1926).
SOURCE: Florian Noetzel Verlag, Wilhelmshaven, Germany.

However, Laban sought to integrate the factor of time in dance notation—as found in musical scores. This could not be accomplished by an analog semiotic system. The solution was kinetography, which, read from bottom to top, allows the depiction of a spatial-temporal system of movement and written dance. In 1927, Laban introduced his first draft of this model at the First German Dance Congress in Magdeburg. By 1928 and the second German Dance Congress in Essen, he had developed his kinetography (figure 49) enough to satisfy the basic needs of *Ausdruckstanz* to record effort, direction, individual movements of the body, and the duration of particular movements. The society for *Schrifttanz* and a journal by the same name were established that same year to provide a forum for the discussion and further reflection of his system. This laid the foundation for a form of dance notation that was later developed further by Laban's students and without which choreography today would not be the same. It has become an indispensable tool for transmitting dance as well as analyzing movement in various fields from theater to dance therapy.

Aside from commonly emphasized components of the notation system, two aspects in particular characterize Laban's concept of *dance writing*: an analytical and a normative side.

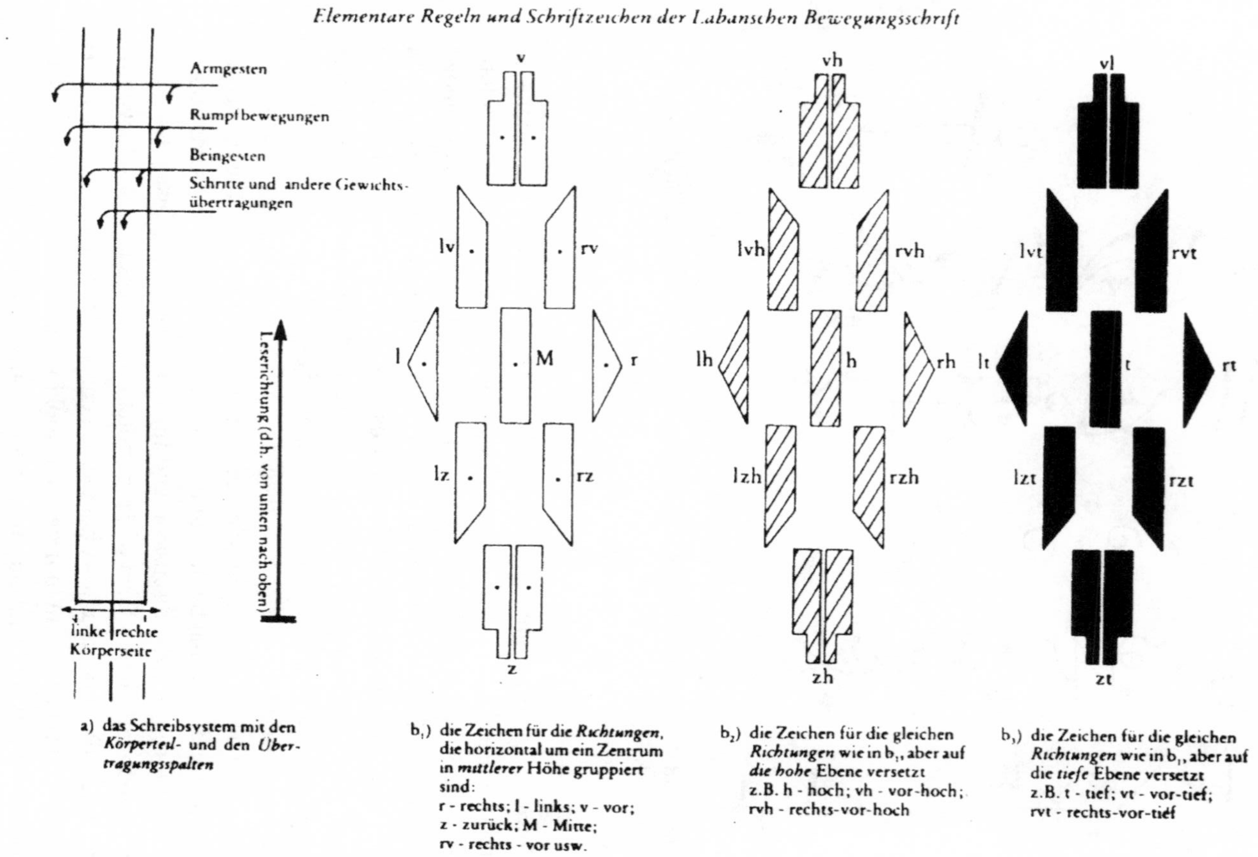

Elementare Regeln und Schriftzeichen der Labanschen Bewegungsschrift

Armgesten

Rumpfbewegungen

Beingesten

Schritte und andere Gewichts-übertragungen

Leserichtung (d.h. von unten nach oben)

linke rechte
linke Körperseite

a) **das Schreibsystem mit den** *Körperteil- und den Über-tragungsspalten*

rt

rvt

rzt

vl

t

zt

lvt

lzt

lt

b₃) *die Zeichen für die gleichen Richtungen wie in b, aber auf* die tiefe *Ebene versetzt* z.B. t - tief; vt - vor-tief; rvt - rechts-vor-tief

rh

rvh

rzh

vh

h

zh

lvh

lzh

lh

b₂) *die Zeichen für die gleichen Richtungen wie in b, aber auf* die hohe *Ebene versetzt* z.B. h - hoch; vh - vor-hoch; rvh - rechts-vor-hoch

r

rv

rz

v

M

z

lv

lz

l

b₁) *die Zeichen für die Richtungen,* die horizontal um ein Zentrum in *mittlerer* Höhe gruppiert sind:

r - rechts; l - links; v - vor;
z - zurück; M - Mitte;
rv - rechts - vor usw.

Figure 49 Rudolf von Laban, "Kinetographie" (1928).
SOURCE: Tanzarchiv, Leipzig, Germany.

The analytical function of kinetography primarily deals with "defining the movement process through analysis and thus freeing it from the kind of vagueness which has made the language of dance appear unclear and monotonous."[30] We have here a distinction between *movement flow* and *movement shape*, between *monolinear* and *polylinear* movements—in other words, a model for reading movement. According to Laban, the reading of dance as a mere movement event not yet defined as a form of expression requires a more corporeal form of seeing than the reading of graphemes, not a digital semiotic operation on the two-dimensional plane of writing (or in the simulated space of films or computers), but rather an act of reading along the sagittal plane of three-dimensionality:

> Our eye sees the invisible axis. A collapsing building, a falling human being, in one word, an alteration in the state of equilibrium already attracts our foreboding attention at the onset of a movement. . . . The eye perceives the volatile state: the onlooker's entire body trembles in response, without altering its position in way that is discernible on the surface. The smallest particles in us vibrate the same dance, as the entire body would when falling.[31]

From this psychophysical pattern of perception, Laban deduces the properties of those symbols that form the basis for reading dance, but also for the reading of the world—hence, the basis of all alphabets, the proto-alphabet: "In all alphabets, the forms of the characters are borrowed from movement: stars, columns, cascades of triangles, rectangles and crystals."[32]

Dance is, as it were, the expression of a holistically defined language and a *universal movement script*.

Laban's philosophical system of choreosophy is divided into three parts: choreography, choreology, and choreutics.[33]

His idea of choreosophy as the wisdom of circles is indebted to Platonic and Pythagorean thinking, namely the assumption that body, movement, space, and the flow of time cannot be comprehended independently from one another. As a mythical form of knowledge, choreosophy is, however, much older. Dance thus means movement, the flow of life in its most general sense. The cycles of

---

30. Laban, "Basic Principles of Movement Notation," in Preston-Dunlop and Lahusen 1990, 32.

31. Laban 1920, 76f. Translation: Elena Polzer.

32. Ibid.

33. Laban explains the differences briefly and clearly in the introduction to his book *Choreutics* (1966).

nature and life and the integration of human movement in these cosmic cycles are considered part of the reference system of micro- and macrocosm. This vitalist aspect of Laban's "danced *Weltanschauung*" invokes Nietzsche, Ludwig Klages, and Henri Bergson: choreosophy as the mythical-danced knowledge of movement as an element in the great cycle of life, the *elán vital*. Havelock Ellis's *The Dance of Life* translates this monism[34] of dance as *Weltanschauung* back into cultural-philosophical dimensions.

Written dance—as the effective model of Laban's dance notation—appears in the choreosophical context not only as a kinetographic system of notation, but also as a medium for creating holistic concepts: "The goal is written dance, and to intellectualize the corporeal and thus liberate the corporeal through notated and composed dance—the desire and intentions of our age!"[35]

Choreography and choreology, as forms of writing (*Schrift*),[36] as acts of writing (*Schreiben*) spatial text, and as the theory and knowledge of movement, are central to the normative function of what written dance means in terms of Laban's more general theory of the "dancer's *Weltanschauung*":

- Choreography as an act of composing and drawing, planning and formulating dance
- Choreology as the "logic or science of circles," and "a kind of grammar or syntax of the language of movement" concerned not only with the external form of movement, but also with its intellectual and emotional content[37]

The individual aspects of choreosophy, choreography, and choreology, which define the comprehensive, holistic meaning of written dance, are ultimately oriented toward *a cultural and pedagogical program defined by dance*.[38] According

---

34. On the problem of totalism and monism in nineteenth- and early twentieth-century literature and philosophy, cf. Gebhard 1984.

35. "Die neue Tanzschrift" (New dance notation), *Schrifttanz* 1 (1928): 16. Translation: Elena Polzer.

36. See note 6 in this chapter on the difference between *Schrift* and *Schreiben* in German.

37. Laban 1966, introduction, viii.

38. It would be interesting here in this context to compare Laban's ideas with Rudolf Steiner's concept of *eurythmy* (a system that consciously distanced itself from the various "eurhythmic" gymnastics and movement theories of the twentieth century, e.g., by altering the "rh" in its spelling). Steiner created his dance alphabet system between 1912 and 1925, roughly at the same time as Laban's experiments with dance theory and kinetography. Unlike Laban, Steiner's "dance writing" eurythmy is neither a notation system nor the development of an independent dance concept. Instead the basic idea behind the eurythmic *semiotic* system is a

to Laban, the path from dance writing to written dance is the only opportunity to "cultivate" dance (and thus also the dancing human being).[39]

This comparison between constructivist-abstract experimentation with the dancing alphabet and the holistic-normative concept delineated by *Schrifttanz* clearly demonstrates the difference between them. The breadth and contrariety of these artistic phenomena make it almost impossible to subsume them under a general terminology of the *modern* in dance.

translation of letters of the alphabet (and later of musical notes; = speech eurythmy and tone eurythmy) into individual, corresponding movement gestures. This movement alphabet can be used to form words, sentences, and "texts": a *literal* transposition of literary texts and music pieces into (choric) movement. This quasi-mediatory character of translation may have been the reason (aside from ideological ones) that Steiner's eurythmy was not recognized as an artistic form of dance by the representatives of free dance and expressionistic dance. For an introduction to the history and ideas of eurythmy in German, cf. Else Klink, in "Eurythmie," in: Bünner/Röthig 1983, 171–81.

39. In *Schrifttanz* 2 (1928): 19f.

Chapter 5

Interruption. Intermediality and Disjunction in the Movement Concepts of Avant-Garde Dance and Theater

Heiner Müller once said that putting his texts on stage was the only possibility of forgetting them.

The disappearance of written text in favor of an increased emphasis on scenic text is one of the main features of classical avant-garde theater, as well as of postmodernism and last but not least of Peter Handke's "piece without words."[1]

There is broad agreement about this in theater studies, as well as about the factors and elements that characterize the redefinition of traditional concepts of scenography and staging theater. The following keywords will play an important role in this chapter:

- *Deliterarization*: the disempowerment of the word, breaking the dominance of language-text by emphasizing other theatrical elements such as body language, lighting effects, music, voice, and sound. Vsevolod Meyerhold and his colleagues once said about Russian constructivist theater that "words in theater are only designs on the canvas of action."[2]

1. See Handke, *The Hour We Knew Nothing of Each Other*, 1996.

2. Cited in Rzhevsky 2009, 16; this sentence seems to have been taken literally in the dance piece *Relâche*, where words, sentences, and names were projected on the backdrop. See the following analysis of *Relâche* (1924).

- *Annulment of the mimetic principle*: the rejection of realism, naturalism, and psychologism in representation and all corresponding scenic elements of illusionary theater.
- *Abstraction*: the construction (and deconstruction), transformation and mechanization, disassociation, and montage of various scenic factors and semiotic levels
- *Mechanization*: the human body analyzed and employed as a "machine," for example, in Nikolai Foregger's *Machine Dances*[3] (1922) or Massine/Prokofiev's *Pas d'Acier* (1927);[4] and correspondingly the integration of objects from modern, technological everyday culture—telephones, cars, photo and video cameras—as in Meyerhold's version of S. Tretiakov's *Earth on End* (1923) or in the ballets *Parade, Le Train bleu, Relâche,* and *Les Mariés de la tour Eiffel*.[5]
- *Perspectivization*: that is, new forms of directing the gaze, multicentric focus, an altered awareness of time and space as influenced by new technologies and media such as film.
- *Accentuation of movement*: in association with the development of new theatrical concepts of time and space, movement as rhythmization, manifestations of new (motoric, dynamic) body and movement patterns.

The concepts of the body, which are most important for the art and the aesthetics of modernity, are those produced—in whatever way—by processes of abstraction, reduction, decomposition, and transformation, often in connection with a specific pattern of movement.[6]

---

3. See Surits 1981.

4. The ballet *Pas d'acier* (*The Steel Step*) by Serge Diaghilev's Ballets Russes premiered on June 7, 1927, in Paris. Choreography, Léonide Massine; music, Sergei Prokofiev; libretto, Georgi B. Jakulow. Technical-constructivist elements (in terms of Soviet Proletkult) are especially evident in the second scene, which is set in a factory: groups of dancers depict the act of working at the machines, while simultaneously embodying the machines themselves. Here is an example of a "mass ornament" (Siegfried Kracauer) that stages the revolutionary pathos of the Industrial Revolution in a ballet (although premiered in the West!), instead of playing with the capitalistic normative principle of the chorus line.

5. These pieces were created in 1923–24, by the Ballets Suédois (*Train bleu* 1924) and the Ballets Russes (*Relâche* 1924).

6. In the work of Futurist, cubist, and constructivist dance and theater makers, body concepts, which were based on abstraction, appeared in the form of an accentuation, as well as elimination of various functions and elements of form; as fragmentation, de-formation (e.g., reshaping with materials, as in the Bauhaus dances of Oskar Schlemmer), mechanization, and also "disappearance" of the body.

In this chapter, I want to take a closer look at one specific concept of the body, which is equally important for both avant-garde theater and dance. This concept of the body is closely associated to the technical function and aesthetics of film.

In his essay "The Work of Art in the Age of Mechanical Reproduction," Walter Benjamin establishes a connection between "profound changes in apperception"[7] and the development of cinematic seeing. The technically mediated gaze leads to a segmented awareness of body and space. The apparatus is incorporated into the gaze step by step. Disruptions, gaps of all kinds in time and space—the principle of interruption characterizes the technical medium of film.

In his theoretical statement "On Montage," Vsevolod Pudovkin emphasizes:

> Acting in front of the camera is considered a continual action, although the images that flow past on the screen are clearly separated from one another, either through spatial or through temporal gaps.[8]

Benjamin defines the illusionary nature of film, its second-degree character, to be the "result of cutting"[9]:

> That is to say, in the studio the mechanical equipment has penetrated so deeply into reality that its pure aspect freed from the foreign substance

7. See Benjamin 2005, section 15: "For the tasks which face the human apparatus of perception at the turning points of history cannot be solved by optical means, that is, by contemplation, alone." Distraction, which "is symptomatic of profound changes in apperception, finds in the film its true means of exercise." Benjamin based his argumentation on the consequences of technical reproduction for the concept of art on a (cultural-sociological-oriented) theory of the transformation of "human sense perception" in the wake of historical developments in technology—a fundamental transformation accompanied by a loss of the "aura" in works of art: "that which withers in the age of mechanical reproduction is the aura of the work of art."

8. Pudovkin 1972, 113–127. Translation from German: Elena Polzer.

9. For my theory of interruption, it is necessary to differentiate between "cut" as editing, i.e., as a secondary process of cutting and assembling camera perspectives, and the primary technical principle of film, i.e., the stroboscopic structure of serial images created by (no longer visible) interruptions. As proper artistic methods, film editing and montage are based on the kinetic stop-and-go principle of the cinematically produced serial image. Therefore, for the sake of terminological clarity, we must first differentiate between the *principle of production* and the *principle of form*. This sheds an interesting light on how both aspects have been mixed or rather identified in film theory, especially in texts concerning early cinematographic experiments in the Soviet Union (as compared to or related to theater; see my comments on Pudovkin and Meyerhold).

of equipment is the result of a special procedure, namely, the shooting by the specially adjusted camera and the mounting of the shot together with other similar ones.[10]

Interruption is primarily a cinematic concept of *perception*. Secondarily, it is an aesthetic and semiotic *model of representation*, adapted and applied by artists for the production of art, that is, editing and montage. Soviet cinematographic film theory has been particularly productive in discussing the issue of *segmentation* and the relationship of editing and montage: especially Meyerhold's concept of *filmization*, as well as the more common translated neologism of a "cinefication of theater,"[11] Sergei Eisenstein's writings on film, and Vsevolod Pudovkin's theory of montage. In his manifesto "A Dialectic Approach to Film Form" (1929), Eisenstein developed a complex system that involved formal and technical factors found in cinematography. Out of a theory of conflict and tension (derived from dialectical materialism, from the driving mechanisms of dialectical contradiction),[12] he formulated an aesthetic that emphasized shot and montage as the basic elements of film because of their rhythmic quality, which is defined by the "interval."

Eisenstein was not interested in the *epic* principle of additive montage (which he accuses Pudovkin's theory of), but rather: "In my opinion . . . montage is an idea that arises from the collision of independent shots—shots even opposite to one another: the "dramatic" principle."[13]

From a poetological point of view, Eisenstein transposed the visual principle of the metaphor onto the confrontation of signs occurring in cinematic montage. In order to illustrate his paradigm of a dynamic confrontation of two semiotic units, thus producing new meaning via "attraction,"[14] Eisenstein

10. Benjamin 2005, section XI.

11. Meyerhold 1988. In his works for the stage from the early 1920s Meyerhold attempted to transfer film techniques to theater as structural factors in the form of dramaturgical elements (in an attempt to make the theatrical production just as mobile as film), concepts of representation (biomechanics), technical and kinetic movement designs, and finally concepts of theater architecture and of audience involvement (by addressing the masses, as accomplished by film).

12. Eisenstein defines the dynamic principle of art as "conflict": "For art is always conflict: (1) according to its social mission, (2) according to its nature, (3) according to its methodology." Eisenstein 1929, 2; and Eisenstein 1977, 46.

13. Eisenstein 1929, 4; Eisenstein 1977, 49.

14. Eisenstein's theory of a "montage of attractions" is directly related to this concept of generating new meaning in art through "conflict"; attractions in the formal sense are compelled to attain a balance of contradictions that resembles chemical osmosis. This applies to both the aggressive and the erotic aspects of this theory of montage, which are aimed at a

referenced the ideographic style of the Japanese artist Sharaku[15]—a method of producing images by placing the singular details of two independent ideograms next to one other and then letting them "explode" into something new. On the basis of this hypothesis of collision through conflict, Eisenstein developed his theory of the *visual counterpoint* as the guiding principle for a dialectical poetics of film.

What I propose here is that these processes of *segmentation*, which are characteristic for film, chronophotography, and editing, were also translated into the body and movement concepts of avant-garde theater and dance.

I would like to call the basic principle that governed this concept of the body and its associated movement patterns the "stroboscopic principle"[16]—a *principle of interruption* that influenced the semiotic dimension of modern dance and theater in numerous ways. In my opinion, this stroboscopic principle of an abstractive concept of the body is linked to a fundamental perceptual constellation that dominated modernity, and that in turn corresponds to two homologous instances of technological development, namely:

- In the field of economics and technology: Taylorism
- In the field of media and technology: film

CINEMATIC SEGMENTATION OF MOVEMENT: CHARLIE CHAPLIN, VSEVOLOD MEYERHOLD, VALESKA GERT

In terms of their segmentation of time and movement, the functional principles of both Taylorism and cinematography are based on a stroboscopic pattern of interruption.

methodology of mise en scène and the relationship of stage and audience. Goethe's allegory of chemical affinity in *Elective Affinities* may also have contributed just as much to this theory of art as did dialectical materialism. Contrary to the semiotic concept here emphasized by myself, Finter (1985) stresses the aspect of "psychotechnique," the "production of affective conditions" in Eisenstein's theory.

15. Eisenstein 1923, 5; 1977, 35. While Eisenstein's recourse to Far Eastern iconography concentrated on dramaturgical issues, Meyerhold's interpretation of Japanese theater models resulted in the triangle of stage (space)—actor—audience.

16. "Stroboscope" = 1. Instrument for determining the frequency of oscillating or rotating systems, a cylinder with evenly spaced holes, which temporarily screens out light; 2. Device to visualize movement: two counter-rotating discs, one of which contains the slits or holes, the other the images; a predecessor of film.

Taylorization is a method of increasing productivity by standardizing worker's movements (assembly line production) and partitioning time in such a way as to decrease effort, while simultaneously improving efficiency.

The basic technical principle underlying *film* is determined by a stroboscopic effect that is, however, not discernible by the naked eye. The illusion of moving images (movies) as movements made by imaginary bodies on screen is created by projecting a sequence of twenty-four (visually blended) images per second and thus disguising the discontinuity of interruption. The prototypes of cinematography, such as the stroboscope and Muybridge's and Marey's chronophotography[17] (figure 50), were already based on this same principle of interruption, that is, a combination of visual and temporal editing and serial montage.

Both models of structuring time through interruption, the stroboscopic principles of Taylorism and of film, greatly influenced avant-garde dance and theater.

Perhaps the most unforgettable example of how *interruption* inscribed itself in the body and in movement is a scene from Charlie Chaplin's *Modern Times* (1936, figure 51): Charlie is a factory worker tightening bolts at a prescribed speed in an assembly line. After work, he takes the mechanical movements with him as he leaves the factory—the broken gestures of a "Taylorized" human being caught up in modern times. Still with a wrench in each hand, Charlie continues to demonically tighten everything that resembles a screw—even the buttons on the dress of a woman walking by. Freed from their original function in the workspace and yet unable to fully detach themselves, the square staccato movements transform into a comical grotesque dance.[18]

The precision of Chaplin's translation of new categories of perception influenced by the developments of technology into an image of the body and a movement language that was distinctly his own gained him the unequivocal admiration of dancers, choreographers, and theater directors alike: among them Vsevolod Meyerhold,[19] Sergei Eisenstein, Valeska Gert,[20] and René

17. See the chapter on Valéry in Part I of this book; see also the chapter "Film" in Kittler 1999.

18. "This scene is one of Chaplin's funniest and wisest 'dance numbers': In it the individual frees himself from the pressures of regulations and simultaneously reveals the appalling damage that he has suffered. Charlie has to go insane in order to re-attain the charm of his gestures, even damaged." Gregor and Patalas 1976, 1: 220. Translation: Elena Polzer. On Chaplin's "Reflection in Modern Times," see Nysenholc 1991.

19. See, on Meyerhold, Chaplin, and his art, *Filmwissenschaftliche Mitteilungen* (*Film Studies Notes*) (Berlin) 1 (1963): 200ff.

20. At the event *Der absolute Film* (*The Absolute Film*) in 1925 in Berlin (where, e.g., Ruttmann's *Opus 2* and René Clair's *Entr'acte* were also screened), Valeska Gert, the famous

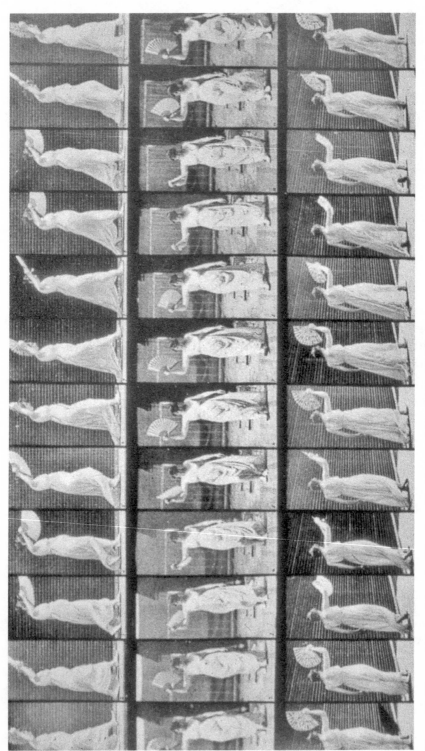

Figure 50 Chronophotographic series "Fan dance" by Eadweard Muybridge (1887).

SOURCE: Eadweard Muybridge: Animal Locomotion, Philadelphia, USA, 1887.

Figure 51 Charlie Chaplin, *Modern Times* (1936).
SOURCE: Keystone Pressedienst GmbH, Hamburg, Germany.

Clair,[21] who once said that Chaplin had made him "into a cinemaniac." Charlie Chaplin, who was for his part an attentive and gifted observer of modern dance,

"grotesque dancer," commented on the genre of the "grotesque film": the grotesque, according to Gert, has become a modern philosophy, and "Now every country will have to start making burlesque films if it wants to be up-to-date. Every country will exaggerate those things that are most important to it. For the Americans, it is motion. Hence its burlesque films tinker with grotesque varieties of motion (Chaplin, Buster Keaton, Harold Lloyd)." *Film-Kurier* 240 (October 12, 1925), online at http://www.filmportal.de/en/material/valeska-gert-on-the-german-burlesque.

21. On René Clair's enthusiasm for Charlie Chaplin, see Wehmeyer 1974, 281; Chaplin was himself, as Gregor and Patalas (1976, 1: 151) note, inspired to his famous portrayal in *Modern Times* (1935) by a comical assembly line sequence in Clair's film *A nous la liberté* (1931).

especially of Nijinsky's art,[22] became the preferred source of cinematic concepts of the body and movement for avant-garde theater and dance makers. His distinctly funny and touching style of walking and gesturing, of clothing and character predestined him for this role. Yvan Goll dedicated his cinematically influenced one-act play *The Chapliniade* (1920)[23] to him. And the "American girl" in Massine, Cocteau, and Satie's cubist ballet *Parade* (1917) cites multiple elements from Charlie Chaplin's typical movement repertoire[24] in a long solo section of her "parade."

Meyerhold's complementary theories about the *Taylorization of theater* and the *cinefication of theater* both imply that stroboscopic factors formed the basic elements of his theatrical concept. In his writings, the principle of interruption is applied to almost all parameters of scenic representation, such as lighting design and use of space, the dramaturgy of the episodic structure,[25] and the rhythmization of spoken text. The function of the "artificial pause," for example, regulates the rhythmic transition from spoken to silent text.

> The "artificial" pause—which can, without exaggeration, be called a silent text—is probably the greatest achievement of the new director: it brings with it a rhythmic re-evaluation of the text.

So Ivan Faludi in his essay "Rhythmische Momente der modernen Regie" (Rhythmic moments of modern directing).[26]

The interruption, the artificial pause, becomes the dominant structuring factor in various concepts of the body and movement. Meyerhold's translation of

22. Chaplin admired the Ballets Russes, whose performances he had seen in Los Angeles during their America tour. Nijinsky, who had parted company with Diaghilev shortly beforehand, especially sparked his interest. The affinity of these two very different artists is documented not only by conversation between the two during an intermission, a conversation that Chaplin recounts in his memoirs, but also by multiple citations from Nijinsky's dances in Chaplin's work (Robinson 1989, 437).

23. Goll, *The Chapliniade: A Film Poem* (1988).

24. See Wehmeyer 1974, 197: "The music shifts into a syncopated melody and the girl assumes the comical, stilted walk of Charlie Chaplin" (translation: Elena Polzer)—a double parodistic citation, as Chaplin's waddling walk with large, turned-out feet/shoes here appears in the context of a "cubist," i.e., disassembled "ballet" and as a parody of the "en dehors" in classical ballet.

25. Regarding dramaturgy, *cinefication of theater* means that the dramaturgical structure of a theatrical representation is modulated by the episodic structure of film. The goal is therefore to modify the segmentation: not into units of action, but into scenic units, which follow one after another "with cinematographic speed" as in the perceptual perspective of film.

26. Faludi 1991, 8. Translation: Elena Polzer.

Taylorism and of the segmentation of the image from film to theater is directly related to the theory and methods of biomechanics. The famous analogy in which Meyerhold compares the movements of a factory worker to those of a dancer[27] resulted in a list of the basic principles governing the biomechanical practice of representation. The biomechanically trained actor has exceptional body control, which he has acquired through acrobatic training. He is fully able to consciously shift between movement and standstill: a stroboscopic movement technique as a physio-mechanical qualification for the creation of constructivist theater.

VALESKA GERT: "CINEMATIC DANCE" AND THE GROTESQUE

In dance, it was Valeska Gert—who was awarded the honorary title of "biogenetic dancer"[28] by Meyerhold during her tour to Moscow (1920)—who achieved a comparable *cinefication* of movement. Interrupted movement flow is a stylistic element that Gert consciously used to differentiate her work from the expressionistic dance of, for example Mary Wigman.[29] With a few exceptions such as Wigman's *Witch Dance* or Kurt Jooss's works of the late 1920s, expressionistic dance favored flowing movements and emphasized aspects such as tension, countertension, and the dynamics produced by bodyweight and momentum—all

27. See the section on Valéry and the "Dancer as inspiratrice" in Part I of this book for more on Meyerhold's *Biomechanics*.

28. See Gert: "Meyerhold was of the opinion that I am 'the bio-genetic dance'" (Gert 1978, 54); it is not clear whether Gert parodied Meyerhold's "biomechanics" in her use of the term "bio-genetic."

29. See Gert: "Woe be the dancer who in Germany has an erotic appeal, and woe to that dancer whose sprit dares cut capers. Spirit is here considered to be intellectual. . . . A dance performance has to smell like sour sweat, be ethical, befuddled, mental, and boring. Ingenuity is less welcome than solidity . . . Mary Wigman fulfills these expectations of the educated middle class and therefore has acquired a national reputation." (Translation here and below, Elena Polzer, last sentence cited in Dils and Albright 2001, 221.) Of herself Gert wrote: "[I have] expressed all manifestations and excesses of our age that can be represented by the body." "[I have] flung modern dance among the audience's hoots and jeers . . . onto the scene under the enthusiastic recognition of a troop of modern Europeans"; for modern dance is "the transition from the old to a new theater." In *Der Querschnitt* (*Cross-Section*) 6 (1926): 361ff. In her book *I Am a Witch*, she compares the established dance form of German expressionistic dance with her own ideas about avant-garde dance: "Mary Wigman . . . danced the pseudoclassical movements with energy, the floor of the podium trembled. She gave her dances abstract names: 'Der Ruf,' 'Das Zeichen.' But a work of art is only then abstract, when it reveals the structure of a topic. She only managed, like many 'Abstracts,' to confuse what is clear, instead of clarifying confusion" (Gert 1978, 43).

entirely contrary to Gert's concept of interruption. The density and excerpt-like quality of her socially critical dance vignettes demonstrate that cinematic style of representation which Eisenstein attempted to define as "micro dramatics" and "montage of attractions." In dances such as *Traffic, Sports, Circus, Boxing Match,* and *Varieté,* she addressed various issues of modern big-city life in a critical, satirical, and "grotesque" fashion; the epithet of the grotesque became the main characteristic of her movement code.[30] Fragmentary allusions to scenes from the streets of Berlin and the representation of disassociation dominated her choice of subject matter and how she chose to present the body. The laconic quality of her movements, the garish boldness of her presentation, surpassed the aspirations of other forms of "contemporary dance satire" (Schikowski)[31] (figure 52). Gert used dance to diagnose an era characterized by movement as a new, decisive quality of experiencing time: tempo, acceleration, dynamics, and segmentation of time. The temporal and movement structure of Gert's dances features editing techniques, the fragmentation of units of movements, and abbreviations of revue-like scenarios. This pattern of segmentation was most pronounced in her piece *Cinema,* in which she danced a movie, parts of a newsreel, a military parade, a film diva, a marathon man, a bicyclist, and the cranking film operator[32]—"all tempo and intensity."

In 1928, Gert formulated a kind of manifesto of her cinematic concept of the body in answer to the Futurist artist Bragaglia.[33] The brothers Arturo and Anton Giulio Bragaglia (the inventors of Futurist photography)[34] had developed "photodynamism" in opposition to Marey's chronophotography. The Bragaglias rejected

30. The emphasis on the grotesque also links Gert's concept of the body and movement to Meyerhold's ideas (however, only those from before the October Revolution). Meyerhold's idea of the grotesque developed as part of his theory on "conditional theater," which is largely based on elements of traditional commedia dell'arte and Russian Balagan theater; as in the case of Gert, central elements of his theory are alienation, the gestural, and forms of presentation such as the revue and the parade (which allows direct communication with the audience). J. Fiebach (1991, 131ff.) sees in Meyerhold's concept of the grotesque (to which I would like to add: and in particular in Gert's grotesque dances!) "perhaps the most significant attempt in theater in the first third of the century to incorporate multidimensionality, comprehensive contradiction, and permanently dissonant mobility." (Translation: Elena Polzer.)

31. Schikowski 1926, 152f.: He describes her dance as "outrageously saucy, grimly impious spoofs, contemporary dance satire."

32. Gert 1978, 43. Translation: Elena Polzer.

33. Gert, "Antwort an Bragaglia" (Answer to Bragaglia), *Der Querschnitt* 8 (1928): 358.

34. One of the most famous photographic works of this Futurist "photodynamism" is *Le Fumeur* (1913), the photograph of a man smoking in which the dynamics of the movement are depicted—the hand turning as it holds the cigarette and the curling smoke merge. The manifesto of the Bragaglia brothers, *La Photographie du Mouvement* (1913), contradicted in

Figure 52 Valeska Gert, *Dance grotesque*
(around 1922).
SOURCE: Deutsches Tanzarchiv Köln / (c)Deutsches
Tanzarchiv Köln, Cologne, Germany

Marey's typical method of analytically decomposing movement into segmented image sequences (a method also found in the disjunction principle of Gert's dances). Instead, they sought to visualize the dynamics of movement, the transitory quality of gesture in photography. Rather than recording the kinetics of the body in its sequential phases, as chronophotography did, the Futurists attempted to disintegrate the solid body into movement by means of the "photo bougée" technique and thus capture a continuum of simultaneously occurring movement in a single image. The Futurists' concept of "photodynamism" clearly contains an homage to gestural vitalism—in terms of Bergson's *élan vital*[35] and Nietzsche's philosophy. Such dynamism ran counter to Gert's concept of dance as well as to the various forms of Futurist theater that were developing in the 1920s.

several aspects theories of Futurist painting and so finally led to a falling-out with Marinetti and his circle.

35. See Lista 1988, 49ff.

In her "Antwort an Bragaglia" (Answer to Bragaglia), Gert criticized the attempts of postwar Futurists to define theater as an "art méchanique," to move the scenery as machinery and replace dancers and actors with marionettes and kinetic objects. Gert's understanding of dance as grotesquerie ran completely counter to that form of abstraction which Prampolini presented in his *Pantomime futuriste* (Paris 1927–28) as a grotesque exaggeration of danced "dynamism." Opposed to eliminating dancers and actors, she argued that the "renewal of the theater" must come from "productive actors." A new concept of the body was required "in order to force the audience to see." This implied the need for the creation of a style of theatrical representation that corresponded to the cinematic techniques of close-up and slow motion, namely in the form of a technologically facilitated magnification (distortion and reduction) of the body. The result is a leaning toward the monumental and the grotesque, according to Gert: an alienation effect with the help of which the actors (and dancers) "appear as fantastically moving monuments of themselves" aided by mirrors, shadows, lighting, and cinematic effects.

Eisenstein integrated Gert's concept of the body into his theories on film and theater. Gert likewise incorporated aspects of Eisenstein's films and his cinematic aesthetic into her dances. In an essay on Gert,[36] Eisenstein described her dances as "unique in their articulation of movement."[37] Characteristic for this articulation of movement was the "syncope," meaning nothing other than the dislocation, interruption, and shifting of metric and rhythmic temporal structures. Eisenstein's concept of a "montage of attractions" is based on the dynamics of syncopation (which as a symbol of the 1920s was closely connected to the fascination exerted by jazz)—the association and the conflicting correlations of semiotic and medial systems, especially those of theater and film.

The dramatic tension between these two media found an outlet in the various cinematographic-kinetic experiments of the cinematic avant-garde. The contrast between corporeal presence in theatrical representation and the "real presence" of cinema tempted artists to exploit these dynamics by confronting them with each other. Representatives of *cinema pur* tended to afford absolute importance to the segmentary structure of film—the pure "filmic rhythm" as

36. Sergei Eisenstein, "Im Weltmass-Stab über Valeska Gert" (On a world scale about Valeska Gert), in Peter 1987, 121.

37. Sergei Eisenstein in Peter 1987, 121. Articulation and motion here appear as elements of movement poetics: "We see that tonal intonation is movement, which we tend to forget in our coloraturas. We see that intonation is the acrobatics of tone articulating limbs." All translation in text and note: Elena Polzer.

technically produced by "lens and film reel." Kinetic games and experiments of speeding up or slowing down images influenced, for example, the "text" of Fernand Léger's *Ballet mécanique* (1924). The title alludes to that artistic medium which had hitherto staged pure movement, namely theatrical dance, as "ballet" (for which Léger designed sets in collaboration with Diaghilev's Ballets Russes that same year).[38] However, in the film it is "objects" taken out of context—pots, pans, faces—that move in a rhythmic dance. Images and movement sequences are dismantled in shot and reverse shot and presented in repetition.

The reflection of time and patterns of interruption in the temporal flow, achieved here by the film, were also central to the music: George Antheil's *Ballet mécanique*, specially composed for Léger's film, is "the first *time-form* on earth,"[39] according to the composer in a manifesto published in *Querschnitt* 1925. The piece, whose "orchestra" was made up of, for example, four pianos, a battery of noise instruments, car horns, and a thundering airplane motor, incorporated the Bruitist experiments of the Futurists, and aspired toward "a new fourth dimension of music," namely time itself as a fundamental principle of movement: "My Ballet Mécanique has under no circumstances, and at no point a single motion or movement that does not come out of *time*."[40]

This theoretical concept of a temporality that is not oriented along the guide-lines of an organic-rhythmic model of musical aesthetics here links film and music in a ballet mécanique. The music is likewise governed by the mechanical, and by the technical principle of the stroboscope as a way of structuring time in conjunction with the movement concept of "modern times."[41]

RELÂCHE: INTERRUPTION AS A STRUCTURAL PRINCIPLE IN DANCE, THEATER, AND FILM

On the basis of the dance theater piece *Relâche* (1924), I would like to now sum-marize how the principle of interruption expressed itself as a cinematic and tech-nical principle of movement on various levels of a single work.

38. In 1924, the piece *Le Train bleu* (choreography, Bronislawa Nijinska; scenario, Jean Cocteau; music, Darius Milhaud) premiered on a "cubist" stage designed by Léger.

39. Antheil 1925.

40. Ibid., 791.

41. Antheil elaborated this concept even further in his opera *Transatlantik* (1930), whose formal composition was strongly influenced by film technique (flashbacks and flash for-wards, scenic polyphony, slow-motion sequences) and revue (spotlights, jazz ballet) and whose soundscape was based on media such as telephones, whirring telegraph poles, and clattering typewriters.

Relâche—a Ballets Suédois production under Rolf de Maré—premiered in Paris on December 4, 1924. The choreography was by Jean Börlin, the music by Erik Satie, and the overall concept by Francis Picabia.[42] The piece can be analyzed on three levels, each of which features typical structures of interruption of its own:

1. The avant-garde aesthetic program
2. The macrostructure
3. The microstructure, from which I will single out just one sub-component and examine the work's implicit concept of movement and the body

Although the Dada movement had, in 1924, already been declared "dead" for over two years and been replaced by surrealism, *Relâche* is still entirely influenced by Picabia's nihilistic accentuated concept of Dada. One characteristic aspect of his approach is his commitment to nonsense. On the front page of the program notes, which Picabia drew up himself, were the words: "When will we lose the habit of explaining everything?"[43] Another typical aspect of Picabia's work was his rejection of theatrical, even cultural, tradition: the "contempt of yesterday," the "only thing that counts is the present" (Picabia). Last, but not least, a distinguishing feature of his pieces was the affront to the institution of the theater as a temple of bourgeois culture. *Relâche*, according to Picabia, is "a rest from all the pretentious eccentricities of contemporary theater." This affront also included a provocative attack on the audience, not only in the form of the typical abusive language,[44] but also in an annihilation of the accustomed theatrical framework.

The title and subtitle of the "ballet," or to be more precise, of the "antiballet," provide decisive clues to the technique of "the pause," of interruption. The title *Relâche* means "Closed—No Performance Tonight" and thus plays with the same theatrical and institutional framework that it simultaneously dispenses with. In

---

42. See Häger 1989; Wehmeyer 1974; Volta 1992, 85ff.

43. Quoted in sleeve notes by S. W. Bennett on E. Satie et al. (1968), *Homage to Erik Satie: Original Works for Orchestra and Orchestrations* (New York: Vanguard).

44. See Wehmeyer 1974, 258; the title of the piece already signals noncompliance with audience expectations of the performative, the re-presentation of theater. The piece played with expectations even more, shortly before the world premiere. The guests arrived in their formal evening attire for the announced grand opening and were refused entry at the door of the Théâtre des Champs-Elysées by a sign saying "Relâche." Of course, no one took it seriously, as they were all already expecting Picabia's provocations and had heard of the "topic" of the evening. However, the theater really did remain closed (Jean Börlin, the choreographer and main dancer had fallen sick). The first show took place one week later, on December 4, 1924. See Häger 1989, 52–56.

Relâche, the negation of dance and theater is contextualized and at the same time brushed aside in an act of nonacting. *Relâche* moreover abandons the context of theater as a theatrical one. In his commentary on *Relâche*, Picabia emphasized the panorama of life in the big city: "city lights"—assembled into short, cinematically segmented sequences of images. *Relâche*, according to Picabia,

> is life, life as I love it, life lived as if there's no tomorrow . . . headlights, pearl necklaces, round and slender female forms, going out in public, music, cars, men in tuxedos, movement, noise, play.[45]

This affirmation of the unspectacular, constantly reemerging quotidian moment can also be interpreted as an annotation of the subtitle of the piece *Relâche*: namely *ballet instantanéiste*. *Instantaneism* stands for a perceptual concept that emphasized instantaneousness as the manifestation of movement.[46] The instantaneist concept of movement and individual movement details transferred the stroboscopic principle of media technology (chronophotography, cinematography) onto the body and onto the act of making theater.

Satie likewise based his composition of the music for *Relâche* on an instantaneist pattern. It was put together as a detailed modular system, in juxtapositions of melodic turns, with simple children's songs—"everyday" and "lewd" music, as Satie explained.[47] The music, its abbreviated citations and rhythmic patterns of interruption, seems to allude to a specific corporeal concept: the lewdness references the obscene as an act of both revealing and concealing the body. In the piece this associative treatment of the obscene takes on an additional dimension—not only that of provocation, but also that of calling into question theater itself. Satie's experimentation with the discontinuous schemata of the cut, cutting off, "interruptio" even extended into *Relâche*'s erotic-semantic level.

---

45. Francis Picabia in an interview with Rolf de Maré, *La Danse*, November–December 1924, cited in Wehmeyer 1974, 262. Translation from German: Elena Polzer.

46. Picabia, who founded *instantanéisme* as a final offshoot of Dada in November 1924 together with Duchamp and Dermée as an artistic movement only concerned with the moment, dedicated the last edition of his magazine *391* to *instantaneism*: the title was "Journal de l'Instantanéisme—pour quelque temps. L'Instantanéiste est un être exceptionnel cynique et indecent." What followed was a manifesto of *instantaneism* saying, e.g., "Instantaneism is something exceptional: cynical and indecent. Instantaneism: does not want yesterday. Instantaneism: does not want tomorrow," etc.; see Wehmeyer 1974, 262 and http://chrisjoseph.org/after391/; on this and on the history of Picabia's Dada magazine *391*, see also Picabia 1988.

47. Satie said: "The music of Relâche? I depicted people at a fair. That is why I used everyday melodies. These melodies are very lewd . . . yes, very lewd." (Translation: Elena Polzer; see Wehmeyer 1974, 274.)

Satie discarded elements of the allegedly "obscene." He sent a few bars of the music that accompanied the appearance of the woman, "Rentrée de la Femme," to Milhaud, for his young fiancée. Toward the end of the musical excerpt, he wrote: "Relâche (Ballet obscène)."[48]

Here the temporal segmentation of the musical composition reflects the ballet's body concept. The woman (and later also the men) undressing on stage, shedding their everyday clothes, and performing the quotidian body in tight skin-colored leotards appeared obscene—precisely because they were not clearly designated as "dancing bodies." However, here is another reference to the title of the piece, this time from the perspective of corporeality: Relâche is a game with what happens behind the scenes, behind closed curtains ("ob-scena") (figure 53). The bodies disappearing and reappearing in a specific temporal rhythm thus appear to be an extension of the subject of "interruption."

The temporal tact of the music steered the concept, not only via rhythm and meter, but by what was played behind the scenes, as "background music": the "musique d'ameublement," as Satie called the *gestus* of his composition. In other words, it was an aesthetic of episodically assembled *ambient music*. The cuts, the loose association of melodic and rhythmic elements, seemed more or less static and were not arranged into an elaborated theme—this "instantaneist" structure of the music corresponded, on *Relâche*'s macro- and microlevel, with equivalent units of movement composition.

The piece was divided into two parts, each with eleven short scenes. A film that Picabia had specially commissioned for this purpose separated these two parts: *Entr'acte* by René Clair.[49]

According to Picabia, *Entr'acte* "is a film that interprets our dreams and the unrealized events that take place in our brain."[50] *Entr'acte* is "a real entr'acte, an intermission in the monotonous boredom of life." The image of "resting" (another alternative reading of *Relâche*) corresponds to the meaning "intermission"—an interruption of the theater piece that is spent in the foyer, in other words, time during which the audience can relax and present itself. It coincides with the old tradition of the "entr'acte," that is, the intermezzi, which characterized the origins of opera buffa and one-act plays, as interspersions in opera and dramas, as disjunctive intarsia of other media.[51]

---

48. Wehmeyer 1974, 284.

49. On René Clair, his contribution to *cinéma pur*. and his oeuvre, see Gregor and Patalas 1976, 1: 71–75 and 149–52; on *Entr'acte* and Satie's music for it, which was not illustrative, contrary to the custom of silent movies, see Wehmeyer 1974, 279–89.

50. Cited in Trippet 2007: 562–63.

51. Regarding the dramaturgy of "interruption" in intermezzos, as concerns the genre of one-act plays, see Döhring and Kirsch 1991.

Figure 53 *Relâche* (1924). The play with the "framework" curtain and the "interruption" of the levels is apparent in the stage setting.
SOURCE: Bibliothèque de l'Opéra, Paris, France.

The interruption of the scenic text by the film, the mutual disruption and conflicting disjunction of dance, theater, and film took on a stroboscopic quality in the greater structure of *Relâche*, which also influenced the structure on a micro-level. The written film scenario lists 346 camera shots, of which René Clair subsequently implemented 292. Clair himself identified "interruption" as the basis of *Entr'acte*: the film is "a visual stammer of regulated harmony."[52] The scenic action on stage appeared similarly fragmented into a micro-rhythm. For his film scenario, Picabia meticulously listed the segmentation of the camera angles in a cinematic way and specified the exact length of the individual scenes in seconds.[53] The resulting succession of loosely associated, not logically or even functionally connected scenes—images of big-city life, a firefighter passing by smoking a cigarette, a woman in an evening gown walking through the

52. Mitry 1960, 18. Translation: Elena Polzer. "Clair attempted a rhythmic orchestration of images and sequences, which were only utilized for their movement value." Gregor and Patalas (1976, 1: 73) here describe the avant-garde intention behind this seminal work of *cinéma pur* and caution against attributing "a precise meaning to 'Entr'acte' and the rhythmic rotation of its leitmotifs—the dancer, the egg dancing on a fountain of water, the roller coaster and the funeral procession."

53. Picabia's description meticulously specifies the timing of the music; see Häger 1989, 250.

auditorium, a group of men undressing—follows a basic principle: that of disjunction, as a pattern of interruption created by editing and montage. The result was various forms of separation, isolation, and overlapping cross- and intersections of movement parameters. The film featured the same typical kinetic style of quick, "narrative" stops (and pauses) that Fernand Léger described in his review of the piece as the cheerful, imaginative "minuterie du geste, du mouvement, des projecteurs."[54] Here the term *minuterie*, which also means "minute light" (or timer), translates the pattern of interruption onto the bodies, forms of movement, and the play of light[55] in *Relâche* from another perspective, namely from that of a mechanical *rhythm of light*.

Disjunction also concerned the separation of image and sound and accordingly, the contrasts between movement and nonmovement: those same semiotic systems traditionally constitutive for ballet and dance theater (but also for music and straight theater) in their integral *connectedness*. In *Relâche*, the music fell silent when the bodies moved and vice versa. The movements—for example by the woman in the evening dress—were interrupted when the music set in.

The disjunction, separation, and quasi-lateral relocation of traditionally synthetic coordinated levels of images and sound, of moving bodies and interruption of movement, shifted from theater to film and from screen to stage. The film, whose structure would require an aesthetical cinematic analysis of its own,[56] encoded movement and its associated concepts of the body, by deconstructing conventional codes: the bodies appeared

54. Fernand Léger, "Vive Relâche," *Der Querschnitt*, 1925, 132ff. In this review, Léger celebrates *Relâche* as the final defeat of traditional ballet. He emphasizes its proximity to the extravaganza of music hall, the merging of stage and auditorium, and the conjunction of different media: "musique lumineuse, électrique, cinématographique." In particular, he stresses the novel aspect of the temporal structure, the patterns of interruption and cinematic movement in the scenic text: "Devant le chronomètre, la seconde, le quart de seconde, le dixième de seconde, il va jouer toute cette jolie fantaisie qui a l'air de ne pas être réglée du tout, qui en a l'air . . . car tout est réglé—voulu—minuterie du geste, du mouvement, des projecteurs."

55. The projection of text and images onto the drop curtain or as fade-ins was very important for both the piece and the film (cited from Wehmeyer 1974, 262): "The curtain rises and reveals a drop curtain with the names of the creators of the piece, Satie and Picabia, in transparent letters that seem illuminated from behind. The names keep constantly reappearing and are thus reminiscent of a bundle of electrical signs as can be found along the main streets of every big modern city. The drop curtain is replaced by a film [not yet *Entr'acte*, G.B.], followed by cinematographic opening credits, which show a series of brief images: they hint at the dance, but follow no logic in the order of their sequence" (translation: Elena Polzer). This is a description of the opening scenario of *Relâche* as action that consisted of projected solitary moments.

56. See Wehmeyer 1974 and Gregor and Patalas 1976.

- *Fragmented* (e.g., in the film excerpt of the "Chaplinesque," moving boxing gloves)
- *Particularized* (head, hair, limbs in the wake of the funeral procession)
- *Mechanized* (as puppets, "mistaken for" and confronted with chess pieces) and over and over again
- *Deleted* in alternating moments of fading and returning; thus almost playfully "rehearsing" the act of disappearing, after pistol and cannon shots, into coffins, disintegrating into thin air—the magical effects of the celluloid medium.

The structural formula of interruption thus provided the framework for a confrontation between the movement and corporeal concepts of film and theater. The woman entered the stage not as a dancer, but as a lady from the audience. She was mirrored by the ballerina in the film, dancing on a pane of glass in a tutu (figure 54). However, this ballerina—or rather the conventional corporeal signs indicating "dancer"—was likewise ambivalent: the dance atop the transparent surface lighted from below was a homage to a dancer, who did not become famous as a physically attractive ballerina, but rather as an inventor of experimental abstract movement, namely Loïe Fuller.[57] The voyeuristic perspective of the camera—"under the skirt" of the dancer—played with parallel patterns on stage, where a woman undressed until she was left with no more than a tight skin-colored leotard. She re-presented nakedness—"playing" with those images of the body already present in the minds of the audience. The scene examined the disappearance and appearance, the representation and deconstruction, of body imagery. Here, both the acts of displaying and the acts of concealing the body signified "obscenity."

Finally, the entire, seemingly mimetic medium of film revealed itself to be an illusion—especially its representations of the body and encoded movement; the female dancer was actually male. The choreographer Jean Börlin himself abruptly abandoned his movement disguise and once more interrupted the only ostensively clean-cut image of the classical female dancer's body.

At this point, I would like to draw a few general hypothetical conclusions. In terms of its function for the development of avant-garde aesthetics, the technical-cinematic structure of interruption (of editing, of rhythmically

---

57. See Brandstetter and Ochaim 1989. Fuller's famous *Fire Dance* was performed on top of a glass panel illuminated in red and orange from below. Since its presentation in Paris in 1892, it has been considered one of Fuller's greatest successes. The quotation is probably an homage by René Clair, since she was the one who pointed him to film, when he was still a budding young author, by giving him the leading male role in Fuller's "Ballet cinématographique," *Le Lys de la vie* (1920); for more about the film and Fuller's concept, see Brandstetter and Ochaim 1989, 69–72.

Figure 54 René Clair: *Entr'acte* (1924), film still of
the scene with the ballerina dancing on a glass plate.
SOURCE: Archives de la Fondation Erik Satie, Paris,
France.

repetitive disjunction) as it affects concepts of the body and movement in the
fields of dance and theater, reveals the following aspects that are worth noting:

> Interruption—fragmentation of the flow of time and perception—is a
> prerequisite of that moment of self-reflection which is characteristic for
> modern art. Inter-ruption, as the suspension of time, but also—more poi-
> gnantly—as a temporal rift, creates a distance of understanding, a point of
> intersection that allows a confrontation of heterogeneous elements and a
> gap,[58] into which inversions and antithetical readings can enter.

If we regard the principle of interruption from a perspective of movement
analysis and thereby take into account such aspects as kinetics and dynamics, we will find issues of power, (body) control, and orientation to be the

58. See Brandstetter 1991c.

main factors of its movement typology. In the alternation of movement and pauses, of staccato and legato, of the flow and halt of motion, self-awareness and awareness of others brings up—from a perspective of psychological movement analysis[59]—issues of control and autonomy. The interruption of movement is a crucial element in the development of a functional concept of the body organized around oriented action, movement in space, and body control. The ability to punctuate, segment, and recoordinate movement coincides with the ability to orient, contain, and control motor skills as a prerequisite for functional action. Seen in this light, the translation and accentuation of the principle of interruption in the body and movement aesthetics of avant-garde dance and theater indicates a reaction and answer to the (new) complexity of modernity. The rapid and incomprehensible developments of modern technology and media, which threatened the integrity of the subject (and which also led to a demonization of technology and the abandonment of civilization by other strands of modernity), generated a model of orientation and of control based on exactly those technical principles of movement that simultaneously influenced the structures of the development and transformation in modernity's models of knowledge and representation. By transporting interruption as a temporal rhythm and editing technique out of the techniques and structures of modern media technology into concepts of the body, of movement, and of staging theater, avant-garde dance and theater reflected (regardless of contents and presentation), on a profound structural level, various models of autonomy and self-determination as strategies of playing and coping with complexity.[60]

Of course—and this is crucial to understanding the various ambiguities of avant-garde art—the term *reflection* does not signify a conciliatory form of integrative self-assertion. Instead, interruption, for example, in the provocative self-referential manifestos of the avant-garde, appears as a hiatus of the conflict.

I therefore draw the following hypothetical conclusion from the fragmentary pattern of interruption:

> Avant-garde theater and avant-garde dance no (longer) meant a *synthesis* of the arts, for example, in terms of a *Gesamtkunstwerk*. Nor did such an aesthetic mean conjunction and integration of art and life. Instead,

59. I am here referring to the model of movement analysis developed by Cary Rick (1989).

60. This is not, however, a seamless continuation of nineteenth-century notions of aesthetic autonomy: by revoking tradition and integrating new media, "autonomy"—as an element of *avant-garde aesthetics*—emphasizes other aspects. The principle of interruption seeks to adapt and transform discursive practices and techniques of knowledge production, rather than merely separate art from life. For a discussion on the aesthetics of autonomy and the avant-garde in system theory as pertains to the issue of complexity, see Jäger 1991.

the artistic idea derived from a pattern of perception based on interruption evoked the idea of *conflict* between separate, isolated art forms. As *Relâche* clearly demonstrates, this also led to conflicting reciprocal interruptions by the various scenic parameters and media. The medium of film interrupted—as *Entr'acte*—the action on stage, which was in turn "interrupted" by events in the auditorium (the entering and exiting "pedestrians"). Action and commentary thus unfolded in the interruption as a form of medial interaction. The conflict—as collision and interruption—hence incites creative friction, which is passed on to the audience as shock and provocation. The audience is not addressed as recipients, but as producers of meaning. They are forced to assemble a form of mental montage out of the interrupted patterns, creating, as it were, the piece in their own imagination.

Conclusion

Over the course of this book, I have traced the avant-garde "Poetics of Dance" by demonstrating the way dance and literature converged in an intricate choreography of interdependence and autonomy at the turn of the century. The interaction of "speaking body" and "moving text" in this relationship reveals the unresolved dialectic between these two art forms. The constellation of both art systems is here revisited at a prominent point in cultural history— that critical moment in European culture which is frequently described as the period of decadence that brought on a crisis of perception around 1900. This crisis was a semiotic one. A rapid succession of emergent artistic patterns of perception and representation—naturalism, impressionism, expressionism, Futurism, and finally *Neue Sachlichkeit*—led to experiences of disassociation that brought to light fresh ways of comprehending oneself and the world. Most importantly, this semiotic crisis drew increased attention to a latent conflict between the semiotics of the body and the semiotics of text. This simultaneously exposed a major difference between two cultural techniques: the ability of the written word to stand the test of time, as contrasted with the moving body of dance and its transient, impermanent signs. As I have shown in my analysis, this difference is most evident in the interpretation of "images of the body" (*Körperbilder*): iconographic patterns—formulas both for perceiving and for representing the body—that mediate between the dancing body and its representation in literature.

This configuration of dance and literature involves various systemic and historical issues: first of all, the question of *myth and memory* as the *narrative patterns* of culture per se. Moreover, forms of *temporality* in culture: the *single moment* versus *history*. And finally, the *movement, concretization, and spatialization* of the body as a *topological formula* of culture—fundamental aspects of aesthetic representation and the determination of the aesthetic qualities as they relate to intuition (*Anschauung*), space, and time.

In the introduction, I described Lafcadio Hearn's tale "Of a Dancing Girl" as a paradigmatic encounter between moments of performance and perception in a foreign culture, an encounter between a dancer and a painter, who is also her reader. This narrative constellation reveals the problematics of corporeal signs and their movement patterns, which is in other terms a conflict of perception and representation that is of crucial cultural—and by this I mean cultural semiotic—importance. This conflict is the symptom of a long chain of such encounters and "readings."

To conclude my thoughts on the patterns of reading dance, I wish to recontextualize the pivotal period of avant-garde art at the turn of the century. On the basis of Rahel Varnhagen's "dance dreams," I will first describe the transition from nineteenth-century romanticism to fin de siècle, and then close with a short look at the "dance ready-mades" of the 1990s.

In her *Traumbuch* (*Dream Book*, ca. 1812),[1] the famous nineteenth-century author and Berlin socialite Rahel Varnhagen described the following dream in her idiosyncratic narrative style. She recalls being in a hall with high ceilings, statues, busts, and paintings, as well as portraits of "all sculptors and painters living or known" (16). A large group of artists and aficionados has convened in this fantastic archive of art history "to appraise these works of art: a kind of last judgment of art!" (17)—a "l'ultima scena" of traditional patriarchal art history. The dreamer Varnhagen attempts to find her way among the multitude of modes and fashions. Then she discovers—accompanied by a cry of "the ideal!"—among this cultural tribunal composed exclusively of men

a young man of around twenty years of age in ordinary clothes, hatless, standing there in a blue dress coat; holding his hands clasped before him; eyes forced downward; rather handsome, with red cheeks and although standing as if ashamed, stifling his laughter: the others cannot see it; I call out, look, he's human, he lives; he cannot hold his laughter in any longer: whereupon the artists again all cry out, the ideal! It is the ideal! (18f.)

Her *other* (female) gaze makes it possible for Varnhagen to discern that the reputed ideal is not mounted on a marble pedestal, but contained in a living human being. The subsequent shared "moment" between the "dis-covered ideal" and his "reader," the smile and the laughter, and her touch and his awakening are Pygmalion-like gestures translated into feminine desire. The transformation from statue to lover begins with laughter and ends in a shared dance:

I tapped him on the shoulder and said, I see that you live, you can hardly stifle your laughter; whereupon he raised his hand; embraced me with

---

1. See Hahn 1990. Further citations with page numbers in the text. All translations: Elena Polzer.

both arms; and we began to waltz in the most cheerful way. With great pleasure, unabashedly, merry. (19)

In Varnhagen's dream, this dance of man and woman in the hall of statues, the erotic swirl of the waltz through the archive of art history, becomes the epitome of a utopian vision, a utopia in which both the restrictions of normative concepts of art and the barriers of social conventions seem suspended. The living embodiment of freedom and equality resists the petrified "ideal." The new ideal is an "artwork in process," snatched from the sediments of the past by the immediacy of the body. Here we gradually have the contours of an aesthetic concept emerging that anticipates the remote future of twentieth-century avant-garde aesthetics. In this vision, dance becomes the utopian art form par excellence. Varnhagen describes the dance as

the most beautiful art! That art in which we ourselves become the material of art, in which we declare ourselves free, happy, healthy, complete; self-contained, elegant, modest, naive, innocent, attuned to our true nature, free from misery, constraints, struggle, limitations, and weaknesses.[2]

Varnhagen thus formulates the idea of a free, "mobile" subject—the image of a "happy human being." It is a dance-dream, whose text has always yet to be written. Dreaming and dancing appear as never-ending processes, movements seeking an "object" that has already disappeared in the text—in the narrative of the dream, as well as in the embodied choreography. The transformations of desire and the "I" of memory in stories and history reappear again in the cycle of writing and reading. Varnhagen notes: "The word *narration* already contains all that storytelling is and can be; to fathom what a story can be, and not to list what happened, is what makes a story."[3]

Yet despite her many doubts concerning existing storytelling conventions, she has not yet lost faith in the general narratability of history. By writing and reading, by telling her story as history, her self constructs its own identity.

Around 1900, this attitude changes completely. The avant-garde's critical approach to the narrative as such and its many subsequent attempts at finding new solutions to problems of perception and representation is the very subject of this book.

To conclude, I will now take a look at the very different situation of the 1990s. In this period, many of the same questions concerning the "text of history" and the

2. Varnhagen 1983, 2: 572.

3. Hahn 1990, 64.

dichotomy of remembering versus forgetting, order versus destruction, reemerged in contemporaneous dance and theater productions. Once again, artists sought models and rules for constructing the relationship between the subject and its position in society. However, the discussion took on an entirely new form. The body was viewed as "material," concepts of space were modeled on virtual reality; time and movement appeared increasingly as merely simulated entities.

Dance and choreography explored these perception formulas in very different directions. William Forsythe's "fractal choreographies" dealt with the new complexity by choreographically reflecting the "lost center" (*In the Middle Somewhat Elevated*, 1988), the loss of order (*The Loss of Small Detail*, 1991), and insurmountable alienation (*Alie/n A(c)tion*, 1993).

Meg Stuart's *Thought Object, ready made* (1992) and *No longer readymade* (1993) both examined the lack of connection between the self and its own history. In the solo *Thought Object, ready made*, the "dancer" stands facing the audience, dressed only in a long, oversize jacket and boots. Her movements consist of "trans-actions." She rummages around in one of the big side pockets of the jacket, takes out all kinds of objects, looks them over one at a time and then carelessly stuffs them back into her other pocket: travel documents, crumpled letters, dried-up flowers, ribbons, tickets. She transfers this detritus of memories slowly and then with more hastily from one pocket to the other until almost everything is strewn sadly across the floor. We watch her attempts to affirm her history with a random collection of mementos, but her actions lack a cohesive thread. Again and again, the dancer tries to coax the objects to guarantee a (his)story, something like a "stable and stationary" identity. But the "freestanding figure" fails to relate the detritus of the past to itself in the key moment of threading things together. The body on display is ultimately no more than an empty clothes rack. The traces of memory fail to locate a subject. The movements of "memoria" appear impersonal, merely scattered in the context—"ready-mades" no longer able to reveal their history.

In the subsequent piece *No longer readymade*, Stuart revisits the same subject. At first, the title seems to promise a solution to the situation, but the attempt fails. We see a man and a woman with various mementos applied to their naked torsos: family photos, scraps of letters, flowers, and other things—fragments and images of their private history. A peculiar form of tattooing: memory is not inscribed in the bodies, but rather applied and fastened to the skin. All our expectations are directed at their imminent encounter. But the dialogue between the bodies clearly reveals that their stories cannot be told; the details of memory do not speak. The only discernible thing is a void.

We are left with the question of whether choreography—the momentary (al)location of movements in time and space—is still able to set this story in motion by wresting memory from the void of oblivion even, if just for a moment, by redirecting the traces and repositioning the images, by forming both the text and con-text of a "no longer ready-made." The options of a future avant-garde are open. Impermanence, anticipation, and reversal as processes of self-similarity are already visible. And so I end with the words of choreographer William Forsythe: "One of the first goals of performance is not to know what one has done."[4]

4. William Forsythe in an interview with Johannes Odenthal, in Odenthal 2005, 22.

BIBLIOGRAPHY

Acocella, Joan R. 1984. *The Reception of Diaghilev's Ballets Russes by Artists and Intellectuals in Paris and London, 1909–1914.* Ann Arbor.

Adorno, Theodor W. 1997. *Aesthetic Theory.* Trans. Robert Hullot-Kentor. Minneapolis.

Akarova. 1988. *Spectacle et Avant-Garde, 1920–1950.* Brussels.

Alewyn, Richard. 1958. *Über Hugo von Hofmannsthal.* Göttingen.

Alighieri, Dante. 2004. *The Vision of Hell.* Trans. H. F. Cary. Project Gutenberg.

Allan, Maud. 1908. *My Life and Dancing.* London.

Allemann, Beda. 1961. *Zeit und Figur beim späten Rilke: Ein Beitrag zur Poetik des modernen Gedichts.* Pfullingen.

Andritzky, Michael, and Thomas Rautenberg, eds. 1989. *"Wir sind nackt und nennen uns Du": Von Lichtfreunden und Sonnenkämpfern. Eine Geschichte der Freikörperkultur.* Gießen.

Androgyn. 1987. *Sehnsucht nach Vollkommenheit.* Catalogue. Ed. Ursula Prinz. Berlin.

Anselm, Sigrun. 1987. *Triumph und Scheitern in der Metropole: Zur Rolle der Weiblichkeit in der Geschichte Berlins.* Ed. Barbara Beck. Berlin.

Antheil, George. 1925. "My Ballet mécanique: What It Means." *Der Querschnitt* 5.9: 789ff.

Anz, Thomas. 1982. *Expressionimsus: Manifeste und Dokumente zur deutschen Literatur, 1910–1920.* Ed. Michael Stark. Stuttgart.

Apollonio, Umbro. 1972. *Der Futurismus: Manifeste und Dokumente einer künstlerischen Revolution, 1909–1918.* Cologne.

Aschengreen, Erik. 1986. *Jean Cocteau and the Dance.* Copenhagen.

Assmann, Aleida, and Dietrich Harth, eds. 1991a. *Kultur als Lebenswelt und Monument.* Frankfurt am Main.

Assmann, Aleida, and Dietrich Harth, eds. 1991b. *Mnemosyne: Formen und Funktionen der kulturellen Erinnerung.* Frankfurt am Main.

Assmann, Jan, and Tonio Hölscher, eds. 1988. *Kultur und Gedächtnis.* Frankfurt am Main.

Astruc, Gabriel. 1929. *Le Pavillon des fantômes.* Paris.

Aufmuth, Ulrich. 1979. *Die deutsche Wandervogelbewegung unter soziologischem Aspekt.* Göttingen.

Austin, Gerhard. 1981. *Phänomenologie der Gebärde bei Hugo von Hofmannsthal.* Heidelberg.

Aveline, Claude, and Michel Dufet. 1969. *Bourdelle et la Danse: Isadora et Nijinsky.* Paris.

Azari, Fedele. 1970. "Futurist Aerial Theatre" (1919). *Drama Review* 15: 127–30.

Bablet, Denis. 1965. *Edward Gordon Craig.* Cologne.

Bablet, Denis. 1986. "Les peintres et le théâtre." *Théâtre en Europe* 11: 6–100.

Bachelard, Gaston. 1964. *The Psychoanalysis of Fire*. Trans. Alan C. M. Ross. Boston.

Bachelard, Gaston. 1975. *Poetik des Raumes*. Frankfurt am Main.

Bahr, Hermann. 1981. *Das unrettbare Ich*. In *Die Wiener Moderne*, ed. by Gotthard Wunberg. Ditzingen.

Bakhtin, Michail M. 1969. *Literatur und Karneval: Zur Romantheorie und Lachkultur*. Munich.

Balász, Béla. 1972. "Zur Kunstphilosophie des Films" (1938). In *Theorie des Kinos: Ideologiekritik der Traumfabrik*, ed. Karsten Witte, 149–70. Frankfurt am Main.

Ball, Hugo. 1996. *Flight Out of Time: A Dada Diary*. Ed. John Elderfield. Berkeley.

Ballets Suédois. 1931. *Les Ballets Suédois dans l'Art Contemporain*. Paris.

Banes, Sally. 1980. *Terpsichore in Sneakers: Post-modern Dance*. Boston.

Banville, Théodore de. 1926. *Choix de Poésies*. Ed. Charles Morrice. Paris.

Barta-Fliedl, Ilsebill. 1992. *Die Beredsamkeit des Leibes: Zur Körpersprache in der Kunst*. Exhibition catalog from the Albertina, Vienna. Ed. Ilsebill Barta-Fliedl and Christoph Geissmar. Salzburg.

Barta-Fliedl, Ilsebill. 1992. "Vom Triumph zum Seelendrama: Suchen und Finden oder Die Abentheuer eines Denklustigen. Anmerkungen zu den gebärdensprachlichen Bilderreihen Aby Warburgs." In *Die Beredsamkeit des Leibes: Zur Körpersprache in der Kunst*, ed. Ilsebill Barta-Fliedl and Christoph Geissmar, 165–70. Salzburg.

Barta, Ilsebill, Zita Breu, Daniela Hammer-Tugendhat, et al., eds. 1987. *Frauen. Bilder. Männer. Mythen: Kunsthistorische Beiträge*. Berlin.

Barthes, Roland. 1975. *The Pleasure of the Text*. Trans. Richard Miller. New York.

Barthes, Roland. 1988. *Das semiologische Abenteuer*. Frankfurt am Main.

Barthes, Roland. 1990. *The Fashion System*. Trans. Matthew Ward and Richard Howard. Berkeley.

Battersby, Martin. 1969. *The Decorative Twenties*. London.

Baudelaire, Charles. 1954. *Oeuvres complètes*. Ed. Y.-G. Le Dantec. Paris.

Baudelaire, Charles. 1964. "The Painter of Modern Life." In *The Painter of Modern Life and Other Essays*, trans. Jonathan Mayne. London. Also online at http://www.idehist. uu.se/distans/ilmh/pm/baudelaire-painter.htm.

Bauer, Oswald Georg. 1985. "Das *Tannhäuser*-Bacchanal." In *Wagnerliteratur— Wagnerforschung: Bericht über das Wagner-Symposion in München* (1983), ed. Carl Dahlhaus and Egon Voss, 215–23. Mainz.

Bauer, Roger. 1991. "Altes und Neues über die Décadence." *Literaturwissenschaftliches Jahrbuch der Görresgesellschaft* 32: 149–73.

Bauer, Sibylle, ed. 1968. *Hugo von Hofmannsthal*. Wege der Forschung, no. 183. Darmstadt.

Baumgarth, Christa. 1966. *Geschichte des Futurismus*. Reinbek.

Baur, Uwe. 1989. "Horváth und die Sportbewegung der Zwanzigerjahre: Seine Sportmärchen im Kontext der Münchner Nonsense-Dichtung." In *Horváths Prosa*, ed. Traugott Krischke, 75–97. Frankfurt am Main.

Baxmann, Inge. 1991. "Traumtanzen oder die Entdeckungsreise unter die Kultur." In *Paradoxien, Dissonanzen, Zusammenbrüche: Situationen offener Epistemologie*, ed. Hans Ulrich Gumbrecht and K. Ludwig Pfeiffer, 316–40. Frankfurt am Main.

Bayerdörfer, Hans-Peter. 1976. "Eindringlinge, Marionetten, Automaten: Symbolische Dramen und die Anfänge der modernen Literatur." *Jahrbuch der Deutschen Schillergesellschaft* 20: 504–38.

Bayerdörfer, Hans-Peter. 1990. "Probleme der Theatergeschichtsschreibung." In *Theaterwissenschaft Heute: Eine Einführung*, ed. Renate Möhrmann, 41–64. Berlin.

Bayerdörfer, Hans-Peter, Karl Otto Conrady, and Helmut Schanze, eds. 1978. *Literatur und Theater im Wilhelminischen Zeitalter*. Tübingen.

Beauvoir, Simone de. 2010. *The Second Sex*. Trans. Constance Borde and Sheila Malovany-Chevallier. New York.

Becker, Marie-Luise. 1903. "Tanz." *Die Schönheit* 1: 277–90.

Becker, Peter. 1987. "Steigerung und Knappheit: Zur Kontingenzformel des Sportsystems und ihren Folgen." In *Sport und Höchstleistung*, ed. Peter Becker, 17–37. Reinbek.

Beckers, Edgar. 1991. "Erziehung durch und in Bewegung." *Tanzforschung, Jahrbuch* 2: 18–36.

Beer-Hofmann, Richard. 1980. *Der Tod Georgs*. Ed. Hartmut Scheible. Stuttgart.

Behringer, Wolfgang, and Constance Ott-Koptschalijski. 1991. *Der Traum vom Fliegen: Zwischen Mythos und Technik*. Frankfurt am Main.

Benjamin, Walter. 1977. *Illuminationen: Ausgewählte Schriften*. Frankfurt am Main.

Benjamin, Walter. 2005. "On the Concept of History" (1940). Trans. Dennis Redmond. Online at http://www.marxists.org/reference/subject/philosophy/works/ge/benjamin.htm.

Benois, Alexandre. 1941. *Reminiscences of the Russian Ballet*. London.

Bentivoglio, Leonetta. 1984. *Danza e futorismo in Italia: 1913–1933*. In *La Danza Italiana*, Vol. 1, 61–82. Rome.

Berber, Anita, and Sebastian Droste. 1923. *Tänze des Lasters, des Grauens und der Ekstase*. Vienna.

Bergius, Hanne. 1989. *Das Lachen Dadas: Die Berliner Dadaisten und ihre Aktionen*. Gießen.

Bergson, Henri. 1912. *Schöpferische Entwicklung*. Jena.

Bernal, Martin. 1992. *Schwarze Athene: Die afroasiatischen Wurzeln der griechischen Antike; wie das klassische Griechenland erfunden wurde*. Munich.

Bernhard, Thomas. 1997. *The Voice Imitator*. Trans. Kenneth J. Northcott. Chicago.

Bernheimer, Charles. 1989. "Degas's Brothels: Voyeurism and Ideology." In *Misogyny, Misandry, and Misanthropy*, ed. R. Howard Bloch and Frances Ferguson, 158–86. Berkeley.

Bie, Oscar. 1905. "Der Tanz als Kunstwerk." In *Die Kunst*, vol. 42. Berlin.

Bie, Oscar. N.d. "Das Ballett." In *Die Literatur*, vol. 15. Berlin.

Billetta, Rudolf. 1950. "Carl Sternheim." Diss. Vienna.

Birdwhistell, Ray. 1970. *Kinesis and Context*. Philadelphia.

Blamberger, Günter. 1991. *Das Geheimnis des Schöpferischen oder: Ingenium est ineffabile?* Stuttgart.

Blanchot, Maurice. 1982. *The Siren's Song: Selected Essays*. Ed. Gabriel Josipovici. Trans. Sacha Rabinovitch. Bloomington.

Blass, Ernst. 1921. *Das Wesen der neuen Tanzkunst*. Weimar. 2nd ed., Weimar, 1922.

Bloch, Ernst. 1959. *Das Prinzip Hoffnung*. 3 vols. Frankfurt am Main.

Blüher, Hans. 1911–1913. *Wandervogel: Geschichte einer Jugendbewegung.* 3 vols. Charlottenburg. Reprint Frankfurt am Main, 1976.

Blumenberg, Hans. 1981. *Die Lesbarkeit der Welt.* Frankfurt am Main.

Blumenberg, Hans. 1981. *Wirklichkeiten in denen wir leben: Aufsätze und eine Rede.* Stuttgart.

Boehn, Max von. 1918. *Bekleidungskunst und Mode.* Munich.

Boehn, Max von. 1925. *Der Tanz.* Berlin.

Böhme, Fritz. 1926. *Der Tanz der Zukunft.* Munich.

Bohrer, Karl Heinz. 1981. *Plötzlichkeit. Zum Augenblick des ästhetischen Scheins.* Frankfurt a.M.

Bomers, Jost. 1991. *Der Chandosbrief: Die Nova Poetica Hofmannsthals.* Stuttgart.

Borchardt, Rudolf. 1957. *Gedichte.* Ed. Marie Luise Borchardt and Herbert Steiner. Stuttgart.

Borchmeyer, Dieter. 1982. *Das Theater Richard Wagners: Idee—Dichtung—Wirkung.* Stuttgart.

Borchmeyer, Dieter. 1989. "Nietzsches Begriff der Décadence." In *Die Modernisierung des Ich: Studien zur Subjektkonstitution in der Vor- und Frühmoderne,* ed. Manfred Pfister, 84–95. Passau.

Borchmeyer, Dieter. 1992. *Die Götter tanzen Cancan: Richard Wagners Liebesrevolten.* Heidelberg.

Borel, France. 1992. *La vêtement incarné: Les métamorphoses du corps.* Paris.

Bornscheuer, Lothar. 1976. *Topik: Zur Struktur der gesellschaftlichen Einbildungskraft.* Frankfurt am Main.

Bouvier, Nicolas. 1983. *Boissonnas: Une dynastie de photographes, 1864–1983.* Lausanne.

Bovenschen, Silvia. 1980. *Die imaginierte Weiblichkeit: Exemplarische Untersuchungen zu kulturgeschichtlichen und literarischen Präsentationsformen des Weiblichen.* Frankfurt am Main.

Bovenschen, Silvia, ed. 1986. *Die Listen der Mode.* Frankfurt am Main.

Brandenburg, Hans. 1917. *Der moderne Tanz.* 2nd ed. Munich. 1st ed., 1913.

Brandenburg, Hans. 1921. *Der moderne Tanz.* 3rd ed. Munich.

Brandstetter, Gabriele. 1984. "Elevation und Transparenz: Der Augenblick im Ballett und modernen Bühnentanz." In *Augenblick und Zeitpunkt: Studien zur Zeitstruktur und Zeitmetaphorik in Kunst und Wissenschaft,* ed. Christian W. Thomsen and Hans Holländer, 475–92. Darmstadt.

Brandstetter, Gabriele. 1988. "Körper im Raum und Raum im Körper": Zu Carl Einsteins Pantomime "Nuronihar." In *Carl Einstein (Internationales Einstein-Kolloquium, 1986),* Bayreuther Beiträge zur Literaturwissenschaft, no. 12, ed. Klaus H. Kiefer, 115–38. Frankfurt am Main.

Brandstetter, Gabriele. 1991a. "'La Destruction fut ma Béatrice'—zwischen Moderne und Postmoderne: Der Tanz Loïe Fullers und seine Wirkung auf Theater und Literatur." In *Avantgarde und Postmoderne: Prozesse struktureller und funktioneller Veränderungen,* ed. Erika Fischer-Lichte and Klaus Schwind, 191–208. Tübingen.

Brandstetter, Gabriele. 1991b. "Der Traum vom anderen Tanz: Hofmannsthals Ästhetik des Schöpferischen im Dialog 'Furcht.'" In "Hugo von Hofmannsthal: Dichtung als Vermittlung der Künste," *Freiburger Universitätsblätter* 112: 37–60.

Brandstetter, Gabriele. 1991c. "Intervalle: Raum, Zeit und Körper im Tanz des 20. Jahrhunderts." In *Zeit-Räume: Zeiträume—Raumzeiten—Zeitträume*, ed. Martin Bergelt and Hortensia Völckers, 225–78. Munich.

Brandstetter, Gabriele. 1992. Psychologie des Ausdrucks und Ausdruckstanz: Aspekte der Wechselwirkung am Beispiel der "Traumtänzerin Magdeleine G." In *Ausdruckstanz: Eine mitteleuropäische Bewegung der ersten Hälfte des 20. Jahrhunderts* (International Symposium "Ausdruckstanz," Thurnau, 1986), ed. Gunhild Oberzaucher-Schüller in cooperation with Alfred Oberzaucher and Thomas Steiert, 199–211. Wilhelmshaven.

Brandstetter, Gabriele, and Brygida M. Ochaim. 1989. *Loïe Fuller: Tanz, Licht-Spiel, Art Nouveau*. Freiburg.

Braun, Edward. 1978. *Meyerhold on Theatre*. Rev. ed. Methuen Drama. Bertrams Print on Demand.

Brauneck, Manfred. 1984. *Theater im 20. Jahrhundert. Programmschriften, Stilperioden, Reformmodelle*. Reinbek.

Brecht, Bertolt. 1967. *Gesammelte Werke*. 20 vols.+ 4 Supplement vols. Frankfurt am Main.

Brinkmann, R. 1961. *Hofmannsthal und die Sprache*, in: *Deutsche Vierteljahresschrift für Literaturwissenschaft und Geistesgeschichte* 35, 69–95.

Broch, Hermann. 1974. *Hofmannsthal und seine Zeit: Eine Studie*. 1st ed. Frankfurt am Main.

Brod, Max. 1990. "Die Frau und die neue Sachlichkeit." In *Die Frau von morgen wie wir sie wünschen: Eine Essaysammlung aus dem Jahre 1929 mit einem Essay von Silvia Bovenschen*, ed. F. M. Huebner, 47–54. Frankfurt am Main.

Broich, Ulrich. 1985. *Intertextualität: Formen, Funktionen, anglistische Fallstudien*. Ed. Manfred Pfister. Tübingen.

Bücher, Karl. 1896. *Arbeit und Rhythmus (Work and Rhythm) (1896)*. Trans. Reference and Research Department, Music Education Division, of the New York WPA Music Project.

Bucher, Willi, and Klaus Pohl, eds. 1986. *Schock und Schöpfung: Jugendästhetik im 20. Jahrhundert*. Darmstadt.

Buonaventura, Wendy. 1990. *Die Schlange vom Nil: Frauen und Tanz im Orient*. Hamburg.

Buonaventura, Wendy. 1994. *Serpent of the Nile: Woman and Dance in the Arab World*. London.

Buckle, Richard, ed. 1971. *Nijinsky on Stage*. London.

Buckle, Richard. 1975. *Nijinsky*. London. Reprinted with revisions, 1980.

Buckle, Richard. 1979. *Diaghilev*. London.

Burke, Peter. 1990. *Die Renaissance*. Berlin.

Bügner, Torsten, and Gerhard Wagner. 1991. "Die Alten und die Jungen im Deutschen Reich: Literatursoziologische Anmerkungen zum Verhältnis der Generationen 1871–1918." *Zeitschrift für Soziologie* 20.3: 177–90.

Bünner, Gertrud, and Peter Röthig, eds. 1983. *Grundlagen und Methoden der rhythmischen Erziehung*. 4th ed. Stuttgart.

Bürger, Peter. 1974. *Theorie der Avantgarde*. Frankfurt am Main.

Butler, Judith. 1989. *Gender Trouble. Feminism and the subversion of identity*. New York.

Caillois, Roger. 1961. *Man, Play and Games*. Trans. Meyer Barash. New York.

Calvesi, Maurizio. 1975. *Futurismus*. Munich.

Carlson, Marvin. 1990. *Theatre Semiotics: Signs of Life*. Bloomington.

Casini Ropa, Eugenia. 1988. *La danza e l'agitprop: I teatri-non-teatrali nella cultura del primo Novecento*. Bologna.

Castro, E. de. 1934. *Salome*. Trans. Margarete Kühne. Coimbra.

Challet-Haas, Jacqueline. 1987. *Terminologie de la danse classique: Description des pas et des termes usuels analogies, différences et notions génerales*. Paris.

Chalupt, René. 1956. *Ravel au miroir de ses lettres*. Paris.

Charcot, Jean Martin, and Paul Richer. 1988. *Die Besessenen in der Kunst*. Ed. Manfred Schneider. Göttingen.

Cherniavsky, Felix. 1983a. "Maud Allan, Part I: The Early Years, 1873–1903." *Dance Chronicle* 6.1: 1–36.

Cherniavsky, Felix. 1983b. "Maud Allan, Part II: First Steps to a Dancing Career, 1904–1907." *Dance Chronicle* 6.3: 189–227.

Cherniavsky, Felix. 1984a. "Maud Allan, Part III: Two Years of Triumph, 1908–1909." *Dance Chronicle* 7.2: 119–58.

Cherniavsky, Felix. 1984b. "Maud Allan, Part IV: The Years of Touring, 1910–1915." *Dance Chronicle* 8.1–2: 1–50.

Cherniavsky, Felix. 1991. *The Salome Dancer: The Life and Times of Maud Allan*. Toronto.

Chladek, Rosalia. 1980. *Tänzerin, Choreographin, Pädagogin Rosalia Chladek*. Ed. Gerda Alexander and Hans Groll. 3rd ed. Vienna. 1st ed., 1965.

Christout, Marie-Françoise. 1972. "Cocteau et la Danse." *Les saisons de la danse*, May: 18–19.

Chujoy, Anatole, ed. 1949. *The Dance Encyclopedia*. New York.

Clausberg. Karl. 1988. "Organ-Projektionen: Der 'ekstatische Flug' und der 'technische Flug.'" In *Fin de Siècle: Hundert Jahre Jahrhundertwende*, 58–63. Berlin.

Cocteau, Jean. 1921. "Cape of Good Hope." *Little Review*, Autumn. Online at http://www.archive.org/stream/littlereview08mcke/littlereview08mcke_djvu.txt.

Coghlan, Brian. 1985. "The Whole Man Must Move at Once: Das Persönlichkeitsbild des Menschen bei Hofmannsthal." *Hofmannsthal-Forschungen* 8: 29–47.

Cohen, Selma Jeanne. 1965. *The Modern Dance: Seven Statements of Belief*. Middletown, CT.

Cohen, Selma Jeanne. 1974. *Dance as a Theatre Art*. New York.

Cohen, Selma Jeanne. 1982. *Next Week, "Swan Lake."* Middletown, CT.

Copeland, Roger and Marshall Cohen. 1983. *What is Dance? Readings in Theory and Criticism*. New York.

Cossart, Michael de. 1978. *The Food of Love: Princesse Edmond de Polignac (1865–1943) and Her Salon*. London.

Cossart, Michael de. 1987. *Ida Rubinstein (1885–1960): A Theatrical Life*. Liverpool.

Cox, Richard. 1979. *Figures of Transformation: Rilke and the Example of Valéry*. London.

Curtius, Ernst Robert. 1952. *Marcel Proust*. Berlin.

Curtius, Ernst Robert. 1967. *Europäische Literatur und Lateinisches Mittelalter*. 6th ed. Bern.

Curtius, Ernst Robert. 1991. "Paul Valéry." In *Herausforderung der Moderne*, ed. K. H. Buchner and E. Köhn. Frankfurt am Main.

Dahlhaus, Carl. 1991. "Die Tragödie als Oper: 'Elektra' von Hofmannsthal und Strauss." In *Geschichte und Dramaturgie des Operneinakters*, ed. Winfried Kirsch and Sieghard Döhring, 277–84. Laaber.

Dahms, Sibylle. 1984. "Der Einfluß von Wagners Werk und Kunsttheorie auf Tanz und Ballett." In *Richard Wagner 1883-1983: Die Rezeption im 19. und 20. Jahrhundert. Gesammelte Beiträge des Salzburger Symposions*, 249-76. Stuttgart.

Dällenbach, Lucien, and Christiaan L. Hart Nibbrig, eds. 1984. *Fragment und Totalität*. Frankfurt am Main.

D'Annunzio, Gabriele. 1910. *Vielleicht—vielleicht auch nicht*. Trans. Karl Vollmoeller. Leipzig.

D'Annunzio, Gabriele. 1946. *Correspondance accompagnée de 12 Sonnets Cisalpins*. Paris.

D'Annunzio, Gabriele. 1964. *Forse che sì forse che no*. In Tutte le opere di Gabriele D'Annunzio, ed. Egidio Bianchetti, *Prose di romanzi*, 2: 863-1180. Verona.

Dedner, Burghard. 1975. "Aufklärungskomödien im 'Massenzeitalter': Über Carl Sternheims Beziehungen zum Publikum." *Jahrbuch der Deutschen Schillergesellschaft* 19: 284-305.

Delius, Rudolf von. 1926. *Tanz und Erotik: Gedanken zur Persönlichkeitsgestaltung der Frau*. Munich.

de Man, Paul. 1979. *Allegories of Reading: Figural Language in Rousseau, Nietzsche, Rilke, and Proust*. New Haven.

de Man, Paul. 1984. *The Rhetoric of Romanticism*. New York.

Demetz, Peter. 1990. *Worte in Freiheit: Der italienische Futurismus und die deutsche Avantgarde, 1912-1934. Mit einer ausführlichen Dokumentation*. Munich.

Depero. 1988. *Katalog der Ausstellung in Rovereto und Düsseldorf*. Ed. Maurizio Fagiolo dell'Arco and Nicoletta Boschiero. Milan.

Derrida, Jacques. 1972. *La Dissémination*, Paris.

Derrida, Jacques. 1976. *Randgänge der Philosophie*. Frankfurt am Main.

Derrida, Jacques. 1981. *Dissemination*. Trans. Barbara Johnson. Chicago.

Derrida, Jacques. 1986. *Mémoires: For Paul de Man*. New York.

Deschodt, Anne Marie, Sacha Van, and Mariano Fortuny. 1979. *Un magicien de Venise*. Paris.

Deutsche Gesellschaft für Schrifttanz. 1928-1931. *Schrifttanz: Eine Vierteljahresschrift*. Vienna.

Dierks, Manfred. 1972. *Studien zu Mythos und Psychologie bei Thomas Mann: An seinem Nachlaß orientierte Untersuchungen zum "Tod in Venedig," zum "Zauberberg" und zur "Joseph"-Tetralogie*. Bern.

Diethe, Carol. 1991. "The Dance Theme in German Modernism." *German Life and Letters* 44.4: 330-52.

Dils, Ann, and Ann Cooper Albright. 2001. *Moving History / Dancing Cultures: A Dance History Reader*. Middletown, CT.

Diringer, A. 1899. *Die Tanzkunst: Kunsthistorische Skizzen mit Tanzlexikon. Die Tänze der einzelnen Völker und Die praktische Lehre der modernen Salon-Tänze*. 3rd ed. Munich.

Doerry, M. 1986. *Übergangsmenschen: Die Mentalität der Wilhelminer und die Krise des Kaiserreichs*. Weinheim.

D'Offay, Anthony, ed. 1991. *Freundschaften. Cunningham, Cage, Johns*. Bonn.

Dorival, Bernard, and Sonja Delaunay. 1980. *Sa vie, son oeuvre 1885-1979*. Paris.

Douglas, Mary. 2003. *Natural Symbols: Explorations in Cosmology*. 3rd ed. New York. 1st ed. 1970.

Dresdner, Albert. 1903. "La danse comme art plastique." *La Musique en Suisse 2.38* (May 15): 218–21; 2.39 (June 1): 233–35; 2.40 (June 15): 247–49.

Drews, Axel, Ute Gerhard, and Jürgen Link. 1985. "Moderne Kollektivsymbolik: Eine diskurstheoretisch orientierte Einführung mit Auswahlbibliographie." In *Internationales Archiv für Sozialgeschichte der deutschen Literatur*, special issue, "Forschungsreferate," 256–357. Tübingen.

Duncan, Elizabeth. 1912. *Elizabeth-Duncan-Schule Marienhöhe/Damstadt*. Jena.

Duncan, Irma. 1937. *The Technique of Isadora Duncan*. New York.

Duncan, Irma, and Allan Ross MacDougall. 1929. *Isadora Duncan*. London.

Duncan, Isadora. 1903. *Der Tanz der Zukunft (The Dance of the Future): Eine Vorlesung*. Trans. Karl Federn. Leipzig.

Duncan, Isadora. 1927. *My Life*. Boni & Liveright: New York.

Duncan, Isadora. 1928a. *The Art of the Dance*. Ed. Sheldon Cheney. Toronto.

Duncan, Isadora. 1928b. *Memoiren*. 1928b. Trans. C. Zell. Zurich.

Dyserink, Hugo. 1988. "*Komparatistische Imagologie: Zur politischen Tragweite einer europäischen Wissenschaft von der Literatur.*" In *Europa und das nationale Selbstve rständnis: Imagologische Probleme in der Literatur, Kunst und Kultur des 19. und 20. Jahrhunderts*, ed. H. Dyserink and Karl Ulrich Syndram, 13–37. Aachener Beiträge zur Komparatistik, vol. 8. Bonn.

Eco, Umberto. 1985. *Einführung in die Semiotik*. 5th ed. Munich.

Eco, Umberto. 1988. "Das Zeichen im Theater." In *Über Spiegel und andere Phänomene*, 62–70. Munich.

Eichstedt, Astrid, and Bernd Polster. 1985. *Wie die Wilden: Tänze auf der Höhe der Zeit*. Berlin.

Einstein, Carl. 1980, 1981, 1985. *Werke. Vol. 1, 1908–1918*. Ed. Rolf-Peter Baacke in cooperation with Jens Kwasny. Vol. 2, 1919–1928. Ed. Marion Schmid in cooperation with Henriette Beese and Jens Kwasny. Vol. 3, 1929–1949. Ed. Marion Schmid and Liliane Meffre. Berlin.

Einstein, Carl. 2004. "Negro Sculpture." Trans. Charles W. Haxthausen and Sebastian Zeidler. *October* 107 (Winter): 122–38.

Eisenstein, Sergei. 1929. "A Dialectic Approach to Film Form." Online at http://interactive2.usc.edu/blog-old/wp-content/uploads/2010/08/Film_Form.pdf.

Eisenstein, Sergei. 1977. *Film Form: Essays in Film Theory*. Ed. and trans. Jay Leyda. San Diego.

Eksteins, Modris. 1989. *Rites of Spring: The Great War and the Birth of the Modern Age*. Boston.

Eksteins, Modris. 1990. *Tanz über Gräben: Die Geburt der Moderne und der Erste Weltkrieg*. Reinbek.

Eksteins, Modris. 2000. *Rites of Spring: The Great War and the Birth of the Modern Age*. Boston.

Ellis, Havelock. 1923. *The Dance of Life*. Boston.

Ellis, Havelock. 1928. *Der Tanz des Lebens*. Trans. Eva Schumann. Leipzig.

Eltz, Johanna. 1986. "Der italienische Futurismus in Deutschland, 1912–1922: Ein Beitrag zu seiner Rezeptionsgeschichte." In *Bamberger Studien zur Kunstgeschichte und Denkmalpflege*, vol. 5. Bamberg.

Emmanuel, Maurice. 1895. *La Danse Grecque antique d'après les monuments figurés.* Paris. Reprint Geneva, 1987.

Emmanuel, Maurice. 1916. *The Antique Greek Dance after Sculptured and Painted Figures.* Trans. Harriet Jean Beauley. New York.

Emmanuel, Maurice. 1985. *Grete Wiesenthal: Die Schönheit des Körpers im Tanz.* Ed. Martin Lang. Salzburg.

Engler, Balz. 1988. *Das Festspiel: Formen, Funktionen, Perspektiven.* Ed. Georg Kreis. Willisau.

Fagiolo dell'Arco, Maurizio. 1988. *Balla: The Futurist.* New York.

Faludi, Ivan. 1991. "Rhythmische Momente der modernen Regie." In *Die russische Avantgarde und die Bühne 1890–1930,* ed. Heinz Spielmann. Catalog. Schleswig.

Fiebach, Joachim. 1991. *Von Craig bis Brecht,* 3rd ed. Berlin

Fiedler, Leonhard M. 1972. "Hofmannsthals Ballettpantomime 'Die grüne Flöte': Zu verschiedenen Fassungen des Librettos." *Hofmannsthal-Blätter* 8–9: 113–45.

Finter, Helga. 1980. *Semiotik des Avantgardetextes: Gesellschaftliche und poetische Erfahrung im italienischen Futurismus.* Stuttgart.

Finter, Helga. 1985. *Das Kameraauge des postmodernen Theaters.* In C. W. Thomsen, ed. *Studien zur Ästhetik des Gegenwartstheaters,* 56–70. Heidelberg.

Finter, Helga. 1990. *Der subjektive Raum.* Vol. 1: *Die Theaterutopien Stéphane Mallarmés,* Alfred Jarrys und Raymond Roussels: Sprachräume des Imaginären. Tübingen.

Fischer, Hans W. 1924. *Das Tanzbuch (mit drei Tanzspielen).* Munich.

Fischer, Hans W. 1928. *Körperschönheit und Körperkultur: Sport, Gymnastik, Tanz.* Berlin.

Fischer, Hans W. 1935. *Menschenschönheit: Gestalt und Antlitz des Menschen in Leben und Kunst. Ein Bildwerk in sieben Schau-Kreisen.* Berlin.

Fischer, Jens Malte. 1978. *Fin de siècle: Kommentar zu einer Epoche.* Munich.

Fischer-Lichte, Erika. 1983. *Semiotik des Theaters.* 3 vols. Tübingen.

Fischer-Lichte, Erika. 1989a. "Der Körper des Schauspielers im Prozess der Industrialisierung: Zur Veränderung der Wahrnehmung im Theater des 20. Jahrhunderts." In *Literatur in einer industriellen Kultur,* ed. Götz Großklaus and Eberhard Lämmert, 468–86. Veröffentlichungen der Deutschen Schillergesellschaft, vol. 44. Stuttgart.

Fischer-Lichte, Erika. 1989b. "Wandel theatralischer Kodes: Zur Semiotik der interkulturellen Inszenierung." *Zeitschift für Semiotik* 11.1: 63–85.

Fischer-Lichte, Erika. 1989c. "Zum kulturellen Transfer theatralischer Zeichen." In *Literatur und Theater: Traditionen und Konventionen als Problem der Dramenübersetzung,* ed. Brigitte Schultze et al., 35–62. Tübingen.

Fischer-Lichte, Erika. 1991. "Die Entdeckung des Zuschauers: Paradigmenwechsel auf dem Theater des 20. Jahrhunderts." In *Zeitschrift für Literaturwissenschaft und Linguistik,* vol. 81, "Theater im 20. Jahrhundert," 13–37.

Fischer-Lichte, Erika, and K. Schwind, eds. 1991. *Avantgarde und Postmoderne: Prozesse struktureller Veränderungen.* Tübingen.

Fisher, Adrian. 1990. *Labyrinth: Solving the Riddle of the Maze.* New York.

Flaubert, Gustave. 1982. *Drei Erzählungen / Trois Contes.* Trans. Cora van Kleffens and André Stoll. Frankfurt am Main.

Flaubert, Gustave. N.d. *Hérodias*. Online at http://www.pagebypagebooks.com/Gustave_Flaubert/Herodias/.

Fokine, Michel. 1961. *Memoirs of a Ballet Master*. London.

Fonteyn, Margot. 1984. *Pavlova: Portrait of a Dancer*. London.

Fortuny e Caramba. 1987. *La moda a teatro. Costumi di scena, 1906–1936*. Cataloghi Marsilio. Venice.

Foster, Susan Leigh. 1986. *Reading Dancing: Bodies and Subjects in Contemporary American Dance*. Berkeley.

Foucault, Michel. 1965. *Madness and Civilization: A History of Insanity in the Age of Reason*. New York.

Foucault, Michel. 1976. *Discipline and Punish: The Birth of the Prison*. New York.

Frank, Manfred, Gérard Raulet, and Willem van Reijen, eds. 1988. *Die Frage nach dem Subjekt*. Frankfurt am Main.

Frèches, Claire, and José Frèches. 1992. *Toulouse-Lautrec: Les lumières de la nuit*. Paris.

Frecot, Janos, Johann Friedrich Geist, and Diethart Kerbs. 1972. *Fidus 1868–1948: Zur ästhetischen Praxis bürgerlicher Fluchtbewegungen*. Munich.

Freud, Sigmund. 1965. *New Introductory Lectures on Psychoanalysis*. "Lecture 33: Femininity." *College Edition*, 22: 112–35. New York.

Freud, Sigmund. 1980. *Werke*. Study ed. 10 vols. and supplemental volume. Frankfurt am Main.

Freud, Sigmund. 1989. *Civilization and Its Discontents*. Trans. James Strachey. New York.

Freund, Liesel, ed. 1929. *Monographien der Ausbildungsschulen für Tanz und Tänzerische Körperbildung*. Vol. 1. Berlin.

Fricke, Richard. 1906. *Bayreuth vor dreißig Jahren: Erinnerungen an Wahnfried und aus dem Festspielhause (mit unveröffentlichten Briefen von Richard Wagner)*. Dresden. Reprinted as *Richard Wagner auf der Probe: Das Bayreuther Tagebuch des Ballettmeisters und Hilfsregisseurs Richard Fricke*. Stuttgarter Arbeiten zur Germanistik, no. 128. Stuttgart, 1983.

Fritz, Helmut. 1980. *Die erotische Rebellion: Das Leben der Franziska Gräfin zu Reventlow*. Frankfurt am Main.

Frizot, Michael, ed. 1984. *La chronofotographie: Temps, photographie et movement autour de E. J. Marey*. Exhibition catalogue. Beaune.

Frühwald, Wolfgang. 1988. "Zwischen Arkadien und Babylon: Münchner Literatur in der Zeit des Prinzregenten Luitpold." In *Munich—Musenstadt mit Hinterhöfen: Die Prinzregentenzeit 1886–1912*, ed. Friedrich Prinz and Marita Krauss, 258–66. Munich.

Fuchs, Georg. 1906. *Der Tanz. Flugblätter für künstlerische Kultur*, 6. Stuttgart.

Fuchs, Georg. 1936. *Sturm und Drang in Munich um die Jahrhundertwende*. Munich.

Fülleborn, Ulrich. 1973. *Das Strukturproblem der späten Lyrik Rilkes: Voruntersuchung zu einem historischen Rilke-Verständnis*. 2nd ed. Heidelberg.

Fuller, Loïe. 1908. *Quinze ans de ma vie*. Paris.

Fuller, Loïe. 1913. *Fifteen Years of a Dancer's Life*. Boston.

Gallwitz, Esther, ed. 1981. *Istanbul*. Frankfurt am Main.

Gebhard, Walter. 1984. *"Der Zusammenhang der Dinge": Weltgleichnis und Naturverklärung im Totalitätsbewußtsein des 19. Jahrhunderts*. Hermea. Germanistische Forschungen, vol. 47. Tübingen.

Gebhard, Walter. 1988. "Genies und Geniesser: Carl Einstein über die Kunst des frühen japanischen Holzschnitts." In *Carl Einstein Colloquium, 1986*, ed. Klaus H. Kiefer, 67–113. Frankfurt am Main.

Germain, André. 1954. *La vie amoureuse de D'Annunzio.* Paris.

Gert, Valeska. 1925. "Burlesque Film." Film-Kurier no. 240, October 12. Online at http://www.filmportal.de/en/material/valeska-gert-on-the-german-burlesque.

Gert, Valeska. 1931. *Mein Weg.* Leipzig.

Gert, Valeska. 1978. *Ich bin eine Hexe: Kaleidoskop meines Lebens.* Reinbek. (Originally published in 1968 by Schneekluth, Munich.)

Gert, Valeska. 1995. "From 'I Am a Witch.'" In *Twentieth Century Theater: A Sourcebook*, ed. Richard Drain, 33–34. New York.

Giertz, Gernot. 1975. *Kultus ohne Götter: Emile Jaques-Dalcroze und Adolphe Appia. Der Versuch einer Theaterreform auf der Grundlage der Rhythmischen Gymnastik.* Munich.

Giese, Fritz. 1920. *Weibliche Körperbildung und Bewegungskunst.* Ed. Hedwig Hagemann. Munich.

Giese, Fritz. 1924. *Körperseele: Gedanken über persönliche Gestaltung.* Munich. 2nd ed., Munich, 1927.

Giese, Fritz. 1925. *Girlkultur: Vergleiche zwischen Amerikanischem und Europäischem Rhythmus- und Lebensgefühl.* Munich.

Goebel, Gerhard. 1978. "Mode und Moderne: Der Modejournalist Mallarmé." *Germanisch-Romnische Monatsschrift* 28: 36–49.

Goethe, Johann Wolfgang von. 1827. *Wilhelm Meister's Travels.* In *German Romance—Specimens of Its Chief Authors*, vol. 4: Goethe. London.

Goffman, Erving. 1974. *Frame Analysis: An Essay on the Organization of Experience.* New York.

Goffman, Erving. 1976. *Gender Advertisements.* New York.

Golücke, Dieter. 1984. *Bernhard Hoetger: Bildhauer, Maler, Baukünstler, Designer.* Worpswede.

Gombrich, Ernst H. 1970. *Aby Warburg: An Intellectual Biography.* London.

Gombrich, Ernst H. 1984. *The Sense of Order: A Study in the Psychology of Decorative Art.* Ithaca, NY.

Gomez Carillo, Enrique. 1927. *Mata Hari. Das Geheimnis ihres Lebens und ihresTodes.* Leipzig.

Göttner-Abendroth, Heide. 1982. *Die tanzende Gött: Prinzipien einer matriarchalen Ästhetik.* Munich.

Gregor, Ulrich, and Enno Patalas. 1976. *Geschichte des Films.* 2 vols. Reinbek.

Grimm, Jürgen. 1982. *Das avantgardistische Theater Frankreichs 1895–1930.* Munich.

Großklaus, Götz, and Ernst Oldemeyer, eds. 1983. *Natur als Gegenwelt: Beiträge zur Kulturgeschichte der Natur.* Karlsruhe.

Guest, Ivor. 1976. *Le Ballte de l'Opéra de Paris.* Paris.

Gumbrecht, Hans-Ulrich and Ursula Link-Heer, eds. 1985. *Epochenschwellen und Epochenstrukuren im Diskurs der Literatur- und Sprachhistorie*, Frankfurt a.M.

Günther, Dorothee. 1962. *Der Tanz als Bewegungsphänomen: Wesen und Werden.* Reinbek.

Günther, Helmut. 1969. *Grundphänomene und Grundbegriffe des afrikanischen und des afroamerikanischen Tanzes.* Graz.

Günther, Helmut. 1983. "Historische Grundlinien der deutschen Rhythmusbewegung." In *Grundlagen und Methoden der rhythmischen Erziehung*, 4th ed., ed. Gertrud Bünner and Peter Röthig, 33–72. Stuttgart.

Häger, Bengt. 1989. *Les Ballets Suédois*. Paris.

Hahn, Barbara, ed. 1990. "Im Schlaf bin ich wacher". *Die Träume der Rahel Levin Varnhagen*. Frankfurt am Main.

Halbe, Max. 1976. *Jahrhundertwende, Erinnerungen an eine Epoche (1935)*. Munich.

Hamburger, Michael. 1961. "Hofmannsthals Bibliothek: Ein Bericht." *Euphorion* 55: 15–76.

Hamburger, Michael. 1964. *Hugo von Hofmannsthal: Zwei Studien*. Göttingen.

Handke, Peter. 1996. *Voyage to the Sonorous Land, or, The Art of Asking / The Hour we Knew Nothing of Each Other: Two Plays*. New Haven, CT.

Hardt, Manfred, ed. 1989. *Literarische Avantgarden*. Darmstadt.

Hart Nibbrig, Christiaan L. 1981. *Rhetorik des Schweigens: Versuch über den Schatten literarischer Rede*. Frankfurt am Main.

Haskell, Arnold. 1955. *Diaghileff: His Artistic and Private Life*. London.

Haskell, Arnold. 1977. *Ballettomania Then and Now*. London.

Haug, Walter, and Rainer Warning, eds. 1989. *Das Fest. Poetik und Hermeneutik*, vol. 14. Munich.

Hausmann, Ulrich. 1991. "Kleine Nike an der Schulter des Helden." *Blätter der Rilke-Gesellschaft* 18, "Rilke, Goethe und die Deutschen," 79–93.

Haverkamp, Anselm, and Renate Lachmann. 1991. *Gedächtniskunst: Raum—Bild—Schrift. Studien zur Mnemotechnik*. Frankfurt am Main.

Hearn, Lafcadio. *Glimpses of an Unfamiliar Japan*. 1894. Online at http://www.fullbooks.com/Gimpses-of-an-Unfamiliar-Japanx39063.html.

Heine, Heinrich. 1987. *Historisch-kritische Gesamtausgabe der Werke*. Ed. Manfred Windfuhr. Vol. 9: *Elementargeister, Die Göttin Diana, Der Doktor Faust, Die Götter im Exil*. Ed. Ariane Neuhaus-Koch. Hamburg.

Heine, Heinrich. N.d. a. *Atta Troll*. Trans. Daniel Platt. Online at http://davidsbuendler. freehostia.com.

Heine, Heinrich. N.d. b. *Pomare*. Online at http://www.heinrich-heine.net/haupt.htm.

Heinse, Wilhelm. 1975. *Ardinghello und die glückseligen Inseln*. Critical ed., Ed. Max L. Baeumer. Stuttgart.

Henkel, Arthur. 1983. *Der Zeiten Bildersaal: Studien und Vorträge. Kleine Studien 2*. Stuttgart.

Hepp, Corona. 1987. *Avantgarde: Moderne Kunst, Kulturkritik und Reformbewegung nach der Jahrhundertwende*. Munich.

Herbert-Muthesius, Angelika. 1985. *Bühne und bildende Kunst im Futurismus: Bühnengestaltungen von Balla, Depero und Prampolini (1914–1929)*. Heidelberg.

Hermand, Jost, ed. 1977. *Lyrik des Jugendstils*. Stuttgart.

Hermand, Jost, and Frank Trommler. 1988. *Die Kultur der Weimarer Republik*. Frankfurt am Main.

Herzog, Reinhart, and Reinhard Koselleck, eds. 1987. *Epochenschwelle und Epochenbewußtsein*. München.

Heym, Georg. 1964. *Dichtungen und Schriften*. Ed. Karl Ludwig Schneider. 3 vols. Munich.

Hillach, Ansgar. 1971. "'Die Schule von Uznach' oder der 'romantische' Sternheim." *Jahrbuch der Deutschen Schillergesellschaft* 15: 441–64.

Hilmes, Carola. 1990. *Die Femme Fatale: Ein Weiblichkeitstypus in der nachromantischen Literatur.* Stuttgart.

Hirsch, Rudolf. 1972. Ein Vorspiel zum Ballett "Die grüne Flöte." *Hofmannsthal-Blätter* 8–9: 95–112.

Hirsch, Rudolf. 1981. "Hugo von Hofmannsthal und das Ballett: Zwei unbekannte Entwürfe für das russische Ballett und Zeugnisse zur Entstehung der 'Josephslegende.'" *Neue Zürcher Zeitung* 24–25 (January): 69.

Hirschbach, Denny, and Rick Takvorian, eds. 1990. *Die Kraft des Tanzes: Hilde Holger.* Vienna.

Hoffman, Kaye. 1984. *Tanz, Trance, Transformation.* Munich.

Hofmann, André, and Vladimir Hofmann. 1981. *Le Ballet.* Paris.

Hofmann, Werner. 1979. *Gegenstimmen: Aufsätze zur Kunst des 20. Jahrhunderts.* Frankfurt am Main.

Hofmann, Werner, ed. 1986. *Eva und die Zukunft: Das Bild der Frau seit der französischen Revolution.* Catalogue. Munich.

Hofmannsthal, Hugo von. 1910. *Elektra: Tragedy in One Act.* Trans. Alfred Kalisch. Music by Richard Strauss (op. 58). Berlin.

Hofmannsthal, Hugo von. 1923. "On Pantomime." *English Review* 36: 261.

Hofmannsthal, Hugo von. 1937. *Briefe 1900–1909.* Wien.

Hofmannsthal, Hugo von. 1948. "Brief an Grete Wiesenthal vom 18. 6. 1910." *Neue Rundschau*: 215–17.

Hofmannsthal, Hugo von. 1952. *Selected Prose.* Trans. Mary Hottinger, Tania Stern, and James Stern. New York.

Hofmannsthal, Hugo von. 1966. *Three Plays.* Trans. Alfred Schwarz. Waynebooks Series, no. 23. Detroit.

Hofmannsthal, Hugo von. 1968. "Her Extraordinary Immediacy." Trans. David Berger. *Dance Magazine*, September.

Hofmannsthal, Hugo von. 1975–. *Sämtliche Werke.* Critical ed., Ed. Heinz Otto Burger, Rudolf Hirsch, Clemens Köttelwesch, et al. Frankfurt am Main.

Hofmannsthal, Hugo von. 1979. *Gesammelte Werke in 10 Bänden.* Ed. Bernd Schoeller in cooperation with Rudolf Hirsch. Frankfurt am Main.

Hofsmannsthal, Hugo von. 1986. *The Lord Chandos Letter. Trans.* Russell Stockman. Marlboro, VT.

Hofmannsthal, Hugo von. 2008a. "Moments in Greece" (1908–1914). Trans. Tania Stern and James Stern. In *The Whole Difference: Selected Writings of Hugo von Hofmannsthal,* ed. J. D. McClatchy. Princeton.

Hofmannsthal, Hugo von. 2008b. *The Whole Difference: Selected Writings of Hugo von Hofmannsthal,* ed. J. D. McClatchy. Princeton.

Hofmannsthal, Hugo von. N.d. *The Letter of Lord Chandos.* English translation online at http://depts.washington.edu/vienna/documents/Hofmannsthal/Hofmannsthal_ Chandos.htm.

Hofmannsthal, Hugo von, and Harry Graf Kessler. 1968. *Briefwechsel 1898–1929.* Ed. Hilde Burger. Frankfurt am Main.

Hofmannsthal, Hugo von, and Helene von Nostiz. 1965. *Briefwechsel.* Ed. Oswalt von Nostiz. Frankfurt am Main.

Hofmannsthal, Hugo von, and Richard Strauss. 1990. *Briefwechsel.* Ed. Willi Schuh. 5th ed. Munich.

Homer. 2000. *The Essential Homer: Selections from the "Iliad" and the "Odyssey."* Trans. Stanley Lombardo. Indianapolis.

Huxley, Michael, and Noel Witts, eds. 2002. *The Twentieth Century Performance Reader.* 2nd ed. New York: Routledge.

Huysmans, Joris-Karl. 2006. *Against the Grain.* Trans. John Howard. Echo Library. Middlesex.

Ingold, Felix Philipp. 1980. *Literatur und Aviatik: Europäische Flugdichtung, 1909–1927.* Frankfurt am Main.

Ingold, Felix Philipp. 1988. *Das Buch im Buch.* Berlin.

Ingold, Felix Philipp, and Wunderlich, Werner, ed. 1992. *Fragen nach dem Autor. Positionen und Perspektiven.* Konstanz.

Irigaray, Luce. 1985. *This Sex Which Is Not One.* Trans. Catherine Porter. Ithaca, NY.

Irmer, Hans-Jochen. 1982. "Die Stellung Rudolf von Labans in der Theatergeschichte." In *Positionen der Vergangenheit und Gegenwart des modernen Tanzes: Laban, Wigman, Palucca, Weidt, Rudolph, Schilling,* 13–17. Arbeitshefte der Akademie der Künste, no. 36. Berlin.

Iser, Wolfgang. 1991. *Das Fiktive und das Imaginäre: Perspektiven literarischer Anthropologie.* Frankfurt am Main.

Israel, Lucien. 1983. *Die unerhörte Botschaft der Hysterie,* München.

Jansen, Wolfgang. 1987. *Glanzrevuen der zwanziger Jahre.* Berlin.

Jäger, Georg. 1991. *Die Avantgarde als Ausdifferenzierung des bürgerlichen Literatursystems. Eine systematische Gegenüberstellung des bürgerlichen und des avantgardistischen Literatursystems mit einer Wandlungshypothese.* In ed. Michael Titzmann. *Modelle des literarischen Strukturwandels,* 221–244. Tübingen.

Jaques-Dalcroze, Émile. 1911. In *Der Rhythmus.* Ein Jahrbuch, ed. Bildungsanstalt Jaques-Dalcroze, Dresden Hellerau, vol. 1, Jena 1911.

Jeschke, Claudia. 1983. *Tanzschriften. Ihre Geschichte und Methode. Die illustrierte Darstellung eines Phänomens von den Anfängen bis zur Gegenwart.* Bad Reichenhall.

Jolizza, W. K. von. 1907. *Die Schule des Tanzes: Leichtfaßliche Anleitung zur Selbsterlernung moderner und alter Gesellschaftstänze.* Vienna.

Jonas, R. A. 1985. *Art and Entertainment: German Literature and the Circus, 1890–1933.* Reihe Siegen, vol. 50. Heidelberg.

Jowitt, Deborah. 1988. *Time and the Dancing-Image.* Berkeley.

Junk, Victor. 1930. *Handbuch des Tanzes.* Stuttgart.

Junk, Victor. 1948. *Grundlegung der Tanzwissenschaft.* Reprint Hildesheim, 1991.

Kaes, Anton, ed. 1983. *Weimarer Republik: Manifeste und Dokumente zur deutschen Literatur, 1918–1933.* Stuttgart.

Kafitz, Dieter, ed. 1991. *Drama und Theater der Jahrhundertwende.* Mainzer Forschungen zu Drama und Theater, vol. 5. Tübingen.

Kaiser, Gerhard. 1973. "Walter Benjamins 'Geschichtsphilosophische Thesen': Zur Kontroverse der Benjamin-Interpreten." In *Antithesen: Zwischenbilanz eines Germanisten,* 1970–1972, 197–273. Frankfurt am Main.

Kaiser, Gerhard. 1981. *Gottfried Keller: Das gedichtete Leben.* Frankfurt am Main.

Kamper, Dietmar. 1972. *Geschichte und menschliche Natur: Die Tragweite gegenwärtiger Anthropologiekritik.* Munich.

Kamper, Dietmar. 1976. *Zur Geschichte des Körpers: Perspektiven der Anthropologie*. Ed. Volker Rittner. Munich.

Kamper, Dietmar. 1982. *Die Wiederkehr des Körpers*. Ed. Christoph Wulf. Frankfurt am Main.

Kamper, Dietmar. 1984. *Das Schwinden der Sinne*. Ed. Christoph Wulf. Frankfurt am Main.

Kamper, Dietmar. 1989. *Der Schein des Schönen*. Ed. Christoph Wulf. Göttingen.

Kamper, Dietmar, and Christoph Wulf, eds. 1989. *Transfigurationen des Körpers: Spuren der Gewalt in der Geschichte*. Berlin.

Keay, Julia. 1987. *The Spy Who Never Was: The Life and Loves of Mata Hari*. London.

Kendall, Elizabeth. 1979. *Where She Danced*. New York.

Kerényi, Karl. 1950. *Labyrinth-Studien: Labyrinthos als Linienreflex einer mythologischen Idee*. 2nd ed. Zurich.

Kern, Hermann. 2000. *Through the Labyrinth*. Munich.

Kessler, Harry Graf. 2005. *Das Tagebuch 1880–1937*. Vol. 4: 1906–1914. Ed. Roland S. Kamzelak and Ullrich Ott. Stuttgart.

Kiefer, Klaus H., ed. 1988. *Carl-Einstein-Kolloquium, 1986*. Bayreuther Beiträge zur Literaturwissenschaft, no. 12. Frankfurt am Main.

Kiefer, Klaus H. 1991. "Erster Weltkrieg und Avantgarde—Ein Projekt." In *Krieg und Literatur: Beiträge des 2. Internationalen Symposions, 140–56*. Osnabrück.

Kirby, E. T. 1972. *The Delsarte Method: 3 frontiers of actor training*. In The Drama Review, Nr. 53 (1972), 55–69.

Kirsch, Winfried, and Sieghard Döhring, eds. 1991. *Geschichte und Dramaturgie des Operneinakters*. Laaber.

Kittler, Friedrich A. 1985. *Aufschreibesysteme 1800/1900*. Munich.

Kittler, Friedrich A. 1999. *Gramophone, Film, Typewriter*. Trans. Goeffrey Wintrop-Young and Michael Wutz. Stanford, CA.

Kleemann, Elisabeth. 1985. *Zwischen symbolischer Rebellion und politischer Revolution: Studien zur deutschen Boheme zwischen Kaiserreich und Weimarer Republik—Else Lasker-Schüler, Franziska Gräfin zu Reventlow, Frank Wedekind, Ludwig Derleth, Arthur Moeller van den Bruck, Hans Johst, Erich Mühsam*. Würzburger Hochschulschriften zur neueren deutschen Literaturgeschichte, vol. 6. Frankfurt am Main.

Klein, Gabriele. 1992. *FrauenKörperTanz: Eine Zivilisationsgeschichte des Tanzes*. Berlin.

Kleinschmidt, Erich. 1982. "Döblin-Studien." *Jahrbuch der Deutschen Schillergesellschaft* 26: 383–427.

Kleinschmidt, Erich. 1992. *Gleitende Sprache: Sprachbewußtsein und Poetik in der literarischen Moderne*. Munich.

Kleinspehn, Thomas. 1989. *Der flüchtige Blick: Sehen und Identität in der Neuzeit*. Reinbek.

Klink, Else. 1983. "Eurythmie." In *Grundlagen und Methoden der rhythmischen Erziehung*, 4th ed., ed. Gertrud Bünner and Peter Röthig, 171–81. Stuttgart.

Klooss, Reinhard, and Thomas Reuter. 1980. *Körperbilder: Menschenornamente in Revuetheater und Revuefilm*. Frankfurt am Main.

Kobel-Bänninger, Verena. 1991. "Wilhelm Lehmann und Paul Valéry: Ein Beispiel deutsch-französischer Literaturbeziehungen im 20. Jahrhundert." *Arcadia* 26.2: 172–89.

Koch, Hans-Albrecht. 1989. *Hugo von Hofmannsthal. Erträge der Forschung*, vol. 265. Darmstadt.

Koch, Manfred. 1987. "'Und wenn man tief bohrt, schwindet die Bildlichkeit'— Erinnerung, Selbstgefühl und Reflexion im Frühwerk Hofmannsthals." In *Sinnlichkeit in Bild und Klang: Festschrift für Paul Hoffmann*, ed. Hansgerd Delbrück, 327–50. Stuttgarter Arbeiten zur Germanistik, no. 189. Stuttgart.

Kochno, Boris. 1970. *Diaghilev and the Ballets Russes*. London.

Koebner, Thomas, Rolf-Peter Janz, and Franz Trommler, eds. 1985. *"Mit uns zieht die neue Zeit": Der Mythos Jugend*. Frankfurt am Main.

Koegler, Horst. 1980. "Vom Ausdruckstanz zum 'Bewegungschor' des deutschen Volkes: Rudolf von Laban." In *Intellektuelle im Bann des Nationalsozialismus*, ed. Karl Corino, 165–79. Hamburg.

Köhler, Michael. 1985. *Das Aktfoto: Ansichten vom Körper im fotografischen Zeitalter* Ed. Gisela Barche. Katalog des Municher Stadtmuseums. Munich.

Köhne-Kirsch, Verena. 1990. *Die "schöne Kunst" des Tanzes: Phänomenologische Erörterung einer flüchtigen Kunstart. Europäische Hochschulschriften Reihe 20*, vol. 315. Frankfurt am Main.

Koopmann, Helmut, ed. 1990. *Thomas Mann-Handbuch*. Regensburg.

Koppen, Erwin. 1973. *Dekadenter Wagnerismus, Studien zur europäischen Literatur des Fin de Siècle*. Berlin.

Krabbe, Wolfgang R. 1989. "'Die Weltanschauung der Deutschen Lebensreform-Bewegungist der Nationalsozialismus': Zur Gleichschaltung einer Alternativströmung im Dritten Reich." *Archiv für Kulturgeschichte* 71.2: 431–61.

Kracauer, Siegfried. 1995. *The Mass Ornament: Weimar Essays*. Cambridge, MA.

Kramer-Lauff, Dietgard. 1969. *Tanz und Tänzerisches in Rilkes Lyrik*. Munich.

Krell, Max, ed. 1923. *Das deutsche Theater der Gegenwart*. Munich.

Küpper, Peter. 1987. Hugo von Hofmannsthal—Der Chandos-Brief. In *Zur Wende des Jahrhunderts*, 71–92. Amsterdam.

Laban, Rudolf von. 1920. *Die Welt des Tänzers*. Stuttgart.

Laban, Rudolf von. 1926a. *Choreographie*. Jena.

Laban, Rudolf von. 1926b. *Gymnastik und Tanz*. Oldenburg.

Laban, Rudolf von. 1926c. "Tanztheater und Tanztempel." In *Die Schönheit*, vol. 1: *Viertes Rhythmusheft: Rudolf von Laban I*, 42–48. Dresden.

Laban, Rudolf von. 1927. "Tanztheater und Bewegungschor." In *Tanz und Reigen*, ed. Ignaz Gentges. Berlin.

Laban, Rudolf von. 1928a. *Schrifttanz: Methodik Orthographie, Erläuterungen*. Vienna.

Laban, Rudolf von. 1928b. *Vom Sinn der Bewegungschöre*. Hamburg.

Laban, Rudolf von. 1935. *Ein Leben für den Tanz*. Dresden.

Laban, Rudolf von. 1966. *Choreutics*. Ed. Lisa Ullmann. London.

Lachmann, Renate, ed. 1982. *Dialogizität*. Munich.

Lachmann, Renate, ed. 1990. *Gedächtnis und Literatur: Intertextualität in der russischen Moderne*. Frankfurt am Main.

Lachmeyer, Herbert, Silvia Mattl-Wurm, and Christian Gargerle, eds. 1991. *Das Bad: Eine Geschichte der Badekultur im 19. und 20. Jahrhundert*. Salzburg.

Landes, Brigitte, ed. and trans. 1989. *"Es gibt keinen Hund": Das futuristische Theater. 61 theatralische Synthesen von Marinetti und anderen.* Edition text und kritik: Frühe Texte der Moderne. Munich.

Landmann, Robert. 1979. *Ascona—Monte Verità: Auf der Suche nach dem Paradies.* Frankfurt am Main.

Langer, Susanne K. 1953. *Feeling and Form: A Theory of Art.* New York.

Langer, Susanne K. 1983. "From: Feeling and Form." In *What Is Dance? Readings in Theory and Criticism*, ed. Roger Copeland and Marshall Cohen, 28–47. New York.

Laqueur, Thomas. 1990. *Making Sex: Body and Gender from the Greeks to Freud.* Cambridge, MA.

Le Bret, Henri. 1923. *Essai sur Valentine de Saint-Point: Notes sur une Évolution, Gestes Métachoriques de Valentine de Saint-Point, Bois gravés de F. Cappatti.* Nizza.

Legendre, Pierre. 1978. *La passion d'être un autre: Étude pour la danse.* Paris.

Leiris, Michel. 1983. *Das Band am Hals der Olympia.* Frankfurt am Main.

Leonhard, Rudolf. 1919. *Katilinarische Pilgerschaft (1913–1916).* Munich.

Le Rider, Jacques. 1985. "Modernismus/Feminismus—Modernität/Virilität: Otto Weiniger und die asketische Moderne." In *Ornament und Askese: Im Zeitgeist de Wien der Jahrhundertwende*, ed. Alfred Pfabigan, 242–60. Vienna.

Le Rider, Jacques. 1993. *Modernity and Crises of Identity: Culture and Society in Fin-De-Siecle.* Trans. Rosemary Morris. Vienna.

Lesure, François, ed. 1980. *"Le Sacre du Printemps": Igor Stravinsky.* Dossier de Presse, no. 1. Geneva.

Lethen, Helmut. 1975. *Neue Sachlichkeit, 1924–1932: Studien zur Literatur des "Weißen Sozialismus."* 2nd ed. Stuttgart.

Lever, Maurice. 1988. *Primavera. Tanz und Leben der Isadora Duncan.* München.

Levinson, André. 1923. *Meister des Balletts.* Potsdam.

Levinson, André. 1971. *Bakst: The Story of the Artist's Life.* New York.

Levinson, André. 1983. *Zum Ruhme des Balletts: Léon Bakst in Wort und Bild* Ed. Eva E. Fischer. Dortmund. Reprint of Léon Bakst, 1922.

Lindner, Ines. 1987. "Die rasenden Mänaden: Zur Mythologie weiblicher Unterwerfungsmacht." In *Frauen, Bilder, Männer, Mythen: Kunsthistorische Beitrage*, ed. Ilsebill Barta, Zita Breu, Daniela Hammer-Tugendhat, et al., 282–303. Berlin.

Lindner, Ines, et al., eds. 1989. *Blick-Wechsel: Konstruktionen von Männlichkeit und Weiblichkeit in Kunst und Kunstgeschichte.* Berlin.

Lippe, Rudolf zur. 1974. *Naturbeherrschung am Menschen. Vol. 1: Körpererfahrung als Entfaltung von Sinnen und Beziehungen in der Ära des italienischen Kaufmannskaptials. Vol. 2: Geometrisierung des Menschen und Repräsentation des Privaten im französischen Absolutismus.* Frankfurt am Main.

Lista, Giovanni, ed. 1973. *Futurisme: Manifestes, Documents, Productions.* Lausanne.

Lista, Giovanni, ed. 1976. *Théâtre futuriste italien.* 2 vols. Lausanne.

Lista, Giovanni. 1977. *Marinetti et le futurisme.* Lausanne.

Lista, Giovanni. 1988. *Les Futuristes.* Paris.

Loers, Veit. 1987. *Alfons Muchas gnostische Botschaft. Vom Paternoster zu den Medien.*

Lorenz, Otto. 1989. *Schweigen in der Dichtung: Hölderlin—Rilke—Celan. Studien zur Poetik deiktisch-elliptischer Schreibweisen.* Palaestra, vol. 284. Göttingen.

Louppe, Laurence, ed. 1991. *Danses Tracées: Dessins et Notation des Chorégraphes. Catalogue of the exhibition in Marseille*, 1991. Paris.

Löwith, Karl. 1991. *Kritik der Geschichte und der Geschichtsschreibung.* In C. H. Buchner and E. Köhn (Ed.). *Herausforderung der Moderne. Annäherungen an Paul Valéry.* Frankfurt a.M.

Lüdke, W. Martin, ed. 1976. *"Theorie der Avantgarde": Antworten auf Peter Bürgers Bestimmung von Kunst und bürgerlicher Gesellschaft.* Frankfurt am Main.

Maenz, Paul. 1974. *Art Deco. 1920–1940: Formen zwischen zwei Kriegen.* Cologne.

Magnin, Emile. 1904. *"Magdeleine": Étude sur le geste au moyen de l'hypnose.* Geneva.

Magnin, Emile. 1905. *L'Art et l'hypnose: Interpretation plastique d'oeuvres littéraires et musicales.* Geneva.

Magriel, Paul, ed. 1977. *Nijinsky, Pavlova, Duncan: Three Lives in Dance.* New York.

Mallarmé, Stephane. 1945. *Oeuvres complètes.* Ed. H. Mondor and G. Jean-Aubry. Paris.

Mallarmé, Stephane. 1985. *Ecrits sur Le Livre (Chiox de textes).* Ed. Henri Meschonnic. Paris.

Mallarmé, Stephane. 2001a. "Another Dance Study." In *Mallarmé in Prose*, ed. Mary Ann Caws, trans. Jill Emerson, 114–17. New York.

Mallarmé, Stephane. 2001b. "Ballets." In *Mallarmé in Prose*, ed. Mary Ann Caws, trans. Jill Emerson, 108–13. New York.

Mallarmé, Stephane. 2007. *Divagations.* Trans. Barbara Johnson. Cambridge, MA.

Mann, Heinrich. 1929. *Diana.* Trans. Erich Posselt and Emmet Glore. New York.

Mann, Heinrich. 1969. *Die Göttinnen oder Die drei Romane der Herzogin von Assy.* Vol. 2: Das Buch Minerva. München.

Mann, Thomas. 2001. *Collected Stories.* London.

Mariano Fortuny 1871–1949: Der Magier des Textilen Design. 1985. Catalogue of the exhibition at the Hochschule für Angewandte Kunst, Vienna. Vienna.

Marin, Louis. 1992. "Zu einer Theorie des Lesens in den bildenden Künsten: Poussins 'Arkadische Hirten.'" In *Der Betrachter ist im Bild: Kunstwissenschaft und Rezeptionsästhetik*, ed. Wolfgang Kemp. Berlin. 142–68.

Marinetti, Filippo Tommaso. 1909. "The Futurist Manifesto." Trans. James Joll. Online at http://cscs.umich.edu/~crshalizi/T4PM/futurist-manifesto.html.

Marinetti, Filippo Tommaso. 1917. "Manifesto of the Futurist Dance." Online at http://antipastimermaids.edublogs.org/2011/03/24/manifesto-of-the-futurist-dance-by-f-t-marinetti-july-8-1917/.

Marinetti, Filippo Tommaso, Emilio Settimelli, and Bruno Corra. 1915. "The Futurist Synthetic Theatre." Online at http://www.391.org/manifestos/19150218marinetti.htm.

Massine, Léonide. 1968. *My Life in Ballet.* Ed. Phyllis Hartnoll and Robert Rubens. London.

Maur, Karin von. 1977. *Oskar Schlemmer.* Catalogue of the exhibition in Stuttgart. Stuttgart.

Mauser, Wolfram. 1961. *Bild und Gebärde in der Sprache Hofmannsthals.* Österreichische Akademie der Wissenschaften. Phil.-hist. Klasse. Sitzungsberichte. Vol. 238, diss. 1. Graz.

Mauser, Wolfram. 1977. *Hugo von Hofmannsthal: Konfliktbewältigung und Werkstruktur. Eine psycho-soziologische Interpretation.* Kritische Information, no. 59. Munich.

Mauser, Wolfram 1981. "Hofmannsthals 'Triumph der Zeit': Zur Bedeutung seiner Ballett- und Pantomimen-Libretti." *Hofmannsthal-Forschungen* 6: 141–50.

Mayer, Mathias. 1993. *Hugo von Hofmannsthal*. Stuttgart.

McCarren, Felicia M. 1998. *Dance Pathologies: Performance, Poetics, Medicine*. Stanford, CA.

Merkel, Kerstin. 1990. *Salome: Ikonographie im Wandel*. Frankfurt am Main.

Metken, Günter. 1974. *Die Präraffeliten. Ethischer Realismus im Elfenbeinturm des 19. Jahrhunderts*. Köln.

Meyerhold, Vsevolod. 1969. "The Actor of the Future and Biomechanics." In *Meyerhold on Theatre*, ed. Edward Braun. New York.

Meyerhold, Vsevolod. 1974. *Theaterarbeit, 1917–1930*. Ed. Rosemarie Tietze. Munich.

Meyerhold, Vsevolod. 1979. *Schriften, Aufsätze, Briefe, Reden, Gespräche*. Ed. A. W. Fewealski. 2 vols. Berlin.

Meyerhold, Vsevolod. 1988. "The Cinefication of Theatre." In *The Film Factory*, ed. Richard Taylor and Ian Christie, 271–74. London.

Michelsen, Peter. 1974. "Zeit und Bindung: Zum Werk Hugo von Hofmannsthals." *Euphorion* 68: 270–85.

Mitry, Jean. 1960. *René Clair*. Paris.

Mitchell, Yvonne. 1979. *Colette: Eine Biographie*. Frankfurt am Main.

Moeller-Bruck, Arthur. 1902. *Das Varieté*. Berlin.

Mohrbutter, Alfred. 1904. *Das künstlerische Kleid der Frau*. Reprint 1985. Darmstadt.

Money, Keith. 1982. *Anna Pavlova: Her Life and Art*. London.

Müller, Hedwig. 1986. *Mary Wigman: Leben und Werk der großen Tänzerin*. Berlin.

Müller, Hedwig, Frank-Manuel Peter, and Garnet Schuldt. 1992. *Dore Hoyer: Tänzerin*. Berlin.

Müller-Seidel, Walter. 1985. "Hofmannsthal und Munich: Zur literarischen Moderne im deutschen Sprachgebiet." *Hofmannsthal-Forschungen* 8: 181–216.

Munro, Thomas. 1956. "'The Afternoon of a Faun' and the Interrelation of the Arts." In *Toward Science in Aesthetics: Selected Essays*, 342–63. New York.

Musil, Robert. 1978. "Ansätze zu neuer Ästhetik: Bemerkungen zu einer Dramaturgie des Films." In *Gesammelte Werke*, ed. Adolf Frisé, vol. 8: *Essays und Reden, 1925*, 1137–54. Reinbek.

Mustacchi, Marianna M. 1981. "Flaubert in the Orient: From Myth to Creativity." *Dance Scope* 15.2: 37–46.

Muybridge, Eadweard. 1881–1885. *Animal Locomotion*. Philadelphia.

Nectoux, Jean Michel, ed. 1989. *Mallarmé—Débussy—Nijinsky—De Meyer: "Nachmittag eines Fauns." Dokumentation einer legendären Choreographie*. Munich.

Nehring, Wolfgang. 1991. "'Elektra' und 'Ödipus': Hofmannsthals 'Erneuerung der Antike' für das Theater Max Reinhardts." In *Hugo von Hofmannsthal: Freundschaften und Begegnungen mit deutschen Zeitgenossen*, ed. Ursula Renner and Gisela Bärbel Schmid, 123–42. Würzburg.

Neubauer, John. 1992. *The Fin-de-Siècle Culture of Adolescence*. New Haven.

Neumann, Gerhard. 1993a. "'L'Inspiration qui se retire'—Musenanruf, Erinnern und Vergessen in der Poetologie der Moderne." In *Memoria: Vergessen und Erinnern*, ed. Anselm Haverkamp and Renate Lachmann, 433–55. Poetik und Hermeneutik, no. 15. Munich.

Neumann, Gerhard. 1993b. "'Ut apes geometriam': Zu Lichtenbergs Schöpfungstheorie und zur Geschichte des Topos-Begriffs." In *Gesellige Vernunft: Zur Kultur literarischen Aufklärung*, ed. Ortrud Gitjahr, Wilhelm Kühlmann, and Wolf Wucherpfennig, 187–210. Würzburg.

Niehaus, Max. 1959. *Himmel, Hölle und Trikot: Heinrich Heine und das Ballett.* Munich.

Niehaus, Max. 1981. *Isadora Duncan: Leben, Werk, Wirkung.* Wilhelmshaven.

Nietzsche, Friedrich. 1997. *Untimely Meditations.* Ed. Daniel Breazeale. Trans. R. J. Hollingdale. Cambridge Texts in the History of Philosophy. Cambridge.

Nietzsche, Friedrich. 2011. *The Complete Works of Friedrich Nietzsche: The First Complete and Authorized English Translatio.* Ed. Oscar Levy. Digital reproduction. Ithaca, NY.

Nijinsky. 1990. Catalogue of the Musée-Galerie de la Seita. Paris.

Nin, Joaquin. 1938. "Comment est né le 'Boléro' de Ravel." *Revue Musicale*, special issue, December.

Nitschke, August. 1989. *Körper in Bewegung: Gesten, Tänze und Räume im Wandel der Geschichte.* Stuttgart.

Nostitz, Helene von. 1979. *Aus dem alten Europa: Menschen und Städte.* Ed. Oswalt von Nostitz. 2nd ed. Frankfurt am Main.

Nostitz, Oswalt von. 1991. *Muse und Weltkind: Das Leben der Helene von Nostitz.* Munich.

Novalis. 1997. *Philosophical Writings.* Ed. and trans. Margaret Mahony Stoljarp. Albany.

Novalis. 2005. *The Novices of Sais.* Trans. Ralph Manheim. Brooklyn.

Nysenholc, Adolphe, ed. 1991. *Charlie Chaplin: His Reflection in Modern Times.* Approaches to Semiotics, no. 101. Berlin.

Oberthür, Mariel, ed. 1992. *Le Chat Noir, 1881–1897.* Catalogue of the exhibition at the Musée d'Orsay. Paris.

Oberzaucher-Schüller, Gunhild, ed., in cooperation with Alfred Oberzaucher and Thomas Steiert. 1992. *Ausdruckstanz: Eine mitteleuropäische Bewegung der ersten Hälfte des 20. Jahrhunderts.* Publikation der Beiträge des Symposions "Ausdruckstanz" in Thurnau, 1986. Wilhelmshaven.

Odenthal, Johannes. 2005. *Tanz Körper Politik.* Berlin.

Osma, Guillermo de. 1980. *Mariano Fortuny: His Life and Work.* New York.

Panofsky, Erwin. 1963. "The Ideological Antecedents of the Rolls-Royce Radiator." *Proceedings of the American Philosophical Society* 107: 273–88.

Panofsky, Erwin. 1972. *Studies in Iconology: Humanistic Themes in the Art of the Renaissance.* New York.

Panofsky, Erwin. 1991. "Ikonographie und Ikonologie." In *Ikonographie und Ikonologie: Theorien—Entwicklung—Probleme*, ed. Ekkehard Kaemmerling, 5th ed., 207–25. Cologne.

Pastori, Jean-Pierre. 1980. *L'Homme et la Danse: Le Danseur du XVIe au XXe Siècle.* Fribourg.

Pater, Walter. 1876. "A Study of Dionysus: The Spiritual Form of Fire and Dew." Online at http://www.readbookonline.net/readOnLine/38076.

Pater, Walter. 1878. "The Bacchanals of Euripides." Online at http://www.readbookonline.net/readOnLine/38077.

Pater, Walter. 2002. *Greek Studies: A Series of Essays* (1904). Honolulu, HI.

Pavis, Patrice. 1988. *Semiotik der Theaterrezeption*, Tübingen.

Pavlova, Anna. 1928. *Tanzende Füße: Der Weg meines Lebens*. Dresden.

Perniola, Mario. 1989. "Erotik des Schleiers und Erotik der Bekleidung." In *Transfigurationen des Körpers: Spuren der Gewalt in der Geschichte*, ed. Dietmar Kamper and Christoph Wulf, 427–51. Berlin.

Perrot, Philippe. 1984. *Le travail des apparances: Le corps féminin du XVIIIe–XIXe siècle*. Paris.

Perrottet, Suzanne. 1989. *Ein bewegtes Leben*. Bern.

Pestalozzi, Karl. 1958. *Sprachskepsis und Sprachmagie im Werk des jungen Hofmannsthal*. Zürcher Beiträge zur deutschen Sprach- und Stilgeschichte, no. 6. Zurich.

Peter, Frank-Manuel. 1987. *Valeska Gert: Tänzerin, Schauspielerin, Kabarettistin*. 2nd ed. Berlin.

Peters, Kurt, ed. 1979. *Laban*. In *Die Tanzarchiv-Reihe*, nos. 19–20. Cologne.

Pfabigan, Alfred, ed. 1985. *Ornament und Askese im Zeitgeist des Vienna der Jahrhundertwende*. Vienna.

Pfister, Manfred, ed. 1989. *Die Modernisierung des Ich: Studien zur Subjektkonstitution in der Vor- und Frühmoderne*. Passau.

Picabia, Francis. 1988. *Aphorismen*. Hamburg.

Plumpe, Gerhard. 1978. *Alfred Schuler: Chaos und Neubeginn. Zur Funktion des Mythos in der Moderne*. Berlin.

Pollig, Hermann. 1987. *Exotische Welten: Europäische Phantasien*. Catalogue of the exhibition of the same name. Stuttgart.

Poppenberg, Felix. 1907–08. "Dekorative Variationen." *Der Türmer* 1: 741–45.

Preston-Dunlop, Valerie, and Susanne Lahusen. 1990. *Schrifttanz: A View of German Dance in the Weimar Republic*. London.

Priddin, D. 1992. *The Art of Dance in French Literature from Théophile Gautier to Paul Valéry*. London.

Prokop, Dieter. 1971. *Materialien zur Theorie des Films: Ästhetik—Soziologie—Politik*. Munich.

Pronko, L. 1962. *C. Avant-Garde: The Experimental Theater in France*. Berkeley.

Proust, Marcel. 1979. *Auf der Suche nach der verlorenen Zeit*. Trans. Eva Rechel-Mertens. 10 vols. Frankfurt am Main.

Proust, Marcel. 2003. *The Prisoner and The Fugitive*. Ed. Christopher Prendergast and trans. Carol Clark and Peter Collier. New York.

Prudhommeau, Germaine. 1965. *La Danse Grecque Antique*. 2 vols. Paris.

Prütting, Lorenz. 1971. *Die Revolution des Theaters: Studien über Georg Fuchs*. Municher Beiträge zur Theaterwissenschaft, no. 2. Weichsenried.

Pudovkin, Vsevolod. 1972. "Über die Montage." In *Theorie des Kinos: Ideologiekritik der Traumfabrik*, ed. Karsten Witte, 113–27. Frankfurt am Main.

Puffett, Derrick. 1989. *Richard Strauss: "Elektra."* Cambridge Opera Handbooks. New York.

Puni, Ivan. 1892–1956, *Berlin 1993* (catalogue of the Berlinische Galerie).

Rabenalt, Arthur Maria. 1965. *Das provokative Musiktheater der zwanziger Jahre: Ein Rückblick*. Munich.

Rainey, Lawrence, Christine Poggi, and Laura Wittmann, eds. 2009. *Futurism: An Anthology*. New Haven.

Rasch, Wolfdietrich. 1967. "Tanz als Lebenssymbol im Drama um 1900." In *Zur deutschen Literatur seit der Jahrhundertwende: Gesammelte Aufsätze*. Stuttgart.

Rasch, Wolfdietrich. 1986. *Die literarische Dekadenz um 1900*. Munich.

Reboul, Jacques. 1912. *Notes sur la morale d'une "annonciatrice."* Paris.

Redfern, Betty. 1983. *Dance, Art and Aesthetics*. London.

Reed, Thomas J. 1983. *Thomas Mann: "Der Tod in Venedig." Text, Materialien, Kommentar*. Munich.

Renner, Rolf Günter. 1987. *Das Ich als ästhetische Konstruktion: "Der Tod in Venedig" und seine Beziehung zum Gesamtwerk Thomas Manns*. Freiburg im Breisgau.

Renner, Ursula. 1991. "'Das Erlebnis des Sehens': Zu Hofmannsthals produktiver Rezeption bildender Kunst." In *Hugo von Hofmannsthal: Freundschaften und Begegnungen mit deutschen Zeitgenossen*, ed. Ursula Renner and G. Bärbel Schmid, 285–305. Würzburg.

Requadt, Paul. 1955. "Sprachverleugnung und Mantelsymbolik im Werke Hugo von Hofmannsthals." *Deutsche Vierteljahresschrift für Literaturwissenschaft und Geistesgeschichte* 29: 255–83.

Reventlow, Franziska Gräfin zu. 1987. *Herrn Dames Aufzeichnungen oder Begebenheiten aus einem merkwürdigen Stadtteil*. Ed. Else Reventlow. Frankfurt am Main.

Rick, Cary. 1989. *Tanztherapie: Eine Einführung in die Grundlagen*. Stuttgart.

Riedel, Ingrid. 1985. *Formen—Kreis, Kreuz, Dreieck, Quadrat, Spirale*. Stuttgart.

Riesz, János. 1976. "Deutsche Reaktionen auf den italienischen Futurismus." *Arcadia* 2: 256–71.

Riesz, János. 1983. "Der Untergang als 'spectacle' und die Erprobung einer 'écriture fasciste' in F. T. Marinettis 'Mafarka le Futuriste' (1909)." In *Aspekte des Erzählens in der modernen italienischen Literatur*, ed. Ulrich Schulz-Buschhaus, 85–99. Tübingen.

Rilke, Rainer Maria. 1955–66. *Sämtliche Werke*. Ed. Ernst Zinn, 6 vols. Frankfurt am Main.

Rilke, Rainer Maria. 1962. *Translations from the Poetry of Rainer Maria Rilke*. Trans. M. D. Hrefer Norton. New York.

Rilke, Rainer Maria. 1995. *Ahead of All Parting: The Selected Poetry and Prose of Rainer Maria Rilke*. Ed. and trans. Stephen Mitchell. New York.

Rilke, Rainer Maria. 2004a. *Auguste Rodin*. Trans. Daniel Slager. New York.

Rilke, Rainer Maria. 2004b. *Sonnets to Orpheus*. Trans. Edward Snow. New York.

Rilke, Rainer Maria. 2010. *The Inner Sky: Poems, Notes, Dreams*. Trans. Damion Searls. Boston.

Rilke, Rainer Maria. N.d. "Spanish Dancer." Online at http://www.poemhunter.com/poem/the-spanish-dancer.

Ritter-Santini, Lea. 1971. *Die Verfremdung des optischen Zitats. Anmerkungen zu Heinrich Manns Roman ,Die Göttinnen'*, in: Jb. d. Dt. Schiller-Gesellschaft, H. 15.

Rittner, Volker. 1983. "Zur Soziologie körperbetonter sozialer Systeme." *Kölner Zeitschrift für Soziologie und Sozialpsychologie, Sonderheft 25*: "Gruppensoziologie: P erspektiven und Materialien," ed. Friedhelm Neidhardt, 233–55 Cologne.

Robinson, David. 1989. *Chaplin: Sein Leben, seine Kunst*. Zurich.

Rochowanski, L. W. 1923. *Der Tanzende Schwerpunkt*. Zurich.

Rohde, Erwin. 1925. *Psyche: The Cult of Souls and the Belief in Immortality among the Greeks.* Trans. W. B. Hillis. Routledge. Reprint 2000–01.

Rolland, Romain. 1903. *Le théâtre du peuple.* Paris.

Rosemont, Franklin, ed. 1983. *Isadora Speaks: Isadora Duncan.* San Francisco.

Roth, Joseph. 1975–76. *Werke.* Ed. Hermann Kesten. 4 vols. Amsterdam.

Rothe, Wolfgang. 1979. *Tänzer und Täter: Gestalten des Expressionismus.* Frankfurt am Main.

Rzhevsky, Nicholas. 2009. *The Modern Russian Theater: A Literary and Cultural History.* M. E. Sharpe.

Sachs, Curt. 1933. *Eine Weltgeschichte des Tanzes.* Berlin.

Saint-Point, Valentine de. 1905. *Poèmes de la Mer et du Soleil.* Paris.

Saint-Point, Valentine de. 1906. *Un Amour.* Paris.

Saint-Point, Valentine de. 1907–1911. *Trilogie de l'Amour et de la Mort, I–III.* Paris.

Saint-Point, Valentine de. 1910. *Une Femme et le Désir.* Paris.

Saint-Point, Valentine de. 1912. *La Guerre: Poème héroique.* Paris.

Sakharoff, Alexander. 1953. *Réflexions sur la Danse et la Musique.* Paris.

Sasportes, José. 1988. *La scoperta del corpo: Percorsi della danza nel Novecento.* Bari.

Sasportes, José. 1989. *Pensare la danza: Da Mallarmé a Cocteau.* Bologna.

Saße, Günter. 1977. *Sprache und Kritik: Untersuchungen zur Sprachkritik der Moderne. Palaestra*, vol. 267. Göttingen.

Schäfers, Bernhard. 1983. "Gruppenbildung als Reflex auf gesamtgesellschaftliche Entwicklungen am Beispiel der deutschen Jugendbewegung." In *Kölner Zeitschrift Für Soziologie und Sozialpsychologie, Sonderheft 25: "Gruppensoziologie: Perspektiven und Materialien,"* ed. Friedhelm Neidhardt, 106–25.

Schaps, Regina. 1982. *Hysterie und Weiblichkeit. Wissenschaftsmythen über die Frau,* Frankfurt a.M.

Schechner, Richard. 1990. *Theater-Anthropologie: Spiel und Ritual im Kulturvergleich.* Reinbek.

Scheerbart, Paul. 1909–10. "Riesenpantomime mit Fesselballons." *Das Theater* 1: 92.

Scheper, Dirk. 1988. *Oskar Schlemmer: Das Triadische Ballett und die Bauhausbühne.* Schriftenreihe der Akademie der Künste, vol. 20. Berlin. Cologne.

Schikowski, John. 1926. *Geschichte des Tanzes.* Berlin.

Schlemmer, Oskar. 1961. "Man and Art Figure" (1925). In *The Theater of the Bauhaus,* ed. Walter Gropius, 17. Middletown, CT.

Schlemmer, Oskar. 1969. "The Mathematics of the Dance." In Hans M. Wingler, *The Bauhaus: Weimar, Dessau, Berlin, Chicago,* trans. Wolfgang Jabs and Basil Gilbert, ed. Joseph Stein. Cambridge, MA.

Schlemmer, Oskar. 1986. "Der theatralische Kostümtanz." *In Künstlerische Schriften der 20er Jahre. Dokumente und Manifeste aus der Weimarer Republik,* ed. Uwe M. Schneede, 274–277. Köln.

Schlemmer, Oskar. 1990. "Misunderstandings: A Reply to Kállai." In *Schrifttanz: A View of German Dance in the Weimar Republic,* ed. Valerie Preston-Dunlop and Susanne Lahusen, 18. London. First published Schrifttanz 4.2 (October 1931).

Schlemmer, Oskar. 2002. "Man and Art Figure" (1925). In *The Twentieth Century Performance Reader,* ed. Michael Huxley and Noel Witts, 2nd ed., 359–70. New York.

Schlötterer, Reinhold. 1986. "Elektras Tanz in der Tragödie Hofmannsthals." *Hofmannsthal-Blätter* 33: 47–58.

Schlundt, Christena L. 1962. *The Professional Appearances of Ruth St. Denis and Ted Shawn: A Chronology and Index of Dances, 1906–1932.* New York.

Schmid, Gisela Bärbel. 1985. "Amor und Psyche: Zur Form des Psyche-Mythos bei Hofmannsthal." *Hofmannsthal-Blätter* 31–32: 58–64.

Schmid, Gisela Bärbel. 1986. "'Das unheimliche Erlebnis eines jungen Elegants in einer merkwürdigen visionären Nacht': Zu Hofmannsthals Pantomime 'Das fremde Märchen.' *Hofmannsthal-Blätter* 3: 47–57.

Schmid, Gisela Bärbel. 1987. "Psychologische Umdeutung biblischer Archetypen im Geiste des Fin de siècle: Zur Entstehung der 'Josephslegende.'" *Hofmannsthal-Blätter* 35–36: 105–13.

Schmid, Gisela Bärbel. 1991. "Der Tanz macht beglückend frei." In *Hugo von Hofmannsthal: Freundschaften und Begegnungen mit deutschen Zeitgenossen,* ed. Ursula Renner and Gisela Bärbel Schmid, 251–60. Würzburg.

Schmidt, Siegfried J., ed. 1991. *Gedächtnis: Probleme und Perspektiven der interdisziplinären Gedächtnisforschung.* Frankfurt am Main.

Schmidt-Aleman, Heinz P., ed. and trans. 1951. *Anna Pawlowa: Die Ballerina des Zaren.* Berlin.

Schmidt-Radefeldt, Jürgen. 1986. "Paul Valéry." In *Französische Literatur des 20. Jahrhunderts: Gestalten und Tendenzen. Zur Erinnerung an Ernst Robert Curtius,* ed. Wolf-Dieter Lange, 163–84. Bonn.

Schmitz, Walter. 1990. *Die Münchner Moderne: Die literarische Szene in der "Kunststadt" um die Jahrhundertwende.* Stuttgart.

Schneider, Manfred. 1985. "Hysterie als Gesamtkunstwerk." In *Ornament und Askese im Zeitgeist des Wien der Jahrhundertwende,* ed. Alfred Pfabigan, 212–29. Vienna.

Schneider, Manfred, ed. 1988. *Jean-Martin Charcot / Paul Richer: Die Besessenen in der Kunst.* Göttingen.

Schneider, Manfred. 1989. "Gesellschaftliche Modernisierung und Literatur der Moderne." In *Zur Terminologie der Literaturwissenschaft: Akten des IX. Germanistischen Symposions der Deutschen Forschungsgemeinschaft Würzburg, 1986,* ed. Christian Wagenknecht, 393–413. Stuttgart.

Schuh, Willy. 1983. "Hofmannsthal, Kessler und die 'Josephslegende.'" *Hofmannsthal-Blätter* 27: 48–55.

Schultz, Joachim. 1981. *Literarische Manifeste der "Belle Epoque": Frankreich 1886–1909.* Bayreuther Beiträge zur Literaturwissenschaft, no. 2. Frankfurt am Main.

Schultze-Naumburg, Paul. 1910. *Die Kultur des weiblichen Körpers als Grundlage der Frauenkleidung.* Leipzig.

Schwalbe, Jürgen. 1971. *Sprache und Gebärde im Werk Hugo von Hofmannsthals.* Studien zur deutschen Sprache und Literatur 2. Freiburg im Breisgau.

Schwerte, Hans. 1991. *Auflösung einer Republik. Über einen Roman von Frank Theiß: Der Zentaur, 1931.* In *Jahrbuch der deutschen Schillergesellschaft,* 35, 275–93.

Scott, Jill. 2005. *Electra after Freud: Myth and Culture.* Ithaca, NY.

Séché, Alphons. 1909. *Les Muses Français: Anthologie des femmes-poètes (XX. siècle).* Paris.

Severini, G. 2009. "Plastic Analogies of Dynamism" (1913). In *Futurism: An Anthology*, ed. Lawrence Rainey, Christine Poggi, and Laura Wittmann, 165–69. New Haven.

Shawn, Ted. 1954. *Every Little Movement: A Book about François Delsarte*. Pittsfield, MA.

Shelton, Suzanne. 1981. *Divine Dancer: A Biography of Ruth St. Denis*. Garden City, NY.

Shercliff, Jose. 1953. *Jane Avril vom Moulin Rouge: Der Roman der berühmten Tänzerin*. Hamburg.

Siegele-Wenschkewitz, Leonore. 1990. *Frauen und Faschismus in Europa: Der faschistische Körper*. Ed. Gerda Stuchlik. Frauen in Geschichte und Gesellschaft, vol. 6. Paffenweiler.

Simmen, Jeannot. 1990. *Vertigo: Schwindel der modernen Kunst*. Munich.

Simmen, Jeannot, ed. 1991. *Schwerelos: Der Traum vom Fliegen in der Kunst der Moderne*. Catalogue of the exhibition 1991–92 in Berlin. Stuttgart.

Soden, Kristine von. 1988. *Neue Frauen. Die zwanziger Jahre*, ed. Maruta Schmidt. Berlin.

Soeffner, Hans-Georg. 1989. *Auslegung des Alltags—Der Alltag der Auslegung, zur wissenssoziologischen Konzeption einer sozialwissenschaftlichen Hermeneutik*. Frankfurt a.M.

Sorell, Walter. 1985. *Der Tanz als Spiegel der Zeit: Eine Kulturgeschichte des Tanzes*. Wilhelmshaven.

Sorell, Walter. 1986. *Mary Wigman: Ein Vermächtnis*. Wilhelmshaven.

Spielmann, Heinz. 1991. *Russische Avantgarde und die Bühne, 1890–1930*. Schleswig.

Stanciu-Reiss, Françoise. 1991. "Glanz und Elend des Waslaw Nijinsky." *Ballett International* 3: 11–15.

St. Denis, Ruth. 1939. *An Unfinished Life*. New York.

Stebbins, Genevieve. 1885. *Delsarte System of Expression*. New York.

Stebbins, Genevieve. 1893. *Dynamic Breathing and Harmonic Gymnastics*. New York.

Steinbeck, Dietrich. 1981. "Probleme der Dokumentation von Theaterkunstwerken." In *Theaterwissenschaft im deutschsprachigen Raum: Texte zum Selbstverständnis*, ed. Helmut Klier, 179–91. Darmstadt.

Steinberg, Cobbett, ed. 1980. *The Dance Anthology*. New York.

Steiner, George. 1989. *Real Presences*. Chicago.

St. Elia, Antonio. 1914. "Manifesto of Futurist Architecture." Online at http://www.unknown.nu/futurism/architecture.html.

Stephens, Anthony R. 1971. "Rilkes Essay 'Puppen' und das Problem des geteilten Ich." In *Rilke in neuer Sicht*, ed. Käte Hamburger, 159–72. Stuttgart.

Stephens, Anthony R. 1974. *Rilkes Malte Laurids Brigge: Strukturanalyse des erzählerischen Bewußtseins*. Bern.

St.-Johnston, Reginald. 1906. *A History of Dancing*. London.

Stöckemann, Patricia. 1991. *Lola Rogge: Pädagogin und Choreographin des Freien Tanzes*. Wilhelmshaven.

Stokes, John, Michael R. Booth, and Susan Bassnett. 1988. *Bernhardt, Terry, Duse: The Actress in Her Time*. New York.

Stokes, John, Michael R. Booth, and Susan Bassnett. 1991. *Sarah Bernhardt, Ellen Terry, Eleonora Duse: Ein Leben für das Theater*. Weinheim.

Straten, Roelof van. 1989. *Einführung in die Ikonographie*. Berlin.

Strauß, Botho. 1992. *Beginnlosigkeit: Reflexionen über Fleck und Linie*. Munich.

Stüber, Werner J. 1984. *Geschichte des modern dance: Zur Selbsterfahrung und Körperaneignung im modernen Tanztheater*. Wilhelmshaven.

Surits, Elisabeth. 1981. "Triumph der Technik oder Menschen als tanzende Maschinen: Das Sowjetische Ballett der zwanziger Jahre und der Einfluß des Konstruktivismus." In *Ballett: Chronik und Bilanz des Ballettjahres*, ed. Hartmut Regitz and Horst Koegler, 24–33. Velber.

Symons, Arthur. 1924. *Collected Works*. Vols. 2 and 3: *Poems*. London. Reprint 1973.

Symons, Arthur. 1899. *Images of Good and Evil*. London. Online at http://www.archive. org/stream/imagesgoodandev01symogoog#page/n40/mode/2up.

Symons, Arthur 2003. *Selected Writings*. Ed. Roger Holdsworth. New York: Routledge.

Szeemann, Harald, ed. 1980. *Monte Verità: Berg der Wahrheit. Lokale Anthropologie als Beitrag zur Wiederentdeckung einer neuzeitlichen sakralen Topographie. Catalogue of the exhibition at the Museum Villa Stuck, Munich*. Munich.

Taeger, Annemarie. 1987. *Die Kunst, Medusa zu töten: Zum Bild der Frau in der Literatur der Jahrhundertwende*. Bielefeld.

Täubrich, Hans-Christian. 1991. *Unter Null: Kunsteis, Kälte und Kultur*. Catalogue of the exhibition of the Centrum Industriekultur Nürnberg and the Stadtmuseum Munich. Ed. Jutta Tschoeke. Munich.

Theweleit, Klaus. 1982. *Männerphantasien*. 2 vols. Reinbek.

Thieß, Frank. 1920. *Der Tanz als Kunstwerk: Studien zu einer Ästhetik der Tanzkunst*. Munich.

Thieß, Frank. 1929. *Erziehung zur Freiheit: Abhandlungen und Auseinandersetzungen*. Stuttgart.

Thieß, Frank. 1931. *Der Zentaur*. Stuttgart.

Thomsen, Christian W., ed. 1985. *Studien zur Ästhetik des Gegenwartstheaters*. Heidelberg.

Thomson, Richard. 1992. "The Dance-Halls and the Chahut, 1886–1892." In *Toulouse-Lautrec*, ed. Marianne Ryan, 238ff. London.

Toulouse-Lautrec, Henri. 1992. *Catalogue of the exhibition in London, 1991 / Paris, 1992*. Ed. Marianne Ryan. London.

Trettin, Käthe. 1978. *Philosophie des Tanzes: Hinweise auf ein Begehren*. Berlin.

Trippet, David. 2007. "Composing Time: Zeno's Arrow, Hindemith's Erinnerung, and Satie's Instantanéisme." *Journal of Musicology* 24: 522–80.

Turner, Victor. 1982. *From Ritual to Theatre: The Human Seriousness of Play*. New York.

Ubersfeld, Anne. 1978. *Lire le théâtre*. Paris.

Vaget, Hans Rudolf. 1985. "Thomas Mann und die Neuklassik: "Der Tod in Venedig" und Samuel Lublinskys Literaturauffassung." In *Stationen der Thomas Mann-Foschung: Aufsätze seit 1970*, ed. Hermann Kurzke, 41–60. Würzburg.

Valéry, Paul. 1948. *Degas Dance Drawing*. Trans. Helen Burlin. New York.

Valéry, Paul. 1951. *Dance and the Soul*. Trans. Dorothy Bussy. London.

Valéry, Paul. 1957–1961. *Cahiers*. Facsimile ed. 29 vols. Paris.

Valéry, Paul. 1958. "Dialoques." In *Paul Valéry: Collected Works*. London.

Valéry, Paul. 1960. *Oeuvres*. Ed. Jean Hytier. 2 vols. Paris.

Valéry, Paul. 1964a. "Philosophy of the Dance." In Paul Valéry, *Aesthetics*, trans. Ralph Manheim. New York.

Valéry, Paul. 1964b. *Dance and the Soul*. Trans. Dorothy Bussy. In *Selected Writings of Paul Valéry*, 184–98. New York.

Valéry, Paul 1989. *Degas, Manet, Morisot*. Trans. David Paul. Princeton.

Van Vaerenbergh, Leona. 1991. *Tanz und Tanzbewegung: Ein Beitrag zur Deutung deutscher Lyrik von der Dekadenz bis zum Frühexpressionismus*. Frankfurt am Main.

Van Vechten, Carl. 1977. "The New Isadora". In Magriel, Paul, ed. 1977. *Nijinsky, Pavlova, Duncan: Three Lives in Dance*, S. 27–35. New York.

Varnhagen, Rahel. 1983. *Gesammelte Werke*. Ed. Konrad Feilchenfeldt, Uwe Schweikert and Rahel E. Steiner, 10 vol. München.

Vasari, Ruggero. 1990. "Flugmalerei—Moderne Kunst und Reaktion" (1934). In *Peter Demetz, Worte in Freiheit: Der italienische Futurismus und die deutsche Avantgarde, 1912–1934. Mit einer ausführlichen Dokumentation*, 381ff. Munich.

Vaydat, Pierre, ed. 1991. *Die "Neue Sachlichkeit"—Lebensgefühl oder Markenzeichen?* Germanica, no. 9. Lille.

Verdone, Mario. 1969. *Teatro del tempo futurista*. Rome.

Vergine, Lea, ed. 1980. *L'altra metà dell'avanguardia, 1910–1940: Pittrici e scultrici nei movimenti delle avanguardie storiche*. Milan.

Veroli, Patricia, ed. 1991. *Clotilde e Alexandre Sakharoff: Un mito della danza fra teatro e avanguardie artistiche*. Bologna.

Vierneisel, Klaus, and Bert Kaeser, eds. 1990. *Kunst der Schale—Kultur des Trinkens*. Catalogue of exhibition. Munich.

Vietta, Egon. 1938. *Der Tanz: Eine kleine Metaphysik*. Frankfurt am Main.

Villany, Adorée. 1912. *Tanzreform und Pseudo-Moral*. Paris.

Virilio, Paul. 1989. *War and Cinema: The Logistics of Perception*. Trans. Patrick Camiller. London.

Volta, Ornella. 1992. *Satie et la Danse*. Paris.

Vondung, Klaus, ed. 1976. *Das Wilhelminische Bildungsbürgertum: Zur Sozialgeschichte seiner Ideen*. Göttingen.

Waagenaar, Sam. 1964. *The Murder of Mata Hari*. London.

Wagner, Nike. 1987. *Geist und Geschlecht: Karl Kraus und die Erotik der Viennaer Moderne*. Frankfurt am Main.

Wagner, Richard. 1917. *Tagebuchblätter und Briefe 1853–1871*. Ed. Wolfgang Golther. Leipzig.

Wagner, Richard. 1988. *Gesammelte Schriften und Dichtungen*. Leipzig.

Walser, Robert. 1966. *Das Gesamtwerk*. Ed. Jochen Greven. Hamburg.

Walser, Robert. 2012. *Berlin Stories*. Ed. Jochen Greven. Trans. Susan Bernofsky et al. New York.

Walter, H. 1980. *Pans Wiederkehr: Der Gott der griechischen Wildnis*. Munich.

Wanner, Hans. 1976. *Individualität, Identität und Rolle. Das frühe Werk Heinrich Manns und Thomas Manns Erzählungen 'Gladius Dei' und 'Der Tod in Venedig'*. München.

Warburg, Aby. 1932. *Gesammelte Schriften*. Ed. Gertrud Bing in cooperation with Fritz Rougemont. 2 vols. Leipzig.

Warburg, Aby. 1979. *Ausgewählte Schriften und Würdigungen*. Ed. D. Wuttke and C. G. Heise. Baden-Baden.

Warburg, Aby. 2009. "The Absorption of the Expressive Values of the Past." Trans. Matthew Rampley. *Art in Translation 1.2*: 273–83.

Warner, Marina. 1985. *Monuments and Maidens: The Allegory of the Female Form.* London.

Wehmeyer, Grete. 1974. *Erik Satie.* Regensburg.

Weininger, Otto. 2005. *Sex and Character (1903).* Trans. Robert Willis. 2nd ed. Online at http://www.theabsolute.net/ottow/geschlecht.pdf.

Weisgerber, Jean, ed. 1984. *Les Avant-Gardes Littéraires au XXe Siècle.* Vol. 2: Théorie. Budapest.

Whitford, Frank. 1992. *The Bauhaus: Masters and Students by Themselves.* Woodstock, NY.

Wiese, Benno von. 1976. *Signaturen: Zu Heinrich Heine und seinem Werk.* Berlin.

Wiesenthal, Grete. 1909. "Unsere Tänze." *Der Merker* 1: 65–68.

Wiesenthal, Grete. 1919. *Der Aufstieg.* Vienna. Reprint entitled Die ersten Schritte, Vienna, 1947.

Wiesenthal, Grete. 1951. *Iffi—Roman einer Tänzerin.* Vienna.

Wigman, Mary. 1966. *The Language of Dance.* Trans. Walter Sorell. Middletown, CT.

Wilhelm, Hermann. 1993. *Die Münchner Bohème—von der Jahrhundertwende bis zum ersten Weltkrieg.* Munich.

Wind, Edgar. 1980. *Pagan Mysteries in the Renaissance.* Rev. ed. Oxford.

Wind, Edgar. 1981. *Heidnische Mysterien in der Renaissance.* Trans. Christa Münstermann with the assistance of Bernhard Buschendorf und Gisela Heinrichs. Frankfurt am Main.

Winther, Fritz. 1914. *Körperbildung als Kunst und Pflicht.* Munich.

Winther, Fritz. 1920. *Lebendige Form: Rhythmus und Freiheit in Gymnastik, Sport und Tanz.* Karlsruhe.

Winther, Fritz. 1922. *Der rhythmische Mensch.* Rudolstadt.

Witte, Karsten, ed. 1972. *Theorie des Kinos: Ideologiekritik der Traumfabrik.* Frankfurt am Main.

Woeckel, G. 1970. "The Spirit of Ecstasy: Die Rolls-Royce-Autokühlerfigur von Charles Sykes." 2 parts. *Alte und moderne Kunst* 15.108: 19–27, 15.109: 24–31.

Wolff, Eugen. 1976. "Die jüngste deutsche Literaturströmung und das Prinzip der Moderne." In *Modernism*, ed. Malcolm Bradbury and James McFarlane, 41–42. Harmondsworth.

Worbs, Michael. 1983. *Nervenkunst: Literatur und Psychoanalyse im Vienna der Jahrhundertwende.* Frankfurt am Main.

Wosien, G. 1972. *Das Mukabele der Mevlevi-Derwische.* Icking.

Wunberg, Gotthart. 1965. *Der frühe Hofmannsthal: Schizophrenie als dichterische Struktur. Mit einer umfassenden Bibliographie zur Sekundärliteratur.* Sprache und Literatur, no. 25. Stuttgart.

Wunberg, Gotthart. 1989. "Chiffrierung und Selbstversicherung des Ich: Die Antikenfiguration um 1900." In *Die Modernisierung des Ich: Studien zur Subjektkonstitution in der Vor- und Frühmoderne*, ed. Manfred Pfister, 190–202. Passau.

Zepler, M. 1906. *N. Erziehung zur Körperschönheit: Turnen und Tanzen. Ein Beitrag zur Mädchenerziehung.* Berlin.

Zglinicki, Friedrich von. 1979. *Der Weg des Films.* Hildesheim.

Ziegler, Ulf Erdmann. 1990. *"Nackt unter Nackten": Utopien der Nacktkultur, 1906–1942.* Berlin.

Zima, Peter V. 1991. *Literarische Ästhetik: Methoden und Modelle der Literaturwissenschaft.* Tübingen.

Zimmermann, Hans-Joachim, ed. 1984. *Antike Tradition und Neuere Philologien: Festschrift für Rudolf Sühnel.* Heidelberg.

Žmegač, Victor. 1978. "Bemerkungen zur Rezeptionsgeschichte Rilkes." In *Literatur und Theater im Wilhelminischen Zeitalter,* ed. Hans-Peter Bayerdörfer, Karl Otto Conrady, and Helmut Schanze, 62–77. Tübingen.

Žmegač, Victor. 1989. "Die Realität ahmt die Kunst nach: Zu einer Denkfigur der Jahrhundertwende." In *Die Modernisierung des Ich: Studien zur Subjektkonstitution in der Vor- und Frühmoderne,* ed. Manfred Pfister, 180–89. Passau.

Žmegač, Victor. 1990. *Der europäische Roman: Geschichte seiner Poetik.* 2nd ed. Tübingen.

Zorn, Friedrich Albert. 1887. *Grammatik der Tanzkunst: Theoretischer und praktischer Unterricht in der Tanzkunst und Tanzschreibkunst oder Choreographie. Nebst Atlas mit Zeichnungen und musikalischen Uebungs-Beispielen mit choreographischen Bezeichnungen und einem besonderen Notenheft für den Musiker.* 3 vols. Leipzig.